# Core Text Series

- Written with authority by leading subject experts
- Takes a focussed approach, leading law students straight to the heart of the subject
- Clear, concise, straightforward analysis of the subject and its challenges

**Series Editor:** Nicola Padfield

**Company Law:** Alan Dignam and John Lowry

**Constitutional and Administrative Law:** Neil Parpworth

**Criminal Law:** Nicola Padfield

**Employment Law:** Robert Upex, Richard Benny and Stephen Hardy

**European Union Law:** Margot Horspool and Matthew Humphreys

**Evidence:** Roderick Munday

**Family Law:** Mary Welstead and Susan Edwards

**Intellectual Property Law:** Jennifer Davis

**Land Law:** Kevin Gray and Susan Francis Gray

**Medical Law:** Jonathan Herring

**The Law of Contract:** Janet O'Sullivan and Jonathan Hilliard

**The Law of Trusts:** James Penner

**The Legal System:** Kate Malleson, Richard Moules

**Tort:** Stephen Hedley

For further information about titles in the series,
**please visit www.oup.co.uk/series/cts**

OXFORD
UNIVERSITY PRESS

CORE TEXT SERIES

# Constitutional and Administrative Law

*Seventh Edition*

## NEIL PARPWORTH

Principal Lecturer in Law

De Montfort University

Series Editor

## NICOLA PADFIELD

Fitzwilliam College, Cambridge

OXFORD
UNIVERSITY PRESS

# OXFORD
UNIVERSITY PRESS

Great Clarendon Street, Oxford, OX2 6DP
United Kingdom

Oxford University Press is a department of the University of Oxford.
It furthers the University's objective of excellence in research, scholarship,
and education by publishing worldwide. Oxford is a registered trade mark of
Oxford University Press in the UK and in certain other countries

© Oxford University Press 2012

The moral rights of the authors have been asserted

Fourth Edition copyright 2006
Fifth Edition copyright 2008
Sixth Edition copyright 2010

Impression: 1

Public sector information reproduced under Open Government Licence v1.0
(http://www.nationalarchives.gov.uk/doc/open-government-licence/
open-government-licence.htm)

Crown Copyright material reproduced with the permission of the
Controller, HMSO (under the terms of the Click Use licence)

British Library Cataloguing in Publication Data

Data available

Library of Congress Cataloging in Publication Data

Library of Congress Control Number: 2012932001

ISBN 978-0-19-969833-2

Printed in Great Britain by
Ashford Colour Press Ltd, Gosport, Hampshire

# Preface

The purpose of this book is to introduce the reader to the fundamental principles and concepts of Constitutional and Administrative Law, or Public Law as it is sometimes also called. Given the size of the book and the ethos of the Core Text series, the treatment accorded to each topic does not claim to be exhaustive. It is hoped, however, that readers will find that it accords them access to the core of the subject and that they will make good use of the 'Further Reading' lists (at the end of each chapter) to enhance their knowledge and understanding. Much of the material referred to therein will be especially useful to those who are required to write essays, especially those who wish to be able to demonstrate that their learning has been gleaned from more than a textbook and their lecture notes.

An underlying intention of the Core Text series is that the titles in the series should appear in new editions on a regular basis so that readers can be confident that they are consulting up-to-date information. Nevertheless, since Constitutional and Administrative Law is a dynamic subject, the reader ought to utilize the Online Resource Centre which accompanies OUP's Public Law titles. This will make you aware of important developments which occur between editions.

The Blair and Brown Labour Governments pursued a reformist agenda when it came to the constitution. The present coalition Government appears minded to do likewise. Since the May 2010 general election, therefore, several important developments have taken place, including the enactment of the Parliamentary Voting System and Constituencies Act 2011 and the Fixed-term Parliaments Act 2011. Reform of the House of Lords remains on the agenda, as evidenced by the publication of a draft Bill. Legislation to provide for the recall of MPs is a further commitment set out in the coalition agreement which is likely to be introduced before too long. These continue to be interesting times for the student of Constitutional and Administrative Law.

As with several of its predecessors, the task of producing a new edition of this book began with OUP commissioning reviews of the previous edition. The comments which the anonymous reviewers provided were, as ever, very helpful. I am grateful to them for taking the time and trouble to be part of the process. I am also grateful to the law publishing staff at OUP for the efficient way in which they have handled all aspects of the publication of this seventh edition. The year 2000, when the first edition appeared, seems a long time ago now. It is very pleasing that there has been a demand for the title in the years that have followed.

Thanks are also owed in great measure to my partner and colleague, Katharine Thompson, and to our two children, Catriona and Calum. Since none of them would want me to write anything which embarrasses them, I shall just say that I love you all very much!

I would like to dedicate this edition to the memory of John and Olive May, who were much loved and are much missed parents, grandparents and great-grandparents.

*Neil Parpworth*
January 2012

# Contents

Table of statutes    xvi

Table of statutory instruments    xxiii

Table of cases    xxiv

Table of European conventions, directives, and treaties    xlv

Guide to using the book    xlvii

**PART I    Fundamental Principles of the Constitution**    **1**

**1    The meaning of a constitution**    **3**

What is a constitution?    3

Classifying constitutions    6

Do written constitutions have any value?    8

The unwritten nature of the UK constitution    9

Does the UK have a constitution?    11

Sources of the UK constitution    12

The changing nature of the UK constitution    12

Should the UK have a written constitution?    13

FURTHER READING    15

SELF-TEST QUESTIONS    16

**2    Separation of powers**    **18**

Introduction    18

Montesquieu and *L'Esprit des Lois*    19

Is there a separation of powers in the UK constitution?    20

FURTHER READING    31

SELF-TEST QUESTIONS    33

**3    Rule of law**    **34**

Meaning of the rule of law    34

Laws should be prospective    36

Laws should be open and clear                                37

Natural justice                                              38

Access to the courts                                         39

Dicey and the rule of law                                    40

Equality before the law                                      42

The principle of legality                                    43

The rule of law and the criminal law                         44

The contemporary significance of the rule of law             45

FURTHER READING                                              49

SELF-TEST QUESTIONS                                          50

**4   The royal prerogative                                  52**

Introduction                                                 52

Some examples of prerogative power                           54

Prerogative and statute                                      57

Adapting prerogative powers                                  59

The prerogative and the courts                               60

Reform                                                       66

FURTHER READING                                              68

SELF-TEST QUESTIONS                                          70

**5   The legislative supremacy of Parliament                71**

Sovereignty of Parliament                                    71

The traditional view                                         71

The doctrine of implied repeal                               77

Entrenchment                                                 79

The new view or the manner and form argument                 79

The Parliament Acts 1911 and 1949                            81

The Union legislation                                        85

Legislative supremacy and the EU                             86

Legislative supremacy and devolution                         89

Legislative supremacy and the Human Rights Act               89

FURTHER READING                                              103

SELF-TEST QUESTIONS                                          105

**PART II    The Institutional Framework of the Constitution    107**

**6    Parliament    109**

House of Commons    109

Composition of the House of Commons    114

Officers of the House of Commons    117

The life of Parliament    118

House of Commons sittings    118

The committee system    121

House of Lords    125

Reform of the House of Lords    126

Parliamentary privilege    129

FURTHER READING    136

SELF-TEST QUESTIONS    137

**7    The European Community and the European Union    139**

The European Communities    139

The European Union    141

The institutions of the Union    141

The European Council    142

The Council of Ministers    143

The Commission    145

The Parliament    148

The Court of Justice of the EU and the General Court    150

FURTHER READING    153

SELF-TEST QUESTIONS    154

**8    The structure of the United Kingdom and devolution    156**

The structure of the United Kingdom    156

Devolution    160

Welsh devolution    161

National Assembly for Wales    161

Welsh Assembly Government    162

Law-making powers    163

Committees                                              165

Developing devolution in Wales                          165

Scottish devolution                                     166

The Scottish Parliament                                 167

The Executive                                           168

Legislative powers                                      168

Acts of Union                                           170

Developing devolution in Scotland                       170

Northern Ireland Assembly                               172

The Belfast Agreement                                   172

Legislative power                                       172

The Northern Ireland Executive                          173

The English Question                                    175

Memorandum of Understanding                             176

FURTHER READING                                         179

SELF-TEST QUESTIONS                                     180

**PART III    Sources of Public Law**                   **181**

**9    Primary and secondary legislation**               **183**

Public General Bills                                    183

The parliamentary stages                               186

House of Lords stages                                  188

A new stage?                                            188

Private Bills                                           191

Hybrid Bills                                           192

Private Members' Bills                                  193

Consolidation Bills                                    195

Delegated legislation                                  196

General types of delegated legislation                 197

Specific types of delegated legislation                198

Statutory instruments                                  201

Quasi-legislation                                      203

FURTHER READING                                        204

SELF-TEST QUESTIONS                                    205

| 10 | EU law | 206 |
|---|---|---|
| | The treaties | 206 |
| | Legislative acts | 206 |
| | Direct applicability | 208 |
| | Direct effect | 209 |
| | EU law and the English courts | 221 |
| | FURTHER READING | 226 |
| | SELF-TEST QUESTIONS | 227 |

| 11 | Constitutional conventions and judge-made law | 228 |
|---|---|---|
| | Constitutional conventions | 228 |
| | The nature of constitutional conventions | 229 |
| | Examples of constitutional conventions | 230 |
| | Enforcing conventions | 234 |
| | Establishing the existence of a convention | 235 |
| | The draft Cabinet Manual | 235 |
| | The courts and conventions | 236 |
| | Can conventions be made into laws? | 237 |
| | Codification | 238 |
| | Conventions and devolution | 239 |
| | Judge-made law | 240 |
| | The common law | 241 |
| | Interpreting Acts of Parliament | 242 |
| | FURTHER READING | 246 |
| | SELF-TEST QUESTIONS | 247 |

| PART IV | Judicial Review of Administrative Action | 249 |
|---|---|---|
| 12 | The nature of judicial review | 251 |
| | The jurisdiction | 251 |
| | Procedural reform | 254 |
| | The rule in *O'Reilly v Mackman* | 255 |
| | The public law/private law distinction | 260 |
| | Collateral challenge | 263 |

Exclusion of judicial review                                          267

The procedure for judicial review                                     269

FURTHER READING                                                       278

SELF-TEST QUESTIONS                                                   279


**13   The grounds for judicial review                                281**

Introduction                                                          281

Illegality                                                            282

Relevant/irrelevant considerations                                    283

Fiduciary duty                                                        285

Fettering of a discretion                                             286

Improper purpose                                                      288

Bad faith                                                             290

Irrationality                                                         291

Proportionality                                                       294

Procedural impropriety                                                298

Natural justice                                                       300

Legitimate expectations                                               302

The right to a fair hearing                                           307

Reasons                                                               309

The rule against bias                                                 312

FURTHER READING                                                       319

SELF-TEST QUESTIONS                                                   320


**14   Judicial review remedies                                       322**

Introduction                                                          322

Damages                                                               323

Prescriptive or permissive?                                           324

A quashing order                                                      324

A prohibiting order                                                   326

A mandatory order                                                     327

Declaration                                                           328

Injunctions                                                           329

Interim declaration                                                   330

Substitutionary remedy                                                          330

Other public law remedies                                                       331

FURTHER READING                                                                 331

SELF-TEST QUESTIONS                                                             332

**PART V    Alternative Means of Redress                                        333**

**15    Tribunals, inquiries, and the ombudsmen remedy                          335**

The distinction between tribunals and inquiries                                 335

Tribunals                                                                       336

The statutory framework                                                         339

Reforming the tribunal system                                                   339

The Administrative Justice and Tribunals Council (AJTC)                         343

Inquiries                                                                       345

The origins of ombudsmen                                                        347

The Parliamentary Commissioner                                                  347

Ombudsmen of the devolved institutions                                          359

The Health Service Commissioner                                                 360

The Local Government Commissioners                                              362

Ombudsmen and the courts                                                        365

Reform                                                                          367

European Ombudsman                                                              368

FURTHER READING                                                                 371

SELF-TEST QUESTIONS                                                             372

**PART VI    Civil Liberties                                                    375**

**16    Freedoms and liberties in the UK                                        377**

Human rights and civil liberties distinguished                                  377

Political and social or economic rights                                         378

The traditional means of protecting civil liberties in the UK                   379

European Convention on Human Rights                                             380

Incorporation of the Convention into English law: the judges' view             395

Judicial deference/discretionary area of judgment                               409

A Bill of Rights?                                                               413

FURTHER READING 415

SELF-TEST QUESTIONS 417

**17** | Freedom of expression 419

Control of obscenity and indecency 419

Publication of obscene matter 420

Test of obscenity 421

Defences 425

Powers of search and seizure 426

A new criminal offence? 427

Further statutory provision for obscenity and indecency 428

The common law 430

Contempt of court 432

FURTHER READING 445

SELF-TEST QUESTIONS 446

**18** | Police powers 448

Police discretion 448

The Police and Criminal Evidence Act 1984 (PACE) 450

Codes of Practice 450

Police powers of stop and search 451

Arrest 457

Powers to enter property 466

Assault on or wilful obstruction of a police officer 478

FURTHER READING 482

SELF-TEST QUESTIONS 482

**19** | Freedom of assembly and public order 484

Rights and freedoms 484

Breach of the peace 485

Public Order Act 1986 497

Racially or religiously aggravated public order offences 507

Processions and assemblies 510

Demonstrations in the vicinity of Parliament 518

FURTHER READING 519

SELF-TEST QUESTIONS 520

Index 523

# Table of statutes

*Paragraph references in **bold** indicate that the text is reproduced in full*

Acquisition of Land (Assessment of
  Compensation) Act 1919, s 2 . . . 5.22
Act of Union 1706 . . . 5.44, 8.6, 8.9
  art I . . . 5.42, 5.43
  art XVIII . . . 5.43
Adoption Act 1976, s 51 . . . 11.50, 11.51
Administration of Justice (Miscellaneous
  Provisions) Act 1933 . . . 14.1
Administration of Justice (Miscellaneous
  Provisions) Act 1938 . . . 14.1
Ancient Monuments and Archaeological
  Areas Act 1979 . . . 12.61
Animal Heath Act 1981, s 73(a) . . . 11.48
Animal Health (Amendment)
  Act 1998 . . . 8.43
Anti-social Behaviour Act 2003,
  s 57 . . . 19.77
Anti-terrorism, Crime and Security
  Act 2001 . . . 16.118
  s 23 . . . 3.35, 13.35
Agricultural Marketing Act 1958,
  s 19(3)(b) . . . 12.4
Army Act 1955, s 94(2) . . . 17.69

Betting, Gaming and Lotteries
  Act 1963 . . . 18.3
Bill of Rights 1689 . . . 5.7, 5.8, 5.58, 13.17
  art 1 . . . 3.21, 4.3
  art 2 . . . 3.21, 4.3
  art 4 . . . 4.3
  art 9 . . . 6.82, 6.85, 6.90, 6.91, 6.93, 15.106
Bribery Amendment Act 1958 . . . 5.28
Building Societies (Distributions) Act
  1997 . . . 9.43

Canada Act 1982 . . . 5.16
Clean Air Act 1993, s 31 . . . 9.55
Colonial Laws Validity Act 1865 . . . 4.36
  s 5 . . . 5.28
Consolidation of Enactments (Procedure) Act
  1949, s 1(1) . . . 9.48

Constitution Act 1902 . . . 5.28
Constitutional Reform Act 2005 . . . 2.33, 12.3
  s 1 . . . 3.41, 3.43
  s 2(1) . . . 2.10
  s 2(2) . . . 2.10
  s 2(2)(e) . . . 2.10
  s 3 . . . 2.13, 2.17
  s 3(1) . . . 2.12
  s 3(2) . . . 2.13
  s 3(5) . . . 2.14
  s 3(6) . . . 2.15, 2.16
  s 3(7) . . . 2.13
  s 4 . . . 2.13
  s 6 . . . 2.11
  s 11 . . . 2.11
  s 17 . . . 2.11
  s 18 . . . 2.11
  s 24 . . . 2.36
  s 26 . . . 2.36
  s 33 . . . 2.20
  s 61 . . . 2.19
  Sch 6 . . . 2.11
  Sch 12 . . . 2.11
Constitutional Reform and Governance
  Act 2010 . . . 4.43
Consumer Protection Act 1987, s 11 . . . 9.57
Contempt of Court Act 1981 . . . 17.38, 17.49
  s 1 . . . **17.50**
  s 2 . . . 17.53
  s 2(2) . . . **17.50, 17.52**, 17.63
  s 3 . . . 17.54
  s 4 . . . 17.78
  s 4(1) . . . 17.55
  s 4(2) . . . 17.55, **17.58**, 17.60–17.67
  s 5 . . . 17.56, 17.78
  s 6 . . . **17.76**
  s 11 . . . **17.59**, 17.68–17.74
  Sch 1 . . . 17.53
Counter-terrorism Act 2005 . . . 17.47
Courts and Legal Services Act
  1990 . . . 15.44

Crown Proceedings Act 1947, s 11 . . . 4.19
Crime and Disorder Act 1998 . . . 12.41
   s 28 . . . 19.70
   s 28(5) . . . 19.74
   s 31(1) . . . 19.67
Crime (Sentences) Act 1997
   s 2 . . . 5.64–5.66
   s 29 . . . 5.73, 5.81
Criminal Injuries and Compensation Act
   1995, s 5(1) . . . 15.23
Criminal Justice Act 1987, 2(13) . . . 17.65
Criminal Justice Act 1988 . . . 4.21
   s 139 . . . 18.19
   s 159(1)(a) . . . 17.64
   s 160 . . . 17.30
   s 171 . . . 4.20
Criminal Justice Act 2003 . . . 13.83
Criminal Justice (Scotland) Act 1980,
   s 78(1) . . . 5.45
Criminal Justice and Immigration Act 2008,
   s 63 . . . 17.23, 17.24
Criminal Justice and Police Act 2001 . . . 18.94
   s 50 . . . 18.95
   s 51 . . . 18.95
   s 54 . . . 18.95
   s 55 . . . 18.95
Criminal Justice and Public Order Act 1994
   s 60 . . . 18.10, 18.12
   s 60(8A) . . . 18.11
Criminal Law Act 1977, s 5(3) . . . 17.37
Criminal Procedure and Investigations Act
   1996, s 29 . . . 5.68
Criminal Proceedings etc (Reform)
   (Scotland) Act 2007 . . . 8.51
Crown Proceedings Act 1947, s 21 . . . 13.87

Data Protection Act 1998 . . . 10.34
   s 28(4) . . . 15.23
   s 28(6) . . . 15.23
Declaratory Act 1720 . . . 8.9
Defamation Act 1996, s 13 . . . 6.87
Defence of the Realm Consolidation Act
   1914 . . . 11.52
Deregulation and Contracting Out Act 1994,
   s 1 . . . 9.61
Divorce (Religious Marriages) Act 2002 . . .
   9.43

Education (No 2) Act 1986, s 38 . . . 13.19
Emergency Powers Act 1920, s 2 . . . 9.58

Equal Pay Act 1970 . . . 10.54, 10.57
European Communities Act 1972 . . . 5.47,
   5.58, 5.60, 8.49, 8.64
   s 2(1) . . . 5.43, 10.10, 10.50
   s 2(2) . . . 9.55, 9.57, 9.58, 10.4
   s 2(4) . . . 5.25, 5.48, 5.49, 5.51, 5.57, 10.50,
   10.64
   Sch 2, para 1A . . . 9.57
European Parliamentary Elections Act
   1999 . . . 5.35
European Parliamentary Elections Act
   2002 . . . 7.31
European Union Act 2011
   s 6(1) . . . **7.7**
   s 6(5)(e) . . . **7.7**
   s 18 . . . **5.52**
European Union (Amendment) Act
   2008 . . . 7.11
Explosive Substances Act 1883, s 4 . . . 19.46
Extradition Act 2003
   s 161 . . . 18.86
   s 162 . . . 18.86
   s 164 . . . 18.86

Firearms Act 1968–97 . . . 8.56
Fixed-term Parliaments Act 2011 . . . 6.71
   s 3 . . . 4.23
   s 3(2) . . . 4.23
Foreign Compensation Act 1950,
   s 4(4) . . . 12.43, 12.44
Freedom of Information Act 2000,
   s 60(1)(4) . . . 15.23

Government of Ireland Act 1914 . . . 5.35
Government of Ireland Act 1920 . . . 8.12
   s 4 . . . 8.11
Government of Wales Act 1998 . . . 8.28, 8.35
   s 111 . . . 15.85
   Sch 9 . . . 15.85
Government of Wales Act 2006 . . . 5.58, 8.38
   Pt 3 . . . 8.30
   Pt 4 . . . 8.32
   s 1 . . . 8.20
   s 2 . . . 8.21
   ss 6–9 . . . 8.22
   s 7 . . . 8.23
   s 45 . . . 8.20, 8.24
   s 47 . . . 8.25
   s 48 . . . 8.25
   s 49 . . . 8.26

s 50 . . . 8.27
s 51 . . . 8.27
s 93 . . . 8.30
s 95 . . . 8.30, 9.58
s 107 . . . 8.32
s 107(5) . . . 5.53
Sch 5 . . . 8.30
Sch 7 . . . 8.34, 8.39

Health Service Commissioners Act 1993 . . .
   9.47, 15.87
s 18ZA . . . 15.109
Health Service Commissioners (Amendment)
   Act 2000 . . . 15.88
Health and Social Care Act 2008,
   s 145 . . . 16.95
Highways Act 1959 . . . 12.46
House of Commons Disqualification Act
   1975 . . . 6.18
s 2 . . . 2.7
Sch 1, Pt II . . . 6.19
Sch 1, Pt III . . . 6.19
House of Commons (Removal of
   Clergy Disqualification) Act 2001,
   s 1(2) . . . 6.20
House of Lords Act 1999 . . . 6.24, 6.65
Household Waste Recycling Act 2003,
   s 5(2) . . . 9.50
Housing Act 1925, s 46 . . . 5.22
Housing Act 1957 . . . 12.33
Housing Act 1985, s 32 . . . 13.17
Housing Act 1988, s 21(4) . . . 16.84
Housing (Homeless Persons) Act
   1977 . . . 12.16
Human Rights Act 1998 . . . 2.33, 2.37, 5.55,
   5.56, 5.58, 5.60, 8.49, 8.64, 11.43, 16.74–124
s 1 . . . 16.75
s 2 . . . 16.77, 16.114
s 2(1) . . . 16.78
s 3 . . . 5.64–5.80, 6.9, 10.62, 11.56, 15.32
s 3(1) . . . 5.63, 5.71, 5.73, 5.82, 5.88
s 4 . . . 3.35, 5.77, 5.82, 5.84
s 6 . . . 12.31, 15.32, 16.83, 16.86, 16.96
s 6(1) . . . 4.35, 5.76, **16.82**, 16.98, 16.101
s 6(3)(a) . . . 16.82
s 6(3)(b) . . . 16.85–16.94
s 6(5) . . . 16.82
s 6(6) . . . 6.9
s 7 . . . 16.104
s 7(1)(b) . . . 5.86

s 7(3) . . . 16.105
s 7(11) . . . 16.112
s 8 . . . 16.112
s 8(1) . . . 16.76
s 8(2) . . . 16.113
s 8(3) . . . **16.113**
s 9(3) . . . 16.116
s 10 . . . 6.50, 9.69, 16.90
s 10(1)(a) . . . 16.117
s 11 . . . 16.106
s 12 . . . 16.80
s 12(4) . . . 16.80
s 13 . . . 16.80, 16.81
s 14 . . . 16.118
s 15 . . . 16.120
s 18 . . . 9.51
s 19 . . . 5.77–5.80, 6.6
s 20 . . . 9.51
s 21(1)(f)(i) . . . 4.35
s 21(5) . . . 9.51
s 22(2) . . . **9.51**
s 22(3) . . . **9.51**
s 22(4) . . . 5.86–5.88
Sch 2 . . . 6.50, 16.90, 16.117
Hunting Act 2004 . . . 5.35

Immigration Act 1971, s 33(5) . . . 4.19
Immigration and Asylum Act 1999 . . . 5.77
Indecent Displays (Control) Act 1981,
   s 1 . . . 17.32
Industrial Training Act 1964, s 1(4) . . . 13.39
Inquiries Act 2005 . . . 4.7
s 1(1)(a) . . . 15.38
s 1(1)(b) . . . 15.38
s 10(5) . . . 15.40
Ireland Act 1949, s 2 . . . 8.11
Irish Church Disestablishment Act
   1869 . . . 5.9

Judicial Pensions and Retirement Act
   1993 . . . 2.20
Justice (Northern Ireland) Act 2002,
   s 1 . . . 2.13

Laws in Wales Act 1536 . . . 8.2
Legislative and Regulatory Reform Act
   2006 . . . 9.61
s 1(1) . . . 9.62
s 1(2) . . . 9.62
s 3 . . . 9.63, 9.64

s 3(2) . . . **9.63**
s 5 . . . 9.66
ss 12–18 . . . 9.65
Life Peerages Act 1958 . . . 6.60, 6.62
Local Government Act 1972,
  s 120(1)(b) . . . 13.7
Local Government Act 1974 . . . 13.15, 15.104,
  15.105
  Pt III . . . 15.94
  s 26(4) . . . 15.96
  s 26(5)(a) . . . 15.96
  s 26(5)(b) . . . 15.96
  s 26(6)(a) . . . 15.97
  s 26(6)(b) . . . 15.97
  s 26(7) . . . 15.97
  s 26(8) . . . 15.97
  s 33ZA . . . 15.109
  Sch 5 . . . 15.98, 15.99
Local Government Act 1988 . . . 15.95
Local Government Finance Act 1982,
  s 20(1) . . . 13.8
Local Government and Housing Act 1989,
  s 33 . . . 12.31

Magistrates' Courts Act 1980,
  s 115 . . . 19.25
Marriage Act 1949 . . . 9.61
  s 1 . . . 16.117
  Sch 1 . . . 16.117
Matrimonial Causes Act 1973,
  s 11(c) . . . 5.81
Medical Act 1983, s 37(1)(a) . . . 13.74
Mental Health Act 1983, s 73 . . . 5.83
Merchant Shipping Act 1988 . . . 86, 10.43
Military Lands Act 1892 . . . 12.36
Misuse of Drugs Act 1971 . . . 8.49, 18.75
  s 5 . . . 5.87
  s 23(2) . . . 18.9
Municipal Corporations Act 1882,
  s 191(4) . . . 13.46

National Assistance Act 1948
  s 21 . . . 16.85
  s 26 . . . 16.85
National Health Service Act 2006 . . . 9.47
National Health Service Reorganisation Act
  1973 . . . 15.86
National Health Service (Scotland) Act
  1972 . . . 15.86
New Towns Act 1946 . . . 13.45

Northern Ireland Act 1974 . . . 8.12
Northern Ireland Act 1998 . . . 8.59
  s 1 . . . 8.60
  s 5(6) . . . 5.53, 8.62
  s 6 . . . 8.62
  s 7 . . . 8.64
  s 9 . . . 8.63
  s 16 . . . 8.66
  s 17 . . . 8.66
  s 18(5) . . . 8.66
  s 19 . . . 8.66
  s 20 . . . 8.66
  s 24 . . . 8.62
  s 30 . . . 8.69
  s 83 . . . 8.65
  Sch 2 . . . 8.62
  Sch 3 . . . 8.63
  Sch 4 . . . 8.67, 8.68
Northern Ireland Constitution Act
  1973 . . . 8.12, 11.36

Obscene Publications Act 1959 . . . 17.1
  s 1(1) . . . **17.5**, 17.14
  s 1(2) . . . **17.4**
  s 1(3) . . . **17.3**
  s 2 . . . **17.2**, 17.17, 17.22
  s 2(1) . . . **17.2**
  s 2(4) . . . **17.33**
  s 3 . . . 17.21
  s 4 . . . 17.18, 17.19, 17.37
Obscene Publications Act
  1964 . . . 17.1
  s 1(2) . . . 17.2
  s 1(5) . . . **17.2**

Parliament Act 1911 . . . 4.11, 5.20, 5.30–5.40,
  6.64, 9.21, 11.10
  s 2(1) . . . 5.35, 5.37, 5.38
Parliament Act 1949 . . . 4.11, 5.30–5.40, 9.21,
  11.10
Parliamentary Commissioner Act
  1967 . . . 15.94
  s 5 . . . 15.55, 15.60
  s 5(1) . . . 15.103
  s 6(3) . . . 15.70
  s 7(1) . . . 15.73
  s 9 . . . 15.74
  s 10 . . . 15.75
  s 10(3) . . . 15.76
  s 10(4) . . . 15.84

s 11ZAA . . . 15.109
Sch 2 . . . 15.53
Sch 3 . . . 15.55, 15.57, 15.86
Parliamentary Constituencies Act 1986,
    Sch 2 . . . 6.17
Parliamentary Standards Act 2009 . . . 6.91, 9.3
    s 1 . . . 6.92
Parliamentary Voting System and
    Constituencies Act 2011
    s 1(7) . . . **6.15**
    s 11 . . . 6.17
Peerage Act 1963 . . . 6.22, 6.23, 11.11
Pharmacy Act 1954 . . . 4.22
Police Act 1964
    s 41 . . . 4.24
    s 51 . . . 18.96
    s 51(3) . . . 19.19
Police Act 1996
    s 89 . . . 18.96, 18.102
    s 89(1) . . . 18.98, 18.101, 18.103, 18.105
    s 89(2) . . . 16.11, 18.99–18.101, 18.105
Police (Appeals) Act 1927 . . . 13.46
Police and Criminal Evidence Act
    1984 . . . 18.1
    s 1 . . . 18.19
    s 2 . . . 18.11
    s 2(1) . . . 18.21
    s 2(9)(a) . . . 18.23
    s 3(1) . . . 18.24
    s 8 . . . 18.66, 18.67
    s 8(1)(d) . . . 18.69
    s 8(1)(e) . . . 18.70
    s 9(2) . . . 18.72
    s 10 . . . 18.70
    s 15 . . . 18.68
    s 15(2) . . . 18.66
    s 15(3) . . . 18.66
    s 16 . . . 18.68
    s 16(3B) . . . 18.68
    s 17 . . . 18.76, 18.77
    s 17(1) . . . 18.79
    s 17(1)(d) . . . 18.78
    s 17(1)(e) . . . 18.79–18.82
    s 17(6) . . . 18.65, 18.86
    s 18 . . . 18.83, 18.86
    s 18(2) . . . 18.90
    s 18(5) . . . 18.85
    s 19 . . . 18.89, 18.92
    s 19(2) . . . 18.90, 18.91
    s 19(3) . . . 18.90, 18.91

s 19(4) . . . 18.91
s 23 . . . 18.90
s 24 . . . 18.31–18.40, 18.58
s 24(5) . . . 18.35, 18.36, 18.51
s 24(5)(e) . . . 18.35, 18.36
s 24(6) . . . 18.36
s 24A . . . 18.34, 18.49
s 25 . . . 18.32
s 28 . . . 18.52, 18.53, 18.56, 18.57
s 28(3) . . . 18.55, 18.57
s 32(2)(b) . . . 18.87
s 50 . . . 18.94
s 60 . . . 18.7
s 66 . . . 18.7
s 67(8) . . . 18.8
s 67(10) . . . 18.8
s 117 . . . 18.58
Sch 1 . . . 18.71
Codes A–H . . . 18.7
Code A . . . 18.20
Code B . . . 18.93
Police Reform Act 2002, s 46 . . . 18.96
Police Reform and Social Responsibility
    Act 2011 . . . 19.103
    s 141 . . . 19.99
    ss 141–149 . . . 19.100
    s 143 . . . 19.102
Post Office Act 1953 . . . 17.27
    s 11(1)(b) . . . 17.26
Postal Services Act 2000
    s 85(3) . . . 17.28
    s 85(3)(a) . . . 17.25
    s 85(3)(b) . . . 17.25
    s 85(4) . . . 17.25, 17.28
Powers of Criminal Courts (Sentencing)
    Act 2000
    s 109 . . . 5.64
Prevention of Crime Act 1953,
    s 1 . . . 19.46
Prevention of Terrorism Act 2005 . . . 3.37,
    17.47
    s 16(2)(a) . . . 16.118
Prevention of Terrorism (Temporary
    Provisions) Act 1984, s 12(1) . . . 18.41
Prison Act 1952, s 47(1) . . . 11.53, 13.32
Private Hire Vehicles (Carriage Guide Dogs
    etc) Act 2002 . . . 9.43
Protection of Children Act 1978,
    s 1 . . . 17.29
Public Order Act 1936, s 1 . . . 19.36

Public Order Act 1986 . . . 19.35
  s 1 . . . 19.39
  s 3 . . . 19.44, 19.45
  s 3(3) . . . 19.44
  s 3(4) . . . 19.75
  s 4 . . . 19.37, 19.41, 19.47–19.53, 19.58–19.69
  s 4(2) . . . 19.49
  s 4A . . . 19.37, 19.47, 19.53, 19.62–19.69
  s 5 . . . 19.37, 19.47, 19.53–19.69
  s 5(3) . . . 19.60
  s 6(3) . . . 19.48
  s 7(3) . . . 19.41
  s 8 . . . 19.66
  s 9 . . . 19.37
  s 11 . . . 19.78
  s 11(2) . . . 19.79
  s 11(3) . . . 19.80
  s 11(7)–(9) . . . 19.81
  s 12 . . . 19.82, 19.85, 19.90, 19.93
  s 12(1) . . . 19.83
  s 13 . . . 19.84
  s 13(7)–(9) . . . 19.88
  s 14 . . . 19.90, 19.92, 19.93
  s 14A . . . 19.94
  s 14A(1) . . . 19.95
  s 14B . . . 19.94
  s 14B(1)–(3) . . . 19.95
  s 14C . . . 19.94
  s 16 . . . 19.75, 19.77
Public Order (Amendment) Act 1996 . . . 9.43
Public Services Ombudsman (Wales) Act 2005 . . . 15.85

Race Relations Act 1976 . . . 13,11
Radioactive Substances Act 1960,
  s 6(1) . . . 12.61
Referendums (Scotland and Wales) Act 1997 . . . 8.19
Registered Establishments (Scotland) Act 1998 . . . 8.7
Regulatory Reform Act 2001 . . . 9.61, 15.108
Rent Act 1977 . . . 5.74
Repatriation of Prisoners Act 1984 . . . 4.33
Representation of the People Act 1983
  s 1 . . . 6.2
  s 1(2)(a) . . . 6.4
  s 3(1) . . . 6.6
  s 4 . . . 6.3

Representation of the People Act 2000 . . . 6.3
  s 1 . . . 6.2
Road Traffic Act 1988 . . . 8.51
Royal Assent Act 1967, s 1(2) . . . 9.24

Scotland Act 1978 . . . 5.45, 5.58, 8.50
  s 28(7) . . . 5.53
Scotland Act 1998 . . . 8.8, 8.41, 8.45, 8.50, 8.51, 11.37, 13.87
  s 1 . . . 8.42
  s 10(2) . . . **8.52**
  s 28(7) . . . 8.47
  s 29(2) . . . 8.47
  s 31 . . . 8.58
  s 31(1) . . . 8.52
  s 37 . . . **8.53**
  Sch 5 . . . 8.48
  Sch 5, Pt II . . . 8.49
Scottish Enterprise Act 1999 . . . 8.7
Scottish Parliament (Constituencies) Act 2004 . . . 8.43
  Sch 4 . . . 8.49
Senior Courts Act 1981
  s 11(3) . . . 2.20
  s 11(8) . . . 2.20
  s 11(9) . . . 2.20
  s 30 . . . 14.7
  s 31 . . . 12.16, 12.36, 12.72, 14.26
  s 31(3) . . . 12.60
  s 31(4) . . . 14.2
  s 31(5)(b) . . . 14.29, 14.30
  s 31(6) . . . 12.70, 12.73, 14.14
  s 31(7) . . . 12.72
  s 31A . . . 15.25
Serious Organised Crime and Police Act 2005 . . . 19.15
  s 110(2) . . . 18.32
  ss 132–138 . . . 19.97, 19.99
Sex Discrimination Act 1975 . . . 10.24, 10.65
  s 6(4) . . . 10.53
Sexual Offences (Amendment) Act 2000 . . . 5.35
South Africa Act 1909 . . . 5.35
  s 35(1) . . . 5.28
  s 152 . . . 5.28
Southern Rhodesia Act 1965 . . . 5.10
Statute of Westminster 1931
  s 4 . . . **11.29**
Statutory Instruments Act 1946, s 1 . . . 9.70

Taxes Management Act 1970, s 20C . . . 3.31,
3.32
Telecommunications Act 1984 . . . 12.16
Terrorism Act 2000 . . . 18.26
s 41 . . . 18.46
s 44 . . . 18.12, 18.15
ss 44–47 . . . 18.16
s 45 . . . 18.12, 18.14
ss 47A–47C . . . 18.16
Test Act 1673 . . . 4.2
Theatres Act 1968, s 2 . . . 17.25
Theft Act 1968 . . . 9.45
s 17 . . . 6.94
Town and Country Planning Act
1990 . . . 12.40
s 70(2) . . . 13.9
s 78 . . . 15.35
Sch 8, Pt I . . . 15.35
Town Police Clauses Act 1847, s 37 . . .
13.50
Transport Act 1962, s 67(1)(c) . . . 12.38
Transport (London) Act 1969, s 1 . . . 13.12
Tribunals, Courts and Enforcement Act
2007 . . . 15.15, 15.18,
s 2(3)(a)–(d) . . . 15.22
s 3 . . . 15.19
s 4(1) . . . 15.21
s 5(1) . . . 15.21
s 7 . . . 15.20
s 9 . . . 15.23
s 10 . . . 15.23
s 13(6) . . . 15.26
ss 15–21 . . . 15.24
s 17(1) . . . 15.24
s 17(2) . . . 15.24
s 18 . . . 15.25
s 19 . . . 15.25
s 22 . . . 15.29
s 43 . . . 15.30

s 141 . . . 14.29
Sch 2 . . . 15.22
Sch 4 . . . 15.22
Sch 4, para 4 . . . 15.20
Sch 5 . . . 15.29
Sch 7 . . . 15.30
Tribunals and Inquiries Act 1992 . . . 15.15,
15.31
s 9 . . . 15.36
s 10 . . . 13.42, 15.27
s 11 . . . 15.28
Sch 1 . . . 15.28
Tribunals of Inquiry (Evidence) Act
1921 . . . 15.38
Triennial Act 1694 . . . 6.34

Union with Scotland Act 1706 . . . 8.5
art 4 . . . 8.49
art 6 . . . 8.49
Union with England Act 1707 . . . 8.5,
8.49
Union with Ireland Act 1800
s 1 . . . 8.9

Wales Act 1978 . . . 8.18, 8.19
War Crimes Act 1991 . . . 3.1, 11.55
War Damage Act 1965 . . . 4.26, 5.35, 11.41
s 1 . . . 3.9
Weights and Measures Act 1985,
s 1 . . . 5.57
Welsh Church Disestablishment Act
1915 . . . 5.35
Welsh Language Act 1967 . . . 8.3

Youth Justice and Criminal Evidence Act
1999
s 41 . . . 5.68, 5.69
s 41(3)(a) . . . 5.68
s 41(3)(c) . . . 5.68–5.70

# Table of statutory instruments

*Paragraph references in **bold** indicate that the text is reproduced in full*

British Nationality (General) Regulations
2003 (SI 2003/548) . . . 14.13

Civil Procedure Rules 1998
(SI 1998/3132) . . . 12.50, 14.1
r 3.1(2)(a) . . . 12.75
r 25.1(b) . . . 14.28
r 40.20 . . . 14.22
r 54.2 . . . 14.7
r 54.3 . . . 14.7
r 54.3(2) . . . 14.2
r 54.5(1) . . . 12.70–12.73
r 54.5(2) . . . 12.75
r 54.7 . . . 12.56
r 54.8 . . . 12.56
r 54.9 . . . 12.56
r 54.10 . . . 12.58
r 54.19 . . . 14.30
r 54.19(2) . . . 14.29
r 54.19(3) . . . 14.29, 14.30
PD 54 . . . 12.56
Control of Pesticides Regulations 1986
(SI 1986/1510) . . . 12.40

Equal Pay (Amendment) Regulations 1983
(SI 1983/1794) . . . 10.54

Human Rights Act (Amendment) Order 2001
(SI 2001/1216) . . . 16.48
Human Rights Act (Amendment) Order 2005
(SI 2005/1071) . . . 16.118
Human Rights Act (Designated Derogation)
Order 2001 (SI 2001/3644) . . . 3.35,
16.118

Local Authority Social Services and National
Health Service Complaints (England)
Regulations 2009 (SI 2009/1768) . . .
15.91

Marriage Act 1949 (Remedial) Order 2007
(SI 2007/438) . . . 16.117

Merchant Shipping (Registration of Fishing
Vessels) Regulations 1988
(SI 1988/1926) . . . 5.46

National Assembly for Wales (Legislative
Competence) (Amendment of Schedule
7 to the Government of Wales Act 2006)
Order 2010 (SI 2010/2968) . . . 8.34

Parliamentary Commissioner Order 2009
(SI 2009/1754) . . . 15.54
Parliamentary Constituencies and Assembly
Electoral Regions (Wales) Order 2006 (SI
2006/1041) . . . 8.21
Pollution Prevention and Control (England
and Wales) Regulations 2000
(SI 2000/1973) . . . 12.64

Regulatory Reform (Collaboration etc
between Ombudsman) Order 2007
(SI 2007/1889) . . . 9.61, 15.96, 15.108
Rules of the Supreme Court (SI 1965/1776)
Ord 53 . . . 12.13, 12.15, 12.16, 12.36, 12.56
Ord 53, r 4(1) . . . 12.71, 12.73, 12.75

Scotland Act 1998 (Transitory and
Transitional Provisions)
(Complaints of Maladministration) Order
1999 (SI 1999/1351) . . . 15.85
Scotland Act 1998 (Transitory and Transitional
Provisions) (Members' Interests) Order 1999
(SI 1999/1350), art 6 . . . 5.54

Town and Country Planning (Inquiries
Procedure) (England) Rules 2000
(SI 2000/1624) . . . 15.35
Toys (Safety) Regulations 2011
(SI 2011/1881) . . . 9.71
Preamble . . . **9.57**
Transfer of Undertakings (Protection of
Employment) Regulations 1981
(SI 1981/1794) . . . 10.56

# Table of cases

## Alphabetical

A v Secretary of State for the Home
Department [2005] UKSIAC
1/2002 . . . 3.35, 5.82, 13.35, 13.88

A v United Kingdom (2003) 36 EHRR 51, 13
BHRC 623, ECtHR . . . 6.88, 6.89

Adender v Ellinikos Organisonos Galaktos
[2006] ECR I-6057, [2007] All ER (EC) 82,
[2006] 3 CMLR 867 . . . 10.35

Adorian v Commissioner of Police for the
Metropolis [2010] All ER (D) 272 (Nov),
[2010] EWHC 3861 (QB) . . . 18.58

A-G for New South Wales v Trethowan [1932]
AC 526, 101 LJPC 158, 76 Sol Jo 511, 47
CLR 97, 147 LT 265, 48 TLR 514, 38 ALR
294, 6 ALJ 79, PC . . . 5.28

A-G of Manitoba v A-G of Canada [1981] 1
SCR 753, 11 MAN R (2d) 1, [1981] 6 WWR
1 . . . 11.22

A-G v BBC [1981] AC 303, [1979] 3 All ER 45,
[1979] 3 WLR 312, 78 LGR 137, 123 Sol Jo
405, CA, revsd [1981] AC 303, [1980] 3 All ER
161, [1980] 3 WLR 109, 78 LGR 529, [1981]
RA 27, 124 Sol Jo 444, HL . . . 15.4, 15.5

A-G v BBC [1997] EMLR 76 . . . 17.51, 17.57,
16.63

A-G v De Keyser's Royal Hotel Ltd [1920]
AC 508, 89 LJ Ch 417, [1920] All ER Rep
80, 64 Sol Jo 513, 122 LT 691, 36 TLR 600,
HL . . . 4.17, 4.19, 4.21

A-G v English [1983] 1 AC 116, [1982] 2 All
ER 903, [1982] 3 WLR 278, 75 Cr App Rep
302, [1982] Crim LR 743, 126 Sol Jo 511,
[1982] LS Gaz R 1175, HL . . . 17.56

A-G v Guardian Newspapers Ltd [1987] 3
All ER 316, [1987] 1 WLR 1248, 131 Sol Jo
1122, [1987] LS Gaz R 2689, [1987] NLJ Rep
785, HL . . . 16.12, 16.71

A-G v Hislop [1991] 1 QB 514, [1991] 1 All ER
911, [1991] 2 WLR 219, CA . . . 17.78

A-G v Jonathan Cape Ltd [1976] QB 752,
[1975] 3 All ER 484, [1975] 3 WLR 606, 119
Sol Jo 696 . . . 11.26

A-G v Leveller Magazine Ltd [1979] AC 440,
[1979] 1 All ER 745, [1979] 2 WLR 247, 68
Cr App Rep 342, 143 JP 260, 123 Sol Jo 129,
HL . . . 17.40, 17.42

A-G v News Group Newspapers [1989] QB
110, [1988] 2 All ER 906, [1988] 3 WLR 163,
87 Cr App Rep 323, 132 Sol Jo 934, [1988]
NLJR 55 . . . 17.77

A-G v Sport Newspapers [1992] 1 All ER 503,
[1991] 1 WLR 1194, 135 Sol Jo LB 28 . . . 17.77

A-G's Reference (No 3 of 1977) [1978] 3 All ER
1166, [1978] 1 WLR 1123, 67 Cr App Rep
393, 143 JP 94, 122 Sol Jo 641, CA . . . 17.19

A-G's Reference (No 5 of 1980) (No 5 of 1980)
[1980] 3 All ER 816, [1981] 1 WLR 88, 72 Cr
App 71, [1981] Crim LR 45, 124 Sol Jo 827,
CA . . . 17.4

A-G's Reference (No 3 of 1999) [2009] UKHL
34 . . . 13.41

A-G's Reference (No 3 of 1999), Re [2009]
UKHL 34 . . . 17.68

Agricultural, Horticultural and Forestry
Industry Training Board v Aylesbury
Mushrooms [1972] 1 All ER 280, [1972] 1
WLR 190, 7 ITR 16, 116 Sol Jo 57 . . . 13.39,
13.40

Ahmed v Bradford Magistrates Court [2008]
EWHC 2934 (Admin) . . . 18.104

Al Fayed v Metropolitan Police Comr [2004]
EWCA Civ 1579, CA . . . 18.39

Al Rawi and others v Security Service and
others [2011] UKSC 34, [2011] 3 WLR 388,
[2012] 1 All ER 1 . . . 17.47

Albert v Lavin [1982] AC 546, [1981] 1 All ER
628, [1981] 2 WLR 1070, 72 Cr App Rep
178, 145 JP 184, 125 Sol Jo 114, [1981] CLR
238, CA, [1982] AC 546, [1981] 3 All ER
878, [1981] 3 WLR 955, 74 Cr App 150, 146
JP 78, 125 Sol Jo 860, HL . . . 18.102, 19.16

Algemene Transporten Expeditie
Onderneming Van Gend en Loos NV v
Nederlandse Administratie der Belastingen
(26/62) [1963] ECR 1, [1963] CMLR 105,
ECJ . . . 10.11

Administratie der Belastingen (26/62) [1963]
    ECR 1, [1963] CMLR 105, ECJ . . . 10.11
Al-Khawaja v UK [2009] All ER (D)
    152 . . . 16.79
Allason v Haines [1996] EMLR 143, [1995]
    NLKR 1576 . . . 6.86
Amsterdam Bulb BV v Produktschap voor
    Siergewassen (50/76) [1977] ECR 137,
    [1977] 2 CMLR 218 . . . 10.17
Anisminic v Foreign Compensation
    Commission [1969] 2 AC 147, [1969] 1 All
    ER 208, [1969] 2 WLR 163, 113 Sol Jo 55,
    HL . . . 12.43, 12.47
Arsenal Football Club v Reed [2003] EWCA
    Civ 696, [2003] 3 All ER 865, [2003] 2
    CMLR 800, [2003] RPC 696, 147 Sol Jo LB
    663, [2003] IP & T 880, [2003] All ER (D)
    289 (May) . . . 7.47
Associated Provincial Picture Houses Ltd v
    Wednesbury Corpn [1948] 1 KB 223, [1947]
    2 All ER 680, 45 LGR 635, 112 JP 55, [1948]
    LJR 190, 92 Sol Jo 26, 177 LT 641, 63 TLR
    623, CA . . . 13.1–13.3, 13.19, 13.21, 13.34,
    13.51, 18.2, 18.38
Aston Cantlow and Wilmcote with Billesley
    Parochial Church Council v Wallbank
    [2003] UKHL 37, [2004] 1 AC 546, [2003]
    3 All ER 1213, [2003] 3 WLR 283, [2003]
    33 LS Gaz R 28, [2003] NLJR 1030, 147
    Sol Jo LB 812, [2003] All ER (D) 360
    (Jun) . . . 5.88, 16.82, 16.84, 16.85, 16.88
Atkin v DPP (1989) 89 Cr App Rep 199, 153
    JP 383, [1989] Crim LR 581 . . . 19.48, 19.49
Atkins v DPP [2000] 2 All ER 425, [2000]
    1 WLR 1427, [2000] 2 Cr App Rep 248,
    [2000] 13 LS Gaz R 42, 144 Sol Jo LB 148,
    DC . . . 17.30
Austin v Metropolitan Police Commissioner
    [2004] EWCA Civ 1067, [2003] EWHC 480
    (QB) 22, [2004] Public Law 829 . . . 19.1,
    19.91
Austin v Commissioner of Police for the
    Metropolis [2009] UKHL 5, [2009] 1 AC
    564, [2009] 2 WLR 372, [2009] 3 All ER
    455 . . . 19.18, 19.22


B v DPP [2008] EWHC 1655
    (Admin) . . . 18.22
Backhouse v Lambeth London Borough
    Council (1972) 116 Sol Jo 802 . . . 13.22

Baron Mereworth v Ministry of Justice [2011]
    EHWC 1589 (Ch) . . . 2.27, 6.95
BBC v Johns [1965] Ch 32, [1964] 1 All ER
    923, [1964] 2 WLR 1071, 41 TC 471, 43
    ATC 38, 10 RRC 239, [1964] TR 45, 108 Sol
    Jo 217, [1964] RVR 579, CA . . . 4.19
Beatty v Gillbanks (1882) 9 QBD 308, JP 789,
    51 LJMC 117, 15 Cox CC 138, [1881–5] All
    ER Rep 559, LT 194 . . . 19.7, 19.30, 19.33,
    19.34
Becker v Finanzamt–Münster Innenstadt
    (8/81) [1982] ECR 53, [1982] 1 CMLR 499,
    ECJ . . . 10.23
Bellinger v Bellinger [2003] UKHL 21, [2003]
    2 AC 467, [2003] 2 All ER 593, [2003] 2
    WLR 1174, [2003] 2 FCR 1, [2003] 1 FLR
    1043, 72 BMLR 147, [2003] NLJR 594, 147
    Sol Jo LB 472, [2004] 1 LRC 42, 14 BHRC
    127, [2003] All ER (D) 178 (Apr) . . . 5.81,
    5.84
Bentley v Brudzinski (1982) 75 Cr App 217,
    [1982] Crim LR 825 . . . 18.103
Bessell v Wilson (1853) 17 JP 567, 1 E&B
    489 . . . 18.18
Blackburn v A-G [1971] 2 All ER 1380, [1971]
    1 WLR 1037, 115 Sol Jo 386, CA . . . 4.31,
    4.32, 14.23
Blackburn v Bowering [1994] 3 All ER 380,
    [1994] 1 WLR 1324, [1995] Crim LR 38,
    CA . . . 18.98
Blench v DPP [2004] EWHC 2717
    (Admin) . . . 18.80
Blum v Secretary of State for the Home
    Department [2006] EWHC 3209
    (Admin) . . . 19.97
Boddington v British Transport Police [1999]
    2 AC 143, [1998] 2 All ER 203, [1998] 2
    WLR 639, 162 JP 455, [1998] NLJR 515,
    HL . . . 9.60, 12.38, 12.39
Bonner v DPP [2004] EWHC 2415
    (Admin) . . . 18.22
Bowles v Bank of England [1913] 1 Ch 57, 6
    TC 136, 82 LJ Ch 124, 57 Sol Jo 43, 108 LT
    95, 29 TLR 42 . . . 5.17
Bradlaugh v Clarke (1883) 8 App Cas 354, 47
    JP 405, 52 LJQB 505, 31 WR 677, 48 LT 681,
    HL . . . 6.83
Bradlaugh v Gossett (1884) 12 QBD 271,
    53 LJQB 209, 32 WR 552, 50 LT 620,
    DC . . . 6.83

Brannigan and McBride v United Kingdom (1993) 17 EHRR 539, ECtHR . . . 16.59

Brasserie du Pêcheur SA v Germany (C-46/93 & C-48/93) [1996] QB 404, [1996] 2 WLR 506, [1996] All ER (EC) 301, [1996] ECRI-1029, [1996] 1 CMLR 889, [1996] IRLR 267, ECJ . . . 10.41

Bribery Comr v Ranasinghe [1965] AC 172, [1964] 2 All ER 785, [1964] 2 WLR 1301, 108 Sol Jo 441, PC . . . 5.28, 5.30

British Railways Board v Pickin [1974] AC 765, [1974] 1 All ER 609, [1974] 2 WLR 208, 118 Sol Jo 134, HL . . . 5.19

Britton v DPP [1996] CLY 1486 . . . 17.8, 17.18

Broadwith v Chief Constable of Thames Valley Police [2000] Crim LR 924, DC . . . 19.92

Bromley London Borough Council v Greater London Council [1983] 1 AC 768, [1982] 1 All ER 129, [1982] 2 WLR 62, 80 LGR 1, [1982] RA 47, 126 Sol Jo 16, HL . . . 13.12

Brown v Stott [2003] 1 AC 681 . . . 16.40

Brutus v Cozens [1973] AC 854, [1972] 2 All ER 1297, [1972] 3 WLR 521, 56 Cr App Rep 799, 136 JP 636, 116 Sol Jo 647, HL . . . 17.28, 19.53

Bryan v United Kingdom (1995) 21 EHRR 342, [1996] 1 PLR 47, [1996] 2 EGLR 123, [1996] 28 EG 137, [1996] JPL 386, ECtHR . . . 5.85

Buchanan v Jennings (2005) UKPC 36, [2005] 2 All ER 273 . . . 6.81

Buckley v Chief Officer of the Thames Valley Police [2009] EWCA Civ 356 . . . 18.42, 18.47

Bugg v DPP [1993] QB 473, [1993] 2 All ER 815, [1993] 2 WLR 628, [1993] Crim LR 374 . . . 12.36–12.38

Burmah Oil v Lord Advocate [1965] AC 75, [1964] 2 All ER 348, [1964] 2 WLR 1231, 109 Sol Jo 401, 1964 SC (HL) 117 . . . 2.12, 4.25, 4.26, 11.41

Byrne v The Motor Insurance Bureau [2007] EWHC 1268, QB . . . 10.59

C v DPP [2003] All ER (D) 37 (Nov), DC . . . 18.104

Campbell v MGN Ltd [2005] UKHL 61, [2004] UKHL 22, HL . . . 16.103

Cannock Chase District Council v Kelly [1978] 1 All ER 152, [1978] 1 WLR 1, 76

LGR 67, 36 P & CR 219, 142 JP 113, 121 Sol Jo 593, CA . . . 13.19

Canon Selwyn, ex p (1872) 36 JP 54 . . . 5.9

Carltona Ltd v Works Comrs [1943] 2 All ER 560, CA . . . 11.27

Case of Proclamations (1611) 12 Coke's Reports, 74 . . . 4.2

Castle and others v Commissioner of Police for the Metropolis [2011] EWHC 2317 (Admin), (2011) 161 NLJ 1252 . . . 19.24

Castorina v Chief Constable of Surrey (1988) 160 LG Rev 241, [1988] NLJR 180, CA . . . 18.36

Caswell v Dairy Produce Quota Tribunal for England and Wales [1990] 2 AC 738, [1990] 2 All ER 434, [1990] 2 WLR 1320, [1990] 25 LS Gaz R 36, [1990] NLJR 742, HL . . . 12.73

Central Independent Television plc, Re [1991] 1 All ER 347, [1991] 1 WLR 4, 92 Cr App Rep 154, 134 Sol Jo 1369, [1990] NLJR 1641, CA . . . 17.67

Chambers and Edwards v DPP [1995] Crim LR 896 . . . 19.58, 19.59

Chapman v United Kingdom (2001) 33 EHRR 399, 10 BHRC 48, ECtHR . . . 5.85

Chester v Bateson [1920] 1 KB 829, 18 LGR 212, 84 JP 65, 89 LJKB 387, 26 Cox CC 591, 122 LT 684, 36 TLR 225 . . . 11.52

Chief Constable of Cleveland Constabulary v McGrogan [2002] EWCA Civ 86, [2002] 1 FLR 707 . . . 19.17

Chief Constable of Thames Valley Police v Hepburn [2002] EWCA Civ 1841 . . . 18.75

Christie v Leachinsky [1947] AC 573, [1947] 1 All ER 567, 45 LGR 201, 111 JP 224, [1947] LJR 757, 176 LT 443, 63 TLR 231, HL . . . 18.52

Clark v University of Lincolnshire and Humberside [2000] 3 All ER 752, [2000] 1 WLR 1988, [2000] ELR 345, [2000] NLJR 616, 144 Sol Jo LB 220, [2000] Ed CR 553, CA . . . 12.21–12.23

Cocks v Thanet District Council [1983] 2 AC 286, [1982] 3 All ER 1135, [1982] 3 WLR 1121, 81 LGR 81, 6 HLR 15, 126 Sol Jo 820, [1984] RVR31, HL . . . 12.16

Collins v Wilcock [1984] 3 All ER 374, [1984] 1 WLR 1172, 79 Cr App Rep 229, 148 JP 692, [1984] Crim LR 481, 128 Sol Jo 660, [1984] LS Gaz R 2140 . . . 18.101

Confédération Nationale des Producteurs de Fruits et Legumes v EEC Council (16–17/62) [1962] ECR 471, [1963] CMLR 160, ECJ . . . 10.7

Congreve v Home Office [1976] QB 629, [1976] 1 All ER 697, [1976] 2 WLR 291, 119 Sol Jo 847, CA . . . 13.17

Cooper v HM Attorney General [2008] EWHC 2285 (QB), [2008] WLR (D) 303 . . . 10.47

Cooper v Wandsworth Board of Works (1863) 14 CBNS 180, 32 LJCP 185, 9 Jur NS 1155, 2 New Rep 31, 11 WR 646, 143 ER 414, 8 LT 278, [1861–73] All Rep Ext 1554 . . . 13.45

Council of Civil Service Unions v Minister for the Civil Service [1985] AC 374, [1984] 3 All ER 935, [1984] 3 WLR 1174, [1985] ICR 14, 128 Sol Jo 837, [1985] LS Gaz R 437, [1985] LRC (Const) 948 . . . 4.27, 4.43, 13.1, 13.4, 13.6, 13.21, 13.27, 13.38, 13.50

Covent Garden Community Association Ltd v Greater London Council [1981] JPL 183 . . . 14.8

Cowan v Metropolitan Police Comr [2000] 1 All ER 504, sub nom Cowan v Condon [2000] 1 WLR 254, CA . . . 18.86, 18.90

Cumming v Chief Constable of Northumbria Police [2003] EWCA Civ 1844, [2004] 04 LS Gaz R 31, [2003] All ER (D) 305 (Dec) . . . 18.44

Cyprus v Turkey (2001) 11 BHRC 45, ECtHR . . . 16.52

D v DPP [2010] EWHC 3400 (Admin), [2011] 1 WLR 882 . . . 18.96

Dallison v Caffrey [1965] 1 QB 348 . . . 18.51

Darbo v DPP [1992] Crim LR 56, [1992] COD 65 . . . 17.21

Darnel's Case; Case of the Five Knights (1627) 3 State Tr 1 . . . 4.2

Davidson v Scottish Ministers (No 2) 2005 SC (HL) 7, [2004] UKHL 34, [2004] HRLR 34 . . . 13.76, 13.83, 13.87

Davis v Lisle [1936] 2 KB 434, [1936] 2 All ER 213, 34 LGR 253, 100 JP 280, 105 LJKB 593, 30 Cox CC 412, 80 Sol Jo 409, 155 LT 23, 52 TLR 475, DC . . . 18.63, 18.64

Day v Savadge (1614) Hob 85 . . . 5.5

de Freitas v Permanent Secretary of Ministry of Agriculture [1999] 1 AC 69, [1998] 3 WLR 675, 142 Sol Jo LB 219, PC . . . 13.34

Defrenne v Sabena (43/75) [1981] 1 All ER 122n, [1976] ECR 455, [1976] 2 CMLR 98, [1976] ICR 547, ECJ . . . 10.15, 10.24, 10.51

Dhesi v Chief Constable of West Midlands (2000) *The Times*, 9 May, CA . . . 18.55

Diennet v France (1995) 21 EHRR 554 . . . 17.48

Dillon v O'Brien (1887) 16 Cox CC 245, 20 LR Ir 300 . . . 18.86

Doughty v Rolls-Royce plc [1992] 1 CMLR 1045, [1992] IRLR 126, [1992] ICR 538, CA . . . 10.30

Douglas v Hello! Ltd [2001] QB 967, [2001] 2 All ER 289, [2001] 2 WLR 992, [2001] 1 FLR 982, [2001] EMLR 199, [2000] All ER (D) 2435, CA . . . 16.80, 16.103

DPP of Jamaica v Mollison [2003] UKPC 6, [2003] 2 AC 411, [2003] 2 WLR 1160, [2003] 11 LS Gaz R 32, [2003] 2 LRC 756, [2003] All ER (D) 206 (Jan) . . . 2.24

DPP v A and B C Chewing Gum Ltd [1968] 1 QB 159, [1967] 2 All ER 504, [1967] 3 WLR 493, 131 JP 373, 111 Sol Jo 331 . . . 17.7

DPP v Avery [2001] EWHC Admin 748 [2002] 1 Cr App Rep 409, 165 JP 789, [2002] Crim LR 142 . . . 18.11

DPP v Baillie [1995] Crim LR 426 . . . 19.90

DPP v Clarke (1991) 94 Cr App Rep 359, 156 JP 267, 135 Sol Jo LB 135 . . . 19.60

DPP v Haw (2007) EWHC 1931 (Admin) . . . 19.98

DPP v Hawkins [1988] 3 All ER 673, [1988] 1 WLR 1166, 88 Cr App Rep 166, 152 JP 518, [1988] Crim LR 741, 132 Sol Jo 1460, [1988] 45 LS Gaz R41 . . . 18.54

DPP v Humphrey [2005] EWHC 822 (Admin) . . . 19.71

DPP v Hutchinson [1990] 2 AC 783, [1990] 2 All ER 836, [1990] 3 WLR 196, 89 LGR 1, 155 JP 71, 134 Sol Jo 1041, [1990] NLJR 1035, HL . . . 19.93

DPP v Jones [1999] 2 AC 240, [1999] 2 All ER 257, [1999] 2 WLR 625, [1999] 2 Cr App Rep 348, 163 JP 285, [1999] Crim LR 672, [1999] 11 LS Gaz R 71, [1999] 13 LS Gaz R 31, [1999] EGCS 36, 143 Sol Jo LB 98, HL . . . 19.95

DPP v Jones [2002] EWHC 110 (Admin) [2002] All ER (D) 157 (Jan) . . . 19.93

DPP v Jordan [1977] AC 699, [1976] 3 All ER 775, [1976] 3 WLR 887, 64 Cr App Rep 33, 141 JP 13, 120 Sol Jo 817, HL . . . 17.19

DPP v L (1999) *The Times*, 1 February . . . 18.56

DPP v McFarlane [2002] EWHC 485 (Admin), [2002] All ER (D) 78 (Mar) . . . 19.69, 19.71

DPP v Meaden [2003] EWHC 3005 (Admin) . . . 18.75

DPP v Orum [1988] 3 All ER 449, [1989] 1 WLR 88, 88 Cr App Rep 261, 153 JP 85, [1988] Crim LR 848, 132 Sol Jo 1637 . . . 19.56

DPP v Pal [2000] Crim LR 756, DC . . . 19.72

DPP v Whyte [1972] AC 849, [1972] 3 All ER 12, [1972] 3 WLR 410, 57 Cr App 74, 136 JP 686, 116 Sol Jo 583, HL . . . 17.6, 17.9, 17.11, 17.12

Dr Bonham's Case (1610) 8 Co Rep 107a . . . 5.5

D'Souza v DPP [1992] 4 All ER 545, [1992] 1 WLR 1073, 96 Cr App 278, 10 BMLR 139, [1992] NLJR 1540, HL . . . 18.78

Duke v GEC Reliance Ltd [1988] AC 618, [1988] 1 All ER 626, [1988] 2 WLR 359, [1988] 1 CMLR 719, [1988] ICR 339, [1988] IRLR 118, 132 Sol Jo 226, [1988] 11 LS Gaz R 42, HL . . . 10.63, 10.64

Dumbell v Roberts [1944] 1 All ER 326, CA . . . 18.40

Duncan v Jones [1936] 1 KB 218, 33 LGR 491, 99 JP 399, 105 LJKB 71, 30 Cox CC 279, [1935] All ER Rep 710, 79 Sol Jo 903, 154 LT 110, 52 TLR 26, DC . . . 19.30, 19.32, 19.33

Duport Steels Ltd v Sirs [1980] IRLR 112; revsd [1980] 1 All ER 529, [1980] 1 WLR 142, [1980] ICR 161, [1980] IRLR 116, 124 Sol Jo 133, HL . . . 2.23, 11.45

EC Commission v Italy (39/72) [1973] ECR 101, [1973] CMLR 439, ECJ . . . 10.17

Edinburgh and Dalkeith Rly Co v Wauchope (1842) 8 Cl & Fin 710, 3 Ry & Can Cas 232, HL . . . 5.18, 5.45

Edwards v DPP (1993) 97 Cr App 301, [1993] Crim LR 854, [1993] COD 378, DC . . . 18.53

Ellen Street Estates Ltd v Minister of Health [1934] 1 KB 590, 32 LGR 233, 98 JP 157, 103 LJKB 364, [1934] All ER Rep 385, 150 LT 468, CA . . . 5.23

Emohare v Thames Magistrates Court [2009] EWHC 689 (Admin), (2009) 173 JP 303 . . . 19.29

Enterprise Inns plc v Secretary of State for the Environment, Transport and the Regions (2000) 81 P & CR 236, [2000] 4 PLR 52, [2000] 20 LS Gaz R 47, [2000] EGCS 58, [2000] JPL 1256 . . . 12.48

Entick v Carrington (1765) 2 Wils 275, 19 State Tr 1029 1065, [1558–1774] All ER Rep 41 . . . 3.26, 3.29, 11.41, 16.11, 18.59

European Ombudsman v Lambert (C-234/02 P) [2004] ECR I-2803 . . . 15.123

Evans v Secretary of State for the Environment, Transport and Regions and Pfeiffer [2005] All ER (EC) 763, (2005) All ER (EC) 763, ECJ . . . 10.60

Factortame Ltd v Secretary of State for Transport [1989] 2 All ER 692 . . . 14.26, 14.27

Farrell v Alexander [1977] AC 59, [1976] 2 All ER 721, [1976] 3 WLR 145, 32 P & CR 292, 120 Sol Jo 451, HL . . . 9.46

Farrell v Whitty [2008] IEHC 124, [2008] EuLR 603 . . . 10.60

Firma Alfons Lütticke GmbH v Hauptzollamt Saarelouis (57/65) [1966] ECR 205, [1971] CMLR 674, ECJ . . . 10.14

Fletcher's Application, Re [1970] 2 All ER 527n, CA . . . 15.103

Flockhart v Robinson [1950] 2 KB 498, 48 LGR 454, sub nom Flockhart v Robertson [1950] 1 All ER 1091, 114 JP 304, 66 (pt 2) TLR 89, DC . . . 19.75

Floe Telecom Ltd v Office of Communications [2009] EWCA Civ 47, [2009] Bus LR 1116 . . . 10.61

Foster v British Gas plc (C-188/89) [1991] QB 405, [1990] 3 All ER 897, [1991] WLR 258, [1990] ECR I-3313, [1990] 2 CMLR 833, [1991] ICR 84, [1990] IRLR 353, ECJ . . . 10.26

Foulkes v Chief Constable of the Merseyside Police [1998] 3 All ER 705, [1999] 1 FCR 98, [1998] 2 FLR 798, [1998] Fam Law 661, CA . . . 19.9, 19.13

Fox v Stirk and Bristol Electoral Registration Officer [1970] 2 QB 463, [1970] 3 All ER 7,

[1970] 3 WLR 147, 68 LGR 644, [1970] RA 330, 134 JP 576, 114 Sol Jo 397, CA . . . 6.3

Fox, Campbell and Hartley v United Kingdom (1990) 13 EHRR 157 . . . 18.48, 18.57

Francovich and Bonifaci v Italy (C-6, 9/90) [1991] ECRI-5357, [1993] 2 CMLR 66, [1995] ICR 722, [1992] IRLR 84, ECJ . . . 10.34, 10.38, 10.41, 10.44

Franklin v Minister of Town and Country Planning [1948] AC 87, [1947] 2 All ER 289, 45 LGR 581, 111 JP 497, [1947] LJR 1440, 63 TLR 446, HL . . . 13.45

Friswell v Chief Constable of Essex [2004] EWHC 2009, QB . . . 18.80

Frodl v Austria [2010] ECHR 508, (2011) 52 EHRR 5 . . . 6.10

Fry, ex p [1954] 2 All ER 118, [1954] 1 WLR 730, 52 LGR 320, 118 JP 313, 98 Sol Jo 318, CA . . . 14.11

Fullard and Roalfe v Woking Magistrates' Court [2005] EWHC 2922 (Admin) . . . 18.62


Garland v British Rail Engineering [1983] 2 AC 751, [1982] 2 All ER 402, [1982] 2 WLR 918, [1982] ECR 359, [1982] 1 CMLR 696, [1982] ICR 420, [1982] IRLR 111, ECJ; apld [1983] 2 AC 751, [1982] 2 All ER 402, [1982] 2 WLR 918, [1982] ECR 555, [1982] 2 CMLR 174, [1982] ICR 420, [1982] IRLR 257, 126 Sol Jo 309, HL . . . 10.53

Gascor v Ellicott [1997] 1 VR 332, Victoria SC . . . 13.79

General Medical Council v BBC [1998] 3 All ER 426, [1998] 1 WLR 1573, 43 BMLR 143, [1998] 25 LS Gaz R 32, [1998] NLJR 942, 142 Sol Jo LB 182, [1998] EMLR 833, CA . . . 17.57

Ghaidan v Godin-Mendoza [2004] UKHL 30, [2004] 3 WLR 113, HL . . . 5.74, 5.82, 10.62

Ghani v Jones [1969] 3 All ER 720, [1969] 3 WLR 1158, 113 Sol Jo 775, [1970] 1 QB 693, [1969] 3 All ER 1700, 134 JP 166, 113 Sol Jo 584, CA . . . 18.86

Gibson v Lord Advocate [1975] 1 CMLR 563, 1975 SC 136, 1975 SLT 134, Ct of Sess . . . 5.43, 5.44

Gilham v Breidenbach [1982] RTR 328n, DC . . . 18.63

Gillan and Quinton v UK (App No 4158/05), (2010) 50 EHRR 45 . . . 18.13, 18.27

Gillies v Secretary of State for Work and Pensions (2006) UKHL 2 . . . 13.83

Godden v Hales (1686) 2 Show 475, 11 State Tr 1166 . . . 4.2, 5.6

Gold Star Publications Ltd v DPP [1981] 1 WLR 732; [1981] 2 All ER 257, HL . . . 17.21

Goodwin v United Kingdom [2002] IRLR 664, [2002] 2 FCR 577, [2002] 2 FLR 487, [2002] Fam Law 738, 13 BHRC 120, 67 BMLR 199, [2002] NLJR 1171, [2002] All ER (D) 158 (Jul), ECtHR . . . 5.84

Governor & Company of the Bank of Scotland v A Ltd [2001] EWCA Civ 52, [2001] 1 WLR 751, [2001] 3 All ER 58 . . . 14.21, 14.28

Grad v Finanzamt Traunstein (9/70) [1970] ECR 825, [1971] CMLR 1, ECJ . . . 10.18

Grand Junction Canal Co v Dimes (1852) 3 HL Cas 759, 8 State Tr NS 85, 17 Jr 73, 10 ER 301, 19 LTOS 317, HL . . . 13.84

Greens v UK [2010] ECHR 1826, (2011) 53 EHRR 21 . . . 6.9

Griffin v South West Water Services Ltd [1995] IRLR 15 . . . 10.27

Griffith v The Queen, sub nom R v Griffith (Tennyson Winston) [2005] HCA Trans 167, [2004] UKPC 58, [2005] 2 WLR 581, PC . . . 2.24


Hall & Co Ltd v Shoreham-by-Sea UDC [1964] 1 All ER 1, [1964] 1 WLR 240, 62 LGR 206, 15 P & CR 119, 128 JP 120, 107 Sol Jo 1001, CA . . . 13.22

Halliday v Nevill (1984) 155 CLR 1, 57 ALR 331, 59 ALJR 124 . . . 18.60, 18.61

Hamilton v Al Fayed [2001] 1 AC 395, [2000] 2 All ER 224, [2000] 2 WLR 609, 144 Sol Jo LB 157, [2000] EMLR 531, HL . . . 6.79, 6.87

Hammond v DPP [2004] EWHC 69 (Admin), [2004] All ER (D) 50 (Jan) . . . 19.53

Handyside v United Kingdom (1976) 1 EHRR 737, ECtHR . . . 16.58

Hashman and Harrup v United Kingdom (1999) 30 EHRR 241, [2000] Crim LR 185, 8 BHRC 104, ECtHR . . . 19.28

Hayes v Chief Constable of Merseyside
Constabulary [2011] EWCA Civ 911,
[2011 WLR (D) 269, [2011] 2 Cr App R
30 . . . 18.36

Hills v Ellis [1983] QB 680, [1983] 1 All ER
667, [1983] 2 WLR 234, 76 Cr App Rep
217, 148 JP 379, [1983] Crim LR 182, 126
Sol Jo 768, [1983] LS Gaz R 153, 133 NLJ
280 . . . 18.99, 18.100

Hipperson v Newbury District Electoral
Registration Officer [1985] QB 1060, [1985]
2 All ER 456, [1985] 3 WLR 61, 83 LGR
638, 129 Sol Jo 432, CA . . . 6.3

Hirst v United Kingdom (No 2) [2004] NLJR
553, 16 BHRC 409, [2004] All ER (D) 588
(Mar), ECtHR . . . 6.6

Hobson v Chief Constable of the Cheshire
Constabulary [2003] EWHC 3011
(Admin), 168 JP 111, [2003] All ER (D) 264
(Nov) . . . 18.59

Holgate-Mohammed v Duke [1984] AC 437,
[1984] 1 All ER 1054, [1984] 2 WLR 660, 79
Cr App Rep 120, [1984] Crim LR 418, 128
Sol Jo 244, [1984] LS Gaz R 1286, [1984]
NLJ Rep 523, HL . . . 18.28

Holloway v DPP [2004] EWHC 2621, [2004]
All ER (D) 278 (Oct) . . . 19.54

Hough v Chief Constable of the Staffordshire
Constabulary [2001] EWCA Civ 39, [2001]
All ER (D) 63 (Jan) . . . 18.43, 18.45

Hubbard v Pitt [1976] QB 142, [1975] 3 All
ER 1, [1975] 3 WLR 201, [1975] ICR 308,
119 Sol Jo 393, 236 Estates Gazette 343,
CA . . . 19.1

Humphries v Connor (1864) 171
CLR1 . . . 19.30–19.32

Hussein v Chong Fook Kam [1970] AC 942,
PC . . . 18.36

I, M and H v DPP [2000] 1 Cr App Rep 251,
[2000] Crim LR 45 . . . 19.45, 19.46

Inter-Environnement Wallonie ASBL v
Region Wallonie (C-129/96) [1997] ECR
I-7411 . . . 10.35

International Transport Roth GmbH
v Secretary of State for the Home
Department [2002] EWCA Civ 158, [2002]
All ER (D) 325 (Feb) . . . 16.107

IRC v National Federation of Self-Employed
and Small Businesses Ltd [1982] AC 617,

[1981] 2 All ER 93, [1981] 2 WLR 722,
[1981] STC 260, 55 TC 133, 125 Sol Jo 325,
HL . . . 12.61

IRC v Rossminster Ltd [1980] AC 952,
[1980] 1 All ER 80, [1980] 2 WLR 1, 70 CR
App 157, [1980] STC 42, 52 TC 160, 191,
[1979] TR 309, 124 Sol Jo 18, L (TC) 2753,
HL . . . 3.31

Ireland v United Kingdom (1978) 2 EHRR 25,
ECtHR . . . 16.48, 16.52

J H Smith (Hale) Ltd v Macclesfield Borough
Council, unreported, 1998 . . . 13.20

Jackson v Attorney General [2005] EWHC 94
(Admin), [2005] EWCA 126, CA . . . 5.13,
5.20, 5.35–5.41, 5.45, 5.48

Jeffrey v Black [1978] QB 490, [1978] 1 All ER
555, [1977] 3 WLR 895, 66 Cr App Rep 81,
142 JP 122, [1977] Crim LR 555, 121 Sol Jo
662, DC . . . 18.84

Johnston v Chief Constable of the Royal
Ulster Constabulary (222/84) [1987] QB
129, [1986] 3 All ER 135, [1986] 3 WLR
1038, [1986] ECR 1651, [1986] 3 CMLR 240,
[1987] ICR 83, [1986] IRLR 263, 130 Sol Jo
953, [1987] LS Gaz R 188, ECJ . . . 10.28

Kanda v Government of Malaya [1962] AC
322, [1962] MLJ 169 . . . 13.48

Kaye v Robertson [1991] FSR 62, CA . . .
11.42

Ken Lane Transport Ltd v North Yorkshire
County Council [1995] 1 WLR 1416, [1995]
3 CMLR 140, 160 LG Rev 477, [1996] RTR
335, 160 JP 91, [1996] Crim LR 189 . . .
11.48

Kenlin v Gardiner [1967] 2 QB 510, [1966] 3
All ER 931, [1967] 2 WLR 129, 131 JP 91,
110 Sol Jo 848 . . . 18.101, 18.103

Kent v Metropolitan Police Comr (1981) *The
Times*, 15 May, CA . . . 19.86

Khan v Metropolitan Police Commissioner
[2008] EWCA Civ 723, [2008] All ER (D)
27 (Jun) . . . 18.83

Knuller v DPP [1973] AC 435, [1972] 2 All ER
898, [1972] 3 WLR 143, 56 Cr App Rep 633,
136 JP 728, 116 Sol Jo 545, HL . . . 17.30,
17.33

Köbler v Austria [2003] All ER (D) 73 (Oct),
ECJ . . . 10.45–10.47

L v UK [2005] ECtHR 584, [2006] 1 FLR 35 . . . 16.117

Laker Airways v Department of Trade [1977] QB 643, [1976] 3 WLR 537, 120 Sol Jo 646; affd [1977] QB 643, [1977] 2 All ER 182, [1977] 2 WLR 234, 121 Sol Jo 52, CA . . . 4.27, 4.28

Lawal v Northern Spirit [2004] EWCA Civ 208, 148 Sol Jo LB 263, [2004] All ER (D) 319 (Feb) . . . 13.82, 13.83

Leigh v Cole (1853) 6 Cox CC 329 . . . 18.18

Lewis v Chief Constable of South Wales Constabulary [1991] 1 All ER 206, CA . . . 18.29, 18.54

Lewis v Cox [1985] QB 509, [1984] 3 All ER 672, [1984] 3 WLR 875, 80 Cr App Rep 1, 148 JP 601, [1984] Crim LR 756, 128 Sol Jo 596, [1984] LS Gaz R 2538 . . . 18.99

Lewisham London Borough Council, ex p Shell UK Ltd [1988] 1 All ER 938, [1990] PLR241 . . . 13.11

Lindley v Rutter [1981] QB 128, [1980] 3 WLR 660, 72 Cr App Rep 1, 124 Sol Jo 792 . . . 18.1

Litster v Forth Dry Dock and Engineering Co Ltd [1990] 1 AC 546, [1989] 1 All ER 1134, [1989] 2 WLR 634, [1989] ICR 341, [1989] IRLR 161, 133 Sol Jo 455, [1989] NLJR 400, HL . . . 10.56

Liverpool v DPP [2008] EWHC 2540 (Admin) . . . 19.52

Liversidge v Anderson [1942] AC 206, [1941] 3 All ER 338, 110 LJKB 724, 85 Sol Jo 439, 166 LT 1, 58 TLR 35, HL . . . 11.27, 12.3

Liyanage v R [1967] 1 AC 259, [1966] 1 All ER 650, [1966] 2 WLR 682, 110 Sol Jo 14, PC . . . 2.25

Lloyd v McMahon [1987] AC 625, [1987] 1 All ER 1118, [1987] 2 WLR 821, 85 LGR 545, 131 Sol Jo 409, [1987] LS Gaz R 1240, [1987] NLJ Rep 265, [1987] RVR 58, HL . . . 13.47

Locabail (UK) Ltd v Bayfield Properties Ltd [1999] 20 LS Gaz R 39, [1999] NLJR 1793, 143 Sol Jo LB 148; affd [2000] QB 451, [2000] 1 All ER 65, [2000] 2 WLR 870, [2000] IRLR 96, [2000] UKHRR 300, 7 BHRC 583, CA . . . 13.86

London and Clydeside Estates Ltd v Aberdeen District Council [1979] 3 All ER 876, [1980] 1 WLR 182, 39 P & CR 549, 124 Sol Jo 100, 253 Estates Gazette 1011, 1980 SC (HL) . . . 13.41

M v Home Office [1994] 1 AC 377, [1993] 3 WLR 433, [1993] 37 LS Gaz R 50, [1993] NLJR 1099, 137 Sol Jo LB 199 . . . 3.27, 3.28, 11.41, 14.24–14.27, 17.38

Macarthys Ltd v Smith [1979] 3 All ER 325, [1979] 1 WLR 1189, [1979] 3 CMLR 44, [1979] ICR 785, [1979] IRLR 316, 123 Sol Jo 603, CA; refd [1981] QB 180, [1981] 1 All ER 111, [1980] 3 WLR 929, [1980] ECR 1275, [1980] 2 CMLR 205, [1980] ICR 672, [1980] IRLR 210, 124 Sol Jo 808, ECJ; apld [1981] QB 180, [1981] 1 All ER 111, [1980] 3 WLR 929, [1980] 2 CMLR 217, [1980] ICR 672, [1980] IRLR 210, 124 Sol Jo 808, CA . . . 10.50, 10.51

MacCormick v Lord Advocate (1953) SC 396, 1953 SLT 255 . . . 5.43, 5.44

Maclaine Watson & Co Ltd v Department of Trade and Industry [1990] 2 AC 418, [1989] 3 All ER 523, [1989] 3 WLR 969, [1990] BCLC 102, 5 BCC 872, 133 Sol Jo 1485, HL . . . 4.32

Malone v Metropolitan Police Comr [1979] 2 All ER 620, [1979] 2 WLR 700, 69 Cr App Rep 168, 123 Sol Jo 303 . . . 11.42

Mangawaro Enterprises v A-G [1994] 2 NZLR 451 . . . 5.79

Manuel v A-G [1983] Ch 77, [1982] 3 All ER 822, [1982] 3 WLR 821, 126 Sol Jo 642, 79 LS Gaz 1411, CA . . . 5.16

Marbury v Madison (1803) 1 Cranch 137 . . . 1.6

Marleasing SA v La Comercial Internacional de Alimentación SA (C-106/89) [1990] ECRI-4135, [1992] 1 CMLR 305, [1993] BCC 421, 135 Sol Jo 15, ECJ . . . 3.15, 10.33–10.36, 10.58–10.62

Marshall v Southampton and South West Hampshire Area Health Authority (Teaching) (152/84) [1986] QB 401, [1986] 2 All ER 584, [1986] 2 WLR 780, [1986] ECR 723, [1986] 1CMLR 688, [1986] ICR 335, [1986] IRLR 140, 130 Sol Jo 340, [1986] LS Gaz R 1720, ECJ . . . 10.24–10.26, 10.30

Martin v HM Advocate [2010] UKSC 10, 2010 SLT 412, 2010 SCCR 401 . . . 8.47, 8.50, 8.51

Mauritius v Khoyratty (2006) UKPC 13
PC . . . 1.9

McArdle v Egan (1933) 32 LGR 85, 98 JP 103,
30 Cox CC 67, [1933] All ER Rep 611, 150
LT 412, CA . . . 18.40

McCall v Poulton [2009] RTR 11, [2008]
EWCA Civ 1313 . . . 10.60, 10.61

McCann v United Kingdom (1995) 21 EHRR
97, ECtHR . . . 16.24, 16.49

McConnell v Chief Constable of Greater
Manchester Police [1990] 1 All ER 423,
[1990] 1 WLR 364, 91 Cr App Rep 88, 154
JP 325, 134 Sol Jo 457, CA . . . 19.10

McInnes v Onslow Fane [1978] 3 All ER 211,
[1978] 1 WLR 1520, 142 JP 590, 122 Sol Jo
844 . . . 13.55, 13.56, 13.68

McKerr, Re [2004] UKHL 12, [2004] 2 All ER
409, [2004] 1 WLR 807, [2004] All ER (D)
210 (Mar) . . . 5.88, 5.89

McLeod v Metropolitan Police Comr [1994] 4
All ER 553, CA . . . 19.7, 19.8

McQuade v Chief Constable of Humberside
Police [2001] EWCA Civ 1330, [2002] 1
WLR 1347, [2001] 35 LS Gaz R 33 . . . 19.11,
19.13

McWhirter v Attorney General [1972] CMLR
882 . . . 4.32

Medicaments and Related Classes of Goods
(No 2), Re [2001] 1 WLR 700, [2001] ICR
564 . . . 13.80

Mepstead v DPP (1995) 160 JP 475,
[1996] Crim LR 111, [1996] COD 13 . . .
18.101

Mercury Communications Ltd v Director
General of Telecommunications [1996] 1
All ER 575, [1996] 1 WLR 48, HL . . . 12.16,
12.20, 12,21

Merkur Island Shipping Corpn v Laughton
[1983] 2 AC 570, [1983] 1 All ER 334, [1983]
2 WLR 45, [1983] 1 Lloyd's Rep 154, [1983]
ICR 178, [1983] IRLR 26, 126 Sol Jo 745,
CA, [1983] 2 AC 570, [1983] 2 All ER 189,
[1983] 2 WLR 778, [1983] ICR 490, [1983]
IRLR 218, 127 Sol Jo 306, HL . . . 3.12

Metropolitan Police Comr v Kay [2007]
EWCA Civ 477 . . . 19.75, 19.78

MGN Pension Trustees v Bank of America
National Trust and Savings Association
[1995] 2 All ER 355, [1995] EMLR
99 . . . 17.61, 17.67

Michaels v Highbury Corner
Magistrates Court [2009] EWHC 2928
(Admin) . . . 18.22

Minister of the Interior v Harris (1952) (4) SA
769 (A) . . . 5.28

Moase v City of Westminster Magistrates
Court [2008] EWHC 2309 (Admin), [2009]
EWCA Civ 1545 . . . 19.97

Molyneaux, ex p [1986] 1 WLR 331, 130 Sol Jo
243, [1986] LS Gaz R 1314 . . . 4.32

Moss v McLachlan [1985] IRLR 76, 149 JP
167 . . . 19.19, 19.20

National Union of Teachers v Governing
Body of St Mary's Church of England
(Aided) Junior School [1997] ICR
334, [1997] IRLR 242, [1997] ELR 169,
CA . . . 10.29

North Dorset DC v Trim [2010] EWCA Civ
1446, [2011] 1 WLR 1901 . . . 12.24

Norwood v DPP [2003] EWHC 1564
(Admin), [2003] Crim LR 888, [2003] All
ER (D) 59 (Jul) . . . 19.74

Nottinghamshire County Council v Secretary
of State for the Environment [1986] AC
240, [1986] 1 All ER 199, [1986] 2 WLR 1,
84 LGR 305, 130 Sol Jo 36, [1985] NLJ Rep
1257, HL . . . 13.21

Office of Government Commerce v
Information Commissioner [2008] EWHC
737 (Admin), [2008] EWHC 774 . . . 2.27

Officier van Justitie v Kolpinghuis Nijmegen
(80/86) [1987] ECR 3969, [1989] 2 CMLR
18, ECJ . . . 3.15, 10.33

O'Hara v Chief Constable of the Royal Ulster
Constabulary [1997] AC 286, [1997] 1 All
ER 129, [1997] 2 WLR 1, [1997] 1 Cr App
447, [1997] Crim LR 432, [1997] 02 LS Gaz
R 26, [1996] NLJR 1852, 141 Sol Jo LB 20,
HL . . . 18.41, 18.43, 18.45

O'Kelly v Harvey (1883) 14 LR Ir 105 . . .
19.23

O'Loughlin v Chief Constable of Essex
(1998) . . . 18.77

Olympian Press Ltd v Hollis [1998] 1 WLR
374, CA . . . 17.18

O'Moran v DPP [1975] QB 864, [1975] 1 All
ER 473, [1975] 2 WLR 413, 139 JP 245, 119
Sol Jo 165, DC . . . 19.36

O'Reilly v Mackman [1983] 2 AC 237, [1982] 3 All ER 680, [1982] 3 WLR 604, 126 Sol Jo 578, CA; affd [1983] 2 AC 237, [1982] 3 All ER 1124, [1982] 3 WLR 1096, 126 Sol Jo 820, HL . . . 12.15–12.24

Osman v Southwark Crown Court (1999) Transcript No CO/2318/98 . . . 18.11, 18.22

Padfield v Minister of Agriculture, Fisheries and Food [1968] AC 997, [1968] 1 All ER 694, [1968] 2 WLR 924, 112 Sol Jo 171, HL . . . 12.4–12.6, 13.68

Palacegate Properties Ltd v London Borough of Camden (2000) 82 P & CR 199, [2000] 4 PLR 59 . . . 12.40

Paponette and others v Attorney General of Trinidad and Tobago [2010] UKPC 32, [2010] WLR (D) 323, [2011] 3 WLR 219 . . . 13.52

Peach Grey & Co v Sommers [1995] 2 All ER 513, [1995] ICR 549, [1995] IRLR 363, [1995] 13 LS Gaz R 31 . . . 17.57

Pepper v Hart [1993] AC 593, [1993] 1 All ER 42, [1992] 3 WLR 1032, [1992] STC 898, 65 TC 421, [1993] ICR 291, [1993] IRLR 33, NLJR 17, [1993] RVR 127, [1993] 2 LRC 153, HL . . . 6.84, 12.5

Percy v DPP [1995] 3 All ER 124, [1995] 1 WLR 1382, 159 JP 337, [1995] Crim LR 714, [1995] 09 LS Gaz R 38 . . . 19.61

Pett v Greyhound Racing Association [1969] 1 QB 125, [1968] 2 All ER 545, [1968] 2 WLR 1471, 112 Sol Jo 463, CA . . . 13.66

Pfeiffer (C-379/01–403/01) [2004] ECR I-8835 . . . 10.32

Phillips v Eyre (1870) LR 6 QB 1, 10 B & S 1004, 40 LJQB 28, 22 LT 869, Ex Ch . . . 3.8

Pickering v Liverpool Daily Post and Echo Newspapers plc [1991] 2 AC 370, [1991] 1 All ER 622, [1991] 2 WLR 513, HL . . . 17.57

Pickstone v Freemans plc [1989] AC 66, [1987] 3 All ER 756, [1987] 3 WLR 811, [1987] 2 CMLR 572, [1987] ICR 867, [1987] IRLR 218, 131 Sol Jo 538, [1987] NLJ Rep 315, CA; affd [1989] AC 66, [1988] 2 All ER 803, [1988] 3 WLR 265, [1988] 3 CMLR 221, [1988] ICR 697, [1988] IRLR 357, 132 Sol Jo 994, [1988] NLJR 193, HL . . . 10.54, 10.55

Police v Reid [1987] Crim LR 702 . . . 19.92, 19.93

Poole v HM Treasury [2006] EWHC 2731 (Comm), [2007] 1 All ER (Comm) 255, [2007] Lloyds Rep IR 114 . . . 10.39

Poplar Housing and Regeneration Community Association Ltd v Donoghue [2001] EWCA Civ 595, [2002] QB 48, [2001] 4 All ER 604, [2001] 3 WLR 183, 33 HLR 823, [2001] 19 LS Gaz R 38, 145 Sol Jo LB 122, [2001] 19 EG 141 (CS) . . . 5.66, 5.67, 16.84

Porter v Magill [2001] UKHL 67, [2002] 2 AC 357, [2002] 1 All ER 465, [2002] 2 WKR 37, [2002] LGR 51, [2001] All ER (D) 181 (Dec) . . . 13.17, 13.81, 13.83, 13.87

Prebble v Television New Zealand [1995] 1 AC 321, [1994] 3 All ER 407, [1994] 3 WLR 970, [1994] 39 LS Gaz R 38, [1994] NLJR 1131, 138 Sol Jo LB 175, [1994] 1 LRC 122, PC . . . 5.79, 6.85, 6.86

Prescott v Birmingham Corpn [1955] Ch 210, [1954] 3 All ER 698, 53 LGR 68, 119 JP 48, 98 Sol Jo 886, CA . . . 13.12

Pubblico Ministero v Ratti (148/78) [1979] ECR 1629, [1980] 1 CMLR 96, ECJ . . . 10.21–10.23

R (Alconbury Developments and others) v Secretary of State for the Environment, Transport and the Regions [2003] 2 AC 295 . . . 16.77

R (Association of British Civilian Internees (Far East Region)) v Secretary of State for Defence (2003) *The Times*, 19 April, CA . . . 13.37

R (Bancoult) v Secretary of State for Foreign and Commonwealth Affairs (No 2) [2008] UKHL 61, [2008] WLR (D) 322 . . . 4.35–4.38

R (Beer (t/a Hammer Trout Farm)) v Hampshire Farmers' Markets Ltd [2003] EWCA Civ 1056 [2004] 1 WLR 233 . . . 12.31

R (Bradley and others) v Secretary of State for Work and Pensions [2008] EWCA Civ 36, [2008] 3 WLR . . . 15.81

R (C) v Secretary of State for Justice [2008] EWCA Civ 882, [2009] QB 657, [2009] 2 WLR 1039 . . . 14.10

R (Cavanagh) v Health Service Commissioner for England (2006) EWCA Civ 1578 . . . 15.90

R (Dhadly) v London Borough of Greenwich [2001] EWCA Civ 1822 . . . 14.30

R (Gillan) v Metropolitan Police Commissioner (2006) UKHL 12, [2006] 2 Cr App R 36, HL . . . 18.12, 18.26

R (Greenfield) v Secretary of State for the Home Department [2005] UKHL 14, [2005] 1 WLR 673 . . . 16.115

R (Haw) v Secretary of State for the Home Department (2006) EWCA Civ 532 . . . 19.97

R (International Transport Roth GmbH) v Secretary of State for the Home Department [2001] 02 LS Gaz R 27, 146 Sol Jo LB 5 . . . 5.77

R (Kurdistan Workers Party) v Secretary of State for the Home Department [2002] EWHC 644, [2002] ACD 99 . . . 14.2

R (Mahmood) v Pharmaceutical Society of Great Britain [2001] EWCA Civ 1245, [2002] 1 WLR 879, [2001] 37 LS Gaz R 39, 145 Sol Jo LB 217, [2001] All ER (D) 462 (Jul) . . . 4.22, 4.23

R (Mohamed) v Secretary of State for Foreign and Commonwealth Affairs (No 2) (Guardian News and Media Ltd intervening) [2010] 3 WLR 554 . . . 17.44

R (on the application of Abbasi) v Secretary of State for Foreign and Commonwealth Affairs [2002] EWCA Civ 1598, [2003] 3 LRC 297, [2002] All ER (D) 70 (Nov) . . . 4.30

R (on the application of Alconbury Developments Ltd) v Secretary of State for the Environment, Transport and Regions [2001] UKHL 23, [2001] 2 All ER 929, [2001] 2 WLR 1389, 82 P & CR 513, [2001] 2 PLR 76, 145 Sol Jo LB 140 . . . 5.85, 13.36

R (on the application of Amraf Training plc) v Department of Education and Training [2001] ELR 125 . . . 13.19

R (on the application of Anderson) v Secretary of State for the Home Department [2002] UKHL 46, [2003] 1 AC 837, [2002] 4 All ER 1089, [2002] 3 WLR 1800, [2003] 1 Cr App Rep 523, [2003] 03 LS Gaz R 31, [2002] NLJR 1858, 146 Sol Jo LB 272, 13 BHRC 450, [2003] 2 LRC 703, [2002] All ER (D) 359 (Nov) . . . 5.73, 5.81

R (on the application of Anufrijeva) v Secretary of State for the Home Department [2003] UKHL 36, [2003] 3 WLR 252, HL . . . 3.19

R (on the application of B) v Worcestershire County Council [2009] All ER (D) 51 (Apr) . . . 13.22

R (on the application of Balchin) v Parliamentary Comr for Administration (No 3) [2002] EWHC 1876 (Admin), [2002] All ER (D) 449 (Jul) . . . 15.107

R (on the application of BAPIO Action Ltd) v Secretary of State for the Home Department [2008] UKHL 27, [2008] All ER (D) 410 (Apr) . . . 13.59

R (on the application of Bhatt Murphy (a firm)) v Independent Assessor [2008] EWCA Civ 755 . . . 13.59

R (on the application of Bibi) v Newham LBC [2001] EWCA Civ 607, CA . . . 13.58

R (on the application of Bradley) v Secretary of State for Work and Pensions [2007] EWHC 242 (Admin) . . . 6.90, 15.80

R (on the application of Brehony) v Chief Constable of Greater Manchester Police [2005] EWHC 640 (Admin) . . . 19.92

R (on the application of Bulger) v Secretary of State for the Home Department [2001] EWHC Admin 119, [2001] 3 All ER 449 . . . 12.65

R (on the application of Burkett) v London Borough of Hammersmith and Fulham [2001] 3 PLR 1, [2001] JPL 775, [2000] All ER (D) 2257, CA . . . 12.74

R (on the application of Cart) v Upper Tribunal (Public Law Project and another intervening) [2011] 3 W.L.R. 107 (Supreme Ct); [2011] QB 120 . . . 15.3, 15.20, 15.26

R (on the application of Chester) v Secretary of State for Justice and Wakefield Metropolitan District Council [2010] EWCA Civ 1439, [2011] 1 WLR 1436 . . . 6.8

R (on the application of Corner House Research) v Director of the Serious Fraud Office [2008] UKHL 60, [2008] EWHC 1354 (Admin) . . . 3.39, 3.40

R (on the application of the CPS) v Blaydon Youth Court [2004] EWHC 2296 (Admin), (2004) 168 JP 638 . . . 19.69

R (on the application of Edwards) v
Environment Agency [2004] EWHC
736 (Admin), [2004] All ER (D) 43
(Apr) . . . 12.64

R (on the application of English Speaking
Board (International) Ltd) v Secretary of
State for the Home Department [2011]
EWHC 1788 (Admin) . . . 14.13

R (on the application of Faulkner) v Secretary
of State for Justice and the Parole Board
[2010] EWCA Civ 1434, [2011] HRLR
7 . . . 16.115

R (on the application of GC) v Commissioner
of Police of the Metropolis (Liberty
and another intervening) [2011] UKSC
21, [2011] 1 WLR 1230, [2011] 3 All ER
859 . . . 5.63

R (on the application of H) v Mental Health
Review Tribunal for North and East
London Region [2001] EWCA Civ 415
[2002] QB 1, [2001] 3 WLR 512, [2001] 21
LS Gaz R 40 . . . 5.83

R (on the application of H) v Secretary
of State for Justice [2008] EWHC 2590
(Admin) . . . 13.63

R (on the application of Hawkes) v DPP
[2005] EWCA 3046 (Admin) . . . 19.14

R (on the application of Heather) v Leonard
Cheshire Foundation [2002] EWCA Civ
366, [2002] 2 All ER 936, [2002] HLR
893, 69 BMLR 22, [2002] All ER (D) 326
(Mar) . . . 16.84, 16.94

R (on the application of Hewitson) v Chief
Constable of Dorset Police & Government
of France (Interested Party) [2003]
3296 (Admin), [2003] All ER (D) 344
(Dec) . . . 18.86

R (on the application of Laporte) v Chief
Constable of the Gloucestershire
Constabulary [2004] EWHC 253 (Admin),
[2004] 2 All ER 874, [2004] NLJR 308,
[2004] All ER (D) 313 (Feb) . . . 19.18, 19.22

R (on the application of M) v Secretary
of State for Health [2003] EWHC 1094
(Admin), [2003] 3 All ER 672n, [2003] All
ER (D) 307 (Apr) . . . 5.84

R (on the application of M) v The
Commissioner for Local Administration
in England [2006] EWHC
2847(Admin) . . . 15.99

R (on the application of Moos and another) v
Commissioner of Police of the Metropolis
[2011] All ER (D) 146 (Apr), [2011] EWHC
957 (Admin), [2011] HRLR 24 . . . 19.24

R (on the application of Niazi) v Secretary of
State for the Home Department [2008] QB
836, [2008] EWCA Civ 755 . . . 13.59

R (on the application of Page) v Secretary
of State for Justice (2007) EWHC
(Admin) . . . 4.32, 4.33

R (on the application of Pearson) v Secretary
of State for the Home Department [2001]
EWHC Admin 239, [2001] All ER (D) 22
(Apr) . . . 6.6

R (on the application of Power-Hynes) v
Norwich Magistrates Court [2009] EWHC
1512 (Admin) . . . 18.74

R (on the application of Prolife Alliance) v
BBC [2003] UKHL 23, [2003] 1 AC 185,
HL . . . 16.108

R (on the application of Rottman) v
Metropolitan Police Comr [2002] UKHL
20, [2002] 2 AC 692, [2002] 2 All ER 865,
12 BHRC 329, [2002] All ER (D) 238
(May) . . . 18.86

R (on the application of Senior-Milne) v
The Parliamentary and Health Service
Ombudsman [2009] EWHC 2240
(Admin) . . . 15.60, 15.107

R (on the application of Shields) v Secretary
of State for Justice [2008] EWHC 3102
(Admin) . . . 4.33, 4.34

R (on the application of Telegraph Group
Plc) v Sherwood [2001] EWCA Crim 1075,
[2001] 1 WLR 1983, [2002] EMLR 10,
CA . . . 17.62, 17.64

R (on the application of Thames Water
Utilities Ltd) v Bromley Magistrates' Court
[2005] EWHC 1231 (Admin) . . . 14.30

R (on the application of Weaver) v London
& Quadrant Housing Trust [2009] EWCA
Civ 587 . . . 16.95

R (on the application of West) v Lloyd's of
London [2004] EWCA Civ 506, [2004] 3
All ER 251 . . . 12.30

R (on the application of Wheeler) v Office of
the Prime Minister [2008] EWHC 1409
(Admin) . . . 2.28, 2.32, 7.10, 13.59

R (Robertson) v Wakefield Metropolitan
District Council [2001] EWHC Admin 915,

[2002] 2 WLR 889, [2002] LGR 286, [2002] 02 LS Gaz R28, 145 Sol Jo LB 267 . . . 10.34

R (Rose) v DPP (2006) CLW 06/06/15, [2006] EWCA Civ 700 . . . 17.35

R (SB) v Governors of Denbigh High School [2006] UKHL 15, [2007] 1 AC 100, [2006] 2 WLR 719, [2006] 2 All ER 487 . . . 16.86

R (Ullah) v Special Adjudicator [2004] UKHL 26, [2004] 2 AC 323 . . . 16.78

R v A (No 2) [2001] UKHL 25 [2002] 1 AC 45, [2001] 3 All ER 1, [2001] 2 WLR 1546, [2001] 2 Cr App Rep 351, 165 JP 609 . . . 5.68–5.72, 5.81, 11.56

R v Abdroikov; R v Green; R v Williamson [2006] 1 Cr App R 1, [2005] 1 WLR 3538, CA . . . 13.83

R v Altrincham Justices, ex p Pennington [1975] QB 549, [1975] 2 All ER 78, [1975] 2 WLR 450, 73 LGR 109, 139 JP 434, 119 Sol Jo 64 . . . 13.77

R v Anderson [1972] 1 QB 304, [1971] 3 All ER 1152, [1971] 3 WLR 939, 56 Cr App 115, 136 JP 97, 115 Sol Jo 847, CA . . . 17.13, 17.14, 17.26

R v Anderson [2008] EWCA Crim 12, [2008] 2 Cr App R (S) 57 . . . 17.36

R v B [2006] EWCA Crim 2692, [2006] All ER (D) 348 (Oct) . . . 17.64

R v Badham [1987] Crim LR 202 . . . 18.85

R v Barnsley Metropolitan Borough Council, ex p Hook [1976] 3 All ER 452, [1976] 1 WLR 1052, 74 LGR 493, 140 JP 638, 120 Sol Jo 182, CA . . . 13.28, 13.29

R v Beck, ex p Daily Telegraph plc [1993] 2 All ER 177, 94 Cr App Rep 376, CA . . . 17.63, 17.66

R v Board of Visitors of HM Prison, The Maze, ex p Hone [1988] AC 379, [1988] 2 WLR 177, 132 Sol Jo 158, [1988] 8 LS Gaz R 35 . . . 13.65

R v Bow Street Metropolitan Stipendiary Magistrates' Court, ex p Pinochet Ugarte (No 2) [2000] 1 AC 119, [1999] 1 All ER 577, [1999] 2 WLR 272, HL . . . 13.84

R v Bremner and Joy (1984) unreported, 20 December, CA . . . 17.26

R v Bristol [2007] EWCA Crim 3214, 172 JP 161, 172 JPN 421, [2007] All ER (D) 47 (Dec) . . . 18.22

R v Broadcasting Complaints Commission, ex p Owen [1985] QB 1153, [1985] 2 All ER 522, [1985] 2 WLR 1025, 129 Sol Jo 349 . . . 13.10

R v Calder & Boyars Ltd [1969] 1 QB 151, [1968] 3 All ER 644, [1968] 3 WLR 974, 52 Cr App Rep 706, 133 JP 20, 112 Sol Jo 688, CA . . . 17.13, 17.18

R v Chaytor [2011] All ER (D) 255, [2011] EWCA Crim 929 . . . 6.94, 6.95

R v Chief Constable of Devon and Cornwall, ex p Central Electricity Generating Board [1982] QB 458, [1981] 3 All ER 826, [1981] 3 WLR 967, 146 JP 91, 125 Sol Jo 745, CA . . . 14.17, 18.4, 19.3, 19.10

R v Chief Constable of Sussex, ex p International Trader's Ferry Ltd [1999] AC 418, [1999] 1 All ER 129, [1998] WLR 1260, [1999] 1 CMLR 1320, [1998] 47 LS Gaz R 29, 142 Sol Jo LB 286, HL . . . 13.21, 18.2

R v Chief Rabbi of the United Hebrew Congregation of Great Britain and the Commonwealth, ex p Wachmann [1993] 2 All ER 249, [1992] 1 WLR 1036, [1991] 3 Admin LR 721 . . . 12.28

R v Civil Service Appeal Board, ex p Cunningham [1991] 4 All ER 310, [1992] ICR 816, [1991] IRLR 297, [1991] NLJR 455, [1992] LRC (Const) 941, CA . . . 13.69

R v Clerkenwell Metropolitan Stipendiary Magistrates, ex p Telegraph plc [1993] QB 462, [1993] 2 WLR 233, 97 Cr App 18, 157 JP 554 . . . 17.65

R v Comr for Local Administration, ex p Croydon London Borough Council [1989] 1 All ER 1033 . . . 15.55, 15.104

R v Comr for Local Administration, ex p H (a minor) [1999] COD 382, 143 Sol Jo LB 39; affd [1999] ELR 314, CA . . . 15.107

R v Comr for Local Administration, for the South, the West, the Midlands, Leicestershire, Lincolnshire and Cambridgeshire, ex p Eastleigh Borough Council [1988] QB 855, [1988] 3 WLR 113, 86 LGR 491, 132 Sol Jo 564 . . . 15.104

R v County of London Quarter Sessions Appeal Committee, ex p Metropolitan Police Comr [1948] 1 KB 670, [1948] 1 All ER 72, 46 LGR 183, 112 JP 118, [1948] LJR 472, 92 Sol Jo 73, 64 TLR 102, DC . . . 19.25

R v Criminal Injuries Compensation Board,
ex p A [1999] 2 AC 330, [1999] COD 244,
143 Sol Jo LB 120, HL . . . 12.73

R v Criminal Injuries Compensation Board,
ex p Lain [1967] 2 QB 864, [1967] 2 All
ER 770, [1967] 3 WLR 348, 111 Sol Jo
331 . . . 4.27

R v Crown Court at Reading, ex p
Hutchinson [1988] QB 384, [1988] 1 All
ER 333, [1987] 3 WLR 1062, 86 LGR 71,
87 Cr App Rep 36, 152 JP 47, [1987] Crim
LR 827, 131 Sol Jo 1455 [1987] LS Gaz R
3172 . . . 12.36

R v Derbyshire County Council, ex p Times
Supplements (1991) 155 LG Rev 123, [1991]
COD 129, [1990] NLJR 1421, 3 Admin LR
241 . . . 13.19

R v Devon County Council, ex p Baker
[1995] 1 All ER 73, 91 LGR 11 BMLR 141, 6
Admin LR 113, CA . . . 13.49

R v Disciplinary Committee of the Jockey
Club, ex p Aga Khan [1993] 2 All ER 853,
[1993] 1 WLR 909, CA . . . 12.26, 12.29

R v Dover Justices, ex p Dover District
Council (1991) 156 JP 433, [1992] Crim LR
371 . . . 17.73

R v DPP [2006] EWHC 1375 (Admin), 171
JPN 140 . . . 19.64

R v DPP, ex p Kebilene [1999] 4 All ER 801,
[1999] 3 WLR 175, [2000] 1 Cr App 275,
[1999] Crim LR 994, revsd [2000] 2 AC
326, [1999] 4 All 801, [1999] 3 WLR 972,
[2000] 1 Cr App Rep 275, [2000] Crim LR
486, [1999] 43 LS Gaz R 32, HL . . . 5.63

R v Duffy (2000) WL 1741395 . . . 19.71

R v E [2004] 21 LS Gaz R 35, 148 Sol Jo
LB 537, [2004] All ER (D) 253 (Apr),
CA . . . 17.60

R v Electricity Comrs, ex p London
Electricity Joint Committee Co (1920) Ltd
[1924] 1 KB 171, 21 LGR 719, 88 JP 13, 93
LJKB 390, [1923] All ER Rep 150, 68 Sol Jo
188, 130 LT 164, 39 TLR 715, CA . . . 14.9

R v Elliott [1996] 1 Cr App Rep 432, [1996]
Crim LR 264, CA . . . 17.13

R v Epping and Harlow General Comrs, ex p
Goldstraw [1983] 3 All ER 257, [1983] STC
693, 57 TC 536, CA . . . 12.10

R v Evesham Justices, ex p McDonagh [1988]
QB 553, [1988] 1 All ER 371, [1988] 2 WLR

227, 87 Cr App Rep 28, 152 JP 65, [1988]
Crim LR 181, 131 Sol Jo 1698, [1988] 2 LS
Gaz R 36, [1987] NLJ Rep 757 . . . 17.71,
17.72

R v Fellows [1997] 2 All ER 548, [1997] 1
Cr App Rep 244 [1997] Crim LR 524,
CA . . . 17.29

R v Football Association Ltd, ex p Football
League [1993] 2 All ER 833, [1992] COD
52 . . . 12.29

R v Forbes and Webb (1865) 10 Cox CC
362 . . . 18.98

R v Foster [1984] 2 All ER 679, CA . . . 4.34

R v Francis [2006] EWCA Crim 3323, [2007]
1 WLR 1021 . . . 19.66

R v Gaming Board for Great Britain, ex p
Benaim and Khaida [1970] 2 QB 417, [1970]
2 All ER 528, [1970] 2 WLR 1009, 134 JP
513, 114 Sol Jo 266, CA . . . 13.46, 13.67,
13.69

R v Gibson [1990] 2 QB 619, [1991] 1 All ER
439, [1990] 3 WLR 595, 91 Cr App Rep 341,
155 JP 126, [1990] Crim LR 738, 134 Sol Jo
1123, CA . . . 17.35, 17.37

R v Goring [1999] Crim LR 670, CA . . .
17.15

R v Gough [1993] AC 646, [1993] 2 All ER
724, [1993] 2 WLR 883, 97 Cr App Rep
188, 157 JP 612, [1993] Crim LR 886, [1993]
NLJR 775, 137 Sol Jo LB 168, HL . . .
13.76–13.79

R v Governor of Pentonville Prison, ex p
Osman [1989] 3 All ER 701, [1990] 1 WLR
277, 90 Cr App Rep 281, [1988] Crim LR
611, 134 Sol Jo 458 . . . 18.86

R v Hamilton [2007] EWCA Crim
2062 . . . 17.35

R v Hampden; Case of Ship Money (1637) 3
State Tr 826 . . . 4.2

R v Hasan [2005] UKHL 22, [2005] 2 WLR
709, HL . . . 17.75

R v Hicklin (1868) LR 3 QB 360, 37 LJMC 89,
11 Cox CC 19, 16 WR 801 . . . 17.5

R v Higher Education Funding Council, ex p
Institute of Dental Surgery [1994] 1 All ER
651, [1994] 1 WLR 242 . . . 13.71, 13.72

R v HM Inspectorate of Pollution, ex p
Greenpeace (No 2) [1994] 4 All ER 329,
[1994] 2 CMLR 548, [1994] COD 116,
[1994] Env LR 76 . . . 12.61, 12.62

R v HM Treasury, ex p British
Telecommunications plc (C-392/93) [1996]
QB 615, [1996] 3 WLR 203, [1996] All
ER (EC) 411, [1996] ECR I-1631, [1996] 2
CMLR 217, [1996] IRLR 300, ECJ . . .
10.42

R v Horncastle [2009] EWCA Crim
964 . . . 16.79

R v Horseferry Road Magistrates' Court, ex p
Bennett [1994] AC 42, [1993] 3 WLR 90, 98
Cr App Rep 114, 137 Sol Jo LB 159 . . . 3.33

R v Horseferry Road Metropolitan
Stipendiary Magistrate, ex p Siadatan
[1991] 1 QB 260, [1991] 1 All ER 324, [1990]
3 WLR 1006, 92 Cr App 257, [1990] Crim
LR 598, [1990] NLJR 704 . . . 19.50

R v Howell [1982] QB 416, [1981] 3 All ER
383, [1981] 3 WLR 501, 73 Cr App Rep 31,
146 JP 13, [1981] Crim LR 697, 125 Sol Jo
462, CA . . . 19.3, 19.4

R v Immigration Appeal Tribunal, ex p
Jeyeanthan [2000] 1 WLR 354, 11 Admin
LR 824 . . . 13.41

R v Independent Television Commission, ex p
TV NI Ltd (1991) The Times, 30 December,
CA . . . 12.71

R v IRC, ex p National Federation of Self-
Employed and Small Businesses Ltd [1982]
AC 617, [1981] 2 All ER 93, [1981] 2 WLR
722, [1981] STC 260, 55 TC 133, 125 Sol Jo
325, HL . . . 12.12

R v Kansal (No 2) [2001] EWCA Crim 1260
[2001] 3 WLR 751, [2001] 2 Cr App Rep
601, [2001] 28 LS Gaz R 43, 145 Sol Jo LB
157, [2001] UKHL 62, [2002] 1 All ER 257,
[2001] 3 WLR 1562, [2002] 1 Cr App Rep
478, [2002] 03 LS Gaz R 25, 145 Sol Jo LB
275, [2002] BPIR 370 . . . 5.87

R v Katinas [2010] EWCA Crim 3171 . . . 19.68

R v Kirk [2006] Crim LR 850 . . . 17.28

R v Lambert [2001] 1 All ER 1014, [2001]
WLR 211, [2001] 1 Cr App Rep 205, [2000]
35 LS Gaz R 36, 144 Sol Jo LB 226, CA;
affd [2001] UKHL 37, [2001] All ER 577,
[2001] 3 WLR 206, [2001] 2 Cr App Rep
511, [2001] 31 LS Gaz R 29, 145 Sol Jo LB
174 . . . 5.86

R v Land [1999] QB 65, [1998] 1 All ER 403,
[1998] 3 WLR 322, [1998] 1 Cr App Rep
301, [1998] 1 FLR 438, [1998] Fam Law 133,

[1998] Crim LR 70, [1997] 42 LS Gaz R 32,
CA . . . 17.29

R v Legal Aid Board, ex p Donn & Co (a firm)
[1996] 3 All ER 1 . . . 12.25

R v Legal Aid Board, ex p Kaim Todner (a
firm) [1999] QB 966, [1998] 3 All ER 541,
[1998] 3 WLR 925, [1998] 26 LS Gaz R
31, [1998] NLJR 941, 142 Sol Jo LB 189,
CA . . . 17.42, 17.74

R v Lewisham London Borough Council, ex
p Shell UK Ltd [1988] 1 All ER 938, (1988)
152 L G Rev 929 . . . 13.18

R v Liverpool Corpn, ex p Liverpool Taxi
Fleet Operators' Association [1972] 2
QB 299, [1972] 2 WLR 1262, 71 LGR
387, 116 Sol Jo 201, [1972] 2 All ER 589,
CA . . . 13.50, 13.53, 13.54, 14.15

R v Lloyd's of London, ex p Biggs [1993] 1
LLR 176, [1993] COD 66 . . . 12.30

R v Local Comr for Administration for the
North and East Area of England, ex p
Bradford Metropolitan City Council [1979]
QB 287, [1979] 2 All ER 881, [1979] 2 WLR
1, 77 LGR 305, 122 Sol Jo 573, [1978] JPL
767, CA . . . 15.47

R v Local Comr for Administration in North
and North East England, ex p Liverpool
City Council [1999] 3 All ER 85, 79 P &
CR 473, [1999] COD 384, [1999] JPL 844, 1
LGLR 614 . . . 13.78

R v Lord Chancellor, ex p Witham [1998] QB
575, [1997] 2 All ER 779, [1998] 2 WLR 849,
[1997] NLJR 378, 141 Sol Jo LB 82 . . . 3.18,
5.57, 11.53

R v Malvern Justices, ex p Evans [1988] QB
540, [1988] 1 All ER 371, [1988] 2 WLR 218,
87 Cr App Rep 19, 152 JP 74, [1988] Crim
LR 120, 131 Sol Jo 1698, [1988] 2 LS Gaz R
36, [1987] NLJ Rep 757 . . . 17.46

R v Mechan [2004] EWCA Crim 388, [2004]
All ER (D) 249 (Mar) . . . 19.41

R v Metropolitan London Rent Assessment
Panel Committee, ex p Properties Co
(FGC) Ltd [1969] 1 QB 577, [1968] 3
WLR 694, 112 Sol Jo 585, [1968] RVR
490 . . . 13.77

R v Metropolitan Police Comr, ex p
Blackburn [1968] 2 QB 118, [1968] 1 All
ER 763, [1968] 2 WLR 893, 112 Sol Jo 112,
CA . . . 14.17, 18.3

R v Metropolitan Police Commissioner, ex p
Blackburn (No 3) [1973] 1 QB 241 . . . 17.9,
17.19

R v Middlesex Crown Court, ex p Khan
(1996) 161 JP 240 . . . 19.29

R v Miller [1999] 2 Cr App Rep (S) 392, [1999]
Crim LR 590, CA . . . 19.68

R v Ministry of Agriculture, Fisheries and
Food, ex p Live Sheep Traders Ltd [1995]
COD 297 . . . 12.10

R v Ministry of Defence, ex p Smith [1996]
QB 517, [1996] 1 All ER 257, [1996] 2 WLR
305, [1996] ICR 740, [1996] IRLR 100,
[1995] NLJR 1689, CA . . . 13.22, 13.23

R v North East Devon Health Authority, ex p
Coughlan [2001] QB 213, [2000] 3 All ER
850, [2000] 3 All ER 850, [2000] 2 WLR
622, 97 LGR 703, 51 BMLR 1, [1999] 31 LS
Gaz R 39, 143 Sol Jo LB 213, [1999] Lloyd's
Rep Med 306, [1999] 2 CCL Rep 285,
CA . . . 13.57

R v NW [2010] EWCA Crim 404, [2010] 1
WLR 1426, [2010] 2 Cr App R 8 . . . 19.40

R v Offen [2001] 2 All ER 154, [2001] 1 WLR
253, [2001] 1 Cr App Rep 372, [2001] 2
Cr App Rep (S) 44, [2001] Crim LR 63,
[2001] 01 LS Gaz R 23, 144 Sol Jo LB 288,
CA . . . 5.64–5.66

R v Olden [2007] EWCA Crim 726 . . . 18.45

R v O'Sullivan [1995] 1 Cr App Rep 455,
CA . . . 17.6, 17.11

R v Panel on Take-overs and Mergers, ex p
Datafin plc [1987] QB 815, [1987] 1 All ER
564, [1987] 2 WLR 699, [1987] BCLC 104, 3
BCC 10, 131 Sol Jo 23, [1987] LS Gaz R 264,
[1986] NLJ Rep 1207, CA . . . 12.27, 12.28

R v Parliamentary Commissioner for
Administration, ex p Balchin (No 1) [1996]
NPC 147, [1997] COD 146, [1996] EGCS
166, [1997] JPL 917 . . . 15.107

R v Parliamentary Commissioner for
Administration, ex p Balchin (No 2) (1999)
79 P & CR 157, [1999] EGCS 78, 2 LGLR
87 . . . 15.107

R v Parliamentary Commissioner for
Administration, ex p Dyer [1994] 1 All ER
375, [1994] 1 WLR 621, [1994] 3 LS Gaz R
47, 137 Sol Jo LB 259 . . . 15.105–15.107

R v Parliamentary Commissioner for
Standards, ex p Al Fayed [1998] 1 All ER

93, [1998] 1 WLR 669, [1997] 42 LS Gaz R
31, CA . . . 5.79, 6.49, 6.93, 15.106

R v Penguin Books Ltd [1961] Crim LR
176 . . . 17.6

R v Perrin [2002] EWCA Crim 747, [2002] All
ER (D) 359 (Mar) . . . 17.9, 17.11

R v Pintori [2007] EWCA Crim 1700 . . .
13.83

R v Port Talbot Borough Council, ex p Jones
[1988] 2 All ER 207, 20 HLR 265 . . . 13.9

R v R [1992] 1 AC 599, [1991] 4 All ER 481,
[1991] 3 WLR 767, 94 Cr App Rep 216,
[1992] 1 FLR 217, [1992] Fam Law 108, 155
JP 989, [1992] Crim LR 207, 135 Sol Jo LB
181, HL . . . 3.10, 3.11

R v Rand (1866) LR 1 QB 230, 30 JP 293, 7 B
& S 297, 35 LJMC 157 . . . 13.84

R v Registrar-General, ex p Smith [1991] 2 QB
393, [1991] 2 All ER 88, [1991] 2 WLR 782,
[1991] FCR 403, [1991] 1 FLR 255, 135 Sol
Jo 52, CA . . . 11.50

R v Reiter [1954] 2 QB 16, [1954] 1 All ER 741,
[1954] 2 WLR 638, 38 Cr App Rep 62, 118
JP 262, 98 Sol Jo 235, CCA . . . 17.16

R v Robinson [1994] 3 All ER 346, 98 Cr App
Rep 370, [1994] Crim LR 356, 18 BMLR
152, [1993] 45 LS Gaz R 40, [1993] NLJR
1643, 137 Sol Jo LB 272, CA . . . 19.44

R v Rogers [2007] UKHL 8, HL . . . 19.73

R v Rowley [1991] 4 All ER 649, [1991] 1
WLR 1020, 94 Cr App Rep 95, 156 JP 319,
[1991] Crim LR 785, 135 Sol Jo LB 84,
CA . . . 17.34

R v Searby [2003] EWCA Crim 1910,
[2003] 3 CMLR 479, [2003] All ER (D) 98
(Jul) . . . 12.40

R v Secretary of State for Education and
Employment, ex p NUT (2000) *The Times*,
8 August . . . 14.10

R v Secretary of State for Employment, ex p
Equal Opportunities Commission [1995]
1 AC 1, [1994] 2 WLR 409, [1995] 1 CMLR
391, 92 LGR 360, [1994] IRLR 176, [1994]
18 LS Gaz R 43, [1994] NLJR 358 . . . 10.52,
14.18, 14.22

R v Secretary of State for the Environment,
ex p Brent London Borough Council [1982]
QB 593, [1983] 3 All ER 321, [1982] 2 WLR
693, 80 LGR 357, 126 Sol Jo 118, [1981] RVR
279 . . . 13.15

R v Secretary of State for the Environment, ex p Hammersmith and Fulham London Borough Council [1991] 1 AC 521, [1990] 3 WLR 898, 89 LGR 129, [1990] RVR 188 . . . 12.7

R v Secretary of State for the Environment, ex p Kirkstall Valley Campaign [1996] 3 All ER 304, [1996] NLJR 478, [1996] JPL 1042 . . . 13.78

R v Secretary of State for the Environment, ex p Ostler [1977] 1 WLR 258, HL . . . 12.46

R v Secretary of State for the Environment, ex p Rose Theatre Trust Co [1990] 1 QB 504, [1990] 1 All ER 754, [1990] 2 WLR 186, 59 P & CR 257, 134 Sol Jo 425, [1990] JPL 360 . . . 12.61, 12.62

R v Secretary of State for Foreign Affairs, ex p World Development Movement Ltd [1995] 1 All ER 611, [1995] 1 WLR 386, [1995] NLJR 51 . . . 12.63

R v Secretary of State for Foreign and Commonwealth Affairs, ex p Everett [1989] QB 811, [1989] 1 All ER 655, [1989] 2 WLR 224, [1989] Imm AR 155, 133 Sol Jo 151, [1989] 8 LS Gaz R 43, CA . . . 4.29, 4.30

R v Secretary of State for Foreign and Commonwealth Affairs, ex p Rees-Mogg [1994] QB 552, [1994] 1 All ER 457, [1994] 2 WLR 115, [1993] 3 CMLR 101, [1993] NLJR 1153, 137 Sol Jo LB 195 . . . 4.29, 4.31, 4.32, 12.63

R v Secretary of State for Foreign and Commonwealth Affairs, ex p Southall [2003] EWCA Civ 1002, [2003] 3 CMLR 562 . . . 11.28

R v Secretary of State for Social Services, ex p Association of Metropolitan Authorities [1986] 1 All ER 164, [1986] 1 WLR 1, 83 LGR 796, 130 Sol Jo 35 . . . 14.12

R v Secretary of State for the Home Department, ex p Asif Khan [1985] 1 All ER 40, [1984] 1 WLR 1337, [1984] FLR 735, [1984] Fam Law 278, [1984] Imm AR 68, 128 Sol Jo 580, [1984] LS Gaz R 1678, CA . . . 13.9, 13.53

R v Secretary of State for the Home Department, ex p Bentley [1994] QB 349, [1993] 4 All ER 442, [1994] 2 WLR 101, [1993] 37 LS Gaz R 49, [1993] NLJR 1025, 137 Sol Jo LB 194, [1993] 4 LRC 15, DC . . . 4.29, 4.32, 4.33, 15.58

R v Secretary of State for the Home Department, ex p Brind [1991] 1 All ER 720, HL . . . 12.9, 13.22, 13.26, 13.30

R v Secretary of State for the Home Department, ex p Cheblak [1991] 1 WLR 890, [1991] 2 All ER 319 . . . 3.36

R v Secretary of State for the Home Department, ex p Daly [2001] UKHL 26, [2001] 2 AC 532, [2001] 3 All ER 433, [2001] 26 LS Gaz R 43, 145 Sol Jo LB 156 13.25, 13.33–13.36 . . . 13.24, 13.32, 13.34

R v Secretary of State for the Home Department, ex p Doody [1994] 1 AC 531, [1993] 3 WLR 154, [1993] NLJR 991 . . . 13.70, 13.71

R v Secretary of State for the Home Department, ex p Fire Brigades Union (1995) [1995] 2 AC 513, [1995] 2 All ER 244, [1995] 2 WLR 464, [1995] NLJR 521, HL . . . 2.26, 4.20

R v Secretary of State for the Home Department, ex p Hosenball [1977] 3 All ER 452, [1977] 1 WLR 766, 141 JP 626, 121 Sol Jo 255, CA . . . 11.14, 11.27, 13.62

R v Secretary of State for the Home Department, ex p Leech (No 2) [1994] QB 198, [1993] 4 All ER 539, CA . . . 3.19, 5.57, 11.53

R v Secretary of State for the Home Department, ex p Northumbria Police Authority [1989] QB 26, [1988] 1 All ER 556, [1988] 2 WLR 590, 132 Sol Jo 125, [1988] 1 LS Gaz R 34, CA . . . 4.24

R v Secretary of State for the Home Department, ex p Pierson [1998] AC 539, [1997] 3 All ER 577, [1997] 3 WLR 492, [1997] 37 LS Gaz R 41 . . . 3.16, 5.57

R v Secretary of State for the Home Department, ex p Ruddock [1987] 2 All ER 518, [1987] 1 WLR 1482, 131 Sol Jo 1551, [1987] LS Gaz R 3335 . . . 13.54

R v Secretary of State for the Home Department, ex p Venables [1998] AC 407, [1997] 3 All ER 97, HL . . . 13.15

R v Secretary of State for Social Services, ex p Association of Metropolitan Authorities [1986] 1 All ER 164, [1986] 1 WLR 1, 83 LGR 796, 130 Sol Jo 35 . . . 14.12

R v Secretary of State for Trade and Industry, exp Greenpeace Ltd [1998] COD 59, [1998] Env LR 415, [1998] EuLR 48 . . . 12.75

R v Secretary of State for Transport, ex p Factortame Ltd (No 2) [1991] 1 AC 603, [1990] 3 WLR 818, [1990] ECR I-2433, [1990] 3 CMLR 1, [1990] 2 Lloyd's Rep 351, [1990] 41 LS Gaz R 33 . . . 5.46–5.48, 5.50, 5.57, 10.52

R v Secretary of State for Transport, ex p Factortame Ltd [1996] QB 404, [1996] 2 WR 506, [1996] All ER (EC) 301, [1996] 1 ECR I-1029, [1996] 1 CMLR 889, [1996] 1 IRLR 267, ECJ . . . 10.41

R v Secretary of State for Transport, ex p Factortame (No 5) [2000] 1 AC 524 . . . 7.46, 10.43

R v Self [1992] 3 All ER 476, [1992] 1 WLR 657, 95 Cr App Rep 42, 156 JP 397, [1992] Crim LR 572, [1992] LS Gaz R 31, 136 Sol Jo LB 88, CA . . . 18.50, 18.51

R v Smethurst [2001] EWCA Crim 772 [2002] 1 Cr App Rep 50, 165 JP 377, [2001] Crim LR 657 . . . 17.29

R v Socialist Worker Printers and Publishers Ltd, ex p A-G [1975] QB 637, [1975] 1 All ER 142, [1974] 3 WLR 801, 118 Sol Jo 791, DC . . . 17.41, 17.69

R v Somerset County Council, ex p Fewings [1995] 3 All ER 20, [1995] 1 WLR 1037, 93 LGR 515, [1995] 16 LS Gaz R 43, [1995] NLJR 450, 139 Sol Jo LB 88, CA . . . 13.7

R v Stamford [1972] 2 QB 391, [1972] 2 All ER 427, [1972] 2 WLR 1055, 56 Cr App Rep 398, 136 JP 522, 116 Sol Jo 313, CA . . . 17.27

R v Sussex Justices, ex p McCarthy [1924] 1 KB 256, 22 LGR 46, 88 JP 3, 93 LJKB 129, [1923] All ER Rep 233, 68 Sol Jo 253 . . . 13.84

R v Thomson Newspapers Ltd, ex p A-G [1968] 1 All ER 268, [1968] 1 WLR 1, 111 Sol Jo 943, DC . . . 17.78

R v Van der Westhuizen (2011) . . . 17.24

R v Waddon (2000) unreported, 6 April, CA . . . 17.4

R v Waltham Forest London Borough Council, ex p Baxter [1988] QB 419, [1987] 3 All ER 671, [1988] 2 WLR 257, 86 LGR 254, 132 Sol Jo 227, [1988] LS Gaz R 36, [1987] NLJ Rep 947, [1988] RVR 6, CA . . . 13.15

R v White [2001] EWCA Crim 216 [2001] 1 WLR 1352, [2001] 1 WLR 1352, [2001] Crim LR 576 . . . 19.70, 19.72

R v Wicks [1998] AC 92, [1997] 2 All ER 801, [1997] 2 WLR 876, 161 JP 433, [1997] 35 LS Gaz R 34, [1997] NLJR 883, [1997] JPL 1049, 141 Sol Jo LB 127, HL . . . 12.38

Raissi v Commissioner of Police of the Metropolis [2008] EWCA Civ 1237 . . . 18.46, 18.47

Redknapp v Commissioner of Police of the Metropolis [2008] EWHC 1177 . . . 18.73

Redmond-Bate v DPP (1999) 163 JP 789, [1999] Crim LR 998 . . . 16.11, 16.12, 19.9, 19.32

Reid v Secretary of State for Scotland [1999] 2 AC 512, [1999] 1 All ER 481, [1999] 2 WLR 28, HL . . . 12.8

Rice v Connolly [1966] 2 QB 414, [1966] 2 All ER 649, [1966] 3 WLR 17, 130 JP 322, 110 Sol Jo 371, DC . . . 18.99, 18.100

Richardson v Chief Constable of the West Midlands Police [2011] EWHC 773 (QB), [2011] 2 Cr App R 1 . . . 18.36

Ridge v Baldwin [1964] AC 40, [1963] 2 All ER 66, [1963] 2 WLR 935, 61 LGR 369, 127 JP 295, 107 Sol Jo 313, HL . . . 12.47, 13.46–13.48, 13.77, 14.10

Riverside Mental Health NHS Trust v Fox [1994] 1 FLR 614 . . . 14.28

Roberts v Hopwood [1925] AC 578, 23 LGR 337, 89 JP 105, 94 LJKB 542, [1925] All ER Rep 24, 69 Sol Jo 475, 133 LT 289, 41 436, HL . . . 13.9

Robson v Hallett [1967] 2 QB 939, [1967] 2 All ER 407, [1967] 3 WLR 28, 51 Cr App Rep 307, 131 JP 333, 111 Sol Jo 254 . . . 18.64

Rost v Edwards [1990] 2 QB 460, [1990] 2 All ER 641, [1990] 2 WLR 1280, [1990] 12 LS Gaz R 42 . . . 6.82

Roy v Kensington and Chelsea and Westminster Family Practitioner Committee [1992] 1 AC 624, [1992] 1 All ER 705, [1992] 2 WLR 239, [1992] IRLR 233, 8 BMLR 9, [1992] 17 LS Gaz R 48, 136 Sol Jo LB 62, HL . . . 12.16

S (a child), Re (Identification: restriction on publication) [2004] EWCA Civ 963, [2004] Fam 43, [2004] UKML 47, CA . . . 17.43, 17.48

S (children: care plan), Re [2002] UKHL 10, [2002] 2 AC 291, [2002] 2 All ER 192, [2002] 2 WLR 720, [2002] LGR 251, [2002] 1 FCR 577, [2002] 1 FLR 815, [2002] 17 LS Gaz 34, [2002] All ER (D) 212 (Mar) . . . 5.72

S v CPS [2008] EWHC 438 (Admin) . . . 19.63

Schmidt v Secretary of State for Home Affairs [1969] 2 Ch 149, [1969] 1 All ER 904, [1969] 2 WLR 337, 133 Sol Jo 16, CA . . . 13.49

Scott v Scott [1913] AC 417, 82 LJP 74, [1911–13] All ER Rep 1, 57 Sol Jo 498, 109 LT 1, 29 TLR 520, HL . . . 17.40, 17.45

Scruttons Ltd v Midland Silicones Ltd [1962] AC 446, [1962] 1 All ER 1, [1962] 2 WLR 186, 106 Sol Jo 34, sub nom Midland Silicones Ltd v Scruttons Ltd [1961] 2 Lloyd's Rep 365, HL . . . 11.47

Secretary of State for the Home Department v GG [2009] EWHC 142 (Admin), [2009] EWCA Civ 786 . . . 18.18

Secretary of State for the Home Department v JJ [2006] 3 WLR 866 . . . 3.37

Secretary of State for the Home Department v Rehman [2001] UKHL 47, [2003] 1 AC 153, HL . . . 3.36

Secretary of State for Social Security v Tunnicliffe [1991] 2 All ER 712, CA . . . 5.86

Sedley's case (1675) Strange 168, [1675] 1 Sid 168 . . . 17.35

Shaw v DPP [1962] AC 220, [1961] 2 All ER 446, [1961] 2 WLR 897, 45 Cr App Rep 113, 125 JP 437, 105 Sol Jo 421, HL . . . 17.33

Sheldrake v DPP [2005] 1 A.C. 264, [2004] 3 WLR 976, [2005] 1 All ER 237 . . . 5.76

Silih v Slovenia [2009] ECHR 571, (2009) 49 EHRR 37 . . . 5.89

Sillars v Smith (1982) SLT 539n . . . 5.45

Sirros v Moore [1975] QB 118, [1974] 3 WLR 459, [1974] 3 All ER 776 . . . 2.21

Smith v DPP [2001] EWHC Admin 55 (2001) 165 JP 432, [2001] Crim LR 735 . . . 18.80, 18.101

Smith v East Elloe RDC [1956] 1 All ER 855, [1956] 2 WLR 888, 54 LGR 233, 6 P & CR 102, 120 JP 263, 100 Sol Jo 282, HL . . . 12.45–12.47

Smith v UK (2000) 29 EHRR 493 . . . 13.23

Snook v Mannion [1982] RTR 321, [1982] Crim LR 601 . . . 18.63

South Bucks District Council v Porter (No 2) [2004] UKHL 33, [2004] UKHL 33, [2004] UKHL 33, [2004] 1 WLR 1953, [2003] 2 AC 558, HL . . . 13.75

Southard v DPP [2006] EWHC 3449 (Admin) . . . 19.57, 19.65

Spicer v Holt [1977] AC 987, [1976] 3 All ER 71, [1976] 3 WLR 398, [1976] RTR 389, 63 Cr App Rep 270, 140 JP 545, [1977] Crim LR 364, 120 Sol Jo 572, HL . . . 18.28

Stancliffe Stone Co Ltd v Peak District National Park Authority [2005] EWCA Civ 747, [2004] EWHC 1475, QB . . . 12.23

Steel v United Kingdom (1998) 28 EHRR 603, [1998] Crim LR 893, 5 BHRC 339, [1999] EHRLR 109, ECtHR . . . 19.4, 19.5, 19.27

Steeples v Derbyshire County Council [1984] 3 All ER 468, [1985] 1 WLR 256, 128 Sol Jo 875, [1985] LS Gaz R 358, [1981] JPL 582 . . . 13.77

Stefan v General Medical Council [1999] 1 WLR 1293, 49 BMLR 161, 143 Sol Jo LB 112, [1999] Lloyd's Rep Med 90, PC . . . 13.74

Stockdale v Hansard (1839) 9 Ad & El 1, 3 State Tr NS 723, 8 LJQB 294, 3 Jur 905, 2Per&Dav1 . . . 5.17, 6.83

Sunday Times v United Kingdom (1979) 2 EHRR 245, ECtHR . . . 17.49

Syed v DPP [2010] EWHC 81 (Admin), [2010] 1 Cr App R 34 . . . 18.81, 18.82

Taylor v Chief Constable of Thames Valley Police [2004] EWCA Civ 858, [2004] 3 All ER 503, CA . . . 18.52, 18.57

Taylor v DPP (2006) 170 JP 485, DC . . . 19.55

Tesco Stores Ltd v Secretary of State for the Environment [1995] 2 All ER 636, [1995] 1 WLR 759, 70 P & CR 184, [1995] 2 EGLR 147, [1995] 24 LS Gaz 39, [1995] NLJR 724, [1995] 27 EG 154, HL

Thoburn v City of Sunderland [2002] EWHC Admin 195, (2002) 166 JP 257, [2002] 15 LS Gaz R 35, [2002] NLJR 312 . . . 1.30, 5.57, 5.60, 10.55, 13.10

Times Newspapers, Re [2008] EWCA Crim 2559, [2009] 1 WLR 1015, [2009] Crim LR 114 . . . 17.69

Timmins v Gormley [2000] QB 451, [2000] 1
All ER 65, [2000] 2 WLR 870, [2000] IRLR
96, CA . . . 13.86

Tovey v Ministry of Justice [2011] EWHC 271,
[2011] HRLR 17 . . . 6.9

Trinity Mirror plc, Re [2008] EWCA Crim
50; [2008] WLR (D) 27 . . . 17.75

Trustees of the Dennis Rye Pension Fund
v Sheffield City Council [1997] 4 All ER
747, [1998] 1 WLR 840, 30 HLR 645,
CA . . . 12.25

Tucker v DPP [2008] EWCA Crim
3063 . . . 19.97

Valentine v DPP [1997] COD 339,
DC . . . 19.51

Van Duyn v Home Office (41/74) [1975] Ch
358, [1975] 3 All ER 190, [1975] 2 WLR 760,
[1974] ECR 1337, [1975] 1 CMLR 1, 119 Sol
Jo 302, ECJ . . . 10.10, 10.19

Vauxhall Estates Ltd v Liverpool Corpn
[1932] 1 KB 733, 30 LGR 22, 95 JP 224, 101
LJKB 779, 75 Sol Jo 886, 146 LT 167, 48
TLR 100 . . . 5.22

Venables v News Group Newspapers Ltd
[2001] Fam 430, [2001] 1 All ER 908, 2
WLR 1038, [2002] 1 FCR 333, [2001] 1 FLR
791, [2001] Fam Law 258, [2001] 12 LS Gaz
R 41, [2001] NLJR 57, 145 Sol Jo LB 43,
[2001] EMLR 255 . . . 16.103

Von Colson and Kamann v Land Nordrhein-
Westfalen (14/83) [1984] ECR 1891, [1986] 2
CMLR 430, 134 NLJ 473, ECJ . . . 10.31

W v DPP [2005] EWHC 1333 (Admin), [2005]
EWCA Civ 1333 . . . 12.41

Waddington v Miah [1974] 2 All ER 377,
[1974] 1 WLR 683, 59 Cr App Rep 149, 138
JP 497, 118 Sol Jo 365, HL . . . 11.54

Wainwright v Home Office [2003] UKHL 53,
[2003] 4 All ER 969, [2003] 3 WLR 1137,
[2004] IP & T 78, [2003] 45 LS Gaz R 30,
147 Sol Jo LB 1208, 15 BHRC 387, [2003]
All ER (D) 279 (Oct) . . . 11.43

Waldron, ex p [1986] QB 824, [1985] 3 WLR
1090, 129 Sol Jo 892, [1986] LS Gaz R 199,
sub nom R v Hallstrom, ex p W [1985] 3
All ER 775, CA . . . 12.11

Walters v WH Smith & Sons Ltd [1914] 1 KB
595 . . . 18.51

Wandsworth London Borough Council v A
[2000] 1 WLR 1246, [2000] LGR 81, [2000]
LGR 81, [2000] ELR 257, [2000] 03 LS Gaz
R 35, 144 Sol Jo LB 47, CA . . . 12.34, 12.35

Wandsworth London Borough Council v
Winder [1985] AC 461, [1984] 3 All ER 976,
[1984] 3 WLR 1254, 83 LGR 143, 17 HLR
196, 128 Sol Jo 838, [1985] LS Gaz R 201,
[1985] NLJ Rep 381, HL . . . 12.33, 12.36

Wason v Walter (1868) LR 4 QB 73, 33 JP 149,
8 B & S 671, 38 LJQB 34, 17 WR 169, 19 LT
409 . . . 6.79

Webb v EMO Air Cargo (UK) Ltd [1992] 2
All ER 43, [1992] 1 CMLR 793, [1992] ICR
445, [1992] IRLR 116, [1992] 10 LS Gaz R
33, [1992] NLJR 16, 136 Sol Jo LB 32, CA,
[1992] 4 All ER 929, [1993] 1 WLR 49,
[1993] 1 CMLR 259, [1993] ICR 175, [1993]
IRLR 27, [1993] 9 LS Gaz R 44, 137 Sol Jo
LB 48, HL

Webb v EMO Air Cargo (UK) Ltd; C-32/93
[1994] QB 718, [1994] 4 All ER 115, [1994]
3 WLR 941, [1994] ECR I-3567, [1994] 2
CMLR 729, [1994] ICR 770, IRLR 482,
[1994] NLJR 1278, ECJ . . . 10.65

Webb v EMO Air Cargo (UK) Ltd (No 2)
[1995] 4 All ER 577, [1995] 1 WLR 1454,
[1996] 2 CMLR 990, [1995] ICR 1021,
[1995] IRLR 645, [1995] 42 LS Gaz R 24,
140 Sol Jo LB 9, HL . . . 10.65

Whalley v Lord Watson of Invergowrie 2000
SC 340, 2000 SLT 475 . . . 5.54

Wheeler v Leicester City Council [1985]
AC 1054, [1985] 2 All ER 1106, [1985]
WLR 335, 83 LGR 725, 129 Sol Jo 558,
[1985] LS Gaz R 3175, [1985] NLJ Rep 781,
HL . . . 13.11, 13.17

White v White and another [2001] UKHL
9, [2001] 2 All ER 43, [2001] PIQR P281,
HL . . . 10.58, 10.61

Williamson v Chief Constable of the West
Midlands Police [2003] EWCA Civ 337,
[2004] 1 WLR 14, 167 JP 181, [2003] All ER
(D) 316 (Feb) . . . 19.4

Wilson v First County Trust Ltd [2003]
UKHL 40, [2004] 1 AC 816, [2003] 4 All ER
97, [2003] 2 All ER (Comm) 491, [2003] 3
WLR 568, [2003] 35 LS Gaz R 39, 147 Sol Jo
LB 872, [2003] All ER (D) 187 (Jul) . . .
5.88

Wise v Dunning [1902] 1 KB 167, 66 JP 212,
71 LJKB 165, 20 Cox CC 121, 50 WR 317,
[1900–3] All ER Rep 727, 46 Sol Jo 152, 85
LT 721, 18 TLR 85, DC . . . 19.30, 19.33, 19.34

YL v Birmingham City Council [2007]
UKHL 27, [2008] 1 AC 95, [2007] 3 WLR
112, [2007] 3 All ER 957 . . . 16.84

Zollman v United Kingdom [2004] ECtHR
361 . . . 6.89

## Numerical

16–17/62 Confédération Nationale des
Producteurs de Fruits et Legumes v EEC
Council [1962] ECR 471, [1963] CMLR 160,
ECJ . . . 10.7

26/62 Algemene Transporten Expeditie
Onderneming Van Gend en Loos
NV v Nederlandse Administratie der
Belastingen [1963] ECR 1, [1963] CMLR
105, ECJ . . . 10.11

57/65 Firma Alfons Lütticke GmbH v
Hauptzollamt Saarelouis [1966] ECR 205,
[1971] CMLR 674, ECJ . . . 10.14

9/70 Grad v Finanzamt Traunstein [1970]
ECR 825, [1971] CMLR 1, ECJ . . . 10.18

39/72 EC Commission v Italy [1973] ECR 101,
[1973] CMLR 439, ECJ . . . 10.17

41/74 Van Duyn v Home Office [1975] Ch
358, [1975] 3 All ER 190, [1975] 2 WLR 760,
[1974] ECR 1337, [1975] 1 CMLR 1, 119 Sol
Jo 302, ECJ . . . 10.10, 10.19

43/75 Defrenne v Sabena [1981] 1 All ER
122n, [1976] ECR 455, [1976] 2 CMLR 98,
[1976] ICR 547, ECJ . . . 10.15, 10.24, 10.51

50/76 Amsterdam Bulb BV v Produktschap
voor Siergewassen [1977] ECR 137, [1977] 2
CMLR 218 . . . 10.17

148/78 Pubblico Ministero v Ratti [1979] ECR
1629, [1980] 1 CMLR 96, ECJ . . . 10.21–10.23

8/81 Becker v Finanzamt–Münster
Innenstadt [1982] ECR 53, [1982] 1 CMLR
499, ECJ . . . 10.23

14/83 Von Colson and Kamann v Land
Nordrhein-Westfalen [1984] ECR
1891, [1986] 2 CMLR 430, 134 NLJ 473,
ECJ . . . 10.31

152/84 Marshall v Southampton and South
West Hampshire Area Health Authority
(Teaching) [1986] QB 401, [1986] 2 All
ER 584, [1986] 2 WLR 780, [1986] ECR
723, [1986] 1CMLR 688, [1986] ICR 335,
[1986] IRLR 140, 130 Sol Jo 340, [1986]
LS Gaz R 1720, ECJ . . . 10.24–10.26,
10.30

222/84 Johnston v Chief Constable of the
Royal Ulster Constabulary [1987] QB 129,
[1986] 3 All ER 135, [1986] 3 WLR 1038,
[1986] ECR 1651, [1986] 3 CMLR 240,
[1987] ICR 83, [1986] IRLR 263, 130 Sol Jo
953, [1987] LS Gaz R 188, ECJ . . .
10.28

80/86 Officier van Justitie v Kolpinghuis
Nijmegen [1987] ECR 3969, [1989] 2 CMLR
18, ECJ . . . 3.15, 10.33

C-106/89 Marleasing SA v La Comercial
Internacional de Alimentación SA [1990]
ECRI-4135, [1992] 1 CMLR 305, [1993]
BCC 421, 135 Sol Jo 15, ECJ . . . 3.15,
10.33–10.36, 10.58–10.62

C-188/89 Foster v British Gas plc [1991]
QB 405, [1990] 3 All ER 897, [1991] WLR
258, [1990] ECR I-3313, [1990] 2 CMLR
833, [1991] ICR 84, [1990] IRLR 353,
ECJ . . . 10.26

C-6, 9/90 Francovich and Bonifaci v
Italy [1991] ECRI-5357, [1993] 2 CMLR
66, [1995] ICR 722, [1992] IRLR 84,
ECJ . . . 10.34, 10.38, 10.41, 10.44

C-46/93 & C-48/93 Brasserie du Pêcheur SA
v Germany [1996] QB 404, [1996] 2 WLR
506, [1996] All ER (EC) 301, [1996] ECRI-
1029, [1996] 1 CMLR 889, [1996] IRLR 267,
ECJ . . . 10.41

C-392/93 R v HM Treasury, ex p British
Telecommunications plc [1996] QB 615,
[1996] 3 WLR 203, [1996] All ER (EC) 411,
[1996] ECR I-1631, [1996] 2 CMLR 217,
[1996] IRLR 300, ECJ . . . 10.42

C-129/96 Inter-Environnement Wallonie
ASBL v Region Wallonie [1997] ECR
I-7411 . . . 10.35

C-379/01–403/01 Pfeiffer [2005] All ER (EC)
763, (2005) All ER (EC) 763, ECJ . . . 10.32

C-234/02 P European Ombudsman v
Lambert [2004] ECR I-2803 . . . 15.123

# Table of European conventions, directives, and treaties

*Paragraph references in **bold** indicate that the text is reproduced in full*

## *Directives*

Dir 64/221//EEC . . . 10.10
  Art 3 . . . 10.19
Dir 73/239//EEC Insurance
  Directive . . . 10.39
Dir 75/117 Equal Pay Directive . . . 10.54
Dir 76/207//EEC Equal Treatment
  Directive . . . 10.24, 10.63, 10.65
Dir 77/187//EEC Acquired Rights
  Directive . . . 10.56
Dir 80/987//EEC . . . 10.38
Dir 84/5/EEC Second Motor Insurance
  Directive . . . 10.58, 10.59
Dir 89/104/EEC Trade Mark
  Directive . . . 7.47
Dir 95/46//EC Data Protection Directive, Art
  14 . . . 10.34

## *Treaties and Conventions*

Amsterdam Treaty . . . 7.34
Anglo-Irish Treaty 1922 . . . 8.11

Convention on the Transfer of Sentenced
  Persons 1983 . . . 4.33

European Coal and Steel Community Treaty
  1951 . . . 7.2
EC Treaty . . . 7.3, 7.6
  Art 5 . . . 10.38
  Art 10 . . . 10.31
  Art 12 . . . 10.11, 10.12
  Art 19 (now Art 157 of the TFEU) . . . 10.15
  Art 48 (now Art 45 of the TFEU) . . . 10.19
  Art 90(3) (now Art 110 of the TFEU) . . . 10.14
  Art 119 (now Art 157 of the
    TFEU) . . . 10.50, 10.53
  Art 177 (now Art 267 of the TFEU) . . . 10.24
  Art 177(3) . . . 10.11

European Convention on Human Rights
  1950 . . . 16.7
  Art 2 . . . 16.24, 16.39, 16.42, 16.47, 16.84
  Arts 2–12 . . . 16.75
  Art 3 . . . 5.64, 13.87, 14.10, 16.39, 16.42,
    16.47, 16.52, 16.84
  Art 4 . . . 16.39, 16.42
  Art 4(1) . . . 16.47
  Art 5 . . . 3.35, 3.37, 5.64, 16.39, 16.42, 16.52,
    16.116, 18.12, 18.26, 18.27, 19.5, 19.23
  Art 5(1) . . . 5.83, 18.12, 18.13, 18.48
  Art 5(1)(b) . . . 19.28
  Art 5(1)(c) . . . 18.48, 19.4
  Art 5(1)(f) . . . 3.35, 16.118
  Art 5(2) . . . **18.57**
  Art 5(3) . . . 16.48, 16.118
  Art 5(4) . . . 5.83, 16.115
  Art 5(5) . . . 16.116
  Art 6 . . . 5.68, 5.83, 13.82, 13.83, 16.39
  Art 6(1) . . . 5.81, 5.85, 6.88, 6.89
  Art 6(2) . . . 5.87, 6.89
  Art 7 . . . 3.9, 3.11, 5.64, 11.54, 16.39, 16.47
  Art 8 . . . 5.81, 6.88, 6.89, 11.43, 13.23, 14.10,
    16.39, 16.84, 17.29, 18.12, 18.14, 19.8
  Art 8(1) . . . 18.12
  Art 8(2) . . . 18.14
  Arts 8–11 . . . 16.42, 16.43
  Art 9 . . . 16.39, 18.12
  Art 10 . . . 6.6, 13.30, 16.39, 17.29, 18.12,
    19.97, 19.98
  Art 10(2) . . . 17.9, 19.28
  Art 11 . . . 16.39, 18.12, 19.97, 19.98
  Art 12 . . . 5.81, 16.39, 16.117
  Art 13 . . . 6.88, 16.39, 16.75
  Art 14 . . . 3.35, 6.6, 16.3916.75
  Art 15 . . . 3.35, 16.47, 16.48, 16.59
  Art 17 . . . 19.74
  Art 21 . . . 16.20, 16.37, 16.38
  Art 22 . . . 16.21

Art 24 . . . 16.21, 16.51, 16.52

Art 26 . . . 16.25

Art 28 . . . 16.26

Art 29 . . . 16.27, 16.54

Art 30 . . . 16.28

Art 31 . . . 16.31

Art 32 . . . 16.32

Art 33 . . . **16.51**, 16.52

Art 34 . . . 16.26, 16.50, 16.85, 16.105

Art 35 . . . 16.53, 16.63

Art 36 . . . 16.33

Art 39(1) . . . 16.55

Art 41 . . . 16.66

Art 43 . . . 16.29, 16.30

Art 45 . . . 16.35

Art 46 . . . 6.7, 16.19, 16.65

Arts 47–49 . . . 16.36

Art 57 . . . **16.119**

Protocol 1, Art 1 . . . 5.83, 5.85

Protocol 1, Art 2 . . . 16.120

Protocol 1, Art 3 . . . 6.6, 6.9

Protocol 1, Arts 1–3 . . . 16.44

Protocol 4 . . . 16.44, 18.13

Protocol 6 . . . 16.44, 16.4516.75

Protocol 7 . . . 16.45

Protocol 11 . . . 16.18, 16.20, 16.46

Protocol 12 . . . 16.44

Protocol 13 . . . 16.45

Protocol 14 . . . 16.19, 16.63, 16.64


Financial Provisions Treaty 1975 . . . 7.4


International Covenant on Civil and Political
   Rights . . . 16.121


Lisbon Treaty 2007 . . . 7.10, 7.34, 10.1


Treaty of Amsterdam . . . 10.1

Treaty on European Union 1992 (Maastricht
   Treaty) . . . 4.29, 7.3, 10.1

Treaty on European Union 2007 (Lisbon
   TEU)
   Art 14(2) . . . 7.32
   Art 15(1) . . . 7.12
   Art 15(5) . . . 7.12
   Art 16 . . . 7.15
   Art 16(4) . . . 7.21

Art 16(6) . . . 7.15

Art 17 . . . 7.25, 7.29, 7.39

Art 17(1) . . . **7.28**

Art 17(2) . . . **7.28**

Art 19 . . . 7.43

Art 19(2) . . . 7.41

Treaty on the Functioning of Europe
   (TFEU) . . . 7.4
   Art 157 . . . 10.50, 10.53, 10.54
   Art 218(11) . . . 7.38
   Art 227 . . . 15.119
   Art 228(1) . . . 15.116, 15.118
   Art 228(2) . . . 15.114
   Art 230 . . . 7.39
   Art 234 . . . 7.27
   Art 238(2) . . . 7.19
   Art 240 . . . 7.22
   Art 247 . . . 7.27
   Art 249(2) . . . 7.38, 7.39
   Art 251 . . . 7.41
   Art 253 . . . 7.43, 7.44
   Art 254 . . . 7.49
   Art 255 . . . 7.43
   Art 256 . . . 7.48
   Art 257 . . . 7.50
   Art 258 . . . 7.29, 7.45, 10.37, 10.38
   Art 259 . . . 7.45
   Art 260 . . . 10.37
   Art 260(2) . . . 7.29
   Art 263 . . . 7.38, 7.48
   Art 265 . . . 7.48
   Art 267 . . . 7.46, 10.45, 10.47
   Art 268 . . . 7.48
   Art 270 . . . 7.48
   Art 272 . . . 7.48
   Art 275 . . . 7.48
   Art 288 . . . 10.2, 10.4, 10.11, 10.17–10.19
   Art 294 . . . 7.35, 10.8
   Art 296 . . . 10.8
   Art 297 . . . 10.8
   Art 297(1) . . . 10.22
   Art 297(2) . . . 10.8, 10.22
Treaty of Nice . . . 7.34, 7.40, 10.1


Universal Declaration of Human Rights
   1948 . . . 16.8
   Art 25(1) . . . 16.8, 16.9

# Guide to using the book

There are a number of features throughout the textbook designed to help you in your studies.

## SUMMARY

The starting point of this chapter is to consider ʌ distinguishes between written and unwritten cʌ dures that may need to be employed in order to ʌ are frequently classified according to their char classifications are therefore explained in this chʌ constitutions have any value; the unwritten natʌ the monarchy under the UK constitution; and wh chapter ends by recognizing that there is an arg

**Chapter summaries** highlight what will be addressed in each chapter, so you are aware of the key learning outcomes for each topic.

## FURTHER READING

Bagehot, W *The English Constitution* (1867).

Barber, N 'Against a Written Constitution' [2008]

Beatson, J 'Reforming an Unwritten Constitution'

Lord Bingham 'A Written Constitution?' The Juc
    available at www.judiciary.gov.uk/Resou
    2004_JSB_Annual_Lecture_2004.pdf.

At the end of each chapter is a list of recommended **further reading**.

These suggestions include books and journal articles, and will help to supplement your knowledge, and develop your understanding of key topics.

## SELF-TEST QUESTIONS

1    What is a constitution?

2    What does entrenchment mean?

3    Do you think that the UK has a constitution?

4    How would you describe the UK's constitutiʌ

5    Professor King has argued that the UK 'has ʌ
     Do you agree?

Each chapter concludes with a selection of **self-test questions**. These allow you to check your understanding of the topics covered, and help you engage fully with the material in preparation for further study, writing essays, and answering exam questions.

# Public Law  Online Resources from Oxford

Visit **www.oxfordtextbooks.co.uk/orc/publiclaw/** for access to a wealth of resources that accompany this book and have been designed to support your study of public law. These resources will help you to keep up-to-date with what is happening in the law and politics, as well as introducing you to key debates and providing a host of links to further material to help you direct your online study.

The following resources are all available on the site free of charge:

- **Regular updates** ensure that you are aware of key legal and political developments, and their significance to the public lawyer, during this time of constitutional change

- An extensive **'library' of web links** is an invaluable resource that directs you immediately to further sources of information on each of the core topics usually taught as part of a public law course, including websites, audio and video clips, blogs, and journal articles

- A **timeline of key dates** in British political history provides a fascinating insight into the events that have influenced the development of constitutional and administrative law in the UK

- **'Oxford NewsNow'** RSS feeds provide constantly refreshed links to the latest relevant news stories

- **Audio podcasts** from expert Oxford authors discuss some key issues in public law and introduce you to their textbooks

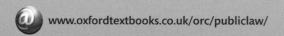

**www.oxfordtextbooks.co.uk/orc/publiclaw/**

**Scan this QR code image with your mobile device to instantly access this site.**
QR Code is registered trademark of DENSO WAVE INCORPORATED

# PART I

# Fundamental Principles of the Constitution

# 1 The meaning of a constitution

## SUMMARY

The starting point of this chapter is to consider what is meant by the term 'constitution'. It distinguishes between written and unwritten constitutions and notes the special procedures that may need to be employed in order to amend written constitutions. Constitutions are frequently classified according to their characteristics. Several of the more common classifications are therefore explained in this chapter. The chapter also considers: whether constitutions have any value; the unwritten nature of the UK constitution; the position of the monarchy under the UK constitution; and whether the UK has a constitution. Finally, the chapter ends by recognizing that there is an argument that the UK should have a written constitution.

## What is a constitution?

1.1 This straightforward question admits of more than one answer depending upon the context in which the word 'constitution' is used. In its broadest sense, a constitution can be defined as being a body of rules which regulates the system of government within a state. It establishes the bodies and institutions which form part of that system, it provides for the powers which they are to exercise, it determines how they are to interact and coexist with one another and, perhaps most importantly of all, it is concerned with the relationship between government and the individual. In his *Five Constitutions*, Finer defined constitutions as:

> codes of rules which aspire to regulate the allocation of functions, powers and duties among the various agencies and officers of government, and define the relationships between them and the public.

And Professor King in his Hamlyn Lecture offered the following definition:

> A constitution is the set of the most important rules that regulate the relations among the different parts of the government of a given country and also the relations between the different parts of the government and the people of the country.

**1.2** In a far narrower sense, a constitution amounts to the written statement of a state or country's constitutional rules in a documentary or codified form. Professor King refers to these as 'Capital-C constitutions' as a means of distinguishing them from 'small-c constitutions', which, he observes, are never written down. Thus the United States has a written constitution, as does Australia, Canada, and virtually every other state with the exception of the UK, Israel, and New Zealand. Constitutional documents are usually the result of some major upheaval in a nation's history. The impetus for the drafting of a constitution may come from a war, whether inter-state or civil, from a revolution, from the grant of independence, or from the creation of a new state following unification or reunification.

**1.3** The 'Capital-C/small-c constitution' distinction identified by Professor King is an interesting one. It provides a clear explanation of the different contexts in which the word 'constitution' may be used. It also enables Professor King to emphasize an important point; that states nearly always have both a small-c and a Capital-C constitution and that, although these constitutions overlap in some respects, they never overlap completely. In other words, small-c constitutions may cover matters not included in the written constitution and vice versa. To illustrate the point, Professor King refers to several examples, including a state's electoral system. As he points out, although an electoral system clearly forms part of a constitution in the small-c sense of the word, written constitutions rarely provide for the means by which a government is elected. Thus it is clear that in states with a written constitution, that constitution is likely to reflect only some of the constitutional arrangements of that state. To get the full picture, therefore, it will be necessary to also look at the state's small-c constitution.

## A superior law

**1.4** Where a constitutional document does exist, it represents a form of law superior to all other laws in the state. This may be implicit, but it is common for it to be stated in the text of the constitution itself. Thus s 2 of the South Africa Constitution (1996) states that:

> This Constitution is the supreme law of the Republic; law or conduct inconsistent with it is invalid, and the obligations imposed by it must be fulfilled.

**1.5** Any law (or conduct) which is in conflict with the constitution may therefore be declared to be unconstitutional by a court of law. Such a declaration will have the effect of rendering the law invalid. The task of determining the constitutionality of legislation is often assigned to a specially constituted Constitutional Court. Thus under the South Africa Constitution, the task of determining constitutional matters may be performed by the Supreme Court of Appeal, a High Court, or other courts of similar status, but it is the Constitutional Court which is the highest court in all constitutional matters. It alone has the competence to decide matters such as: disputes between organs of the state in the national or provincial sphere concerning the constitutional status, powers, or functions of any of those organs of state; the constitutionality of any parliamentary or provincial Bill; the claim that Parliament or the President has failed to fulfil a constitutional obligation; or, the constitutionality of any amendment to the constitution (s 167(4)). The South African courts have the power to make an order concerning the constitutional validity of an Act of Parliament, a provincial Act, or any conduct of the President. However, an order of constitutional invalidity has no force unless it has been confirmed by the Constitutional Court.

**1.6** In the case of the United States, the Supreme Court acts as a guardian of the constitution. However, this role was not allotted to it by the constitution itself. Rather, the court assumed the role: see *Marbury v Madison* (1803). Thus to use Professor King's terminology, here we see an example of the relationship between the small-c and the Capital-C constitutions and how an important development in the rules of the former has facilitated the better protection of the latter.

## Amendment

**1.7** Documentary constitutions often provide for their own amendment. Amendment will sometimes be necessary to reflect the changes that have occurred within society. It therefore prevents the constitution from becoming an historical anachronism. Since the constitution is the supreme law within the nation or state, it is unlikely that it will be capable of being amended in the same way as other laws. Usually, a special procedure will have to be followed in order to effect a change to a documentary constitution. In the case of the Canadian Constitution (1982), the whole of Part V of that document (arts 38–49) is given over to the procedure for amending the constitution. By contrast, the Australian Constitution (1900) and the Indian Constitution (1949) have only one section or article (s 128 and art 368 respectively) that lays down the procedure for constitutional amendment. Amending the Indian Constitution would appear to be a more straightforward process than amending either the Canadian or Australian constitutions. Article 368(2) provides that:

> An amendment of this Constitution may be initiated only by the introduction of a Bill for the purpose in either House of Parliament, and when the Bill is passed in each House by a majority of the total membership of that House and by a majority of not less than two-thirds of the members of that House present and voting, [it shall be presented to the President who shall give his assent to the Bill and thereupon] the Constitution shall stand amended in accordance with the terms of the Bill.

**1.8** Where the intention is to effect particular amendments relating to certain specified articles of the Indian Constitution, or to amend the representation of Indian states in Parliament, a further procedure must be followed. This requires that the amendment is ratified by the legislatures of not less than one-half of the states by resolutions to that effect passed by those legislatures before the amending Bill is presented to the President for assent. An attempt to amend art 368 itself must also comply with this additional procedure. This takes us into the realms of entrenchment and double entrenchment.

## Entrenchment

**1.9** Entrenchment will also be considered in Chapter **5** on the legislative supremacy of
Parliament. For present purposes, it is sufficient to note that the special procedures
for amending documentary constitutions amount to entrenching provisions. In other
words, the fundamental importance of the constitution as the supreme law within a
state dictates that it should not be susceptible to amendment in the same way as other
laws. By creating special procedures for amending the constitution, its drafters are
thereby protecting it against amendment for which there is no concerted support. Thus
in *Mauritius v Khoyratty* (2006), the PC commented that s 1 of the Constitution of
Mauritius which provides that 'Mauritius shall be a sovereign democratic state which
shall be known as the Republic of Mauritius' had been 'deeply entrenched' by the
requirement in s 47(3) of the Constitution that it could not be amended by a Bill unless
that Bill had been approved by at least three-quarters of the electorate in a referendum
held prior to its introduction, and that once introduced, it had been supported at the
final vote by all the members of the Mauritian Assembly. Of course, if the provision
which lays down the special procedure to be followed is not itself protected, it could be
repealed in the usual manner. The net effect would be that the constitution itself would
become subject to amendment in the usual manner. Accordingly, it is not uncommon,
as the example of the Indian Constitution demonstrates, for the provision which lays
down the special procedure to itself be subject to that procedure. This amounts to
entrenching the entrenching provision or double entrenchment.

## Classifying constitutions

### Written or unwritten

**1.10** Constitutions may be classified in a variety of different ways. As we have already seen,
constitutions may be written or unwritten, in the sense that they either exist or do not
exist in a documentary or codified form. This is, however, a rather crude classification.
It says nothing about the actual content of the constitution or the system of government
within the state. Moreover, it does not help us to distinguish between one constitution
and another since, as we have already noted, virtually all constitutions are written.
Therefore, we must look to other ways in which constitutions have been classified.

### Flexible or inflexible

**1.11** One classification commonly used is to refer to constitutions as being either flexible
or inflexible. Flexible constitutions are generally considered to be those which can be
amended or altered with comparative ease. Inflexible constitutions are those where
amendment is rather more difficult. Usually this will be because the constitution

requires that a special procedure is followed, (see para **1.9**). The UK constitution tends to be regarded as a flexible constitution in that it can be amended simply by passing an Act of Parliament: there is no special procedure to be followed. However, even though the process of amending may be straightforward, reform is also dependent upon support for the proposed change. This may not always be forthcoming.

## Monarchical or republican

**1.12**  A further classification which is adopted refers to a constitution as being either monarchical or republican. The UK constitution falls into the former category, although as we shall see in the chapters that follow, the personal powers of the Queen are now somewhat limited. A republican constitution provides for the post of a President. In some states, the President is effectively head of state and head of the government. This is the position in, for example, the United States and South Africa. In other states, however, the President may be the head of state but may not have any real political power. In Ireland, for example, the President is the head of state, but the head of government is the Taoiseach (Prime Minister).

## Parliamentary or presidential

**1.13**  Allied to this classification is that which is made between constitutions that are parliamentary and those that are presidential. In a parliamentary system, the head of the executive branch of government is the Prime Minister. He or she will be a member of the legislature and will be accountable to that body for the actions of the government. The UK is therefore a good example of this system. Under a presidential system, the President will be both head of state and head of the executive branch of government. However, the President will not be a member of the legislature and is therefore not directly accountable to that body. The US system is a frequently cited example of a presidential system in that the elected President is a member of neither the House of Representatives nor the Senate.

## Federal or unitary

**1.14**  Constitutions may also be classified on the basis that they are either federal or unitary. A federal system entails government at both the national (or central) and state levels, with national and state Parliaments, each of which has designated areas of legislative competence under the constitution. The US constitution is therefore a two-tier federal system, as are a number of other constitutions, including those in Australia, Canada, and South Africa. A unitary system, by contrast, provides for government solely at the national level. Although the UK constitution has traditionally been described as unitary, might it be argued that devolution (see Chapter **8**) has meant that it should be reclassified as federal or quasi-federal?

### Quantitative and qualitative classifications

**1.15** The classifications (paras **1.10–1.14**) are those which are most commonly applied to constitutions. In effect, they amount to structural and quantitative classifications. It has been noted by Wolf-Phillips that several writers have sought to apply qualitative classifications to constitutions. These include classifying a constitution as normative or nominal, stable or fragile, public or private. With regard to the latter, the classification is used to distinguish between the specified part of the constitution, the 'public' constitution, and areas of unspecified activity which are termed the 'private' constitution. However, these qualitative classifications need not detain us further. For present purposes, it is enough to be aware of the fact that constitutions can be classified according to their own particular characteristics. Indeed, a single constitution may be capable of being classified in a number of different ways. Thus the UK constitution is unwritten, flexible, monarchical, parliamentary, and quasi-federal(?).

### The uniqueness of constitutions

**1.16** No one constitution will be exactly the same as another constitution. This is because, in the words of Finer:

> *all constitutions contain elements that are autobiographical and correspondingly idiosyncratic . . . Different historical contexts have generated different preoccupations: different preoccupations have generated different emphases.*

However, despite acknowledging that constitutions have their own particular features, it is worth noting that Finer et al have taken the view that at a 'general level' the constitutions of the United States, France, Germany, and Russia 'have much in common'. Common features which they share include: a democratic basis; providing for protection against the abuse of power; according a special role to political parties; and having a version of the separation of powers (see Chapter **2**) and some system of checks and balances. Finally, however, the authors note that:

> *in none of these does the constitution itself give a full or accurate depiction of the polity: each text operates within a matrix of custom, convention, case law, and cautious compromise.*

In other words, to adopt Professor King's terminology once again, the Capital-C constitution for each of these states represents but part of the overall picture. That picture can only be viewed in its entirety by also having regard to each state's small-c constitution.

## Do written constitutions have any value?

**1.17** The short answer to this question is 'yes'. Written constitutions are valuable in the sense that they provide some indication of what actually happens in practice. A constitutional actor may look to the constitution to see what is required of them in a given situation. However, regardless of the length and complexity of a constitution, it is highly unlikely that it will contain all the answers to all the questions. Where a written constitution is silent on a particular matter, the lacuna will be filled by custom, convention, etc.

1.18   Although written constitutions are of value and therefore the comparative study of them is a worthwhile exercise, the actual text of a constitution may be somewhat mis-leading. There may be a wide discrepancy between what it says ought to happen and what actually happens in practice. Constitutions are therefore vulnerable to the whims of those who exercise power within a state. Indeed, it is sometimes argued that this means that the value of a constitution is either negligible or non-existent. If those who exercise power do so with self-restraint, the constitution becomes unnecessary. If they do not, it is argued that the constitution has become worthless. Is there any truth in this argument?

## The unwritten nature of the UK constitution

1.19   If the layman knows anything about the UK constitution, it is that it is unwritten. As we have already seen, however, this is only correct if we further qualify what we mean by 'unwritten'. If we mean that the UK constitution does not exist in documen-tary form, then the statement is correct. If, however, we mean that the rules of the UK constitution are unwritten, then the statement is erroneous. Several of the principal sources of the UK constitution are clearly written. Acts of Parliament are written law as are the principles of the common law which have been established by the courts and subsequently reported.

### The Commonwealth constitution

1.20   Although it is true to say at present that the UK does not have a documentary con-stitution, there is a view that the Commonwealth as it was called (England, Scotland, and Ireland) did have a written constitution following the Civil War (1645–9). In 1653, the Instrument of Government was drafted. This provided that the supreme legisla-tive authority of the Commonwealth resided in the Lord Protector (Oliver Cromwell for life) and Parliament. The executive branch of government consisted of the Lord Protector assisted by a council of between 13 and 21 persons. Following the death of Cromwell, his successors as Lord Protector were to be elected by the council.

1.21   The Instrument of Government made quite detailed provision with regard to the elec-tion of persons to sit in Parliament. It can therefore be excluded from the ambit of Professor King's general observation (noted at para 1.3), that Capital-C constitutions are 'typically silent' on the electoral system. Shire and borough constituencies were identified for England and Wales and the representation for Scotland and Ireland was to be determined by the Lord Protector and his council. A ceiling of 400 was placed on the membership for England and Wales. Scotland and Ireland were to have no more than 30 representatives each. Those who had fought against the parliamentarian cause, ie the Royalists, were disqualified from standing as candidates or from exercising a vote in the following four elections. The franchise was to be exercised by those with any estate, real or personal, to the value of £200. An annual revenue was to be raised for maintaining an army and navy for the defence and security of the nation, and for paying the charges of the administration of justice and other government expenses.

**1.22**  This brief description of several of the main provisions of the Instrument of Government reveals that it was concerned with the regulation of the system of government during the Interregnum. In this sense, therefore, it would seem to merit being described as a constitution. What Lord Bingham has called a 'characteristically imaginative and forward-looking constitution' ceased to have effect, however, with the restoration of the monarchy in 1660.

## The position of the monarchy under the UK constitution

**1.23**  The UK is often referred to as a constitutional monarchy. In short, this means that the Queen is head of state and that she reigns in accordance with the constitution. The word 'reigns' has been used in preference to 'rules' since, as Professor Bogdanor has noted, in modern times a 'constitutional monarchy is also a limited monarchy'. By 'limited monarchy' we mean in accordance with the constitution. We also use the word 'limited' to signify the fact that, in practice, there is very little that the Queen can do of her own volition; it is Her Majesty's government rather than Her Majesty personally which makes the important decisions and exercises real executive power. Thus as Lord Bingham has observed:

> The political power of the monarch has diminished to vanishing point, since the personal directions which remain are very limited, must be exercised according to clearly-understood principles and cannot be regarded as an exercise of independent power in any ordinary sense.

**1.24**  Walter Bagehot wrote in *The English Constitution* that the sovereign had the right to be consulted, the right to advise, and the right to warn. Such rights are, however, clearly limited. They relate to the influence that the sovereign may exert over her government, rather than to the exercise of monarchical power. In practice, it is virtually impossible to assess how great an influence the Queen has had over her Prime Ministers during the course of her reign. This is because communications between sovereign and PM are confidential. Professor Bogdanor has argued that it would be dangerous for the monarchy if these private communications were ever published. In his opinion, the monarchy 'must remain hidden by an official veil of discretion'. Nevertheless, whilst acknowledging the speculative nature of the exercise, he has offered several thoughts on the influence of the Queen. He considers that her influence is likely to increase with the length of her reign. Many years on the throne brings with it accumulated political experience. Secondly, he suggests that the Queen's influence will be greater 'on matters that are not fundamental to party ideology'. Finally, Professor Bogdanor considers that the Queen's influence 'will be felt most strongly where Commonwealth affairs are at stake because of her position as Head of the Commonwealth'.

1.25  In truth, however, despite the foregoing, it may be unwise to overstate the role of the monarchy in the UK constitution. Professor King has gone so far as to suggest that the monarchy is the most obvious example of a 'peripheral matter'. It has, in his opinion, long since ceased to feature in a significant way in British political life and the importance of the role which it performs under the constitution is in inverse proportion to the substantial volume of scholarly writings on the subject. Do you agree?

## Does the UK have a constitution?

1.26  It is implicit in what has been said thus far that the answer to this question is 'yes'. Although it has been acknowledged that the UK does not have a written constitution, ie a documentary or codified constitution, the UK constitution has been referred to as a recognizable entity. However, whilst this reflects the orthodox view, it is worth noting that there is an alternative view, namely that there is no UK constitution. It has been argued by F F Ridley that the UK does not have a constitution because it fails to exhibit any of the four essential characteristics of a constitution. These are as follows:

- it establishes or constitutes the system of government and is thus not part of it;

- it involves an authority outside and above the order it establishes, ie the constituent power;

- it is a form of law superior to all other laws;

- it is entrenched.

1.27  The first and second characteristics are evident in the following passage taken from Thomas Paine's *The Rights of Man*:

> *A constitution is a thing antecedent to a government, and a government is only the creature of a constitution. A constitution is not the act of a government but of a people constituting a government; and government without a constitution is power without a right.*

1.28  When we look at the nature of Ridley's four characteristics, it is evident that they are likely to be satisfied by a documentary or codified constitution. Conversely, they are unlikely to be satisfied by an unwritten constitution. Thus, the claim that the UK has no constitution rests on the fact that the UK has no written documentary constitution which, in Ridley's analysis, is the only appropriate form in which constitutions exist.

## Sources of the UK constitution

**1.29**  Since it is not possible to take the UK constitution down from the shelf and read its provisions in the way that one could read, for example, the US or Australian constitutions, we have to look to a variety of sources for the content of the UK constitution.

**1.30**  Several such sources have already been mentioned. Acts of Parliament may clearly be constitutional in character. Indeed, it might be argued that a great many of the Acts currently on the statute book are constitutional laws: see *Thoburn v City of Sunderland* (2002), where Laws LJ made a distinction between what he termed 'ordinary statutes' and 'constitutional statutes' (paras **5.57–5.60**).

**1.31**  Decisions of the courts are also a source of the constitution, as are the legislative supremacy of Parliament, the rule of law, the royal prerogative, and constitutional conventions. Each of these will be considered in greater depth later in this book. A final source of the UK constitution is to be found in EU law. Some of the laws that are made by the EU can rightly be described as forming part of the UK constitution. The institutions of the EU will therefore be considered in the second part of this book, as will the legislative procedures and the different types of legal instrument that are provided for under the Treaty on the Functioning of the European Union.

## The changing nature of the UK constitution

**1.32**  Constitutional change may be gradual and barely perceptible. It may affect some actors or institutions within the constitutional framework to a significant degree while leaving others relatively untouched. Traditionally, the development of the UK constitution has been regarded as an incremental evolutionary process. However, this no longer seems to be the case. In the words of Professor King:

> *Although few people seem to have noticed the fact, the truth is that the United Kingdom's constitution changed more between 1970 and 2000, and especially between 1997 and 2000, than during any comparable period since at least the middle of the 18th century.*

In support of this observation Professor King enumerates 12 'important individual changes' that have taken place in the UK constitution since 1970. These are as follows: joining the EEC (as it then was); the use of popular referendums; the changing position of local government; the increasing use of judicial review; the fragmentation of the political party system; the handing over of control over interest rates to the Bank of England; devolution to Scotland and Wales; devolution to Northern Ireland; the creation of a new local authority for London; new electoral systems for electing members of the European and Scottish Parliaments and the Welsh Assembly; the Human Rights Act 1998; and the reform of the House of Lords.

**1.33** Writing several years after Professor King, Professor Bogdanor has argued that 'the years since 1997 have seen an unprecedented and perhaps uncompleted series of constitutional reforms'. His list of reforms, which number 15, is broadly similar to that identified by Professor King with the obvious exception of the significant modifications made to the office of Lord Chancellor and the establishment of a Supreme Court (both discussed in Chapter **2**). In Professor Bogdanor's opinion:

> Any of these reforms would constitute, by itself a radical change. Taken together, they allow us to characterize the years since 1997 as a veritable era of constitutional reform.

Most, if not all, of these reforms will be considered in this book. Their collective effect is that today's UK constitution is profoundly different from that which prevailed for the greater part of the previous century.

## Should the UK have a written constitution?

**1.34** If we were to answer this question bearing in mind Ridley's analysis (paras **1.26–1.28**), presumably the answer would be 'yes' since only then would the UK have a constitution deserving of the name. Indeed, it might be argued, as Lord Bingham did extra-judicially, that it is 'ironic that we should have thought it necessary to bequeath a codified constitution to most of our overseas territories before granting them their independence, while continuing to regard such provision as unnecessary for ourselves'.

**1.35** It is worth noting that the UK's constitutional arrangements have caused a number of individuals and organizations to make the case for a written constitution. Although neither of the two main political parties has adopted a written constitution as official policy, the Liberal Democrats have. Charter 88, an independent campaign rather than a membership organization, has argued for some time that a written constitution should lie at the heart of a programme of constitutional reform for the UK.

**1.36** It has to be acknowledged, however, that the desire for a written constitution is not universal. Those opposed to such a course of action often remark on the fact that the UK's constitutional arrangements have served it well for several hundred years and that, accordingly, change is unnecessary. This may be characterized as the 'if it isn't broken don't fix it' line of reasoning. Thus, for example, Professor Barber has recently contended:

> Britain's constitution has, by and large, been a success. It has produced stable government and – in terms of democracy, transparency, human rights and the provision of social

*welfare – it compares reasonably favourably with many other constitutions…Unless advocates of a written constitution can show a need for systematic change, for a new constitutional settlement, it is hard to see what we will gain by undertaking the exercise.*

There may be some substance in this argument. However, it does not necessarily follow that those who argue for a written constitution consider that the present arrangements are fundamentally flawed. Some may do, but others may take the view that a written constitution would be a way of further improving and clarifying the current position.

## Drafting a constitution

**1.37**   If we accept that there is a need for a written constitution, problems of a practical nature will arise. These relate to the drafting and content of the constitution. The precise content of a constitution would be a difficult question to decide. If it were necessary to do so, it is likely that the task would be performed by a specially constituted constitutional convention of experts and politicians. To some extent, this has already happened. In 1991, the Institute for Public Policy Research (IPPR), an independent charitable organization established in 1988, published *The Constitution of the United Kingdom*. The IPPR had brought together a number of leading academics in the field and, as a result of their discussions and advice, a UK constitution consisting of 129 articles and six Schedules was drafted 'in the conviction that an example would advance the public argument more effectively than further general discussion of the problems which it raises and attempts to resolve'. It should be noted that what the drafters produced was not a codification of the UK's constitutional arrangements which existed at the time. Rather, it was a prescription for what those arrangements ought to be in the future.

**1.38**   More recently, Professors Bogdanor and Vogenauer have considered the problems associated with drafting a constitution for the UK. In addition to the obvious problem of what the constitution should include, the authors draw attention to the difficulties associated with enacting a constitution which has long been uncodified and which is currently based on the doctrine of the legislative supremacy of Parliament (see Chapter **5**). Although they regard these problems as 'formidable', they consider that the enactment of a UK constitution is both 'feasible' and desirable because 'we cannot be said to know what our constitution actually is, much less to understand it, until we have attempted to enact it'. Do you agree?

**1.39**   Lord Bingham also made a significant contribution to the debate on whether the UK should have a codified constitution. Although originally opposed to codification, by 2004 he had 'moved towards agnosticism' on the matter. In his opinion, if a codified constitution were adopted, it should comply with seven 'very important rules'. Thus:

- its adoption should be subject to popular endorsement;
- it should avoid undue detail;

- it should set out the fundamental principles which underpin the state;

- its provisions should be justiciable – ie it should lay down enforceable rights and duties rather than contain expressions of hope and aspiration;

- it should, subject to the constraints of parliamentary supremacy, provide for some degree of entrenchment;

- it should, so far as is achievable, be neutral in terms of politics, and systems of social and economic organization;

- it should not make provision for a constitutional court.

**1.40** With regard to the last rule, it has previously been noted (paras **1.5–1.6**) that states with codified constitutions often have specialist courts to determine important constitutional cases. Lord Bingham believed, however, that 'such a court is alien to our tradition'. He was of the view that the qualities required of a judge in determining a constitutional case do not differ from those 'in other kinds of decision-making', and that 'the line of demarcation between constitutional and other questions would not necessarily be very clear'. Furthermore, he contended that 'it would diminish the standing of the courts if they lacked jurisdiction to determine constitutional issues'. Do you share Lord Bingham's reservations?

## FURTHER READING

Bagehot, W *The English Constitution* (1867).

Barber, N 'Against a Written Constitution' [2008] PL 11.

Beatson, J 'Reforming an Unwritten Constitution' (2010) 126 LQR 48.

Lord Bingham 'A Written Constitution?' The Judicial Studies Board 2004 Annual Lecture – available at www.judiciary.gov.uk/Resources/JCO/Documents/Speeches/Bingham_2004_JSB_Annual_Lecture_2004.pdf.

Bogdanor, V *The Monarchy and the Constitution* (1995) Clarendon Press.

Bogdanor, V 'Our New Constitution' (2004) 120 LQR 242.

Bogdanor, V *The New British Constitution* (2009) Hart.

Bogdanor, V and Vogenauer, S 'Enacting a British Constitution: Some Problems' [2008] PL 38.

Bogdanor, V and Hockman, S 'Towards a Codified Constitution' (2010) Justice Journal 74.

Feldman, D 'None, One or Several? Perspectives on the UK's Constitution(s)' [2005] CLJ 329.

Finer, S E *Five Constitutions* (1979) Penguin Books.

Finer, S E, Bogdanor, V and Rudden, B *Comparing Constitutions* (1995) Clarendon Press.

Goldsworthy, J (ed) *Interpreting Constitutions: A comparative study* (2006) OUP.

Hazell, R 'Reinventing the Constitution' [1999] PL 84.

Hazell, R *Constitutional Futures Revisited: Britain's Constitution to 2020* (2010) Palgrave Macmillan.

Institute of Public Policy Research, *The Constitution of the United Kingdom* (1991).

King, A 'Does the United Kingdom still have a constitution?' (Hamlyn Lecture, 2001) Sweet & Maxwell.

Lewis, J 'The Constitutional Court of South Africa' (2009) 125 LQR 440.

Lyon, A *Constitutional History of the United Kingdom* (2003) Cavendish.

McLean, I *What's Wrong with the British Constitution?* (2010) OUP.

Ministry of Justice, *The Governance of Britain* (Cm 7170) July 2007.

Munro, C *Studies in Constitutional Law* (2nd edn, 1999) Butterworths.

Oliver, D *Constitutional Reform in the UK* (2003) OUP.

Oliver, D and Fusaro, C (eds) *How Constitutions Change: A comparative study* (2011) Hart.

Pollard, D, Parpworth, N, and Hughes, D *Constitutional and Administrative Law: Text with Materials* (4th edn, 2007) OUP.

Ridley, F F 'There is no British Constitution: A Dangerous Case of the Emperor's Clothes' (1988) 41 Parliamentary Affairs 340.

Tomkins, A *Our Republican Constitution* (2005) Hart.

Ward, I *The English Constitution: Myths and Realities* (2004) Hart.

Wicks, E *The Evolution of a Constitution: Eight key moments in British Constitutional History* (2006) Hart.

Wolf-Phillips, L *Constitutions of Modern States* (1968) Pall Mall Press.

## SELF-TEST QUESTIONS

1   What is a constitution?

2   What does entrenchment mean?

3   Do you think that the UK has a constitution?

4   How would you describe the UK's constitution?

5   Professor King has argued that the UK 'has never had a defining constitutional moment'. Do you agree?

6   To what extent, if any, do you agree with Professor Bogdanor's (2004) view that 'the constitutional reforms since 1997 offer a spectacle unique in the democratic world, of a country transforming its uncodified constitution into a codified one, there being neither the political will nor the consensus to do more'?

7   Professor Ward has argued: 'England needs a new constitution, a new politics, a new public philosophy. Our present system of government is rotten, our apology for democracy

feeble, our received visions of unitary constitutionalism no longer credible in the "new world order" in which we live'. Do you agree?

8   What are the arguments both for and against the drafting of a written constitution for the UK?

9   Do you think that Lord Bingham was right when he observed that: 'The existence of a constitutional document would . . . inculcate a constitutional sense and awareness which are now lacking'?

# 2 Separation of powers

## SUMMARY

The separation of powers is an important concept in constitutional law. In this chapter the origins and meaning of the doctrine will be considered. Reference will be made to Montesquieu's *L'Esprit des Lois* which is widely regarded as the most influential exposition of the doctrine. We will then consider whether or not there is a separation of powers in the UK constitution. In so doing, it will be necessary to examine, amongst other things, the reforms set out in the Constitutional Reform Act 2005. It will also be necessary to acknowledge that there is generally a difference of opinion between academics and judges as to the importance of the separation of powers doctrine to an understanding of the UK constitution.

## Introduction

2.1 The 'separation of powers' is a doctrine that has exercised the minds of many. Ancient philosophers, political theorists and political scientists, framers of constitutions, judges and academic writers have all had cause to consider the doctrine through the centuries. Discussion in the UK has tended to focus upon whether or not it can be said that the UK's unwritten or uncodified constitution is based upon a separation of powers. Strong views have been expressed on both sides of the debate, as will become apparent. At this initial stage, however, it needs to be appreciated that in considering this doctrine, we have moved from the discipline of law to that of political theory. The separation of powers is a doctrine not a legal principle.

2.2 It may not be possible to state precisely the origins of the doctrine of the separation of powers. However, if we look to the writings of the Greek philosopher Aristotle, it is possible to discern a rudimentary separation of powers doctrine. Thus in his *Politics*, Aristotle remarked that:

> There are three elements in each constitution in respect of which every serious lawgiver must look for what is advantageous to it; if these are well arranged, the constitution is bound to be well arranged, and the differences in constitutions are bound to

*correspond to the differences between each of these three elements. The three are, first the deliberative, which discusses everything of common importance; second, the officials . . . ; and third, the judicial element.*

**2.3** The English political theorist, John Locke, also envisaged a threefold classification of powers. Writing in *The Second Treatise of Government* (1689), Locke drew a distinction between three types of power: legislative, executive, and federative. In Locke's analysis, the legislative power was supreme and although the executive and federative powers were distinct, the one concerned with the execution of domestic law within the state and the other with a state's security and external relations, he nevertheless took the view that 'they are always almost united' in the hands of the same persons. Absent from his classification is any mention of a separate judicial power. Moreover, the proper exercise of these powers is achieved not through separation but on the basis of trust, ie that a community has entrusted political power to a government. Thus Locke's analysis does not, strictly speaking, amount to the exposition of a doctrine of the separation of powers. For that, we must turn to the writings of Montesquieu.

## Montesquieu and *L'Esprit des Lois*

**2.4** Charles Louis de Secondat, otherwise known as Baron de Montesquieu, was a provincial French nobleman and parliamentary magistrate. His lasting contribution to political theory, *L'Esprit des Lois* (*The Spirit of the Laws*) was the product of his observations whilst travelling in Europe between 1728 and 1731, although the book itself was not published until 1748. Much of Montesquieu's time during this period was spent in England attending the court of George II and moving in political circles. His exposure to English political life and the manner in which government was conducted has accordingly led to speculation as to the extent to which some of the views expressed in his book were formulated by his English experiences.

**2.5** *The Spirit of the Laws* is an eclectic book. It contains writings on many aspects of law and government, including the view that the laws of a state are greatly influenced by certain of the characteristics of that state, such as its climate, terrain, and mores. Writing in the preface to the book, Montesquieu requested a favour of his readership that he feared would not be granted, namely that they 'approve or condemn the book as a whole and not some few sentences'. His fears have subsequently been realized. Attention has tended to focus on particular parts of *The Spirit of the Laws*, most notably in the present context on chapter 6 of Book 11. In this chapter entitled *On the Constitution of England* lies the very core of Montesquieu's exposition of the Separation of Powers. For the author:

*When legislative power is united with executive power in a single person or in a single body of the magistracy, there is no liberty, because one can fear that the same monarch or senate that makes tyrannical laws will execute them tyrannically.*

*Nor is there liberty if the power of judging is not separate from legislative power and from executive power. If it were joined to legislative power, the power over the life and liberty of the citizen would be arbitrary, for the judge would be the legislator. If it were joined to executive power, the judge could have the force of an oppressor.*

*All would be lost if the same man or the same body of principal men, either of nobles, or of the people, exercised these three powers: that of making the laws, that of executing public resolutions, and that of judging the crimes or the disputes of individuals.*

**2.6**  The rationale underlying the separation of powers, to preserve liberty and prevent the abuse of power, is apparent throughout this passage. Speculation has sometimes centred upon whether chapter 6 of Book 11 is a description of the constitutional framework which Montesquieu observed in England, or whether it is his prescription for the features that a constitution ought to exhibit. In addition, questions have arisen as to the extent to which he was influenced by the opinions of others, most notably Viscount Bolingbroke, a contemporary English politician and pamphleteer. Whatever the answers to these questions, the fact remains that Montesquieu has, in the words of the authors of *The Federalist Papers*, come to be seen as 'the oracle who is always consulted and cited on this subject'. In their opinion, 'if he be not the author of this invaluable precept in the science of politics, he has the merit of at least displaying and recommending it most effectually to the attention of mankind'. It is perhaps not surprising, therefore, that M J C Vile has described Montesquieu as the 'father of modern constitutionalism'.

## Is there a separation of powers in the UK constitution?

**2.7**  If by separation we mean a strict separation between the three functions or organs of government, the legislature, the executive, and the judiciary, so that there is no overlap whatsoever, then the simple answer to the question is 'No'. A separation of powers in the purest sense is not, and never has been, a feature of the UK constitution. An examination of the three powers reveals that in practice they are often exercised by persons or bodies which exercise more than one such power. Thus, for example, there is a broad overlap between the legislative and executive in the UK constitution. The PM and his cabinet colleagues are members of both bodies and indeed, as we shall see in Chapter **11**, constitutional convention requires that this is so. Therefore Bagehot's assertion in *The English Constitution* (1867) that there was a 'close union and an almost complete fusion of legislative and executive power' in the constitution is as true today as when those words were originally published. This is despite the fact that s 2 of the House of Commons Disqualification Act 1975 imposes a limit of 95 on the number of ministers entitled to sit and vote in the HC. Not for nothing did the former Lord Chancellor, Lord Hailsham, once describe the British system of government as an 'elective dictatorship'.

**2.8** There are too many examples of overlap between the three functions of government for them all to be included in this book. The following list is therefore not exhaustive, although it does seek to highlight several of the more significant incidences of overlap.

- Parliament exercises a legislative function and to a lesser extent a judicial function in that it is responsible for the regulation of its own internal affairs.

- Government ministers are members of the executive who exercise a legislative function in Parliament and also when they make delegated legislation.

- In addition to exercising a judicial function, courts make law in the sense that they develop principles of the common law.

- Government ministers exercise a judicial function when they determine appeals in relation to disputes arising under, for example, town and country planning legislation.

- Magistrates exercise administrative as well as judicial functions in that they grant licences.

Of all the instances of overlap, however, it was the position of the Lord Chancellor which was traditionally cited in support of the argument that there is no separation of powers in the UK constitution.

## The Lord Chancellor

**2.9** The office of Lord Chancellor has existed for centuries. It has occupied a unique position in the UK constitution in that the incumbent was a member of all three branches of government and therefore exercised all three forms of power: legislative; executive; and judicial. However, on 12 June 2003 the Government announced that it was to dispense with centuries of tradition by abolishing the office of Lord Chancellor. The announcement was received with surprise in many quarters. Rather than being made as the conclusion to a consultation process, the announcement actually set such a process in motion. Accordingly, in the months which followed, the Government published various consultation papers on issues such as the establishment of a new way of appointing judges and the creation of a Supreme Court.

**2.10** The proposal to abolish the office of Lord Chancellor met with a considerable amount of opposition both within and outside Parliament. Accordingly, the Government relented and the office was retained. Section 2(1) of the Constitutional Reform Act 2005 thus provides that 'a person may not be recommended for appointment as Lord Chancellor unless he appears to the Prime Minister to be qualified by experience'. Relevant experience may include any of the following:

- experience as a minister of the Crown;
- experience as a member of either House of Parliament;

- experience as a qualifying practitioner, ie a barrister, advocate, or solicitor with the appropriate rights of audience; or

- experience as a teacher of law in a university.

The PM is under an obligation to 'take into account' the different types of experience referred to in s 2(2). He may, if he so wishes, take into account other experience which he considers relevant (s 2(2)(e)). Thus a PM's hands are not tied by s 2 as to whom to recommend for appointment as Lord Chancellor although, as Lord Bingham has pointed out, 'theoretically at least, the Prime Minister's judgment on this matter is no doubt open to review'. A Lord Chancellor need not have the legal background which has been a prerequisite for previous holders of the office. Neither must he be a member of the HL. The current Lord Chancellor and Secretary of State for Justice, Kenneth Clarke MP, has held various cabinet posts in a long political career, including Home Secretary and Chancellor of the Exchequer.

**2.11** The first part of the long title to the Constitutional Reform Act 2005 states that it is 'An Act to make provision for modifying the office of Lord Chancellor, and to make provision relating to the functions of that office'. The more important of these modifications, and the general effect of the Act on the Lord Chancellor's role, may be summarized as follows:

- The Lord Chancellor has ceased to be head of the judiciary. That role is now performed by the Lord Chief Justice who is also President of the Courts of England and Wales (s 7 of the 2005 Act).

- The automatic link between the Lord Chancellor and the speakership of the HL was broken by the creation of a separate post, Lord Speaker (see Chapter **6**). This may be held by a Lord Chancellor in the future, but this need not necessarily be the case (s 18 and Sch 6).

- The Lord Chancellor does not sit as a judge in the Supreme Court.

- The Lord Chancellor now appoints judges, or recommends to the Queen the appointment of judges, on the basis of a recommendation received from a Judicial Appointments Commission (s 6 and Sch 12).

- The Lord Chancellor is required to take an oath in which the office holder undertakes to respect the rule of law, defend the independence of the judiciary and ensure the provision of resources for the efficient and effective support of the courts (s 17).

As a prelude to these reforms, the Lord Chancellor's Department ceased to exist and was replaced by the Department for Constitutional Affairs (DCA) under the control of the Secretary of State. That department has itself now ceased to exist. It has been replaced by the Ministry of Justice headed by the Secretary of State for Justice and Lord Chancellor with responsibility for the former roles of the DCA as well as the criminal justice functions of the Home Office. Ministries of Justice are a common feature of

European governments. The creation of a Ministry of Justice in the UK, although welcomed by some, was the subject of criticism in other quarters. In part this was due to the manner in which the 'machinery of government change' was made. More importantly, however, there have been concerns expressed about the impact of the change on the perceived independence of the judiciary.

## Judicial independence

**2.12** The judicial power is the weakest of the three governmental powers in the UK constitution. Lord Steyn has argued that it is also the least dangerous department of government. It can be overridden by Parliament because the courts recognize and accept that body as being legislatively supreme: see, for example, *Burmah Oil v Lord Advocate* (1965) (paras **4.25-4.26**). Nevertheless, it is a significant power. In the modern age, where executive decision-making has greatly increased, it is vitally important that there are checks on the exercise of executive discretion. Recourse to the courts, principally by way of a claim for judicial review (see Chapters **12-14**), represents just such a check on the legality if not the merits of executive decisions. Thus the acts of the executive may be declared to be lawful/unlawful by the courts and of course such a power is particularly important in the post-Human Rights Act era. In order for the judiciary to uphold the rule of law (see Chapter **3**) and to discharge their functions generally, it is imperative that they are independent of the other two branches of government. In the past, a vitally important part of the Lord Chancellor's role was to protect the judiciary from the undeserved and unsubstantiated criticisms of the press, the public, and his ministerial colleagues alike. Now, there is also a guarantee of continued judicial independence to be found in s 3(1) of the 2005 Act, which provides:

> *The Lord Chancellor, other Ministers of the Crown and all with responsibility for matters relating to the judiciary or otherwise to the administration of justice must uphold the continued independence of the judiciary.*

**2.13** For the purposes of s 3, the 'judiciary' includes the judiciary of the Supreme Court, any other court established under the law of any part of the UK, and any international court (s 3(7)). Section 3 does not, however, impose a duty which is within the legislative competence of the Scottish Parliament to impose (s 3(2)). In other words, it recognizes that the responsibility for justice is not a devolved matter. Separate provision is also made for Northern Ireland in that s 1 of the Justice (Northern Ireland) Act 2002 is replaced by a new s 1: see s 4 of the 2005 Act.

**2.14** Section 3 imposes further duties for the purpose of upholding continuing judicial independence. Thus by virtue of s 3(5), the Lord Chancellor and other ministers 'must not seek to influence particular judicial decisions through any special access to the judiciary'. In other words, ministers must not attempt to gain any access to the judiciary which is over and above that enjoyed by a member of the public. They may of course continue to seek to influence judicial decisions by the arguments advanced on their behalf in legal proceedings, and by bringing an appeal where they are unhappy with a decision reached by a court.

**2.15**  It is evident, therefore, that despite the reforms to the office of Lord Chancellor, the holder of that post still has important responsibilities in respect of matters relating to the judiciary. These responsibilities are such that the Lord Chancellor (unlike his other ministerial colleagues) is subject to further obligations set out in s 3. Thus s 3(6) provides that the Lord Chancellor 'must have regard to':

- the need to defend judicial independence;
- the need for the judiciary to have the support necessary to enable them to exercise their functions; and
- the need for the public interest in regard to matters relating to the judiciary or otherwise to the administration of justice to be properly represented in decisions affecting those matters.

**2.16**  These duties were created in accordance with a concordat which was agreed between the then Lord Chancellor, Lord Falconer, and the then Lord Chief Justice, Lord Woolf, on 26 January 2004 at a time when it was the Government's intention to abolish the office of Lord Chancellor. The current Lord Chief Justice, Lord Judge, has made clear that the concordat is a public document, not a private agreement. Furthermore, he has speculated before the HL Constitution Committee that 'if the Lord Chancellor of the day offers the Lord Chief Justice money that the Lord Chief Justice is completely satisfied is derisory for the purposes of running the administration of justice', the holder of his post may decide to bring the concordat to an end. In part, the s 3(6) duties reflect the traditional role of the Lord Chancellor, eg to defend the independence of the judiciary. Also, however, they reflect the changing nature of that role by placing an emphasis on the administrative functions of the Lord Chancellor in relation to the judiciary. It might be argued that the tone of s 3(6) also highlights the changing nature of the Lord Chancellor's role. 'Must have regard to' is not a particularly strong obligation to impose in relation to matters as important as the need to defend judicial independence. Primary responsibility for that particular role has transferred to the Lord Chief Justice as head of the judiciary.

**2.17**  In commenting on the 'judicial independence' provisions in the 2005 Act, Professor Woodhouse has drawn attention to the lack of a statutory definition of the phrase and has suggested that it 'may be seen more appropriately as a means to several ends rather than as an end in itself' – those ends being, for example, maintaining public confidence in the justice system and the UK's system of government. The reforms made to the office of Lord Chancellor in terms of eligibility for appointment have, in her opinion, made it less rather than more likely that future Lord Chancellors will be effective defenders of judicial independence, despite s 3 of the 2005 Act. Thus she observes:

> *Because the office holder need not be a member of the legal profession, may be an elected politician, and will no longer have the responsibilities that in the past engendered*

*a particular loyalty to and empathy with the judiciary, the relationship between judges and Lord Chancellor will inevitably change. There will be nothing, other than title and tradition, to make the Lord Chancellor – as compared with any other minister – the uniquely appropriate minister responsible for judicial independence.*

Given the likelihood that future Lord Chancellors are 'more likely to be non-lawyers and career politicians', Professor Woodhouse contends:

*If this is the case, it will be even more difficult for them than it had been for their predecessors to put the interests of judicial independence above those of their party, particularly if this should require them to confront openly a ministerial colleague or disagree publicly with a government policy, a course of action that could jeopardize their ministerial careers.*

## Judicial appointments

**2.18** In a written statement to the HL Committee on the Constitutional Reform Bill (April 2004), the then Lord Chancellor criticized the arrangements for appointing judges as follows:

*There can be no doubt that we are served by judges, tribunal members and magistrates of the very highest calibre. But equally, there can be no doubt that our record of selecting them is no longer acceptable. The selection process should not be entirely in the hands of a single Government Minister. The process should be independent and transparent. In its current form, it is neither. That the process has worked as effectively as it has is a tribute to the integrity and probity of successive Lord Chancellors. But appointments have been as successful as they have despite the selection process, not because of it.*

**2.19** Accordingly, s 61 of the 2005 Act established an independent Judicial Appointments Commission (JAC) which is responsible for selecting candidates to recommend to the Lord Chancellor for judicial appointment. Its existence removes from the executive the day-to-day responsibility for selecting candidates for appointment, and it significantly reduces ministerial discretion in the appointment process. It is clear, however, that despite its name, the JAC is a recommending rather than an appointing body. Its existence does not therefore bring to an end the practice of the executive appointing judges. The justification for the continuing role of the executive in this context was explained to the HL Committee by the then Lord Chancellor as follows:

*[A]ppointing judges is a central function of the State. Parliamentary accountability for the appointments system must therefore be retained, through the Secretary of State. It follows that a Secretary of State who is accountable for appointments should have a real, albeit carefully tempered, discretion in those appointments ... The recommending model also preserves the Constitutional convention that The Queen acts solely on the advice of her Ministers.*

## Tenure

**2.20** Provision for the security of judicial tenure was originally made in the Act of Settlement 1700. Its more recent expression, at least in terms of the judges of the Court of Appeal, High Court, and the Crown Court (collectively the 'Supreme Court') is to be found in the Senior Courts Act 1981. Section 11(3) of this Act provides that judges of the Supreme Court remain in office 'during good behaviour', subject to a power of removal vested in the monarchy on an address presented to it by both Houses of Parliament. A judge of the new Supreme Court also enjoys the same security of tenure: see s 33 of the Constitutional Reform Act 2005. A criminal conviction may therefore be the catalyst for removal from office, although a judge would be more likely to resign in such circumstances. He may be compulsorily retired under s 11(8) and (9) of the 1981 Act where it is evident that he is unable to perform his duties due to infirmity or that incapacity has prevented him from resigning. Under the Judicial Pensions and Retirement Act 1993, the retirement age for judges is set at 70. This may be extended, however, to the age of 75 for an individual judge if it is thought in the public interest to do so.

## Remuneration

**2.21** In addition to security of tenure, judges enjoy security of remuneration. This means that their salaries are protected against being reduced by government order. Moreover, judges are immune from legal proceedings in respect of the discharge of their judicial functions: see *Sirros v Moore* (1975).

## The two camps

**2.22** The debate as to whether or not there is a separation of powers in the UK constitution has, as Professor Munro has noted, led to the establishment of two opposing camps. In the first of these camps can be placed the academic writers on constitutional law. The general consensus amongst them is that there is no separation of powers. Thus, for example, the late Professor S A de Smith contended that: 'No writer of repute would claim that it is a central feature of the modern British constitution'. Similarly W A Robson referred to the doctrine as 'that antique and rickety chariot . . . So long the favourite vehicle of writers on political science and constitutional law for the conveyance of fallacious ideas'. More recently, Professor Barendt has suggested that academics have generally paid scant regard to the separation of powers and that their treatments of the doctrine 'tend to be either brief or dismissive'.

## The view of the judiciary

**2.23** In the opposing camp are the judiciary. On numerous occasions, senior judges have expressed the opinion that the UK constitution is based on a separation of powers.

Thus in *Duport Steels Ltd v Sirs* (1980), Lord Diplock stated that:

> at a time when more and more cases involv[e] the application of legislation which gives effect to policies that are the subject of bitter public and parliamentary controversy, it cannot be too strongly emphasised that the British Constitution, though largely unwritten, is firmly based on the separation of powers; Parliament makes the laws, the judiciary interpret them.

**2.24** Absolute faith in the certainty of this conviction has led the Privy Council (PC) to read a separation of powers into a former colony's constitution on the basis that it has been drafted by persons familiar with the 'Westminster model': see *Hinds v R* (1977) which was subsequently applied in *DPP of Jamaica v Mollison* (2003) and *Griffith v The Queen* (2005). In *Mollison*, Lord Bingham observed:

> Whatever overlap there may be under constitutions on the Westminster model between the exercise of executive and legislative powers, the separation between the exercise of judicial powers on the one hand and legislative and executive powers on the other is total or effectively so. Such separation, based on the rule of law, was recently described…as 'a characteristic feature of democracies'.

**2.25** It should be noted, however, that in a comment on *Hinds* published under the heading 'A Constitutional Myth: separation of powers', Professor Hood Phillips remarked: 'But one rubs one's eyes when one reads that the concept of the separation of powers was developed in the unwritten constitution of the United Kingdom.' Nevertheless, in the earlier case of *Liyanage v R* (1967), where the PC declared invalid legislation made in Ceylon (now Sri Lanka) which had been amended in order to ensure that the unsuccessful plotters of a coup were convicted, the court did so on the basis of the separation of powers.

**2.26** In *R v Secretary of State for the Home Department, ex p Fire Brigades Union* (1995) (para **4.20**), a case concerned with the alleged abuse of prerogative power, Lord Mustill observed in his dissenting judgment that:

> It is a feature of the peculiarly British conception of the separation of powers that Parliament, the executive and the courts have each their distinct and largely exclusive domain. Parliament has a legally unchallengeable right to make whatever laws it thinks right. The executive carries on the administration of the country in accordance with the powers conferred on it by law. The courts interpret the laws, and see that they are obeyed.

**2.27** In *Office of Government Commerce v Information Commissioner* (2008), in commenting on the separation of powers, Burnton J observed that in the UK's constitution, the principle is 'restricted to the judicial function of government, and requires the executive and the legislature to abstain from interference with the judicial function, and conversely requires the judiciary not to interfere with or to criticize the proceedings of the legislature'. More recently, in *Baron Mereworth v Ministry of Justice* (2011), Lewison J remarked that 'The separation of powers, although not in quite the pure form that Montesquieu imagined, has always been part of our constitution'.

**2.28** Judicial belief in the existence of a separation of powers in the UK's constitution was also evident in a case where the claimant sought the court's assistance to make the Government give effect to a promise to hold a referendum prior to ratifying a European treaty.

> *R (on the application of Wheeler) v Office of the Prime Minister* **(2008):** In October 2004, the EU member states signed the Treaty establishing a Constitution for Europe. The then PM, Tony Blair, promised a referendum on whether the UK should ratify it. The treaty fell, however, after being rejected by referendums held in France and the Netherlands. After a period of reflection, the EU brought forward a new treaty, the Lisbon Treaty. The UK Government publicly stated that it did not intend to hold a referendum on this treaty, principally because it did not regard the Lisbon Treaty as having equivalent effect to the Constitutional Treaty. The claimant contended that the promise to hold a referendum in respect of the Constitutional Treaty involved an implied representation that a referendum would be held in respect of any treaty having equivalent effect, thus giving rise to a legitimate expectation that such a referendum would be held. DC held: dismissing the claim, that the promise made related specifically to the Constitutional Treaty and not the Lisbon Treaty, which on any view was a distinct and different treaty. There was no room for reading into the original promise an implied promise that there would be a referendum in respect of any treaty having equivalent effect.

**2.29** In reaching this decision, Richards LJ was of the view that an assessment of the substantive or material differences between the two treaties depended on a 'political perspective and political judgment'. Moreover, 'the subject-matter, nature and context of a promise of this kind place it in the realm of politics, not of the courts, and the question whether the government should be held to such a promise is a political rather than a legal matter'. In short, the matter was regarded as non-justiciable due to judicial adherence to the doctrine of the separation of powers.

**2.30** Extra-judicial observations on the separation of powers have also been voiced by senior members of the judiciary. Thus before his retirement as a Law Lord, Lord Steyn stressed the importance of the doctrine thus:

> When the government has a massive majority in the House of Commons the executive becomes all powerful and parliamentary scrutiny of the acts and intentions of the executive is not always as careful as it ought to be. That is when the constitutional principle of the separation of powers becomes important.

In a subsequent lecture Lord Steyn remarked:

> It used to be said that the doctrine of separation of powers is a comparatively weak principle in the English constitution. As between the legislature and the executive

*that is still so . . . But the separation of powers as between the legislature and executive, on the one hand, and the judiciary, on the other hand, has been greatly strengthened.*

And later observed:

*Under our constitution the separation of powers protecting judicial independence is now total and effectively so. This constitutional principle exists not to eliminate friction between the executive and judiciary. It exists for this reason only: to prevent the rise of arbitrary executive power.*

## A partial separation of powers

**2.31** Faced with opposing views as to the importance of the separation of powers doctrine to the UK constitution, the inevitable question is 'Which one is correct?'. The answer, however, is rather less straightforward. As we have seen, the incidences of overlap between the various powers even post the Constitutional Reform Act 2005 are such that it is impossible to claim that there is an absolute separation of powers in the UK constitution. Indeed, an absolute separation would in practice be counterproductive in that it would prevent the abuse of power by preventing the exercise of power. Government could not operate if this were the case.

**2.32** It is significant that a body of persons which exercises one of the three powers, the judiciary, believe that there is a separation of powers. That Parliament makes the laws and the judiciary interpret them has become something of a judicial mantra. It may be argued, as Professor Barendt has done, that these statements are made 'to reinforce the argument for judicial restraint in interpreting statutes' and that they reflect a belief in a pure or absolute separation of powers. If the judiciary remain of this opinion, and cases such as *R (on the application of Wheeler) v Office of the Prime Minister* (2008) suggest that there is no reason to believe that they will not, then the separation as between the judicial and the other powers will continue to be preserved even if the legislative and executive branches of government become even more entwined. In this sense, therefore, it can be argued that there is a partial separation of powers in the UK constitution.

**2.33** The importance of this partial separation ought not to be overlooked. Neither should such a separation, to borrow the words of Professor Munro, 'be lightly dismissed'. At a time when the courts are hearing cases brought by individuals under the Human Rights Act 1998 in which it is alleged that a public body has breached a Convention right, it is imperative that the judiciary remain separate and independent from the executive if they are properly to fulfil the role accorded to them under the constitution. Arguments such as these explain why the Constitutional Reform Act 2005 was the vehicle for an important institutional reform: the establishment of a Supreme Court.

## The Supreme Court

**2.34** The establishment of a Supreme Court has clear separation of powers implications. Until that event, the most senior judges, the Law Lords as they were known, sat in the legislative chamber of the HL as cross-benchers and were therefore able to exercise a legislative as well as a judicial function. Such arrangements caused confusion in the minds of some because, as the Government's consultation paper, *A Supreme Court for the United Kingdom* (July 2003), pointed out:

> It is not always understood that the decisions of the 'House of Lords' are in practice decisions of the Appellate Committee and that non-judicial members of the House never take part in the judgments. Nor is the extent to which the Law Lords themselves have decided to refrain from getting involved in political issues in relation to legislation on which they might later have to adjudicate always appreciated.

**2.35** It is thus evident that the separation of powers between the legislative and judicial branches of government was achieved in practice by a combination of convention, habit, and custom. Although the arrangements appeared to work in practice, the Government nevertheless felt that reform was necessary. Thus in a written statement to the HL Committee on the Constitutional Reform Bill, the then Lord Chancellor opined:

> The Law Lords are judges and not Legislators; the separation between these two roles should be made explicit. The principle of separation is already established in many other democracies. It is time . . . for our institutional arrangements to reflect the reality of the constitutional position . . . The Government believes strongly that our highest court should be one which others can look to as a beacon of excellence. The quality of the current Law Lords is undisputed. But if our highest court is to be an example to all, it must also be demonstrably independent of the legislature . . . The ECHR, established in English law by the Human Rights Act, stresses that judges must be independent, impartial and free of any prejudice or bias – both real and perceived. For this to be ensured, judicial independence needs not just to be preserved in practice, but also to be buttressed by appropriate and effective constitutional guarantees. The establishment of a Supreme Court will provide those guarantees.

**2.36** The creation of the Supreme Court was thus intended to emphasize the functional separation between Parliament and the courts by putting matters on a more formal footing. This functional separation is accompanied by a physical separation. Thus the first members of the new Supreme Court (the serving Law Lords at the time that the court came into existence (s 24 of the 2005 Act), ie 1 October 2009) are no longer entitled to sit and vote in the HL. The court of final appeal is also no longer situated within one of the chambers of Parliament. Instead, the Justices of the Supreme Court as they are styled (s 26 of the 2005 Act) hear cases in the Middlesex Guildhall opposite the Palace of Westminster.

**2.37** Although these arrangements have clear attractions from a separation of powers perspective, especially when it is appreciated that the growth in judicial review cases over the years and the role of the courts under the Human Rights Act 1998 make the need for an independent judiciary more important than ever, it would be a mistake to think that the establishment of a Supreme Court was universally welcomed. Indeed, in the Law Lords' own response to the Government's consultation paper, there was a distinct lack of unanimity among their Lordships on several issues, including whether there was a need for a Supreme Court at all. A number of serving Law Lords were of the opinion that 'on pragmatic grounds, the procedural change is unnecessary and will be harmful'. It was their belief that:

> the Law Lords' presence in the House is of benefit to the Law Lords, to the House, and to others including the litigants. Appeals are heard in a unique, suitably prestigious, setting for this country's court of final appeal. The 'House of Lords' as a judicial body is recognized by the name throughout the common law world. Overall, it is believed, it has a fine record and reputation.

**2.38** Such views may be contrasted, however, with those of the Law Lords who were in favour of a Supreme Court. Their argument was not that the old arrangements did not work well. Rather, their support for a Supreme Court was based on principle rather than pragmatism. These Law Lords:

> regard the functional separation of the judiciary at all levels from the legislature and executive as a cardinal feature of a modern, liberal, democratic state governed by the rule of law. They consider it important, as a matter of constitutional principle, that this functional separation should be reflected in the major institutions of the state, of which the final court of appeal is certainly one.

**2.39** A final yet important point ought to be made about the creation of the Supreme Court. Despite the new name, the court is not like Supreme Courts in other countries which have the power to strike down primary legislation which is in conflict with the constitution (paras **1.5-1.6**). Instead, the new court has the same appellate jurisdiction as that which was exercised by the Appellate Committee of the HL and the Judicial Committee of the Privy Council.

## FURTHER READING

Allan, T R S *Law, Liberty and Justice: The legal foundations of British Constitutionalism* (1993), chapter 3.

Allison, J W F *The English Historical Constitution* (2007) Cambridge University Press, chapter 4.

Barendt, E 'Separation of Powers and Constitutional Government' [1995] PL 599.

Lord Bingham 'The Old Order Changeth' (2006) 122 LQR 211.

Carolan, E *The New Separation of Powers: A Theory for the Modern State* (2009) OUP.

Lord Cooke 'The Law Lords: an Endangered Heritage' (2003) 119 LQR 49.

Gwyn, W B *The Meaning of the Separation of Powers* (1965) The Hague: Martinus Nijhoff.

Baroness Hale 'A Supreme Court for the United Kingdom' (2004) 24 Legal Studies 36.

Lord Hope 'A Phoenix from the Ashes? Accommodating a new Supreme Court' (2005) 121 LQR 253.

Lord Hope 'Voices from the Past – the Law Lords' Contribution to the Legislative Process' (2007) 123 LQR 547.

House of Lords Constitution Committee, *Relations between the executive, the judiciary and parliament* (2006–7, HL Paper 151).

House of Lords Constitution Committee, *Relations between the executive, the judiciary and parliament* (2007–8, HL Paper 177).

House of Lords Constitution Committee, *Meetings with the Lord Chief Justice and the Lord Chancellor* (2010–11, HL Paper 89).

Lord Mance 'Constitutional Reforms, the Supreme Court and the Law Lords' (2006) 25 CJQ 155.

Lord Phillips 'Constitutional Reform: One Year On', The Judicial Studies Board 2007 Annual Lecture – available at www.judiciary.gov.uk/Resources/JCO/Documents/Speeches/Maltravers_2007_Annual_Lecture.pdf.

Lord Phillips, 'Judicial Independence & Accountability: A view from the Supreme Court' – available at www.supremecourt.gov.uk/docs/speech_110208.pdf.

Munro, C *Studies in Constitutional Law* (2nd edn, 1999) Butterworths, chapter 9.

Pollard, D, Parpworth, N, and Hughes, D *Constitutional and Administrative Law: Text with Materials* (4th edn, 2007) OUP.

Stevens, R 'A Loss of Innocence? Judicial independence and the separation of powers' (1999) 19 OJLS 366.

Lord Steyn 'The Weakest and Least Dangerous Department of Government' [1997] PL 84.

Lord Steyn 'The Case for a Supreme Court' (2002) 118 LQR 382.

Lord Steyn 'Democracy, the Rule of Law and the Role of Judges' [2006] EHRLR 243.

Tucker, A J 'Legitimate Expectations and the Separation of Powers' (2009) 125 LQR 233.

Vile, M J C *Constitutionalism and the Separation of Powers* (1967) Clarendon Press.

White, R 'Separation of Powers and Legislative Supremacy' (2011) 127 LQR 456.

Williams, Sir David 'Bias; the Judges and the Separation of Powers' [2000] PL 45.

Lord Windlesham 'The Constitutional Reform Act 2005: Members, judges and constitutional change: Part 1' [2005] PL 806.

Woodhouse, D *The Office of Lord Chancellor* (2001) Hart.

Woodhouse, D 'The Constitutional and Political Implications of a United Kingdom Supreme Court' (2004) 24 Legal Studies 134.

Woodhouse, D 'The Constitutional Reform Act 2005 – Defending Judicial Independence the English Way' (2007) 5 Int'l J Const L 153.

## SELF-TEST QUESTIONS

1   What was Montesquieu's contribution to the development of the doctrine of the separation of powers?

2   Why do you think that the former Lord Chancellor, Lord Irvine, has referred to the independence of the judiciary as 'a fundamental article of Britain's unwritten constitution' and as 'a critical aspect of the doctrine of separation of powers'? To what extent, if any, do you think that the reforms set out in the Constitutional Reform Act 2005 are likely to lead to the better protection of judicial independence than has hitherto been the case?

3   Do you agree with the view that by the beginning of the 21st century, the office of Lord Chancellor had become a 'constitutional anomaly' which was in need of reform?

4   What are the arguments both for and against the claim that there is no separation of powers within the UK constitution?

5   To what extent, if any, has the establishment of a Judicial Appointments Commission ensured that there are 'significant and powerful fetters on the executive' (per Lord Falconer) in relation to the appointment of judges?

6   With the doctrine of the separation of powers in mind, what were the arguments both for and against the establishment of the Supreme Court?

7   Professor Woodhouse has contended: 'A proactive, open, and accountable Supreme Court is likely to be more effective in protecting and defending judicial independence than a government minister – even one with the exalted title of Lord Chancellor'. Do you agree?

8   Lord Bingham has commented that of all the Government's proposals which were later largely reflected in the Constitutional Reform Act 2005, 'the most eye-catching, the most widely criticized and in the event the most contentious was that to abolish the Lord Chancellor's office'. Why do you think that this was so?

# 3

# Rule of law

## SUMMARY

This chapter considers what is meant by the 'rule of law'. The concept is by no means straightforward and opinions vary as to the content of the rule of law. However, since the rule of law amounts to a means of controlling the abuse of power, its constitutional importance cannot be denied.

## Meaning of the rule of law

3.1 The rule of law is often stated to be one of the fundamental doctrines or principles of the UK constitution. Indeed, Professor Jowell has described it as 'a resilient and effective force behind the evolution of the United Kingdom's constitution'. However, despite its undoubted importance, defining what is meant by 'the rule of law' is no easy task. The difficulty stems from the fact that the rule of law means different things to different people. T R S Allan has noted that: 'In the mouth of a British constitutional lawyer, the term "rule of law" seems to mean primarily a corpus of basic principles and values, which together lend some stability and coherence to the legal order.' In the mouth of the politician, however, the rule of law becomes a stick with which to beat other regimes. For example, in the Report of the War Crimes Inquiry (1989) Cm 744, which preceded the enactment of the War Crimes Act 1991, it was argued, amongst other things, that the jurisdiction to try war criminals for offences committed on foreign soil was being extended to the English courts by the Act because the USSR (as it then was) had no rule of law. More recently, the events in Zimbabwe, where the Government of President Robert Mugabe refused to enforce court orders to eject 'war veterans' from 'white-owned' farms, have been criticized in some parts of the Commonwealth as a denial of the rule of law.

3.2 In a helpful contribution to the debate surrounding the rule of law, Professor Craig has sought to draw a distinction between formal and substantive meanings of the rule of law and, as a corollary, to identify which of these conceptions is favoured by the commentators mentioned in this chapter. Thus he observes:

> *Formal conceptions of the rule of law address the manner in which the law was promulgated (was it by a properly authorised person, in a properly authorised manner,*

*etc); the clarity of the ensuing norm (was it sufficiently clear to guide an individual's conduct so as to enable a person to plan his or her life, etc); and the temporal dimension of the enacted norm (was it prospective or retrospective, etc). Formal conceptions of the rule of law do not however seek to pass judgment upon the actual content of the law itself. They are not concerned with whether the law was in that sense a good or a bad law . . . Those who espouse substantive conceptions of the rule of law seek to go beyond this. They accept that the rule of law has the formal attributes mentioned above, but they wish to take the doctrine further. Certain substantive rights are said to be based on, or derived from, the rule of law. The concept is used as the foundation for those rights, which are then used to distinguish between 'good' laws, which comply with such rights, and 'bad' laws which do not.*

**3.3** Although the rule of law has generally been seen as a characteristic feature of western liberal democracies, the former Law Lord, Lord Steyn, has commented:

> *In the light of Guantanamo Bay, Abu Graib, Fallujah, the other horrors of the Iraq war, and the continuing revelations about so-called extraordinary rendition – a fancy phrase for kidnapping – the Muslim world may not be over impressed with protestations about the rule of law.*

**3.4** Raz has observed that the rule of law:

> *. . . is not to be confused with democracy, justice, equality (before the law or otherwise), human rights of any kind or respect for the dignity of man. A non-democratic legal system, based on the denial of human rights, on extensive poverty, on racial segregation, sexual inequalities and religious persecution may, in principle, conform to the requirements of the Rule of Law better than any of the legal systems of the more enlightened western democracies.*

**3.5** Lord Steyn implicitly agreed with these remarks when he identified Nazi Germany, South Africa, and Chile as regimes which show that 'strict adherence to legality is no guarantee against tyranny'. However, the former senior Law Lord, the late Lord Bingham, argued against Raz's contention. Although he acknowledges its 'logical tone', he was of the view that:

> *A state which savagely repressed or persecuted sections of its people could not . . . be regarded as observing the rule of law, even if the transport of the persecuted minority to the concentration camp or the compulsory exposure of female children on the mountainside were the subject of detailed laws duly enacted and scrupulously observed.*

In Lord Bingham's opinion, Raz's view infringes the 'fundamental compact' that underpins the rule of law; the compact between the individual and the state, the governed and the governor, whereby both parties 'sacrifice a measure of the freedom and power which they would otherwise enjoy' for the benefit of all.

**3.6** Instead of striving to formulate a definition of the rule of law, the wiser course of action may be to consider the 'corpus of basic principles and values' which it encapsulates. Raz has suggested that 'there is little point in trying to enumerate them all' since they will vary in content and importance from one society to the next. However, he identifies some of the more important principles as follows:

- all laws should be prospective, open, and clear;
- laws should be relatively stable;
- the making of particular laws should be guided by open, stable, clear, and general rules;
- the independence of the judiciary must be guaranteed;
- the principles of natural justice must be observed;
- the courts should have review powers over the implementation of the other principles;
- the courts should be easily accessible; and
- the discretion of the crime-preventing agencies should not be allowed to pervert the law.

**3.7** Allan has argued that the rule of law 'encompasses principles of procedural fairness and legality, equality and proportionality'. In his analysis, these principles are given a substantive content by the courts via the development of the common law. More recently, Lord Bingham has contended that the principle of the rule of law can be broken down into eight sub-rules, a number of which overlap with the principles identified by Raz. In the next part of this chapter, we shall consider some of the principles which have been identified by either Raz, Allan, or Lord Bingham.

## Laws should be prospective

**3.8** If laws should be prospective, it follows that they must not be retrospective. Retrospectivity is widely condemned, especially in the context of criminal statutes, because its effect is to render unlawful that which was lawful at the material time. In *Phillips v Eyre* (1870), Willes J remarked that:

> *Retrospective laws are, no doubt, prima facie of questionable policy, and contrary to the general principle that legislation by which the conduct of mankind is to be regulated ought, when introduced for the first time, to deal with future acts, and ought not to change the character of past transactions carried on upon the faith of the then existing law.*

**3.9** Retrospective legislation is also contrary to art 7 of the European Convention on Human Rights (ECHR). When interpreting an Act of Parliament, therefore, English courts have presumed that the measure does not have retrospective effect. However, this presumption is capable of being rebutted by the express words of the statute, as was the case with the War Damage Act 1965 (see paras **4.25–4.26**). Section 1 of that Act abolished the right at common law to compensation for damage done to or the destruction of property in time of war 'before or after the passing of this Act'. Might it be argued, however, as Lord Rodger has, that the effect of art 7 of the ECHR has been to transfer what were formerly nothing more than 'rules of interpretation' into a 'fundamental principle of our law'?

**3.10** Despite the fact that retrospective legislation is said to be contrary to the rule of law, arguably it is quite commonplace. The common law is retrospective in the sense that it may be developed and stated by a court after the event. Thus the man who raped his wife was not committing an offence that was known to the law at the material time, but the HL subsequently decided that a husband no longer had immunity from prosecution: see *R v R* (1992). Allan argues, however, that:

> In another sense, the common law is not truly retrospective in operation. It attempts to apply previously articulated principles to new instances; and in its earlier development it gave concrete expression to understandings which, though implicit in previous practice or settled understandings, had not before been settled authoritatively.

**3.11** The postscript to the decision in *R v R* (1992) was that the European Commission of Human Rights found that art 7 of the ECHR had not been violated. It did so on the basis that prior to the HL decision, there were clear indications that the law was developing in such a way as to impose criminal liability for marital rape. It may be counter-argued, however, that it was not until the HL decision that the law was authoritatively stated on this point, ie that legal certainty was established.

## Laws should be open and clear

**3.12** Related to the idea that laws should be prospective is the notion that the law should be open and clear. In order for people to understand what it is that the law requires them to do, or to refrain from doing, it is necessary that the law is free from ambiguity and uncertainty. Thus in *Merkur Island Shipping Corpn v Laughton* (1983), where the CA had to consider the effect of three Acts concerned with trade union relations in determining whether participation in industrial action gave rise to liability in tort, Lord Donaldson MR observed that:

> The efficacy and maintenance of the rule of law, which is the foundation of any parliamentary democracy, has at least two prerequisites. First, people must understand that it is in their interests, as well as in that of the community as a whole, that they

*should live their lives in accordance with the rules and all the rules. Second, they must know what those rules are. Both are equally important.*

**3.13** The case was subsequently heard by the HL. In giving judgment, Lord Diplock expressed complete agreement with the opinion expressed by Lord Donaldson MR. He then added his own observation: 'Absence of clarity is destructive of the rule of law; it is unfair to those who wish to preserve the rule of law; it encourages those who wish to undermine it.'

**3.14** The need for clear and intelligible laws applies to both the law made by Parliament and the common law principles developed by the courts. Excessive judicial activism in relation to the latter thus gives rise to difficulties since, as Lord Bingham has pointed out: 'It is one thing to alter the law's direction of travel by a few degrees, quite another to set it off in a different direction.' Indeed, it may not be overstating the case to say that if judges were to consistently seek to be excessively adventurous or innovative in their judgments, the rule of law would be seriously weakened and perhaps even fatally wounded as a result.

**3.15** The principles of legal certainty and non-retroactivity have been recognized by the Court of Justice of the European Communities (ECJ) as principles of EU law. Thus in Case 80/86: *Officier van Justitie v Kolpinghuis Nijmegen* (1987), the ECJ observed that the obligation placed on national courts to interpret national law in the light of the wording of EU law was limited by the general principles of law which form part of EU law and in particular the principles of 'legal certainty and non-retroactivity'. However, since that case was decided, the importance of the interpretative obligation has been further emphasized: see Case C-106/89: *Marleasing SA v La Comercial Internacional de Alimentación SA* (1990) (paras **10.33-10.36**). If domestic courts are to interpret a national law as being in accordance with an EU measure, even where the words used are clearly inconsistent, can it be argued that the national law is uncertain and hence contrary to the rule of law?

## Natural justice

**3.16** Turning to the fifth principle identified by Raz, that the principles of natural justice must be observed, both Professor Jowell and Lord Bingham have argued that this is one of the central features of the rule of law. In *R v Secretary of State for the Home Department, ex p Pierson* (1998), Lord Steyn encapsulated the view thus:

> Unless there is the clearest provision to the contrary, Parliament must be presumed not to legislate contrary to the rule of law. And the rule of law enforces minimum standards of fairness, both substantive and procedural.

**3.17** By the principles of natural justice it is meant that individuals have the right to a fair hearing and that there should be an absence of bias in the decision-making process.

These principles, which in modern judicial parlance are reflected in the 'duty to act fairly', will be considered more fully later in this book (Chapter **13**). For present purposes, it need only be noted that their importance is highlighted by the fact that the courts have shown themselves willing to require that they are complied with even where a statute has made no provision for the procedure to be followed.

## Access to the courts

**3.18**  Access to justice is, not surprisingly, regarded by the judges as being a fundamental principle of the English legal system. Accordingly, they jealously guard the principle and take a dim view of any measure which attempts to erode access. Thus in *R v Lord Chancellor, ex p Witham* (1998), the applicant sought to challenge an order made by the Lord Chancellor under a statutory power which increased the fees for issuing writs. It was claimed by the applicant, who was on income support, that this had the effect of denying him access to justice because he could not pay the increased fee and because legal aid was not available in respect of his claim for defamation. In granting a declaration that part of the order was ultra vires, Laws J observed:

> Access to the courts is a constitutional right; it can only be denied by the government if it persuades Parliament to pass legislation which specifically – in effect by express provision – permits the executive to turn people away from the court door. That has not been done in this case.

**3.19**  Access to justice may of course be denied in other ways, such as where a prisoner who was contemplating bringing various civil actions was denied access to his solicitor by a prison governor: see *R v Secretary of State for the Home Department, ex p Leech (No 2)* (1994). A more subtle denial of access to justice took place in a case which reached the HL.

> *R (on the application of Anufrijeva) v Secretary of State for the Home Department* (2003): A was an asylum seeker who was awarded income support on her arrival to the UK. Subsequently, however, the Home Office (HO) determined that she was not an asylum seeker. Her entitlement to income support therefore ceased. The HO's decision was communicated to the Benefits Agency, which terminated further payments. Its decision was not, however, communicated directly to A. A challenged the decisions to treat her asylum claim as determined before she was notified of it and to withdraw her income support. The HCt refused her claim for judicial review and the CA upheld that decision. A further appealed. HL held: by a majority of four to one, that the appeal be allowed. In the opinion of the majority, constitutional principle required an adverse administrative decision to be communicated to a person, thereby affording them the opportunity to challenge it in the courts. Moreover, in the absence of express language or necessary implication to the contrary, statutory words could not override fundamental rights and would be presumed

by the court to be subject to them. Since Parliament had not legislated to the contrary effect in the present case, the adverse asylum decision against A did not take effect until it had been properly notified to her. A was thus entitled to income support up until the date of notification.

During the course of his opinion in *Anufrijeva*, Lord Steyn referred to 'the constitutional principle requiring the rule of law to be observed'. His Lordship continued:

> That principle requires that a constitutional state must accord to individuals the right to know of a decision before their rights can be adversely affected . . . I accept, of course, that there must be exceptions to this approach, notably in the criminal field, eg arrests and search warrants, where notification is not possible. But it is difficult to visualize a rational argument which could even arguably justify putting the present case in the exceptional category.

## Dicey and the rule of law

**3.20**   Part II of *Introduction to the Study of the Law of the Constitution* is concerned with what Dicey considered to be one of the two features characterized by the political institutions of England since the days of the Norman Conquest, the rule of law. For Dicey, the rule of law was 'one of the most marked peculiarities of English life'. It was, in the words of Lord Bingham, 'the second great rock on which his constitutional edifice was founded', the other being the legislative supremacy of Parliament (see Chapter **5**). However, despite the frequency with which the expression was used, Dicey considered that the concept remained 'full of vagueness and ambiguity' for many. Accordingly, in Part II of his book, he set out to define what was meant by the 'rule of law'.

### The three elements

**3.21**   In Dicey's opinion, the rule of law comprised three elements. The first was that no man was punishable except for a distinct breach of the law established in an ordinary manner before the ordinary courts of the land. This entailed an absence of arbitrary, discretionary, or prerogative powers of restraint vested in the executive. Put simply, Dicey considered that the rule of law reflected the predominance of regular law as opposed to the influence of arbitrary power. Thus, he was making a case against the suspending or dispensing powers which had been exercised by the Stuart monarchs and which were made illegal by arts 1 and 2 of the Bill of Rights 1689 (see para **4.3**).

**3.22**   The second aspect of the Diceyean conception of the rule of law was that no man was above the law. A different but related feature of this second aspect was that 'every man, whatever be his mark or condition, is subject to the ordinary law of the realm and amenable to the jurisdiction of the ordinary tribunals'. Thus the rule of law applied to every official 'from the Prime Minister down to a constable or collector of taxes' in the same way that it did to any other citizen. It sought to ensure that there was equality before the law. For Dicey, this idea of legal equality was no mere abstract notion. Rather, it had practical application as was evidenced by the law reports which 'abound with cases in which officials have been brought before the courts, and made, in their personal capacity, liable to punishment, or to the payment of damages, for acts done in their official character but in excess of their lawful authority'.

**3.23** Dicey's third aspect of the rule of law was that the general principles of the constitution, by which he meant such things as the right to personal liberty, were the result of judicial decisions determining the rights of private persons in cases brought before the courts. In short, the constitution was 'judge made' and it bore on its face 'all the features, good and bad, of judge-made law'.

## Criticisms of Dicey

**3.24** Dicey's opinions on the rule of law have subsequently been analysed and criticized by writers on constitutional law. Professor Jennings took Dicey to task on a number of points, including the idea that the rule of law was inconsistent with or contradictory to the existence of discretionary powers. In *The Law and the Constitution*, Professor Jennings listed a number of discretionary powers which both existed and were capable of being exercised at the time that Dicey first published his thoughts. Indeed, in the years that have passed since this observation was made, there has been a continued growth in the volume and extent of discretionary powers that are available to the executive. As we shall see later, statutory and non-statutory discretionary power is what enables the government of the day to perform many of its various tasks and functions. Jennings offered an explanation as to why Dicey may have overlooked the existence of discretionary power. It is based on the political views of the latter which were those of a liberal subscriber to the doctrine of *laissez faire*. In Jennings's opinion, Dicey imagined that the constitution was 'dominated' by this doctrine and thus he talked in terms of the rights of the individual as opposed to the powers possessed by public authorities.

**3.25** Further criticisms have been levelled at Dicey's understanding of the rule of law. In particular, these relate to the second aspect of the rule of law, that the laws apply equally to all men irrespective of their rank or status. In formulating this proposition, Dicey was prepared to make an exception for soldiers and clergymen of the established Church. In his opinion, these two categories of persons were subject to laws which did not affect the rest of the nation and they were also subject to the jurisdiction of tribunals, by which he meant courts martial and ecclesiastical courts, which had no jurisdiction in respect of the ordinary man. Nevertheless, Dicey considered that their position was not inconsistent with the rule of law in that they were still subject to the same duties as the ordinary citizen. The flaw in Dicey's reasoning here is that he only acknowledges those subject to additional legal obligations; he fails to take account of those for whom special provision or immunity has been made. Thus children are not treated in the same way as adults by the criminal law: below the age of 10, a child is *doli incapax* (ie incapable of committing a crime). Foreign diplomats enjoy immunity from the operation of the criminal law. A more limited immunity is enjoyed by judges who cannot be sued for the way in which they have dealt with a case, and by Members of Parliament who cannot be sued for defamation in respect of things said whilst within the precincts of the Palace of Westminster (see paras **6.79–6.80**).

**3.26** Dicey derived support for the assertion that no man is above the law from the law reports. He noted that many cases had been heard by the courts in which officials had been held to be subject to the laws of the land. One such case, *Entick v Carrington* (1765) has been described by Keir and Lawson as 'perhaps the central case in English constitutional law'.

> *Entick v Carrington* (1765): E brought an action for trespass after his house had been broken into by King's Messengers and certain papers had been seized as evidence of seditious writings. The defendants argued that their actions were justified by a warrant issued by the Secretary of State. The case therefore turned on the legality of the warrant. Held: the power claimed by the Secretary of State to issue the warrant was not supported by any of the extant law books. Lord Camden CJ: 'If it is law, it will be found in our books. If it is not to be found there, it is not law.' The warrant was illegal and void and the entry had therefore been a trespass.

## Equality before the law

**3.27** A more recent example of Dicey's second proposition regarding the rule of law is to be found in a HL decision on the question whether or not a government minister acting in his official capacity could be guilty of contempt of court.

> *M v Home Office* (1994): M was a citizen of Zaire. He arrived in the UK seeking political asylum. He was interviewed and subsequently informed that his claim had been rejected by the Home Secretary (HS). His position was later reconsidered, but it was still decided that he did not qualify for asylum. The decision to refuse asylum was taken on the basis that the Home Office did not believe M's account of events. Directions for his removal from the UK were made. M applied for leave to move for judicial review of the decision to refuse him asylum. Leave was refused. A renewed application for leave to move was made to the CA on the day that he was scheduled to be removed from the UK. The renewed application was dismissed. Immediately thereafter, new lawyers acting on M's behalf applied to the HCt for leave to move for judicial review on fresh grounds. Garland J, who was in chambers, wished M's departure to be postponed so that the application could be made the following day. He believed that he had received an undertaking from counsel for the HS to this effect. However, M was deported back to Zaire via Paris. Whilst en route to Zaire, Garland J became aware of the situation and made a mandatory order requiring the HS to return M to the UK.

On the basis of legal advice and the underlying belief that the asylum decision had been correct, the HS decided not to comply with the order. Travel arrangements for the return of M were cancelled. Garland J subsequently discharged his own order on the basis that he had not had the jurisdiction to make it. M's lawyers applied to have the HS committed for contempt of court. Simon Brown J dismissed the motion. The CA allowed M's appeal to the extent of holding that the HS had personally been in contempt of court. The HS appealed. HL held: dismissing the appeal, that Garland J's order had been properly made. A finding of contempt could not be made against the Crown directly, but it could be made against a government department or a minister either personally, or acting in his official capacity. Since it was the department for which he was responsible which was guilty of contempt, the finding of contempt would be made against the HS in his official capacity rather than against him personally.

**3.28**  The principal judgment in *M v Home Office* (1994) was delivered by Lord Woolf. He observed, amongst other things, that the court's purpose in making findings of contempt was to ensure that 'the orders of the court are obeyed'. Moreover, Lord Woolf considered that the 'object of the exercise' in a case such as the present 'is not so much to punish an individual as to vindicate the rule of law by a finding of contempt'. Here, therefore, lies the importance of *M v Home Office*. This was the first occasion on which a government minister had been found guilty of contempt of court. The decision of the HL thus underlines the point that nobody, not even the executive, is above the law. In the words of Lord Templeman in the case itself:

> the argument that there is no power to enforce the law by injunction or contempt proceedings against a minister in his official capacity would, if upheld, establish the proposition that the executive obey the law as a matter of grace and not as a matter of necessity, a proposition which would reverse the result of the Civil War.

## The principle of legality

**3.29**  The principle which emerges from *Entick v Carrington* (1765) (para **3.26**) is that interference with the rights of the individual, in that case the right of property, can only be justified on the basis of some lawful authority. In other words, entering a person's house or seizing his property requires lawful authority, whether it be in the form of a statutory or common law power. This is sometimes referred to as the principle of legality.

**3.30**  The principle of legality is but one aspect of the wider concept of the rule of law. Nevertheless, its presence helps to ensure that the rule of law acts as a safeguard against the violation of an individual's rights. In the words of Allan, the rule of law:

> is a crucial strand in the constitutional tapestry for the protection of liberty: it excludes arbitrary or discriminatory action by the powerful against the powerless by erecting the general law as bulwark or barrier between the two.

**3.31** However, the protection which the rule of law affords in this context has distinct limits. Provided that the lawful authority to interfere with an individual's rights exists, the rule of law represents an ineffective weapon in the hands of the judiciary. It requires the existence of legal authority, but it imposes no strictures on the quality of that authority. Recently Professor Jowell has praised Dicey for having recognized 'that the rule of law is not concerned with the necessary qualities of law, of "good" law, of the legal system, or of adjudication'. Thus all that the courts can do when faced by authority in the form of a statutory power or the common law is to interpret the relevant power in a way which interferes as little as possible with the rights of individuals. However, in the case of statutory powers, the courts cannot impede or restrict the working of legislation.

> ***IRC v Rossminster Ltd* (1980):** Inland Revenue officers suspected that the company had committed tax fraud. They obtained warrants to search the premises under s 20C of the Taxes Management Act 1970. The warrants did not specify the particular offences being investigated. A search was conducted and the officers seized anything which they believed to be evidence relating to tax fraud. The company sought judicial review. HL held: that the appeal against an order of the CA to quash the warrants would be granted. The courts have a duty to supervise the legality of any purported exercise of powers to enter a person's premises. However, since the warrants followed the exact wording of the statute, the company had no answer to them.

**3.32** The *Rossminster* case thus demonstrates the weakness of the requirement that interference with an individual's rights must be based on lawful authority where Parliament is prepared to enact very wide powers justifying such an interference. In the CA, Lord Denning observed that s 20C of the 1970 Act was 'drawn so widely that in some hands it might be an instrument of oppression'. Moreover, Lord Scarman in the HL considered that what was permitted under the statute amounted to 'a breath-taking inroad upon the individual's right of privacy and right of property'. Nevertheless, since Parliament had created the power and it had been lawfully exercised, the courts could not intervene.

## The rule of law and the criminal law

**3.33** Judicial responsibility for the maintenance of the rule of law extends beyond overseeing executive action and ensuring that statutory powers are properly exercised. It also arises in the field of criminal law where the courts may take the view that the police have abused their power to such an extent that they should be prevented from bringing a prosecution.

> ***R v Horseferry Road Magistrates' Court, ex p Bennett* (1994):** B, a New Zealand citizen, was wanted by the UK police for a series of offences alleged to have been committed.

He was arrested in South Africa and placed on a flight to London by the South African police, despite the fact that there was no extradition treaty between the two countries. On his arrival, B was arrested by the UK police and, subsequently, magistrates committed him for trial. B applied for judicial review of the magistrates' decision. He contended that the circumstances of his arrival in the UK would make it an abuse of the process of the court if the prosecution against him were to proceed. HL held: reversing the decision of the DC, that the most basic principle of any system of law was the maintenance of the rule of law. It was unacceptable that the court should ignore executive lawlessness beyond the frontiers of its own jurisdiction. The whole proceeding was tainted and accordingly the case should be remitted to the DC for further consideration.

## The contemporary significance of the rule of law

**3.34** Despite the difficulties associated with defining what is meant by the 'rule of law', it is clear that the principles which it encompasses act as a restraint on the exercise of power by governments. In the UK, this function of the rule of law is especially important given that there is no codified constitution against which the conduct of government can be judged. In terms of the practical application of the rule of law, therefore, it may be argued, as Professor Jowell has done, that this is achieved by means of judicial review (see Chapters **12–14**). Speaking extra-judicially, Lord Woolf has put forward a radical thesis; that an Act of Parliament which violated the rule of law could be disobeyed by the courts (see para **5.11**). Similar views have been expressed by Allan in a recent contribution to the academic debate on the rule of law.

**3.35** The contemporary significance of the rule of law has of course increased as a result of the Human Rights Act 1998. The shift in English law from a reliance on residual rights and liberties to the assertion of positive rights under the Act has meant that government actions are now potentially subject to rather more intense judicial scrutiny than was previously the case. It is no longer sufficient that executive action has been judged to be reasonable; it must also have been proportionate. The willingness of the judiciary to uphold the rule of law has been evident in a number of different contexts post 1998. Most notably, however, it has been evident in relation to the legislative measures taken to deal with the perceived terrorist threat following Al-Qaeda's attacks in the USA on 11 September 2001.

*A v Secretary of State for the Home Department* **(2005):** A and the other appellants were non-UK nationals who were resident in the UK and who were considered to pose a threat to the safety of the nation. They could not be deported to their countries of origin because they faced the prospect of being tortured or treated inhumanely. Accordingly, Parliament passed the Anti-terrorism, Crime and Security Act 2001. Section 23 of the Act provided for the detention without trial of individuals such as the appellants. Since the provision was contrary to art 5(1)(f) of the ECHR, the Government sought to enter a derogation under art 15 of the ECHR on the ground that there was a 'public emergency threatening the life of the nation': see the Human Rights Act (Designated Derogation) Order 2001, SI 2001/3644. The appellants appealed to the Special Immigration Appeals Commission. It concluded that s 23 of the 2001 Act was discriminatory and so in breach of art 14 of the ECHR in that it applied to non-UK nationals only. It therefore quashed the 2001 derogation order and issued a declaration of incompatibility under s 4 of the Human Rights Act 1998 in respect of s 23 of the 2001 Act. The CA allowed an appeal by the Secretary of State. The appellants appealed. HL held: by a majority of 8 to 1, that there was insufficient evidence to show that the Secretary of State had been wrong in taking the view that there was a public emergency threatening the life of the nation. However, that threat came from both foreign and UK nationals. Section 23 of the 2001 Act was therefore discriminatory in that it allowed non-UK suspected terrorists to leave the country and British suspected terrorists to remain at large whilst providing for the indefinite detention of others such as A. It was also not strictly required within art 15 of the ECHR and was therefore disproportionate. The 2001 designation order was therefore quashed, and s 23 of the 2001 Act was declared to be incompatible with arts 5 and 14 of the ECHR.

**3.36** The decision in *A* represents an important development in the relationship between the courts and the executive. Indeed, the now retired Law Lord, Lord Steyn, has contended that the decision 'goes to the very heart of our democracy' and 'anchors our constitutional system on the rule of law'. Whereas the courts had on previous occasions shown themselves rather too willing to accept the word of government as to what was necessary in the interests of national security (see, for example, *R v Secretary of State for the Home Department, ex p Cheblak* (1991) and *Secretary of State for the Home Department v Rehman* (2001)), in *A* we see the HL prepared to consider: whether there was a public emergency threatening the life of the nation; and whether the power to detain without trial was strictly required by the exigencies of the situation. Although the majority accepted the government view that there was a public emergency, Lord Hoffmann did not. For the majority, the existence of that public emergency did not, however, justify detention without trial for non-UK nationals. In the words of Lord Nicholls, 'indefinite detention without charge or trial is anathema in any country which observes the rule of law'. For Lord Hoffmann:

> *such a power in any form is not compatible with our constitution. The real threat to the life of the nation, in the sense of a people living in accordance with its traditional laws and political values, comes not from terrorism but from laws such as these. That is the true measure of what terrorism may achieve. It is for Parliament to decide whether to give the terrorists such a victory.*

**3.37** Following the ruling in *A*, it was necessary for the then Labour Government to replace the detention without trial provisions in the 2001 Act with new powers which would enable it to exercise control over all persons suspected of being involved in terrorist-related activity. Its response was to introduce the control order regime under the

Prevention of Terrorism Act 2005. The scope of a non-derogating control order, ie a control order which was compatible with art 5 of the ECHR, was very wide. Thus restrictions could be placed on a person's freedom of association, freedom of movement, access to the means of communication etc. The control order regime fared little better than its predecessor before the courts. Thus, for example, in *Secretary of State for the Home Department v JJ* (2006), the CA held that control orders which obliged their subjects to, amongst other things, remain in a one bedroom flat for 18 hours a day, amounted to a deprivation of liberty contrary to art 5 of the ECHR. The orders were also the subject of criticism by the independent statutory reviewer of the 2005 Act, Lord Carlile of Berriew. In its *Review of Counter-Terrorism and Security Powers* (2011) Cm 8004, the coalition Government concluded, amongst other things, that 'the current control order regime can and should be repealed'. Accordingly, at the time of writing, the Home Office sponsored Terrorism Prevention and Investigation Measures Bill is before Parliament.

3.38 The Bill seeks to repeal the 2005 Act and empower the Secretary of State to impose a 'TPIM' notice on a specified person. It is intended that the threshold for imposing such a notice will be higher than that which exists in relation to control orders. Thus the Secretary of State will need to have a reasonable belief (rather than a reasonable suspicion) that the person is or has been involved in terrorist-related activity before serving a TPIM notice. It is also intended that the measures imposed under a TPIM notice will be more circumscribed than under a control order, and that they should be subject to a two-year time limit, beyond which they will not remain in force unless there is evidence of further involvement in terrorist-related activity.

3.39 The terrorist threat to the UK also provided the background to a further recent HL case where the rule of law was at issue.

*R (on the application of Corner House Research) v Director of the Serious Fraud Office* **(2008):** In 2004, the Director of the SFO began an investigation into allegations of corruption against a UK company, BAE systems. As part of that investigation, the SFO looked into an arms contract between the company and the Saudi Arabian Government. It was claimed by the company that the disclosure of information required by a statutory notice served on it by the SFO would adversely affect diplomatic relations between the UK and Saudi Governments, and jeopardize the arms contract. Nevertheless, the investigation continued. Later, when it became apparent that the SFO wished to investigate Swiss bank accounts to determine whether or not the company had made payments to Saudi public officials, the Saudi authorities made it clear that if the investigation continued, their government would: withdraw from bi-lateral counter-terrorism agreements with the UK; withdraw cooperation from the UK in relation to its strategic objectives in the Middle East; and end negotiations for the purchase of military aircraft. The Director of the SFO subsequently decided to discontinue the investigation. The claimants sought judicial review. They contended that the Director had acted unlawfully by yielding to the Saudi threats. The DC quashed the Director's decision. He appealed. HL held: in allowing the appeal, that in determining the case, the DC had erred in asking itself whether there had been no alternative course of action open to the Director. Instead, the issue was whether in deciding that the public interest in pursuing an investigation into alleged corruption was outweighed by the public interest in protecting lives, the Director had made a decision outside the scope of his powers. Since the evidence revealed that the Director had taken the decision to discontinue the investigation with extreme reluctance, and only after consulting others, he had therefore acted lawfully.

**3.40** The decision in *Corner House Research* is significant for a number of reasons, not least of which is that it further illustrates the general reluctance of the courts to intervene in respect of decisions to investigate or prosecute alleged criminal activity, save in exceptional circumstances. The Saudi Government's threats were regarded as posing a real risk to 'British lives on British streets', and the HL accepted that it was concerns about public safety rather than commercial interests which had led to the decision not to continue the investigation. Of course, as Baroness Hale pointed out, 'it is extremely distasteful that an independent public official should feel himself obliged to give way to threats of any sort'. Indeed, in the DC, the Director's decision to submit to the threat had been held to be contrary to the rule of law. Patently, however, the HL applied a less exacting standard than the DC had earlier done when determining the lawfulness of the Director's decision.

## Constitutional Reform Act 2005

**3.41** The Constitutional Reform Bill as originally introduced said nothing expressly about the rule of law. However, during the Bill's report stage in the HL (7 December 2004), the then Lord Chancellor moved an amendment which inserted a new clause. In so doing, Lord Falconer explained:

> The Government have no problem in accepting that the rule of law must and does guide the actions of Ministers and all public officials. It is also clear that Ministers and other public officials must comply with the law. That obligation is enforceable in the courts. So, if a Minister went beyond his powers or used them for a purpose other than that for which they were intended, he may have his actions overturned by the courts [Hansard, HL, Vol 667, col 738].

Continuing on this same theme, Lord Falconer sought to outline 'two fundamental issues that need to be addressed in the attempt to legislate with respect to the rule of law'. The first of these was that 'the notion of the rule of law cannot be expressed in the form of an ordinary legal rule . . . Such a rule must be open to the interpretation that it is referring to standards that lie outside – and, in a sense, above – the law'. The second was that 'the success of the rule of law in our system has never been dependent on grand statutory exhortations'. The clause which Lord Falconer introduced provoked much debate in the HL and the issue was revisited when he moved a further amendment at the Bill's third reading. This revised version of the clause is now reflected in s 1 of the 2005 Act. It provides that:

> This Act does not adversely affect – (a) the existing constitutional principle of the rule of law, or (b) the Lord Chancellor's existing constitutional role in relation to that principle.

**3.42** This declaratory provision applies to the 'existing' principle of the rule of law and the Lord Chancellor's role in respect of the principle. However, neither what is meant by the 'rule of law' nor the nature of the Lord Chancellor's role in this context is defined by the Act. Nevertheless, in moving the amendment, Lord Falconer commented:

> We all agreed that we do not want to change the Lord Chancellor's existing role in relation to the rule of law. That role goes further than simply respecting the rule of law in discharging his ministerial functions. It includes being obliged to speak up in Cabinet or as a Cabinet Minister against proposals that he believes offend the rule of law. That role does not require him proactively to police every act of government. The role is not one that is enforceable in the courts [Hansard, HL, Vol 667, col 1538 (20 December 2004)].

**3.43** In commenting upon s 1 of the 2005 Act in an extra-judicial capacity, Lord Bingham expressed the contradictory view that the Lord Chancellor's role in relation to the rule of law 'would no doubt be susceptible, in principle, to judicial review'. In his opinion, although the drafters of the 2005 Act may have refrained from defining the rule of law on the basis that it was 'thought to be too clear and well-understood to call for statutory definition', it was more likely that they 'recognised the extreme difficulty of formulating a succinct and accurate definition suitable for inclusion in a statute, and preferred to leave the task of definition to the courts if and when the occasion arose'. At the time of writing, that occasion has yet to materialize.

## FURTHER READING

Allan, T R S *Law, Liberty and Justice: The Legal Foundations of British Constitutionalism* (1993) Clarendon Press.

Allan, T R S 'The Rule of Law as the Rule of Reason: Consent and Constitutionalism' (1999) 115 LQR 221.

Allan, T R S *Constitutional Justice: a Liberal Theory of the Rule of Law* (2001) OUP.

Bedner, A 'An Elementary Approach to the Rule of Law' [2010] HJRL 48.

Bellamy, R (ed) *The Rule of Law and the Separation of Powers* (2005) Ashgate Publishing.

Lord Bingham 'Dicey Revisited' [2002] PL 39.

Lord Bingham 'The Rule of Law' [2007] CLJ 67.

Lord Bingham, *The Rule of Law* (2010) Allen Lane.

Craig, P 'Formal and Substantive Conceptions of the Rule of Law: an Analytical Frame-work' [1997] PL 467.

Ekins, R 'Judicial Supremacy and the Rule of Law' (2003) 119 LQR 127.

House of Lords, Constitution Committee, *Relations between the executive, the judiciary and parliament* (2006–7, HL Paper 151), especially Appendix 5 by Professor P Craig.

House of Lords, Constitution Committee, *Relations between the executive, the judiciary and parliament: Follow-up report* (2007–8, HL Paper 177).

Jennings, Sir Ivor *The Law and the Constitution* (5th edn, 1959) University of London Press.

Jowell, J 'The Rule of Law's Long Arm: Uncommunicated decisions' [2004] PL 246.

Jowell, J 'The Rule of Law and its Underlying Values' in Jowell and Oliver (eds) *The Changing Constitution* (7th edn, 2011) OUP.

Larkin, S 'Debunking the Idea of Parliamentary Sovereignty: The controlling factor of legality in the British constitution' (2008) 28 OJLS 709.

Pollard, D, Parpworth, N, and Hughes, D *Constitutional and Administrative Law: Text with Materials* (4th edn, 2007) OUP.

Raz, J 'The Rule of Law and its Virtue' (1977) 93 LQR 195.

Lord Rodger 'A Time for Everything under the Law: Some Reflections on Retrospectivity' (2005) 121 LQR 57.

Sir Philip Sales 'A Comparison of the Principle of Legality and Section 3 of the Human Rights Act 1998' (2009) 125 LQR 598.

Sampford, C *Retrospectivity and the Rule of Law* (2006) OUP.

Lord Steyn, 'Democracy, the Rule of Law and the Role of Judges' [2006] EHRLR 243.

Tamanaha, B *On the Rule of Law* (2004) Cambridge University Press.

Tomkins, A 'Readings of *A v Secretary of State for the Home Department*' [2005] PL 259.

Turpin, C and Tomkins, A *British Government and the Constitution: Text and Materials* (7th edn, 2011) Cambridge University Press.

Lord Woolf, 'The Rule of Law and a Change in the Constitution' [2004] CLJ 317.

## SELF-TEST QUESTIONS

1   What is the constitutional significance of the rule of law?

2   Having regard to the distinction between formal and substantive meanings of the rule of law, which do you think is favoured by Raz, Dicey, Allan, and Lord Bingham? Which do you prefer? Is there a middle way between the two meanings?

3    Do you agree with the view that *Entick v Carrington* (1765) demonstrates all three aspects of Dicey's conception of the rule of law?

4    What is the inherent weakness apparent in the principle of legality?

5    Professor Jowell has referred to the 'elasticity' of the rule of law. To what extent, if any, do any of the cases referred to in this chapter demonstrate that elasticity?

6    In finding against the Government in *A v Secretary of State for the Home Department*, do you think that the HL applied a formal or substantive conception of the rule of law?

7    To what extent, if any, can it be argued that the decision in *A v Secretary of State for the Home Department* caused the Government to respond in a way which has actually increased the repressive measures which the state is able to take against suspected terrorists?

8    When national security is at risk, Lord Bingham has argued that 'governments understandably go to the very limit of what they believe to be their lawful powers to protect the public'. Do you agree with him that in such circumstances 'the duty of the judges to require that they go no further must be performed if the rule of law is to be observed'?

9    To what extent, if any, do you agree with Lord Steyn that 'a series of decisions of the House of Lords in the last few years have breathed new life into the rule of law'?

# 4

# The royal prerogative

## SUMMARY

This chapter considers the nature of prerogative power and the manner of its exercise. It identifies some examples of prerogative powers and considers how certain personal or reserve powers of the monarch might be exercised in practice. The chapter also explores the relationship between prerogative power and statute and focuses on how the courts have dealt with the prerogative. Traditionally this involved determining the nature and extent of a prerogative power. More recently, the courts have shown a willingness to review the exercise of certain prerogative powers. The chapter concludes by looking at several ways in which the prerogative could be reformed.

## Introduction

**4.1** The royal prerogative is an important source of power within the UK constitution. In his *Commentaries on the Laws of England,* Blackstone wrote that the royal prerogative was:

> that special pre-eminence which the King hath, over and above all other persons, and out of the ordinary course of the common law, in right of his regal dignity.

From this passage, it is evident that the prerogative is legal in nature and that it is unique to the Crown. This uniqueness is further evident from Blackstone's later observation that 'if once any prerogative of the Crown could be held in common with the subject, it would cease to be prerogative any more'.

**4.2** Although it is correct to talk in terms of the 'royal prerogative', we should take care when considering what is meant by these words. If we were to step back in time prior to the 'Glorious Revolution' of 1688 (see paras **5.6–5.8**), we would see that some, but by no means all, of the power vested in the monarch was exercised at the monarch's discretion. In the 17th century, a number of cases were heard by the courts which concerned measures taken under the prerogative. In the *Case of Proclamations* (1611), the judges sought to identify the limits on the monarch's prerogative powers. Thus it was held that the King could not change the law by proclamation. In particular, he did not have the power to 'make a thing unlawful, which was permitted by the law before'. In other words, new criminal offences could not be created by proclamation. Subsequently in *Darnel's Case*, or the *Case of the Five Knights* (1627), it was accepted that the King had the power to imprison five knights who had refused to contribute towards a forced loan. Similarly in *R v Hampden* or the *Case of Ship Money* (1637), the Exchequer Chamber ruled by seven to five that the King was entitled to impose a charge on his subjects for providing ships without the common consent of Parliament. Finally, in *Godden v Hales* (1686), the question at issue was whether or not the King had the power to dispense with the requirement in the Test Act 1673 that an army officer had to take certain oaths of supremacy and allegiance. Eleven of the 12 judges who gave judgment ruled that the King did have the power under the prerogative to dispense in this case. The decision was based on a number of grounds which were stated by Herbert CJ as follows:

> *(1) that the kings of England are sovereign princes; (2) that the laws of England are the king's laws; (3) that therefore tis an inseparable prerogative in the kings of England to dispense with penal laws in particular cases and upon particular necessary reasons; (4) that of those reasons and those necessities, the king himself is sole judge; and then which is consequent upon all, (5) that this is not a trust invested in, or granted to, the king by the people, but the ancient remains of the sovereign power and prerogative of the kings of England; which never yet was taken from them, nor can be.*

**4.3** The term 'royal prerogative' thus originated at a time when the monarch's personal power was far greater than it is today; when the Crown was not fettered by the shackles of a constitutional monarchy. Those shackles were originally attached in 1689 by the Bill of Rights. The significance of this document will be discussed more fully in Chapter **5**. For present purposes, however, it should be noted that the Bill of Rights curtailed certain of the prerogatives of the Crown. It declared in arts 1, 2, and 4 respectively:

> *That the pretended power of suspending of laws or the execution of laws by regall authority without consent of Parlyament is illegal.*

> *That the pretended power of dispensing with laws or the execution of laws by regal authority as it hath been assumed and exercised of late is illegal.*

> *That levying money for or to the use of the Crowne by pretence of prerogative without grant of Parlyament for longer time or in other manner than the same is or shall be granted is illegal.*

**4.4** Today, therefore, although the books and the courts still refer to the 'royal prerogative', much of the power that can be so described is in reality vested in the hands of the executive. With the exception of certain personal prerogatives, such as the grant of particular honours, eg The Order of the Garter, prerogative power is exercised in the name of the Crown by and on the advice of the government of the day. This modern-day usage of the prerogative caused Dicey to define it as 'every act which the Executive government can lawfully do without the Authority of an Act of Parliament'.

**4.5** Dicey's definition is, however, rather wide. There are certain things that the Crown can lawfully do, such as entering into contracts, which although they are done without the authority of an Act of Parliament, cannot be said to amount to an exercise of prerogative power. The late Sir William Wade has argued, therefore, that Blackstone's is the preferred definition of the prerogative. Applying the 'Blackstone test', Sir William has questioned whether cancelling a designation under an international agreement, the issue or withdrawal of passports, or the appointment or dismissal of ministers has anything to do with the prerogative. However, as we shall see, the courts have regarded such acts as involving the exercise of prerogative power.

## Some examples of prerogative power

**4.6** It is a widely held view among academics, the judiciary, and the Government, that the exact limits of prerogative power are not capable of precise definition. Indeed, it was only in 2003 that the Labour Government published for the first time a non-exhaustive list of prerogative powers in response to a demand made by the HC Public Administration Select Committee. More recently, the Government published *The Governance of Britain, Review of the Prerogative Powers: Final Report* (2009). The Annex to the Report is of particular interest since it contains the results of an internal scoping exercise relating to executive prerogative powers. Government departments were asked to identify those areas where prerogative powers are relied upon, or had been relied upon in the recent past. The survey thus provided an illustration of the contemporary use of ministerial prerogative powers although like the 2003 list, it disavowed any claim to be exhaustive. Ministerial prerogative powers were grouped into five categories: Government and the civil service; justice system and law and order; powers relating to foreign affairs; powers relating to armed forces, war and times of emergency; and miscellaneous.

**4.7** For present purposes, it should be noted that the power to appoint QCs and the prerogative of mercy fell into the second category, whereas the powers to make and ratify treaties, conduct diplomacy, and issue, refuse, or withdraw passports were 'foreign affairs' prerogatives. Powers relating to the armed forces etc included the right to make war or peace or institute hostilities falling short of war, and the deployment and use of armed forces overseas. The 'miscellaneous' category included the power to establish corporations by Royal Charter, and the power to hold public inquiries not covered by the Inquiries Act 2005 (see para **15.38**).

**4.8** The Annex to the 2009 Report also listed what it termed 'other prerogative powers' which were themselves grouped into four categories: constitutional/personal prerogatives; powers exercised by the Attorney-General; archaic prerogative powers; and legal prerogatives of the Crown. For present purposes, the first of these categories is the most important. It includes: the appointment and removal of ministers; the appointment of the PM; the power to dismiss a government; the power to summon, prorogue, and

dissolve Parliament; assent to legislation; and the power to legislate under the prerogative by Order in Council. In practice, constitutional convention (see Chapter **11**) regulates the way in which these powers are exercised.

## Royal Assent

**4.9** In order for a Bill to become an Act of Parliament it is necessary that, on the completion of its various stages in Parliament, the measure receives the Royal Assent. In
practice, Royal Assent is regulated by convention and has therefore become something
of a formality. This is evidenced by the fact that it was last refused during the reign of
Queen Anne in the first decade of the 18th century, and only then on the advice of her
government. Nevertheless, the monarch retains the right to refuse Royal Assent. In
theory, the monarch could refuse her Assent to any Bill to which she took exception. If
she was acting on the advice of her ministers in so doing, her action would be relatively
free from controversy. If, however, the refusal was in direct opposition to the wishes of
her government, controversy would abound. Such a course of action is therefore highly
unlikely, save in the most exceptional of circumstances.

**4.10** One such exceptional circumstance may be, as Professor Brazier has noted, where the
monarch refused Assent to a Bill which had failed to comply with a procedural requirement relating to its enactment. If, for example, a measure required that a referendum
be held before a particular event could take place and a Bill seeking to bring about that
event was passed without a referendum having first taken place, the monarch might be
justified in refusing Royal Assent. In so doing, the monarch would be ensuring that the
correct manner and form for legislating had been complied with. This example presup-
poses that Parliament is able to impose procedural restrictions on its successors. As we
shall see in Chapter **5**, views differ as to whether or not this is in fact possible.

**4.11** Alternatively, Royal Assent might be refused where Parliament sought to extend its
own life beyond the five years stipulated in the Parliament Acts 1911 and 1949 for no
good reason, or where the government of the day sought to alter the franchise or the
boundaries of the Westminster electoral constituencies in such a way as to make it all
but impossible to remove it from office at a general election. At a more personal level, a
Bill to abolish the monarchy might not be assented to, although it is extremely unlikely
that such a Bill would be introduced before Parliament without the prior knowledge
and approval of the monarch.

## The appointment of ministers

**4.12** Although the government of the day is Her Majesty's government and the ministers
that make up that government are accordingly Her Majesty's ministers, the monarch's
role in their appointment is essentially formal. Political patronage lies not with the
monarch but with the PM. Thus ministerial appointments are made on the basis of

prime ministerial nomination; the monarch is no longer in a position whereby she could reject a nomination and doubtless this is the message that would be conveyed by advisers were it thought otherwise. The position with regard to the appointment of a PM is, however, a little different.

**4.13** In theory, the monarch is able to choose a PM, although in practice that choice is limited by two factors: first, by the constitutional convention that the chosen candidate should be the person who is capable of commanding the confidence of the majority of members of the HC; and, secondly, that in the modern political age, party leaders are elected by their party membership. With regard to the latter, Professor Brazier has argued that: 'As a matter of strict law, party elections can neither preclude nor pre-empt the prerogative of choice'. Whilst the truth of this assertion cannot be denied, it would be highly unlikely that a monarch would ignore the results of a party election save where there was a very good reason for doing so. At a time when the main party leaders are elected by the broad membership of the party rather than just the parliamentary party, it is conceivable that a party leader may not be able to command the confidence of his or her party at Westminster, whereas another colleague may be able to do so. In those circumstances, the prerogative of choice would entitle the monarch to pass over the party leader in favour of the alternative candidate. Whether the membership of a political party would be prepared to accept such an outcome is, however, a different matter.

**4.14** Following the general election held on 6 May 2010, no one political party had a majority of seats in the HC. In other words, there was a 'hung' parliament for the first time in many years. The appointment of a PM therefore depended upon which of the political parties, Conservative or Labour, could convince the Liberal Democrats to form a coalition government. Negotiations took place over a period of five days between the Conservatives and the Liberal Democrats, and between Labour and the Liberal Democrats, before a Conservative and Liberal Democrat coalition was formed. During this period, various conventions appear to have been followed. These were identified some 36 years previously in a memorandum written by Robert (now Lord) Armstrong who was the Principal Private Secretary to the PM, Edward Heath, at the time of the 1974 hung parliament. Professor Blackburn has commented:

> Stated simply, these conventions are, first, that the incumbent Prime Minister has the first opportunity to continue in office and form an administration; secondly, that if he is unable to do so...then the Leader of the Opposition is appointed Prime Minister; and thirdly, it is for the political parties to negotiate any inter-party agreement for government among themselves without royal involvement.

**4.15** The appointment of David Cameron as PM in May 2010 did not occur, therefore, as a result of royal involvement or preference. Instead, it was the culmination of confidential inter-party negotiations following the general election.

## An alternative view

**4.16** From this discussion of some of the more important personal prerogatives or reserve powers of the monarch it will have become apparent that the sovereign retains a measure of personal discretionary power which has the potential to be used in exceptional circumstances. However, this orthodox view has recently been challenged by Professor Blackburn. He argues that whilst it may have been true in the past, it is a view which is now an anachronism since it fails to reflect the modern constitutional reality. In a thought-provoking article Professor Blackburn examines the main personal prerogatives and argues that in respect of each there is in fact far less room for royal activism than some commentators have argued. In his opinion, some constitutional writers have been guilty of 'talking up' the discretionary role of the monarch in these matters. He therefore 'seeks to bury, not praise, future references and talk about the "personal prerogatives" of the monarch'. Whether or not his comments will achieve this end remains to be seen. For present purposes, however, it is sufficient to draw attention to them in order to demonstrate that on this matter as in so many other constitutional law matters, there is ample room for differences of opinion.

## Prerogative and statute

**4.17** Prerogative power is, as has been noted already, something which is unique to the Crown. It is derived from the common law and as such is clearly distinct from statute. Nevertheless, there may be instances when prerogative and statutory powers overlap. In such circumstances, which is to prevail – the prerogative or statute? This was the point at issue in a case decided shortly after the conclusion of the First World War.

> *A-G v De Keyser's Royal Hotel Ltd* **(1920):** The Crown took possession of a hotel in May 1916 and made it available to personnel of the Royal Flying Corps. It was claimed that this had been done under the Defence of the Realm Regulations. The owners of the hotel later sought a declaration that they were entitled to be paid rent for the use and occupation of the hotel, or alternatively, that they should be compensated for the act of possession. It was counter-argued by the Crown that possession had been effected under the prerogative power to take property for the defence of the realm and that, accordingly, the hotel owners had no right to be compensated. HL held: where Parliament passes an Act empowering the Crown to do a certain thing which it could formerly have done under the prerogative, it is the statutory power, subject to whatever conditions and limitations have been attached to it, which must be exercised thereafter.

**4.18** The principle which emerges from this case is clear. In the event of a conflict between the prerogative and a statutory power, it is the latter which prevails. Were it otherwise, the effect would be to deny the legislative supremacy of Parliament. The Crown can be said to have acquiesced in the further reduction of its prerogative power by assenting to the Act which is the source of the statutory power. In these circumstances, the fate of the prerogative power needs to be considered.

**4.19** In the *De Keyser's* case, Lord Atkinson rejected suggestions that the prerogative power to take property for the defence of the realm would be 'merged' into the statute. Instead, he preferred the view that it would be held in 'abeyance'. This would mean, therefore, that the prerogative power might be capable of being exercised once again at some later date following the repeal of the statutory power that superseded it. This conjecture is based on the assumption that the statute is silent as to the fate of the prerogative power. A prerogative power may, however, be abolished by the express words of the statute or by necessary implication. Alternatively, it may be expressly preserved: see, for example, s 11 of the Crown Proceedings Act 1947 and s 33(5) of the Immigration Act 1971. Neither statute nor the Crown nor the courts can, however, create new prerogative powers for as Lord Diplock observed in *BBC v Johns* (1965):

> It is 350 years and a civil war too late for the Queen's courts to broaden the prerogative. The limits within which the executive government may impose obligations or restrictions on citizens of the United Kingdom without any statutory authority are now well settled and incapable of extension.

**4.20** The relationship between the prerogative and statute was once again at issue before the HL in a case concerned with the operation of the Criminal Injuries Compensation Scheme.

> ***R v Secretary of State for the Home Department, ex p Fire Brigades Union* (1995):**
> A statutory scheme for compensating the victims of violent crime was established under the Criminal Justice Act 1988. It replaced an existing scheme operated under prerogative power. However, by virtue of s 171 of the Act, the Secretary of State (SoS) was entitled to bring the scheme into force on a date of his choosing. He decided not to do so and hence the old prerogative scheme continued to operate. Later, using the prerogative power, the SoS established a new tariff system which was very different to the statutory scheme. The practical consequence of his decision was that some victims of crime would receive considerably smaller payments than they would have done under either the old prerogative scheme or the statutory scheme. Representatives of those likely to be affected sought judicial review of the SoS's actions. HL held: by a majority of three to two, that the decision whether or not to bring the statutory provisions into force was a matter for the discretion of the SoS. He was not under any duty to bring the scheme into effect. However, he was under a duty to consider from time to time whether or not to bring the scheme into force. By stating in a White Paper that he had no intention of bringing the statutory scheme into force and then establishing a new tariff scheme under the prerogative, the SoS had acted unlawfully. The prerogative power had been abused in that it had been used to frustrate the will of Parliament.

**4.21** The *De Keyser's* principle did not apply in the *Fire Brigades* case because the relevant provisions of the Criminal Justice Act 1988 were not in force at the material time. Had they been, they would have precluded the possibility of using the prerogative to establish the tariff scheme. It has been suggested by Professor Barendt that in using the prerogative power to introduce the new tariff scheme, the SoS 'was trying to legislate'. Accordingly, he is of the opinion that the HL 'should have simply held it was unconstitutional for the executive to legislate'. Do you agree?

**4.22** In the later case of *R (Mahmood) v Pharmaceutical Society of Great Britain* (2002), where it was argued that a bye-law made under the authority of a royal charter (ie issued under the prerogative) was ultra vires because it had been replaced or curtailed by a statutory power to make bye-laws under the Pharmacy Act 1954, the CA held that the bye-law was not ultra vires. In the words of Kennedy LJ:

> I cannot find anything in the 1954 Act which expressly or by implication extinguished the power granted by paragraph 17 of the charter to make byelaws such as byelaw 29 . . . Where a power is given directly by statute then of course statutory power must be used, but for the rest there is no hint of any curtailment of the powers granted by the charter.

**4.23** The position in *Mahmood* may thus be contrasted with what has happened in relation to the prerogative power to dissolve Parliament. Formerly, this was a power exercised by the Queen on the advice and consent of the PM of the day. As such, it enabled the Government to seek a general election at the most opportune moment, subject to the monarch's right to refuse a dissolution. Now, however, as a consequence of the Fixed-term Parliaments Act 2011, the power to dissolve Parliament no longer vests with the monarch. Instead, a dissolution will ordinarily occur at a fixed point in time in accordance with s 3 of the Act. Although the Act does not declare that 'The prerogative power to dissolve Parliament is hereby abolished', it does provide in s 3(2) that 'Parliament cannot otherwise be dissolved'. If not expressly then at least by implication, the prerogative power of dissolution has been extinguished by the 2011 Act.

## Adapting prerogative powers

**4.24** Although new prerogative powers cannot be created, there is scope for the adaptation of existing prerogative powers to meet modern-day needs.

*R v Secretary of State for the Home Department, ex p Northumbria Police Authority* **(1989):** Chief police officers were informed in a Home Office circular that they could be issued with plastic baton rounds and CS gas from a central store maintained by the SoS. It was stated that the supply could take place without the approval of the Police Authority (PA). The PA sought to challenge the validity of part of the circular. The SoS claimed to be acting in accordance with a statutory power to maintain a central store (s 41 of the Police Act 1964) or by virtue of the prerogative power to maintain the peace. The PA claimed that it had the exclusive power (s 4(4) of the Police Act 1964) to equip the police force. The DC refused the application. It held that s 4(4) did not give the PA a monopoly power of supply. Although the SoS did not have the power under s 41 to supply equipment, he did have the power to do so under the prerogative. CA held: s 41 of the 1964 Act did authorize the SoS to supply the equipment. Even if it did not, both it and s 4(4) fell short of an express and unequivocal inhibition on the use of the prerogative power to do all that is necessary to preserve the peace of the realm. Such a prerogative had existed at least since medieval times. It had not been surrendered by the Crown in the process of assenting to the creation of independent police forces for the purposes of keeping the peace. Nourse LJ remarked that: 'the scarcity of references in the books to the prerogative of keeping the peace within the realm does not disprove that it exists. Rather it may point to an unspoken assumption that it does'.

## The prerogative and the courts

4.25 The relationship between the prerogative and the courts gave rise to some significant constitutional cases which, as we have seen, were decided prior to the constitutional settlement of 1688. In the 300 or so years that have since passed, prerogative power has continued to exercise the minds of the courts. The traditional view expressed by the judges was that whilst they were prepared to determine the existence of a prerogative power and examine its scope and extent, they were not prepared to question how that power had been exercised.

*Burmah Oil v Lord Advocate* **(1965):** The British Government had ordered the destruction of certain oil installations owned by the oil company so as to prevent them falling into the hands of advancing Japanese forces during the Second World War. The company sought compensation from the Government. The HL was therefore required to consider the extent of the prerogative power under which the destruction had taken place and whether or not compensation was payable. HL held: by a majority of three to two, that the prerogative concerned the control of the armed forces, the waging of war, and all those things in an emergency which are necessary for the conduct of war. Such a wide residue of power to govern in time of war was necessary since Parliament may not be able to pass the required legislation in time. The company was entitled to be compensated for the destruction of its installations.

4.26 The effect of the decision in *Burmah Oil* was subsequently nullified by the passage of the War Damage Act 1965. This Act, which had been promised by the Government if it was defeated in the courts, abolished rights at common law to compensation in respect of damage to or the destruction of property in the name of the Crown during wartime. Since the Act had retrospective effect, Burmah Oil failed to obtain their compensation.

This episode therefore demonstrates the ease with which an inconvenient judicial decision may be overcome by a legislatively supreme Parliament under the control of the executive.

**4.27**  The orthodoxy that the exercise of the prerogative could not be subject to legal challenge was at issue in several cases such as *R v Criminal Injuries Compensation Board, ex p Lain* (1967), where it was held that the fact that the Board had been set up under the prerogative did not protect it from the jurisdiction of the courts, and *Laker Airways v Department of Trade* (1977). In this latter case, which concerned the withdrawal of both Laker Airways' licence to operate a service to the United States and its designation as a carrier under the Treaty of Bermuda (made with the United States by the UK Government under the prerogative), Lord Denning took the view that the exercise of the prerogative could be reviewed by the courts. This was because it was a discretionary power not very dissimilar to those vested in the executive by statute. In his opinion, with which the other CA judges who heard the appeal did not agree, the treaty-making power was therefore subject to review. Nevertheless, the orthodoxy prevailed until the landmark decision of the HL in *Council of Civil Service Unions v Minister for the Civil Service* (1985), otherwise known as the *GCHQ* case.

> **The *GCHQ* case:** Under art 4 of the Civil Service Order in Council 1982, made under the prerogative, the Minister for the Civil Service was empowered to make regulations or issue instructions relating to the terms of employment of Civil Service employees. An instruction was issued banning employees at the Government Communications Headquarters (GCHQ) from being members of a trade union since it was feared that industrial action would disrupt the sensitive intelligence work undertaken there. It was believed that this in turn would pose a threat to national security. The established practice was that employees would be consulted prior to an alteration being made to their terms of employment. The applicant sought a declaration that the instruction was invalid due to a failure to consult. HL held: that the instruction was reviewable either as a direct exercise of prerogative power (the majority) or as the exercise of a delegated power conferred by the sovereign under the prerogative. However, although the union had a legitimate expectation to be consulted, this was defeated by the overriding interests of national security.

**4.28**  The principle established in *GCHQ*, that the exercise of prerogative power may be subject to review by the courts, thus puts such powers on a similar footing to statutory discretionary powers. However, not all prerogative powers are thereby subject to the supervisory jurisdiction of the courts. In giving judgment in *GCHQ*, Lord Roskill felt that the view expressed by Lord Denning in *Laker Airways*, that the prerogative was reviewable where it had been exercised improperly or mistakenly, was 'far too wide'. In his opinion, the right of challenge was not unqualified. It depended 'upon the subject matter of the prerogative power which is exercised'. Accordingly, there were, as Lord Roskill put it, certain 'excluded categories' of prerogative powers, the exercise of which would not be subject to review by the courts. These included: the treaty-making power; the defence of the realm; the prerogative of mercy; the grant of honours; and the appointment of ministers. Since several such powers clearly involve the exercise of political judgment and are matters of high policy, it would be very difficult for the courts to review their exercise without transgressing the doctrine of the separation of powers. Matters involving the exercise of political judgment are for the executive rather than the courts.

4.29 In the years that have passed since *GCHQ* was decided, several applicants for judicial review have sought to apply the principle established in that case to the facts of their own particular situation.

---

*R v Secretary of State for Foreign and Commonwealth Affairs, ex p Everett* **(1989):** The applicant (E) who was living in Spain was the holder of a British passport which was due to expire. A form for a new passport was completed and lodged with the British Embassy in Madrid. However, a new passport was not forthcoming. This accorded with the Foreign Office policy that passports would not be issued overseas to persons for whom an arrest warrant had been issued in the UK. Such a warrant had been issued in respect of E, although none of its particulars were known to him. E sought an order to quash the decision not to issue him with a new passport and a mandatory order to require his passport application to be considered in a proper and lawful manner. CA held: the issue or withdrawal of a passport involved the exercise of prerogative power. A passport was a familiar document to all those who travel in the world and its issue was a normal expectation of every citizen. Its grant or refusal was an administrative decision, not a matter of foreign affairs. Accordingly, the exercise of this prerogative power was subject to judicial review. However, in the circumstances, since E was fully aware of all the details of the arrest warrant by the time that the case came to court, there were no grounds for granting the relief sought.

---

*R v Secretary of the Home Department, ex p Bentley* **(1994):** Derek Bentley (B) and his co-accused, Christopher Craig (C), were convicted of the murder of a policeman. B, a 19-year-old with a mental age of 11, was hanged, but C, who fired the fatal shot, was reprieved on account of his age (16). Concerns were expressed at the safety of B's conviction and his family began a campaign for a posthumous free pardon. In 1992, the Home Secretary (HS) declined to exercise the prerogative of mercy to grant such a pardon on the basis that it was not open to him to do so. B's sister sought to challenge that refusal by making an application for judicial review. DC held: that some aspects of the exercise of the prerogative of mercy are amenable to the judicial process. The HS had misdirected himself in law by believing that he only had the power to grant a free pardon. He had failed to appreciate that the prerogative of mercy was capable of being exercised in many different ways due to its breadth and flexibility. It lay within the HS's power to grant a conditional pardon as a recognition of the fact that a mistake had been made.

---

---

*R v Secretary of State for Foreign and Commonwealth Affairs, ex p Rees-Mogg*
**(1994):** On 7 February 1992 the Treaty on European Union was signed on behalf of the UK
by the Foreign Minister. The applicant sought judicial review of the Treaty's ratification. He
argued, inter alia, that by ratifying Title V of the Treaty which established a common foreign
and security policy among member states, the government would be transferring part of the
prerogative without statutory authority. DC held: Title V did not entail an abandonment or
transfer of prerogative powers. Rather, it entailed an exercise of those powers in relation to
foreign affairs. Thus the applicant's argument failed.

---

**4.30** The distinction which the CA in *Everett* made between an administrative decision (the
issue or withdrawal of a passport) and matters of foreign policy was clearly important because the Government had attempted to argue that its prerogative power in
respect of passports did include foreign policy issues which were non-justiciable. In the
more recent case of *R (on the application of Abbasi) v Secretary of State for Foreign and
Commonwealth Affairs* (2002) the CA noted, inter alia, that the justiciability of a prerogative power depends 'not on general principle, but on subject matter and suitability
in the particular case'. Thus it was 'not an answer to a claim for judicial review to say
that the source of the power of the Foreign Office is the prerogative'. Although subject
matter was therefore the determinative issue, the CA further noted that the authorities
established that a 'court cannot enter the forbidden areas, including decisions affecting
foreign policy'.

**4.31** Of the three applications for judicial review (para **4.29**), the most speculative was *ex p
Rees-Mogg* in that it involved the treaty-making power. It had long been established
prior to *GCHQ* that such a power was not subject to the jurisdiction of the courts. Thus
in *Blackburn v A-G* (1971), where the applicant sought to challenge the UK's signing of
the EC Treaty, Lord Denning observed that:

> The Treaty-making power of this country rests not in the courts, but in the Crown; that
> is, Her Majesty acting on the advice of her ministers. When her ministers negotiate and
> sign a treaty, even a treaty of such paramount importance as this proposed one, they
> act on behalf of the country as a whole. They exercise the prerogative of the Crown.
> Their action in so doing cannot be challenged or questioned in these courts.

**4.32** The authority of *Blackburn v A-G* (1971) was subsequently confirmed in *McWhirter
v Attorney General* (1972), *Ex p Molyneaux* (1986), and *Maclaine Watson & Co Ltd v
Department of Trade and Industry* (1990). The treaty-making power was one of Lord
Roskill's 'excluded categories' from the principle established in *GCHQ*, and the decision in *ex p Rees-Mogg* merely demonstrates that this remains the case. Nevertheless,
it would be wrong to see these 'excluded categories' as a closed list. The decision in *ex p
Bentley* accepted that the exercise of the prerogative of mercy could be subject to review,
and yet this prerogative power also featured in Lord Roskill's list. The jurisdiction to

review the exercise of the prerogative of mercy has subsequently been used in several cases. In *R (on the application of Page) v Secretary of State for Justice* (2007), the Administrative Court held that the Secretary of State had acted unfairly in not exercising the prerogative to release P from prison, where a mistake as to the proper date of his release had been made due to concurrent sentences for various offences and a successful appeal against one of his convictions.

**4.33** The decision in *Page* reflects how the prerogative of mercy may be used in the context of remission. In modern times, the prerogative has also been exercised in relation to the grant of a conditional pardon (*Bentley*), where, as we have seen, it was posthumously recognized that the penalty imposed was not commensurate with B's offending. A third situation in which the prerogative of mercy may be exercised is where it is accepted that a defendant has been wrongly convicted and that there has been a serious miscarriage of justice as a result. In the appropriate circumstances, a free pardon may be granted.

> *R (on the application of Shields) v Secretary of State for Justice* (2008): The claimant (S) had been convicted in Bulgaria of the attempted murder of a bar worker, sentenced to 15 years' imprisonment, and ordered to pay £90,000 in compensation. On appeal, the prison sentence was reduced to 10 years. S was later repatriated to the UK under the Repatriation of Prisoners Act 1984 and the Convention on the Transfer of Sentenced Persons 1983 to serve the balance of his sentence. A public campaign was begun on his behalf on the basis that he had been wrongly convicted. Another UK citizen, who had been arrested by the Bulgarian police but released without charge, had later signed a written confession before his own solicitor. It was therefore argued on S's behalf that the Secretary of State (SoS) ought to exercise the prerogative of mercy and grant a pardon. The SoS was advised, however, that the 1984 Act and the 1983 Convention precluded the grant of a pardon where a person had been transferred to the UK from a foreign prison. S sought judicial review of that decision. Admin Ct held: that although the grant of a free pardon had been little used in modern times, the prerogative to do so undoubtedly remained. It was capable of being exercised in those very rare cases where justice had not been achieved by a concluded court process. The SoS had erred in thinking that he did not have the power or jurisdiction to grant a pardon.

**4.34** Although the outcome in *Shields* was that the court issued a declaration that the Secretary of State did have the power and jurisdiction to issue a pardon, whether or not the power was ultimately exercised in favour of the claimant remained a matter for the minister. As Maddison J pointed out, 'it is not in dispute in this case that the formulation of criteria for the exercise of the prerogative to pardon are entirely matters of policy for the Secretary of State'. In the event, following an investigation by the Merseyside Police and the coming to light of important new evidence, the Secretary of State recommended that the Queen grant a free pardon. S was accordingly released from prison. It should be remembered, however, that the effect of a free pardon is, as was stated by Watkins LJ in *R v Foster* (1984), to remove 'all pains, penalties and punishments whatsoever that from the said conviction may ensue'. Since the prerogative relates to mercy rather than justice, the grant of a free pardon does not eliminate a conviction.

**4.35** An interesting issue concerning the reviewability of the prerogative has been identified by Billings and Pontin. They draw attention to the definition of 'primary legislation' in the Human Rights Act 1998, s 21(1)(f)(i), which encompasses Orders in Council made pursuant to the royal prerogative. The significance of this lies in the fact that the general prohibition on a public authority acting in a way which is incompatible with a Convention right (s 6(1)) does not apply where: (a) as a result of primary legislation that authority could not have acted differently; or (b) the primary legislation cannot be interpreted in such a way as to be compatible with the Convention right and the public authority was acting in order to give effect to or enforce the relevant provision (s 6(2)). The authors therefore wonder whether equating an Order in Council with primary legislation will have the effect of conferring immunity from the 1998 Act's provisions where human rights are adversely affected by the exercise of prerogative power. In *R (Bancoult) v Secretary of State for Foreign and Commonwealth Affairs (No 2)* (2008) (paras **4.36–4.38**), Lord Hoffmann effectively answered the point by observing that the effect of s 21(1)(f)(i) was that an Order in Council 'cannot be overridden by Convention rights'. In the event of a conflict between an order and a Convention right, he was therefore of the view that a court 'can only make a declaration of incompatibility under s 4 of the 1998 Act'. On the facts of *Bancoult*, the HL ruled, amongst other things, that since the ECHR had no application in the Chagos Islands, the Crown's actions could not infringe the terms of the 1998 Act.

**4.36** The validity of two Orders in Council made pursuant to the colonial prerogative power was at issue in judicial review proceedings.

*R (Bancoult) v Secretary of State for Foreign and Commonwealth Affairs (No 2)* **(2008):** The Chagos Islands were ceded to Great Britain by France in 1814. In 1965 they were constituted a separate colony, the British Indian Ocean Territory. In 1971, the inhabitants of the Islands were compulsorily removed under the authority of an Immigration Ordinance because the main island in the archipelago, Diego Garcia, was required by the USA for use as a military base. The 1971 Ordinance was later quashed by the DCt on the ground that it exceeded the scope of the British Indian Ocean Territory Order 1965 under which it was made. The then Secretary of State (SoS) went on record as accepting the court's decision. Later, however, the Government decided that resettlement was not feasible. Since the territory was still wanted for defence purposes, two orders in council were made – the British Indian Ocean Territory (Constitution) Order 2004 and the British Indian Ocean Territory (Immigration) Order 2004. The cumulative effect of the orders was to prevent the Chagossians from returning home. The respondents succeeded in persuading the DCt that the orders were invalid. The SoS appealed on the grounds that: a challenge to the validity of the orders in council made under the prerogative was precluded by the Colonial Laws Validity Act 1865; and that since the orders were made by the monarch, this placed the process outside the court's jurisdiction. The CA held: dismissing the appeal, that the claim was not barred by the 1865 Act because the present dispute was not about whether the 2004 Constitution Order was repugnant to a superior statute or law. Rather, it was about whether it was law. Orders in council are acts of the executive and as such they are amendable to judicial review. The use of the prerogative power of colonial governance did not enjoy a generic immunity from review and there was nothing in the orders themselves which made the issues non-justiciable, eg they were not concerned with issues of national security. The Government's response to the quashing of the 1971 Ordinance had given rise to a legitimate expectation that the Chagossians would be allowed to return home, unless there was a radical change in circumstances. No such change had occurred. The SoS appealed. HL held: that there was no reason in principle why prerogative legislation, like other prerogative acts, should not be reviewable by the courts on ordinary principles of public law, ie legality, irrationality, and procedural impropriety. The power to legislate by Order in Council was therefore subject to judicial review. Moreover, the British Indian Ocean Territory (Constitution) Order 2004 was not a colonial law for the purposes of the 1865 Act and therefore that Act did not preclude review by the courts. However, by a majority of 3:2, it was decided that the vires of s 9 of the 2004 Order could not be challenged on the ground of repugnancy to any fundamental principle of English common law. The decision to prevent resettlement had not been an abuse of power, and the statement made by the SoS had not created a legitimate expectation of resettlement on which the Chagossians were able to rely.

**4.37** Although the majority of the HL in *Bancoult* differed from the DC and the CA on the question whether the Secretary of State had acted unlawfully, all three courts were agreed that prerogative legislation was susceptible to judicial review. Thus Lord Hoffmann explained:

> But the fact that such Orders in Council in certain important respects resemble Acts of Parliament does not mean that they share all their characteristics. The principle of sovereignty of Parliament, as it has been developed by the courts over the past 350 years, is founded upon the unique authority Parliament derives from its representative character. An exercise of the prerogative lacks this quality; although it may be legislative in character, it is still an exercise of power by the executive alone . . . I see no reason why prerogative legislation should not be subject to review on ordinary principles of legality, irrationality and procedural impropriety in the same way as any other executive action.

**4.38** The decision in *Bancoult* is therefore significant in that it would seem to represent an extension of the principle established in the *GCHQ* case. Whereas that case was concerned with the jusiticiability of an executive decision made pursuant to powers conferred by a prerogative order, the present case was concerned with the validity of a prerogative order itself. Although Lord Hoffmann recognized that the cases could therefore be distinguished on their facts, he saw 'no reason for making such a distinction'.

## Reform

**4.39** Reform of the prerogative could occur in a variety of different ways. One possibility might be for all the specific prerogative powers to be put on a statutory footing. The advantage of such an approach would be to remove the uncertainty which still surrounds the prerogative despite the recent publication of the Labour Government's list (paras **4.6–4.8**). The prerogative powers would be clearly defined and their exercise would accordingly be open to parliamentary, judicial, and public scrutiny. It might be argued that this would also represent a significant step on the road to a written constitution. A less radical alternative to codification might be to convert certain prerogative powers to statutory powers, as has happened with the power to dissolve Parliament (para **4.23**) and to manage the civil service. A further alternative to either codification or individual statutory replacement would be to place the exercise of certain prerogative powers under the control of Parliament.

**4.40** In March 2004, the HC Public Administration Select Committee published a report, *Taming the Prerogative: Strengthening Ministerial Accountability to Parliament*, in which it considered the use of prerogative powers by ministers and emphasized the lack of parliamentary approval or scrutiny in relation to their exercise. Although the report recognized that there was a need for this kind of executive power, it felt that there should be a greater and more systematic form of parliamentary oversight. In its opinion, the case for reform was 'unanswerable'. It therefore advocated a new approach which would have entailed placing the government under a statutory duty to draw up a list of the prerogative powers exercised by ministers which would then be considered by a parliamentary committee. Legislation would then follow to provide for statutory safeguards where appropriate.

**4.41** One of the recommendations contained within the committee's report was that 'any decision to engage in armed conflict should be approved by Parliament, if not before military action then as soon as possible afterwards'. Although the Government's response expressed itself to be 'not persuaded' by the recommendation, the HL Constitution Committee nevertheless decided to conduct an inquiry on the use of the royal prerogative to deploy the UK's armed forces. In its subsequent report, *Waging War: Parliament's Role and Responsibility*, the Committee concluded that:

> the exercise of the Royal prerogative by the Government to deploy armed force overseas is outdated and should not be allowed to continue as the basis for legitimate war-making in our 21st century democracy. Parliament's ability to challenge the executive must be protected and strengthened. There is a need to set out more precisely the extent of the Government's deployment powers, and the role Parliament can – and should – play in their exercise.

**4.42** In July 2007, the Labour Government under Gordon Brown published a Green Paper, *The Governance of Britain* (Cm 7170) in which it discussed the reform of several prerogative powers. Thus in relation to the non-justiciable treaty-making power, it recognized the existence of the 'Ponsonby Rule' whereby treaties which come into force on a later date than their signature must first be laid before Parliament as a command paper for a minimum of 21 sitting days. This convention therefore afforded Parliament the opportunity to scrutinize and consider treaties signed by the Government. The

'Ponsonby Rule' was subsequently put on a statutory footing by virtue of Part 2 of the Constitutional Reform and Governance Act 2010.

4.43 Turning to the civil service, the Green Paper stated that 'the Prime Minister, as Minister for the Civil Service, exercises powers in relation to the Civil Service under the royal prerogative'. This view may be contrasted with that of Sir William Wade who, in a comment on the *GCHQ* case, expressed the opinion that the power to appoint and dismiss civil servants 'is not a prerogative power at all, but merely the ordinary power which everyone has to employ servants and to tell them what to do'. Nevertheless, it was apparent from the Green Paper that the Government intended to bring forward legislation to put the civil service on a statutory footing. This was duly achieved by Part 1 of the Constitutional Reform and Governance Act 2010.

4.44 It is noteworthy that the Green Paper did not propose the general abolition and non-replacement of prerogative powers since the Labour Government was firmly of the view that 'the powers currently exercised . . . must continue to be held by someone, with appropriate constraints on their use'. Instead, as part of a wider programme of making government more accountable for its actions, the Green Paper committed it to a process of consultation on various matters such as whether individual prerogative powers ought to be set down in statute.

4.45 The reform of prerogative powers may continue in the future under the present coalition Government. Bringing an end to the prerogative power to dissolve Parliament was a significant first step. It should also be noted that in the case of certain prerogative powers, in particular the appointment and dismissal of ministers, although they are not candidates to be reformed, their exercise has changed under the current administration. They are no longer the exclusive preserve of the PM. Instead, as the *Coalition Agreement for Stability and Reform* (May 2010) makes clear, such powers will only be exercised following consultation with the Deputy PM. Patently, this step has been necessary in order to put the new government on a firm foundation. It is a change of practice which will only last as long as the coalition Government itself.

4.46 The HC Political and Constitutional Reform Committee is, at the time of writing, conducting an inquiry into the role and powers of the PM. Written submissions have been invited to a number of questions, including 'Should the PM's role and powers be codified in statute or otherwise?' and 'Is any further change required with regard to specific powers currently exercised under the royal prerogative, by transferring them to statute or otherwise?' Whether or not its final report acts as a further catalyst for prerogative reform remains to be seen.

## FURTHER READING

Allen, M and Thompson, B *Cases and Materials on Constitutional and Administrative Law* (10th edn, 2011) OUP.

Bennion, FAR 'Modern Royal Assent Procedure at Westminster' [1981] 2 Stat LR 135.

Billings, P and Pontin, B 'Prerogative Powers and the Human Rights Act: Elevating the status of Orders in Council' [2001] PL 21.

Blackburn, R 'Monarchy and the Personal Prerogatives' [2004] PL 546.

Blackburn, R 'The 2010 General Election Outcome and Formation of the Conservative–Liberal Democrat Coalition Government' [2011] PL 30.

Bogdanor, V *The Monarchy and the Constitution* (1995) OUP.

Brazier, R *Constitutional Reform* (2nd edn, 1998) OUP.

Brazier, R *Constitutional Practice: The Foundations of British Government* (3rd edn, 1999) OUP.

Brazier, R '"Monarchy and the Personal Prerogatives": A personal response to Professor Blackburn' [2005] PL 45.

Brazier, R 'Legislating about the Monarchy' [2007] CLJ 86.

Chitty J *Prerogatives of the Crown* (1820) Butterworths.

Cohn, M 'Medieval Chains, Invisible Links: On Non-statutory Powers of the Executive' (2005) 25 OJLS 97.

Craig, P and Tomkins, A (eds) *The Executive and Public Law* (2006) OUP.

Dixon, D '*Godden v Hales* revisited–James II and the Dispensing Power' (2006) 27 J Leg Hist 129.

House of Commons Public Administration Select Committee *Taming the Prerogative: Strengthening Ministerial Accountability to Parliament* (2003–4, HC 422).

House of Lords Constitution Committee *Waging War: Parliament's Role and Responsibility* (2005–6, HL Paper 236-I and II).

House of Lords Constitution Committee *Waging War: Parliament's Role and Responsibility Follow-up* (2006–7, HL Paper 51).

Jennings, Sir Ivor *Cabinet Government* (3rd edn, 1959) Cambridge University Press.

Laws, D *22 Days in May: The Birth of the First Lib Dem-Conservative Coalition* (2010) Biteback Publishing.

Munro, C *Studies in Constitutional Law* (2nd edn, 1999) Butterworths, chapter 8.

Pollard, D, Parpworth, N, and Hughes, D *Constitutional and Administrative Law: Text with Materials* (4th edn, 2007) OUP.

Sunkin, M and Payne, S (eds) *The Nature of the Crown: A Legal and Political Analysis* (1999) OUP.

Tomkins, A *Our Republican Constitution* (2005) Hart.

Twomey, A 'The Refusal or Deferral of Royal Assent' [2006] PL 580.

Wade, Sir William 'Procedure and Prerogative in Public Law' (1985) 101 LQR 180.

Wade, Sir William *Constitutional Fundamentals* (1989) Stevens.

# SELF-TEST QUESTIONS

1   Professor Blackburn has contended that: 'The concept of the royal prerogative raises the nature of the constitution itself, its unwritten nature and its dependency upon the ancient common law.' To what extent, if any, do you agree with this view?

2   Is the Queen entitled to refuse Royal Assent to a Bill? If she did so refuse, what would be the potential consequences?

3   Twomey has contended: 'the history of the exercise of the power to grant Royal Assent … as part of the royal prerogative in the United Kingdom, suggests that an underlying discretion may continue to exist, albeit one that is heavily circumscribed by constitutional convention'. Do you agree?

4   Which is more important, statute or prerogative? Why? Which cases could be used to support your view?

5   How have judicial attitudes towards the prerogative altered with the passage of time?

6   Do you agree with Professor Tomkins that the decision in *ex p Northumbria Police Authority* (1988) is an example of the courts being 'alarmingly lax in their policing of the boundaries of the prerogative'?

7   Is there a case for arguing that the decision in *GCHQ* is more important in terms of principle than practice?

8   Which prerogative powers are reviewable by the courts and why?

9   Do you think that ministerial accountability to Parliament represents an effective safeguard against the arbitrary use of prerogative power?

10   Is reform of the prerogative necessary and if so, what form should it take?

# 5 The legislative supremacy of Parliament

## SUMMARY

This chapter examines the constitutional significance of the doctrine of the legislative supremacy of Parliament. It considers the traditional view of this doctrine which holds that Parliament is legislatively omnicompetent. It also takes into account the new view of the doctrine. Adherents of this view argue that whilst there are no limits on Parliament as to subject matter, Parliament can bind itself in terms of the manner and form of legislating. The chapter also considers the effect on legislative supremacy of the following: the Parliament Acts 1911 and 1949; the Acts of Union; the UK's membership of the EU; devolution; and the Human Rights Act 1998.

## Sovereignty of Parliament

5.1 In many of the standard texts on constitutional and administrative law, there is likely to be a chapter entitled 'The Sovereignty of Parliament' or a variant thereof. 'Sovereignty' was the word which Dicey used to describe the concept of 'the power of law-making unrestricted by any legal limit'. In short, he used it to describe a legal concept. However, as Dicey himself acknowledged, 'sovereignty' is also capable of bearing political meanings. It may be used, for example, to indicate where political power resides in a state. For the avoidance of doubt, the expression 'legislative supremacy' will be used throughout this chapter to signify the law-making power of Parliament.

## The traditional view

5.2 The importance of the principle of the legislative supremacy of Parliament to an understanding of the UK constitution has meant that it has been much written about. Dicey, for example, described the principle as meaning:

> [N]either more nor less than this, namely, that Parliament thus defined has, under the English constitution, the right to make or unmake any law whatsoever; and, further,

> *that no person or body is recognised by the law of England as having a right to override*
> *or set aside the legislation of Parliament.*

**5.3** The Parliament which enjoyed this unlimited legislative authority consisted of the Queen, the HL, and the HC. For Dicey, therefore, the principle of legislative supremacy (or parliamentary sovereignty as he termed it) had both a positive and a negative aspect. On the positive side, it meant that all Acts of Parliament, whatever their purpose, would be obeyed by the courts. On the negative side, it meant that there was 'no person or body of persons who can . . . make rules which override or derogate from an Act of Parliament'. Writing some 70 years later, Wade devoted his attention to the basis of legal sovereignty and concluded that it was to be found in the rule that the courts obey Acts of Parliament. Expanding on this theme more fully, he argued that:

> *The rule is above and beyond the reach of statute . . . because it is itself the source of*
> *the authority of statute. This puts it into a class by itself among rules of common law,*
> *and the apparent paradox that it is unalterable by Parliament turns out to be a truism.*
> *The rule of judicial obedience is in one sense a rule of common law, but in another*
> *sense–which applies to no other rule of common law–it is the ultimate* political *fact*
> *upon which the whole system of legislation hangs. Legislation owes its authority to*
> *the rule: the rule does not owe its authority to legislation. To say that Parliament can*
> *change the rule, merely because it can change any other rule, is to put the cart before*
> *the horse.*

**5.4** Thus at the heart of the discussion of the supremacy of Parliament lies the relationship between Parliament and the courts. Parliament has unlimited legislative authority because the courts recognize this to be the case. H L A Hart considers that the rule of parliamentary supremacy is part of what he terms 'the ultimate rule of recognition'. This is deployed by the courts as a means of identifying what are valid rules of law. An alternative means of describing the legislative supremacy of Parliament would be to say that it is, borrowing from the political theorist Hans Kelsen, the 'grundnorm' of the constitution. In other words, it is the fundamental rule upon which all other rules of the constitution are based.

## The pre-1688 position

**5.5** The notion that Parliament has unlimited legislative authority has not always been accepted by the courts. Thus in *Dr Bonham's Case* (1610), Coke CJ was of the opinion that the common law had the power to control Acts of Parliament and to sometimes declare them to be void. The circumstances in which this might happen were where an Act was 'against common right and reason, or repugnant, or impossible to be performed'. Similarly in *Day v Savadge* (1614), the view was expressed that if an Act was against 'natural equity' in that it made a man a 'judge in his own case', the Act would be 'void in itself'. However, these cases need to be set in their appropriate historical context. They were decided prior to the 'Glorious Revolution' of 1688, from which date the legislative supremacy of Parliament has been recognized by the courts.

## The Glorious Revolution 1688

**5.6** 'Revolution' is an epithet frequently used to describe particular historical events. It implies that there has been some major upheaval within a state with the result that the old order has been replaced by the new. Whilst the events in England in 1688–9 had none of the bloodlust and terror of the events in France a century later, they did bring about a significant change in the relationship between the monarch and Parliament. James II, a Roman Catholic, had succeeded to the thrones of England and Scotland in February 1685 on the death of his brother, Charles II. During the course of the next three years, he clashed with Parliament and the Anglican church as a result of his attempts to use prerogative powers to dispense with laws which discriminated against Catholics (see, for example, *Godden v Hales* (1686), para **4.2**).

**5.7** Eventually, a number of prominent politicians signed a letter which invited William of Orange, the Protestant son-in-law of James II, to intervene. He landed at Torbay in Devon in November 1688 with a force of approximately 15,000 soldiers, most of whom were Dutch. They met with little resistance from the forces still loyal to James II en route to London. They entered the capital in the middle of December, at which point James II fled the country, taking refuge in France. A Convention 'Parliament' was summoned by William of Orange, and it issued a Declaration of Rights in which it condemned the actions of James II. The throne was offered jointly to William and his wife Mary (the elder daughter of James II) on the terms and conditions set out in the Bill of Rights 1689. The rights contained in this document were neither novel nor far-reaching. Thus, for example, art 10 declared 'That excessive bail ought not to be required, nor excessive fines imposed; nor cruel and unusual punishments inflicted.'

**5.8** The Bill of Rights 1689 did not therefore take the form of a conventional 'rights' document. Indeed, it might be argued that it was as much about the 'wrongs' of James II as it was about the 'rights' of the people. However, its constitutional significance lies in the fact that it asserted the supremacy of Parliament over the monarch. From that point onward, matters such as the levying of taxation or the raising or keeping of a standing army could not be done without the grant or consent of Parliament. It was Parliament which now held the purse strings. It was Parliament which now had responsibility for the security of the state. It was Parliament which now had legislative power. And it was to the Acts of Parliament that the courts now owed obedience.

## Judicial obedience to Acts of Parliament

**5.9** Numerous cases can be cited as proof of this judicial obedience to legislation enacted by Parliament. Thus in *Ex p Canon Selwyn* (1872), a case which raised the question of the validity of the monarch's assent to the Irish Church Disestablishment Act 1869, Cockburn CJ stated that:

> [T]here is no judicial body in the country by which the validity of an Act of Parliament could be questioned. An Act of the legislature is superior in authority to any court of

*law. We have only to administer the law as we find it, and no court could pronounce a*
*judgment as to the validity of an Act of Parliament.*

**5.10**   Similarly in *Madzimbamuto v Lardner-Burke* (1969), a case concerned with, inter alia, Southern Rhodesia's Declaration of Independence in 1965 and the subsequent passage of the Southern Rhodesia Act 1965 by the UK Parliament in which it was declared that Southern Rhodesia remained part of Her Majesty's dominions, Lord Reid stated that:

> *It is often said that it would be unconstitutional for the United Kingdom Parliament to*
> *do certain things, meaning that the moral, political and other reasons against doing*
> *them are so strong that most people would regard it as highly improper if Parliament*
> *did these things. But that does not mean that it is beyond the power of Parliament to*
> *do such things. If Parliament chose to do any of them the courts could not hold the Act*
> *of Parliament invalid.*

**5.11**   These examples of judicial obedience to Acts of Parliament have been gleaned from the law reports. It is worth noting, however, that whilst speaking in an extra-judicial capacity, the former LCJ, Lord Woolf, has argued that there may be circumstances in which the courts might no longer be required to obey an Act of Parliament. In his opinion, if Parliament did 'the unthinkable' and passed a law which abolished the court's power of judicial review:

> *then I would say that the courts would also be required to act in a manner which would*
> *be without precedent. Some judges might choose to do so by saying that it was an*
> *unrebuttable presumption that Parliament could never intend such a result. I myself*
> *would consider there were advantages in making it clear that ultimately there are even*
> *limits on the supremacy of Parliament which it is the courts' inalienable responsibility*
> *to identify and uphold. They are limits of the most modest dimensions which I believe*
> *any democrat would accept. They are no more than are necessary to enable the Rule*
> *of Law to be preserved.*

**5.12**   Thus in Lord Woolf's analysis, an Act which contravened the requirements of the rule of law could be disobeyed by the courts. If this were to happen, what would be the consequences for the doctrine of the legislative supremacy of Parliament? Lord Woolf's remarks can be contrasted with those of Lord Steyn. Whilst delivering a lecture in 1996, the latter observed that:

> *The relationship between the judiciary and the legislature is simple and straightforward.*
> *Parliament asserts sovereign legislative power. The courts acknowledge the sovereignty*
> *of Parliament. And in countless decisions the courts have declared the unqualified*
> *supremacy of Parliament. There are no exceptions.*

**5.13**   Significantly, however, in one of the last cases which Lord Steyn heard prior to retiring as a Law Lord, *Jackson v Attorney General* (2005) (paras **5.35–5.41**), his views appeared to have shifted more towards those of Lord Woolf when he observed, albeit obiter, that:

> *The classic account given by Dicey of the doctrine of the supremacy of Parliament, pure and absolute as it was, can now be seen to be out of place in the modern United Kingdom. Nevertheless, the supremacy of Parliament is still the general principle of our constitution. It is a construct of the common law. The judges created this principle. If that is so, it is not unthinkable that circumstances could arise when the courts may have to qualify a principle established on a different hypothesis of constitutionalism. In exceptional circumstances involving an attempt to abolish judicial review or the ordinary role of the courts, the Appellate Committee of the House of Lords or a new Supreme Court may have to consider whether this is a constitutional fundamental which even a sovereign Parliament acting at the behest of a complaisant House of Commons cannot abolish.*

Also in *Jackson* Lord Hope observed:

> *Our constitution is dominated by the sovereignty of Parliament. But Parliamentary sovereignty is no longer, if ever it was, absolute. It is no longer right to say that its freedom to legislate admits of no qualification whatever. Step by step, gradually but surely, the English principle of the absolute legislative sovereignty of Parliament which Dicey derived from Coke and Blackburn is being qualified.*

These remarks are important. They suggest that, for at least some senior members of the judiciary, there are restrictions on Parliament's ability to legislate, such as where Parliament sought to pass a statute which was contrary to the rule of law. In the opinion of Gordon, 'the comments of Lord Steyn and Lord Hope may mark a crucial point in the development of the UK constitution' in that they 'seek to place substantive limitations on the legislative capacity of Parliament through the subjection of legal sovereignty to superior immutable values emanating from the common law'. Whether they will signal a more widespread judicial rejection of the constitutional orthodoxy remains to be seen.

## Non-legal limits on the legislative power of Parliament

**5.14** Lord Reid's remarks in *Madzimbamuto* (para **5.10**) represent a classical formulation of the traditional view that there are no legal limits on the legislative power of Parliament. Under this view, Parliament has the power to make whatever laws it thinks fit, including repressive laws of the most barbarous kind. Thus to take an example deployed by Leslie Stephen, Parliament could, if it so wished, enact a law that all blue-eyed babies should be killed at birth. It possesses the legal power to do so even if the likelihood of such a law being passed is remote in the extreme. In practice, therefore, there is a clear distinction between what Parliament can do and what it will do. Its legislative power is subject to the type of non-legal limits to which Lord Reid referred. Political considerations, for example, play a central role in the determination of a government's legislative programme. Unpopular legislation can have a very damaging effect upon a government, particularly when a general election draws near. Governments may therefore seek to do that which makes them popular with the electorate, or at least refrain from doing that which makes them unpopular.

5.15  A further example of the traditional view of Parliament's legislative power is evident in the writings of Sir Ivor Jennings. In addition to drawing attention to the fact that parliamentary supremacy means that Parliament has the legal power to legislate on whatever subject matter it likes, Jennings suggested that it also meant that 'Parliament can legislate for all persons and all places'. This point was made with the aid of an example: that if Parliament enacted that smoking on the streets of Paris was illegal, it would therefore be an offence to do so. The French police and the French courts would, of course, not recognize such a piece of legislation. However, the English courts would recognize it and they would be able to try a person for the offence, assuming that they had been given the jurisdiction to do so by the Act.

## Parliament and the courts

5.16  This example underlines the vastness of Parliament's legislative power and that the doctrine of the supremacy of Parliament is concerned with the relationship between Parliament and the courts. In particular, it centres upon the obedience which the courts show to Acts of Parliament. In *Manuel v A-G* (1982), where the vires of a UK statute (the Canada Act 1982) was challenged, Sir Robert Megarry V-C observed that he had:

> heard nothing in this case to make me doubt the simple rule that the duty of the court is to obey and apply every Act of Parliament, and that the court cannot hold any such Act to be ultra vires. Of course there may be questions about what the Act means, and of course there is power to hold statutory instruments and other subordinate legislation ultra vires. But once an instrument is recognised as being an Act of Parliament, no English court can refuse to obey it or question its validity.

5.17  From this passage it is evident that anything short of an Act of Parliament is not entitled to the same obedience. Thus a resolution of the HC will not be obeyed by the courts because it has not been made by Parliament but merely by one of the constituent parts of that body: see *Stockdale v Hansard* (1839) and *Bowles v Bank of England* (1913).

## Enrolled Bill rule

5.18  On several occasions, it has been argued before the courts that a defect or irregularity in the manner in which an Act of Parliament has been passed means that it ought not to be applied. Thus in *Edinburgh and Dalkeith Rly Co v Wauchope* (1842), it was claimed that the provisions of a Private Act of Parliament should not be applied because it had been passed without W having been given notice of it as was required by Standing Orders. The HL rejected the argument. Lord Campbell observed that:

> all that a court of justice can look to is the parliamentary roll; they see that an Act has passed both Houses of Parliament, and that it has received the Royal Assent, and no court of justice can inquire into the manner in which it was introduced into Parliament, what was done previously to its being introduced, or what passed in Parliament during the various stages of its progress through both Houses of Parliament.

**5.19** Although the comments of Lord Campbell were obiter, they have subsequently been relied upon as the correct statement of the constitutional position. Thus in *British Railways Board v Pickin* (1974), where P claimed that the Board had misled Parliament with a false recital in the preamble to a Private Act which deprived him of an interest in land, Lord Reid observed that:

> The function of the court is to construe and apply the enactments of Parliament. The court has no concern with the manner in which Parliament or its officers carrying out its standing orders perform these functions.

**5.20** It should be noted, however, as Lord Hope did in *Jackson v Attorney General* (2005) (paras **5.35-5.41**), that 'an Act passed under the 1911 Act does not measure up to that test'. In other words, the enrolled Bill rule does not apply to an Act passed using the Parliament Act 1911 procedure (paras **5.31-5.35**) since by definition such a measure has not been passed by both Houses of Parliament.

## The doctrine of implied repeal

**5.21** Since one aspect of the orthodox view of the supremacy of Parliament is that Parliament is unable to bind its successors, it follows that legislation enacted by one Parliament is not immune from amendment or repeal by legislation enacted by a later Parliament. In this sense, supremacy can be said to be a continuing attribute of Parliament. Where there is an inconsistency between Acts of Parliament or an earlier Act is no longer required because a new Act has been passed, provisions in the earlier Act or indeed the whole Act itself may be amended or repealed. The extent of the amendment or repeal will be stated in the later Act and will take legal effect once that Act or the relevant provision has come into force. This amounts to an express repeal of the earlier provision.

**5.22** There may be occasions, however, when an inconsistency between Acts of Parliament has escaped the attention of the legislative draftsman (parliamentary counsel). In such circumstances, the doctrine of implied repeal holds that the later Act will impliedly repeal the earlier Act to the extent to which the two are inconsistent with one another.

*Vauxhall Estates Ltd v Liverpool Corpn* **(1932):** Section 2 of the Acquisition of Land (Assessment of Compensation) Act 1919 provided for the assessment of compensation where land had been compulsorily purchased by a public authority. Section 7(1) of the same Act sought to preserve the provisions of the 1919 Act by declaring that provisions of other Acts had effect subject to the 1919 Act and that if they were inconsistent, they will cease to have or shall have no effect. Section 46 of the Housing Act 1925 also provided for the assessment of compensation, but in different terms. The question for the court, therefore, was whether the 1919 Act was able to protect itself from later repeal or amendment. DC held: the suggestion that the hands of Parliament could be tied so that it could not subsequently enact provisions inconsistent with the 1919 Act was contrary to the principle of the UK constitution. No Act of Parliament could effectively provide that no future Act shall interfere with its provisions.

**5.23**  The issue arose once again in respect of the same statutory provisions in *Ellen Street Estates Ltd v Minister of Health* (1934). In that case, where the CA reached the same conclusion as the DC had in the earlier case, Maugham LJ stated that:

> *The legislature cannot, according to our constitution, bind itself as to the form of subsequent legislation, and it is impossible for Parliament to enact that in a subsequent statute dealing with the same subject-matter there can be no implied repeal. If in a subsequent Act Parliament chooses to make it plain that the earlier statute is being to some extent repealed, effect must be given to that intention just because it is the will of the Legislature.*

**5.24**  If an Act of Parliament was able to prevent its future repeal by a later Act, then clearly there would be a restriction or limit on the supremacy of Parliament: Parliament would be able to legislate as it thought fit provided that it did not enact legislation inconsistent with earlier Acts. In this way, later Parliaments would be bound by the laws made by earlier Parliaments with the result that the scope for legislating would become progressively reduced. Eventually a point might be reached at which there was little need for further enactment because the statute book was full of unrepealable laws. This would be absurd. Accordingly, the doctrine of implied repeal prevents this from happening by holding that in the event of inconsistency between two Acts, that which is the most recent expression of Parliament's will and legislative intent prevails.

## Implied repeal and the European Communities Act 1972

**5.25**  A constitutionally important challenge to the doctrine of implied repeal is to be found in s 2(4) of the European Communities Act 1972. This provides that 'any enactment passed or to be passed . . . shall be construed and have effect subject to the foregoing provisions of this section'. Section 2 of the 1972 Act makes provision for, inter alia, the supremacy of EU law over national law. Accordingly, s 2(4) seems to suggest that a later Act of Parliament must be construed and given effect in such a way as to be consistent with EU law. Does this mean, therefore, that we must confine the doctrine of implied repeal to matters of domestic law only? Issues such as this will be considered later in this chapter when we turn our attention to the impact that the UK's membership of the EU has had upon the legislative supremacy of Parliament (paras **5.46–5.52**).

## Entrenchment

**5.26** To say that a provision has been entrenched signifies that the amendment or repeal of that provision has been made more difficult by the requirement that it must be accomplished in a particular manner or in conformity with a prescribed procedure. Thus, for example, a specified majority of the legislature may be required before a change can be effected, or the electorate may have to approve of the reform via a referendum. Since entrenchment affords a measure of protection for the provision in question, it is often reserved for a state's fundamental laws. Constitutions and Bills of Rights are, as we saw in Chapter **1**, often only capable of being altered in accordance with a prescribed special procedure.

**5.27** Entrenchment therefore represents a restriction on the way in which a legislature can operate. Because one aspect of the traditional view of supremacy is that Parliament cannot bind its successors, it follows that for those who adhere to this view, entrenched provisions would have no binding effect. A later Parliament would be free to disregard the prescribed special procedure and legislate in the normal manner. However, an alternative view exists which recognizes that entrenched provisions would have to be complied with.

## The new view or the manner and form argument

**5.28** The traditional view of the legislative supremacy of Parliament continues to have, as we have seen, a number of adherents. However, a competing view has been put forward by several academics, including Professors Jennings, Heuston, and Marshall. This 'new' view or the 'manner and form' argument as it is sometimes called, holds that whilst there are no limits on the subject matter upon which Parliament may legislate, the manner and form in which Parliament may legislate may be circumscribed. Thus special procedures for making legislation may be established, such as requiring that a Bill on a particular subject is preceded by a referendum or that a specified majority of both Houses of the Legislature must have voted in its favour before it can be said that a Bill has been passed. If such procedures have not been complied with, the new view of supremacy holds that an injunction could be sought to prevent the further passage of the measure or that the monarch would be justified in refusing the Bill Royal Assent. Alternatively, if Royal Assent were given, the resulting 'Act' may be declared void by the courts. In support of this view, several cases are often cited.

***A-G for New South Wales v Trethowan (1932):*** By virtue of s 5 of the Colonial Laws Validity Act 1865, the NSW legislature (the Legislative Assembly and the Legislative Council) was empowered to legislate for the state provided that any such laws were made in the correct manner and form. In 1929, an amendment was made to the Constitution Act 1902. This required that a Bill to abolish the Council could not be presented for Royal Assent unless it had first gained the approval of the majority of the electorate in a referendum. A change of government resulted in a change of policy with regard to the Council. Bills to abolish both it and the referendum requirement were passed by the legislature without a referendum having been held. Members of the Council sought a declaration that the Bills could not therefore be presented for Royal Assent and injunctions to prevent this from happening. PC held: the NSW legislature had the power to alter the Constitution Act 1902 so as to require specific kinds of legislation to be passed in a prescribed manner. A Bill to abolish the Council which received the Royal Assent without having been approved by the electorate in a referendum would not be a valid Act. It would be ultra vires s 5 of the 1865 Act.

***Minister of the Interior v Harris (1952):*** The South Africa Act 1909 created the Union of South Africa and established its Parliament. The UK Parliament, which passed the Act, wished to protect the voting rights of the 'Cape Coloured' voters. Therefore, by virtue of s 35(1) of the 1909 Act, the right to vote was not to be removed by the Union Parliament on the grounds of race or colour save where the Bill had been passed by both Houses of Parliament sitting together and where, at the third reading, it had been agreed by at least two-thirds of the total number of members of both Houses. This provision itself could only be repealed in the same manner (s 152). In 1948, by which time South Africa had become an independent state, the government introduced apartheid. As part of this policy, Cape Coloureds were deprived of their existing voting rights by legislation not passed in accordance with the provisions of ss 35(1) and 152. A number of the disqualified voters challenged the validity of the later Act. Appellate Division of the Supreme Court of SA held: that although the Union had acquired legislative sovereignty as a result of The Statute of Westminster 1931, the entrenched clauses of the 1909 Act remained in force. Accordingly, the courts had the power to declare an Act invalid where it was not passed in conformity with those provisions. The Separate Representation of Voters Act was therefore void.

***Bribery Comr v Ranasinghe (1965):*** The Bribery Commission was responsible for bringing prosecutions before the Bribery Tribunal established under the Bribery Amendment Act 1958. R was convicted and sentenced to a term of imprisonment and a fine by the tribunal. An appeal to the Supreme Court was successful on the basis that the persons comprising the tribunal were appointed in a manner that was inconsistent with the Ceylon Constitution. Under s 29(4) of the Constitution, any amendments to it, such as those made by the 1958 Act, required a two-thirds majority in the House of Representatives and a Speaker's certificate endorsing the Bill. The 1958 Act had not complied with either requirement. PC held: the English cases had taken a narrow view of the court's power to look behind an Act to examine the manner in which it was passed. However, in the UK constitution there was

> no governing instrument which prescribed the law-making powers and how they were to be exercised. Since the Ceylon Constitution did prescribe the procedure for law-making and that procedure had not been followed, the 1958 Act was thereby invalid.

**5.29** Collectively these cases demonstrate the manner and form argument in practice. However, they must be treated with caution. Their initial attraction should not be allowed to obscure the fact that they are Commonwealth cases and, as such, are not decisions that are binding on English courts. A more fundamental objection relates to the constitutional framework within which the cases arose. In each case, the procedure for legislating was prescribed by a higher law. Failure to comply with that procedure therefore amounted to an unconstitutional act, and hence justified the intervention by the courts. In none of the three examples, therefore, were the legislatures supreme in the way that the UK Parliament can be said to be legislatively supreme.

**5.30** In the UK, as the decision in *Bribery Commissioner v Ranasinghe* confirmed, there is no written documentary constitution in which the procedures for legislating are stated. The nearest that we can get to this are the procedures laid down in the Parliament Acts 1911 and 1949.

## The Parliament Acts 1911 and 1949

**5.31** The collective effect of these two pieces of legislation has been the reduction of the legislative powers of the HL. The 1911 Act came about as a consequence of a constitutional struggle between the two Houses of Parliament. The Liberal Government of the day had secured the passage of its social welfare legislation through the HC only for it to be defeated by a Conservative-dominated HL. Matters came to a head with the peers' rejection of the 1909 Finance Bill, in effect the budget. Two general elections followed in 1910, but with the threat of the creation of enough Liberal peers to secure the passage of the Bill through the upper chamber, the Lords ultimately relented and passed the Parliament Act 1911.

**5.32** The preamble to the 1911 Act is significant in that it clearly states that it was the intention of its drafters to substitute for the HL 'a Second Chamber constituted on a popular instead of hereditary basis'. This is worth remembering when we come to consider reform of the HL (see Chapter **6**). However, in the present context, the importance of the Parliament Acts 1911 and 1949 lies in the fact that they have removed the Lords' power of veto, save in respect of a Bill attempting to extend the life of Parliament beyond its five-year limit. Thus the HL has no power to amend or delay the passage of money Bills (Bills relating to taxation, debt, public money, or loans) for any longer than one month. Other public Bills may receive the Royal Assent, notwithstanding that they have been rejected by the HL, where they have been passed by the HC in two successive sessions and there is at least one year (the 1911 Act originally set the limit at two years) between the second reading in the first session and the date on which the Bill passes the HC in the second session.

**5.33**  A Bill passed in accordance with the Parliament Acts 1911 and 1949 procedure can be identified by looking at the 'enacting formula' of the resulting Act. The standard formula makes reference to the measure having been enacted 'by and with the advice and consent of the Lords Spiritual and Temporal, and Commons'. However, where the Lords have not consented to a Bill, as was the case with the War Crimes Act 1991, the enacting formula appears as follows:

> *Be it enacted by the Queen's most Excellent Majesty, by and with the advice and consent of the Commons, in this present Parliament assembled, in accordance with the provisions of the Parliament Acts 1911 and 1949, and by the authority of the same, as follows.*

**5.34**  Ekins has contended that the absence of any reference to the HL in the enacting formula of an Act passed under the Parliament Acts procedure does not mean that it is only the Queen and the HC that enact such legislation. Rather, he argues that the reference to 'in this present Parliament assembled' signifies a larger body than just the HC. In other words, the HL has played a part in the legislative process which enacts laws under the Parliament Acts procedure. Thus he states:

> *Parliament intended the 1911 Act to serve as a decision-making procedure, enabling the Queen, Lords and Commons to legislate even when the Lords disagreed. If the Act bypassed the Lords altogether, it would be a delegation of authority. The Act that we have, however, resolves the political crisis by enabling the institution to act without unanimity. Thus, the Lords do participate in legislative acts pursuant to the Parliament Acts. The authority they share is exercised to enact legislation and the Lords should understand the resulting Act to be in some sense their Act, in the same way that the minority in the House understands the vote of the majority to settle how the House acts.*

**5.35**  Acts passed under the Parliament Acts procedure are rare. In addition to the War Crimes Act 1991, the Government of Ireland Act 1914, the Welsh Church Disestablishment Act 1915, the Parliament Act 1949, the European Parliamentary Elections Act 1999, the Sexual Offences (Amendment) Act 2000, and the Hunting Act 2004 were passed in this manner. A challenge to the validity of this latter Act, the first to have arisen in respect of legislation made using the Parliament Acts procedure, thus provided the courts with an opportunity to determine an issue which had provoked much academic discussion.

*Jackson and others v Attorney General* **(2005):** The Hunting Act 2004 imposed a ban on hunting wild animals with dogs. The measure was opposed in the HL and it was therefore necessary for it to be passed without the consent of that body using the Parliament Acts procedure. J and others were actively involved in hunting. They brought a challenge against the 2004 Act in which they claimed that it was legally invalid on the basis that it was made under the authority of the Parliament Act 1949 which, they contended, was also invalid. The DC held that the 1949 Act was a valid Act and that the 2004 Act was also therefore valid. In its judgment, the Parliament Acts procedure could be used to make any laws, save for those expressly excluded by s 2(1) of the 1911 Act. The claimants appealed. The CA dismissed their appeal. It did so, however, on different grounds to the DC. In its judgment, the power to make laws under the Parliament Acts procedure was subject to implied as well as express limits. Thus, where it was used to effect 'fundamental constitutional changes', the resultant legislation may be subject to challenge. The 1949 Act was however valid since the modifications which it had made to the 1911 Act were 'of a modest nature'. The claimants appealed. HL held: that the distinction made by the CA between modest and fundamental constitutional changes could not be achieved by a process of interpreting the Act. The Bill which became the Parliament Act 1949 had been within the scope of the 1911 Act. The 1949 Act was therefore a valid Act, as was the 2004 Act.

**5.36** The HL decision in *Jackson* is important for a number of reasons. It has made it clear that legislation passed under the authority of the Parliament Acts procedure is not to be regarded, as some had argued, as being delegated legislation because it has been enacted by only two of the three constituent parts of Parliament. Rather, it is primary legislation which has simply been made using a different procedure to that which is normally used to enact such legislation. It has also made it clear that the 1949 Act is a valid Act of Parliament, even though it effected changes to the limits set out in the Parliament Act 1911 which have made it easier for the HC to legislate in the face of opposition from the HL. There is, therefore, now no need for a Bill like that which the former Master of the Rolls, the late Lord Donaldson, introduced on 8 November 2000 which sought to confirm the validity of the 1949 Act and the Acts subsequently passed under its authority.

**5.37** In another respect, however, the decision in *Jackson* may be said to have muddied the waters. Although their Lordships unanimously rejected the distinction which the CA had made between 'modest' and 'fundamental' constitutional change, a number of obiter comments were made during the course of the various opinions which suggest that there are implicit as well as explicit limits on the legislation which can be made using the Parliament Acts procedure. Thus, for example, several Law Lords expressed the view that the prohibition in s 2(1) of the 1911 Act on using the Parliament Acts to enact a Bill to extend the life of Parliament beyond five years would also apply to a Bill which attempted to use that same procedure to delete the relevant words from s 2(1) itself. In the words of Lord Nicholls:

> *The Act setting up the new procedure expressly excludes its use for legislation extending the duration of Parliament. That express exclusion carries with it, by necessary implication, a like exclusion in respect of legislation aimed at achieving the same result by two steps rather than one.*

**5.38** Thus for Lord Nicholls and a majority of the nine Law Lords who heard the appeal in *Jackson*, 'this implied restriction is necessary in order to render the express restriction effectual'. Accordingly on this analysis, a Bill to remove the exclusion in s 2(1) on a Bill extending the life of Parliament from being subject to the Parliament Acts procedure would have to be passed in the normal way, ie with the consent of both the HC and the HL. This view may be contrasted, however, with that of the former Senior Law Lord, the late Lord Bingham, who observed on this point that:

> *Once it is accepted, as I have accepted, that an Act passed pursuant to the procedures in s 2(1), as amended in 1949, is in every sense an Act of Parliament having effect and entitled to recognition as such, I see no basis in the language of s 2(1) or in principle for holding that the parenthesis in that subsection . . . are unamendable save with the consent of the Lords. It cannot have been contemplated that if, however improbably, the House of Lords found themselves in irreconcilable deadlock on this point, the government should have to resort to the creation of peers.*

Which of these two views do you prefer? The traditional view as expressed by Lord Bingham, or the more radical view expressed by Lord Nicholls? Might it be argued that under Lord Nicholls' view, the prohibition in s 2(1) of the 1911 Act on a Bill to extend the life of Parliament is in a sense entrenched (see paras **5.26–5.27**) in that it cannot be repealed using the Parliament Acts procedure? If this is correct, can it be said that a manner and form limitation has been imposed on successor Parliaments by the Parliaments which made the 1911 and 1949 Acts?

**5.39**  A further point to note about the decision in *Jackson* concerns the views expressed on the question whether there are any further implied restrictions on the use of the Parliament Acts procedure. Thus, for example, could the Parliament Acts procedure be used to abolish the HL? The CA held that such a result could only be achieved by legislation made by Parliament as normally constituted. In apparent agreement with this view Lord Steyn observed:

> *I am deeply troubled about assenting to the validity of such an exorbitant assertion of government power in our bi-cameral system. It may be that such an issue would test the relative merits of strict legalism and constitutional principle in the courts at the most fundamental level.*

**5.40**  Other Law Lords who heard the appeal in *Jackson* were a little more guarded on the issue. Thus, for example, in considering whether the 1911 Act could be used to effect 'a fundamental disturbance of the building blocks of the constitution', Lord Carswell was of the view that whether a legal challenge to the Act in question could succeed was 'a topic on which I should prefer to receive much more specifically directed argument and to give much more profound consideration before reaching a conclusion'. Similarly, Lord Brown was 'not prepared to give such a ruling as would sanction in advance the use of the 1911 Act for all purposes, for example to abolish the House of Lords'.

**5.41**  In the light of these observations, therefore, it would seem that whether or not the Parliament Acts procedure could be used to effect major constitutional change remains a moot point even though the HL rejected the CA's distinction between it and modest constitutional change, which the latter felt could be effected using the procedure. Thus in the unlikely event that a government sought to abolish the HL without the consent of that body, it is perfectly clear that the relevant legislation may be subject to a legal challenge. What is less clear, however, in the light of *Jackson*, is what view the courts would take on the validity of that legislation.

## The Union legislation

5.42 A number of Scottish lawyers have sought to argue that the Acts of Union between Scotland and England (which constituted the new state of Great Britain) contained a number of provisions which were intended to be entrenched by those who framed the legislation. Thus, for example, art 1 of the 1706 Act states that the Union between Scotland and England is to last 'for ever after'. Although there are differences of opinion on this point, closer examination of the Union legislation reveals that many of its provisions have been subject to modification, amendment, and repeal by subsequent Acts of the UK Parliament. At face value, this would seem to suggest that any attempt which may have been made to bind the post-1706 Parliament has failed. Nevertheless, the Scots lawyers contend that restraints have been placed upon Parliament by the Acts of Union and that these restraints have been respected when proposals for changes to the 1706 Act have been considered. Moreover, where change has been effected, they contend that it has taken place at the request and with the consent of those affected by it and that it can therefore be accepted on this basis.

5.43 Two Scottish cases are often cited in support of the argument that parts of the Acts of Union are immutable: *MacCormick v Lord Advocate* (1953) and *Gibson v Lord Advocate* (1975). The former was concerned with an objection raised by several Scottish Nationalists to the designation of the new monarch as Queen Elizabeth the Second when as a matter of fact, the first Queen Elizabeth had been queen of England not of Scotland. This, they contended, amounted to a contravention of art I of the Act of Union. The latter case involved the argument that EEC fishing regulations, which had been made part of UK law by virtue of s 2(1) of the European Communities Act 1972, were contrary to art XVIII of the Act of Union. In both cases, the actions failed on the ground of relevancy. The Act of Union did not make provision for royal titles and the control of fishing in territorial waters was a public law rather than a private law matter. Nevertheless, the cases have been seized upon due to the fact that in certain obiter remarks, several Scottish judges appeared to suggest that there may be provisions in the Acts of Union which could not be repealed by the UK Parliament. If this view is correct, then parts of the Union legislation are binding and thus they amount to a limitation on what Parliament can do.

**5.44** Such arguments raise interesting issues, but they have a tendency to leave many questions unanswered. Thus, for example, as Professor Munro has noted, whilst the proponents of the view argue that the repeal of provisions of the Acts of Union can be explained on the basis that they have been consented to, they fail to explain by whom the consent has been given: the electorate, the elected representatives, or the courts? Moreover, it ought to be borne in mind that the judicial remarks in *MacCormick* and *Gibson* were obiter and that in the years that have followed, no Scottish court has declared an Act of Parliament to be invalid on the basis that it is inconsistent with the Act of Union.

**5.45** In a later Scottish case, *Sillars v Smith* (1982), it was argued by four defendants charged with an offence of vandalism contrary to s 78(1) of the Criminal Justice (Scotland) Act 1980 that the Act was invalid on the basis that the power to legislate for Scotland had been transferred to the Scottish Assembly by virtue of the Scotland Act 1978 (see Chapter **8** on devolution). Applying *Edinburgh and Dalkeith Rly Co* and *MacCormick*, the Lord Justice-Clerk rejected the argument that the vires of an Act of Parliament could be challenged in a Scottish court. Nevertheless, in *Jackson v Attorney General* (2005) (paras **5.35–5.41**), Lord Hope remarked, as previously noted, that 'the English principle of the absolute legislative sovereignty of Parliament which Dicey derived from Coke and Blackstone is being qualified'. Having regard to the Scottish cases he further observed: 'So here too it may be said that the concept of a Parliament that is absolutely sovereign is not entirely in accord with the reality.' Although these comments were obiter, they do suggest that the argument regarding the Acts of Union continues to have important adherents and that it therefore ought not to be lightly dismissed.

## Legislative supremacy and the EU

**5.46** The UK's membership of the EU raises important constitutional questions as to how that membership can be reconciled with the legislative supremacy of Parliament. Later we will see how English courts have responded to the task of interpreting national law in the light of EU law (paras **10.50–10.65**). For the time being, however, we will focus our attention on a case involving some Spanish fishermen.

*R v Secretary of State for Transport, ex p Factortame Ltd (No 2) (1991):* F and others were companies incorporated under UK law. Their directors and shareholders were mostly Spanish nationals. Between them, they owned 95 deep-sea fishing vessels which were registered as British under the Merchant Shipping Act 1894. They could therefore be allotted part of the UK's quota under the EC Common Fisheries Policy. Subsequently, the Merchant Shipping Act 1988 and the Merchant Shipping (Registration of Fishing Vessels) Regulations 1988 came into force. These required that fishing vessels be re-registered. F and the other companies were unable to satisfy the new requirement of predominantly

British ownership because their vessels were managed and controlled from Spain. F and the others sought judicial review of the Act and Regulations as being contrary to the EEC Treaty. The DC sought a preliminary ruling from the ECJ on the substantive questions of EC law. In the meantime, it granted the applicants interim relief and disapplied the relevant part of the 1988 Act and the Regulations. The CA set aside that order. The applicants appealed to the HL which held that, as a matter of English law, the courts did not have the jurisdiction to grant relief disapplying the Act. The HL referred to the ECJ the question whether, as a matter of Community law, the relief could be granted. The ECJ held that it could. If all that prevented interim relief being granted was a national law, that law should be set aside. HL held: that the relief would be granted.

**5.47** In giving judgment in *Factortame (No 2)*, Lord Bridge directly addressed the question of the effect of the decision on the supremacy of Parliament. His remarks are worth stating in their entirety:

> *Some public comments on the decision of the Court of Justice, affirming the jurisdiction of the courts of member states to override national legislation if necessary to enable interim relief to be granted in protection of rights under Community law, have suggested that this was a novel and dangerous invasion by a Community institution of the sovereignty of the United Kingdom Parliament. But such comments are based upon a misconception. If the supremacy within the European Community of Community law over the national law of member states was not always inherent in the EC Treaty it was certainly well established in the jurisprudence of the Court of Justice long before the United Kingdom joined the Community. Thus, whatever limitation of its sovereignty Parliament accepted when it enacted the European Communities Act 1972 was entirely voluntary. Under the terms of the 1972 Act it has always been clear that it was the duty of a United Kingdom court, when delivering final judgment, to override any rule of national law found to be in conflict with any directly enforceable rule of Community law. Similarly, when decisions of the Court of Justice have exposed areas of United Kingdom statute law which failed to implement Council directives, Parliament has always loyally accepted the obligation to make appropriate and prompt amendments. Thus there is nothing in any way novel in according supremacy to rules of Community law in those areas to which they apply and to insist that, in the protection of rights under Community law, national courts must not be inhibited by rules of national law from granting interim relief in appropriate cases is no more than a logical recognition of that supremacy.*

**5.48** The decision in *Factortame (No 2)* has provoked much academic discussion. To those who have consistently espoused the traditional view of the supremacy of Parliament, *Factortame (No 2)* has come to be regarded as a denial of the orthodoxy that Parliament cannot bind its successors. Since provisions in the 1988 Act were 'disapplied' under the terms of s 2(4) of the European Communities Act 1972, the 1972 Parliament had, in the words of Sir William Wade, 'succeeded in binding the Parliament of 1988 and restricting its sovereignty, something that was supposed to be constitutionally impossible'.

Accordingly, Sir William suggested that this amounts to a 'revolutionary' development and that if it cannot be so described, then 'constitutional lawyers are Dutchmen'.
More recently, in *Jackson v Attorney General* (2005) (paras **5.35-5.41**), in considering
the qualifications on the 'English principle' of the absolute legislative supremacy of
Parliament, Lord Hope suggested that 'Part I of the European Communities Act 1972
is perhaps the prime example'. In seeking to explain the point, Lord Hope observed:

> Although Parliament was careful not to say in terms that it could not enact legislation
> which was in conflict with Community law, that in practice is the effect of s 2(1) when
> read with s 2(4) of that Act. The direction in s 2(1) that Community law is to be recognised
> and available in law and is to be given legal effect without further enactment, which
> is the method by which the Community Treaties have been implemented, concedes the
> last word in this matter to the courts. The doctrine of the supremacy of Community law
> restricts the absolute authority of Parliament to legislate as it wants in this area.

**5.49**  An alternative, less radical, explanation of the decision is that it is not so much a revolution as the application of a rule of construction laid down in s 2(4) of the 1972 Act. As
we have already seen (para **5.25**), this provides that:

> any enactment passed or to be passed, other than one contained in this Part of this Act,
> shall be construed and have effect subject to the foregoing provisions of this section.

**5.50**  The effect of this provision has been summed up by Sir John Laws in his extra-judicial writings. He contends that it establishes 'a rule of construction for later statutes,
so that any such statute has to be read (whatever its words) as compatible with rights
accorded by European law'. In his view, therefore, *Factortame (No 2)* demonstrates the
rule being applied by a HL that accepted that it must be followed unless or until it had
been expressly repealed.

**5.51**  While this argument recognizes that membership of the EU has to some extent curtailed the legislative supremacy of the UK Parliament, it also acknowledges that this is
so because Parliament has said that it shall be the case in s 2(4) of the 1972 Act. In this
sense, therefore, it could be argued that the principle of the legislative supremacy of
Parliament is being upheld.

**5.52**  Section 18 of the European Union Act 2011 states that:

> Directly applicable or directly effective EU law (that is, the rights, powers, liabilities,
> obligations, restrictions, remedies and procedures referred to in section 2(1) of the
> European Communities Act 1972) falls to be recognised and available in law in the
> United Kingdom only by virtue of that Act or where it is required to be recognised and
> available in law by virtue of any other Act.

This declaratory provision seeks to make clear the exiting legal position, i.e. that EU
law enjoys primacy over national law because the 1972 Act (and other Acts or subordinate legislation) so provide. Its purpose, therefore, is to counter suggestions that the

supremacy of Parliament may be further eroded in future by ways other than the will of Parliament, e.g. by decisions of the courts which, since they recognise that the EU constitutes a superior legal order, seek to give effect to laws and principles in the UK independent of statutory incorporation.

## Legislative supremacy and devolution

5.53 The devolution legislation will be considered more fully in Chapter **8**. For present purposes, it must be noted that devolution raises a number of important questions, not least of which is what effect does it have upon the legislative supremacy of the UK Parliament? In answering this question, it is first necessary to be clear as to what the devolution legislation entitles the assemblies to do. Despite the fact that all the devolved legislatures now have primary law-making powers, the UK Parliament retains the power to legislate for each country: see s 107(5) of the Government of Wales Act 2006, s 28(7) of the Scotland Act 1998, and s 5(6) of the Northern Ireland Act 1998. The legislative supremacy of the UK Parliament is also underlined in the Memorandum of Understanding between the UK Government and the devolved administrations (paras **8.75–8.80**). Moreover, the subordinate nature of the devolved legislatures is further evidenced by the fact that Acts made by them may be held to be invalid by the courts where they exceed the legislative competence of the relevant legislature.

5.54 In the Scottish case of *Whalley v Lord Watson of Invergowrie* (2000), the petitioners (individuals in hunting-related occupations) sought interdict (an injunction) to prevent an MSP from presenting a Bill to the Scottish Parliament seeking to ban hunting with dogs. They did so on the basis that he had received legal, administrative, and other assistance in preparing the Bill from an anti-hunting group in alleged contravention of art 6 of the Scotland Act 1998 (Transitory and Transitional Provisions) (Members' Interests) Order 1999. In hearing the case, the Lord President drew attention to 'the fundamental character of the Parliament as a body which – however important its role – has been created by statute and derives its powers from statute'. His Lordship continued:

> As such, it is a body which, like any other statutory body, must work within the scope of those powers. If it does not do so, then in an appropriate case the court may be asked to intervene and will require to do so, in a manner permitted by the legislation. In principle, therefore, the Parliament like any other body set up by law is subject to the law and to the courts which exist to uphold that law.

## Legislative supremacy and the Human Rights Act

5.55 The Human Rights Act 1998 received Royal Assent on 9 November 1998. Many of its provisions did not enter into force, however, until 2 October 2000. For present purposes, it should be noted that the Act was passed in the same manner according to the same procedures as the other Public General Acts passed during the 1998–9 Parliamentary session. Since it is not entrenched, it follows that its provisions may be amended or repealed in the normal manner. Nevertheless, Professor Feldman argued:

> Although the Act is not entrenched, it will have a special status. As a matter of practical politics, it will progressively achieve a symbolic (even iconic) status which will make amendments to it politically more controversial than amendments to ordinary legislation. This will become an increasingly significant constraint on those who want to restrict the rights as a generation of citizens is educated in its provisions and grows to maturity under its influence.

5.56 The 'special status' of the HRA 1998 has not protected it against calls for its repeal, most notably from the present Home Secretary, Theresa May MP. However, assuming that this does not happen, what effect will the Act's status have upon the possibility of the implied repeal of any of its provisions? In other words, is the HRA 1998 immune from implied repeal or does it fall within the scope of that doctrine?

5.57 In view of the fact that the legislative supremacy of Parliament is concerned with the relationship between Parliament and the courts, it is necessary to have regard to what the courts have said either expressly or by implication on this matter. If we were to recall the decision in *Factortame (No 2)* (paras **5.46–5.51**) it is clear from that case that the conflict between the European Communities Act 1972 and the Merchant Shipping Act 1988 was resolved by the HL in favour of the former. In other words, although the point was not argued, s 2(4) of the European Communities Act 1972 was not impliedly repealed by the later Act. A similar conclusion was reached by the DC in four appeals relating to offences committed under weights and measures legislation: see *Thoburn v Sunderland City Council* (2002). In reaching the conclusion that the 1972 Act could not be impliedly repealed by the Weights and Measures Act 1985, s 1, Laws LJ acknowledged that in recent years the common law had created a class or type of legislative provision which could not be repealed by mere implication. In the light of the recognition by the courts of certain fundamental rights (see, for example, *R v Secretary of State for the Home Department, ex p Pierson* (1998), *R v Secretary of State for the Home Department, ex p Leech* (1994), and *R v Lord Chancellor, ex p Witham* (1998)), Laws LJ contended that the courts should also recognize 'a hierarchy of Acts of Parliament'. That hierarchy involved making a distinction between what he termed 'ordinary statutes' and 'constitutional statutes'. In Laws LJ's opinion, a constitutional statute was a statute which:

> (a) conditions the legal relationship between citizen and state in some general, overarching manner, or (b) enlarges or diminishes the scope of what we would now regard as fundamental constitutional rights.

5.58 Applying these criteria, Laws LJ cited the following as examples of constitutional statutes: Magna Carta; the Bill of Rights 1689; the Acts of Union; the Reform Acts; the

European Communities Act 1972; the Scotland Act 1998; the Government of Wales Act 1998; and, the Human Rights Act 1998.

**5.59** The legal significance of being classified as a constitutional statute is that whereas ordinary statutes may be impliedly repealed, constitutional statutes may not. For the repeal of a constitutional statute (or the abrogation of a fundamental right) to be effected, Laws LJ observed that:

> the court would apply this test: is it shown that the legislature's actual – not imputed, constructive or presumed – intention was to effect the repeal or abrogation? I think that the test could only be met by express words in the later statute, or by words so specific that the inference of an actual determination to effect the result contended for was irresistible. The ordinary rule of implied repeal does not satisfy this test. Accordingly, it has no application to constitutional statutes.

**5.60** This development of the common law was described by Laws LJ as being both 'benign' and 'highly beneficial'. In his opinion:

> It gives us most of the benefits of a written constitution, in which fundamental rights are accorded special respect. But it preserves the sovereignty of the legislature and the flexibility of our uncodified constitution. It accepts the relation between legislative supremacy and fundamental rights is not fixed or brittle: rather the courts (in interpreting statutes, and now, applying the HRA) will pay more or less deference to the legislature, or other public decision-maker, according to the subject in hand.

Thus it would seem that in the light of the decision in *Thoburn*, constitutional statutes such as the European Communities Act 1972 and the Human Rights Act 1998 are not immune from express repeal, but that they are, contrary to the constitutional orthodoxy in respect of ordinary statutes, immune from implied repeal.

**5.61** Sir John Laws has returned to the issue of designating statutes as being either 'constitutional' or 'ordinary' in an extra-judicial capacity. He has argued that since the common law already recognizes certain basic or fundamental constitutional rights as 'part of the legal furniture', eg the right of free expression, with the consequence that such rights cannot be abrogated or overridden by Parliament save by the clear and unambiguous words of a statute, the same principle can be applied to the laws made by Parliament by the 'disapplication of implied repeal in the case of constitutional statutes'. Sir John explains the impact of this new rule of construction on the legislative supremacy of Parliament thus:

> It would not mean the loss of sovereignty. It would merely specify the conditions in which Parliament could change the constitutional law. And the conditions would be just the same as those which presently apply if Parliament seeks to change constitutional principles established by the common law. So we can see that this adjustment of the doctrine of implied repeal really does no more than replicate an approach already taken

*by the courts to common law constitutional principles. And that approach is taken without apparent offence to any aspect of the doctrine of Parliamentary sovereignty.*

**5.62**   As Sir John Laws himself acknowledges, the establishment of such a principle 'requires much more than a judgment of the Divisional Court', ie the decision in *Thoburn* (para **5.57**). At the very least, it requires acceptance by the higher courts, in particular the new Supreme Court. Moreover, even if the doctrine of implied repeal ought to be modified in the way in which he proposes, there are issues which need to be addressed, such as devising a clearer and more comprehensive test for the identification of a constitutional statute, and determining who is to apply the test, Parliament or the courts?

## Judicial interpretation

**5.63**   Section 3(1) of the HRA 1998 provides that:

> *So far as it is possible to do so, primary legislation and subordinate legislation must be read and given effect in a way which is compatible with Convention rights.*

In effect, therefore, this section imposes an interpretative obligation on the courts, and an obligation on all public authorities to give effect to Convention rights: see *R (on the application of GC) v Commissioner of Police of the Metropolis (Liberty and another intervening)* (2011). The obligations are, however, subject to qualification. The courts will only be required to interpret primary and secondary legislation as being compatible with Convention rights 'so far as it is possible to do so'. In other words, if it is not possible to interpret the relevant legislation in a way which is compatible with a Convention right, a judge should not do so and should instead make a declaration of incompatibility (see paras **5.80–5.85**). Thus in *R v DPP, ex p Kebilene* (1999), Lord Steyn observed:

> *It is crystal clear that the carefully and subtly drafted Human Rights Act 1998 preserves the principle of parliamentary sovereignty. In a case of incompatibility, which cannot be avoided by interpretation under section 3(1), the courts may not disapply the legislation. The court may merely issue a declaration of incompatibility which then gives rise to a power to take remedial action: see section 10.*

**5.64**   Subsequent cases decided after s 3 came into force illustrate how the courts have responded to the interpretative obligation contained in that section.

*R v Offen* **(2001):** Section 2 of the Crime (Sentences) Act 1997 (now s 109 of the Powers of Criminal Courts (Sentencing) Act 2000) provided that where a person had previously been convicted of a serious offence and was subsequently convicted of another serious offence after the commencement of s 2, then if that person was over 18 at the time of the commission of the second offence, a court must impose a life sentence unless it was of the view that there were exceptional circumstances relating to either of the offences or to the offender which justified it not doing so. In each of the five appeals before the CA, D had either pleaded guilty to or had been convicted of a second serious offence within the meaning of s 2 of the 1997 Act. In four of the cases, a life sentence had been imposed on the basis that there were no exceptional circumstances justifying a failure to do so. In the fifth case, the A-G challenged the trial judge's decision not to impose a life sentence on the grounds of exceptional circumstances. The appellants contended that either: (i) the interpretation of s 2 of the 1997 Act was affected by s 3 of the HRA 1998; or (ii) s 2 was incompatible with their rights under arts 3, 5, and 7 of the ECHR. CA held: dismissing four of the appeals and imposing a life sentence in respect of the A-G's appeal, that s 2 of the 1997 Act established a norm, ie that those who commit two serious offences are a danger or risk to the public. Construing s 2 in accordance with the duty imposed by s 3 of the HRA 1998, that section did not contravene Convention rights (arts 3 and 5) if the courts applied it so that it did not result in offenders being sentenced to life imprisonment when they did not constitute a significant risk to the public. As regards art 7, the imposition of the automatic life sentence did not contravene the prohibition on imposing a penalty heavier than one that was applicable when an offence had been committed because the life sentence related to the second not the first serious offence.

**5.65** In reaching this conclusion in *Offen*, Lord Woolf CJ described the effect of s 3 of the HRA 1998 on s 2 of the 1997 Act thus:

> *The objective of the legislature . . . will be achieved, because it will be mandatory to impose a life sentence in situations where the offender constitutes a significant risk to the public. Section 2 of the 1997 Act therefore provides a good example of how the HRA 1998 can have a beneficial effect on the administration of justice, without defeating the policy which Parliament was seeking to implement.*

**5.66** It is clear from the foregoing passage that the CA in *Offen* considered that s 3 of the HRA 1998 enabled the court to interpret s 2 of the 1997 Act in a way that was Convention-compatible and which gave effect to the underlying purpose of the section. The fine line which exists between interpretation and legislating had not therefore been transgressed. The importance of this distinction was considered by Lord Woolf in certain obiter remarks made in *Poplar Housing and Regeneration Community Association Ltd v Donoghue* (2001). In that case his Lordship observed:

> *The most difficult task which courts face is distinguishing between legislation and interpretation. Here practical experience of seeking to apply s 3 will provide the best guide. However, if it is necessary in order to obtain compliance to radically alter the effect of legislation this will be an indication that more than interpretation is involved.*

**5.67** These remarks in *Poplar* were preceded by a consideration of the importance of s 3 which Lord Woolf felt was 'difficult to overestimate'. Although these remarks were also obiter, they merit attention due to the insight that they provide on the interpretative obligation imposed on the courts by that section. In the words of Lord Woolf:

> When the court interprets legislation usually its primary task is to identify the intention of Parliament. Now, when s 3 applies, the courts have to adjust their traditional role in relation to interpretation so as to give effect to the direction contained in s 3. It is as though legislation which predates the HRA 1998 and conflicts with the Convention has to be treated as being subsequently amended to incorporate the language of s 3.

Lord Woolf then proceeded to identify the following 'probably self-evident' points in respect of the interpretative obligation:

- unless the legislation would otherwise be in breach of the ECHR, s 3 can be ignored;

- where a court has to rely on s 3, it should limit the extent of the modified meaning to that which is necessary to achieve compatibility;

- s 3 does not entitle the court to legislate;

- the views of the parties and of the Crown with regard to a 'constructive' interpretation cannot modify the task of the court; and

- where it is not possible to use s 3 to achieve a result which is compatible with the Convention, the court has a discretion as to whether or not to grant a declaration of incompatibility.

**5.68** The HL response to the interpretative obligation in s 3 has been evidenced in several cases.

> **R v A (No 2) (2001):** A was charged with rape. His defence was that sexual intercourse had taken place with the complainant's consent, or, alternatively, he believed that she had consented. At a preparatory hearing pursuant to s 29 of the Criminal Procedure and Investigations Act 1996, counsel for A applied for leave to cross-examine the complainant about an alleged previous sexual relationship between her and A in the three weeks prior to the alleged rape. In reliance on s 41 of the Youth Justice and Criminal Evidence Act 1999, the trial judge ruled, inter alia, that an act of consensual sexual intercourse with a friend of A could be put to the complainant in cross-examination, but that the complainant could not be cross-examined about her alleged sexual relationship with A. Since the trial judge considered that such a ruling constituted a prima facie breach of art 6 of the ECHR, he gave A leave to appeal. The CA allowed the appeal on the basis that: the trial judge had been in error to give leave to cross-examine the complainant about sexual intercourse with A's friend; and, because although the questioning and evidence in relation to the alleged prior sexual relationship between A and the defendant was admissible under s 41(3)(a) of the 1999 Act in relation to A's belief that the complainant had consented, it was inadmissible on the issue whether the complainant in fact consented. To direct a jury in such a way might, the CA felt,

lead to an unfair trial. The Crown was granted leave to appeal. HL held: dismissing the appeal, that under s 41(3)(c) of the 1999 Act construed where necessary in the light of s 3 of the HRA 1998, the test of admissibility was whether the evidence and the questioning relating to it was so relevant to the issue of consent as to make its exclusion endanger the fairness of the trial contrary to art 6. If such a test were satisfied, the evidence should not be excluded.

**5.69**  In reaching such a conclusion in *R v A (No 2)* (2001), Lord Steyn sought to provide a general explanation as to the potential effect of s 3 on the words of a statute. In his Lordship's opinion:

> *In accordance with the will of Parliament as reflected in s 3 it will sometimes be necessary to adopt an interpretation which linguistically may appear strained. The techniques to be used will not only involve the reading down of express language in a statute but also the implication of provisions. [emphasis added]*

Applying such an approach to the particular case before the HL, Lord Steyn opined:

> *In my view s 3 of the HRA 1998 requires the court to subordinate the niceties of the language of s 41(3)(c) of the 1999 Act . . . to broader considerations of relevance judged by logical and commonsense criteria of time and circumstances. After all, it is realistic to proceed on the basis that the legislature would not, if alerted to the problem, have wished to deny the right to an accused to put forward a full and complete defence by advancing truly probative material. It is therefore possible under s 3 . . . to read s 41 of the 1999 Act, and in particular s 41(3)(c), as subject to the implied provision that evidence or questioning which is required to ensure a fair trial under art 6 of the convention should not be regarded as inadmissible. The result of such a reading would be that sometimes logically relevant sexual experiences between a complainant and an accused may be admitted under s 41(3)(c). On the other hand, there will be cases where previous sexual experience between a complainant and an accused will be irrelevant, eg an isolated episode distant in time and circumstances . . . On this basis a declaration of incompatibility can be avoided. If this approach is adopted, s 41 will have achieved a major part of its objective but its excessive reach will have been attenuated in accordance with the will of Parliament as reflected in s 3 of the HRA 1998. [emphasis added]*

**5.70**  Thus in recognition of the fact that the then Lord Chancellor, Lord Irvine, had asserted during the progress of the Human Rights Bill through Parliament that 'in 99 per cent of the cases that will arise, there will be no need for judicial declarations of incompat- ibility', the HL in *R v A (No 2)* (2001) demonstrated an extremely creative approach to the interpretation of s 41(3)(c) of the Youth Justice and Criminal Evidence Act 1999. It is questionable, however, whether implying provisions into a section in order to achieve compatibility with a Convention right can appropriately be described as interpretation rather than legislating. Might it not be argued that *R v A (No 2)* (2001) is an example of their Lordships legislating, albeit on the basis that it was with the implicit approval of

Parliament? It should be noted in this context that while Lord Hope approved of the test of admissibility laid down by Lord Steyn, his Lordship did remark (echoing the views of Lord Woolf in *Poplar*) that he:

> would find it very difficult to accept that it was permissible under s 3 of the HRA 1998 to read into s 41(3)(c) of the 1999 Act a provision to the effect that evidence or questioning which was required to ensure a fair trial under art 6 of the convention should not be treated as inadmissible. The rule of construction which s 3 lays down is quite unlike any previous rule of statutory interpretation. There is no need to identify an ambiguity or absurdity. Compatibility with convention rights is the sole guiding principle. That is the paramount object which the rule seeks to achieve. But the rule is only a rule of interpretation. It does not entitle the judges to acts as legislators. *[emphasis added]*

**5.71** The interpretative methodology which was adopted in *R v A* has been criticized in some academic quarters. However, as the subsequent case law has shown, the senior judiciary have endorsed the approach which a unanimous HL applied. Thus in *Ghaidan v Godin-Mendoza* (2004) (para **5.74**), although Lord Millett dissented on the question whether s 3(1) could be applied in that case, he nevertheless commented in relation to *R v A* that he had 'no difficulty with the conclusion which the House reached in that case'. Might it be argued, therefore, as Kavanagh has done, that the criticisms of *R v A* owe more to the subject matter and outcome of the decision than to the HL's approach to the use of s 3(1)? In other words, do they relate to matters such as the controversial issue of sexual history evidence in rape cases where there are concerns about the civil liberties of both the victim and the defendant, or the fact that unlike earlier cases, the HL in *R v A* was dealing with legislation which had been enacted post the HRA 1998?

**5.72** In several cases since *R v A*, the HL has sought to further clarify the limits of the interpretative obligation under s 3 of the HRA 1998. Thus in *Re S (children: care plan)* (2002), Lord Nicholls observed that:

> Section 3 is concerned with interpretation. This is apparent from the opening words of s 3(1) . . . The side heading of the section is 'Interpretation of Legislation'. Section 4 (power to make a declaration of incompatibility) and, indeed, s 3(2)(b) presuppose that not all provisions in primary legislation can be rendered convention compliant by the application of s 3(1) . . . In applying s 3 courts must be ever mindful of this outer limit. The HRA 1998 reserves the amendment of primary legislation to Parliament. By this means the HRA 1998 seeks to preserve Parliamentary sovereignty. The HRA 1998 maintains the constitutional boundary. Interpretation of statutes is a matter for the courts; the enactment of statutes, and the amendment of statutes, are matters for Parliament.

**5.73** In the later case of *R (on the application of Anderson) v Secretary of State for the Home Department* (2002) (see para **5.81**) where the HL was invited to construe s 29 of the Crime (Sentences) Act 1997 in a manner that was compatible with the ECHR by reading it as precluding participation by the Secretary of State in the fixing of a tariff for a convicted murderer, Lord Bingham observed:

> To read s 29 as precluding participation by the Home Secretary, if it were possible to do so, would not be judicial interpretation but judicial vandalism: it would give the section an effect quite different from that which Parliament intended and would go well beyond any interpretative process sanctioned by s 3 of the HRA 1998.

And Lord Steyn opined:

> It would not be interpretation but interpolation inconsistent with the plain legislative intent to entrust the decision to the Home Secretary . . . Section 3(1) is not available where the suggested interpretation is contrary to express statutory words or is by implication necessarily contradicted by the statute.

**5.74**  In a further recent case, the HL demonstrated what may be accomplished by complying with the interpretative obligation contained in s 3(1).

---

*Ghaidan v Godin-Mendoza* **(2004):** The defendant lived with his same-sex partner for many years prior to the partner's death. In 1983 the couple moved into a flat owned by the claimant. D's partner was the statutory tenant under the Rent Act 1977. Following the partner's death, the claimant brought possession proceedings against D in the county court. The judge held that D had succeeded to an assured rather than a statutory tenancy because he had not been his partner's spouse. That type of tenancy was less advantageous to D. D appealed. CA held that he was entitled to succeed to a statutory tenancy. The claimant appealed. HL held: by a majority of four to one, that the word 'spouse' in para 2 of Sch 1 to the 1977 Act which allowed the spouse of a protected tenant to succeed to the tenancy on the tenant's death was to be read so that 'spouse' included the survivor of a same-sex relationship.

---

In delivering his judgment in *Ghaidan*, Lord Nicholls sought to explain the effect of s 3 as follows:

> It is now generally accepted that the application of s 3 does not depend upon the presence of ambiguity in the legislation being interpreted. Even if, construed according to the ordinary principles of interpretation, the meaning of the legislation admits of no doubt, s 3 may none the less require the legislation to be given a different meaning . . . From this it follows that the interpretive obligation decreed by s 3 is of an unusual and far-reaching character. Section 3 may require a court to depart from the unambiguous meaning the legislation would otherwise bear. In the ordinary course the interpretation of legislation involves seeking the intention reasonably to be attributed to Parliament in using the language in question. Section 3 may require the court to depart from this legislative intention, that is, depart from the intention of the Parliament which enacted the legislation.

**5.75**   Although Lord Millett dissented in relation to the application of the relevant principles to the facts of the case, his comments on the effect of s 3 would appear to reflect those of other senior judges. Thus for Lord Millett:

> *even if, construed in accordance with ordinary principles of construction, the meaning of the legislation admits of no doubt, s 3 may require it to be given a different meaning. It means only that the court must take the language of the statute as it finds it and give it a meaning which, however unnatural or unreasonable, is intellectually defensible. It can read in and read down; it can supply missing words, so long as they are consistent with the fundamental features of the legislative scheme; it can do considerable violence to the language and stretch it almost (but not quite) to breaking point.*

**5.76**   In the later case of *Sheldrake v DPP* (2005), Lord Bingham referred to the 'illuminating discussion' which had occurred in *Ghaidan* concerning the import of s 3. In his judgment, although the opinions expressed therein could not be briefly summarized, they did 'leave no room for doubt on four important points':

> *First, the interpretation obligation under s 3 is a very strong and far reaching one, and may require the court to depart from the legislative intention of Parliament. Secondly, a Convention-compliant interpretation under s 3 is the primary remedial measure and a declaration of incompatibility under s 4 an exceptional course. Thirdly, it is to be noted that during the passage of the Bill through Parliament the promoters of the Bill told both Houses that it was envisaged that the need for a declaration of incompatibility would rarely arise. Fourthly, there is a limit beyond which a Convention-compliant interpretation is not possible, such limit being illustrated by* Anderson...*and* Bellinger v Bellinger.

## Ministerial statement

**5.77**   In interpreting legislation passed after the HRA 1998, the courts are further assisted by the terms of s 19. This requires that a minister in charge of a Bill must make a statement prior to its second reading that, in his opinion, its provisions are either compatible with Convention rights or, if they are not, that the Government nevertheless wishes to proceed. Clearly a statement that a Bill is compatible with Convention rights will provide the courts with a further justification to be creative in the way that they carry out their interpretative function. However, s 19 statements of compatibility do not pre-determine that a provision is Convention-compliant. As Lord Hope pointed out in *R v A*, such statements are 'no more than expressions of opinion by the Minister'. Thus they do not necessarily protect legislative provisions from subsequent declarations of incompatibility under s 4 of the HRA 1998: see the decisions of the DC and CA in *R (International Transport Roth GmbH) v Secretary of State for the Home Department* (2001) in respect of the Immigration and Asylum Act 1999.

**5.78**   An interesting question with regard to s 19 is whether or not it is judicially enforceable. In considering this matter, Bamforth has argued that it might be enforceable if it were regarded as a constraint on the manner in which Parliament can legislate. Applying the manner and form argument (paras **5.28–5.29**), a Bill could not become a valid Act of Parliament in the absence of a ministerial statement. However, he suggests two possible ways in which the argument that s 19 is enforceable might be defeated. The first of these is to reject the manner and form argument as being in error, and instead to rely upon the traditional Diceyean notion of legislative supremacy. The problem with this account, however, is that whilst it explains the nature of the relationship between Parliament and the courts, it also recognizes that the relationship may change. If a revolution were to take the form of the judicial recognition of procedural restrictions on Parliament's ability to legislate, s 19 would be enforceable. Therefore, Bamforth prefers an alternative way of demonstrating that s 19 is judicially unenforceable.

**5.79** This regards the s 19 requirement as a proceeding in Parliament which the courts would be prevented from examining due to parliamentary privilege in the form of art 9 of the Bill of Rights 1689. In support of this argument, Bamforth cites *Prebble v Television New Zealand* (1995) (para **6.85**) and *R v Parliamentary Comr for Standards, ex p Al Fayed* (1998) (para **15.106**) as evidence of the English courts' continuing unwillingness to interfere with the proceedings in Parliament. Moreover, he refers to the New Zealand case of *Mangawaro Enterprises v A-G* (1994) where it was held that the equivalent of s 19, s 7 of the New Zealand Bill of Rights Act 1990, was an obligation which fell within the term 'proceedings in Parliament'. In Bamforth's opinion, therefore, if an English court was asked to enforce the s 19 requirement, it is unlikely that it would depart from the 'self-denying ordinance in relation to interfering with the proceedings of Parliament' (per Lord Woolf in *ex p Al Fayed*).

## Declaration of incompatibility

**5.80** Despite ss 3 and 19 of the HRA 1998, if a court reaches the conclusion that either primary or subordinate legislation is incompatible with a Convention right and that a Convention-compliant interpretation is not possible, s 4 of the Act empowers it to issue a declaration to that effect. Such a declaration 'does not affect the validity, continuing operation or enforcement of the provision in respect of which it is given' (s 4(6)(a)). It is, therefore, in the words of Professor Gearty, 'politically potent but legally irrelevant'. The HRA 1998 thus preserves the legislative supremacy of Parliament by choosing not to confer on the courts a power to strike down primary legislation.

**5.81** In *R v A*, Lord Steyn remarked that a 'declaration of incompatibility is a measure of last resort' which 'must be avoided unless it is plainly impossible to do so'. In other words, it is only to be used when inconsistencies between legislative provisions and Convention rights cannot be reconciled by means of interpretation. Since October 2000, declarations of incompatibility have been made by the highest court in a number of contexts.

---

*R (on the application of Anderson) v Secretary of State for the Home Department*
**(2002):** A was serving a mandatory life sentence for murder. Both the trial judge and the
Lord Chief Justice recommended that he serve a minimum of 15 years in prison, but the SoS
set the tariff at 20 years. A could not be considered for release on life licence by the Parole
Board until the tariff had been served. The power to release A was exercisable by the SoS,
on the Board's recommendation, under s 29 of the Crime (Sentences) Act 1997. A applied
for judicial review of the SoS's decision. The DC dismissed his application and the CA confirmed that decision. A appealed to the HL. He contended that the SoS's power to fix the
tariff for a convicted murderer was incompatible with the right under art 6(1) of the ECHR
to have a sentence imposed by an independent and impartial tribunal. The SoS contended
that, rather than imposing a sentence, he was administering a sentence already imposed. HL
held: allowing the appeal, that the role of the SoS in fixing the sentence was objectionable
because he was not independent of the executive. The rule of law depended upon a functional separation between these two branches of government. A declaration of incompatibility would be made in respect of s 29 of the 1997 Act since it was not possible to interpret
that provision as being compatible with A's right under art 6(1) of the ECHR without doing
violence to the language of the statute.

---

*Bellinger v Bellinger* **(2003):** Mrs B was, at birth, classified and registered as male. However, since 1975 she had lived and dressed as a woman. In 1981, she underwent gender reassignment surgery. In May of that year, she went through a ceremony of marriage with Mr B.
Section 11(c) of the Matrimonial Causes Act 1973 provides that a marriage is void unless the
parties are 'respectively male and female'. In the proceedings, Mrs B sought a declaration
that the marriage was valid at its inception and that it was subsisting. The trial judge refused
to make the declaration, as did the CA. Before the HL, Mrs B advanced an alternative claim;
that s 11(c) was incompatible with arts 8 and 12 of the ECHR. HL held: that a person whose
sex had been correctly classified at birth could not later become a person of the opposite
sex for the purposes of s 11(c). It followed that the marriage ceremony had been invalid.
However, in the light of the ECtHR decision in *Goodwin v United Kingdom* (2002), the non-
recognition of gender reassignment for the purposes of marriage was not compatible with
arts 8 and 12 of the ECHR. Accordingly, a declaration of incompatibility would be made in
respect of s 11(c) of the 1973 Act.

---

5.82   A further example of the HL issuing a declaration of incompatibility pursuant to s 4 is
to be found in *A v Secretary of State for the Home Department* (2005) (paras **3.35–3.36**).
In *Ghaidan*, Lord Steyn returned to the issue of declarations of incompatibility. In his
Lordship's opinion, the frequency of such declarations suggested that there had been 'a
misunderstanding of the remedial scheme of the 1998 Act'. That scheme was such that
'interpretation under s 3(1) is the prime remedial remedy and that resort to s 4 must
always be an exceptional course'.

5.83   Declarations of incompatibility have not been the sole preserve of the HL. Thus in *R (on
the application of H) v Mental Health Review Tribunal for North and East London Region*

(2001), the CA declared that s 73 of the Mental Health Act 1983 was incompatible with the applicant's rights under art 5(1) and (4) of the ECHR. Moreover, in *International Transport Roth GmbH v Home Office* (2001) QBD (2002) CA, both courts were in agreement that a civil penalty regime under the Immigration and Asylum Act 1999 which made carriers liable for clandestine entrants arriving in the UK, was incompatible with art 6 and art 1 of Protocol No 1 to the ECHR. As of 8 August 2011, 27 declarations of incompatibility have been made. Of these, eight have been overturned on appeal and 19 have become final in whole or in part: see *Responding to human rights judgments* (2011) Cm 8162.

5.84 The jurisprudence on s 4 of the HRA 1998 reveals a number of important points, not least of which is the willingness of the courts to grant a declaration of incompatibility even where the government has sought to argue that such a course of action would serve no useful purpose. Thus in *Bellinger v Bellinger* (2003), Lord Nicholls stressed that the decision whether or not to make a s 4 declaration involved an exercise of discretion on the part of a court having regard to all the circumstances of the case. While he acknowledged that the Government had not questioned the decision in *Goodwin v United Kingdom* (2002), and that it was committed to giving effect to that decision, he was nevertheless of the view that: 'when proceedings are already before the House, it is desirable that in a case of such sensitivity this House, as the court of final appeal in this country, should formally record that the present state of statute law is incompatible with the convention'. In *R (on the application of M) v Secretary of State for Health* (2003), Maurice Kay J rejected various submissions advanced on behalf of the Government as to why he ought not to make a s 4 declaration. These included: that the Government had already publicly acknowledged that the relevant legislation was incompatible with art 8 of the ECHR; that the Strasbourg court had been content for the matter to be resolved by way of a friendly settlement; and that a proposed Mental Health Bill would resolve the problem.

5.85 A further point to note from the jurisprudence on s 4 is that judicial views as to the appropriateness of making a declaration of incompatibility have not always converged.

*R (on the application of Alconbury Developments Ltd) v Secretary of State for the Environment, Transport and Regions* (2001): It was contended in conjoined applications that powers of the Secretary of State relating to planning matters, compulsory purchase, railways, and highways were incompatible with art 6(1) of the ECHR. The essence of the applicant's argument was that when a decision was taken by the SoS himself rather than by an inspector appointed by him, the role of the SoS in determining government policy meant that he had an interest in the decision which prevented him from being an independent and impartial tribunal. The DC accepted the force of these submissions as well as those which contended that the availability of judicial review in respect of an impugned decision was not sufficient to render the procedure compatible with art 6(1) of the ECHR. Accordingly, the DC granted a declaration of incompatibility. The SoS appealed. HL held: allowing the appeal, that there was no incompatibility between the various powers of the

SoS and art 6(1). In the opinion of their Lordships, although the SoS did not himself amount to an independent and impartial tribunal for the purposes of art 6(1), the judicial review jurisdiction of the HCt was such as to provide a sufficient review of the legality of the decisions and the procedures followed. Their Lordships found support for such a finding in the jurisprudence of the Strasbourg institutions which had held on more than one occasion that the requirements of art 6 were satisfied by the availability of judicial review in respect of an impugned decision: see, for example, *Bryan v United Kingdom* (1995) and *Chapman v United Kingdom* (2001).

In *Wilson v First County Trust Ltd* (2003), the HL reversed a decision of the CA that s 127(3) of the Consumer Credit Act 1974 was incompatible with art 6(1) and art 1 of Protocol No 1 to the ECHR. Moreover, in *R (on the application of H) v Secretary of State for Health* (2005), the HL reversed an earlier CA ruling when it held that it was possible for s 29(4) of the Mental Health Act 1983 (which provides for the indefinite detention of a patient) to be operated so as to be compatible with a patient's rights under art 5 of the ECHR via the mechanism of referring the case to a mental health review tribunal or challenging the lawfulness of the detention in judicial review proceedings.

## Does the Human Rights Act have retrospective effect?

5.86 It is a principle of English law that statutory provisions are presumed not to have retrospective effect, unless the relevant Act provides otherwise: see, for example, the remarks of Staughton LJ in *Secretary of State for Social Security v Tunnicliffe* (1991). Following the enactment of the HRA, whether or not it applied retrospectively was therefore an issue of some practical importance. The Act itself was not as clear as it might have been. Thus by virtue of s 7(1)(b), a person who claims that a public authority has acted (or proposes to act) in a way which is incompatible with a Convention right may rely on the Convention right(s) concerned in any legal proceedings, provided that that person either is or would be the victim of the unlawful act. However, s 22(4) of the Act provides:

> Paragraph (b) of subsection (1) of section 7 applies to proceedings brought by or at the instigation of a public authority whenever the act in question took place; but otherwise that subsection does not apply to an act taking place before the coming into force of that section.

5.87 In *R v Lambert* (2001), the issue for the HL to consider was whether an appellant could rely on the HRA at the time of his appeal, when the Act was in force, despite the fact that at the time of his conviction for an offence contrary to s 5 of the Misuse of Drugs Act 1971, where it was alleged that the trial judge's direction to the jury had violated the presumption of innocence in art 6(2) of the ECHR, the HRA had not been in force. Their Lordships concluded by a majority (four to one) that the appellant was not able to rely on the alleged breach of his Convention rights at his trial. However, in the later case of *R v Kansal (No 2)* (2002), the HL held by a majority (three to two) that *Lambert* had been erroneously decided with regard to the meaning of s 22(4). Nevertheless, due to the fact that the earlier case was very recent, and because it had been a clear-cut decision, their Lordships declined to overrule it.

5.88   More recently, in *Aston Cantlow and Wilmcote with Billesley Parochial Church Council v Wallbank* (2003) (para **16.84**), Lord Hope remarked that 'the question whether, and if so in what circumstances, effect should be given to the HRA 1998 where relevant events occurred before it came into force is far from easy'. Lord Nicholls seemed to have provided some clarification in *Wilson v First County Trust Ltd* (2003), when he observed that 'in general the principle of interpretation set out in s 3(1) does not apply to causes of action accruing before the section came into force'. Later, in *Re McKerr* (2004), he commented:

> It is now settled, as a general proposition, that the HRA 1998 is not retrospective. The Act itself treats s 22(4) as an exception.

5.89   The decision in *Re McKerr* was not applied, however, in *Re McCaughey's Application for Judicial Review* (2011). In this case, the SC accepted that although the HRA did not apply retrospectively in relation to a state's procedural obligation to investigate a death which occurred before the Act came into force, where the decision had already been taken to hold an inquest, the judgment of the ECtHR in *Silih v Slovenia* (2009) confirmed that a freestanding obligation arose to ensure that the requirements of art 2 of the ECHR were complied with.

# FURTHER READING

Allan, T R S 'Parliamentary Sovereignty: Law, Politics, and Revolution' (1997) 113 LQR 443.

Bamforth, N 'Parliamentary Sovereignty and the Human Rights Act 1998' [1998] PL 572.

Bogdanor, V 'Our New Constitution' (2004) 120 LQR 242.

Bradley, A 'The Sovereignty of Parliament–Form or Substance?' in Jowell and Oliver (eds) *The Changing Constitution* (7th edn, 2011) OUP.

Lord Cooke 'A Constitutional Retreat' (2006) 122 LQR 224.

Dicey, A V *Introduction to the Study of the Law of the Constitution* (10th edn, 1959) Macmillan.

Ekins, R 'Acts of Parliament and the Parliament Acts' (2007) 123 LQR 91.

Elliott, M 'Bicameralism, Sovereignty and the Unwritten Constitution' (2007) 5 Int'l J Const L 370.

Emmerson, B and Friedman, D 'Retrospectivity under the Human Rights Act' (2002) Matrix Public Law Seminar (www.matrixlaw.co.uk).

Ford, J D 'The Legal Provisions in the Acts of Union' [2007] CLJ 106.

Gearty, C A 'Reconciling Parliamentary Democracy and Human Rights' (2002) 118 LQR 248.

Goldsworthy, J *The Sovereignty of Parliament: History and Philosophy* (1999) Clarendon Press.

Goldsworthy, J *Parliamentary Sovereignty: Contemporary Debates* (2010) Cambridge University Press.

Gordon, M 'The Conceptual Foundations of Parliamentary Sovereignty: Reconsidering Jennings and Wade' [2009] PL 519.

Heuston, R V F *Essays in Constitutional Law* (2nd edn, 1964) OUP.

Kavanagh, A 'Unlocking the Human Rights Act: The "Radical" Approach to Section 3(1) Revisited' [2005] EHRLR 259.

Larkin, S 'Debunking the Idea of Parliamentary Sovereignty: The controlling factor of legality in the British constitution' (2008) 28 OJLS 709.

Laws, Sir John 'Law and Democracy' [1995] PL 57.

Laws, Sir John 'Constitutional Guarantees' [2008] Stat LR 1.

Lord Lester 'The Art of the Possible: Interpreting Statutes under the Human Rights Act' [1998] EHRLR 665.

McLean, I and McMillan, A 'Professor Dicey's Contradictions' [2007] PL 435.

Mead, D 'Rights, Relationships and Retrospectivity: The impact of Convention rights on pre-existing private relationships following *Wilson* and *Ghaidan*' [2005] PL 459.

Munro, C *Studies in Constitutional Law* (2nd edn, 1999) Butterworths.

Nicol, D 'Gender Reassignment and Transformation of the Human Rights Act' (2004) 120 LQR 194.

Pollard, D, Parpworth, N, and Hughes, D *Constitutional and Administrative Law: Text with Materials* (4th edn, 2007) OUP.

Lord Rodger 'A Time for Everything under the Law: Some Reflections on Retrospectivity' (2005) 121 LQR 57.

Sir Philip Sales 'A Comparison of the Principle of Legality and Section 3 of the Human Rights Act 1998' (2009) 125 LQR 598.

Sir Philip Sales, and Ekins, R 'Rights-consistent Interpretation and the Human Rights Act 1998' (2011) 127 LQR 217.

Sir Stephen Sedley 'The Rocks or the Open Sea: Where is the Human Rights Act Heading?' (2005) 32 J of Law & Soc 3.

Lord Steyn 'The Weakest and Least Dangerous Department of Government' [1997] PL 84.

Lord Steyn '2000–2005: Laying the Foundations of Human Rights Law in the United Kingdom' [2005] EHRLR 349.

Wade, H W R 'The Legal Basis of Sovereignty' [1955] CLJ 172.

Wade, H W R 'Sovereignty–Revolution or Evolution?' (1996) 112 LQR 568.

Wicks, E 'A New Constitution for a New State? The 1707 Union of England and Scotland' (2001) 117 LQR 109.

Wicks, E *The Evolution of a Constitution* (2006) Hart.

Lord Woolf 'Droit Public–English Style' [1995] PL 57.

Young, A *Parliamentary Sovereignty and the Human Rights Act* (2008) Hart.

# SELF-TEST QUESTIONS

1   In *British Railways Board v Pickin* (1974), Lord Reid commented that: 'The idea that a court is entitled to disregard a provision in an Act of Parliament on any ground must seem strange and startling to anyone with any knowledge of the history and law of our constitution'. To what extent, if any, do these remarks still reflect the attitude of the courts towards laws made by Parliament?

2   Does it follow that if Parliament can make it easier to legislate, ie legislation made in accordance with the Parliament Acts 1911 and 1949, it can also make it harder to legislate as de Smith and Brazier have contended?

3   In a comment on the *Jackson* case Elliott has argued that it 'graphically illustrates the fluidity of the British Constitution and the contested nature of its fundamental aspects'. With reference to the opinions delivered in the HL, what do you think he meant by this?

4   To what extent, if any, do you agree with the view expressed by Professor Bogdanor that the referendum in the UK has become 'an instrument of entrenchment since it prevents the powers of Parliament from being transferred without the approval of the people'?

5   Are you convinced by the manner and form argument? Why?

6   Does the Act of Union 1706 impose limitations on what future Parliaments can do?

7   How far has the UK's membership of the EU altered the traditional understanding of the legislative supremacy of Parliament?

8   Having regard to the characteristics of a 'constitutional statute' identified by Laws LJ in *Thoburn v Sunderland City Council,* can you think of an instance of (a) that is not also an instance of (b)?

9   To what extent, if any, does the Human Rights Act 1998 impose practical limitations on the legislative supremacy of Parliament?

10   Although the jurisprudence in relation to s 3 of the Human Rights Act 1998 suggests that the judiciary are mindful that they must interpret rather than legislate under the provision, to what extent, if any, might it be argued that the 'real area of difficulty lies in identifying the limits of interpretation in a particular case' (per Lord Nicholls in *Re S (children: care plan)*)?

11 What do you think Lord Steyn meant when he observed extra-judicially in relation to the decisions in *Anderson* and *Bellinger* that: 'Both may be regarded as examples falling in the forbidden territory'?

12 Writing extra-judicially about the Human Rights Act 1998, Sir Stephen Sedley has commented: 'But if a conservative use of the s 4 power is harnessed to an equally conservative use of the s 3 power, Parliament's great scheme of permeating the statute book with human rights values may start to falter.' Does the case law evidence a 'conservative use' of either s 3 or s 4?

# PART II

## The Institutional Framework of the Constitution

# 6 Parliament

## SUMMARY

This chapter is concerned with the two chambers which, with the Queen, collectively form Parliament. The composition of both Houses is considered in this chapter. The electoral franchise is discussed and attention is focused upon two important issues: electoral reform and the reform of the House of Lords. The chapter concludes by considering what is meant by 'parliamentary privilege'.

## House of Commons

### The election of the House of Commons

**6.1** 'Electoral law' is an extensive and at times complex area of the law. It is not possible within the confines of this book to deal with all of its aspects and intricacies. For present purposes, therefore, we will consider two issues which are constitutionally important: the franchise; and, the electoral system.

### The franchise

**6.2** The UK is a democracy by which it is meant that the government is elected by the people. In the past, however, a variety of different qualifications relating to the ownership of land and property meant that the franchise was limited to a very small proportion of the population. Successive Reform Acts passed during the 19th century broadened the franchise, but universal adult suffrage was only established in 1928 when women over the age of 21 were given the vote. Today, whether or not a person is entitled to vote in a parliamentary election is governed by the terms of s 1 of the Representation of the People Act 1983 (as substituted by s 1 of the Representation of the People Act 2000). This provides that for a person to be able to vote in a constituency, they must:

- be registered in the register of parliamentary electors for that constituency;
- not be subject to any legal incapacity to vote (age apart);

- be either a Commonwealth citizen or a citizen of the Republic of Ireland; and

- be of voting age (18 years or over).

**6.3** The franchise for parliamentary elections is wide and is based on residence: see s 4 of the RPA 1983 (as substituted by the RPA Act 2000). Whether or not a person is resident is a question of fact to be determined according to the circumstances. Thus in *Hipperson v Newbury District Electoral Registration Officer* (1985), the CA held that women who had camped on highway land and common land at Greenham Common Air Base for in excess of two years, and who had received their mail there, were resident for the purposes of the RPA 1983. The situation would have been different, however, had it been shown, which it was not, that their residence was illegal. In *Fox v Stirk and Bristol Electoral Registration Officer* (1970), where students appealed against refusals to place them on electoral registers for the towns where they attended university, the CA accepted that there was a sufficient degree of permanence in their stay in the towns for them to be said to be resident. The fact that they were there for at least half of a year converted simple occupation into residence.

**6.4** Those who hold the franchise are entitled to exercise one vote in a parliamentary election (s 1(2)(a) of the RPA 1983). Voting in more than one constituency at a general election is prohibited. Thus although a student may be entered on electoral registers both at home and at a university town, they may only vote in one of the two constituencies.

**6.5** A person is disqualified from voting in a parliamentary election, even though they are on the electoral register, if they:

- are in prison serving a sentence, or they have escaped from prison;

- have been convicted of an election offence; or

- lack the mental capacity to vote.

**6.6** The disqualification relating to prisoners has been the subject of legal challenge both in the national courts and before the ECtHR. In *R (on the application of Pearson) v Secretary of State for the Home Department* (2001), the three claimants were all convicted prisoners serving periods of imprisonment. They had applied for their names to be put on the electoral register but their applications had been refused. Accordingly, they each sought a declaration that their disenfranchisement by virtue of s 3(1) of the RPA 1983 was incompatible with art 14 and art 3 of Protocol No 1 to the ECHR. Their applications were dismissed. In so doing, the HCt noted that a working group on electoral procedures had been established to consider changes to electoral law and practice following the enactment of the RPA 1983, and that its recommendation that remand prisoners and mental patients (other than those who had been convicted and placed in custody) should be entitled to vote had been given effect in the Representation of the People Act 2000. In the court's opinion, the disenfranchisement of prisoners reflected the prevailing view that a loss of rights was part of a convicted prisoner's punishment and that the removal from society entailed a loss of society's privileges, including the right to vote. It was also noted that the practice in Europe on this issue was varied with eight countries, including the UK, not allowing prisoners to vote, 20 not disenfranchising prisoners, and eight imposing a more restricted disenfranchisement. One of the applicants accordingly applied to the ECtHR.

---

*Hirst v United Kingdom (No 2) (2005):* The applicant submitted that rather than being a privilege, the right to vote was one of the fundamental rights which underpinned a truly democratic society. It was further argued that the disqualification from voting did not pursue any legitimate aim, and that it was disproportionate, arbitrary and impaired the essence of the right. On behalf of the Government it was submitted that under art 3 of Protocol No 1 to the ECHR, the right to vote was not absolute and that a wide margin of appreciation was to be allowed to contracting states in determining the conditions under which the right was exercised. The policy of disqualification had been adhered to over many years with the explicit approval of Parliament (the RPA 2000 had been accompanied by a statement of compatibility under s 19 of the HRA 1998). It was further argued that the disqualification pursued the legitimate aim of preventing crime and punishing offenders and enhancing civic responsibility and respect for the rule of law, and that it was proportionate since it only affected those who were serving a custodial sentence for the duration of that sentence. Chamber held: that its own case law established that art 3 of Protocol No 1 to the ECHR guarantees individual rights, including the right to vote and stand for election and that, although contracting states had a wide margin of appreciation in this matter, it was for the ECtHR to determine in the last resort whether the requirements of the Convention had been complied with. The ECHR organs had emphasized in a number of different contexts that the fact that a convicted person had been deprived of his liberty did not mean that he had lost the protection of the other Convention rights, eg the right to correspond, have access to a lawyer or court, and have access to his family and practise his religion. Although it was unnecessary to decide whether disqualification met legitimate aims, it was the case that the blanket ban on voting was indiscriminate and disproportionate. Accordingly, it breached art 3 of Protocol No 1 to the ECHR. The UK Government appealed: Grand Chamber held: by a majority of 12 votes to 5, that there had been a violation of art 3 of Protocol No 1, and unanimously that no separate issue arose under either arts 10 or 14 of the ECHR. In agreeing with the Chamber's judgment, the Grand Chamber accepted that the franchise was an area in which a wide margin of appreciation should be granted to a national legislature. However, it was also of the view that the 'rights guaranteed under art 3 of Protocol No 1 are crucial to establishing and maintaining the foundations of an effective and meaningful democracy governed by the rule of law'. Section 3(1) of the 1983 Act was therefore a 'blunt instrument' in that it amounted to an automatic and indiscriminate restriction on a vitally important Convention right.

---

**6.7**   The UK Government is under an obligation by virtue of art 46 of the ECHR to implement or 'execute' the judgments of the ECtHR. In the case of prisoner voting, however, it has procrastinated. Thus the previous Labour Government consulted on the issue on two occasions: see 'Voting Rights of Convicted Prisoners Detained within the United

Kingdom', CP 29/06 (14 December 2006); and CP 6/09 (8 April 2009). In the latter consultation, it was suggested that a prisoner's right to vote ought to depend upon the length of sentence imposed.

**6.8** After *Hirst*, there have been further domestic and ECtHR cases on the same issue. Thus in *R (on the application of Chester) v Secretary of State for Justice and Wakefield Metropolitan District Council* (2010), the Court of Appeal affirmed an earlier decision rejecting a claim for judicial review of a prisoner's statutory disenfranchisement. It did so on the basis that what the claimant sought was in effect an advisory opinion from the court as to the content of legislation necessary to comply with the ruling in *Hirst*. Given the controversial nature of the subject, that was a matter for Parliament rather than the courts. In *Hirst* itself, the ECtHR had noted that there was no evidence that Parliament had ever really 'sought to weigh the competing interests or to assess the proportionality of a blanket ban'. It is noteworthy, therefore, that on 11 February 2011, the HC held a debate on this very issue. In a free vote, back benchers passed a motion by 234: 22 to the effect that legislative decisions were a matter for Parliament, not the ECtHR, and that there was support for the current position regarding the disenfranchisement of prisoners.

**6.9** The ECtHR returned to the issue of the UK's blanket ban on prisoner voting in *Greens v UK* (2011), where it held (in a pilot judgment), that once again, the UK was in breach of art 3 of Protocol No 1 to the ECHR. Importantly, the judgment of the court directed the UK Government to introduce amending legislation within a six-month period (by 11 October 2011). Following *Greens*, the issue was the subject of further domestic litigation in *Tovey v Ministry of Justice* (2011), where a claim for damages for being prohibited from voting in the May 2010 general election or the European Parliament election, and a declaration that rights under art 3 of Protocol No 1 had been breached, was struck out. Although the UK Government had patently failed to amend the 1983 Act in the light of *Hirst*, it was held that such failure did not give rise to a cause of action in domestic law since s 6(6) of the Human Rights Act 1998 expressly excludes legislative inactivity from the ambit of unlawful acts. Moreover, Langstaff J was of the view that it was not possible under s 3 of the 1998 Act to read s 3 of the 1983 Act in such a way as to comply with the ruling in *Hirst*, since to do so would accord the relevant statutory words the exact opposite of their actual meaning.

**6.10** Patently, the uncertainty surrounding the issue of prisoners' voting rights is unsatisfactory. That uncertainty has been added to by a further decision of the ECtHR in *Frodl v Austria* (2011). Here, the court appeared to narrow the scope of a state's margin of appreciation in relation to the franchise as referred to in *Hirst* by suggesting that a decision on disenfranchisement should be taken by a judge, and that the sanction should only be imposed in respect of offenders serving a lengthy term of imprisonment where there was a direct link between their offence and disenfranchisement. In other words, it would be a sanction confined to those who commit electoral offences.

**6.11** Clarification may come in *Scoppola v Italy*, which was due to be heard by the Grand Chamber of the ECtHR in early November 2011. The UK Government has succeeded in getting the time limit specified in *Greens* extended. It will thus have six months from the date of the decision in *Scoppola* to comply with its obligations under art 46 of the ECHR. It has also sought leave of the ECtHR to intervene in that case because the issues which arise are analogous to those in *Hirst* and *Greens*: see *Responding to human rights judgments* (2011) Cm 8162.

## The electoral system

**6.12** The system which operates for elections to the Westminster Parliament (see Chapter **8** in respect of the devolved Assemblies) is often referred to as 'first past the post'. In other words, the successful candidate will be the person who records the most votes at the polls. It is often the case, therefore, that a candidate who is elected the MP for a particular constituency has in fact recorded less than half the votes cast by the electorate. Sometimes a candidate may record much more than half of the votes cast. Anomalies may also exist at the national level. The party which wins the election and forms the government need not necessarily have recorded the most votes at the polls. For example, the Labour Government which was elected in February 1974 secured fewer votes than the outgoing Conservative Government (11.64m to 11.91m). Moreover, in the 1983 general election, although there was little difference between the percentage share of the votes cast nationally for both the Labour and Liberal/Social Democrat Party Alliance (27.6% and 25.4% respectively), there was a huge difference in terms of the number of seats that those votes secured (209 compared to 23).

**6.13** These disparities have given rise to concerns that our present electoral arrangements do not properly reflect the views and opinions of the electorate, especially those held by minorities. Accordingly, the issue of voting reform has been considered from time to time. In order to give the debate on electoral reform a clearer focus, and for the purpose of recommending an alternative system to be put before the people in a referendum, the Labour Government set up an Independent Commission on the Voting System under the chairmanship of the late Lord Jenkins of Hillhead in December 1997. It considered a number of alternative voting systems, including: second ballot; supplementary vote; the additional member system; single transferable vote; and the party list system.

**6.14** It might be argued that there are almost as many voting systems as there are democratic countries. Each has its own particular characteristics and its own subtle nuances. One such system is the alternative vote (AV) system which is used to elect the House of Representatives in Australia. The advantage of this system over the first past the post system is that in order to be elected, a successful candidate must secure at least 50% of the votes cast. The system operates in single member constituencies. Voters are required to rank the candidates in order of preference. If none of the candidates has an absolute majority at the first count, the candidate with the fewest votes is eliminated. The second preference votes for this candidate are then redistributed amongst the remaining candidates. This process is continued until one of the candidates does have an absolute majority.

**6.15** The AV system was made the subject of only the second UK-wide referendum held on 5 May 2011. Section 1(7) of the Parliamentary Voting System and Constituencies Act 2011 stated:

> At present, the UK uses the 'first past the post' system to elect MPs to the House of Commons. Should the 'alternative vote' system be used instead?

The holding of the referendum saw the fulfilment of a further commitment set out in the coalition Government's *The Coalition: Our programme for government* (May 2010). The result was an overwhelming rejection of AV. Thus of the 42.2% of the electorate who voted, very nearly 68% answered the referendum question in the negative. In other words, less than one third of voters were in favour of a change to AV. In the light of this result, it seems unlikely that electoral reform will occupy a high position on the political agenda in the foreseeable future.

## Composition of the House of Commons

**6.16** Currently, there are 650 seats in the HC. As of 1 July 2011, these were divided amongst the parties as follows: Conservative (305); Labour (256); Liberal Democrats (57); Democratic Unionist Party (8); Scottish National Party (6); Sinn Fein (5); Independent (1); Plaid Cymru (3); Social Democratic & Labour Party (3); Alliance (1); Green (1); the Speaker and Deputies (4). These figures reveal, therefore, that there are three main political parties in the HC: Conservative, Labour, and the Liberal Democrats. Moreover, they show that the present coalition Government has a majority of 74 which is in truth a working majority of 83 given that the five Sinn Fein MPs have not taken their seats and are therefore not entitled to vote, and discounting the Speaker and the three Deputies.

**6.17** In the coalition Government's *The Coalition: Our programme for government* (May 2010), a commitment was made to introduce legislation to create 'fewer and more equal sized constituencies'. Section 11 of the Parliamentary Voting System and Constituencies Act 2011 achieves this by substituting a new Sch 2 in the Parliamentary Constituencies Act 1986. As a result, a future House of Commons will have 600 MPs. The number chosen by the coalition Government was criticized in Parliament as being arbitrary. It was further criticized on the basis that it would reduce the ability of the Commons to hold the executive to account since there is no proportionate reduction in the number of MPs on the government payroll. Although the reduction in size is likely to save £12 million per annum it has necessitated the redrawing of the parliamentary constituencies by the Boundary Commission. This controversial and time-consuming process will need to be completed in time for the May 2015 general election.

## Disqualification from membership

**6.18** Holders of certain offices and places are disqualified from membership of the HC by virtue of the House of Commons Disqualification Act 1975. These include:

- judges (eg Court of Appeal, High Court, circuit judges, county court judges, and stipendiary magistrates);
- civil servants;
- members of the armed forces;
- members of police forces;
- members of the National Criminal Intelligence Service or the National Crime Squad; and
- members of foreign legislatures.

**6.19** In addition to the offices referred to, the holders of certain other offices described in Parts II and III of Sch I to the 1975 Act are also disqualified from membership of the HC. Thus, for example, membership of the Commission for Equality and Human Rights disqualifies an individual as does membership of the Administrative Justice and Tribunals Council, the Environment Agency, the Law Commission, and the Parole Board, to name but a few. Similar disqualification provisions apply in respect of the Scottish Parliament and the Welsh Assembly.

**6.20** It was formerly the case that the clergy were also disqualified from sitting in the HC. However, as a result of the House of Commons (Removal of Clergy Disqualification) Act 2001, that disqualification no longer applies. A person who has been ordained or who is a minister of any religious denomination may therefore sit in the HC. The disqualification still applies, however, to a Lord Spiritual (para **6.59**): s 1(2) of the 2001 Act.

## Membership by peers

**6.21** It was long accepted that a peer was disqualified from sitting in the HC. Thus an MP who had been made a life peer ceased to be eligible to sit in the HC as did an MP who had succeeded to an hereditary peerage. In the case of Tony Benn, the death of his father in 1960 meant that he became Viscount Stansgate, and he therefore ceased to be a member of the HC. However, he subsequently stood in the by-election brought about by his own succession and was returned for the Bristol South East constituency, as he had been at the 1959 general election. His defeated opponent in the by-election instituted legal proceedings and in *Re Bristol South East Parliamentary Election* (1961), the QBD held that Benn's status as a peer disqualified him from being elected. Accordingly, the votes cast for him had been wasted and his opponent was therefore duly elected as MP for the constituency.

**6.22** There have been two postscripts. The first of these was the passing of the Peerage Act 1963. This provides that any person who succeeds to a peerage may disclaim the peerage for life. This is achieved by an instrument of disclaimer delivered to the Lord Chancellor within 12 months of the date of succession, or within 12 months of attaining the age of 21. Where an MP succeeds to a peerage, the period of disclaimer is one month. During that month he is not disqualified from membership of the HC, although he will not be entitled to sit or vote in the House. The disclaimer of a peerage is irrevocable, but it does not affect the succession to the title.

**6.23** The former PM Sir Alec Douglas Home took advantage of the Peerage Act to disclaim his hereditary peerage in order that he could become PM (see further para **11.11**). Where a peerage has been disclaimed, no other hereditary peerage can be conferred on the disclaimer. Thus when Sir Alec ceased to be PM, he was able to return to the HL by being made a life peer.

**6.24** The second postscript concerns the disqualification of hereditary peers from sitting in the HC. This has now been ended as a consequence of the House of Lords Act 1999. Thus an hereditary peer who has ceased to be a member of the HL by virtue of the Act may nevertheless be returned to the HC via the ballot box. The Liberal Democrat MP John Thurso was the first hereditary peer to be so elected. Life peers continue to be disqualified from membership.

## Resignation

**6.25** An MP vacates a seat in the HC when elevated to the peerage, when Parliament is dissolved, on being expelled, or on their death. However, by virtue of a resolution of the HC passed on 2 March 1624, an MP is constitutionally debarred from resigning their seat. What happens, therefore, when an MP wishes to resign?

**6.26** The answer lies in a rather quaint process known as applying for the Chiltern Hundreds. In fact, two offices, Crown Steward and Bailiff of the three Chiltern Hundreds of Stoke, Desborough, and Burnham, and of the manor of Northstead, have been retained for the purpose of circumventing the prohibition on resignation. In effect, an MP who wishes to resign applies to the Chancellor of the Exchequer for one of the offices. Since they were once offices of profit under the Crown, although they now no longer attract a salary, a successful applicant is thereby disqualified from continuing to serve as an MP.

**6.27** The practice of applying for the Chiltern Hundreds has existed for more than 260 years. An applicant will invariably be successful and will hold the office until it is granted to another or they apply to be released from it. In more recent times, the stewardship has been held by, amongst others, John Stonehouse, Roy Jenkins, Neil Kinnock, Betty Boothroyd, and Tony Blair. Appointees to the Stewardship of Northstead have included the Rev Ian Paisley, Enoch Powell, Leon Brittan, the former Speaker, Michael Martin,

Gerry Adams, and Sir Peter Soulsby. The latter gave up his seat in the Commons in order that he could become Leicester's first elected mayor.

## Officers of the House of Commons

### The Speaker

**6.28** The Speaker of the HC is the chamber's presiding officer. The post itself dates back to the 13th century, although the first 'Speaker' was appointed in 1377. A Speaker is elected at the beginning of each new Parliament or on the death or retirement of the previous holder of the post. The electorate consists of current MPs and the election itself is presided over by the Father of the House (see para **6.33**). The successful candidate is an MP and must remain so in order to continue to hold the post. However, once elected, a Speaker ceases to play an active role with regard to the political issues of the day. He or she must be above political controversy and must act in a completely independent and impartial manner in the discharge of the Speaker's functions. A Speaker who stands at the general election does so as the Speaker seeking re-election rather than as a member of a political party. The present speaker is John Bercow MP.

**6.29** The primary and highly visible role of the Speaker is to act as chairperson of the HC during the course of debates. MPs are called to speak by the Speaker. Government ministers and their 'shadows' on the opposition benches will invariably be called. Backbench MPs may find it more difficult to be called even though they may have a particular interest in the subject matter of a debate. Rather than simply relying on their ability to 'catch the Speaker's eye' in the chamber by rising out of their seat, an MP may indicate a desire to speak in advance of the debate. Nevertheless, the Speaker retains a discretion as to which MPs are called.

**6.30** While a debate is being held, the Speaker (or his deputies) are responsible for ensuring that the proceedings are conducted in accordance with the rules of the HC. An MP who uses unparliamentary language, eg calling a fellow MP a liar, or who makes an allegation against another MP, may be required to withdraw the remark by the Speaker. A failure to do so or a more serious flouting of the rules of the House may result in an MP being 'named' by the Speaker. Where this takes place, a motion requesting that the MP be suspended is voted on by the House. If the motion is approved, the named MP will be suspended from the House for a specified period.

**6.31** The Speaker does not preside over all the debates which take place in the HC. The workload is spread between the Speaker and several deputies, although in the case of Prime Minister's Questions and the more important debates, it is normally the Speaker who presides. Where, however, the House is listening to the Chancellor's budget speech and in the subsequent debate on the provisions of the Finance Bill, the House sits in

Committee form and is therefore presided over by the Chairman of Ways and Means, a deputy speaker, rather than by the Speaker.

**6.32** In a division (see para **6.39**) following a debate, neither the Speaker nor the deputies vote. In the event of a tied vote, however, the Speaker has the casting vote. Convention dictates that this is exercised in favour of the government of the day.

### The Father of the House

**6.33** The title 'Father of the House' is bestowed on the most senior member of the HC. This is determined by the length of unbroken service in the HC. The principal function performed by the Father of the House is to preside over the election of a Speaker. In addition, the Father may be called upon to speak where historical or ceremonial matters are being considered by the House. During the course of the 20th century, five former PMs held the title, including David Lloyd George, the former Liberal PM, whose 15-year period as Father of the House (1929–44) was the longest in that century. The present Father of the House is Sir Peter Tapsell MP who was first elected to the HC in 1959, but who has enjoyed unbroken membership since the 1966 general election.

## The life of Parliament

**6.34** Prior to the Triennial Act 1694, there was no time limit placed on the life of a Parliament; it could continue for as long as the Crown desired. The Septennial Act of 1715 imposed a seven-year time limit which was subsequently reduced to five years by an amendment made by the Parliament Act 1911. Now, however, as a consequence of the Fixed-term Parliaments Act 2011, the life of Parliament is no longer expressed in terms of a maximum. Instead, it has been fixed at five years. There are, however, exceptions. Thus it is possible for the PM to extend the fixed-term period by up to two months in appropriate but unspecified circumstances. Also, more importantly, an early general election may be held where the HC has either passed a motion in favour of such an event by a two-thirds majority, or has passed a motion of no confidence in the government of the day and has failed to pass a motion of confidence in an alternative government within a 14-day period.

## House of Commons sittings

**6.35** At the time of writing, the House of Commons Procedure Committee is carrying out a review of the sittings of the House and the Parliamentary calendar. The parliamentary day which it is investigating is a varied one. In the light of recommendations made by the Select Committee on Modernisation of the HC in December 2001 and further changes implemented after the May 2005 general election, the hours of Parliament were adjusted to 'make better use of the earlier hours of the day'. Accordingly, in the Main Chamber, the hours are as follows: Monday and Tuesday (2.30 pm–10.30 pm); Wednesday (11.30 am–7.30 pm); Thursday (10.30 am–6.30 pm); and Friday (9.30 am–3.00 pm). Other than on a Monday and Tuesday, therefore, the House will normally rise rather earlier than was formerly the case when sittings long into the night were not uncommon. It should be noted, however, that the HC may sit beyond the stated times if it wishes. Since November 1999, the HC also sits in a further chamber known as Westminster Hall. Sittings in this chamber take place on Tuesdays, Wednesdays, and Thursdays. The hours for Tuesdays are 9.30 am– 2.00 pm. On a Wednesday, the chamber sits from 9.30 am–5.00 pm, and on a Thursday, it only sits in the afternoon (2.30 pm–5.30 pm).

**6.36** The HC does not generally sit at the weekends. From time to time during the course of the last century, it has however sat on a Saturday. Such sittings have tended to take place in response to a major event, such as the outbreak of the Second World War or the invasion of the Falkland Islands.

**6.37** The length of a parliamentary session has hitherto been flexible. Where a general election was called other than in the autumn, it resulted in a short session followed by a long session. Now, however, as a consequence of the Fixed-term Parliaments Act 2011, future parliamentary elections will ordinarily be held on the first Thursday in May. The present Leader of the House of Commons, Sir George Young MP, has commented in a written minister statement (13 September 2010) that the parliamentary timetable will be more certain as a result. In the past, a session typically began in November with the State Opening of Parliament and the Queen's Speech, and continued until Parliament was prorogued. In future, however, it seems likely that a parliament will consist of five 12-month sessions each of which will begin and end in the spring. In order to ensure a relatively smooth transition, the coalition Government has indicated that the present session will run until Easter 2012.

**6.38** Parliament does not sit during each week of a session. Instead, there are recesses for Christmas, Easter, and the summer. Also, more recently, recesses have been introduced to reflect school half-term holidays. For the 2002–03 session, the then Leader of the House took the unprecedented step of publishing the entire sessional calendar at the beginning of the session, rather than announcing individual recesses shortly before they were due to take place. This approach has been followed ever since. Occasionally, the House may be recalled where events demand that it should meet. This is what happened in September 1956, when Parliament was recalled for several days to discuss the Suez Crisis. Parliament was also recalled in August 2011 to discuss the rioting that had taken place in London and other cities.

## Voting

**6.39** Unlike most legislatures, including the Scottish Parliament, voting at Westminster does not take place electronically. The HC votes by having a division. In short, MPs register their vote to a motion by passing through either the 'Aye' or the 'No' lobbies situated either side of the Speaker's chair. As an MP passes through a lobby, their name is ticked off the division list by a clerk. Two MPs, who act as tellers, stand at the exit doors of the lobby and count the MPs who pass by them. A division is heralded by the ringing of division bells throughout the Palace of Westminster. These enable MPs who were not present at the conclusion of the debate to make their way to the chamber to cast their vote. Eight minutes after the Speaker put the original question on which the MPs are voting, the entrances to the lobbies are locked. On completion of the vote, the tellers return to the chamber and stand facing the Speaker with the table between them and the Speaker's chair. One of the tellers announces the number of votes cast and these are read out once again by the Speaker. The result of the vote is confirmed when the Speaker announces 'So the Ayes/Noes have it'.

## Abstaining

**6.40** There is no formal mechanism by which an MP can register an abstention in a vote; the voting system only takes account of Ayes and Noes. Nevertheless, if an MP wishes to abstain, this can be signified by remaining in the chamber when a division is called.

## Nodding through

**6.41** Occasionally, poor health or physical infirmity may prevent an MP actually walking through a lobby to cast a vote. In these circumstances, provided that they are in the precincts of the Palace of Westminster, they can be nodded through. This entails the clerks and tellers being informed by the Whips of the way in which the member wishes to vote on the motion, after the member's intentions have been ascertained. Nodding through ought only to be necessary where it is envisaged that a vote will be close. The Labour Governments of 1964–6 and 1976–9 had very small majorities and therefore it was necessary from time to time for stricken MPs to be brought to the palace by ambulance.

## Pairing

**6.42** Pairing is a rather more civilized voting practice. Essentially it is an arrangement between two MPs from opposing parties, agreed to by the Pairing Whips, whereby in certain less important votes, neither casts a vote. Had they voted they would only have cancelled one another out. Their joint absence has no effect on the size of the majority either for or against the motion. It merely means that the total number of votes cast on the motion is less than it would otherwise have been.

**6.43** Although electronic voting does not currently take place in the Westminster Parliament (see para **6.39**), the Select Committee on Modernisation of the HC has raised the possibility of its introduction. However, as the following passage indicates, the reform that the Committee envisaged would combine the benefits of the current system of voting with the advantages to be gained from the utilization of modern technology:

> *Members greatly value the informal contacts that arise when the House gathers for a division. The requirement for all Members to gather for a vote is important for the cohesion of Parliament and provides a valuable opportunity for MPs and Ministers to mingle. Any acceptable form of electronic voting must still require Members to attend the division. However, the introduction of an electronic method of recording their vote would enable Members to vote on multiple divisions at the same time, and to reduce time lost through divisions when a number of votes are taken in succession.*

## The committee system

**6.44** Much important work is carried out in the HC by committees. These committees are numerous and they are established to perform a variety of different functions. Thus there are: Committees of the whole House; Public Bill and General Committees; Select Committees (and Joint Select Committees); Departmental Select Committees; and other committees, such as Business Committees and the Ecclesiastical Committee. Within these classifications, further distinctions can be made. Thus the following are all examples of General Committees: Public Bill Committees; Committees on Delegated Legislation; the European Standing Committee; and the Welsh and Northern Ireland Grand Committees.

**6.45** Space does not permit a detailed consideration of each of these different types of committee. In the case of Committees on Public Bills, which are concerned with a detailed, clause-by-clause examination of Public Bills referred to them after their second reading, more will be said in Chapter **9** (see para **9.15**). For present purposes, therefore, attention will focus on the Select Committee structure which exists in the HC.

### Select Committees

**6.46** There are a number of different Select Committees within the HC. Indeed, some are more correctly described as being Joint Select Committees where they represent the union of a HC and a HL Select Committee under one chairperson. Although there is much variety, Select Committees share a common feature. They are permanent committees. The membership of Select Committees will vary with time. New members are appointed by the Selection Committee and existing members eventually cease to serve on the committee. However, the committee itself will continue to exist.

## Domestic committees

**6.47** Formerly there were five domestic committees which considered the provision of services within the HC. As from July 2005, however, these were replaced by a single committee, the Administration Committee. Further examples of domestic committees include: the Liaison Committee, the Modernisation of the HC Committee, and the Standards and Privileges Committee. The Liaison Committee was appointed to consider and advise the HC on matters relating to the work and functioning of Select Committees. Its membership is made up of one member from each of the Select Committees (usually the chairperson) and it is often chaired by a senior government backbencher. In March 1997, the Liaison Committee produced a *Report on The Work of Select Committees* (HC 323, 1996–7 session). It concluded that:

> 40. Scrutiny of the activities of the Executive is one of the traditional and most important roles of any democratic Parliament. In a House of over 650 members the only effective way such scrutiny can be carried out in a substantial and comprehensive manner is through the Select Committee system. These are not our views, they are the views of many informed commentators on the workings of Parliament. A similar awareness of the value of the Committee system is growing throughout the Westminster-model Parliaments of the Commonwealth, from large and established Parliaments like Canada and Australia to the newly emerging multiparty democracies in Africa.

**6.48** One of the important functions which the Liaison Committee performs is to hear evidence from the PM on matters of public policy. The former PM, Tony Blair, has described the experience of appearing before the Committee as being 'extremely tough'. He has also compared it favourably with PM's Questions, which in his opinion is 'very adversarial' and 'almost like a debating joust every week'.

**6.49** The Committee on Standards and Privileges is perhaps one of the best known domestic committees. It was appointed in November 1995 and one of its functions is to oversee the work of the Parliamentary Commissioner for Standards. Its role in this respect is important given that the decisions of the commissioner are not susceptible to judicial review: see *R v Parliamentary Comr for Standards, ex p Al Fayed* (1998). The committee is also concerned with matters of privilege which are referred to it as well as with the conduct of MPs.

**6.50** Several committees are concerned with the scrutiny of proposed legislation. These include the Regulatory Reform Committee, the European Scrutiny Committee, the Statutory Instruments Committee, the Consolidation Bills Committee, and the Human Rights Committee. The last three are examples of Joint Committees of the HC and the HL. The role of the first of these Joint Committees will be considered in Chapter **9** (see paras **9.77-9.79**). The Consolidation Bills Committee is concerned with legislation which generally restates the existing law in a more accessible and convenient form. Consolidation is a process which will also be considered in Chapter **9** (see paras **9.46-9.49**). The Human Rights Committee is concerned with, inter alia, matters relating to human rights in the UK (but not individual cases) and proposals for remedial orders made under s 10 and laid under Sch 2 to the Human Rights Act 1998.

## Departmental Select Committees

**6.51**  A system of Departmental Select Committees was originally established in 1979. The leader of the HC at the time, Norman St John-Stevas, introduced the proposals to the House as:

> *a necessary preliminary to the more effective scrutiny of government . . . an opportunity for closer examination of the departmental policy . . . an important contribution to greater openness in government, of a kind that is in accord with our parliamentary arrangements and our constitutional tradition.*

More recently in its First Report for the 2001–2 session (HC 224-I), the Select Committee on Modernisation of the HC described the role of departmental select committees thus:

> *One of the chief means which the House employs to conduct the scrutiny of Ministers and Government policy are the departmental select committees. These have proved successful vehicles for scrutiny in the twenty years or so since they were set up. They enable Members to develop an expertise and authority in specialised areas of public policy. They provide a forum for detailed examination of Ministers at length which is not always practical in the full Chamber. At their best they enable Members from both sides of the House to examine the issues in a non-partisan environment and to assess what is in the interest of the public not the advantage of the party.*

**6.52**  Departmental Select Committees mirror government departments. Thus a change in the structure of a government department by, for example, amalgamation with another department or sub-division into two departments, will be reflected at the committee level. The following are examples of Departmental Select Committees: Defence Committee; Business, Innovation and Skills Committee; Environment, Food and Rural Affairs Committee; Foreign Affairs Committee; Health Committee; Home Affairs Committee; Transport Committee; and the Treasury Committee. Each Select Committee has the power to appoint a sub-committee and the Environment, Food and Rural Affairs Committee has the power to appoint two subcommittees: see Standing Order No 152(2) and (3) of the Rules of the HC.

**6.53**  Departmental Select Committees are appointed 'to examine the expenditure, administration and policy of the principal government departments . . . and associated public bodies' (Standing Order No 152(1)). They do not generally concern themselves with draft legislation, unless the committee stage of a Bill has been referred to them by the HC (see para **9.15**). However, given the greater emphasis now being placed on pre-legislative scrutiny (see paras **9.8–9.11**), Departmental Select Committees are likely to play more of a role in the legislative process in the future. In the conduct of its investigations, a Departmental Select Committee is empowered by Standing Order No 152(4)(a) 'to send for persons, papers and records, to sit notwithstanding any adjournment of the House, to adjourn from place to place, and to report from time to time'. The membership of these committees essentially consists of backbench MPs, taking account of the strength of the political parties within the chamber. A practice has arisen whereby government ministers, Parliamentary Private Secretaries, and Opposition front bench spokespersons are not nominated for committee membership. The chairperson of a Departmental Select Committee is chosen by the membership of the committee. This means, therefore, that although a chairperson may be a member of the party in government, this need not necessarily be the case.

## Reform of the Select Committees

**6.54** In February 2002 the Select Committee on Modernisation of the HC published a report (HC 224-I) on how Parliament's scrutiny role through the Select Committee system could be strengthened and improved. This followed work carried out by the Liaison Committee (*Shifting the Balance: Select Committees and the Executive*, HC 300 of Session 1999–2000), the Hansard Society (*The Challenge for Parliament: Making Government Accountable*, 2001), and a Commission chaired by Lord Norton (*Strengthening Parliament*, 2000). Although space does not permit a full consideration of the recommendations made by the Committee, it should be noted that the Committee proposed, inter alia, 'a new system of nomination which will be transparent and will enhance the independence of the select committees'. Essentially this would have entailed the selection of nominations to the places allocated to each party initially taking place within the party itself (as is presently the case), followed by a consideration of those nominations by a Committee of Nomination chaired by the Chairman of Ways and Means and consisting of nine other senior members of the HC. When the report was debated in the HC (14 May 2002), a separate motion to establish a Committee of Nomination was defeated.

**6.55** The Select Committee on Modernisation of the HC also proposed, inter alia, that Departmental Select Committees should have a clearer remit. To this effect, it recommended that there should be an agreed statement of the core tasks of such committees. These included:

- to consider major policy initiatives;
- to consider the government's response to major emerging issues;
- to conduct pre-legislative scrutiny of draft Bills;
- to take evidence from each minister at least annually; and
- to examine treaties within their subject areas.

# House of Lords

## Composition

**6.56** The House of Lords was, until the passing of the House of Lords Act 1999, essentially composed of three groups of peers: hereditary peers; archbishops and bishops; and life peers. Together these three groupings constituted the 'Lords Spiritual and Temporal' referred to in the enacting formula of an Act of Parliament.

## Hereditary peers

**6.57** Hereditary peers have, generally speaking, inherited the title that they hold from an ennobled ancestor. A small number of hereditary peers in the HL had their titles conferred directly upon them, but it has been the practice in more recent times to refrain from conferring hereditary peerages, save in exceptional circumstances, eg where the individual has no heirs. There were something in the region of 760 hereditary peers in the HL at the beginning of 1999 and hence they constituted the majority of the second chamber. The majority of the hereditary peers were supporters of the Conservative Party.

**6.58** Despite the fact that the term 'peers' means equal, there are five ranks within the peerage: duke, marquess, earl, viscount, and baron. Hereditary titles normally occupy one of the first four ranks.

## Archbishops and bishops

**6.59** The lords spiritual, the archbishops and bishops, are a comparatively small group within the HL. They sit in the upper chamber by virtue of the Bishoprics Act 1878. This provides that the Archbishops of Canterbury and York, together with the Bishops of London, Durham, and Winchester, and the next 21 most senior of the diocesan bishops are entitled to sit in the HL. In total, therefore, they number 26. Unlike hereditary or life peers, the bishops are ex officio members of the HL in that they sit in the chamber by virtue of the post that they hold. On retirement from his See, a bishop ceases to be a member of the HL. He may, however, return to the upper chamber in the event of being made a life peer, as was the case with the former Archbishop of Canterbury, Lord Carey of Clifton.

## Life peers

**6.60** The third group within the HL are the life peers. The creation of peerages for life, which are personal to those on whom they are conferred and which do not therefore pass to a successor, is a relatively recent development. It dates back to the Life Peerages Act 1958 which accorded the monarch the power to confer life peerages on both men and women. A life peer ranks as a baron and as such is entitled to attend and vote in the HL. In the 50 or so years since the passage of the 1958 Act, the power to create life peers has been much used. Currently, there are something in the region of 670 life peers in the HL.

6.61 Life peers are drawn from a variety of backgrounds, interests, professions, and political affiliations. Elevation to the upper chamber is considered desirable by the government on the basis that the new life peer has some particular expertise, experience, or knowledge which will be valuable to the chamber in the performance of its functions. Since 1958, it has not been uncommon for former senior government ministers, including former PMs, to have had life peerages conferred on them.

6.62 Prior to the passage of the Life Peerages Act 1958, a special form of life peerage did in fact exist. It was conferred on individuals who were collectively known as the Law Lords. These individuals carried out the judicial functions of the HL. Now that the new Supreme Court is operational (see Chapter 2), the link between the legislature and the highest court in the legal system has been broken. It is therefore no longer possible for the UK's most senior judges to be part of the law-making process in Parliament.

### The Lord Speaker

6.63 One of the reforms that has been made to the office of Lord Chancellor (see Chapter 2) is that the holder of the post no longer acts as Speaker of the HL. The Woolsack is therefore now occupied by the Lord Speaker. Unlike the Lord Chancellor, the Lord Speaker is not appointed by the PM. Neither does the holder of the office have charge of a government department. Instead, the Lord Speaker is elected for a period of up to five years at a time although they may serve a second term. The principal roles of the Lord Speaker include: offering procedural advice to the HL; taking the Chair in Committee of the whole House; acting as an ambassador for the HL both in the UK and overseas; and being responsible for security in the HL part of the Parliamentary Estate. Unlike the Speaker in the HC, the Lord Speaker does not call the HL to order or rule on points of order. Neither does the Lord Speaker call members of the House to speak.

## Reform of the House of Lords

6.64 As was noted previously (para 5.32), the preamble to the Parliament Act 1911 states, in part, that its drafters ultimately intended to 'substitute for the House of Lords as it at present exists a Second Chamber constituted on a popular instead of hereditary basis'. In the hundred years since these words first appeared on the statute book, reform of the

House of Lords has occupied various positions on the political agendas of successive governments. The Labour governments of Tony Blair and Gordon Brown succeeded in carrying through many constitutional reforms of note (see paras **1.32-1.33**). Reform of the House of Lords could best be described, however, as a work in progress at the time of Labour's defeat in the May 2010 general election. The House of Lords Act 1999 had reduced the number of hereditary peers in the second chamber to 92. Moreover, it had established an Appointments Commission responsible for making recommendations to the PM regarding the appointment of life peers.

6.65 The Labour Governments had also established a Royal Commission to look into the matter under the chairmanship of Lord Wakeham. Its report, *A House for the Future* (Cm 4534), was published in January 2000. It made a number of recommendations, including that a reformed second chamber:

- should act as a 'constitutional long-stop'; ensuring that changes are not made to the constitution without full and open debate and an awareness of the consequences;

- should be authoritative, but that its authority should not be such as to challenge the ultimate democratic authority of the HC;

- should be broadly representative of British society as a whole.

6.66 The Wakeham Commissions' recommendations were broadly supported by the Labour Government. It made its own contribution to the debate by publishing various official documents. These included three White Papers, *The House of Lords – Completing the Reform* (Cm 5291) (2001), *The House of Lords: Reform* (Cm 7027) (2007), and *An Elected Second Chamber: Further Reform of the House of Lords* (Cm 7438) (2008), and a consultation document, *Constitutional Reform: Next Steps for the House of Lords* (2003). There were also parliamentary debates on matters such as a partly-elected and partly-appointed second chamber. It was noteworthy that whilst the HC voted in favour of a fully-elected and an 80% elected 20% appointed second chamber, the only reform option to secure a majority in the HL was a fully-appointed House.

6.67 Since it was formed, the coalition Government has also demonstrated its willingness to address the issue of House of Lords reform. Following the establishment of a cross-party Committee to consider the various issues, it published its own White Paper, *House of Lords Reform Draft Bill* (Cm 8077) (2011) which, as its title indicates, is accompanied by a draft Bill setting out the Government's proposals in legislative form. A Joint Committee of Parliament has also been appointed to consider and report on the Bill by 29 February 2012.

6.68 It should be noted, initially, that the Government's proposals retain the name 'House of Lords' for the purposes of the pre-legislative scrutiny. This is not because the intention is to call the reformed chamber by the same name as its predecessor. Rather, it is because the Government 'does not want discussion of the name to be a distraction from the more fundamental issues of the composition of the second chamber'.

**6.69** With regard to functions, the intention is that these should be the same in the reformed second chamber as they are in the present HL. The Government also believes that 'the change in the composition of the second chamber ought not to change the status of that chamber as a House of Parliament or the existing constitutional relationship between the two Houses of Parliament'. Thus there is no intention to amend the Parliament Acts so as to alter the balance of power between the two Houses of Parliament. A reformed second chamber would remain subordinate to the HC.

**6.70** The White Paper notes that hitherto, the relationship between the two Houses of Parliament has largely been governed by convention. This has helped to produce a 'delicate balance which has evolved over the years'. Accordingly, although clause 2 of the draft Bill stops a long way short of codifying the relevant conventions, it does make clear that nothing in the Bill affects them. They would therefore continue to operate in the event that the second chamber is reformed. Thus, for example, a second chamber would, like the HL before it, have to think very carefully about rejecting a Bill which the Commons had passed.

**6.71** Earlier reform proposals envisaged a second chamber consisting of 540–600 members. Currently, the total membership of the HL is 788. However, the White Paper notes that during the 2009–10 session, the average daily attendance was 388. Thus it is argued that the size of the 'working house' is considerably smaller than the total number of members. It is also argued that 'in most other countries the second chamber is substantially smaller than the first chamber'. The Government therefore proposes that the reformed second chamber will have 300 full-time Parliamentarians as members. They will be eligible to serve a single non-renewable membership of 15 years, with elections to be held every five years at the same time as general elections for the HC under the Fixed-term Parliaments Act 2011. The elections to the second chamber would be staggered so that a third of the elected seats (80) would be contested at each election. Thus it would take three election cycles for the new second chamber to fully emerge from the old HL. During the transitional period, existing peers would remain but would be reduced in number in direct proportion to the increase in newly elected or appointed members.

**6.72** Although the Government proposes that the second chamber should be 80% elected 20% appointed, it does not reject the possibility of a completely elected chamber. The proportional voting system which it prefers is the single transferable vote (STV). This would entail voters ranking the candidates on the ballot paper in order of preference. To be elected, a candidate would need to achieve one vote more than the 'quota' (calculated on the basis of the number of votes cast divided by the number of seats available). Once this has happened, any surplus votes would be transferred to the other candidates in accordance with the voters' preferences. This process of vote transfer would continue until all the seats in an electoral district were filled. The franchise for the reformed second chamber would be the same as for the HC (see paras **6.2–6.11**).

**6.73**   The White Paper considers that in a reformed second chamber, there should continue to be a role for the established Church. However, given its reduced size, it is proposed that 12 rather than 26 archbishops and bishops should be appointed. All members of the reformed chamber, excluding the bishops, would be paid a taxable salary and would be able to claim allowances for costs incurred in connection with their parliamentary duties. It is proposed that the level of salary ought to be lower than for an MP, but more than a member of one of the devolved legislatures to reflect the fact that members of the second chamber 'would have responsibilities for UK-wide legislation but would not have constituency duties'.

**6.74**   Three final points relating to the Government's proposals are worthy of mention. The first concerns the issue of expulsion or suspension for misconduct. It is proposed that a reformed second chamber would have the power to make standing orders allowing it to suspend or expel members other than the bishops. Expulsion would result in a permanent loss of membership. The second point relates to resignation. Members of the second chamber would be entitled to resign at any time by giving written notice to the Clerk of the Parliaments. Vacancies which arose as a result would be filled in accordance with the relevant clauses of the draft Bill so as to maintain a constant level of membership.

**6.75**   The final point to note concerns the possibility that some members of the reformed second chamber may regard it as a stepping-stone to the HC; as an environment in which to lay the foundations of a political career before moving to the principal chamber. The Government therefore proposes that a time restriction should exist to disqualify former members of the reformed second chamber from being elected to the HC for a specified period of time after they cease to be members. Thus it would not be possible to resign from the second chamber so as to immediately stand for election to the HC. Instead, the former member would only be eligible to stand at the next scheduled general election. A similar disqualification would apply to a member of the second chamber who had resigned some time in advance of a general election. Former MPs would, however, be treated differently. For them, there would be no period of disqualification if they sought to become members of the reformed second chamber.

**6.76**   The Government's intention is that the first elections to the reformed second chamber will take place in 2015. Although there is strong parliamentary support for the principle of reform of the HL, it remains to be seen how closely any new arrangements will resemble the proposals set out in the White Paper and the accompanying draft Bill.

## Parliamentary privilege

**6.77**   The origins of parliamentary privilege can be traced to a time long before that body can be said to have possessed real power within the constitution. Essentially, parliamentary privilege evolved at the insistence of monarchs that they should have free access to their advisers as and when they wanted. Accordingly, those advisers, many of whom sat in Parliament, were protected from molestation, arrest, and imprisonment on their journeys to and from Parliament and were thus in a position to advise as required. Originally the enforcement of such a privilege lay with the Crown. However, this jurisdiction was subsequently transferred to Parliament in the reign of Henry VIII, where it has remained ever since.

6.78   Today, 'parliamentary privilege' means something more than the mere freedom from molestation, arrest, or imprisonment. The notion has a wider meaning, encompassing matters such as freedom of speech, committal for contempt, and Parliament's regulation of its own internal proceedings. 'Parliamentary privilege' is thus a term for what is in truth a collection of privileges.

6.79   The privileges of Parliament 'belong to the House and not to the individual': per Lord Browne-Wilkinson in *Hamilton v Al Fayed* (2001) (para **6.87**). Thus, for example, the jurisdiction to commit members or 'strangers' for contempt is exercised by the House as a whole rather than by individual members. Freedom of speech is a particularly important privilege in that it enables members of either House to participate fully and with complete candour in the business of Parliament without fear of subsequent legal proceedings. It ensures, in effect, that what might otherwise be a libel outside the Palace of Westminster is not regarded as such by the courts where the words are uttered within its precincts. In the words of Lord Cockburn CJ in *Wason v Walter* (1868):

> It is clear that the statements made by Members of either House of Parliament in their places in the House, though they might be untrue to their knowledge, could not be made the foundation of civil or criminal proceedings, however injurious they might be to the interest of a third party.

6.80   The breadth of the immunity enjoyed by Parliamentarians is evident from this passage. It is absolute in relation to things said in Parliament even where the speaker knows them to be false or malicious. In 1997, a joint committee of both Houses was established in order to review the law relating to parliamentary privilege. It concluded:

> We consider it of utmost importance that there should be a national public forum where all manner of persons, irrespective of their power or wealth, can be criticised. Members should not be exposed to the risk of being brought before the courts to defend what they said in Parliament. Abuse of parliamentary freedom of speech is a matter for internal self-regulation by parliament, not a matter for investigation and regulation by the courts. The legal immunity principle is as important today as ever. The courts have a duty not to erode this essential constitutional principle.

6.81   It should be noted, however, that whilst the privilege attaches to things said in Parliament, it does not extend to things said outside Parliament even where they simply report what has been said therein. Extra-parliamentary repetition may well therefore amount to a libel: see the decision of the PC in the New Zealand case, *Buchanan v Jennings* (2005).

**6.82** Freedom of speech is protected by art 9 of the Bill of Rights. This provides that:

> *the freedome of speech and debates or proceedings in Parlyament ought not to be impeached or questioned in any court or place out of Parlyament.*

As with many such statements, the precise meaning of art 9 is unclear. The difficulty centres upon what is meant by 'proceedings in Parliament'. Thus in 1958, where an MP wrote a letter to the Paymaster-General in which certain allegations were made against the London Electricity Board, and the matter was referred by the HC to the Committee of Privileges, that committee's conclusion, that the letter amounted to a 'proceeding in Parliament', was clearly called into question when the House voted against accepting its report. More recently in *Rost v Edwards* (1990), a case involving the alleged libel of an MP, evidence consisting of a letter sent by an opposition MP to the Speaker in which complaints were made against the plaintiff was ruled inadmissible on the basis that it amounted to 'proceedings in Parliament', whereas evidence obtained from the Register of Members' Interests could be heard since it came from a public document.

**6.83** Professor Heuston has contended that 'around parliamentary privilege some of the great battles of the Constitution have been fought'. Two such battles were fought by Messrs Stockdale and Bradlaugh.

---

***Stockdale v Hansard* (1839):** S sued H for a defamatory libel alleged to be contained in a prison inspector's report ordered to be printed and published by the HC. The inspector had suggested that a book published by S was obscene and indecent. In the first action, H argued that the publication was covered by parliamentary privilege and that it was justified. In a second action instituted by S, H relied solely upon the privilege defence. QBD held: whether or not a particular privilege existed was a matter for the courts to determine. The privilege of publication asserted in this case did not exist. The resolution of the HC alone could not alter the law or place the HC beyond the law's control. Only Parliament as a whole could make or unmake the law.

---

***Bradlaugh v Gossett* (1884):** B had been elected to represent Northampton in Parliament. However, as an atheist, he was unable to take the oath required under the Parliamentary Oaths Act 1866. B was willing to take an affirmation in place of the oath, but this was not allowed: see *Bradlaugh v Clarke* (1883). B was re-elected and attempted to take the oath. The HC resolved that he should not be allowed to do so, and that force could be used to exclude him if he attempted to re-enter the House. B argued that the resolution was void and that an injunction should be granted to prevent the Sergeant-at Arms enforcing it. QBD held: the jurisdiction of the Houses over their own members was absolute and exclusive. What was said or done within the walls of Parliament could not be inquired into by the courts. Had the

House resolved to exempt B from any penalties arising under the Act when taking his seat, that would have been a matter that the courts could have determined according to their interpretation of the statute.

6.84 Further instances of parliamentary privilege featuring in proceedings before the courts have occurred since these cases were decided. Thus in the landmark case of *Pepper v Hart* (1993), the HL relaxed a self-imposed rule which had previously excluded it from consulting parliamentary materials when interpreting a statute. To consult *Hansard* when construing an Act was held not to amount to a questioning of the freedom of speech or debate in Parliament and was not therefore contrary to art 9 of the Bill of Rights. Recourse to such interpretative aids would, however, only be permissible in limited circumstances where, for example, the words of a statute were ambiguous or their literal meaning would lead to an absurdity.

6.85 In *Prebble v Television New Zealand Ltd* (1995), a libel case involving allegations made in a television programme to the effect that a former New Zealand Government minister had lied to Parliament, the PC agreed with the New Zealand CA that it would be contrary to art 9 of the Bill of Rights to allow D to rely upon statements made by P in the House of Representatives as proof of the defence of justification. Suggestions that the words used were untrue or misleading was a matter for the House to decide, not the courts. In effect, the PC held that art 9 of the Bill of Rights precluded the use of parliamentary materials either as a sword, ie as the basis for instituting proceedings, or as a shield, ie as a defence to such proceedings.

6.86 The decision in *Prebble* was followed in *Allason v Haines* (1995). In this case A, an MP, brought proceedings for libel in respect of a newspaper article in which it was alleged that he had been banned from naming MPs in a Commons motion whom he claimed were 'agents of influence' for the KGB and in which it was recalled that he had not been stopped from making similar allegations against a journalist in a Commons motion several years previously. The QBD applied *Prebble* and held that parliamentary privilege precluded the defence of justification. However, a stay (known as a 'fair trial stay') was granted in respect of the action on the basis that it would be unjust to deprive the defendants of their only defence and allow A to continue on an unsatisfactory and unfair basis.

6.87 Although it is clear that the rationale for a 'fair trial stay' in defamation proceedings in which parliamentary privilege is an issue is to avoid an injustice being done to the defendant, the grant of a stay may have a detrimental impact upon the claimant. In effect, it will preclude the claimant from having the opportunity to clear his own name. With this in mind, therefore, s 13 of the Defamation Act 1996 entitles a person whose conduct in or in relation to proceedings in Parliament is in issue in defamation proceedings to waive the right to protection from parliamentary privilege. What, however, might be the consequences where an MP chooses to exercise this power?

---

*Hamilton v Al Fayed* **(2001):** H was the former MP for Tatton and A was a very wealthy businessman with numerous interests, including the ownership of Harrods. A contended that he had made substantial cash payments directly to H on a number of occasions between mid-1987 and late 1989 and also that he had given Harrods gift vouchers to H. The cash and vouchers were said to be payments in return for H tabling parliamentary questions and other parliamentary services on behalf of A. In October 1994 a report was published in *The Guardian* newspaper setting out the nature of these allegations. H and others initiated libel proceedings but, in July 1995, May J granted a fair trial stay since parliamentary privilege was involved. On 4 July 1996 the Defamation Act received Royal Assent. In consequence of the passing of the Act, H applied to lift the stay on the action against *The Guardian* having waived his privilege under s 13 of the Act. Shortly before the matter came to trial, however, H and the others withdrew their action amid much publicity. The Committee on Standards and Privileges subsequently asked the Parliamentary Commissioner for Standards (PCS) to investigate the 'cash for questions' allegations to see whether there had been a breach of HC rules. Whilst the PCS's inquiry was still continuing and about a week before A was due to give evidence to the PCS, A appeared on a Channel 4 *Dispatches* programme and repeated the substance of the allegations against H. H instituted libel proceedings in respect of these remarks. A sought either an order dismissing the action as an abuse of the process of the court or a fair trial stay on the grounds of parliamentary privilege. Popplewell J refused A any relief and the CA dismissed A's appeal on different grounds. A appealed (in the meantime, the defamation action had been tried and H's claim had been dismissed). HL held: dismissing the appeal, that it was firmly established that the courts are precluded from entertaining in any proceedings evidence, questioning, or submissions designed to show that a witness in parliamentary proceedings deliberately misled Parliament. To mislead Parliament would be a breach of parliamentary behaviour in respect of which Parliament had exclusive jurisdiction. With regard to s 13 of the 1996 Act, its effect was entirely clear. Had H not waived his parliamentary privilege, it would have been impossible for A to have had a fair trial in the libel action. However, since s 13 did apply to the case it provided a complete answer to the appeal.

---

**6.88** Allegations made on the floor of the HC and repeated in the press were the subject of an application heard by the ECtHR.

---

*A v United Kingdom* **(2003):** An MP initiated a parliamentary debate on the subject of municipal housing policy during which he specifically referred to A several times, giving her name and address and referring to members of her family. Shortly before the debate a press release was issued to a local newspaper and the national *Daily Express*. The press release was subject to an embargo not to publish until the speech had commenced. The newspaper articles included photographs of A and mentioned her name and address. The *Daily Express* article bore the headline 'MP names nightmare neighbour'. As a consequence of the press coverage, A received hate-mail and she was stopped in the street, spat at, and abused. Through her solicitors she wrote to the MP and her letter was referred to the Office of the Speaker. The Speaker's representative replied to the effect that MPs' remarks were protected by parliamentary privilege. A applied to the ECtHR. She argued, inter alia, that the parliamentary immunity enjoyed by the MP violated arts 6(1), 8, and 13 of the ECHR. ECtHR held: that parliamentary immunity preserved the legitimate aims of protecting free speech in Parliament and maintaining the separation of powers between the legislature and the judiciary. In a democracy, it was felt that parliaments are the essential fora for political debate and that very weighty reasons needed to be advanced to justify interference with the freedom of expression exercised therein. In the light of these considerations and the fact that a similar immunity was recognized by rules within other signatory states, the Council of Europe, and the European Union, it followed that the immunity did not impose a disproportionate restriction on the right of access to court under art 6(1). Similar considerations defeated the argument that it was contrary to art 8. With regard to art 13, the ECtHR recalled that it did not go so far as to guarantee a remedy allowing a contracting state's primary legislation to be challenged before a national court on the grounds that it was contrary to the ECHR.

**6.89** The decision in *A v United Kingdom* was later applied in *Zollman v United Kingdom* (2004). In this case where the applicants, Belgian nationals, had been accused by a UK Government minister during the course of a debate in the HC of dealing in diamonds from Angola in contravention of UN sanctions, the ECtHR unanimously dismissed the application as inadmissible. In the judgment of the court, the minister's statement did not violate the presumption of innocence under art 6(2) of the ECHR or attack their reputation contrary to art 8. Neither did the fact that parliamentary privilege precluded an action for defamation violate their right of access to a court under art 6(1) of the ECHR. Indeed, on the basis of the previous decision in *A v United Kingdom*, the ECtHR held that the art 6(1) claim was manifestly ill-founded.

**6.90** In *R (on the application of Bradley) v Secretary of State for Work and Pensions* (2007) (para **15.80**), where the claimants sought judicial review of the Secretary of State's rejection of the Parliamentary Commissioner for Administration's (PCA) finding of maladministration in respect of occupational pension schemes, the Speaker of the HC intervened due to concerns that art 9 of the Bill of Rights 1689 might be infringed if evidence given by the PCA to the HC Public Affairs Select Committee, and the Committee's report, were to be relied upon in the case. Bean J agreed with the Speaker 'that to allow the evidence of a witness to a Select Committee to be relied on in a court would inhibit the freedom of speech in Parliament and thus contravene art 9 of the Bill of Rights'. He therefore did not allow the PCA's oral evidence to be relied upon in court. However, as far as the Committee's report was concerned, Bean J did not consider that citation from it would infringe art 9 because the report bore 'no resemblance to a minister answering supplementary questions or a member of either House speaking in debate'. In the event, reliance was not placed on the report not because of art 9, but because Bean J held that it was for the court rather than the Select Committee to determine whether the Secretary of State had acted unlawfully in rejecting the PCA's findings.

## Parliamentary Standards Act 2009

**6.91**  The catalyst for the Act was the scandal over MPs' allowances and expenses which came to light following the publication of leaked information by the *Daily Telegraph* in May and June 2009. The legislation completed its stages in Parliament in a few short weeks and one of the key reforms which it introduced was that the payment of MPs' salaries and allowances would be administered and regulated by a new body, the Independent Parliamentary Standards Authority. The Bill which was introduced was significantly altered and amended during its passage. For present purposes, it should be noted that the clauses which generated the most vociferous opposition were those which, it was contended, infringed parliamentary privilege. A clause which would have put a code of conduct enshrining the seven principles of public life (selflessness, integrity, objectivity, accountability, openness, honesty, and leadership) on a statutory footing was therefore dropped, and a clause which would have precluded art 9 of the Bill of Rights 1689 from being used to prevent parliamentary proceedings from being admissible in legal proceedings against an MP for an offence contrary to the Act was defeated. In the opinion of the HL Select Committee on the Constitution, the clauses 'threatened to undermine freedoms which are asserted for Parliament to operate properly and risked opening the door to conflict between Parliament and the courts'.

**6.92**  Despite these successes, the Bill's opponents remained unconvinced that the measure would not have a residual impact upon parliamentary privilege, in particular freedom of speech and debate in Parliament. Accordingly, they succeeded in having a clause inserted which is now s 1 of the 2009 Act. This states:

> *Nothing in this Act shall be construed by any court in the United Kingdom as affecting Article IX of the Bill of Rights 1689.*

**6.93**  To some extent, it might be argued that the provision amounts to a 'for the avoidance of doubt' measure. In other words, it states explicitly that which is implicit given the attitude of the courts towards art 9 as evidenced in cases such as *R v Parliamentary Commissioner for Standards, ex p Al Fayed* (1998).

**6.94**  In addition to the 2009 Act, the MPs' allowances and expenses scandal also led to the prosecution of three former MPs and a peer for false accounting offences contrary to s 17 of the Theft Act 1968. In separate trials, each was found guilty and the sentences imposed ranged from 9–18 months' imprisonment. Prior to this, however, the defendants had claimed that they ought not to be the subject of criminal proceedings since their expenses and allowances claims were 'proceedings in Parliament' and hence were protected by parliamentary privilege: see *R v Chaytor* (2011). In dismissing their appeals, the Supreme Court emphasized that the extent of parliamentary privilege is ultimately a matter for the courts to determine. In its judgment, the submission of expenses claims was an incident of the administration of Parliament, not part of its proceedings. Thus Lord Phillips observed:

> *Scrutiny of claims by the courts will have no adverse impact on the core or essential business of Parliament, it will not inhibit debate or freedom of speech. Indeed it will not inhibit any of the varied activities in which Members of Parliament indulge that bear in one way or another on their parliamentary duties. The only thing it will inhibit is the making of dishonest claims.*

Accordingly, the defendants could not rely on art 9. Neither could they show that their prosecutions were precluded by the exclusive cognizance of Parliament to regulate its own internal affairs, since it had long been accepted that the principle was waived where it was alleged that an MP had committed an ordinary crime in the House or its precincts.

**6.95** In *Chaytor*, Lord Phillips explained the principle of exclusive cognizance thus:

> *This phrase describes areas where the courts have ruled that any issues should be left to be resolved by Parliament rather than determined judicially. Exclusive cognizance refers not simply to Parliament, but to the exclusive reach of each House to manage its own affairs without interference from the other or from outside Parliament.*

In *Baron Mereworth v Ministry of Justice* (2011), it was held that the principle meant that the court had no jurisdiction to hear a claim that contrary to s 1 of the House of Lords Act 1999, the claimant had, as a recently ennobled hereditary peer, an entitlement to sit in the HL. Had it been necessary to determine the interpretation issue, Lewison J was of the view that the plain wording of s 1 admitted of no other construction than that hereditary peers were no longer entitled to be a member of the HL by virtue of their peerage.

## FURTHER READING

Briant, S 'Dialogue, Diplomacy and Defiance: Prisoners' voting rights at home and in Strasbourg' [2011] EHRLR 243.

Dickson, B 'The Processing of Appeals in the House of Lords' (2007) 123 LQR 571.

Feldman, D 'Parliamentary Scrutiny of Legislation and Human Rights' [2002] PL 323.

Foster, S 'Reluctantly Restoring Rights: Responding to the prisoner's right to vote' (2009) 9 HRL Rev 489.

Harlow, C, Cramer, F, and Doe, N 'Bishops in the House of Lords: A critical analysis' [2008] PL 490.

House of Commons Research Paper 09/69, *Parliamentary Trends; statistics about Parliament* (29 July 2009).

Jack, Dr M et al *Erskine May's Treatise on the Law, Privileges, Proceedings and Usage of Parliament* (24th edn, 2011) LexisNexis Butterworths.

Leopold, P 'The Application of the Civil and Criminal Law to Members of Parliament and Parliamentary Proceedings' in Oliver and Drewry (eds) *The Law and Parliament* (1998).

Lord Chancellor's Department *The House of Lords – Completing the Reform* (2001) Cm 5291.

Lord Hope 'Voices from the Past – The Law Lords' Contribution to the Legislative Process' (2007) 123 LQR 547.

Ministry of Justice, *An Elected Second Chamber: Further Reform of the House of Lords* Cm 7438 (2008).

Ministry of Justice, *Responding to human rights judgments* Cm 8162 (2011).

Munro, C *Studies in Constitutional Law* (2nd edn, 1999) Butterworths, chapter 4.

Nicol, D 'Legitimacy of the Commons Debate on Prisoner Voting' [2011] PL 681.

Office of the Deputy Prime Minister, *House of Lords Reform Draft Bill* Cm 8077 (2011).

Pannick, D '"Better that a horse should have a voice in the House [of Lords] than that a judge should" (Jeremy Bentham): Replacing the Law Lords by a Supreme Court' [2009] PL 723.

Parpworth, N *Parliamentary Standards Act 2009*, Current Law Annotated Statutes, Sweet & Maxwell.

Parpworth, N 'The Parliamentary Standards Act 2009: A Constitutional Dangerous Dogs Measure?' (2010) 73 MLR 262.

Parpworth, N and Thompson, K *Parliamentary Voting System and Constituencies Act 2011*, Current Law Annotated Statutes, Sweet & Maxwell.

Parpworth, N and Thompson, K *Fixed-term Parliaments Act 2011*, Current Law Annotated Statutes, Sweet & Maxwell.

Pollard, D, Parpworth, N, and Hughes, D *Constitutional and Administrative Law: Text with Materials* (4th edn, 2007) OUP.

Office of the Leader of the House of Commons *The House of Lords: Reform* Cm 7027 (2007).

Oliver, D 'Reforming the United Kingdom Parliament' in Jowell and Oliver (eds) *The Changing Constitution* (7th edn, 2011) OUP.

*Report of the Independent Commission on Electoral Reform* (the Jenkins Report) (1998) Cm 4090.

Royal Commission on Reform of the House of Lords *A House for the Future* (2000) Cm 4534.

Sharland, A and Loveland, I 'The Defamation Act 1996 and Political Libels' [1997] PL 113.

## SELF-TEST QUESTIONS

1   Consider who is excluded from standing as an MP or voting in a parliamentary election. How might these exclusions be justified?

2   Do you think that electoral reform is necessary? What do you think of the voting system proposed by the Jenkins Commission?

3   What are the arguments both for and against the lowering of the voting age in parliamentary and local government elections from the present 18 to 16?

4   Why was the departmental select committee system established in 1979? How effective can these committees be in scrutinizing the conduct of the executive?

5   Why is reform of the House of Lords necessary? What ought to be the role of a reformed second chamber and how should its membership be determined?

6   What does 'parliamentary privilege' mean? How necessary are the privileges which it encompasses?

# 7 The European Community and the European Union

## SUMMARY

The aims of this chapter are threefold: first, it seeks to consider briefly the events that have led to the creation of the European Community and the European Union; secondly, it seeks to introduce the reader to the principal institutions which serve the European Union and to consider the nature and functions of each; and thirdly, it seeks to indicate, where appropriate, the nature of the institutional reforms which will take place following the ratification of the Lisbon Treaty by the member states.

Note: Following the amendments made by the Lisbon Treaty, two treaties are now of key importance in the present context: the Treaty on European Union (TEU) and the Treaty on the Functioning of the European Union (TFEU). The treaty articles referred to in this chapter are therefore from either one of these treaties.

## The European Communities

7.1 By the conclusion of the Second World War, most of Europe lay utterly devastated. The continent as a whole had paid a huge price in terms of its human and natural resources. Nevertheless, such devastation had at least one positive aspect. It made people realize that the events of 1939–45 must not be repeated. This desire to preclude the need for war in the future was the basis for the establishment of a new European order in the non-communist states. Winston Churchill had argued in 1946 that 'we must build a kind of United States of Europe'. In 1950, the then French Foreign Minister, Robert Schuman, published a plan that both he and Jean Monnet had devised. It proposed to place Europe's coal and steel industries, the armourers of nations, under the control of a high authority.

7.2 The Treaty founding the European Coal and Steel Community (ECSC) was concluded in Paris on 18 April 1951. It entered into force on 23 July 1952 following its ratification by the legislatures of the founding states. In 1957, further developments occurred when two new communities, the European Economic Community (EEC) and the European

Atomic Energy Community (Euratom), were established under the Treaties of Rome. There were six original members of the three communities: Belgium, West Germany, France, Italy, Luxembourg, and the Netherlands. In the years that have followed, other states have joined the communities so that the current membership stands at 27. In addition to the original six, Denmark, Ireland, and the UK (1973), Greece (1981), Spain and Portugal (1986), and Sweden, Austria, and Finland (1995) are all member states. A further 10 countries became member states on 1 May 2004. They are: the Czech Republic; Estonia; Cyprus; Latvia; Lithuania; Hungary; Malta; Poland; Slovenia; and Slovakia. Twenty-five became 27 with the accession of Bulgaria and Romania in January 2007. Thus the EU now dwarfs the original community in terms of geographical size and population. Its expansion is likely to continue since accession negotiations either have taken place or may do so with Croatia, Iceland, the Republic of Macedonia, Montenegro, and Turkey.

**7.3**  Despite the developments that have occurred regarding accession, the three communities have continued to exist separately in accordance with their own founding treaties. In 1978, the European Parliament resolved that the three communities should be referred to collectively as 'the European Community'. This change in nomenclature was ultimately achieved by the Treaty on European Union (the Maastricht Treaty) which also renamed the EEC Treaty (Treaty of Rome) the EC Treaty. A further change in nomenclature has taken place following the ratification of the Lisbon Treaty. Although the Treaty on European Union (TEU) has retained its name, the EC Treaty has been renamed the Treaty on the Functioning of the European Union (TFEU). Throughout the two treaties, the word 'community' has been replaced by 'union'.

**7.4**  Originally each community was served by its own separate institutions. However, initiatives such as the Merger Treaty signed on 8 April 1965 succeeded in bringing about the unification of the various institutions which existed at the time. As a result of the reforms effected by the Lisbon Treaty, the institutional framework of the EU can now be stated to comprise: the European Council; the Council; the Commission; the European Parliament; and the Court of Justice of the European Union (ECJ). Strictly speaking there are a further two principal institutions: the Court of Auditors and the European Central Bank. The former was established under the terms of the Financial Provisions Treaty 1975 and achieved institution status by virtue of the TEU. However, as its name implies, its primary role is to examine the accounts of all revenue and expenditure of the Union. The provisions relating to both it and the Central Bank are to be found in the TFEU. Neither institution will be considered in any further detail.

**7.5**  Prior to considering the nature and functions of the EU institutions, we must first consider a further important development in the history of the EC as was: the creation of the European Union.

## The European Union

**7.6** In February 1992, the heads of state or government of the member states signed the TEU at Maastricht in the Netherlands. In addition to the changes in nomenclature, the TEU made substantial changes to the provisions of the EC Treaty itself. These included strengthening the powers of the Parliament and introducing provisions designed to lead to economic and monetary union. The first stage of this process entailed the completion of the single market and the removal of controls on the movement of capital within the EC. The second stage, which began on 1 January 1994, aimed to bring about the convergence of the European economies provided that they satisfied what have become known as the 'convergence criteria' set out in the EC Treaty. The third and final stage has entailed the establishment of a common exchange rate for member states and the use of a common currency, the Euro.

**7.7** Whilst a number of states have been in the vanguard of monetary union, eg France and Germany, not all have opted in. In the UK, for example, European monetary union has proved to be a particularly sensitive political issue. Were the UK to 'opt in', its effect would be that the UK's national currency would be phased out and replaced by the Euro. At present, however, this seems a highly unlikely development. If it were to happen, a referendum would be a necessary prerequisite as a consequence of s 6(1) and (5) (e) of the European Union Act 2011.

## The institutions of the Union

**7.8** The remainder of this chapter is given over to a consideration of the various institutions which serve the EU and to an explanation of the way in which they have been reformed now that the Lisbon Treaty has been formally ratified by the member states.

**7.9** Institutional reform has been on the European agenda for some time. Recent reform proposals included those which were to establish a Constitution for Europe. Although the relevant treaty was signed in October 2004 and subsequently ratified by the majority of the member states, it was rejected in 2005 by the peoples of France and the Netherlands in referenda votes. Since these events prevented the Constitutional Treaty's implementation, the EU embarked upon a period of reflection as to how best to take its reform agenda forward. In June 2006, the European Council requested that the incoming German presidency take the lead on the matter. During the course of that presidency (January–June 2007), various discussions and negotiations were held between member states. The Lisbon Treaty emerged as a result. In the UK, the new text was the subject of heated political debate over the question whether it was in reality very different from the Constitutional Treaty. The matter was of some practical importance not least because whereas the previous Labour Government was committed to holding a referendum on the Constitutional Treaty, it was not of the view that such a course of action was necessary in respect of the Lisbon Treaty on the ground that it did not alter the nature of the relationship between the EU and the member states.

**7.10**   In subsequent judicial review proceedings, the claimant sought a declaration that the Government had acted unlawfully by deciding not to hold a referendum in respect of the Lisbon Treaty. The claim in *R (on the application of Wheeler) v Office of the Prime Minister* (2008) (para **2.28**) was defeated on several grounds, including that promises made in relation to the Constitutional Treaty related specifically to that Treaty, not the Lisbon Treaty, and that the claimant had failed to show that the Lisbon Treaty had equivalent effect to the Constitutional Treaty.

**7.11**   The process of ratifying the Lisbon Treaty was not straightforward. The people of Ireland originally rejected the Treaty in a referendum only to change their minds when they were given a further opportunity to consider the matter. The final obstacle to ratification was removed when the Czech Republic accepted the Treaty, thereby allowing it to enter into force on 1 December 2009. In the UK, ratification of a treaty is achieved by the passing of an Act of Parliament. Thus in the case of the Lisbon Treaty, ratification occurred by virtue of the European Union (Amendment) Act 2008.

## The European Council

**7.12**   One of the key institutional changes effected by the Lisbon Treaty was the division of the former Council of Ministers into two institutions: the European Council and the Council. The former is thus a new EU institution. It is charged with the responsibility to 'provide the Union with the necessary impetus for its development' and to 'define the general political directions and priorities thereof' (art 15(1) TEU). It does not, however, have any legislative functions.

**7.13**   The European Council consists of the heads of state or government of the member states, its President, and the President of the Commission. The High Representative of the Union for Foreign Affairs and Security Policy also takes part in its work. This post and that of the President of the European Council are new creations. The latter is held by a person elected by the European Council by qualified majority vote for a term of two and a half years. The President may serve a maximum of two terms (art 15(5)) and may be removed from office during either term in the event of 'an impediment or serious misconduct' by a qualified majority vote of the European Council. The President is precluded from holding a national office. The holder of the post convenes meetings of the European Council which are held twice every six months. It is the President's role to: chair and drive forward the work of the European Council; ensure the preparation and continuity of the work of the European Council in cooperation with the President of the Commission; endeavour to facilitate cohesion and consensus within the European Council; and present a report to the European Parliament after each of the European Council's meetings. The President also represents the EU externally on issues concerning its common foreign and security policy without prejudice to the powers of the High Representative of the Union for Foreign Affairs and Security Policy.

**7.14** The High Representative of the Union for Foreign Affairs and Security Policy is, like the President, elected by the European Council by a qualified majority vote (art 18). The holder of the post presides over the Foreign Affairs configuration, and is one of the Vice Presidents of the Commission. His or her role is to conduct the Union's common foreign and security policy and to ensure consistency of its external action.

## The Council of Ministers

**7.15** By virtue of art 16 of the TEU, the Council consists of a representative of each member state at ministerial level, authorized to commit the government of that member state. Membership of the Council of Ministers is dependent upon the subject matter under discussion. Currently, there are ten different configurations. If environmental matters are being discussed, for example, then each member state will be represented in the Council by its environment minister.

**7.16** The General Affairs configuration seeks to ensure consistency in the work of the Council, and to prepare and ensure the follow-up to the meetings of the European Council in liaison with its President and the Commission (art 16(6)). The Foreign Affairs configuration seeks to develop EU foreign policy and to ensure that its external actions are consistent.

### Presidency

**7.17** The office of President of the Council is held in turn by each of the member states for a period of six months. Meetings of the Council are convened by the President (the appropriate national minister) on his own initiative, or at the request of a member state or the Commission. The presidency therefore provides a member state with the opportunity to set the agenda for the next six months. Favoured policies or initiatives in areas other than foreign affairs (the responsibility of the High Representative of the Union for Foreign Affairs and Security Policy) can be advanced, although given the brevity of the term of office and the protracted legislative process, it is likely that these will only come to fruition during the presidency of another member state. Nevertheless, the success of a presidency does tend to be judged on the basis of the initiatives brought forward whilst at the helm.

**7.18** The legislative power of the Union essentially resides in the Council although, as we shall see, the European Parliament now has a more important legislative role than was formerly the case. Unless the Treaty provides otherwise, the Council acts by a qualified majority of its members. The need for unanimity amongst the member states before action can be taken at the EU level is therefore now relatively rare. It does still exist in respect of certain sensitive matters, such as the approximation of laws relating to the establishment or functioning of the common market.

## Qualified majority voting

**7.19** Where the Council is required by the Treaty to act by qualified majority, as is often the case, the votes of each of the member states are weighted in accordance with the Protocol on transitional provisions (Protocol No 36), as specified by art 16(5) of the TEU and art 238(2) of the TFEU. Until 31 October 2014, therefore, for acts of the European Council and of the Council requiring a qualified majority vote, member states' votes are weighted as follows: Germany, France, Italy, and the UK (29 votes each); Spain and Poland (27); Romania (14); Netherlands (13); Belgium, Czech Republic, Greece, Hungary, and Portugal (12); Bulgaria, Austria, and Sweden (10); Denmark, Ireland, Lithuania, Slovakia, and Finland (7); Cyprus, Estonia, Latvia, Slovenia, and Luxembourg (4); and Malta (3). In order to be adopted, acts of the Council will require at least 255 votes (out of a total of 345) cast in favour by a majority of the members where the Treaty requires them to be adopted on a proposal from the Commission. In other cases, acts will be adopted where at least 255 votes in favour have been cast by at least two-thirds of the members. A third rule provides that where an act is to be adopted by the European Council or the Council by a qualified majority, a member of the European Council or the Council may request verification that the states voting in favour of the measure represent at least 62% of the Union's total population. If this condition is not met, the act in question must not be adopted. Thus it follows that a state which wishes to block a European Council or Council act must either achieve a blocking minority (91 votes) or rely on what has been termed the 'population safeguard'.

**7.20** The Lisbon Treaty has made further important changes to the system of qualified majority voting which will take effect from 1 November 2014. As from that date, a qualified majority will be defined as at least 55% of the members of the Council, comprising at least 15 of them, and representing at least 65% of the population of the EU (art 16(4) TEU). A blocking minority must include at least four Council members, failing which the qualified majority is deemed to have been attained.

**7.21** By way of derogation from art 16(4) of the TEU, art 238(2) of the TFEU provides that as from 1 November 2014, where the Council does not act on a proposal from the Commission or from the High Representative of the Union for Foreign Affairs and Security Policy, the qualified majority shall be defined as at least 72% of the members of the Council comprising at least 65% of the EU's population. The advantage of this system is that it will remove the need for future negotiations on the allocation of votes to member states and the definition of what amounts to a qualified majority. For the time being, however, the present weighted votes system (para **7.19**) continues to operate.

## COREPER and the Secretariat

**7.22** The Council is by its very nature unable to meet for anything much longer than several days a month. National demands on a minister's time prevent extended gatherings with European ministerial counterparts. Accordingly, the Council is assisted in its tasks by a Committee of Permanent Representatives of the Member States (COREPER) (art 240 TFEU). COREPER, as its name implies, is a permanent body of member state representatives which deals with matters that fall within the Council's remit. The fact that it is a permanent body ensures some measure of continuity in the discharge of the Council's functions, and it also provides a way of dealing with the less important matters that do not require close attention by the Council itself. In addition to COREPER, the Council is assisted by a Secretariat under the stewardship of a Secretary General and a Deputy-Secretary General.

## The Commission

**7.23** If we were to recall the threefold classification of governmental powers referred to in Chapter **2**, it would be fair to describe the European Commission as the executive of the EU. It is the unifying force within the EU, in part because unlike the Council, it is concerned with the promotion of EU as opposed to national interests and policies. The non-partisan nature of the Commission will be considered.

**7.24** Currently, the Commission consists of 27 members who are 'chosen on the grounds of their general competence and whose independence is beyond doubt'. There is therefore one Commissioner for each member state. Formerly the larger member states, France, Germany, Italy, Spain, and the UK, had two Commissioners and the remaining countries had one each. The arrangements were changed, however, due to the process of enlargement. The Commission will continue to evolve so that as from 1 November 2014, its size will be reduced to a number corresponding to two-thirds of member states unless the European Council, acting unanimously, decides to alter the number (art 17(5)). Subject to a system of equal rotation, each successive Commission will be composed so as to satisfactorily reflect the demographic and geographical range of all the member states. Commissioners must be independent in the performance of their duties and must not seek or take instructions from any government or any other body. Clearly, therefore, a Commissioner is not to be regarded as a national representative.

## The President and the Commissioners

**7.25** The President of the Commission and his fellow Commissioners are appointed in accordance with the procedure laid down in art 17 of the TEU. The European Council, acting by a qualified majority, is required to propose a candidate for President of the Commission to the European Parliament. The candidate shall be elected by the European Parliament by a majority of its members. If the candidate does not obtain the required majority, the European Council acting by a qualified majority is required to propose a new candidate to the Parliament within one month. The procedure for appointing the members of the Commission entails the drawing up of a list of persons in accordance with the proposals made by each member state. The list is then adopted by the Council in common accord with the President-elect. The President, the High Representative of the Union for Foreign Affairs and Security Policy, and the other members of the Commission are then subject as a body to a vote of consent by the Parliament. Following its approval, the Commission is appointed by the European Council, acting by a qualified majority.

**7.26** Once in office, a Commissioner will be responsible for a particular area of policy which is not unlike a ministerial portfolio. Commissioners are assisted in their task by a departmental staff and by any of the Directorates-General which fall within their particular area. In addition, the Commission as a whole is further supported by an administrative staff of approximately 25,000, many of whom are translators. Despite this departmental division in accordance with policy areas, the Commission is collectively responsible for its own acts. Decisions are taken on the basis of a simple majority of its members.

**7.27** A Commissioner's term of office lasts for a period of five years, although this may be renewed. He or she must resign, however, if the President so requests. Additionally, a Commissioner may be removed from office where a motion of censure has been passed by the European Parliament in accordance with art 234 of the TFEU (para **7.39**). In such an event, the Commission is required to resign en bloc. Alternatively, the Court of Justice may, on an application by the Council or Commission, compulsorily retire a Commissioner where he or she no longer fulfils the conditions required to perform his or her duties or has been guilty of serious misconduct (art 247 TFEU).

**7.28** Various provisions in the treaties confer upon the Commission a range of executive powers and functions. However, for present purposes, attention will focus upon art 17(1) and (2) of the TEU. These provide that the Commission shall:

- ensure the application of the Treaties, and of the measures adopted by the institutions pursuant to them;
- oversee the application of Union law under the control of the Court of Justice;
- execute the budget and manage progress;

- exercise coordinating, executive, and management functions, as laid down in the Treaties;

- ensure the Union's external representation, with the exception of the common foreign and security policy and save where the Treaties otherwise provide;

- formulate proposals on which Union legislative acts may only be adopted, save where the Treaties provide otherwise.

**7.29** The two key roles which the Commission performs are evident in art 17: the elaboration of EU policy; and the enforcement of EU law. Without seeking to deal in any great detail with the EU's legislative process, it is worth noting, however, that it is the Commission which proposes legislative measures following a process of consultation with interested parties and on the basis of advice received from its legal advisers and Directorates-General. Such proposals may be rejected or considerably amended prior to their becoming law. Nevertheless, it is from the Commission that they originate. In its role as guardian of the Treaties, the Commission has at hand the procedure laid down in art 258 of the TFEU. This entitles the Commission to issue a member state with a reasoned opinion where it believes that the state has failed to fulfil an obligation under the Treaties. Where the member state fails to comply with the reasoned opinion within the prescribed period, the Commission may bring the matter before the ECJ. Although a vast majority of alleged infringements are resolved at the informal reasoned opinion stage of the proceedings, formal referrals to the ECJ are sometimes a necessary means by which a recalcitrant member state can be brought to heel. A member state is required to comply with a ruling of the ECJ. In the event that it fails to do so, the Commission may institute further proceedings against it and the ECJ has the power by virtue of art 260(2) TFEU to impose a lump sum or penalty payment on a member state which has failed to comply with its original ruling.

## Resignation

**7.30** In January 1999, the Commission was subjected to a motion of censure in respect of allegations of fraud. The motion was defeated, but a subsequent resolution of the Parliament called for the fraud allegations to be examined more thoroughly by a committee of experts. The committee's report on *Fraud, Mismanagement and Nepotism in the European Commission* was published on 15 March 1999. It concluded that there were 'instances where Commissioners or the Commission as a whole bear responsibility for instances of fraud, irregularities or mismanagement in their services or areas of special responsibility'. Several members of the Commission, including the President at the time, Jacques Santer, were subjected to particular criticism in the report. The result was that on the evening of 15 March, the Commission took an unprecedented step: it resigned en masse.

## The Parliament

**7.31** The European Parliament is the institution which is representative of the citizens of the member states in that it is directly elected by them to exercise the powers conferred upon it by the TEU and TFEU. However, this was not always the case. Prior to 1979, when direct elections to the Parliament first took place, its members (MEPs) were selected by their national legislatures and were therefore only indirectly representative of their nation's electorate. Elections to the European Parliament are governed, in the UK, by the European Parliamentary Elections Act 2002. The Act provides for a system of proportional representation for the election of MEPs (a regional closed-list system), which is in line with other member states.

**7.32** The size and composition of the Parliament has changed as a consequence of enlargement. Article 14(2) of the TEU provides that the Parliament's membership shall not exceed 750 in addition to the President of the Commission. The representation of EU citizens is digressively proportional with no member state having fewer than six MEPs nor more than 96 seats. Formerly the Treaty itself provided for the distribution of seats amongst member states. That is now subject to an allocation rule.

**7.33** The business of the Parliament is conducted in plenary sessions and committee meetings held variously in Strasbourg, Luxembourg, and Brussels. MEPs sit in the chamber in political rather than national groupings. This practice is considered to promote integration in that the political groupings contribute to the forming of a European awareness and to the expression of the political will of EU citizens. They are formed, according to the Parliament's own procedural rules, by the simple expedient of a statement handed to the President of the Parliament which includes the name of the group and the signatures of its members. To be a recognized grouping in the Parliament, it is necessary to have at least 23 members where they are all nationals of the same member state. Smaller groupings may be recognized where their membership is drawn from different states.

**7.34** The functions of the Parliament were originally limited so that, in truth, it resembled little more than an advisory and supervisory body. However, the advent of direct elections has seen a corresponding increase in the importance and status of the Parliament. This has been further underpinned by the TEU, the Amsterdam Treaty, the Treaty of Nice, and the Lisbon Treaty, all of which have sought to enhance the role of Parliament by increasing its powers. Accordingly, it presently fulfils an advisory and consultative role in respect of a wide range of matters including, for example, the accession of new member states.

**7.35** Although it would be wrong to think of the Parliament as a legislative body in the sense of the Westminster Parliament, its participation in the legislative process has developed through the consultation, cooperation, and co-decision procedures. More recently, the Lisbon Treaty has sought to simplify matters by providing for an 'ordinary legislative procedure' and a 'special legislative procedure'. The former is, in effect, what was previously the co-decision procedure. Where the Treaties refer to the ordinary legislative procedure for the adoption of an act, the procedure set out in art 294 of the TFEU applies. That procedure commences when the Commission submits a legislative proposal to the European Parliament and the Council. It may then, depending upon the extent of agreement between the institutions, involve up to four stages. At first reading, the Parliament adopts its position and communicates it to the Council. If the Council approves the Parliament's position, the act is adopted in accordance with the wording used by the Parliament and the legislative process is complete. If, however, the Council does not approve the Parliament's position, it is required to adopt its own position and communicate it to the Parliament, along with its reasons for adopting its position. At this stage, the Commission is also required to inform the Parliament of its position.

**7.36** The second stage or reading concerns the Parliament. It is able to respond in one of a number of ways within three months of receiving the Council's communication. Thus it may approve the Council's position at first reading, in which case the act will have been adopted in accordance with the Council's wording. The same outcome also occurs if the Parliament fails to reach a decision on the communication during the relevant period. Alternatively, the Parliament may reject the Council's position by a majority of its members, in which case the act will not have been adopted and the Parliament will have effectively vetoed the measure. Finally, the Parliament may, by a majority of its members, propose amendments to the Council's position at first reading. Where this is the case, the amended text is forwarded to the Council and the Commission, which are both required to deliver an opinion on the amendments.

**7.37** Once in receipt of the Parliament's amendments, the Council, acting by a qualified majority, has three months in which to either approve all the amendments or not approve them. Where the amendments are approved, the act in question is deemed to have been adopted. If, however, not all the amendments are approved, the President of the Council, in agreement with the President of the Parliament, is required to convene a meeting of the Conciliation Committee within a six-week period. The Committee is composed of members of the Council and an equal number of members representing the Parliament. Its task is to reach agreement on a joint text. The Commission is required to take part in the Committee's proceedings and 'take all necessary initiatives' to try to reconcile the positions of the Council and Parliament. If a joint text is not approved by the Committee within six weeks of its being convened, the act is deemed not to have been adopted. If, however, the Committee does approve a joint text, both the Council and the Parliament have six weeks from the approval in which to adopt the act in the form of the joint text. A failure to do so also means that the measure has not been adopted.

**7.38** The power of the Parliament is also greater than it was originally in two other important respects. The institution is now on an equal footing with the Council and the Commission (and the member states) in that it can bring proceedings before the Court of Justice to review the legality of a Community act on the grounds of lack of competence, infringement of an essential procedural requirement, infringement of the Treaties or of any rule of law relating to their application, or misuse of powers: see art 263 of the TFEU. Moreover, the Parliament may now also seek a prior opinion from the Court of Justice as to whether an international agreement which is envisaged is compatible with the Treaties: see art 218(11) of the TFEU.

**7.39**   The European Parliament also has a supervisory role in respect of the Commission. By virtue of art 230, the Commission is required to reply orally or in writing to questions put to it by the Parliament or its members. Moreover, the Commission's annual general report on the activities of the EU, as required by art 249(2), must be published not later than one month before the opening of the session of Parliament. However, the most significant way in which the Parliament can supervise the Commission is via a motion of censure. Such a motion which, according to the Parliament's own procedural rules, may be handed to the President of the Parliament by a political group or one-tenth of the current MEPs and which must be supported by reasons, is voted on by Parliament. Article 234 of the TFEU provides that the vote must be open and that it cannot take place until at least three days after the motion of censure has been tabled. Where the vote is carried by a two-thirds majority which itself represents a majority of the MEPs, the members of the Commission must, as previously stated, resign en bloc. This is an important sanction for the Parliament to impose. It should be noted, however, that it does not take immediate effect. A Commission against which a motion of censure has been carried may still continue to transact business until they are replaced in accordance with the procedure laid down in art 17 of the TEU.

## The Court of Justice of the EU and the General Court

**7.40**   Concerns about the increasing workload of the Court of Justice of the European Communities (ECJ) (as it then was), particularly in the light of enlargement, led to reforms being made to the European legal system by the Treaty of Nice. The Lisbon Treaty has also made some further changes, including a change in nomenclature. Thus what was formerly the Court of Justice of the European Communities is now the Court of Justice of the European Union.

**7.41**   The Court of Justice (ECJ) sits in Luxembourg. It consists of one judge per member state (art 19(2) TEU). Although it may sit as a full court, art 251 of the TFEU permits it to sit in chambers or a Grand Chamber in accordance with the rules laid down in the Statute of the Court of Justice of the EU.

### Advocates-General

**7.42**   The Court is assisted in its task of interpreting and applying the EU treaties by eight Advocates-General. As Professor Hartley has noted, 'although not required by law, this normally includes one from each of the big countries'. This number may be increased, however, by the Council of Ministers acting unanimously following a request from the Court. The role of the Advocate-General is thus to provide the Court with reasoned submissions on those cases which it hears. These submissions appear in full when cases are reported in the law reports, although it must be stressed that the Court is under no obligation to decide a case in accordance with the submissions received. The Court can and sometimes does take a different view on a case to that articulated by an Advocate-General.

## Qualifications

**7.43** By virtue of art 19 of the TEU and art 253 of the TFEU, judges and Advocates-General are chosen from persons whose independence and impartiality is beyond doubt. They must possess the qualifications required for appointment to the highest judicial offices in their own countries or be jurisconsults of recognized competence. They are appointed by common accord of the governments of the member states for a term of six years, after consultation with a panel established under art 255 of the TFEU. The panel consists of seven persons, all of whom have previously sat as judges of the Court of Justice and the General Court, or as members of national supreme courts or who are lawyers of recognized competence. The role of the panel is to provide an opinion on a candidate's suitability to perform the duties of a judge or Advocate-General, thus informing the appointment process. Retiring judges and Advocates-General are eligible for reappointment.

**7.44** In order to ensure continuity in the work of the Court, there is a partial replacement of judges and Advocates-General every three years. Thus on such occasions, half of the Court and the Advocates-General will have three years' experience, assuming that they have not already been reappointed, and the remaining half will be new to their posts. The judges of the Court elect a President from among their number who holds the post for three years. He is eligible for re-election. Article 253 of the TFEU further provides that the Court of Justice shall establish its Rules of Procedure and that these will require the approval of the Council acting by a qualified majority.

## Functions and jurisdiction of the ECJ

**7.45** The primary function of the ECJ is to ensure that, in the interpretation and application of the Treaty, the law is observed. In performing this task, the Court may be required to sit in judgment on whether a member state has failed to fulfil an obligation under the Treaty. It may do so where the matter has been brought to its attention by the Commission (art 258 TFEU) or by another member state (art 259 TFEU). Alternatively, the Court has jurisdiction to:

- rule on actions brought by a member state, an institution or a natural legal person;

- give preliminary rulings on the interpretation of Union law or the validity and interpretation of acts adopted by the institutions;

- rule in other cases provided for in the Treaties.

**7.46**  A national court has the discretion to make a referral under art 267 of the TFEU where it considers that a ruling on a point of European law is necessary in order for it to give judgment. If, however, there is no judicial remedy (appeal or review) under national law against the court's decision, art 267 requires that the matter shall be brought before the ECJ. The jurisdiction conferred by art 267 is therefore important in that it represents a means by which European law can be given a consistent interpretation throughout the member states. An art 267 referral is not, however, an invitation to the ECJ to decide a particular case. The national courts retain 'the sole jurisdiction to find the facts in the main proceedings' (per Lord Hope in *R v Secretary of State for Transport, ex p Factortame (No 5)* (1999)). Nevertheless, where a case turns on a point of European law, the ECJ's ruling will clearly affect the outcome reached by the national court.

**7.47**  In the case of *Arsenal Football Club v Reed* (2003), which concerned civil proceedings brought by the football club for infringement of trade mark and passing off, the trial judge made a referral to the ECJ which concerned the construction of the Trade Mark Directive (EEC 89/104). When the case came back before him, however, he concluded that the ECJ had disagreed with the findings of fact which he had made and that since it had thereby 'exceeded its jurisdiction', he was not bound by that court's conclusion. Accordingly, he came to a different conclusion to that reached by the ECJ. On appeal, his decision was reversed by the CA. In the judgment of that court, although the judge had been entitled to disregard any conclusion reached by the ECJ in so far as it was based upon a factual background inconsistent with his judgment, the ECJ had not disregarded his conclusions of fact and had actually considered an issue on which he had not come to any conclusion.

## The General Court

**7.48**  Prior to a change in nomenclature effected by the Lisbon Treaty, the court attached to the ECJ with the jurisdiction to initially hear and determine cases was known as the Court of First Instance. It is now known as the General Court (GC). By virtue of art 256 of the TFEU, the jurisdiction of the General Court relates to:

1. actions or proceedings referred to in arts 263, 265, 268, 270, and 272 of the TFEU (with the exception of those assigned to a specialized court set up under art 257 and those reserved in the Statute for the Court of Justice);

2. actions or proceedings brought against decisions of the specialized courts set up under art 257; and

3. questions referred for a preliminary ruling under art 275, in specific areas laid down by the Statute.

Decisions given by the General Court under (i) may be subject to a right of appeal to the ECJ on a point of law only. Decisions given under (ii) and (iii) may exceptionally be subject to review by the ECJ where there is a serious risk of the unity or consistency of Union law being affected.

**7.49**  By virtue of art 254 of the TFEU, the number of judges of the General Court (GC) is determined by the Statute of the Court of Justice, which may also provide for the GC to be assisted by Advocates-General. The independence of the judges of the GC must be beyond doubt and they must also be persons who possess the ability required for appointment to high judicial office. They are appointed for a term of six years, although retiring members are eligible for reappointment. The members of the GC are required to elect a President from among their number for a period of three years, although he may be re-elected. The GC must also appoint a Registrar and establish its Rules of Procedure in agreement with the ECJ. Such Rules require the approval of the Council, acting by a qualified majority.

## Specialized courts

**7.50**  The reference to 'specialized courts' in (ii) (para **7.48**) hints at a further development in the legal system of the Union: the establishment of specialized courts to hear and determine at first instance certain classes of action or proceeding brought in specific areas (art 257 TFEU). The decision to establish a specialized court will be taken by the European Parliament and the Council acting in accordance with the ordinary legislative procedure either on a proposal from the Commission (and after consulting the ECJ) or at the request of the ECJ (and after consulting the Commission). Article 257 further provides that the regulation establishing a specialized court will lay down the rules on the organization of the court and the extent of its jurisdiction. Members of the specialized courts will be chosen from persons whose independence is beyond doubt and who possess the ability required for appointment to judicial office. Appointments are made by the Council, acting unanimously. Like the GC, the courts will establish their Rules of Procedure in agreement with the ECJ and such rules will require the approval of the Council, acting by qualified majority. Decisions given by the specialized courts may be subject to a right of appeal to the GC on a point of law. However, a right of appeal on matters of fact will also be allowed where the regulation establishing the court so provides.

# FURTHER READING

Arnul, A 'The European Court and Judicial Objectivity: A reply to Professor Hartley' (1996) 112 LQR 411.

Birkinshaw, P 'Constitutions, Constitutionalism and the State' (2005) 11 EPL 31.

Craig, P 'The ECJ and Ultra Vires Action: A conceptual analysis' (2011) 48 CML Rev 395.

Dyèvre, A 'The Constitutionalism of the European Union: Discourse, present, future and facts' (2005) 30 EL Rev 165.

Hartley, T C 'The European Court, Judicial Objectivity and the Constitution of the European Union' (1996) 112 LQR 95.

Hartley, T C *The Foundations of European Union Law* (7th edn, 2010) OUP.

Johnston, A 'Judicial reform and the Treaty of Nice' (2001) 38 CML Rev 499.

Kietz, D and Maurer, A 'The European Parliament in Treaty Reform: Predefining IGCs through Interinstitutional agreements' (2007) 13 ELJ 20.

Kilbey, I 'The Interpretation of Article 260 TFEU (ex 228 EC)' (2010) 35 EL Rev 370.

Kokott, J and Rüth, A 'The European Convention and its Draft Treaty establishing a Constitution for Europe: Appropriate answers to the Laeken questions?' (2003) 40 CML Rev 1315.

Komarek, J 'In the court(s) we trust? On the need for hierarchy and differentiation in the preliminary ruling procedure' (2007) 32 EL Rev 165.

Lenaerts, K, Arts, D, Maselis, I, and Bray, R *Procedural Law of the European Union* (2nd edn, 2006) Sweet & Maxwell.

Lenaerts, K Van Nuffel, P, Bray, R, and Cambien, N *European Union Law* (3rd edn, 2011) Sweet & Maxwell.

Mathijsen, P S R F *A Guide to European Union Law* (10th edn, 2010) Sweet & Maxwell.

Mehde, V 'Responsibility and Accountability in the European Commission' (2003) 40 CML Rev 423.

Munro, C *Studies in Constitutional Law* (2nd edn, 1999) Butterworths, chapter 6.

Pollard, D, Parpworth, N, and Hughes, D *Constitutional and Administrative Law: Text with Materials* (4th edn, 2007) OUP.

Shaw, J 'The Treaty of Nice: Legal and constitutional implications' (2001) 7 EPL 195.

Shaw, J 'Europe's Constitutional Future' [2005] PL 132.

Slynn, G 'The Court of Justice of the European Communities' (1984) 33 ICLQ 409.

Steiner, J and Woods, L *Textbook on EU Law* (10th edn, 2009) OUP.

Tridimas, T 'The Court of Justice and Judicial Activism' (1996) 21 EL Rev 199.

## SELF-TEST QUESTIONS

1 Why were the European Communities formed?

2 What significance lies in renaming the EEC the EC, and then renaming the EC the EU?

3   What is the role of the Commission? To what extent is the Commission accountable for its actions?

4   What is the significance of the voting system used by the Council?

5   How has the legislative role of the European Parliament developed over time?

6   Is it correct to describe the ECJ as being an appeal court?

7   How significant are the Lisbon Treaty reforms to the EU institutions?

# 8 The structure of the United Kingdom and devolution

## SUMMARY

The first part of this chapter traces the historical development of the United Kingdom. In the second part, devolution is considered. This involves describing the events which led to the enactment of the devolution legislation in 1998, and considering the key provisions in that legislation. The chapter concludes by taking account of the mechanisms which have been put in place to ensure efficient working relationships between the UK Government and the devolved administrations.

## The structure of the United Kingdom

**8.1** Much has been written about the constitutional history of the UK. Limits of space, however, preclude anything other than the briefest outline of events which have led to the creation of the UK, ie the union of England, Wales, Scotland, and Northern Ireland.

### Wales

**8.2** For centuries Wales was a country consisting of a number of minor kingdoms united by a common language and culture. Attempts were made by various Welsh leaders to unite the country through military conquest, but all proved to be unsuccessful. The military conquest of Wales, or at least that part under the control of Llewelyn of Gruffudd, was achieved by Edward I in 1283. Thereafter, the principality was ruled in the name of the prince whereas the rest of Wales was under the control of a collection of princes and noblemen. During the next 200 years, English influence over Wales strengthened. However, it was not until the reign of Henry VIII that a union between the two countries was achieved. In 1536, the English Parliament passed the Laws in Wales Act. This guaranteed that the Welsh would enjoy all those freedoms, liberties, rights, and privileges enjoyed by the King's subjects in his other dominions. It provided for the representation of the Welsh constituencies in the HC. The Act also provided that English would be the official language to be used in matters pertaining to the law. In 1543, a further Act was passed which established, in each Welsh county, a county court and a sheriff, coroners, and Justices of the Peace. Courts of Great Sessions were also established to administer English law. The Act made them subject to the jurisdiction of the Council of Wales.

**8.3** In the 19th and 20th centuries, several important events occurred which form the background to Welsh devolution. Welsh nationalism became closely related to the rise of religious nonconformity in Wales during the 19th century. The desire, however, was not to have home rule for Wales. Instead, it was the disestablishment of the Church of England in Wales which was eventually achieved in 1914. In terms of the recognition of Wales as a separate political entity, this started to happen following the Second World War. Thus in 1948, a new Council of Wales was created by the Labour Government to act in an advisory capacity. In 1955, Cardiff was officially recognized as the capital of Wales. The Welsh Office emerged as a separate government department in 1965 along with the post of Secretary of State for Wales. Then in 1967, Parliament passed the Welsh Language Act. This provides that Welsh may be spoken in any legal proceedings in Wales by any of the parties to the proceedings, including witnesses. It further provides that a minister may by order prescribe that a Welsh version or a part-Welsh, part-English version of an official document made under an Act be produced.

**8.4** In the 1970s, Welsh devolution became an important political issue. The background to the present arrangements will be considered (paras **8.18–8.19**).

## Scotland

**8.5** Unlike Wales, Scotland managed to resist English attempts at conquest during the Middle Ages. It retained its independence and its own monarchy until 1603, when James VI of Scotland acceded to the throne of England on the death of Elizabeth I. From that point onward, the Crowns of England and Scotland were united. Despite this royal unification, Scotland retained its own Parliament. That Parliament was, like its English counterpart, prepared to offer the Crown to William and Mary in 1688 provided that the new monarchs accepted that from that point onward, Parliament was supreme. In the years that followed, relations between the Scottish and English Parliaments became increasingly strained. However, as a consequence of negotiations between representatives of the two Parliaments, it was agreed that both the Scottish and English Parliaments should be abolished, and that in their place, there should be established a Parliament of Great Britain. This was achieved by the Union with Scotland Act 1706 (an English statute) and the Union with England Act 1707 (a Scottish statute), collectively known as the Acts of Union.

**8.6** The Acts of Union provided for the union of the two kingdoms of England and Scotland. The throne was to pass to the House of Hanover in the event that Queen Anne died without heirs. The Parliament of Great Britain established by the Union was to include 16 Scottish peers in the HL and 45 elected representatives in the HC. Scottish private law was preserved by the Union as were the Scottish courts. All laws in either kingdom which were contrary to or inconsistent with the articles of the Union were thereby abolished.

**8.7** The Union between England and Scotland which was created in 1707 has continued until the present day. From time to time events such as the Jacobite uprising in 1745 have constituted a threat to the Union, but it has remained intact. In part this may be due to the fact that uniformity has not necessarily been a feature of the Union. Thus in certain important areas such as the legal system, education, and local government, Scotland has remained distinct from England. In order to preserve that distinctiveness, it has been necessary for the Westminster Parliament to pass Acts that apply solely in Scotland. These are apparent from the short title of the Act where Scotland is specifically referred to, eg Scottish Enterprise Act 1999. Sometimes, the reference to Scotland may be in parenthesis, eg Registered Establishments (Scotland) Act 1998. Alternatively, Acts of Parliament may be stated not to apply in Scotland.

**8.8** In terms of the representation of Scottish interests at UK government level, a Secretary of State for Scotland was appointed in the first post-Union government. However, following the events of 1745, that practice was discontinued and effective political power was exercised by the Lord Advocate, the principal law officer in Scotland. In 1885, the office of Secretary for Scotland was re-established and by 1928, the holder of the post enjoyed cabinet status as Secretary of State for Scotland. In the years since this development, the Scottish Office came to play an increasingly important role in matters relating to Scotland. Prior to the Scotland Act 1998, a certain amount of devolution had already occurred, in that the Scottish Office had taken responsibility for matters such as higher education and the arts. However, this was devolution of an administrative rather than a legislative kind.

## Northern Ireland

**8.9** Northern Ireland has only existed as a separate entity since the 1920s when the Irish Free State was established. Prior to this, it formed part of an Ireland which had been subject to English, and following the Acts of Union with Scotland, British influence since the 12th century. In 1720, for example, the British Parliament passed the Declaratory Act in which it was declared that it had the power to legislate for Ireland. The Act was repealed in 1782, but a legislative Union between Britain and Ireland was established at the end of the 18th century. As with the Union between England and Scotland, it was achieved by both the British and Irish Parliaments passing Acts (in the case of the British Parliament, the Union with Ireland Act 1800). By virtue of art 1, the United Kingdom of Great Britain and Ireland was established. Irish representation in what was now the UK Parliament was provided for in arts 3 and 4.

**8.10** During the course of the 19th century, Irish issues were never very far from the top of the political agenda. Catholic emancipation, the disestablishment of the Irish Church, and Home Rule were all much debated in Parliament, as were the Bills which sought to give effect to them. In the case of Home Rule, however, such Bills were invariably defeated.

**8.11** In 1920, Parliament passed the Government of Ireland Act. The purpose of this Act was, according to its long title, 'to provide for the better government of Ireland'. In order to achieve this purpose, the Act established separate Parliaments for Northern and Southern Ireland. Northern Ireland was to consist of: the parliamentary counties of Antrim, Armagh, Down, Fermanagh, Londonderry, and Tyrone and the boroughs of Belfast and Londonderry. Southern Ireland comprised the remainder of Ireland. The legislative powers of the Irish Parliaments were determined by s 4 of the 1920 Act. The Act adopted an approach which has been repeated in more recent devolution legislation, ie to prescribe those matters in respect of which the Parliaments did not have the power to make laws. The Southern Ireland Parliament never came into existence because in 1922 the signing of an Anglo-Irish Treaty resulted in the creation of the Irish Free State. Initially the state was regarded by Britain as having dominion status, although in 1937 Eire was declared to be a sovereign independent state by its own constitution. In 1949 it was decided that Eire would henceforth be known as the Republic of Ireland. In the Ireland Act of the same year, Parliament recognized that the former Eire had now ceased to be part of His Majesty's dominions. Moreover, s 2 of the 1949 Act declared that, despite its independence, the Republic of Ireland was not to be regarded as a foreign country.

**8.12** The dominion status of Northern Ireland was unaffected by Irish independence. The Northern Ireland Parliament continued to legislate in accordance with the powers conferred by the Government of Ireland Act 1920, until the resumption of direct rule by Westminster in 1972. This occurred as a response to the escalation of terrorist violence within Northern Ireland in the late 1960s and early 1970s. In 1973, Parliament passed the Northern Ireland Assembly Act which provided for the establishment of an Assembly and for elections to the assembly. During the same year, it also passed the Northern Ireland Constitution Act 1973 which made provision for the government of Northern Ireland. The status of Northern Ireland was made plain by the terms of s 1 of the Act. This provided that:

> *in no event will Northern Ireland or any part of it cease to be part of Her Majesty's dominions and of the United Kingdom without the consent of the majority of the people in Northern Ireland voting in a poll.*

However, the initiative was short-lived and the Assembly was dissolved the following year by the Northern Ireland Act 1974.

**8.13** Further attempts were made to try and ease the tensions between the Unionist and Nationalist communities in Northern Ireland during the years 1974–85. In 1985, the British and Irish Governments signed the Anglo-Irish Agreement which was designed to encourage constructive dialogue with regard to Northern Ireland. In the years that have followed, considerable progress has been made towards securing peace in

Northern Ireland. In 1994, for example, the IRA and the Unionist paramilitary organizations declared a ceasefire. Successive British Governments sought to get the political parties round the negotiating table. These efforts resulted in the Belfast Agreement being reached (see paras **8.60** and **8.61**).

## Devolution

**8.14** Professor Bogdanor has argued that devolution 'is a peculiarly British contribution to politics'. In support of this view, he contends that devolution was evident in the suggestions made by Edmund Burke in 1774 that the legislatures of the American states could have legislative power in respect of domestic matters whilst remaining subordinate to the Westminster Parliament. Moreover, Home Rule for Ireland, which became W E Gladstone's preferred solution to the Irish Question in the late 19th century, was nothing more than 'the policy of devolution to an Irish legislative body sitting in Dublin'.

**8.15** In more recent times, devolution has been an important issue for the people of Scotland and Wales. It has been the demand of many who have wanted to be governed by a Parliament based within their own country rather than by a Parliament based in London. But what is meant by the term 'devolution'? Professor Bogdanor has contended that:

> The process of devolution involves the dispersal of power from a superior to an inferior political authority. More precisely, it consists of three elements: the transfer to a subordinate elected body on a geographical basis, of functions at present exercised by Parliament. These functions may be either legislative, the power to make laws, or executive, the power to make decisions within an already established legal framework.

**8.16** This definition highlights an important feature of devolution, namely that it involves the transfer of power from the Westminster Parliament to a subordinate legislature. Under this arrangement, the Westminster Parliament remains supreme. The powers of the subordinate legislature are limited; in no sense can they be described as being equal to those of the Westminster Parliament. Although the legal and political implications of devolution are wide-ranging, the effect of the transfer of power is not to create a federal state. For that to happen, there must be a division of supreme power between central and regional government.

**8.17** Professor Bogdanor's definition does not quite tell the full story, however, since as we shall see, devolution may involve the transfer of functions from central government to a subordinate executive in addition to or as an alternative to the transfer of legislative power from one Parliament to another. In other words, devolution may be 'executive', 'legislative', or both.

## Welsh devolution

**8.18** The devolution of power to a Welsh Assembly has occupied positions both high and low on the political agenda in the last 40 years or so. In 1973, the Royal Commission on the Constitution (established in 1969) recommended that there should be some form of devolved power to Wales. Its preferred option was a 100-strong Welsh Senate with legislative powers in respect of certain specified matters. In 1974 and then again in 1975, the Labour Government produced White Papers in which devolution proposals for both Wales and Scotland were discussed. Essentially the proposals for Wales envisaged a directly elected Assembly with executive as opposed to legislative powers. A Bill was subsequently introduced in Parliament and, following its initial defeat, it eventually received Royal Assent in July 1978. However, the Wales Act 1978 never took effect because nearly 80% of those who voted in the ensuing referendum voted against it.

**8.19** The devolution issue was returned to once again by the Labour Party whilst in opposition. In its manifesto prior to the general election of May 1997, the party committed itself to meeting the demand for decentralization of power to Wales. Following its success at the polls, the new Labour Government secured the passage of the Referendums (Scotland and Wales) Act 1997 and published its proposals in a White Paper entitled *A Vote for Wales: The Government's Proposals for a Welsh Assembly*. The turnout of only 50% in the subsequent referendum suggested, perhaps, that attitudes in Wales towards a Welsh Assembly had not really changed very much in the 20 years that had passed since the rejection of the Wales Act in 1978. Nevertheless, since a fraction over half of those who voted did so in support of an Assembly, the Government had a mandate to proceed with Welsh devolution. The Government of Wales Bill was therefore introduced before Parliament and, despite Conservative opposition, it received Royal Assent on 31 July 1998.

## National Assembly for Wales

**8.20** Section 1 of the Government of Wales Act 1998 established a single body corporate known as the National Assembly for Wales or Cynulliad Cenedlaethol Cymru. Originally, therefore, no distinction was made between the legislature and the executive. Although a de facto distinction rapidly emerged in practice following the first election on 6 May 1999, the Richard Commission recommended formally splitting the single body corporate into a National Assembly (deliberative body) and a Welsh Assembly Government (executive body). This has now been achieved by the Government of Wales Act 2006: see ss 1 and 45 of the Act.

**8.21** The Assembly is made up of one member (AM) for each Assembly constituency and four members for each Assembly electoral region. By virtue of s 2 of the 2006 Act, Assembly constituencies are the Welsh Parliamentary constituencies. There are five electoral regions as specified in SI 2006/1041, Sch 2. The Assembly therefore has 60 elected members: 40 representing Assembly constituencies and 20 representing Assembly regions. Unlike the Westminster Parliament, elections for the Assembly take place every four years. The most recent election took place on 5 May 2011.

**8.22** Those entitled to vote in an Assembly constituency have two votes. One vote, the constituency vote, is used to elect an Assembly member for the constituency. The other, the electoral region vote, is used to elect a member of the Assembly for the region. The latter vote may be given for an individual candidate or, in a departure from traditional electoral practice, for a list of candidates not exceeding 12 which has been submitted to the regional returning officer by a registered political party. Constituency Assembly members are elected in accordance with the Westminster model, ie on the basis of a simple majority. A member for an electoral region, however, is elected on the basis of a proportional representation system of voting as described in the 2006 Act (ss 6–9).

**8.23** Formerly it was possible for an unsuccessful constituency candidate to be returned as a regional list member of the Assembly. What Hadfield has termed, a 'back-door' election is now no longer possible because s 7 of the 2006 Act precludes a regional list from containing the name of a person who is also a constituency candidate.

## Welsh Assembly Government

**8.24** Section 45 of the 2006 Act provides that there is to be a Welsh Assembly Government, or Llywodraeth Cynwilliad Cymru, whose members consist of: the First Minister (FM); the Welsh Ministers; the Counsel General to the Welsh Assembly Government; and the Deputy Welsh Ministers. Jones and Williams have noted that the name 'Welsh Assembly Government' caused some controversy in that, ironically, it was seen as blurring the distinction between legislative and executive functions. However, as they point out, the 'difficulty is ameliorated by the collective nomenclature "Welsh Ministers"'.

**8.25** The FM is appointed by the Queen after having been nominated by the Assembly pursuant to s 47 of the 2006 Act. A number of events can act as the catalyst for a nomination. These include: the holding of a general election; the Assembly resolving that the Welsh ministers no longer enjoy its confidence; the resignation of the FM; or his or her death or permanent inability to act as FM. The Presiding Officer of the Assembly is required to recommend the appointment of the nominee to the Queen. The power to appoint the Welsh ministers lies with the FM, subject to the Queen's approval (s 48). The FM also enjoys the power to remove a Welsh minister. Welsh ministers may resign at any time and must do so where the Assembly has resolved that they no longer enjoy its confidence.

**8.26** The Counsel General (CG) is the legal adviser to the Welsh Assembly Government and its representative in the courts. In effect, the holder of the post performs a role equivalent to that of the Attorney-General in the UK Government. The CG is appointed by the Queen on the recommendation of the FM (s 49). He or she may be removed from office by the Queen on the recommendation of the FM. The FM may not recommend either appointment or removal without the agreement of the Assembly. The CG may be a member of the Assembly but there is no legal requirement that they must be. He or she may resign at any time and they will cease to hold office on the appointment of a new FM. They may, however, be reappointed.

8.27  The FM has the power to appoint Deputy Welsh ministers from among the Assembly members to assist the FM, a Welsh minister or the CG in the exercise of their functions subject to the Queen's approval (s 50). A Deputy Welsh minister may be removed from office by the FM and may resign at any time. Resignation must take place where the Assembly has resolved that the Welsh ministers no longer enjoy its confidence. There is a statutory limit of 12 on the number of persons who may be Welsh ministers (either Welsh Ministers or Deputy Welsh ministers) at any one time (s 51). Since the FM and CG are not included in the number, the maximum size of a Welsh Assembly Government is 14.

## Law-making powers

8.28  Under the Government of Wales Act 1998, law-making powers were vested in the Welsh Assembly. They were, however, limited to the making of delegated rather than primary legislation. In the White Paper, *Better Governance for Wales*, it was acknowledged that the Assembly's legislative powers were inadequate. Accordingly, those powers are to be strengthened in what Hazell has termed 'three crabwise steps'.

### Stage one

8.29  This stage was achieved not through legislation but through a revision of Devolution Guidance Note 9, *Post-Devolution Primary Legislation Affecting Wales*. In that document, the UK Government agreed that parliamentary Bills 'should be drafted in a way which gives the Assembly wider and more permissive powers to determine the detail of how the provisions should be implemented in Wales'. In effect, therefore, the intention was to make greater use of framework legislation for Wales at Westminster. This extra-statutory development was undoubtedly important. However, we must also consider stages two and three, both of which have a statutory footing.

### Stage two

8.30  Part 3 of the Government of Wales Act 2006 empowers the Assembly to make a new type of subordinate legislation known as 'Assembly Measures' (s 93). A proposed Assembly Measure is enacted by being passed by the Assembly and approved by Her Majesty in

Council (as opposed to being granted Royal Assent). It may make any provision that could be made by an Act of Parliament. However, it will not be law to the extent to which it falls outside the Assembly's legislative competence (s 94). The scope of that competence is set out in Sch 5 to the 2006 Act. This specifies various 'matters' within 20 'fields' in respect of which the Assembly may legislate. The fields include the following: agriculture, fisheries, forestry and rural development; culture; economic development; education and training; environment; food; health and health services; local government; National Assembly for Wales; public administration; social welfare; tourism; and town and country planning. As originally enacted, Pt I of Sch 5 only specified various 'matters' in relation to one of these 'fields', field 13 on the National Assembly for Wales. 'Matters' may be added to, varied, or removed from Pt I of Sch 5 by Orders in Council, as can 'fields'. In other words, s 95 of the 2006 Act provides a mechanism by which the Assembly's competence to make Assembly Measures can be extended, restricted, or otherwise amended by the making of Legislative Competence Orders in Council.

8.31 Legislative Competence Orders (LCOs) thus represent a new form of Order in Council (see para **9.58**). A proposal for a draft Order may be received from the Welsh Assembly Government, a committee of the National Assembly for Wales, or from an individual AM. The draft will then be subject to scrutiny both at the Assembly and in Westminster by the Welsh Affairs Select Committee. In both cases, the scrutiny focuses upon the scope of the proposed LCO, its clarity and precision, and whether the legislative competence can or should be devolved under the terms of the 2006 Act. As of 4 April 2011, the Welsh Affairs Select Committee had reported on ten proposed LCOs. The HC Justice Committee has noted that there has been some criticism of the scrutiny of draft LCOs, in part because the process is seen as being overly complex: see *Devolution: A Decade On* (2009), HC 529-I. Concerns have also been expressed about the role of the Secretary of State for Wales in that even if a draft LCO has been approved by its scrutineers, he retains the discretion whether or not to lay the Order before both Houses of Parliament. Since the 2006 Act is silent on the matter, the Justice Committee has recommended that the Secretary of State produce a protocol outlining the principles which would inform his decision and setting out a maximum timescale within which a decision should be reached.

## Stage three

8.32 The third stage in the process of enhancing the Assembly's legislative powers is set out in Part 4 of the 2006 Act. This confers a power on the Assembly to make laws known as 'Acts of the National Assembly for Wales'. Proposed Acts will be known as Bills and a Bill will only become an Act of the Assembly once it has been passed by the Assembly and received Royal Assent (s 107). In short, therefore, Pt 4 is concerned with the Assembly's power to make primary legislation.

8.33 The 'Assembly Act' provisions of the 2006 Act did not come into force automatically. Rather, they were subject to the need for a referendum and a majority vote in their favour. This was held on 3 March 2011. Although the turn-out was not high (just over

35%), crucially, nearly 63.5% of those who voted answered the referendum question in the affirmative. Accordingly, the Assembly now has primary law-making powers. In its legislative programme for 2011–12, the Welsh Government was therefore able, unlike its predecessors, to propose the enactment of certain Bills.

**8.34** The legislative competence of the Assembly to make Acts is, however, limited by s 108 of the 2006 Act to the *subjects* specified in Pt 1 of Sch 7 and the exceptions identified therein, as amended by the National Assembly for Wales (Legislative Competence) (Amendment of Schedule 7 to the Government of Wales Act 2006) Order 2010, SI 2010/2968. There are 20 subject areas set out in the Schedule which mirror the 20 'fields' in Sch 5. Not all the subjects have exceptions: see, for example, environment and housing. Others, however, do. Thus, for example, in the case of local government, the National Assembly does not have the power to make Acts in respect of a number of matters, including: local government franchise; electoral registration and administration; anti-social behaviour orders; and Sunday trading.

## Committees

**8.35** The Government of Wales Act 1998 was prescriptive as to the committees which had to be established by the Assembly. Thus, in addition to the Executive Committee, it provided for the establishment of the following statutory committees: subject committees; a subordinate legislation scrutiny committee; an audit committee; and regional committees. The 2006 Act is less prescriptive in that other than an audit committee (s 30), the establishment of committees is made a matter for the Assembly's standing orders (s 28). Committees have the power to appoint sub-committees. The membership, chairing and procedure of both must be specified in standing orders. A non-Assembly member is not permitted to be a member of either type of committee.

**8.36** Given the numbers of committees and Assembly members, it is not uncommon for members to sit on more than one committee. Formerly Welsh ministers were able to sit as a member of a committee. This is now no longer the case. Had the Government accepted an increase in the size of the Assembly from 60 to 80 members as the Richard Commission recommended, the task of scrutinizing the Welsh Assembly Government's actions may have been made a little easier. However, that recommendation was rejected.

## Developing devolution in Wales

**8.37** In a document entitled *Putting Wales First: A Partnership for the People of Wales* (October 2000), the Welsh Assembly Government committed itself to establishing an independent commission into the powers and electoral arrangements of the National Assembly so as to ensure that it was able to operate in the best interests of the Welsh people. In the spring of 2004, that commission, under the chairmanship of Lord Richard, published a report, *The Powers and Electoral Arrangements of the National Assembly for Wales*, in which it set out its vision for further developing devolution in Wales. This included: conferring the power on the Welsh Assembly to make primary legislation in respect of devolved matters and for the Westminster Parliament to legislate for Wales in respect of reserved matters (see the Scottish devolution model); increasing the size of the Assembly from 60 to 80 members; and changing the electoral system to the single transferable vote. Although not all of the Richard Commission's recommendations were accepted by the Government, the report did stimulate further debate on Welsh devolution and led to the publication of a White Paper, *Better Governance for Wales* (Cm 6582), in June 2005. This in turn led to the enactment of the Government of Wales Act 2006.

8.38   Trench has contended that the 2006 Act is a 'carefully-crafted political tool, designed to maximize support for incremental devolution while not going beyond what was acceptable to anti-devolutionists in the Labour Party'. In his opinion, the approach which it takes is the opposite of what the Richard Commission advocated in that:

> While the Richard Commission set out a clear path to a defined goal, the Act opens a door for a journey – but one for which the destination, the duration and even the route to be taken are unknown. Instead of a route map, it is a right to roam.

8.39   Although the third stage of Welsh devolution has now been completed, it remains possible for the Westminster Parliament to continue to legislate for Wales in areas other than the 20 set out in Sch 7. It follows, therefore, that full Welsh devolution can only be achieved by making further statutory provision for additional stages in the process.

## Scottish devolution

8.40   The movement for the devolution of government in Scotland developed in the 1960s along with that which sought devolution for Wales. It received a boost from the Royal Commission on the Constitution 1969–73 which expressed support for devolution in its majority report (the Kilbrandon Report). In 1977, a Labour Government which was dependent upon the support of Liberal and Scottish and Welsh Nationalist MPs to remain in office introduced the Scotland Bill before Parliament. The Bill, which provided for the creation of a Scottish Assembly with devolved legislative powers, received Royal Assent in July 1978. However, devolution did not take immediate effect. Instead, it was only to be instituted following a referendum of the Scottish people. An amendment carried during the passage of the Bill ensured that at least 40% of the electorate had to vote 'yes' for devolution to occur. In the event, although the majority of those who did vote were in favour of devolution, they only constituted 32.9% of the electorate. Thus the Act was repealed by order in June 1979.

**8.41** The desire for change did not cease despite this setback. Instead, energies were channelled into a cross-party campaign for devolution led by the Scottish Constitutional Convention. In 1995, the Convention published a report entitled *Scotland's Parliament: Scotland's Right*, which set out its proposals for a Scottish Parliament. This became a reality following the election of the Labour Government in May 1997 and the subsequent passing of the Scotland Act 1998.

## The Scottish Parliament

**8.42** Section 1 of the Scotland Act 1998 established the Scottish Parliament. As with the Welsh Assembly, it is made up of constituency and regional members. Constituency members are elected by simple majority, whereas regional members are elected under the additional member system of proportional representation. The electoral regions are the eight European parliamentary constituencies, each of which is represented by seven members. The Scottish electorate, like its Welsh counterpart, has two votes to cast at an ordinary election: one vote for a constituency member and one vote for a regional member, the identity of whom is determined either according to a registered political party's regional list, or on the basis that they are an individual regional candidate. The Scottish Parliament therefore consists of 129 members: 73 constituency members and 56 regional members.

**8.43** The Scotland Act 1998, as originally enacted, provided for a direct link between the constituencies for the Scottish Parliament and those for the HC. It followed, therefore, that were the Boundary Commission for Scotland to recommend a reduction in the number of Scottish MPs at Westminster, this would lead to an automatic reduction in the size of the Scottish Parliament. Accordingly in December 2001, the Government launched a public consultation on this issue. The majority of the respondents were in favour of the Scottish Parliament retaining its present size and the Government therefore committed itself to bring forward legislation to ensure that this would happen. The Scottish Parliament (Constituencies) Act 2004 thus removes the link between the constituencies for the Scottish Parliament and the HC and ensures that any future review of the former will take place separately from any review of the latter.

**8.44** Members of the Scottish Parliament (MSPs) are not prohibited by the 1998 Act from having a dual mandate. Thus in addition to being an MSP, they could also be an MP, an MEP, or a local authority councillor. The duration of a Parliament is fixed in law at four years.

### The Parliament's officers

**8.45** The Scotland Act 1998 makes provision for a presiding officer of the Parliament assisted by two deputies. These individuals are elected by the Parliament from among its own members. There is also a Clerk of the Parliament who is appointed by the Scottish Parliamentary Corporate Body. The membership of this body consists of the presiding officer and four members of the Parliament appointed in accordance with standing orders. The proceedings of the Parliament are themselves regulated by standing order.

## The Executive

**8.46**  A Scottish Executive is provided for under the 1998 Act. Its membership consists of: the First Minister (FM) (appointed by the monarch); ministers (appointed by the FM with the agreement of Parliament and with the monarch's approval); and the Lord Advocate and the Solicitor-General for Scotland (recommended by the FM with the agreement of Parliament but appointed by the monarch). The Act also makes provision for the appointment of deputy ministers who assist their more senior colleagues in the exercise of their functions.

## Legislative powers

**8.47**  Unlike the Welsh Assembly, the Scottish Parliament has always had the power to enact primary legislation. Once a Bill has been passed by the Parliament and has received the Royal Assent, it is known as an Act of the Scottish Parliament. Nevertheless, there are limitations upon the Parliament's legislative competence. Chief amongst these is that the power to make law does not affect the power of the UK Parliament to make law for Scotland (s 28(7)). An Act of the Scottish Parliament will be outside its legislative competence if, for example, it would be part of the law of another country other than Scotland or if it is incompatible with any of the Convention rights or with EU law (s 29(2)). In *Martin v HM Advocate* (2010), Lord Hope noted that s 29 'lies at the heart of the scheme of devolution to which the Act gives effect'.

**8.48**  Further restrictions on the Parliament's legislative powers exist in respect of what the Act terms 'reserved matters' and enactments that are protected from modification. Schedule 5 to the Act specifies matters that are subject to a general reservation. These include certain aspects of the constitution, such as the Union between Scotland and England (see para **8.53**), the registration and funding of political parties, and certain other aspects relating to foreign affairs and defence matters.

**8.49**  Part II of Sch 5 to the Act makes more specific reservations under a number of different heads such as Home Affairs, Trade and Industry, Social Security, and Employment. Thus, for example, under Home Affairs, the Scottish Parliament has no legislative competence in respect of the Misuse of Drugs Act 1971 or in respect of elections for membership of the HC, the European Parliament, and the Scottish Parliament itself. This latter reservation explains why the Scottish Parliament (Constituencies) Act 2004 (para **8.43**) is a Westminster statute. Neither can an Act of the Scottish Parliament modify or confer power by delegated legislation to modify the law on reserved matters. Schedule 4 to the Act specifies particular enactments which are protected from modification by an Act of the Scottish Parliament. These include arts 4 and 6 of the Union with Scotland Act 1706, and the Union with England Act 1707, so far as they relate to the freedom of trade, certain specified provisions of the European Communities Act 1972, and the Human Rights Act 1998.

**8.50** Thus the approach adopted in the Scotland Act 1998 is to indicate those reserved matters in respect of which the Parliament does not have legislative competence. Its predecessor, the Scotland Act 1978, took a different approach to this question. It spoke in terms of 'devolved matters' in respect of which the Assembly did have legislative competence and then proceeded to list precisely what those devolved matters were in several of the Schedules to the Act. In *Martin v HM Advocate* (2010), Lord Hope contrasted the provisions under the 1978 and 1998 Acts. He was of the view that 'while the scheme in the 1998 Act may not strike one as a model of clarity, it does appear so far to have achieved the aim of stability'.

**8.51** Since the 1998 Act was enacted, the vast majority of legal disputes over devolution issues have centred on the functions of the Lord Advocate in criminal cases. Whether or not an Act of the Scottish Parliament is within its legislative competence is a matter for the courts to decide. In *Martin v HM Advocate* (2010), Lord Hope explained:

> But the judicial function in this regard has been carefully structured. It is not for the judges to say whether legislation on any particular issue is better made by the Scottish Parliament at Holyrood or by the UK Parliament at Westminster. How that issue is to be determined has already been addressed by the legislators. It must be decided according to particular rules that the Scotland Act 1998 has laid down.

In that case, the SC decided by a majority of 3:2 that a provision in the Criminal Proceedings etc (Reform) (Scotland) Act 2007 which allowed a sheriff to impose the maximum sentence of 12 months for the offence of driving whilst disqualified, when sitting summarily, was within the legislative competence of the Scottish Parliament. For the majority, the impugned enactment did not increase the maximum penalty for the offence as specified in the Road Traffic Act 1988 (a UK statute). Instead, it sought to enlarge the sheriff's sentencing powers in cases such as the present, thereby precluding the need for a more expensive and time-consuming jury trial. In other words, its essential purpose was the reallocation of business within the Scottish court system which was not a reserved matter. Nevertheless, the fact that *Martin v HM Advocate* was decided 3:2 demonstrates that differences of opinion may well occur in respect of legislative competence arguments, and that this is perhaps inevitable given that the 1998 Act does not, and could not, precisely divide reserved and dissolved matters into completely separate compartments.

## Pre-legislative scrutiny

**8.52** Although the Scotland Act 1998 devolves wide-ranging legislative powers to that Parliament, there are, as we have seen, matters which fall outside the Parliament's legislative competence. In order to try to avoid a situation whereby Acts are passed which exceed the extent of this competence, the 1998 Act provides for a system of pre-legislative scrutiny. On or before the introduction of a Bill in the Parliament, the minister in charge is required to state that in his opinion, its provisions are within the legislative competence of the Parliament (s 31(1)). The presiding officer is also required to reach a decision on this matter. The Advocate-General, the Lord Advocate, or the Attorney-General may refer to the SC the question whether a Bill or any of its provisions is within the legislative competence of the Parliament. If, however, despite these safeguards, a provision of a Bill or of an Act of the Scottish Parliament or of legislation made by a member of the Scottish Executive could be read in such a way as to be outside the Parliament's competence or the minister's power, s 10(2) of the 1998 Act states that:

> Such a provision is to be read as narrowly as is required for it to be within competence, if such a reading is possible, and is to have effect accordingly.

## Acts of Union

**8.53** The constitutional position of the Acts of Union has been described in Chapter 5 (paras **5.42–5.45**). For present purposes, it should be noted that the briefest of all the provisions of the Scotland Act 1998, s 37, states that: 'The Union with Scotland Act 1706 and the Union with England Act 1707 have effect subject to this Act'. This provision was described in the Scottish Office guide to the Scotland Bill as being 'a technical clause which will ensure that the Acts of Union are construed in the light of the Scotland Act'. In other words, it is an attempt to ensure that the 1998 Act is not subject to challenge on the ground that it is inconsistent with the Acts of Union.

## Developing devolution in Scotland

**8.54** In April 2008, a commission under the chairmanship of Sir Kenneth Calman was established with a remit as follows:

> To review the provisions of the Scotland Act 1998 in the light of experience and to recommend any changes to the present constitutional arrangements that would enable the Scottish Parliament to serve the people of Scotland better, improve the financial accountability of the Scottish Parliament, and continue to secure the position of Scotland within the United Kingdom.

**8.55** The Commission's final report, *Serving Scotland Better: Scotland and the United Kingdom in the 21st Century*, was published in June 2009. Its authors were of the unanimous opinion that the Scottish Parliament has been 'a remarkable and substantial success' since it enjoys the confidence of the Scottish people and has helped to bring government closer to the people. The report's recommendations were accepted by the previous Labour Government: see the White Paper, *Scotland's Future in the United Kingdom* (Cm 7738). More recently, *The Coalition: Our programme for government* (May 2010), contained a commitment on behalf of the present coalition Government to implement the Calman recommendations. At the time of writing, this is being achieved in the Scotland Bill which has passed all of its stages in the HC and has been sent to the HL.

**8.56** The Bill seeks to strengthen the financial accountability of the Scottish Parliament and to increase its powers and functions. Key provisions include:

- empowering the Scottish Parliament to set the rate of income tax for Scottish taxpayers;
- devolving stamp duty land tax, landfill tax, and aggregate levies as they relate to Scotland;
- empowering the Scottish ministers to borrow for a number of specified purposes, including to fund capital expenditure;
- devolving the power to regulate air weapons under the Firearms Act 1968–97;
- devolving the power to prescribe drink-driving and national speed limits in Scotland.

**8.57** Currently, the Scottish Parliament is financed by way of a block grant from the UK Parliament which is calculated by using the 'Barnett formula'. The same system is also used to finance the Welsh and Northern Ireland Assemblies. It is envisaged that once the new Scottish tax system is in place as from 2015, the Scottish Parliament will become responsible for raising approximately 35% of the revenue which it spends. The remaining 65% will continue to be paid by the block grant.

**8.58** In addition to the foregoing reforms, the Scotland Bill aims to update and improve the devolution settlement in other ways. Thus, for example, it seeks to rename the 'Scottish Executive' the 'Scottish Government' to reflect the increasing use of the latter term. More importantly, it seeks to extend the legislative competence statement currently required of ministers by s 31 so that in future, it will apply to any person in charge of a Bill. Moreover, under the present arrangements, a Bill which has been referred to the Supreme Court for an opinion as to whether or not it is within the Parliament's legislative competence is thereby precluded from receiving Royal Assent. Under new arrangements provided for in the Bill, however, whereas a 'general reference' will have the same consequence, a 'limited reference' will not prevent the Bill being sent for Royal Assent.

## Northern Ireland Assembly

**8.59** Devolution for Northern Ireland is provided for by the Northern Ireland Act 1998. Parts II and III of the Act, which are concerned with the legislative powers of the Northern Ireland Assembly and the establishment and functions of the executive authorities, only took effect when it appeared to the Secretary of State that progress had been made in implementing the Belfast Agreement.

## The Belfast Agreement

**8.60** This agreement, otherwise known as the 'Good Friday Agreement', was the product of multi-party negotiations between the British and Irish Governments and the main political parties in Northern Ireland. It recognizes that Northern Ireland shall continue to be part of the UK and shall not cease to be so without the consent of the majority of the people of Northern Ireland voting in a poll. This part of the agreement has been given statutory effect in s 1 of the 1998 Act. The agreement also involves the amendment of the Irish Constitution so as to reflect the fact that 'a united Ireland shall be brought about only by peaceful means with the consent of a majority of the people, democratically expressed, in both jurisdictions in the island'. In addition, strand one of the agreement provides for a democratically elected Assembly in Northern Ireland, whilst strand two envisaged the creation of a North/South Ministerial Council. This body consists of members of the executives from both Northern Ireland and the Republic of Ireland, and its tasks include cooperation on matters of mutual interest, and the adoption of common policies in areas such as agriculture, education, and the environment.

**8.61** Strand three of the Agreement provides for the establishment of a British-Irish Council (BIC) comprising representatives from the British and Irish Governments, the devolved institutions in Northern Ireland, Scotland and Wales, and the Isle of Man and the Channel Islands. The object of the BIC is 'to promote the harmonious and mutually beneficial development of the totality of relationships among the peoples of these islands'.

## Legislative power

**8.62** As with the other devolved legislatures, the Northern Ireland Assembly has the power to make primary legislation in the form of Acts of the Assembly. This power to legislate does not affect the power of the Westminster Parliament to make laws for Northern Ireland (s 5(6)). However, Acts of the Northern Ireland Assembly may modify an Act of

Parliament in so far as it is part of the law of Northern Ireland. The legislative competence of the Assembly is dealt with by s 6 of the 1998 Act. Thus it is outside the legislative competence of the Assembly to enact a law which deals with an 'excepted matter'. Excepted matters are listed in Sch 2 to the Act. They include the Parliament of the UK, international relations, the defence of the realm, and the control of nuclear, biological, and chemical weapons. It is also outside the legislative competence of the Assembly to make laws which are incompatible with Convention rights or EU law or which discriminate against people 'on the ground of religious belief or political opinion'. Any Act or any provision thereof which is outside the Assembly's legislative competence is therefore not law. Similarly there is no power to make, confirm, or approve subordinate legislation which would be invalid for the same reasons (s 24).

**8.63**  A minister in charge of a Bill is required to make a statement either before or on the Bill's introduction that in his opinion, the Bill would be within the legislative competence of the Assembly (s 9). The presiding officer of the Assembly is required to refer to the Secretary of State any Bill which he considers relates to an excepted or reserved matter. Reserved matters are listed in Sch 3. They include: disqualification from membership of the Assembly; the criminal law; the creation of offences and penalties; prosecutions; the surrender of fugitive offenders between Northern Ireland and Ireland; the establishment, organization, and control of the Police Service of Northern Ireland; civil defence; emergency powers; the administration of justice; import and export controls; financial matters; telecommunications; intellectual property; human genetics; and consumer safety in relation to goods. Any matter which is neither excepted nor reserved is a transferred matter.

**8.64**  Section 7 of the 1998 Act entrenches certain enactments. Thus certain parts of the European Communities Act 1972, the whole of the Human Rights Act 1998, and certain specified parts of the 1998 Act itself are immune from modification by an Act of the Assembly or by subordinate legislation. Any attempt to modify one of these enactments would therefore be outside the legislative competence of the Assembly.

## Interpretation

**8.65**  Where primary legislation could be read as being either within the legislative competence of the Assembly or outside it, s 83 of the Act requires that it is read in a way which makes it within that competence. The same rule of construction is to be applied to subordinate legislation which could be read as either valid or invalid.

## The Northern Ireland Executive

**8.66**  The Executive Committee of Northern Ireland consists of the First Minister (FM), the Deputy First Minister (DFM), and the Northern Ireland ministers (s 20). The FM and

DFM are elected by the Assembly. The candidature is joint. In order to be elected, the candidates must achieve the support of a majority of members voting in the election, and a majority of both the designated Nationalists' and designated Unionists' votes (s 16). The FM and the DFM will determine the number of ministerial offices to be held and the functions to be exercised by each (s 17), although the number of offices shall not exceed 10 unless the Secretary of State so provides. The actual nomination of ministers from among the members of the Assembly is carried out by the political parties. The opportunity to nominate is dependent upon the numerical strength of the party within the Assembly. This is calculated on the basis of a formula set out in s 18(5) of the Act. The political parties are also able to nominate the ministerial office that the nominee is to fill. The FM and the DFM may hold a ministerial office in addition to their roles as FM and DFM. The Act further provides for the appointment of junior ministers in accordance with a determination by the FM and DFM (s 19).

8.67 Each minister, from the FM down to the junior ministers, shall not take up office until he has affirmed the terms of the pledge of office. The pledge appears as Annex A to strand one of the Belfast Agreement and is reproduced in Sch 4 to the 1998 Act. It requires, amongst other things, that a minister shall:

- discharge his duties of office in good faith;
- be committed to non-violence and exclusively peaceful and democratic means;
- serve all the people of Northern Ireland equally and act in accordance with the obligations of government to promote equality and prevent discrimination;
- support and act in accordance with the decisions of the Executive Committee and Assembly; and
- comply with the Ministerial Code of Conduct.

8.68 The Ministerial Code of Conduct is also set out in Sch 4 to the Act. It requires, amongst other things, that ministers 'observe the highest standards of propriety and regularity involving impartiality, integrity and objectivity in relationship to the stewardship of public funds'. Moreover, Assembly ministers are required to follow the seven principles of public life set out by the Committee on Standards in Public Life (the Nolan Committee).

8.69 The Assembly may resolve that a minister no longer enjoys the confidence of the Assembly because he is not committed to peace or because he has failed to observe any of the other terms of the pledge (s 30). Where this is the case, the relevant person is excluded from holding ministerial office for 12 months. A resolution may be passed in respect of a political party for the same reasons and, where this happens, it will have the effect of excluding members of that party from holding ministerial office for 12 months.

8.70 The Northern Ireland Assembly and the Executive has been suspended for a fair amount of its lifetime. During the suspension, responsibility for the direction and control of central government in Northern Ireland rested with the Secretary of State for Northern Ireland and his Northern Ireland Office colleagues who legislated by Order in Council. The Assembly and the Executive was restored on 8 May 2007 following elections held on 7 March 2007.

## The English Question

8.71 Unlike the other nations which comprise the UK, England does not have its own Parliament or Assembly. Devolution in the other countries, particularly in Scotland, has led to the emergence of the 'English Question' or the 'West Lothian Question' after the former MP, Tam Dalyell, who was MP for that constituency when he posed the question in 1978. Essentially the question is concerned with whether it is acceptable, following the introduction of devolution, for Scottish MPs in the Westminster Parliament to continue to be able to speak and vote on certain English matters when English MPs have no corresponding ability to speak and vote on those Scottish matters that have been devolved to the Scottish Parliament in Edinburgh. More recently, those who are opposed to this state of affairs have called for 'English votes on English laws' and have introduced Private Members' Bills in the UK Parliament to this effect: see, for example, the Parliament (Participation of Members of the House of Commons) Bill (2005–6) and the House of Commons (Participation) Bill (2006–7).

8.72 Resolving the anomaly that is the 'English Question' is a very difficult task involving what Professor Hazell has termed both 'technical' and 'political' difficulties. Dealing with the technical aspect first, identifying those laws on which only English MPs would be allowed to vote sounds straightforward but, in practice, such measures may be difficult to identify. Moreover, the position would become more complicated where a Bill did not solely relate to England but varied in its territorial extent. In such a case, MPs for non-English constituencies would be permitted to vote on some clauses of the Bill but not on others. The potential for confusion is clear.

8.73 Turning to the political difficulties associated with 'English votes on English laws', such a policy may undermine the principle of equality among MPs at Westminster. It would mean in effect that there were two classes of MP, with the majority English constituency MPs having the right to vote on all matters and the minority non-English constituency MPs being precluded from voting on purely English matters. In Hazell's opinion, were this to happen, 'it would effectively create a parliament within a parliament'.

8.74 Despite these concerns, the coalition Government has announced (in a written ministerial statement published in *Hansard* on 8 September 2011) that it intends to make good on its earlier commitment to establish a commission to consider the 'West Lothian Question'. The primary role of the commission will be to examine parliamentary business and procedure and consider how Parliament as a whole can deal more effectively with business which relates wholly or primarily to England. The intention is to appoint a small group of independent, non-partisan experts with constitutional, legal, and parliamentary expertise. Formal proposals were to be brought forward in the Autumn of 2011.

## Memorandum of Understanding

**8.75** In October 1999, a series of agreements were reached between the UK Government and the devolved administrations in Scotland and Wales. These set out the principles which underlie the relationships between the various administrations. The principal agreement is the Memorandum of Understanding (MoU). Since it was first issued (Cm 4444) the MoU has been reissued on three further occasions to reflect necessary changes: July 2000 (Cm 4806); December 2001 (Cm 5240); and March 2010 (Cm 7864).

**8.76** Paragraph 2 of the MoU is unequivocal about the document's legal status. It asserts that the MoU:

> is a statement of political intent, and should not be interpreted as a binding agreement. It does not create legal obligations between the parties.

**8.77** All four of the administrations are committed to the principle of good communication with each other. This will involve allowing administrations to make representations to one another in good time for those representations to be fully considered. Consultation is therefore a feature of the relationship between the administrations, although of course, the MoU does not create a legal right to be consulted. Cooperation across a range of areas is also a feature of the relationship.

**8.78** The MoU notes that the UK Parliament retains the right to legislate on any matter, whether devolved or not (para 14). However, in practice, the UK Government will comply with what the MoU terms 'the convention' that the UK Parliament 'would not normally legislate with regard to devolved matters except with the agreement of the devolved legislature' (see para **11.36**).

**8.79** With regard to matters of European law, it is clear that these remain the responsibility of the UK Government. However, the first sentence of para 20 of the MoU states that:

> The UK Government will involve the devolved administrations as fully as possible in discussions about the formulation of the UK's policy position on all EU and international issues which touch on devolved matters.

In the event of a failure to enforce or comply with a European obligation which leads to the imposition of a financial penalty, eg damages awarded in accordance with the *Francovich* principle (paras **10.38–10.49**), the four administrations are agreed that any damages or costs awarded shall be paid by the administration responsible for the failure.

8.80  It is clear from the MoU that most of the contact between the administrations is carried out on a bilateral or multilateral basis, between the departments which have day-to-day responsibility for the issues under consideration. However, given the need for the creation of 'some central co-ordination of the overall relationship', the administrations have agreed to participate in a Joint Ministerial Committee (JMC).

## The Joint Ministerial Committee

8.81  The JMC is the subject of one of the supplementary agreements to the MoU. It consists of UK Government, Scottish, Welsh, and Northern Ireland ministers. Its terms of reference are:

- to consider non-devolved responsibilities which impinge on devolved responsibilities, and devolved matters which impinge on non-devolved responsibilities;

- where the administrations agree, to consider devolved matters if it is beneficial to discuss their respective treatment in the different parts of the UK;

- to keep the arrangements for liaison between the administrations under review; and

- to consider disputes between the administrations.

8.82  The JMC potentially meets in several guises. At its plenary meetings, it is chaired by the PM and its membership consists of the most senior ministers from the other administrations, ie First Ministers or secretaries and their deputies or other ministerial colleagues. The Secretaries of State for Scotland, Wales, and Northern Ireland also attend plenary meetings. The JMC may also meet in other 'functional' formats, eg JMC Europe or JMC Domestic. It should be noted, however, that this formal machinery for inter-governmental relations has not been much utilized. The HC Justice Committee has noted, for example, that the JMC did not meet in plenary form between 2002 and 2008. It would seem to be the case, therefore, that greater use has been made of more informal and bilateral links between the UK Government and the devolved administrations. Perhaps, however, the situation is beginning to improve. Thus the HC Justice Committee has drawn attention to the fact that a full plenary of the JMC was held on 25 June 2008 and that, since that date, there have been further meetings, including one at which an agreement was reached on a UK-wide approach to marine planning.

## Concordats

8.83  In addition to the Agreement on the JMC, the MoU is further supplemented by concordats in areas where it is considered desirable to have uniform arrangements for relations between the administrations. Thus concordats relate to: the handling of matters with an EU dimension; financial assistance to industry; and international relations touching on the responsibilities of the devolved administrations. The concordats are not intended to be legally binding documents. Further concordats or less formal agreements may be drawn up in the future as and when the need for them arises.

## Concordat on coordination of European Union policy issues

8.84  Of the three concordats, it is concordat B which has the greatest constitutional significance. Its purpose is to flesh out the general propositions on EU policy issues which were made in the MoU. It is once again clear from this concordat that the UK Government retains overall domestic responsibility for the formulation of policy on EU issues and for legislating to implement EU obligations throughout the UK. However, the devolved administrations have an important role to play in:

- the discussion and formulation of policy on EU issues;

- scrutinizing EU issues relating to devolved matters to ensure that its interests are properly reflected;

- putting forward the UK negotiating line at Council of Ministers meetings;

- implementing and enforcing new EU obligations which relate to devolved matters;

- drafting responses to the European Commission where infraction proceedings relate solely to implementation in Scotland, Wales, or Northern Ireland; and

- paying the costs and penalties where an adverse ruling by the ECJ against the UK can be attributed to the inactivity of the devolved administration.

8.85  In terms of promoting the UK line to the wider European audience, the concordat states that the composition of the UK team will be decided by the lead UK government minister 'on a case-by-case basis'. Thus, ministers from the devolved administrations are likely to form part of the UK team where the discussion at a meeting of the Council of Ministers centres upon issues that will have a significant impact on their devolved responsibilities.

## Reforming inter-governmental relations

8.86  As part of its inquiry into how devolution is working, the HC Justice Committee examined the present arrangements for relations between the UK Government and the devolved administrations: see *Devolution: A Decade On*, fifth report of 2008–9 session, HC 529-I. It noted, amongst other things, that the MoU and the accompanying concordats have changed little since they were first established and that they have been subject to criticism on the grounds of their non-transparent nature and non-statutory status. It questions whether they are 'fit for purpose' and asserts:

> *The system of devolved government, including governments of different political complexions, requires a set of arrangements which provide opportunity for the*

*expression of legitimate political and territorial differences, negotiation, dialogue and dispute resolution. These arrangements also need to facilitate the co-ordination of action in areas of joint interest, the promotion of common interests and good relations and an effective means of dealing with the consequential effects of decisions taken in the respective jurisdictions. The absence of such a structure is one of the weaknesses of the current devolution settlement.*

**8.87** With regard to the JMC, the Justice Committee welcomed the reconvening of meetings and recommended that it continues to meet on a regular basis. It also envisaged a more active and systematic role for the JMC as 'the central apparatus for inter-governmental relations within the United Kingdom'.

# FURTHER READING

Bogdanor, V *Devolution* (1979) OUP.

Bogdanor, V 'Our New Constitution' (2004) 120 LQR 242.

Brazier, R 'The Scotland Bill as Constitutional Legislation' [1998] Stat LR 12.

Brazier, R 'The Scottish Government' [1998] PL 212.

Burrows, N 'This is Scotland's Parliament; Let Scotland's Parliament Legislate' (2002) Jur Rev 213.

Craig, P and Walters, M 'The Courts, Devolution and Judicial Review' [1999] PL 274.

Crawford, B 'Ten Years of Devolution' (2010) 63 Parliamentary Affairs 89.

Ford, J D 'The Legal Provisions in the Acts of Union' [2007] CLJ 106.

Grice, P 'The Creation of a Devolved Parliament: An overview of the processes and principles involved in establishing the Scottish Parliament' (2001) 7 JLS 1.

Hadfield, B 'The Belfast Agreement' [1998] PL 599.

Hadfield, B 'Devolution, Westminster and the English Question' [2005] PL 286.

Hadfield, B 'Devolution: A National Conversation' in Jowell and Oliver (eds) *The Changing Constitution* (7th edn, 2011) OUP.

Hazell, R 'Reinventing the Constitution: Can the State Survive?' [1999] PL 84.

Hazell, R 'The Continuing Dynamism of Constitutional Reform' (2007) 60 Parliamentary Affairs 3.

Himsworth, C M G 'Devolution and its Jurisdictional Asymmetries' (2007) 70 MLR 31.

House of Commons Justice Committee, *Devolution: A Decade On*, fifth report of session 2008–9, HC 529-I.

Jones, T and Williams, J 'The Legislative Future of Wales' (2005) 68 MLR 642.

Jones, T, Turnbull, J and Williams, J 'The Law of Wales or the Law of England and Wales' [2005] Stat LR 135.

Jones, T and Williams, J *The Government of Wales Act 2006* Annotated Statutes, Sweet & Maxwell.

Lynch, P 'Governing Devolution: Understanding the Office of First Minister in Scotland and Wales' (2006) 59 Parliamentary Affairs 420.

Lyon, *A Constitutional History of the United Kingdom* (2003) Cavendish.

Mitchell, J *Devolution in the UK* (2009) Manchester University Press.

Rawlings, R 'The New Model Wales' (1998) 25 Journal of Law and Society 461.

Rawlings, R 'Concordats of the Constitution' (2000) 116 LQR 257.

Sherlock, A 'Wales: A new devolution settlement for Wales' (2008) 14 EPL 297.

Sherlock, A 'Devolution in Transition in Wales' (2011) 17 EPL 25.

Trench, A 'The Government of Wales Act 2006: The next steps on Devolution for Wales' [2006] PL 687.

Wicks, E 'A New Constitution for a New State? The 1707 Union of England and Scotland' (2001) 117 LQR 109.

## SELF-TEST QUESTIONS

1 What is the difference between 'executive devolution' and 'legislative devolution'?

2 Do the devolution provisions in respect of Wales, Scotland, and Northern Ireland amount to 'executive devolution', 'legislative devolution', or both?

3 What impact has devolution had upon the legislative supremacy of Parliament?

4 To what extent, if any, do you agree with Professor Bogdanor (2004) that 'devolution introduces, for the first time, the federal spirit into the British constitution' with the result that 'Westminster has become a quasi-federal Parliament'?

5 How might the practice of publishing some government Bills in draft be particularly useful in the context of devolution?

6 Professor Rawlings has described Welsh devolution as 'a process not an event'. What do you think he meant by this?

7 Winetrobe has argued in relation to Scottish devolution: 'That the scheme has survived so far relatively unscathed may be due not so much to the quality of the scheme or of its actors, as to the degree of consensus-building that preceded it, and to the generally favourable political, economic, and legal circumstances in which it has operated.' If this view is correct, what circumstances might cause the devolution arrangements between Westminster and Edinburgh to be more severely tested?

8 What do you consider to be the answer to the 'English question'?

# PART III
## Sources of Public Law

# 9 Primary and secondary legislation

## SUMMARY

This chapter is concerned with laws made by Parliament, primary legislation, and laws made by persons or bodies other than Parliament, secondary legislation. It focuses on the various types of Bill which may be introduced before Parliament, and draws distinctions between the processes for enacting Public General Acts and Private Acts of Parliament. The various types of Bills which may be introduced by private members are also considered in this chapter. The second part of this chapter is concerned with delegated or secondary legislation. Mention is made of the various types of delegated legislation that exist, and consideration is given to the way in which such legislation is subject to parliamentary and judicial scrutiny. The chapter concludes by briefly considering what is meant by the term 'quasi-legislation'.

## Public General Bills

9.1 In any one parliamentary session, something in the region of 40 to 50 Public General Acts are passed. The vast majority of these are government-inspired measures. The actual process of legislating involves a number of parliamentary and extra-parliamentary stages which will be discussed. It ought to be noted at this juncture that Bills may be introduced in either the HC or the HL although generally speaking, the more contentious Bills start their life in the HC. In any event, the various stages are essentially the same.

### The impetus for legislation

9.2 Once elected, a government's legislative programme will be announced at the beginning of each parliamentary session during the course of the Queen's speech. The precise content of the government Bills will often be worked out at a later stage, unless they have already been published in draft. The impetus for legislating in particular fields may come from a variety of different sources. Prior to a general election, it is commonplace for the main political parties to state what their legislative intentions are in published manifestos.

**9.3** Some government Bills which are introduced before Parliament may embody the recommendations of a Royal Commission, the Law Commission, or a specially constituted committee. Where this is the case, the form and content of the proposed law is likely to have been much discussed. On other occasions, however, there may not be the opportunity for mature reflection because events dictate that law should be made quickly. Government legislation passed in order to satisfy a pressing need is therefore unlikely to have been prefigured in a manifesto or for that matter the Queen's speech. A good example is the Parliamentary Standards Act 2009 which was enacted in a few short weeks as a direct consequence of the scandal surrounding MPs' allowances and expenses which broke in May and June 2009 following revelations leaked to the *Daily Telegraph* newspaper.

## Preparatory stages

**9.4** Generally speaking, government Bills will have been the subject of much preparatory work prior to their introduction in Parliament. This preparatory work may take a number of different forms. One possibility is that the government of the day may have sought to consult interested parties by producing a Green or White Paper on the subject matter of a future Bill. Thus, for example, on being appointed PM at the end of June 2007, Gordon Brown swiftly published a Green Paper, *The Governance of Britain* (Cm 7170) (July 2007), in which he set out his constitutional reform agenda and invited consultation on a number of key proposals. White Papers in particular often precede important legislative initiatives. A good example is *Rights Brought Home* (Cm 3782) (October 1997), which outlined the Government's intention to give effect to ECHR rights in English law.

**9.5** The life of a government Bill is likely to begin in the sponsoring department. Legislative proposals will be drawn up within that department and then parliamentary counsel will be instructed to work these proposals into a legislative form. The actual drafting of government legislation is therefore carried out by a small cohort of legally qualified senior civil servants. Policy matters are for the sponsoring department, not for parliamentary counsel. However, in order to give proper effect to the department's wishes, counsel will have to have a good grasp of the policy which underlies the proposed legislation and may need to offer up alternative suggestions where the department's intended approach appears not to work. Thus the former First Parliamentary Counsel, Sir Geoffrey Bowman, has commented that:

> The line between offering workable solutions (on the one hand) and making up the policy (on the other hand) is often a fine one. And a great deal of experience is needed to judge where it lies in a given case.

**9.6** In January 2011, the Cabinet Office published a document, *Working with Parliamentary Counsel* which, as its title implies, explains the nature of the relationship between government departments and parliamentary counsel. Much of the document relates to the form and content of the drafting instructions. With regard to the role of counsel in relation to policy-making, it is stated, amongst other things, that the default position 'will be one of cautious detachment'. It is envisaged, however, that there may be circumstances where, even in their normal default role, counsel will be able to make a significant contribution to policy-making with the agreement of the sponsoring department.

**9.7** The actual process of drafting a Bill may take some time, especially where the subject matter is complex or the Bill runs to a great many clauses and schedules. A number of versions of the draft Bill may pass back and forth between parliamentary counsel and the sponsoring department as part of the iterative process before a final version is produced. Once this stage has been reached, the Bill will be ready to be introduced in Parliament.

## Pre-legislative scrutiny

**9.8** A criticism which could be levelled at the procedure outlined in the previous paragraph is that it provides for little, if any, consultation with individual MPs, Parliament, or the wider general public before Bills are introduced. Moreover, it has been observed that:

> Once Bills are introduced they are largely set in concrete. There has been a distinct culture prevalent throughout Whitehall that the standing and reputation of Ministers have been dependent on their Bills getting through largely unchanged. As a result there has been an inevitable disposition to resist alteration, not only on the main issues of substance, but also on matters of detail. [First Report of the HC Modernisation Committee (HC 190), para 7]

**9.9** Therefore, in response to recommendations made by the HC Modernisation Committee in its first report, *The Legislation Process*, (1997–98 session, HC 190), and in accordance with the Government's declared intention, a practice has arisen whereby some Bills have been published in draft form prior to their introduction in Parliament. In the words of the Modernisation Committee, pre-legislative scrutiny:

> provides an opportunity for the House as a whole, for individual backbenchers, and for the Opposition to have a real input into the form of the actual legislation which subsequently emerges, not least because Ministers are likely to be far more receptive to suggestions for change before the Bill is actually published. It opens Parliament up to those outside affected by legislation . . . [A]bove all, it should lead to better legislation and less likelihood of subsequent amending legislation.

**9.10** The Bill to establish the Food Standards Agency was the first draft Bill to be considered by an ad hoc select committee set up for that purpose, the Food Standards Committee. In the 2010–12 parliamentary session the coalition Government has thus far published six draft Bills which include a Draft Detention of Terrorist Suspects (Temporary Extensions) Bill and a Draft House of Lords Reform Bill (see Chapter **6**).

**9.11**   Allied to the publication in draft of particular Bills was a new practice which was instituted by the Labour Government in July 2007: the publication of a draft legislative programme. The purpose underlying this initiative was to re-engage both Parliament and the general public with the legislative process and to make government more accountable to both constituencies. Although it remains to be seen whether the coalition Government will also adhere to this practice, the agreement which is set out in *The Coalition: Our programme for government* (2010), does provide some indication of legislative initiatives which it intends to bring forward during the current parliamentary session. It should be noted, however, that the coalition was roundly criticized for introducing two important constitutional Bills, the Parliamentary Voting System and Constituencies Bill and the Fixed-term Parliaments Bill, in the absence of any pre-legislative scrutiny.

## The parliamentary stages

**9.12**   There are five stages in the parliamentary life of a Bill: first reading; second reading; committee stage; report stage; and third reading. Each of these will be considered in turn.

### First reading

**9.13**   This stage represents the formal presentation of the Bill before Parliament. The short title of the Bill is read out and the House orders that the Bill shall be printed. There is no debate or division on the provisions of the Bill at the first reading.

### Second reading

**9.14**   This stage represents the first opportunity that the House has to consider the principle and detail of the Bill. The debate will be opened by a government minister from the sponsoring department who will set out and explain the Bill's clauses and the thinking behind them. If there is opposition to the Bill, which is often the case, the second reading affords the opportunity to voice that opposition and to generally attack the substance of the Bill. It does not, however, provide an opportunity to amend individual clauses. A Bill may be rejected in its entirety at this stage, but this is a rare occurrence, especially when the government of the day has a working majority in the HC.

### Committee stage

**9.15**   Public Bills which have received a second reading (except those concerned with supply or taxation) will automatically be referred to a Public Bill Committee (formerly a Standing Committee) unless the HC has decided, for example, that the committee stage is to be held on the floor of the House. The committee stage itself entails a clause-by-clause consideration of the Bill. Amendments may be made to the Bill at this stage and new clauses or schedules may be moved by committee members as well as by the minister responsible for the Bill or opposition spokespersons. Normally the committee to which the Bill is referred will be a Public Bill Committee of approximately 20 members which reflects the strength of the political parties within the HC. At any one time, therefore, there may be a number of Public Bill Committees which are established as and when the need for them arises. Very occasionally, a Bill may be considered by the appropriate Select Committee (see paras **6.51–6.53**). The scrutiny which a Bill receives is likely to be even more thorough than that which it receives from a normal Public Bill Committee. Taking the committee stage on the floor of the House is usually reserved for Bills that are of constitutional importance or for those measures that need to be passed quickly. The Bill which first took the UK into the EC and those Bills which have incorporated subsequent EC and EU Treaties into UK law had their committee stages on the floor of the House.

## Report stage

9.16 The report stage entails a detailed consideration of the Bill, as amended in committee, by the whole House. The House is not bound to accept any amendment made to the Bill by a Public Bill Committee. Further amendments may be made to the Bill at the report stage, including the addition of new clauses. Where the committee stage of a Bill took place on the floor of the House and there were no amendments, the Bill will by-pass the report stage and proceed to third reading.

## Third reading

9.17 This final stage of a Bill's progress provides a further opportunity to debate its principles and to consider the amendments made to it either in committee or during the report stage. The Bill cannot be substantively amended at this stage, but it may be opposed and perhaps even defeated where the opposition has numerical strength.

## Monarch's consent

9.18 A Bill which affects the prerogative, hereditary revenues, the personal property or interest of the Crown, the Duchy of Lancaster, or the Duchy of Cornwall must first receive the consent of the monarch before it can be passed. This consent is distinct from Royal Assent which is granted following the completion of a Bill's parliamentary stages (para **9.24**). The consent, which is usually signified at third reading but which may be signified at any stage in the Bill's parliamentary life, has the effect of placing the monarch's prerogative or interest in the hands of Parliament for the purposes of the Bill. A standard form of words is used. Thus at the start of the second reading debate on the Fixed-term Parliaments Bill in the Hl, the Advocate-General for Scotland, Lord Wallace, stated:

> *My Lords, I have it in command from Her Majesty the Queen to acquaint the House that Her Majesty, having been informed of the purport of the Fixed-term Parliaments Bill, has consented to place her Prerogative, so far as it is affected by the Bill, at the disposal of Parliament for the purposes of this Bill. [Hansard, HL, Vol 725 at col 929 (1 March 2011)]*

## House of Lords stages

**9.19** Assuming that a Bill has been introduced in the HC, once it has received a third reading it is then sent to the HL. The legislative process in the HL is much the same as that in the HC. Two differences are, however, worthy of note. First, the committee stage of a Bill in the HL usually takes place on the floor of the House rather than in a committee room. Secondly, amendments to a Bill can be made at the third reading as well as during the committee and report stages.

**9.20** If the HL accepts the Bill as passed by the HC in its entirety, it will then be ready to receive Royal Assent. If, however, the HL amends the Bill, the Bill in its amended form will be sent back to the HC for its consideration. Three courses of action are open to the HC at this juncture:

- agree to the Lords' amendments;
- agree to the Lords' amendments but with further amendments; or
- disagree with the Lords' amendments.

**9.21** Where a Bill has been further amended by the HC, it will be sent back to the Lords with the amendments. If the HC and the HL are unable to agree a final text of the Bill during 'Ping Pong', a stalemate will have been reached. This can be resolved by invoking the Parliament Acts 1911 and 1949 procedure (paras **5.31–5.41**). In short, this will enable the Bill to become an Act despite the absence of the HL consent to the measure. In order for this to happen, the Bill must have been passed by the HC in two successive sessions and one year must have elapsed between the date of the second reading of the Bill in the HC in the first of the two sessions and the date on which the Bill passes in the HC in the second of those sessions.

## A new stage?

**9.22** In its manifesto (*Invitation to Join the Government of Britain*) which was published prior to the 2010 general election, the Conservative Party made a great many commitments, including that it would, if elected, 'introduce a new Public Reading Stage for Bills to give the public an opportunity to comment on proposed legislation online'. In the coalition agreement, *The Coalition: Our programme for government* (2010), the commitment was reiterated and expanded upon. Thus in addition, the coalition Government committed itself to providing for a dedicated 'public reading day' during a Bill's committee stage where the online comments received from members of the public would be debated by the committee.

9.23 A pilot public reading stage was launched on 15 February 2011 in respect of the Protection of Freedoms Bill. It lasted some 3 weeks and elicited in excess of 500 comments. Although there was broad support for this new innovation amongst those that commented, several suggestions were made as to how the stage might be improved. These included that the dedicated website ought to be arranged in such a way as to allow respondents to comment on more than just individual clauses in the Bill. Also, it was felt that provision ought to be made to allow members of the public to propose entirely new clauses for inclusion in the Bill. Although all of the respondents' comments were passed onto the Public Committee, this did not happen until after it had commenced its proceedings. Also, the coalition Government decided that there would not be a 'public reading day' during the committee stage of the Bill. It remains to be seen, therefore, whether this extra-parliamentary stage will become a feature of the legislative process in the future.

## Royal Assent

9.24 A Bill which has passed all its stages in both the HC and the HL will then be presented for Royal Assent. In order for a Bill to become an Act of Parliament, it is imperative that it receives Royal Assent. Although the signification of Royal Assent is now something of a formality, there may be circumstances where a refusal to exercise this prerogative power can be justified (paras **4.9–4.11**). The monarch retains the right to declare the Royal Assent in person in Parliament by virtue of s 1(2) of the Royal Assent Act 1967. However, as *Erskine May* notes, this last occurred on 12 August 1854. The practice nowadays is for the Royal Assent to be notified to the respective Houses by the Speaker, or the Lord Speaker, or by commissioners.

## The fall of a Bill

9.25 If a Bill fails to complete all of its procedural stages by the end of the parliamentary session, it will normally fall. In other words, it will not be possible to return to the Bill in the new session and continue its passage from the stage which had been reached previously unless the HC has agreed that it should be carried over (for the practical details of a 'carryover motion', see HC Standing Order No 80A). From a practical point of view, this rule dictates that few Bills will be introduced late on in a parliamentary session. It also means that the clutch of Bills which are introduced early on in the session have the potential to create legislative congestion which in turn means that the later Bills might not be scrutinized quite as thoroughly as they would otherwise have been.

## Post-legislative scrutiny

**9.26**  More recently, it has been suggested that Bills which have passed all their parliamentary stages and which have become Acts of Parliament ought to be subject to post-legislative scrutiny. This would entail a review of the relevant law in order to determine whether it has met its intended purpose and policy objectives, whether it has had unintended consequences, and whether the wording of the resultant Act is sufficiently clear and unambiguous so as to be workable in practice. In response to a recommendation from the HL Select Committee on the Constitution that legislation should be the subject of post-legislative scrutiny, the Labour Government asked the Law Commission to undertake a study of the matter.

**9.27**  In its subsequent report, *Post-Legislative Scrutiny* (Law Com No 302, Cm 6945) (2006), the Law Commission accepted that there is a strong case for more systematic post-legislative scrutiny. Accordingly, it recommended that the Government consider the establishment of a Parliamentary joint committee on post-legislative scrutiny which would be able to carry out the function where a select committee has decided not to exercise the power. A joint committee would have the discretion to decide which legislation should be reviewed and the timescale for any review that was carried out. In the light of its experience, the Law Commission also felt that there may be scope for the development of Parliamentary post-legislative scrutiny of delegated legislation. Moreover, it was also of the opinion that government departments should routinely consider whether and if so how legislation should be monitored and reviewed.

**9.28**  The Law Commission's report was welcomed by the Government as a 'thoughtful and considered review of this area': see *Post-legislative scrutiny–The Government's Approach* (March 2008), Cm 7320. Although the previous Government was in favour of post-legislative scrutiny, it was also of the view that a scrutiny system must: concentrate on appropriate Acts; avoid re-running policy debates; reflect the circumstances of each Act; and be complementary to the scrutiny which can already take place. It therefore considered that the key role would be performed by the departmental select committees rather than by a specially created joint committee as advocated by the Law Commission. The existing committees would carry out post-legislative scrutiny, normally within 3–5 years of an Act having received Royal Assent, based on a memorandum submitted by the relevant government department. Although the previous Government considered that it would be premature to establish a dedicated system for post-legislative scrutiny of secondary legislation, it did make the point that a review of an Act 'should properly include the consideration of all or much of the delegated legislation made under the Act'.

## Private Bills

**9.29** Unlike Public Acts which are general and apply to everyone, Private Acts of Parliament are limited in their application. They are often concerned with a particular area or undertaking. Historically, the spread of the railways in this country was achieved by a great many Private Acts of Parliament. Similarly, prior to the enactment of national public health legislation in the last quarter of the 19th century, sanitation, etc was provided for at a local level under the terms of improvement Acts petitioned for by local councils.

### Petitioning Parliament

**9.30** The key distinction between a Public and a Private Bill is that whereas the former is presented to Parliament by a minister or sponsor (in the case of a Private Members' Bill), the latter is petitioned for by a particular person or organization. This petition has to be presented to Parliament on or before 27 November in any year. Since Private Bills may confer rights and powers greater than those conferred by Public Bills, it is necessary that they are advertised in the press and that those likely to be affected by their provisions have received proper notification.

**9.31** A petition for a Bill must comply with the conditions laid down in Parliament's Standing Orders for Private Business. Each petition is therefore scrutinized by examiners specially appointed for this purpose. The petitioners or their parliamentary agents are required to appear before the examiners. Parliamentary agents are individuals with particular expertise and knowledge of the Private Bill procedure. There are several firms of such agents who may be employed by a Bill's petitioner to draft the legislation and secure its passage through both Houses of Parliament.

### Parliamentary stages

**9.32** In order to become law, a Private Bill must pass each of the stages that apply to Public Bills. At the committee stage, the proceedings are conducted much as if they were being heard in a court of law. The committee sits in a quasi-judicial capacity and may hear representations from counsel for the Bill's promoters or from counsel representing its opponents. Where the Bill's promoters object to an opponent on the ground that the person does not have locus standi, this will be determined by the Court of Referees, a committee of senior backbenchers.

**9.33** In the case of an opposed Bill, counsel for its promoters will be required to establish the case for the Bill. If they are unable to do so to the satisfaction of the committee, the Bill will be regarded as having been rejected in its entirety. If, however, the case for the Bill has been made out, the committee will then proceed to consider to what extent, if at all, the Bill needs amending. Where a Bill is unopposed at the committee stage, the proceedings will be less court-like and will involve the promoter answering any questions that the committee may wish to ask about the Bill.

9.34 Following its committee stage in the HC, a Bill will be further considered if it has been amended, and it will then proceed to a third reading. Once a Private Bill has passed all its stages in the HC, it will go to the HL where it will go through a similar process. Any amendments made to the Bill by the HL must be considered by the HC. Once the text of the Bill has been agreed by both Houses, it will then be presented for Royal Assent.

## Suspension

9.35 A final point to note about Private Bills concerns their status at the end of a parliamentary session. Whereas Public Bills that fail to complete all their stages within a session are thereby normally deemed to have fallen (para **9.25**), Private Bills may be suspended and resurrected in a new session to complete their remaining stages.

## Hybrid Bills

9.36 Occasionally a Bill may exhibit the characteristics of both a Public and a Private Bill. In other words, whilst applying generally, it may affect a particular private interest in a manner different from other private interests which can be said to fall into the same category or class. Where this happens, the Bill is said to be hybrid. Hybrid Bills often, but not exclusively, are concerned with the carrying out of works in a particular area which are of importance to the nation as a whole. Thus the Bill which provided for the construction of the Channel Tunnel Rail Link was a hybrid Bill.

9.37 The procedure for enacting a hybrid Bill represents a combination of the procedures for Public and Private Bills. The second reading, report stage, and third reading are carried out in the same manner as for Public Bills. Indeed, hybrid Bills are Public Bills for the purposes of numbering and publication following their enactment. After the second reading, however, a hybrid Bill may be committed to a Select Committee if petitions against it have been received. If they have not, the Bill will be recommitted to a Public Bill Committee or it will have its committee stage on the floor of the House.

9.38 Where petitions against the Bill have been received, it is for the committee to determine the locus standi of a petitioner, assuming that this has been challenged by the Bill's promoter. The committee will hear representations from both sides and will then examine the Bill clause by clause. The Bill will then be reported to the House either with or without amendment. Once reported, the Bill will be recommitted to a Public Bill Committee or committee of the whole House and will then complete its remaining stages in the same way as other Public Bills. It will then be sent to the HL, where it may be opposed once again before a Select Committee. The final agreed text of the Bill will receive Royal Assent in the usual way.

## Private Members' Bills

**9.39** In addition to debating government Bills, time is taken up during the course of a Parliamentary session considering Private Members' Bills. These provide an opportunity for individual members to secure the enactment of a piece of legislation which reflects a particular interest that they might have. Private Members' Bills fall into one of four categories: Ballot Bills; Ten Minute Rule Bills; Ordinary Presentation Bills; and Private Members' Bills from the Lords.

**9.40** Private Members' Bills are Public Bills and should not therefore be confused with Private Bills.

### Ballot Bills

**9.41** These are so-called because their sponsor has 'won' the opportunity to bring forward a Bill in a ballot held shortly after the beginning of each parliamentary session. Approximately two-thirds of MPs enter the ballot, but only the first 20 to be drawn out will have the opportunity to put a Bill down for discussion on one of the Fridays set aside for this purpose. Having a particular legislative initiative in mind is not a prerequisite for entering the ballot. If an uncommitted member is successful in securing a good position in the ballot, it is likely that they will be lobbied by pressure groups or other organizations to sponsor a Bill championing a particular cause. Alternatively, an uncommitted member may be offered a 'handout' Bill by the government in respect of which it was unable, for one reason or another, to find a place in its legislative programme for that session. An advantage of such a Bill is that it will have the support of the government, both politically and in terms of resources, and will therefore stand quite a good chance of becoming law.

**9.42** Bills introduced via the ballot procedure have the best chance of success of all the different types of Private Members' Bills. In the 1996–97 session, for example, 14 of the 22 Private Members' Bills which received Royal Assent were Ballot Bills. In the 1997–98 session, Ballot Bills accounted for half of the 10 Private Members' Bills which became Acts and in the 2002–03, 2003–04, 2005–06, and 2007–08 sessions, all the Private Members' Bills which became Acts were Ballot Bills (13, 5, 3, and 2, respectively).

### Ten Minute Rule Bills

**9.43** As its name implies, a Ten Minute Rule Bill does not occupy very much parliamentary time. This type of Bill may be introduced by any member on a Tuesday or Wednesday afternoon after Question Time. The rule in Standing Order No 23 states that the Bill may be accompanied by a brief speech introducing it to the House and by a speech opposing the motion. Bills introduced in this manner do not have a very good chance of success. Between 1985 and 1992, not one Ten Minute Rule Bill was enacted. Between 1995 and 1998, only one such Bill was enacted in each of the three parliamentary sessions: the Public Order (Amendment) Act 1996; the Building Societies (Distributions) Act 1997; and the Animal Health (Amendment) Act 1998, respectively. Since 1999, only two Ten Minute Rule Bills have been enacted: the Divorce (Religious Marriages) Act 2002; and the Private Hire Vehicles (Carriage Guide Dogs etc.) Act 2002. Nevertheless, despite this very low level of success, the procedure does provide a means by which particular issues or concerns can be raised in the House and can thereby be more widely publicized.

## Ordinary Presentation Bills

9.44 Every Member of Parliament is entitled under Standing Order No 57 to introduce a Bill on any subject they wish, provided that they have given notice of their intention to do so. However, given that Ordinary Presentation Bills rank lower than Ballot Bills, they often do not receive sufficient parliamentary time in which to be debated. In the 1996–97 session, none of the 23 Bills introduced in this manner was enacted. In the last 35 or so years, the most productive session for this type of Bill was 1990–91, when eight out of the 48 Bills introduced became law. These included the Badgers (Further Protection) Bill, the Breeding of Dogs Bill, the Football (Offences) Bill, and the Smoke Detectors Bill. Since 1999, only two Ordinary Presentation Bills have become law (both in the 2008–09 session).

## Private Members' Bills from the Lords

9.45 These are Bills which have been introduced in the HL by a backbench peer and which have passed all their stages in that House. A sponsor for them may then be found in the HC. In the 1996–97 session, all seven Bills first presented in the HL became law. Interestingly two of these, the Land Registration Bill and the Theft (Amendment) Bill, were originally presented by Lords Browne-Wilkinson and Goff respectively, both of whom were Law Lords at the time. Under normal circumstances, a Law Lord would have refrained from introducing a Bill since if he were subsequently to hear an appeal relating to the interpretation of the resultant Act, it might be argued that he was acting contrary to the separation of powers (Chapter 2). However, neither of these Acts was controversial. The former was introduced to give effect to recommendations for reform made by the Law Commission, and the latter was passed to fill certain gaps in the law of obtaining by deception under the Theft Act 1968. Of course, the establishment of a Supreme Court (paras **2.34–2.39**) which is separate from the legislature ensures that now, no serving member of that court is able to sponsor legislation in this way.

## Consolidation Bills

**9.46** Consolidation is, in the words of Lord Simon of Glaisdale in *Farrell v Alexander* (1977), a process 'designed to bring together in a more convenient, lucid and economical form a number of enactments related in subject-matter (and often by cross-reference) previously scattered over the statute Book'. It can therefore be distinguished from codification which involves the drafting of a code reflecting both statutory and common law principles in a particular subject area. There are several types of consolidation:

- 'pure' consolidation, ie the Bill simply re-enacts without amendment the previous law;

- consolidation under the Consolidation of Enactments (Procedure) Act 1949 – this allows 'corrections and minor improvements' to be made in the Bill;

- consolidation with Law Commission amendments.

**9.47** It will be apparent from the long title of the Act which of these three categories the consolidating measure falls into. Thus the National Health Service Act 2006 is 'An Act to consolidate certain enactments relating to the health service', whereas the Health Service Commissioners Act 1993 is:

> *An Act to consolidate the enactments relating to the Health Service Commissioners for England, for Wales and for Scotland with amendments to give effect to recommendations of the Law Commission and the Scottish Law Commission.*

**9.48** Since the process of consolidation involves the re-enactment of previous law rather than the enactment of new law, the progress of a consolidation Bill is different to that of a normal Bill. Where the Lord Chancellor considers that a consolidating Bill is necessary, but that corrections and minor improvements ought to be made to the enactments, then in accordance with s 1(1) of the Consolidation of Enactments (Procedure) Act 1949, he may lay before Parliament a memorandum proposing those corrections and minor improvements. A notice specifying from where such a memorandum may be obtained must be published in the *London Gazette*.

**9.49** Consolidation Bills are introduced in the HL and will be referred to a Joint Committee of both Houses. The Joint Committee will consider the Bill, the memorandum, and any representations which have been received. It must not approve any corrections or minor improvements unless it is satisfied that they do not make changes to the existing law that are of such importance as to require separate enactment. The report stage and the third reading in the HL take place without debate, as do the various stages in the HC.

### Is it in force?

**9.50** This question, which will often be asked of an Act of Parliament or of a provision therein, is not always easily answered. The fact that an Act has passed all of its parliamentary stages and has received Royal Assent is no guarantee that it is actually in force. Some Acts will take effect immediately. Others, however, may specify a date on which they will enter into force. For example, s 5(2) of the Household Waste Recycling Act 2003 states that:

> *This Act comes into force at the end of the period of two months beginning with the day on which it is passed.*

**9.51**   Yet another alternative is that the Act will be brought into force, either wholly or partly, by the issuing of commencement orders. The Human Rights Act 1998 provided a good example of a statute which applied several of these approaches to its provisions. By virtue of s 22 of the Act:

> *(2) Sections 18, 20 and 21(5) and this section come into force on the passing of this Act.*
>
> *(3) The other provisions of this Act come into force on such day as the Secretary of State may by order appoint; and different days may be appointed for different purposes.*

**9.52**   The reader of a statute must therefore take care to ensure that the relevant provisions are in force. Some assistance can be gained from a section which is usually at the end of the Act and which is generally entitled 'Short title, commencement and extent'. However, if that section provides for the making of commencement orders, additional care is required. It may even be necessary to inquire of the government department concerned whether or not a particular commencement order has been made.

## Delegated legislation

**9.53**   Acts of Parliament are, as we have seen, primary legislation passed by Parliament. However, given the volume of legislation which needs to be passed in any one year and the relatively limited amount of parliamentary time available for this purpose (see Chapter **6**), it is simply not possible for all the necessary legislation to be enacted by Parliament. Accordingly, a further type of legislation exists which is variously known as delegated, secondary, or subordinate legislation.

**9.54**   In the *Report of the Committee on Ministers' Powers* (Donoughmore Committee, 1932) (Cmd 4060), several reasons were given for the committee's belief that a system of delegated legislation was 'both legitimate and constitutionally desirable for certain purposes, within certain limits, and under certain safeguards'. In addition to the pressure on parliamentary time, the committee considered that delegated legislation was necessary because:

- the technical nature of some modern legislation made its inclusion in a Bill inappropriate – it could not be effectively discussed in Parliament;

- in the case of large and complex schemes of reform, it would be difficult to work out the administrative machinery in time to insert it into a Bill – often it is only possible to do this at a later date;

- it allows for flexibility – adaptation can take place without the need for amending legislation; and

- it can provide a quick response where there is a need for urgent legislative action.

**9.55** The term 'delegated' legislation signifies that the power to make legislation has been delegated to a person or body other than Parliament by Parliament. The power to make delegated legislation is provided for in an Act of Parliament commonly referred to as the 'enabling' or 'parent' Act. The most noteworthy form of delegated power is that conferred on ministers of the Crown. Thus, for example, s 2(2) of the European Communities Act 1972 confers a general power to make delegated legislation in order to give effect to the UK's EU obligations. Other enabling Acts may confer a power to make more specific delegated legislation. Thus s 31 of the Clean Air Act 1993 confers a power on the Secretary of State to make regulations in order to 'impose limits on the sulphur content of oil fuel which is used in furnaces or engines'.

**9.56** In addition to ministers of the Crown, other bodies with the power to make delegated legislation include local authorities, which have the power to make bye-laws, and the court rule committees which have the power to make Rules of Court relating to procedure.

**9.57** Where delegated legislation is published in the form of a statutory instrument (paras **9.70–9.72**), the preamble to the statutory instrument will state the authority under which it has been made. Thus the preamble to the Toys (Safety) Regulations 2011 states that;

> *The Secretary of State makes regulations 1 to 39 in exercise of the powers conferred by section 11 of the Consumer Protection Act 1987, and paragraph 1A of Schedule 2 to the European Communities Act 1972, and all other regulations in exercise of the powers conferred by section 2(2) of, and paragraph 1A of Schedule 2 to, the European Communities Act 1972.*

## General types of delegated legislation

### Orders in Council

**9.58** These are a form of delegated legislation made by the Privy Council in the exercise of powers conferred by a parent Act. Thus, for example, s 2 of the Emergency Powers Act 1920 empowers the Privy Council to make Orders in Council in the event that a proclamation of emergency has been made. Similarly, s 2(2) of the European Communities

Act 1972 provides for the making of Orders in Council so that the UK may meet its obligations under EU law. In the context of devolution, s 95 of the Government of Wales Act 2006 provides for the making of Legislative Competence Orders which may extend the legislative competence of the National Assembly for Wales in respect of the specified 'fields' or 'matters' (see para **8.30**).

### Regulations, orders, directions, rules

**9.59** These terms tend to be used interchangeably in enabling Acts. However, the Donoughmore Committee (1932) made the case for a more precise use of the terminology. In its view:

> The expression 'regulation' should be used to describe the instrument by which the power to make substantive law is exercised, and the expression 'rule' to describe the instrument by which the power to make law about procedure is exercised. The expression 'order' should be used to describe the instrument of the exercise of (a) executive power, (b) the power to take judicial and quasi-judicial decisions.

The power to make these forms of delegated legislation is often conferred on a government minister. However, as has already been noted, the court rule committees have the power to make Rules of Court which relate to procedure.

### Bye-laws

**9.60** Bye-laws are rules made by local authorities, public corporations, and certain non-governmental independent bodies. The power to make bye-laws is conferred by an Act of Parliament. However, before a bye-law becomes effective, it will first need to be confirmed by a Secretary of State. Where a bye-law has been made, it will be binding on all persons within the relevant locality, or in respect of the area or organization to which it relates. Thus, for example, passengers on a train are obliged to comply with a bye-law which prohibits smoking in carriages: see *Boddington v British Transport Police* (1999). Where a bye-law has not been complied with, the body which made it can enforce it by pursuing criminal proceedings. Breach of a bye-law will often result in the imposition of a financial penalty, although an injunction may be obtainable to prevent further breaches of the bye-law.

## Specific types of delegated legislation

### Regulatory reform orders

**9.61** Successive Conservative and Labour Governments have pursued deregulation agendas that have led to the enactment of three pieces of legislation: the Deregulation and

Contracting Out Act 1994; the Regulatory Reform Act 2001; and the Legislative and Regulatory Reform Act 2006. Under s 1 of the 1994 Act, a minister of the Crown had the power to amend or repeal any provision made by primary legislation enacted before or during the 1993–94 session where he was of the opinion that its effect was to impose a burden on any person carrying on a trade, business, or other profession. It was used on 48 separate occasions to make orders which, for example, amended the Marriage Act 1949 so as to allow bookings at registry offices to be made 12 months in advance of a wedding instead of three months. However, the limited scope of the power (it did not apply to post-1994 legislation) led the Government to consult on how it might be amended. The result, ultimately, was the Regulatory Reform Act 2001 that provided for a potentially more extensive use of regulatory reform orders: see, for example, the Regulatory Reform (Collaboration etc between Ombudsman) Order 2007, SI 2007/1889 (paras **15.108–15.109**).

**9.62** The law is now to be found in the Legislative and Regulatory Reform Act 2006. By virtue of s 1(1) and (2) of the Act, a minister has the power to make a provision the purpose of which is to remove or reduce any burden, or the overall burdens, on any person, which result either directly or indirectly from any legislation. In short, s 1 provides members of the executive with the power to amend or repeal primary and secondary legislation by the expedient of secondary legislation. The 'burden' referred to in s 1 is any of the following:

- a financial cost;

- an administrative inconvenience;

- an obstacle to efficiency, productivity, or profitability; or

- a sanction, criminal or otherwise, which affects the carrying on of any lawful activity.

**9.63** The scope of the power is potentially very broad indeed. It is, however, subject to various 'restrictions' as specified in Pt I of the 2006 Act. Of these, the most important is to be found in s 3, which provides that a minister may not make a provision unless he considers that certain preconditions are satisfied in relation to that provision. These are stated in s 3(2) as follows:

- the policy objective intended to be secured by the provision could not be satisfactorily secured by non-legislative means;

- the effect of the provision is proportionate to the policy objective;

- the provision, taken as a whole, strikes a fair balance between the public interest and the interests of any person adversely affected by it;

- the provision does not remove any necessary protection;

- the provision does not prevent any person from continuing to exercise any right/ freedom which that person might reasonably expect to continue to exercise;

- the provision is not of constitutional significance.

**9.64** For present purposes it is preconditions five and six which are of greatest interest. As Burns has pointed out in an annotation to s 3, the fifth precondition is concerned with protecting legitimate expectations to existing rights and freedoms, such as those set out in the ECHR (see Chapter **16**). The sixth precondition must be read carefully. It does not prevent a constitutional statute (see Chapter **5**) from being amended by a provision made under the 2006 Act. Rather, it requires that the amending provision is not of itself of 'constitutional significance'. Quite what this expression means in the present context is unclear.

**9.65** The importance of the preconditions is reinforced by the procedure for making an order under the Act: see ss 12–18. As part of that process that also involves consultation and the laying of a draft order before Parliament, a minister must also provide Parliament with an explanatory document setting out, amongst other things, the reasons for making the provision. An important part of the explanatory document is an explanation from the minister as to why he considers that the relevant preconditions are satisfied.

**9.66** Further 'restrictions' on the power to make provisions under the 2006 Act include that they may not be made to 'impose, abolish or vary any tax' (s 5) or to create new criminal offences where the proposed punishments exceed levels specified in the Act. Section 5 thus preserves Parliament's exclusive control over the levying of taxation as set out in the Bill of Rights 1689.

**9.67** As indicated (para **9.65**), the procedure for making an order under the 2006 Act involves a consultation process which precedes the laying of a draft order before Parliament. The minister is able to recommend which parliamentary procedure will be used for making the order. Although recommendations that either the negative or affirmative resolution procedures be used may be subject to a process of Parliamentary approval, the recommendation that the super-affirmative procedure be followed is binding on Parliament.

**9.68** The Regulatory Reform Committee examines and reports on all draft legislative reform orders proposed under the 2006 Act. In addition, the committee has the power to report more widely on matters relating to regulatory reform. Thus, for example, on 21 July 2009 it published *Themes and Trends in Regulatory Reform*, HC 329-I.

## Remedial orders

**9.69** Under s 10 of the Human Rights Act 1998, a minister of the Crown has the power to make a remedial order where a provision of an Act has been declared by a court to be incompatible with a Convention right. The way in which such orders are made and their legal effect is considered in Chapter **16**.

## Statutory instruments

**9.70** By virtue of s 1 of the Statutory Instruments Act 1946, where a power to make, confirm, or approve orders, rules, regulations, or other subordinate legislation has been conferred on a minister and is stated to be exercisable by statutory instrument (SI), any document by which that power is exercised is known as a statutory instrument. Similarly, a power conferred on Her Majesty and expressed to be exercisable by Order in Council takes the form of an SI. Statutory instruments are therefore a particular species of delegated legislation.

**9.71** Statutory instruments are made rather than enacted. The text of an SI will state the date on which it was made, the date that it was laid before Parliament, and the date on which it comes into force. For the purposes of identification, in addition to having a title, each SI is numbered. The citation for an SI comprises the year in which it was made together with its number. Therefore the Toys (Safety) Regulations referred to in para **9.57** may be cited as 2011/1881. In any one year, approximately 3,500 SIs are issued by the Stationery Office.

**9.72** Unlike Acts of Parliament which are drafted by parliamentary counsel, the text of an SI is normally drafted by lawyers within the relevant government department. SIs may vary quite considerably in terms of length and complexity. Some SIs may be brief whereas others may extend to a great many pages and provisions. In terms of complexity, SIs are quite commonly used as the vehicle for dealing with detailed technical matters that would otherwise clutter up a Bill. However, given that SIs have the force of law in the same way that Acts of Parliament do, it is necessary to consider the procedure for making them, the extent to which they are subject to scrutiny, and the attitude of the courts towards them.

### Parliamentary procedure

**9.73** SIs are not subject to the same parliamentary stages as a Bill. In the case of some SIs, such as commencement orders which are employed to bring into force the whole or part of an Act, they may take effect as soon as they are made and hence not be subject to any parliamentary approval whatsoever. However, the more contentious SIs will be subject to one of two procedures provided for in the Statutory Instruments Act 1946: the negative procedure; or the affirmative procedure. Precisely which procedure applies will depend upon what the parent Act says.

### Negative procedure

**9.74** Under this procedure, an SI laid before Parliament will come into effect (normally 40 days from the day on which it was so laid), unless either House passes a motion calling for its annulment within the relevant time. The effect of such a motion is that the SI will not become law. This negative procedure is more commonly used than the affirmative procedure. Where neither House passes a motion calling for its annulment, it may be argued that the SI has been approved by Parliament, albeit indirectly.

## Affirmative procedure

**9.75**   A rather more direct form of parliamentary approval is apparent in the affirmative procedure. This requires that a motion approving the SI has to be passed by both Houses in order for it to take effect. Usually the motion will have to be passed within 28 days of the SI being laid before Parliament. The advantage of this procedure in terms of parliamentary control is that the measure must be discussed in Parliament before it can become law.

**9.76**   Whichever of the two procedures is used, it ought to be noted, however, that unless the parent Act provides otherwise, the SI cannot be amended by either House. In short, it must be accepted in its entirety as laid before Parliament if it is to become law.

## Parliamentary scrutiny

**9.77**   In addition to the procedures previously described, a measure of parliamentary scrutiny is achieved by: the HC Select Committee on Statutory Instruments; the HL Select Committee on the Merits of Statutory Instruments; and the Joint Select Committee on Statutory Instruments. The latter has the broadest remit of the three committees. It is appointed to consider all those instruments which are required to be laid before Parliament together with other SIs that are not, with a view to determining whether the special attention of the House should be drawn to any of them. There are a number of grounds which would justify this course of action in respect of an SI. These include that:

- it imposes a charge on the public revenues or requires payments to be made to central or local government in respect of licences or consents;
- it is made in pursuance of an enactment containing specific provisions excluding it from challenge in the courts;
- it purports to have retrospective effect although this is not expressly provided for in the parent Act;
- there appears to have been an unjustifiable delay in the publication or in the laying of it before Parliament;
- there is doubt as to whether it is intra vires or that it appears to make an unusual or unexpected use of the powers conferred by the parent Act; or
- its drafting appears to be defective.

**9.78** What the Joint Select Committee must not consider are the merits of the SI or the policy on which it is based. In order to perform its functions, the committee has the power to appoint one or more sub-committees. It has the power to sit notwithstanding any adjournment of the House, and may require any concerned department to submit a memorandum explaining the SI under consideration or to depute a representative to appear as a witness before it to explain the SI. Where the committee considers that an SI falls into any of the categories (see para **9.77**), it is required to report the matter to the House.

**9.79** The Joint Select Committee produces a large number of reports on SIs in each parliamentary session. Thus in the 2005–06 session, it produced 37 reports. At the time of writing, the committee has published 27 reports during the 2010–12 session. In the last of these, which was published on 19 July 2011, four SIs were reported to the House for defective drafting.

**9.80** Unlike the Joint Select Committee, the HL Select Committee on the Merits of SIs patently does have the authority to consider the merits of SIs. It may draw an instrument, draft, or proposal to the attention of the HL on one of several grounds. These include that it is politically or legally important, or gives rise to issues of public policy likely to be of interest, or that it may inappropriately implement EU legislation.

## Judicial scrutiny

**9.81** It will be remembered that in respect of statutes dealing with purely domestic law matters, the courts have no power to declare such Acts to be invalid. The doctrine of the legislative supremacy of Parliament prevents such an eventuality (see Chapter **5**). However, the position is somewhat different with regard to delegated legislation. As a result of the ultra vires doctrine, a court may strike down delegated legislation where it exceeds the power under which it was made. In so doing, the courts are upholding the will of Parliament by quashing delegated legislation which goes beyond that which Parliament intended. The legality rather than the merits of delegated legislation is thus subject to the supervisory jurisdiction of the courts. This jurisdiction is invoked by the procedure known as a claim for judicial review. Judicial review will be considered more fully in Chapters **12–14**.

## Quasi-legislation

**9.82** 'Quasi-legislation' is a term which is used to cover what Professor Ganz has referred to as 'a wide spectrum of rules whose only common factor is that they are not directly enforceable by the courts'. Thus into this category fall such things as: circulars, codes of guidance, codes of practice, guidance notes, planning policy statements, and planning policy guidance notes. Given the generic nature of the term 'quasi-legislation', it is not surprising that the instruments that it encompasses do not necessarily share the same characteristics. However, Professor Ganz has identified several features common to quasi-legislation. These include:

- the use of non-technical language which is easily understood by lay persons;
- the documents are flexible and can therefore easily be drawn up and replaced;
- the documents are often designed to ensure that those to whom they are addressed exercise the powers which they have in common in a uniform manner;
- the documents are a manifestation of the belief that persuasion rather than compulsion is the way to achieve an objective; and
- the documents represent an acceptable compromise between legislating on a particular matter or doing nothing.

## FURTHER READING

Bates, T St J N 'Post-Legislative Scrutiny' (2006) 27 Stat LR iii.

Bowman, Sir Geoffrey 'The Art of Legislative Drafting' (2005) 7 Eur J L Reform 3.

Bowman, Sir Geoffrey 'Why is there a Parliamentary Counsel Office' (2005) 26 Stat LR 69.

Burns, S *Legislative and Regulatory Reform Act 2006* Current Law Annotated Statutes, Sweet & Maxwell.

Cabinet Office, *Working with Parliamentary Counsel* (January 2011).

Committee on Ministers' Powers Report (1932), Cmd 4060.

First Report of the Modernisation Committee of the HC, *The Legislation Process*, 1997–98 session (HC 190).

Ganz, G *Quasi-Legislation: Recent Developments in Secondary Legislation* (1987) Sweet & Maxwell.

The Hansard Society *Making the Law* (1993).

The Hansard Society, *Making Better Law: Reform of the legislative process from policy to Act* (2010).

Hazell, R 'Who is the guardian of legal values in the legislative process: Parliament or the Executive?' [2004] PL 495.

House of Commons Factsheet L3 (Legislative Series), *The Success of Private Members' Bills* (Revised June 2010).

Jack, Dr M et al *Erskine May's Treatise on the Law, Privileges, Proceedings and Usage of Parliament* (24th edn, 2011) LexisNexis Butterworths.

Kennon, A 'Pre-Legislative Scrutiny of Draft Bills' [2004] PL 477.

Korris, M 'Standing up for Scrutiny: How and why Parliament should make better law' (2011) 64 Parliamentary Affairs 564.

The Law Commission, *Post-Legislative Scrutiny* (Law Com No 302, Cm 6945) (2006).

Marsh, D and Read, M *Private Members' Bills* (1988) Cambridge University Press.

Office of the Leader of the House of Commons *The Governance of Britain – The Government's Draft Legislative Programme* (Cm 7175) (July 2007).

Office of the Leader of the House of Commons *Post-legislative Scrutiny – The Government's Approach* (Cm 7320) (March 2008).

Pollard, D, Parpworth, N, and Hughes, D *Constitutional and Administrative Law: Text with Materials* (4th edn, 2007) OUP.

Samuels, A 'Consolidation: A Plea' (2005) 26 Stat LR 56.

de Waal, H ' "There ought to be a law": A look at Private Members Bills' (1990) 11 Stat LR 18.

Zander, M *The Law-making Process* (6th edn, 2004) Cambridge University Press.

## SELF-TEST QUESTIONS

1    Is there a case for making the pre-legislative scrutiny of government Bills compulsory? When might pre-legislative scrutiny be impracticable?

2    How important a development is the annual publication of a draft legislative programme? Is there a case for arguing that a 'draft' Queen's speech will tie the hands of a government?

3    Do you agree with Bennion that publishing government Bills in draft is a 'misconceived reform' which 'ensures that a proposal goes off half-cock' and which results, due to the lack of parliamentary explanation, in the measure being 'inevitably misunderstood'?

4    The PM has stated that 'our new public reading stage will improve the level of debate and scrutiny of Bills by giving everyone the opportunity to go online and offer their views on any new legislation'. Is this an example of misplaced optimism, or a fair comment on the likely effect of the innovation?

5    In the consultation paper *Post-Legislative Scrutiny* (Law Com Consultation Paper No 178) that preceded the publication of its final report, the Law Commission argued that 'it would be far more preferable to have effective review of a few pieces of legislation a year rather than a perfunctory review of many Acts'. Do you agree?

6    What arguments can be advanced in favour of the making of delegated legislation?

7    When might it be inappropriate to legislate by exercising delegated powers?

8    What purpose does quasi-legislation serve?

# 10  EU law

## SUMMARY

The institutions of the EU and the functions that they perform have already been discussed in Chapter **7**. In this chapter, therefore, the focus is primarily upon EU laws (primary and secondary) and the doctrines of: direct applicability, direct effect, and indirect effect. The latter two doctrines have emerged from the jurisprudence of the ECJ, as has the principle of state liability in damages for a breach of EU law, which will also be considered. The chapter concludes with a consideration of how English courts have responded to the task of interpreting national law in the light of EU law.

Note: Following the amendments made by the Lisbon Treaty, two Treaties are now of key importance in the present context: the Treaty on European Union (TEU) and the Treaty on the Functioning of the European Union (TFEU). The Treaty articles referred to in this chapter are therefore from these treaties as indicated.

## The treaties

10.1 The treaties are the primary law of the EU. In addition to the treaties which originally established the three European Communities (para **7.2**), a number of other treaties have subsequently been made. These include the Treaty on European Union (the Maastricht Treaty), the Treaty of Amsterdam, the Treaty of Nice, and the Lisbon Treaty, all of which have made important amendments to the foundation treaties. Following its eventual ratification, the Lisbon Treaty has become the fifth amending treaty since the UK joined the EU in 1973. A number of the reforms which it has made have been considered in Chapter 7. For present purposes, it will be necessary to consider its impact on the laws which can be made at the EU level.

## Legislative acts

10.2 Article 288 of the TFEU confers legislative power on the Union's institutions to make secondary legislation in accordance with the provisions of the Treaty. This secondary legislation may take one of a number of different forms: regulations, directives, decisions, recommendations, and opinions.

## Regulations

10.3 Regulations are of general application to the member states of the EU . They are binding in their entirety and are directly applicable in all member states. In other words, regulations become part of national law without any need for further enactment.

## Directives

10.4 Directives are binding on those member states to which they are addressed, at least in terms of the objective which they require to be achieved. However, unlike regulations, they are not directly applicable. In order for a directive to take effect in national law, it is necessary for it to be implemented by the member state. Article 288 confers a discretion upon the national authorities as to how implementation is to be achieved in practice. In the UK, a general power to make secondary legislation to give effect to EU obligations is to be found in s 2(2) of the European Communities Act 1972. Thus an EU directive could be implemented domestically by way of national secondary legislation. This is by far the most common means by which the UK meets its EU obligations. Alternatively, however, an EU directive could be implemented in the form of an Act of Parliament or as part of such an Act. This less common approach is likely to be reserved for very important measures, or where an appropriate Bill is before Parliament at the relevant time.

## Decisions

10.5 Decisions are binding in their entirety on those to whom they are addressed. Unlike directives, they may be addressed to individuals as well as to member states. In either case, a decision has the force of law and must therefore be complied with.

## Recommendations and opinions

10.6 Both these forms of secondary legislation have no binding force and hence no legal effect. They are merely persuasive.

## Nomenclature

10.7 Despite the titles of these various legal instruments, it does not automatically follow that because, for example, an instrument has been labelled a 'regulation' it is therefore a regulation in law. What matters is not the official title of the measure but its 'object and content' (see *Confédération Nationale des Producteurs de Fruits et Legumes v EEC*

*Council*: 16–17/62 (1962)). Thus where the legality of an EU act has been challenged, it may be necessary for the ECJ to examine the measure closely in order to determine its object and content and hence its true legal status.

## Reasons for making secondary legislation

**10.8** In addition to having binding effect, regulations, directives, and decisions are also distinguishable from recommendations and opinions on two further grounds: reasons and publicity. Article 296 of the TFEU states that legal acts, ie regulations, directives, and decisions, must state the reasons on which they are based. Additionally, they must refer to any proposals, initiatives, recommendations, requests, or opinions required by the treaties. It would seem that these requirements include the need to state the legal basis for a Union act in its preamble. A statement of reasons serves a useful purpose in that it is a record of the basis upon which the EU institutions felt that it was necessary to act. Moreover, those reasons may, where they are too vague or imprecise, or indeed where they are non-existent, entitle the ECJ to strike down the legislation.

## Publicity

**10.9** Article 297 of the TFEU makes provision for the publication of certain types of EU legal instrument that have been adopted in a particular manner. Regulations, directives, and decisions adopted in accordance with the ordinary legislative procedure referred to in art 294 are signed by the President of the European Parliament and by the President of the Council and are published in the *Official Journal of the European Union*. Regulations and directives which are addressed to all member states are also published in the *Official Journal*, as are decisions which do not specify to whom they are addressed. In all these cases, the relevant legal instrument enters into force on the date specified therein, or where no date is specified, 20 days after publication. Directives and decisions which do not fall into any of these categories are required by art 297(2) to be notified to those to whom they are addressed. They take effect upon notification.

## Direct applicability

**10.10** Of the various EU legal instruments, only regulations are, according to art 288, directly applicable. In other words, only regulations take effect in domestic law without any need for further enactment. Section 2(1) of the European Communities Act 1972 recognizes the existence of directly applicable provisions when it refers to provisions which 'are without further enactment to be given legal effect or use in the United Kingdom'. The concept of direct applicability thus appears to be relatively straightforward. However, there has sometimes been a tendency for the ECJ and national courts to use the terms 'direct applicability' and 'direct effect' interchangeably. Thus, for example, in *Van Duyn v Home Office*: Case 41/74 (1975) (see para **10.19**), the ECJ's judgment referred to 'direct applicability' when it had been asked whether Directive 64/221 was capable of having direct effect. For present purposes, therefore, 'directly applicable' shall be taken to mean nothing other than the characteristic of becoming law without the need for domestic enactment.

## Direct effect

**10.11** Whereas art 288 of the TFEU (and its predecessors) specifically mentions the concept of direct applicability, it is silent as to the concept of direct effect. This is because the doctrine was established not by legislative means but by a decision of the ECJ.

---

**Case 26/62:** *Algemene Transporten Expeditie Onderneming Van Gend en Loos NV v Nederlandse Administratie der Belastingen* **(1963)**: Van Gend en Loos imported a certain amount of a chemical substance into the Netherlands from the former West Germany. The Dutch revenue authorities applied an import charge of 8% and the company appealed. It claimed that it ought to have been charged a duty of only 3% and that by increasing the import duty after the entry into force of the EC Treaty, the Dutch Government had acted contrary to art 12 of the Treaty. Its appeal was dismissed. Van Gend en Loos therefore applied to the Tariefcommissie at Amsterdam. In accordance with what was then art 177(3) of the EC Treaty, the Tariefcommissie referred two questions to the ECJ: whether art 12 created rights capable of being enforced by the individual before a national court; if the answer to this question was 'yes', whether the 8% import duty was contrary to art 12. ECJ held: art 12 had direct effect within the territory of a member state.

---

**10.12** In reaching this decision, the ECJ dismissed objections from the Dutch and Belgian Governments that it did not have jurisdiction to examine the internal effects of art 12. With regard to the merits of the first question posed, the ECJ noted that the Treaty was 'more than an agreement creating only mutual obligations between the contracting parties'. Confirmation of this fact was to be found in the Treaty's preamble which refers to individuals as well as to governments. In an important passage which has since been much quoted, the ECJ observed that:

> the Community constitutes a new legal order in international law, for whose benefit the States have limited their Sovereign rights, albeit within limited fields, and the subjects of which comprise not only the member-states but also their nationals. Community law, therefore, apart from legislation by the member-states, not only imposes obligations on individuals but also confers on them legal rights. The latter arise not only when an explicit grant is made by the Treaty, but also through obligations imposed, in a clearly defined manner, by the Treaty on individuals as well as on member-states and the Community institutions.

**10.13** Thus a Treaty article was capable of conferring legally enforceable rights on an individual: it could have direct effect. Whether or not it did have direct effect depended, however, on whether the article was: clear and unconditional; and did not require further legislative intervention by the state. If these criteria were satisfied, the article was directly effective.

**10.14** It rapidly became apparent that the direct effect doctrine was not limited to Treaty articles which imposed negative obligations. Thus in Case 57/65: *Firma Alfons Lütticke GmbH v Hauptzollamt Saarelouis* (1966), the ECJ held that the positive obligation imposed on member states by art 90(3) (now art 110 of the TFEU) to repeal or amend national provisions for the imposition of differential taxation did have direct effect.

**10.15** The position with regard to Treaty articles is therefore clear. They can have direct effect provided that they satisfy the conditions laid down in *Van Gend en Loos*. The two examples that have been referred to illustrate the enforcement of a legal right as against the state, ie vertical direct effect. However, in Case 43/75: *Defrenne v Sabena* (1976), the ECJ held that art 119 of the EU Treaty (now art 157 of the TFEU), which establishes the principle that men and women should receive equal pay for equal work, was directly effective in proceedings brought by an individual against a private company. Treaty articles can therefore be said to have horizontal direct effect as well.

**10.16** Once it was accepted that Treaty articles could have direct effect, it became necessary to consider whether the other legal instruments referred to in what is now art 288 of the TFEU could also have direct effect.

## Regulations and direct effect

**10.17** The wording of art 288 by itself implies that regulations do have direct effect. Since a regulation is binding in its entirety and directly applicable, it follows that it can create legally enforceable rights. This was confirmed by the ECJ in Case 39/72: *EC Commission v Italy* (1973). In the later Case 50/76: *Amsterdam Bulb BV v Produktschap voor Siergewassen* (1977), the ECJ spoke in terms of direct effect being 'inherent in regulations and other rules of Community law'.

## Decisions and direct effect

**10.18** It will be remembered that art 288 provides that decisions are binding in their entirety on those to whom they are addressed. Unlike regulations, decisions are not directly applicable. Nevertheless, in Case 9/70: *Grad v Finanzamt Traunstein* (1970), the ECJ ruled that decisions relating to taxes and VAT satisfied the criteria for direct effect. In delivering its judgment, the court observed that:

> It would be incompatible with the binding effect attributed to decisions by Article 189 [now art 288] to exclude in principle the possibility that persons affected may

*invoke the obligation imposed by a decision. Particularly in cases where, for example, the Community authorities by means of a decision have imposed an obligation on a Member State or all the Member States to act in a certain way, the effectiveness ('l'effet utile') of such a measure would be weakened if the nationals of that state could not invoke it in the courts and the national courts could not take it into consideration as part of Community law.*

## Directives and direct effect

**10.19**  The doctrine of direct effect is perhaps of greatest significance when considered in the context of directives. Article 288 makes it clear that in order for a directive to enter into force in domestic law, it is necessary for the member state to implement the Union law. In other words, directives are not directly applicable. Moreover, given that one of the criteria for direct effect as laid down in *Van Gend en Loos* is that the measure must not require further legislative intervention by the state, it would seem, on the face of it, that directives cannot have direct effect. Nevertheless, such an obstacle has not been allowed to stand in the way of the direct effect of directives.

> **Case 41/74: *Van Duyn v Home Office* (1975)**: Miss Van Duyn was a Dutch national. She was offered employment in the UK as a secretary with the Church of Scientology. The British Government regarded the activities of the church as contrary to public policy. It was described by the Minister of Health in the HC as 'a pseudo-philosophical cult' that was socially harmful. Although the law could not be used to prohibit the practice of Scientology, it could be used to prevent foreign nationals from entering the UK to study Scientology. When Miss Van Duyn arrived at Gatwick Airport, she was refused leave to enter the UK. Relying on art 48 of the EC Treaty (now art 45 TFEU) and art 3 of Directive 64/221, Miss Van Duyn claimed that the refusal of leave to enter was unlawful. She sought a declaration from the HCt that she was entitled to stay in the UK. Under art 177 (now art 267 TFEU), the HCt sought a preliminary ruling from the ECJ on several matters. These included whether Directive 64/221 had direct effect. ECJ held: that it would be incompatible with the binding nature of a directive to exclude the possibility that it may have direct effect. Whether or not a particular directive had direct effect depended upon the nature, general scheme, and wording of the provision. Directive 64/221 did confer rights on the individual which were legally enforceable before a national court. Despite the ECJ's preliminary ruling on the question of direct effect, the UK Government was entitled to exclude Miss Van Duyn from the UK on the grounds of public policy relating to her personal conduct, ie the fact that she was a Scientologist.

**10.20**  The decision in *Van Duyn* is a good example of judicial activism on the part of the ECJ. In order to ensure that directives have the full force of law, the ECJ was prepared to rule that they were capable of having direct effect. However, the decision was not universally welcomed. For some member states, it represented the ECJ overstepping the legitimate bounds of the judicial function. It was argued that if directives were to create legally enforceable rights, that was a matter for primary legislation rather than the determination of the ECJ.

**10.21** In Case 148/78: *Pubblico Ministero v Ratti* (1979), the direct effect of directives was further considered by the ECJ. It concluded that where an individual had acted in accordance with EU directives as yet unimplemented by the state, the state could not be allowed to rely upon its own failure to perform the obligations where the measure was pleaded against it. Its own inactivity precluded or 'estopped' it from raising such a defence.

**10.22** The decision in *Ratti* is of further interest in that it establishes that directives will only have direct effect once the time limit for their implementation has expired. Up until this point, a member state which has not implemented a directive could claim that it was exercising its discretion as to how best to do so. Once the time limit has expired, however, it has failed to comply with an obligation and ought not to be allowed to benefit from such a failure. Where a time limit for implementation is not identified in a directive, it enters into force on the 20th day following publication (art 297(1) and (2)).

**10.23** In *Ratti*, R was prosecuted by the state for a breach of a national law which was incompatible with unimplemented EU law. The practical effect of the ECJ's decision was that he was able to rely upon this incompatibility as a defence to the prosecution. In Case 8/81: *Becker v Finanzamt–Münster Innenstadt* (1982), the ECJ accepted that a state's failure to comply with the obligations arising under a directive within the specified time limit could form the basis of an action against the state as well as a defence to proceedings brought by the state. As in previous cases, the ECJ stressed that the 'practical effectiveness' of a directive would be weakened if individuals could not rely upon it before a national court.

## Horizontal and vertical direct effect

**10.24** Despite the factual differences between the 'directive cases', they share a common theme: they involve proceedings between the state and the individual. In other words, when the ECJ held in each of these cases that the relevant directive created legally enforceable rights, it was asserting that it had vertical direct effect. We have already seen in *Defrenne v Sabena* that a regulation may have horizontal direct effect. Can directives also have horizontal direct effect?

> **Case 152/84: *Marshall v Southampton and South West Hampshire Area Health Authority (Teaching)* (1986):** Miss M was employed by the AHA as a senior dietician. She was dismissed approximately four weeks after reaching the age of 62 despite her stated willingness to work until she was 65. The sole reason for her dismissal was that she had passed the retirement age for women applied by the AHA, ie when social security payments became payable. Miss M brought proceedings before an Industrial Tribunal. She claimed that the AHA had discriminated against her on the grounds of sex contrary to the Sex

Discrimination Act 1975 and Community law. The tribunal dismissed her claim under the 1975 Act because s 6(4) allowed such discrimination where it arose out of 'provision in relation to retirement'. It upheld her claim that the principle of equality of treatment laid down in Directive 76/207 had been infringed. On appeal to the Employment Appeal Tribunal, the decision on the second point was set aside. An individual could not rely on the violation of the principle of equality of treatment before a UK court or tribunal. Miss M appealed to the CA which sought a preliminary ruling from the ECJ under art 177 (now art 267 TFEU). ECJ held: in response to the CA's first question, that the dismissal of Miss M solely because she had attained the age for a state pension amounted to discrimination on the grounds of sex contrary to the directive. On the second question, whether the Equal Treatment Directive had direct effect, the ECJ ruled that it did.

**10.25**  In reaching its conclusion on the second question, the ECJ accepted the argument that since a directive imposes obligations on the state rather than the individual, a provision of a directive could not be relied upon against an individual. In other words, the court concluded that directives could not have horizontal direct effect. Directives could be relied upon, however, against the state regardless of the capacity in which it was acting, ie as public authority or employer. The practical effect of such a ruling is worth noting. It meant that a state employee could seek to enforce a directive as against his employer, where the state had not implemented or had incorrectly implemented the provision, whereas the employee of a private company was unable to do likewise. This anomaly was drawn to the attention of the ECJ by the UK Government in *Marshall*, but the court's response was to observe that the 'distinction may easily be avoided if the member-state concerned has correctly implemented the directive in national law'. If it has done this, all employees, whether public or private, would enjoy the same rights which would be capable of being enforced before the national courts.

## What is an emanation of the state?

**10.26**  The restriction placed upon the direct effect of directives by the decision in *Marshall* meant that for the individual seeking to rely upon a directive a further hurdle had to be overcome; it would have to be established that the other party to the proceedings was the state or an emanation of the state. In *Marshall* itself, the ECJ accepted that the AHA was an organ of the state. Subsequently, what constitutes an emanation of the state for the purpose of enforcing directives has received a broad but imprecise interpretation. Thus in Case C-188/89: *Foster v British Gas plc* (1991), the ECJ held in a preliminary ruling that the British Gas Corporation (BGC), the controlling body of a nationalized industry, was an emanation of the state. The factors which had led to this decision were that:

- the BGC provided a public service;
- it was under the control of the state in that the state could dictate its policies and retain its surplus revenue; and
- the BGC had special powers beyond those which result from the normal rules applicable to relations between individuals.

**10.27** Applying these conditions to the facts in *Griffin v South West Water Services Ltd* (1995), Blackburne J concluded that SWW, a privatized water company, was an emanation of the state against which directives were capable of being enforced. Professor Craig has argued that this ruling is 'of real significance, given the number of privatized undertakings which now exist'. Undoubtedly this must be correct. Prior to the decision, there had been suggestions that the privatized utilities may be beyond the reach of the direct effect doctrine. The decision in *Griffin* demonstrates that this is not the case.

**10.28** In Case 222/84: *Johnston v Chief Constable of the Royal Ulster Constabulary* (1987), where J sought to challenge the chief constable's policy of not allowing policewomen to be armed which had resulted in her contract of employment not being renewed, the ECJ observed that the chief constable was:

> an official responsible for the direction of the police service. Whatever its relations may be with other organs of the state, such a police authority, charged by the state with the maintenance of public order and safety, does not act as a private individual. It may not take advantage of the failure of the state, of which it is an emanation, to comply with Community law.

**10.29** Furthermore, in *National Union of Teachers v Governing Body of St Mary's Church of England (Aided) Junior School* (1997), the CA reversed a decision of the Employment Appeal Tribunal that the governing body of the school was not an emanation of the state. It did so on the basis of several factors. These included that education was a public service, and that the Secretary of State and local authorities had powers with regard to the provision of education which satisfied the requirement of state control laid down in *Foster*.

**10.30** The case which runs contrary to the general trend of according 'state authority' or 'emanation of the state' a wide definition, is *Doughty v Rolls-Royce plc* (1992). Here the CA concluded that although it could be assumed that Rolls-Royce was under state control at the relevant time, the company could not be said to provide a public service and neither was there any evidence that it exercised special powers of the type enjoyed by the BGC. Nevertheless, according 'state authority' a wide definition has been one means by which the strictures of the *Marshall* decision have been circumvented. An alternative means has been the development of the doctrine of indirect effect.

## Indirect effect

**10.31** The doctrine of indirect effect (sometimes referred to as the 'duty of purposive interpretation') which emerged from Case 14/83: *Von Colson and Kamann v Land Nordrhein-Westfalen* (1984) (a decision which in fact predates *Marshall*) amounts to an interpretative obligation placed on national courts. It is based on the duty formerly imposed by art 10 of the EC Treaty on all member states to take all appropriate measures to ensure the fulfilment of their EC obligations. It requires that in the event that a directive does not fulfil the criteria for direct effect, a national court is nevertheless obliged to 'interpret their national law in the light of the wording and the purpose of the directive'. This has the appearance of a strong, unequivocal obligation. However, at the conclusion of the ruling in *Von Colson*, the ECJ stated that:

> It is for the national court to interpret and apply the legislation adopted for the implementation of the directive in conformity with the requirements of Community law, in so far as it is given discretion to do so under national law.

**10.32** The interpretative obligation is evidently qualified by the inclusion of 'in so far as it is given discretion to do so under national law'. Thus it would appear that the obligation is not such as to require a national court to cross the boundary between interpretation and legislating. In the words of Drake, it 'is not designed to give national courts a legislative function to allow them to re-write national law'. In the joined Cases C-379/01–403/01: *Pfeiffer* (2004), the ECJ somewhat belatedly stated the legal basis of the principle of indirect effect as follows:

> the argument for national law to be interpreted in conformity with Community Law is inherent in the system of the Treaty, *since it permits the national court, for matters within its jurisdiction, to ensure the full effectiveness of Community law when it determines the dispute before it. [emphasis added]*

**10.33** In subsequent cases, the *Von Colson* principle has been further refined. Thus in Case 80/86: *Officier van Justitie v Kolpinghuis Nijmegen* (1987) the ECJ held that the obligation on a national court to take into account a directive as an aid to the interpretation of national law was 'limited by the general principles of law which form part of Community law and in particular the principles of legal certainty and non-retroactivity'. In Case C-106/89: *Marleasing SA v La Comercial Internacional de Alimentación SA* (1990), where there was a conflict between the Spanish Civil Code and an unimplemented EC Directive, the fact that the litigation was between private parties precluded the possibility of direct effect. However, the ECJ stated the nature of the interpretative obligation thus:

> in applying national law, whether the provisions in question were adopted before or after the directive, the national court called upon to interpret it is required to do so, as far as possible, in the light of the wording and purpose of the directive in order to achieve the result pursued by the latter.

**10.34** The interesting feature of this statement on the nature of the interpretative obligation is that it is stated to apply to all national legislation, irrespective of whether it was made before or after the relevant directive. The late Lord Slynn stated, extra-judicially, that he was one of those who felt that 'there may have been reasons for thinking that it might not be appropriate to extend the obligation to measures adopted before a directive existed'. Certainly it does seem a little odd that national law enacted many years previously should be interpreted in the light of a more recent directive. Nevertheless, this is what *Marleasing* requires and this is what the QBD did in *R (Robertson) v Wakefield Metropolitan District Council* (2001). Here it was argued that the refusal by an electoral return officer to accede to the claimant's request that his name and address as stated on the electoral register should not be supplied to commercial organizations amounted to, inter alia, a failure to comply with art 14 of EC Directive 95/46 on data protection. In allowing the claim, Maurice Kay J observed that in the light of *Marleasing* and *Francovich* (paras **10.33** and **10.38**) it was incumbent on the court to construe regulations made both before and after the directive came into effect in a manner that was 'Directive-compliant and consistent with the Data Protection Act 1998'.

**10.35** In *Adender v Ellinikos Organisonos Galaktos* (2006) the Grand Chamber of the ECJ gave a preliminary ruling on a matter over which there had previously been some doubt – the time from which national courts are required to interpret rules of domestic law in conformity with the provisions of a directive that do not have direct effect where the directive has been transposed belatedly. In considering the matter the ECJ noted that by virtue of its own earlier decision in Case C-129/96: *Inter-Environnement Wallonie ASBL v Region Wallonie* (1998), member states could not be reproached for not having adopted implementing measures where the period for transposing a directive was yet to expire. It did not accept, however, that the interpretive obligation arose from the date on which the national implementing measures actually entered into force since such a concession 'would be liable seriously to jeopardize the full effectiveness of Community law and its application'. Instead, it held that:

> where a directive is transposed belatedly, the general obligation owed by national courts to interpret domestic law in conformity with the directive exists only once the period for its transposition has expired.

The ECJ also emphasized in *Adender* that during the period prescribed for the transposition of a directive, member states to which the directive was addressed must refrain 'from taking any measures liable seriously to compromise the attainment of the results prescribed by it'. That obligation also applied to national courts. Accordingly, once a directive had entered into force:

> The courts of the member states must refrain as far as possible from interpreting domestic law in a manner which might seriously compromise, after the period for transposition has expired, attainment of the objective pursued by that directive.

**10.36** The decision in *Marleasing* has attracted what Maltby has described as a 'deluge of comment'. This is not so very surprising if one takes the view that the case represents the acceptance of horizontal direct effect via the back door. For present purposes, however, it is unnecessary to recite academic opinion on the subject. Instead, we shall focus our attention on how the decisions in *Von Colson* and *Marleasing* have been received by the English courts. Prior to doing so, however, it is necessary to refer to another important development which has emerged from the jurisprudence of the ECJ: the principle of state liability in damages.

## State liability

**10.37** Non-implementation of directives has been a Community-wide problem. Member states have failed to implement directives correctly, or they have implemented them in an incomplete manner, or not at all. Whatever the failing, the result is the same: non-implementation means that EU law is not applied uniformly throughout the Community and the harmonization of laws is not achieved. Recalcitrant member states may be brought to heel if they are made the subject of art 258 TFEU proceedings by the Commission. Such proceedings may result in an adverse ruling by the ECJ against the member state. However, prior to the amendment made to what is now art 260 of the TFEU, the ECJ had no power to impose a sanction on a member state that had failed to comply with an EU obligation and had then failed to comply with a court ruling to that effect. Now a sanction does exist in the form of a lump sum or penalty payment.

**10.38** Article 258 proceedings are, generally speaking, rather cumbersome and time-consuming. A number of years may pass between the original identification of a failure to implement a directive and a ruling of the court to that effect. Even where the ECJ ruled against a member state, there was no direct benefit for the individual adversely affected. Compensation payable to the individual for a state's failure to comply with an EU obligation is not provided for under the TEU or TFEU, although it is in respect of damage caused by a Union institution resulting from non-contractual liability. Thus it has been left to the ECJ to fill the lacuna.

---

**Cases C-6, 9/90:** *Francovich and Bonifaci v Italy* **(1991)**: EC Directive 80/987 made provision for, amongst other things, the payment of employed workers' salaries in the event that their employer became insolvent. Italy failed to implement the directive and was the subject of an adverse ruling by the ECJ following art 169 (now 258) proceedings. Both F and B were employees of companies that had become insolvent. Since the payment of their outstanding salaries could not be obtained from their former employers, they brought proceedings against Italy for either the unpaid remuneration or monetary compensation. The national courts sought a preliminary ruling from the ECJ as to whether the directive had direct effect, and whether a state could be liable for loss and damage resulting from a breach of its obligations under Community law. ECJ held: that the directive did not satisfy the test for direct effect; the relevant provisions were not sufficiently precise and unconditional. However, the full effectiveness of Community rules would be impaired and the protection of the rights that they grant would be weakened if individuals were unable to obtain redress when such rights had been infringed due to a breach of EU law for which the state was responsible. State liability in damages was inherent in the system of the Treaty. It could also be based upon art 5 of the EC Treaty which, amongst other things, obliged a member state to nullify the unlawful consequences of a breach of EU law.

---

**10.39** *Francovich* thus establishes the principle of state liability in damages where a member state has failed to comply with an EU obligation. It also prescribes the circumstances in which that liability gives rise to a right to reparation. Three conditions must be fulfilled:

- the purpose of the directive must be to grant rights to individuals;
- the content of those rights should be capable of being identified on the basis of the provisions of the directive; and
- there must be a causal link between the breach of the state's obligation and the loss and damage suffered by the individual.

A failure to satisfy any of these conditions will defeat a *Francovich* claim. Thus in *Poole v HM Treasury* (2006), for example, it was held by the Commercial Court that Directive 73/239 (the Insurance Directive) did not confer rights on the claimants to achieve the purpose of the directive, ie to facilitate the development of an open market in the provision of direct insurance and to harmonize existing national supervisory provisions. In short, the claim fell at the first hurdle.

10.40 Where the conditions are fulfilled, however, a state must make reparation for the loss or damage suffered in accordance with domestic rules on civil liability. Thus, although the right to reparation is founded on EU law, the actual payment of compensation is governed by domestic law. The criteria for determining the extent of reparation must not be less favourable than that which applies to similar claims or actions based on domestic law. Moreover, it must not be such as to make it impossible or excessively difficult to obtain reparation.

10.41 In joined Cases C-46/93 and C-48/93: *Brasserie du Pêcheur SA v Germany* and *R v Secretary of State for Transport, ex p Factortame Ltd* (1996), the ECJ applied a modified form of the *Francovich* criteria for establishing a right to reparation. Whilst conditions 1 and 3 were the same as those stated in *Francovich*, condition 2 stated that the breach of EU law must be sufficiently serious. These joined cases can be further distinguished on the basis that state liability arose not due to a failure to implement a directive, but because the state had legislated contrary to EU law. In other words, the state was punished for an act rather than an omission.

10.42 In Case C-392/93: *R v HM Treasury, ex p British Telecommunications plc* (1996), the ECJ noted that its own case law revealed that a breach of EU law is sufficiently serious where 'in the exercise of its legislative powers, an institution or member state has manifestly and gravely disregarded the limits on the exercise of its powers'. Whether or not a breach is sufficiently serious is a matter for a national court to decide, as is the question whether there is a direct causal link between the breach of EU law and the damage sustained by the individual: Case C-5/94: *R v Ministry of Agriculture, Fisheries and Food, ex p Hedley Lomas (Ireland) Ltd* (1997).

10.43 In *R v Secretary of State for Transport, ex p Factortame* (1999), the HL held that the requirements in the Merchant Shipping Act 1988 relating to the nationality, domicile, and residence of the shareholders of fishing vessels registered as British for the purposes of the Act clearly amounted to a sufficiently serious breach of Community law. Indeed, in the words of Lord Hope:

> If damages were not to be held to be recoverable from this case, it would be hard to envisage any case, short of one involving bad faith, where damages would be recoverable.

**10.44** One issue which has not been touched upon thus far concerns the meaning to be ascribed to 'state' in the present context. As Anagnostaras has noted, the 'state' can have both a horizontal and a vertical dimension: horizontally it encompasses the three branches of government–legislative, executive, and judicial; vertically it applies to decentralized entities and emanations which operate in the public domain. Such distinctions may have important practical consequences where the *Francovich* principle is invoked. Thus although it may be accepted that a violation of Community law has taken place, it may not always be that easy to determine to whom that violation is attributable – the legislature, the executive, or a decentralized entity? Moreover, even where the violation can be attributed to any one of the components of the state, the question remains whether liability should attach to the central state or to the component part. If it is the former, what Anagnostaras terms the 'dissuasive function of *Francovich*' will be enhanced. However, if liability attaches to a decentralized entity, it is open to argument whether the dissuasive function or deterrent effect of *Francovich* has been thereby undermined. Thus far, as Anagnostaras notes, the ECJ has taken the view that 'the issue falls within the ambit of the national procedural autonomy that the states enjoy in the field of application of Community law'. It is perfectly possible, therefore, that the central state may escape the financial consequences of *Francovich* by transferring 'the obligation to make good damages to bodies operating under statutory duties and possessing funds of their own'. Whilst this accords with the notion that the wrongdoer should be punished and whilst it ought also to ensure that the national treasury is not regarded by a decentralized entity as a compensation fund for its own violations of EU law, do you consider that it is right that the central state is potentially able to avoid liability in this way?

**10.45** In *Köbler v Austria* (2003), the ECJ held that the principle of state liability is sufficiently broad to cover breaches of EU law which have been committed by national courts which act as a court of last instance. Liability could arise where: the relevant EU law which has been infringed confers rights on individuals; there is a direct causal link between the breach of the rule and the damage suffered; and there must be a 'manifest infringement' of the relevant EU law. With regard to determining whether or not the last condition has been met, the ECJ noted that it depended on factors such as:

> The degree of clarity and precision of the rule infringed, whether the infringement was intentional, whether the error of law was excusable or inexcusable, the position taken, where applicable by a Community institution and non-compliance by the court in question with its obligation to make a reference for a preliminary ruling under the third paragraph of Article [267].

**10.46** The decision in *Köbler* was subsequently confirmed by the ECJ in *Traghetti del Mediterraneo v Italy* (2006). In giving judgment, the ECJ stated:

> Community law precludes national legislation which excludes state liability, in a general manner, for damage caused to individuals by an infringement of Community law attributable to a court adjudicating at last instance by reason of the fact that the infringement in question results from an interpretation of provisions of law or an assessment of facts or evidence carried out by that court. Community law also precludes national legislation which limits such liability solely to cases of intentional fault and serious misconduct on the part of the court, if such a limitation were to lead to exclusion of the liability of the member state concerned in other cases where a manifest infringement of the applicable law was committed . . .

**10.47** The HCt decision in *Cooper v HM Attorney General* (2008) was the first case in the UK in which a claimant sought an award of damages on the ground that a court adjudicating at last instance had made an error in applying EU law. It was claimed that damage had been suffered in consequence of two judgments of the CA refusing the Council for the Protection of Rural England judicial review of certain planning decisions made by a local authority. More specifically, it was claimed that the CA's reasoning had been contrary to subsequent ECJ decisions relating to the Environmental Impact Assessment Directive, and that it had erroneously failed to seek a preliminary ruling under what is now art 267 of the TFEU. In the opinion of Plender J, although the CA judgments did disclose errors of law, none of them were such as to give rise to liability pursuant to the principle established in *Köbler*. In a postscript to his judgment, Plender J observed:

> Any contention that a court adjudicating at last instance can be said to have made a manifest error of Community law when its judgment is, in some respect, inconsistent with a later judgment of the ECJ is as misconceived as it is inconsistent with the judgment in Köbler. Community law is a system in the process of constant development . . . This being the case, inconsistencies between national decisions and subsequent decisions of the Court of Justice can be expected to arise. Claims based on the Köbler case are to be reserved for exceptional cases, involving errors that are manifest; and in assessing whether this is the case, account must be taken of the specific characteristics of the judicial function, which entails the application of judgment to the interpretation of provisions capable of bearing more than one meaning.

**10.48** In the light of these remarks, do you agree with Davis that 'it will be difficult to establish that a national court of last resort will have committed a "sufficiently serious" breach in the light of the very wide discretion accorded to the judicial branch of government in the normal exercise of its functions'?

**10.49** In the context of devolution, it will be recalled that one of the concordats to the Memorandum of Understanding, the *Concordat on co-ordination of European Union policy issues*, makes it clear that a devolved administration will be responsible for paying any costs or penalties which result from a ruling by the ECJ which is attributable to the administration's own inactivity (see paras **8.84–8.85**).

## EU law and the English courts

**10.50** Since the UK's entry into what was the EC, the question of the relationship between national and European law has regularly been considered by the English courts. We have already seen that s 2(1) of the European Communities Act 1972 gives effect to directly applicable Community law. Thus in *Macarthys Ltd v Smith* (1979), Lord Denning MR was of the view that in interpreting a provision of the Equal Pay Act 1970, the court was bound to look to art 119 of the EC Treaty (now art 157 of the TFEU). In his opinion, the process of construing a domestic statute would take effect thus:

> we are entitled to look to the Treaty as an aid to construction; but not only as an aid but as an overriding force. If on close investigation it should appear that our legislation is deficient or inconsistent with Community law by some oversight of our draftsman then it is our bounden duty to give priority to Community law. Such is the result of s 2(1) and (4) of the European Communities Act 1972.

**10.51** The remainder of the CA in *Macarthys* preferred to interpret the 1970 Act according to the ordinary canons of construction. These required that the words in the statute be given their ordinary and natural meaning and that the court should refrain from reading into the statute words which were not there, or from looking outside the Act to art 119 as an aid to construction. On a referral to the ECJ on questions concerning the interpretation of art 119, the ECJ reiterated that in the light of *Defrenne v Sabena*: 43/75 (1976), art 119 was directly effective. It therefore took priority over domestic law which was inconsistent with its terms. In the words of Lord Denning MR in *Macarthys Ltd v Smith* (1981):

> That priority is given by our own law. It is given by the European Communities Act 1972 itself. Community law is now part of our law; and, whenever there is any inconsistency, Community law has priority. It is not supplanting English law. It is part of our law which overrides any other part which is inconsistent with it.

**10.52** Since the judgment in *Macarthys*, it is possible to identify several approaches which English courts have taken to the task of interpreting national law in the light of EU law. These have involved: disapplying an Act of Parliament which is inconsistent with EU law; reading words into domestic law which has been passed to give effect to EU law; and applying the normal canons of construction where national law was not passed to implement EU law. The first of these approaches, which was evident in *Factortame* (1991) and *R v Secretary of State for Employment, ex p Equal Opportunities Commission*

(1995) (para **14.22**), has already been considered in Chapter 5 (paras **5.46–5.52**). The following discussion therefore focuses upon the second and third approaches.

## The purposive approach

**10.53** The second approach involves interpreting a domestic provision in a purposive manner. If the purpose for which the legislation was enacted, made, or amended was to give effect to EU law, then English courts have shown themselves willing to interpret it so as to give effect to EU law, even where this means straining the literal meaning of the words used. Thus in *Garland v British Rail Engineering* (1983), where, following a referral to the ECJ, the HL held that the words in s 6(4) of the Sex Discrimination Act 1975 should be construed in the light of art 119 of the EC Treaty (now art 157 of the TFEU), Lord Diplock observed that:

> it is a principle of construction of United Kingdom statutes, now too well established to call for citation of authority, that the words of a statute passed after the Treaty has been signed and dealing with the subject matter of the international obligation of the United Kingdom, are to be construed if they are reasonably capable of bearing such a meaning, as intended to carry out that obligation, and not to be inconsistent with it.

**10.54** A purposive approach has been adopted by the HL on several other occasions.

---

*Pickstone v Freemans plc* **(1989):** The applicants were employed as warehouse operatives. They were paid the same as a male warehouse operative. They claimed that their work was of an equal value to that done by a male warehouse checker who was paid more than they were. The applicants invoked the Equal Pay Act 1970 before an industrial tribunal, together with art 119 (now art 157 of the TFEU) and Directive 75/117. Their complaint was dismissed and this decision was upheld on appeal by the Employment Appeal Tribunal. On a further appeal by the applicants, the CA held that they were entitled to claim under art 119. The employers appealed to the HL. HL held: dismissing the appeal, that s 1(2) of the 1970 Act, as amended by the Equal Pay (Amendment) Regulations 1983, had been enacted to implement the UK's obligations on equal pay under art 119 and EC Directive 75/117 and to comply with a ruling of the ECJ. With that purpose in mind, it should be construed accordingly, supplying by implication words appropriate to meet the UK's EC obligations, even though the literal meaning of the words used suggested that the UK was in fact in breach of those obligations.

---

**10.55** In the later appeal in *Thoburn v Sunderland City Council* (2002) (paras **5.57–5.60**), Laws LJ described *Pickstone* as 'a case which illustrates the lengths our courts will go to in construing Acts of Parliament to uphold the supremacy of substantive Community rights'.

**10.56** The precedent established by *Pickstone v Freemans* was subsequently applied in *Litster v Forth Dry Dock and Engineering Co Ltd* (1990). Here the HL interpreted the Transfer of Undertakings (Protection of Employment) Regulations 1981 in a purposive manner so as to give effect to EC Directive 77/187. Their Lordships were prepared to imply into the 1981 regulations the words necessary to secure domestic compliance with both the directive and various decisions of the ECJ. Had they interpreted the regulations literally, the employees would have been denied the protection accorded to them by EU law in the event of the transfer of a business from one owner to another.

**10.57** *Pickstone* and *Litster* are therefore examples of the HL acting in accordance with the interpretative obligation formulated by the ECJ in *Von Colson*. In both cases, the HL interpreted domestic laws in a purposive manner. Indeed, in *Pickstone*, their Lordships were prepared to consult *Hansard* to determine the purpose underlying the amendment to the Equal Pay Act 1970, even though at that time the exclusionary rule against the use of *Hansard* was still being applied. The case therefore represented an important development in this regard which culminated in the relaxation of the rule by the HL in *Pepper v Hart* (1993).

**10.58** A purposive approach was not adopted, however, by the HL in *White v White and another* (2001). This case involved the interpretation of the Second Council Directive (EEC) 84/5 on the approximation of laws of the member states relating to insurance against civil liability in respect of the use of motor vehicles and amendments to various agreements between the Secretary of State and the Motor Insurers' Bureau which had been made in order to give effect to the directive. Although the claimant won his case through the application of national law, the important part of the judgment in the present context relates to Lord Nicholls' observations in respect of *Marleasing*. In his Lordship's judgment, the *Marleasing* principle did not apply to the present case because *White* was not concerned with legislation. Thus he opined:

> The rationale of the Marleasing *case is that the duty of member states under art 5 is binding on all the authorities of member states, including the courts. The courts must apply national law accordingly, whenever the law was enacted or made. But it is one matter to apply this principle to national law. Whatever form it may take, law is made by authorities of the state. It is quite another to apply this principle to contracts made between citizens. The* Marleasing *principle cannot be stretched to the length of requiring contracts to be interpreted in a manner that would impose on one or other of the parties' obligations which, the* Marleasing *case apart, the contract did not impose. This is so even where one of the parties is an emanation of government, here, the Secretary of State.*

**10.59** In *Byrne v The Motor Insurance Bureau* (2007), Flaux J observed in relation to *Marleasing*:

> The application of this principle in English courts leads to a broad approach to statutory interpretation way beyond what would be permissible under domestic law . . . The only real limit to this approach to interpretation seems to be that, although the approach

> may change the meaning of legislation, it must not conflict with a fundamental feature
> of the legislation.

Flaux J had been asked to apply the *Marleasing* principle to an Untraced Drivers Agreement made between the Motor Insurance Bureau and the Secretary of State so as to ensure that the Agreement was compatible with the Second Motor Insurance Directive 84/5. He concluded that the principle did not apply to a private law agreement such as the Untraced Drivers Agreement on the basis of the earlier CA decision in *Mighell v Reading* (1999). Had he been free from authority, Flaux J expressed the obiter view that the *Marleasing* principle would have justified writing into the Agreement additional words to ensure compatibility 'notwithstanding that normal English law principles of construction would not permit that interpretation'.

**10.60** In the later case of *McCall v Poulton* (2009), the CA held that despite the decisions of the HL in *White v White* and Flaux J in *Byrne*, it was arguable on the basis of the ECJ decisions in *Evans v Secretary of State for the Environment, Transport and Regions* and *Pfeiffer* (2004), that the ECJ would say that the *Marleasing* principle ought to apply in the context of an agreement entered into by the state in order to fulfill an EU obligation. Accordingly, since they were issues of some general importance, the CA felt it desirable to seek a preliminary ruling from the ECJ as to whether *Marleasing* applied to the Motor Insurance Bureau Agreement, and whether that body was an emanation of the state, especially since the Irish courts had already held that it was in *Farrell v Whitty* (2008). In effect, therefore, the CA was of the view that the impact of *Pfeiffer* had not been taken into account by the court in *Byrne*. With regard to the application of the *Marleasing* principle, Waller LJ observed in *McCall* that:

> If the Marleasing *principle applies, the national court goes much further in interpreting the enactment than it could conceivably go by the ordinary rules of interpretation. As [counsel] put it, the court can use a 'cleaver' and simply strike out provisions that do not comply with the directive.*

**10.61** More recently, in *Floe Telecom Ltd v Office of Communications* (2009), the CA held that the *Marleasing* principle does not apply in the context of a mobile telephone company's operating licence. Thus in distinguishing *McCall v Poulton* and applying *White v White*, Mummery LJ observed:

> In this case the licence is a permission granted on terms laid down by the Secretary of State and accepted by Vodafone. The fact that it is granted under and in accordance with legislation does not make it legislation or any other form of law . . . The licence, which binds only the parties to it and can even be revoked for non-payment of the fees provided for in it, cannot reasonably be described as law caught by the Marleasing *principle . . .*

**10.62** Collectively these decisions serve to underline the evolving nature of the jurisprudence surrounding the application of the *Marleasing* principle. That jurisprudence is now also much influenced by the approach which the courts have taken to the interpretation of 'so far as possible' in s 3 of the Human Rights Act 1998. Thus the HL decision in *Ghaidan v Godin-Mendoza* (2004) (para **5.74**) has been applied in the context of EU law on a number of occasions: see, for example, *HMRC v IDT Card Services Ireland Ltd* (2006) and *EBR Attridge Law LLP v Coleman* (2010).

## Normal canons of construction

**10.63** The third approach adopted in relation to the interpretation of domestic law, applying the normal canons of construction, was evident in yet another case concerned with the equality of treatment of men and women.

---

*Duke v GEC Reliance Ltd* **(1988):** D was employed by GEC. Following her sixtieth birthday she was required to retire in accordance with company policy. She claimed that she had been unlawfully discriminated against on the grounds of sex contrary to the Sex Discrimination Act 1975, and she sought damages for wrongful dismissal. The industrial tribunal dismissed her claim. That decision was upheld by both the Employment Appeal Tribunal and the CA. D appealed to the HL. She argued that European law required that the Equal Pay Act 1970 and the 1975 Act be construed so as to give effect to the Equal Treatment Directive (76/207). HL held: neither the 1970 Act nor the 1975 Act was passed to give effect to Directive 76/207. Since both Acts were intended to preserve discriminatory retirement ages, GEC was not liable to D under English law. Moreover, since Directive 76/207 did not have horizontal direct effect, GEC was not liable to D under European law either.

---

**10.64** In *Duke*, Lord Templeman stressed that the court would construe national law in a purposive manner where it was passed to give effect to EU law. However, in his opinion, the facts of the present case did not call for such a construction. Moreover, he observed that:

> Section 2(4) of the European Communities Act 1972 does not in my opinion enable or constrain a British court to distort the meaning of a British statute in order to enforce against an individual a Community directive which has no direct effect between individuals. Section 2(4) applies and only applies where Community provisions are directly applicable.

**10.65** In *Webb v EMO Air Cargo (UK) Ltd* (1992), Lord Templeman's dictum was cited with approval by Lord Keith. However, the HL sought a preliminary ruling from the ECJ as to whether it would be discriminatory on the grounds of sex, contrary to EC Directive 76/207, for an employer to dismiss an employee on the basis that her pregnancy would prevent her from being available for work at a time when her services were particularly required. On the basis of that ruling, the HL held that the relevant terms of the Sex Discrimination Act 1975 could be construed in the light of the directive: *Webb v EMO Air Cargo (UK) Ltd (No 2)* (1995). In so doing, their Lordships reached an interpretation which was actually contrary to their original interpretation.

# FURTHER READING

Anagnostaras, G 'The Allocation of Responsibility in State Liability Actions for Breach of Community Law: A modern gordian knot' (2001) 26 EL Rev 139.

Anagnostaras, G 'Erroneous Judgments and the Prospect of Damages: The scope of the principle of governmental liability for judicial breaches' (2006) 31 EL Rev 735.

Betlem, G 'The Doctrine of Consistent Interpretation – Managing Legal Uncertainty' (2002) 22 OJLS 397.

Beutler, B 'State Liability for Breaches of Community Law by National Courts: Is the requirement of a manifest infringement of the applicable law an insurmountable obstacle?' (2009) 46 CML Rev 773.

Craig, P 'Directives: Direct Effect, Indirect Effect and the Construction of National Legislation' (1997) 22 EL Rev 519.

Craig, P 'Britain in the European Union' in Jowell and Oliver (ed) *The Changing Constitution* (7th edn, 2011) OUP.

Davis, R 'Liability in Damages for a Breach of Community Law: Some Reflections on the question of whom to sue and the concept of the "State" ' (2006) 31 EL Rev 69.

Dougan, M 'The Disguised Vertical Direct Effect of Directives?' (2000) 59 CLJ 586.

Drake, S 'Twenty Years after *Von Colson*: The impact of "indirect effect" on the protection of the individual's Community rights' (2005) 30 EL Rev 329.

Granger, M-P 'National Applications of *Francovich* and the Construction of a European Administrative ius commune' (2007) 32 EL Rev 157.

Harlow, C and Rawlings, R 'Accountability and Law Enforcement: The centralized EU enforcement procedure' (2006) 31 EL Rev 447.

Hartley, T C *The Foundations of European Union Law* (7th edn, 2010) OUP.

Klamert, M 'Judicial Implementation of Directives and Anticipatory Indirect Effect: Connecting the dots' (2006) 43 CML Rev 1251.

Lackhoff, K and Nyssens, H 'Direct Effect of Directives in Triangular Situations' (1998) 23 EL Rev 397.

Lenz, M 'Horizontal What? Back to Basics' (2000) 25 EL Rev 509.

Maltby, N '*Marleasing*: What is All the Fuss About?' (1993) 109 LQR 301.

Pollard, D, Parpworth, N, and Hughes, D *Constitutional and Administrative Law: Text with Materials* (4th edn, 2007) OUP.

Ross, M 'Beyond *Francovich*' (1993) 56 MLR 55.

Schaeffer, A 'Linking *Marleasing* and s 3(1) of the Human Rights Act 1998' (2005) 10 JR 72.

Lord Slynn 'Looking at European Community Texts' [1993] Stat LR 12.

Steiner, J 'From Direct Effects to Francovich: Shifting means of enforcement of Community Law' (1993) 18 EL Rev 3.

Steiner, J 'The Limits of State Liability for Breach of European Community Law' [1998] EPL 69.

Tridimas, T 'Liability for Breach of Community Law: Growing up and mellowing down' (2001) 38 CML Rev 301.

Winter, T A 'Direct Applicability and Direct Effects' (1972) 9 CML Rev 425.

# SELF-TEST QUESTIONS

1   What is the difference between direct applicability and direct effect? Which EU legal instruments can have both characteristics?

2   Why did the ECJ decide that directives should have direct effect?

3   Explain what Professor Craig meant by the following statement: 'Direct effect spreads the workload of enforcing Community law, and its supremacy, across all the individuals and the national courts of the EC.'

4   In developing the doctrine of direct effect and the principle of state liability in damages, has the ECJ exceeded the proper bounds of the judicial function?

5   To what extent, if any, can it be argued that the practical effect of the decisions in *Von Colson* and *Marleasing* is that directives can now have horizontal direct effect?

6   Professor Hartley has contended: 'In recent years, the European Court seems to be doing everything within its power to emphasize the importance of indirect effect, though it never forgets to include the words "so far as possible" in its rulings.' By reference to decided cases, consider the accuracy of this statement.

7   Has membership of the EU resulted in British judges having to be more creative/radical when interpreting domestic legislation?

8   Although the *Francovich* principle represents an attempt by the ECJ to make EU law more effective, to what extent is the effectiveness of the remedy dependent upon the attitude of the national courts?

9   Do you agree with Drake that the HL's reasoning in *White v White* (2001) as to why it should not apply the *Marleasing* principle to private law agreements is 'unsatisfactory'?

# 11 Constitutional conventions and judge-made law

## SUMMARY

Several sources of the UK constitution have been considered in previous chapters. In this chapter, it is necessary to turn our attention to two further sources which are important: constitutional conventions, which are a non-legal source of the constitution; and judge-made law, which clearly is a legal source of the constitution.

## Constitutional conventions

11.1 Any analysis of the sources of the UK constitution would be deficient if it failed to refer to constitutional conventions, once described by J S Mill in *Representative Government* as the 'unwritten maxims' of the constitution. Much has been written about conventions so that in the words of Hood Phillips:

> [M]ore than a dozen constitutional historians, political theorists and lawyers made their cumulative contributions prior to Dicey. Men such as John Locke, Edmund Burke, William Hearn and Edward Augustus Freeman all expressed views on what the latter referred to as 'a whole code of political maxims' which had grown up 'without leaving among the formal acts of our legislature any traces of the steps by which it grew'.

Nevertheless, it is to Dicey's *Introduction to the Study of the Law of the Constitution* to which we must turn for the distinction between constitutional law and the conventions of the constitution since as Munro has contended, although the dichotomy between legal and convention rules 'was a notion which had been previously grasped', it had never been 'so forcefully nor so influentially expressed'. Although this dichotomy has subsequently been described by Sir Ivor Jennings as being 'by no means free from difficulty', it is worth noting that in Dicey's opinion, 'constitutional law' was 'the proper subject of legal study'. Hence much of his work is devoted to the study of the sovereignty of Parliament and the rule of law. However, in Part III of his *Introduction*, Dicey turned his attention to the connection between these two principles and the conventions of the constitution.

## The nature of constitutional conventions

**11.2** For Dicey, conventions amounted to 'understandings, habits or practices which, though they may regulate the conduct of . . . officials, are not in reality laws at all since they are not enforced by the courts'. Latterly in the same work, he referred to them as 'customs, practices, maxims or precepts which are not enforced or recognised by the courts'. Munro has defended Dicey against those who claim that his proposition that conventions are not recognized by the courts is in fact contradicted by those cases in which they have been considered. He argues that Dicey used the phrase 'not enforced or recognised by the courts' to mean 'not enforced or recognised as legal rules by the courts'. Developing the point further, Munro contends:

> *Such an interpretation is supported by common sense. Dicey recognised that extra-legal rules existed and were important, described them in considerable detail, and criticised the 'unreality' of the lawyer's view of the constitution. He is scarcely likely to have suggested that the judiciary were unaware of the existence of such rules.*

**11.3** A critique of Dicey's distinction between laws and conventions is strictly beyond the scope of this book. However, it is worth noting at this juncture that it rests upon the issue of enforceability: laws are enforced by the courts whereas conventions are not. This may be an over-simplification since, in truth, the enforcement of laws is not the exclusive preserve of the courts. Administrative tribunals may be said, for example, to enforce the law in accordance with powers conferred upon them by Parliament. Nevertheless, it is a distinction which is not completely devoid of merit, as will be discussed.

**11.4** Later writers have offered their own definitions as to what is meant by the term 'constitutional convention'. Writing in his *Modern Constitutions*, Wheare defined a convention as 'a binding rule, a rule of behaviour accepted as obligatory by those concerned in the working of the constitution'. The binding nature of conventions is therefore important. Since they are non-legal rules, obedience to them is important if they are to have any constitutional value.

**11.5** Prior to considering some examples of constitutional conventions, it seems only right to draw attention to recent criticisms of the coverage that has been accorded to constitutional conventions by academic writers. Jaconelli has argued in a forthright manner that writers on this subject have tended to be too imprecise when discussing constitutional conventions. He is of the opinion that they have tended to focus too much on identifying purported examples of conventions (even though some may not be deserving of the description) and too little on the nature of constitutional conventions. In his analysis, he makes a self-confessed trite point which is nevertheless important: that genuine or real constitutional conventions are conventions that are constitutional in nature. For Jaconelli:

*Matters constitutional are those which regulate the manner in which the business of government is to be conducted in such areas as . . . relations between the government as a whole and Parliament; relations between the two Houses of Parliament; relations between the United Kingdom and the member countries of the Commonwealth.*

**11.6** How then does Jaconelli define a constitutional convention? He argues that in essence they are social rules, although he is quick to point out that not all social rules therefore qualify as constitutional conventions. In his opinion, 'constitutional conventions form only a sub-class of the genus social rule'. Constitutional conventions may therefore be distinguished from habits which, irrespective of the length of their existence, do not have normative consequences, ie they are not the basis for making a judgment as to what ought to have been done in a given situation.

**11.7** More recently, Barber has argued that the distinctions between laws and conventions which are often canvassed, eg that laws are enforced whereas conventions are not, are unsustainable. Accordingly, he is of the opinion that:

*Constitutional conventions and laws are two brands of social rule which differ in the extent of their formalization. Laws and constitutional conventions behave in similar ways and share many common qualities. This makes it possible for courts, as well as legislatures, to transform conventions into laws on occasion. Furthermore, because the difference between conventions and laws is a soft one, it can sometimes be hard, perhaps even impossible, to state decisively whether a rule should be thought of as a constitutional convention or a law.*

## Examples of constitutional conventions

**11.8** There are many examples of constitutional conventions in the UK constitution. Marshall has suggested that they are essentially concerned with the constitutional relationships between the various actors in the constitution. For him, the 'existence of rules of a conventional character is evident' in relations between:

- the cabinet and the PM;
- the government as a whole and Parliament;
- the two Houses of Parliament;
- ministers and the Civil Service;
- ministers and the machinery of justice; and
- the UK and the member countries of the Commonwealth.

**11.9** Neither the office of PM nor the cabinet is prescribed by law. Thus, for example, it is a long recognized and well understood convention that when exercising the prerogative power to appoint a PM, the monarch will appoint the person who enjoys the confidence of the majority of MPs in the HC. Following the inconclusive result in the May 2010 general election, compliance with this convention could only be achieved once coalition talks between Labour and the Liberal Democrats, and the Conservatives and the Liberal Democrats, had been completed and the Liberal Democrats had agreed to form a coalition Government with the Conservatives.

**11.10** A further example of a convention relating to the PM is that the holder of the office should be a member of the HC. The explanation for this is that electoral reform in the 19th and 20th centuries, coupled with the enactment of the Parliament Acts 1911 and 1949, has ensured that the HC is now the dominant chamber in the UK's bicameral legislature. The principle of democracy requires, therefore, that the PM should be directly accountable to the elected chamber for his government as a member of that chamber.

**11.11** The need to comply with this convention was illustrated by the events of 1963. Harold Macmillan, the then PM, resigned from office on the grounds of ill health and, after several potential leaders of the Conservative Party expressed their willingness to succeed him, it was eventually decided that his successor would be Lord Home. However, in order to comply with the convention, Lord Home relinquished his title under the Peerage Act 1963 so that he could take a seat in the HC. A similar convention does not appear to exist in respect of other cabinet ministers. Nevertheless, in the post-Second World War period, the most senior ministerial posts, the Chancellor of the Exchequer, the Home Secretary, and the Foreign Secretary, have almost without exception been held by members of the HC. On one of the rare occasions when this was not the case, when Lord Carrington was the Foreign Secretary in the first Thatcher Government (1979–83), the advent of the Falklands War led to concerns that because he was a member of the HL, he was unable to account for events before the HC, the task falling to a ministerial deputy.

**11.12** A convention does exist, however, whereby government ministers are required to be parliamentarians. Accordingly, where a PM wishes to appoint to a ministerial post a person who is outside Parliament at the relevant time, two courses of action are available: have the Party's Chief Whip find a 'safe seat' for them in the HC; or, alternatively, have a peerage conferred upon them. The former strategy entails a degree of risk in that even if a sitting MP can be persuaded to stand down, there is no guarantee that the minister-designate will win the resulting by-election. The electorate of the relevant constituency may not act as Party managers would wish, as was the case in 1964 when the London Borough of Leyton rejected Patrick Gordon Walker, Harold Wilson's chosen Foreign Secretary. Thus the Foreign Secretary designate suffered the misfortune of two defeats at the polls in the same year. In more recent times, both Conservative and Labour Governments have tended to opt for the low-risk strategy of having the chosen candidate made a life peer. Thus when Gordon Brown formed his Government at the end of June 2007, several of the junior ministerial appointees, including the former Director General of the CBI, Sir Digby Jones, were non-Parliamentarians who were ennobled in order to comply with the convention.

## Ministerial responsibility

**11.13**　A further example of a convention is the doctrine of ministerial responsibility. In essence it comprises two limbs: that the minister is individually responsible to Parliament for the policy and administration of his department; and that the cabinet of which he is a member is collectively responsible to Parliament and of course the electorate for the policies and administrative decisions of the government. A third limb which may exist is that a minister is individually responsible for his own personal conduct. Thus he may be required to resign from his post where a 'scandal' has arisen in his private life such as an adulterous or inappropriate relationship or where there has been financial impropriety. Jaconelli has argued, however, that this is not a matter of constitutional convention because it 'fails to meet the threshold requirement of governmental consequence'. In response to the view that personal misconduct of this type does have a constitutional dimension in that it raises questions as to an individual's suitability to hold office, he points out that, if this is indeed the case, account would also have to be taken of an individual's conduct prior to their appointment. That this does not appear to happen in practice is evident from an example that Jaconelli uses, the career of the late Alan Clarke MP, a self-confessed adulterer.

## Individual ministerial responsibility

**11.14**　Individual ministerial responsibility for what is done in an official capacity by those employed in the minister's department is an important convention although as the former Cabinet Secretary, Sir Richard (now Lord) Wilson has pointed out, it only 'tends to come into play when something has gone wrong and mud is being thrown around'. Being called to account before Parliament, whether on the floor of either chamber or in the committee room, for the exercise of ministerial powers is an important means of ensuring that such powers are not abused. Indeed, the very idea of ministerial responsibility to Parliament is sometimes regarded by the courts as rendering judicial review either unnecessary or inappropriate. Admittedly the argument is most commonly used in respect of a decision that is deemed to be non-justiciable. Thus in *R v Secretary of State for the Home Department, ex p Hosenball* (1977), where H, an American citizen and investigative journalist, sought to challenge a decision to deport him from the UK, the CA noted that the case involved a conflict 'between the interests of national security on the one hand and the freedom of the individual on the other'. It concluded that achieving a balance between the two was a matter for the Home Secretary rather than the court, although in the words of Lord Denning MR, the Home Secretary was 'answerable to Parliament as to the way in which he did it and not to the courts here'.

**11.15**　Ministerial responsibility thus entails a recognition of the democratic principle, that a minister is responsible to the Parliament elected by the people. It is also a way of emphasizing the distinction between a minister's overtly political opinion on the one hand and the political neutrality of the Civil Service on the other. However, the doctrine of ministerial responsibility does pose some practical difficulties, not least of which concerns the appropriate response by a minister when there have been failings within their department.

**11.16** Traditionally, departmental inefficiencies and failings have, where the matter has been sufficiently important, resulted in the resignation of the minister. Thus in 1954 the then Minister of Agriculture, Sir Thomas Dugdale, resigned over what became known as the 'Crichel Down Affair'. Although he had no personal involvement in the matter, it was enough that his department had been guilty of maladministration in its dealings with the former owners of a farm which had been transferred to the Ministry once it was no longer required by the Air Ministry for use as a bombing range. In Jaconelli's analysis, this would be a clear case of the operation of a constitutional convention since 'the governmental consequences are obvious enough'. Similarly in 1982, the then Foreign Secretary, Lord Carrington, resigned amid public criticism that his department had failed to comprehend the true nature of the threat posed to the Falkland Islands by Argentinian forces.

**11.17** Ministerial resignations such as these can, however, be balanced against examples where a minister did not resign. Thus in 1968, the Foreign Secretary, George Brown, did not resign from office even though a report by the Parliamentary Commissioner for Administration had found his department guilty of maladministration in its handling of a number of compensation claims under a scheme designed to compensate those who had been detained in the Sachsenhausen concentration camp. More recently, it has become possible to discern an increasing reluctance on the part of ministers to resign. In 1994, for example, the then Home Secretary, Michael Howard, refused to comply with demands for his resignation over the escape of prisoners from Whitemore jail. In his defence, he argued that as a minister he was responsible for policy and that responsibility for operational matters lay with the Director-General of Prisons. The fact that he was able to remain in office suggests that he had not lost the confidence of either the backbench MPs in his party or, more importantly still, the PM. In the opinion of Lord Wilson, it is this which is 'the acid test, not some rule of automatic resignation in the event of a serious mishap'.

## Collective cabinet responsibility

**11.18** Collective cabinet responsibility, the second limb of the convention of ministerial responsibility, requires of the cabinet that it present a united front to the world at large. In other words, differences of opinion which may have surfaced at the formative stage of government policy during the course of cabinet discussions are not to be acknowledged in any public pronouncements. Once a policy has been decided upon at cabinet level, the members of the cabinet are obliged to support and defend that policy whenever and wherever it is necessary to do so. If they feel unable to meet this obligation, the convention requires them to resign. Such a course of action is considered necessary since division within the cabinet can have a destabilizing effect upon the government. Resignation was the chosen course of action by the then Secretary of State for Trade and

Industry, Michael Heseltine, when in 1986 he felt unable to support the Government's decision to promote a rival bid to that which he favoured for the rescue of the Westland Helicopters company. More recently, in 2003, the then Leader of the HC, the late Robin Cook, resigned from the second Blair Government on account of his opposition to the war in Iraq.

**11.19** A minister's disagreement with cabinet policy may, however, be manifested in ways other than resignation. As J P Mackintosh has noted, by the actions and statements of a minister's closest political confidante, his Parliamentary Private Secretary, it may be possible to surmise that the minister was defeated in cabinet. Alternatively, ministerial dissent may be registered by way of an unattributed leak to the press. Where there is deep division within a cabinet over a policy matter, one way of dealing with it may be to actually suspend or waive the convention of collective cabinet responsibility. This was the rather unusual course of action chosen by the then PM, Harold Wilson, when in 1975 it was decided to hold a referendum on the question whether the UK should remain a member of the European Economic Community (as it then was). The initiative worked and the cabinet held together even after a positive vote was cast in the referendum.

## Enforcing conventions

**11.20** A characteristic of all these conventions which was identified by Dicey and which was referred to earlier is that they are not enforced by the courts. There are, however, some commentators who argue that this is in fact not the case or that, if it is, it is conceivable that the position may change. Thus T R S Allan has argued that by recognizing conventions the courts are in effect enforcing them. For his part, Elliott is of the view in relation to conventions which limit the legislative supremacy of Parliament that as a result of them having been long observed, it is possible that at some point in the future they will be enforced by the courts. Both arguments have, however, been criticized by Jaconelli. In an important contribution to the academic debate on this subject, he considers the question whether or not constitutional conventions bind. Jaconelli takes the view, albeit tentatively, that those to whom conventions apply are under a moral obligation to follow them as a result of 'a system of reciprocal acts and forbearances'. In other words:

> [T]he party that is in power at the moment respects the constraints that are imposed on it by constitutional conventions in the expectation that the opposition parties, when they attain office, will likewise respect the same constraints.

In a sense, therefore, as Munro has pointed out, 'a principle no higher than political self-interest accounts for the observance of conventions'.

**11.21** A failure to comply with a convention may result in the convention ceasing to exist. Conventions can thus wither and die when they are no longer felt to be necessary or appropriate. Alternatively, new conventions may grow and develop to reflect changing constitutional relationships. The difficulty may often lie in identifying when a new convention has come into being or when an old convention has been altered or abolished. Nevertheless, in the words of Jennings, conventions 'provide the flesh which clothes the dry bones of the law; they make the legal constitution work; they keep it in touch with the growth of ideas'.

## Establishing the existence of a convention

**11.22** The evolution of a convention may be a slow process, but in order to determine whether or not a convention has become established, Professor Jennings suggested that three questions had to be asked:

> First, what are the precedents; secondly, did the actors in the precedents believe that they were bound by a rule; and thirdly, is there a reason for the rule?

A satisfactory answer to each of these questions establishes the existence of a convention. The Jennings 'test' has been described by Jaconelli as a 'crude amalgam of precedents and reasons'. However, in *A-G of Manitoba v A-G of Canada* (1981), the Canadian Supreme Court applied the test and thereby recognized the existence of a number of conventions. This case demonstrates another important feature of constitutional conventions: they are not unique to the UK. They exist in states with written constitutions as well as those without. Indeed, Munro has argued that conventions ought perhaps to play a larger role in countries with written constitutions since 'the greater the degree of constitutional rigidity, the greater is the need for the benefits of informal adaptation which conventions bring'.

## The draft Cabinet Manual

**11.23** In early 2010, the then PM, Gordon Brown, requested the Cabinet Secretary 'to lead work to consolidate the existing unwritten, piecemeal conventions that govern the way central government operates under our existing constitution into a single written document'. The project was later supported by the coalition Government and a draft Cabinet Manual was published in December 2010. It is expected that the final version of the document will appear in early 2012.

**11.24** The draft Manual purports to be 'a guide to laws, conventions, and rules on the operation of government'. It consists of eleven chapters and three annexes. The chapters are concerned with: the sovereign; elections and government formation; the executive; collective cabinet decision-making; ministers and Parliament; ministers and the law; ministers and the Civil Service; relations with the devolved administrations and local government; relations with the EU and other international institutions; government finance and expenditure; and official information. Essentially, the draft Manual has been produced in order to assist the cabinet, ministers, and civil servants. It has no legal status as such, and the coalition Government has denied that it amounts to a first step towards a codified constitution. Nevertheless, it is certainly of interest.

**11.25** The HL Select Committee on the Constitution produced a report, *The Cabinet Manual* (12 Report of session 2010–11), HL Paper 107, in which the draft Manual was subject to a number of criticisms. For present purposes, it should be noted that the committee felt that the Manual's definition of a convention ('rules of constitutional practice that are regarded as binding in operation but not in law'), was correct in so far as it went, but that it failed to 'capture the nuances which exist in determining whether, how and to what extent a convention is binding'. Although it was of course necessary for the draft Manual to set out particular conventions, the committee felt that these ought to have been stated more precisely, where possible, or, if it was not possible so to do, uncertainties as to the extent of a convention ought to have been acknowledged. Criticism was also levelled at the draft Manual for referring to conventions concerned with the relationship between the two Houses of Parliament, such as the Salisbury-Addison convention, since it was felt that although it was important for ministers to be aware of such conventions, it was not appropriate for the Cabinet Office to attempt to define them; that was a matter for the two Houses.

## The courts and conventions

**11.26** Judicial recognition of conventions has also taken place in the English courts.

*A-G v Jonathan Cape Ltd (1976):* Richard Crossman, a cabinet minister between 1964 and 1970, kept a political diary. Following his death in 1974, the first volume was ready for publication. It was sent to the Cabinet Secretary for approval, but this was refused on the ground that publication would be contrary to the public interest in that it would breach the doctrine of collective responsibility. Later, the author's literary executors allowed extracts of the diary to be published in *The Sunday Times*. The Attorney-General sought injunctions against the publishers, the executors, and the newspaper to prevent further publication. CA held: the injunctions would be refused. There was overwhelming evidence that the doctrine of joint responsibility was generally understood and equally strong evidence that it was sometimes ignored. The court should intervene only in the clearest cases where the continuing confidentiality of the material could be demonstrated. Publication would not inhibit future free and open discussion in cabinet.

**11.27** Further examples of English judges taking account of constitutional conventions are apparent in *Liversidge v Anderson* (1942), *Carltona Ltd v Works Comrs* (1943) and, of course, *ex p Hosenball* (1977). In the *Carltona* case, Lord Greene MR observed that:

> The duties imposed upon ministers and the powers given to ministers are normally exercised under the authority of the ministers by responsible officials of the department. Public business could not be carried on if that were not the case. Constitutionally, the decision of such an official is, of course, the decision of the minister. The minister is responsible. It is he who must answer before Parliament for anything that his officials have done under his authority, and, if for an important matter he had selected an official of such junior standing that he could not be expected to competently perform the work, that minister would have to answer for that in Parliament.

**11.28** More recently, the CA has held that it could not be seriously argued that a constitutional convention existed whereby no Act of Parliament could be proposed which altered the UK constitution in a fundamental way without prior electoral approval. Thus in *R v Secretary of State for Foreign and Commonwealth Affairs, ex p Southall* (2003), the CA refused leave to appeal against an earlier refusal of leave to apply for judicial review where the applicant had sought various declarations relating to the draft treaty establishing a European constitution (see Chapter 7). In the words of Schiemann LJ, the applicant:

> has not put before us material capable of sustaining that any such convention has the force of law. There is material which indicates that referendums . . . have been held of late prior to some constitutional changes. However, these referendums have been the result of Acts of Parliament rather than preconditions for the lawfulness of any Act of Parliament . . . We are therefore not persuaded that it is arguable that there is any constitutional convention of the breadth asserted by [counsel].

The CA in *ex p Southall* also drew attention to the fact that the applicant was asking it to embark upon a novel course of action by making a declaration as to a constitutional convention. In the opinion of the court, this would be constitutional change of some importance and even if it was accepted (which it was not) that such a principle should now be recognized by the courts, it would not be appropriate to make a declaration in the present case given the uncertain position regarding the draft treaty on an EU constitution.

## Can conventions be made into laws?

**11.29** The simple answer to this question is 'yes'. If Parliament passed an Act which incorporated a constitutional convention, then it would have ceased to be a convention and would thereafter be a legal rule. One example which is commonly referred to is s 4 of the Statute of Westminster 1931. This provides that:

> No Act of Parliament of the United Kingdom passed after the commencement of this Act shall extend, or be deemed to extend, to a Dominion as part of the law of that Dominion unless it is expressly declared in that Act that the Dominion has requested, and consented to, the enactment thereof.

Strictly speaking, this was the enactment of a modified form of the actual convention governing the relationship between the UK Parliament and the Dominions. This had provided that laws made by Parliament for the Dominions had to be consented to by the latter. The distinction is subtle: s 4 accepts an Act's assertion that it has been consented to by a Dominion; the convention required nothing less than actual consent.

**11.30** Statutory enactment is therefore one way in which a convention may become law. There is also a view sometimes expressed in the academic literature to suggest that constitutional conventions may 'crystallize' into law without the intervention of Parliament. Barber describes the process as being 'a gradual one' and contends that 'the Ministerial Code is an instance of a set of conventions which are in the process of crystallization'. The Code, which was published in 1992 and later reissued in a revised form in 2007, covers many of the more important aspects of the convention of ministerial responsibility. Barber argues that over the years it has 'grown in political strength' to the extent that when it is alleged that ministers have acted improperly, reference is often made to the Code having been breached. In his opinion, therefore, a new convention has emerged: that ministers are under a duty to follow the rules set out in the Code. However, he also argues that 'this new convention does not fit into our traditional model of constitutional conventions' because 'it is a rule which identifies a formalized set of rules [the Code], and which, by recognizing them, renders them constitutionally obligatory'.

## Codification

**11.31** If it is accepted that conventions have an important role to play in the UK constitution, why not codify them? Marshall and Moodie have drawn up a 'balance sheet' of what codification could/could not achieve. They argue, for example, that codification could not make obedience to a convention any more enforceable than it is at present. Moreover, they suggest that codification 'could not prevent dispute about what the rules ought to be'. Defining the precise nature of a particular constitutional convention would inevitably be a difficult task. There is always the danger that a statutory definition may not reflect the constitutional reality but instead what the drafters believe that reality ought to be. In other words, codification may prescribe rather than describe. Although it is possible to argue that a particular convention 'may acquire greater legitimacy and authority by its transformation into law', the argument may not have the same force when applied generally.

**11.32** In Australia, there has been an attempt to incorporate all constitutional conventions into a single text. The form and content of the conventions was determined by a Constitutional Convention of politicians. They were concerned with a number of matters, such as the constitutional powers of the Queen in Australia and the powers of the Governor-General to appoint and dismiss ministers. C J G Sampford has noted that the criteria adopted by the Convention for recognizing a convention 'were precedent and the likelihood of general support'. Evidently there is some similarity here with the 'Jennings test'. Interestingly, despite the authoritative nature of the text, it was not legally binding.

**11.33** The process of codification raises important questions as to the effect that it would have upon those conventions that have been recognized and declared and those that have not. Given that it is widely accepted that conventions evolve, would provision need to be made for the updating and amending of an authoritative text?

**11.34** On 22 May 2006 a Joint Committee on Conventions was established to consider the practicality of codifying the key conventions on the relationship between the two Houses of Parliament. In particular, the committee was to consider:

- the Salisbury-Addison convention whereby the HL does not vote against measures included in a governing party's election manifesto;
- conventions regarding secondary legislation;
- the convention that government business in the HL should be considered in reasonable time;
- conventions relating to the exchange of amendments to legislative proposals between both Houses.

**11.35** Its final report, *Conventions of the UK Parliament* (HL Paper 265-I, II HC Paper 1212-I, II), was welcomed by the Labour Government as 'a valuable source of information on the origins, development and meaning of the various conventions which give life to the relationship between the two Houses of Parliament'. The fact that both Houses debated and passed resolutions approving the report was significant in that it demonstrated agreement as to the current scope and operation of the relevant conventions. Assuming that further reforms are made to the HL (see Chapter **6**), it is likely that the current conventions will be called into question. Whether they will survive compositional change remains to be seen.

## Conventions and devolution

**11.36** The advent of devolution (Chapter **8**) provides yet further evidence of the importance of conventions. Conventions feature in, for example, the relations between: the three executives and the devolved Assemblies; the Assembly ministers and the Civil Service;

the UK Parliament and the devolved Assemblies; and the UK Government and the devolved administrations. With regard to the convention of collective cabinet responsibility (paras **11.18-11.19**), Munro has noted that whilst this is likely to be applied in Scotland and Wales, in Northern Ireland it has been put on a statutory footing (Sch 4 to the Northern Ireland Act 1998). In terms of the relationships between the UK Government and the devolved administrations, these are regulated by a Memorandum of Understanding (MoU) and various concordats (paras **8.75-8.80** and **8.83-8.85**). For present purposes, the non-legal nature of these agreements should be noted as should the MoU's express reference to a 'convention', whereby legislation on devolved matters would not normally be passed by the UK Parliament without the agreement of the devolved legislature.

**11.37** In Scotland, this 'convention' has become known as the 'Sewell Convention' after the Scottish Office Minister, Lord Sewell, who referred to it during the course of the parliamentary debates on the Bill which became the Scotland Act 1998. It would appear that since the devolution settlement took effect, the Convention has been applied far more often than was originally anticipated even though the party in control at Westminster has, until 2007, been the same as the ruling party in Edinburgh. Burrows has argued, therefore, that 'the repeated use of the Sewell Convention has the potential to undermine the devolution settlement'. Do you agree?

**11.38** In its fifth report for the 2008–09 session, *Devolution: A Decade On* (2009), HC 529-I, the HC Justice Committee noted, amongst other things, that there are those who believe that there should be a clear set of principles established which clarify the circumstances in which the Sewell Convention is likely to be invoked. Since the Committee heard evidence from the Scottish Executive that it envisaged the convention remaining a key part of the constitutional arrangements relating to devolution, it therefore recommended the publication by the UK and Scottish Governments of their agreed understanding of those principles.

## Judge-made law

**11.39** It will be remembered that for Dicey, the constitution was the product of judge-made law. However, for some considerable time, judges were anxious to play down their law-making function. In the words of Lord Reid:

> There was a time when it was thought almost indecent to suggest that judges make law–they only declare it. Those with a taste for fairy tales seem to have thought that in some Aladdin's cave there is hidden the Common Law in all its splendour and that on a judge's appointment there descends on him knowledge of the magic words Open Sesame. Bad decisions are given when the judge muddles the password and the wrong door opens. But we do not believe in fairy tales any more.

Today, however, it is widely accepted that judge-made law is a reality. It may take one of two main forms: the development of the common law; and the interpretation of statutes.

## The common law

**11.40**  This body of law comprises the rules and principles that have been declared to be the law by the courts. Rather like statute law, the common law straddles the divide between private law, eg contract and tort, and public law.

**11.41**  In the present context, we have already seen several examples of what may be properly described as judicial law-making. Thus in *Entick v Carrington* (1765), the courts established the principle that interference with an individual's property required prior authorization by the law (see paras **3.26** and **3.29**). That which was done without lawful authority was therefore unlawful. In *Burmah Oil v Lord Advocate* (1965), the HL held that the oil company had a common law right to be compensated for the destruction of its installations by British forces which were acting under the prerogative. Admittedly that right was subsequently extinguished by the terms of the War Damage Act 1965 (see paras **4.25-4.26**). Nevertheless, the case does illustrate how the courts may develop the common law in order to take account of new situations. More recently, in *M v Home Office* (1994), the HL showed itself willing to hold that a minister of the Crown could be in contempt of court for failing to comply with a court order (see paras **3.27-3.28**).

**11.42**  These examples reflect the development of the common law in a way which holds the executive to account. They show the courts performing their traditional role of protecting the rights of the individual against state interference. However, not every plea to extend the common law is met with a favourable response. Thus in the context of the right to privacy, the courts have, on several occasions, shown themselves unwilling to declare that such a right exists at common law. In *Kaye v Robertson* (1991), for example, where a well-known actor was lying sedated in a hospital bed recovering from brain surgery when a journalist both interviewed and photographed him, the CA recognized that this amounted to 'a monstrous invasion of privacy'. However, in the words of Bingham LJ (as he then was), that invasion 'however gross, does not entitle him to relief in English law'. Similarly in *Malone v Metropolitan Police Comr* (1979), where M challenged the legality of the tapping of his telephone, the Chancery Division was not prepared to recognize a right of privacy in respect of telephone conversations. Sir Robert Megarry V-C reflected on the fact that there was an absence of authority on the point, but then observed that that in itself should not deter a court from recognizing a right. However, he opined that:

> On the other hand, it is no function of the courts to legislate in a new field. The extension of the existing laws and principles is one thing, the creation of an altogether new right

*is another. At times judges must, and do, legislate; but as Holmes J once said, they do so interstitially, and with molecular rather than molar motions. Anything beyond that must be left for legislation. No new right in the law, fully-fledged with all the appropriate safeguards, can spring from the head of a judge deciding a particular case: only Parliament can create such a right.*

**11.43** The development of a separate tort of privacy was considered to be a likely consequence of the enactment of the Human Rights Act 1998. Nevertheless, in *Wainwright v Home Office* (2003), the HL declined to adopt 'some high level principle of privacy' and rejected the argument that such a development would be necessary in order to comply with art 8 of the ECHR. In the words of Lord Hoffmann:

> *For the reasons so cogently explained by Sir Robert Megarry in Malone . . . this is an area which requires a detailed approach which can be achieved only by legislation rather than the broad brush of common law principle.*

**11.44** Where Parliament does legislate, the doctrine of the legislative supremacy of Parliament prevents the courts from ruling on the validity of an Act of Parliament. However, it is by no means an easy task to draft clear and unequivocal laws. Accordingly, the courts play a vital role in interpreting the laws made by Parliament.

## Interpreting Acts of Parliament

### Rules of interpretation

**11.45** When interpreting an Act, the judges strive to ensure that effect is given to the will of Parliament. The doctrine of the separation of powers demands this and, as we saw in *Duport Steels Ltd v Sirs* (1980) (para **2.23**), it is sometimes invoked to remind judges of the need for judicial restraint. To help them in their task, the judges have developed a number of rules of statutory interpretation. Thus, from time to time reference may be made to the literal rule, the golden rule, or the mischief rule. The problem with such rules, however, is that they rarely provide a conclusive answer to the question of interpretation under consideration. Moreover, the answer may be different depending on the rule which is applied.

**11.46** Broadly speaking, the courts tend to follow one of two approaches when interpreting Acts of Parliament. They will either apply a literal approach, in which case they focus on the words used in the statute and accord those words their ordinary and natural meaning. Alternatively, the courts may adopt a purposive approach to interpretation. This requires the courts to look beyond the wording of the statute and have regard to the purpose for which the relevant law was made.

**11.47** The literal approach has had some notable advocates in the past. Thus in *Scruttons Ltd v Midland Silicones Ltd* (1962), Viscount Simonds observed that the 'first duty' of the judge was 'to administer justice according to law, the law which is established for us by Act of Parliament or the binding authority of precedent'. Similarly, when considering the role of the judge, Lord Devlin wrote that:

> Judges, I have accepted, have a responsibility for the common law, but in my opinion they have none for statute law; their duty is simply to interpret and apply it and not to obstruct. I remain unconvinced that there is basically anything wrong with the rule of construction that words in a statute should be given their natural and ordinary meaning . . . But in the end the words must be taken to mean what they say and not what their interpreter would like them to say: the statute is the master and not the servant of the judgment.

**11.48** However, more recently, the purposive approach has become increasingly common, especially in the context of interpreting laws that have been made to give effect to EU obligations. Where this is the case, the courts have been willing to read words into a statute or delegated legislation in order to ensure that there is consistency between the national law and an EU law which the national law was passed to implement.

---

***Ken Lane Transport Ltd v North Yorkshire County Council* (1995):** The Welfare of Animals during Transport Order 1992 was intended to implement Directive 91/628/EEC. It provided that during a journey, the person in charge of transported animals was to ensure that they were watered, fed, and rested at suitable intervals. The interval between waterings, etc was not to exceed 15 hours. The company transported calves from Yorkshire to the south of France without watering them, etc despite the fact that the journey took more than 15 hours. The company was convicted of an offence contrary to s 73(a) of the Animal Health Act 1981. DC held: dismissing the appeal against conviction, that the 1992 Order was to be construed so as to accord with the Directive. The definition of 'journey' in the Order was of no assistance. Accordingly, the court would read into the Order the Directive's definition of 'journey', in which case, the whole transit from Yorkshire to France was one journey of more than 15 hours duration.

---

**11.49** The purposive approach to statutory interpretation has been considered in the context of European legislation in Chapter **10**. For present purposes, it must be acknowledged that by interpreting legislation in this way, the courts are correcting drafting errors or oversights. Whether this is an appropriate task for the courts to perform is a moot point. In defence of the approach, it might be argued that the courts are merely seeking to give the legislation the meaning that Parliament intended. If the courts prove to have been mistaken as to Parliament's intention, that body has the means at hand to clarify the legal position by amending the relevant statutory provisions.

**11.50** Judicial activism of this sort does not only occur in the context of the interpretation of national laws passed to implement European law. Occasionally, the courts have felt it necessary to give a domestic law a meaning which seems to conflict with the actual wording of the statute.

> *R v Registrar-General, ex p Smith* (1991): S was detained in a secure mental hospital following his conviction for the murder of a complete stranger and the manslaughter of his cell mate. He had been adopted at a very young age and had expressed hatred for his adoptive parents. The cell mate had been killed during a psychotic bout when S believed that he was killing his adoptive mother. S did not know who his natural parents were. He applied for a copy of his birth certificate under s 51 of the Adoption Act 1976. The Registrar-General refused to supply that information on the basis of medical advice. S sought judicial review of that decision. He argued that s 51 conferred on him an absolute right to the information. The DC refused his application. CA held: dismissing his appeal, that the Registrar-General had not acted unlawfully. Public policy grounds required that statutes should not be interpreted so as to require the performance of a duty if to do so would enable a person to commit a serious crime.

**11.51** The rather disturbing nature of the facts in *ex p Smith* helps to explain why the CA reached this conclusion. In effect, the judges accepted that there was an implied limitation on what was, to all intents and purposes, an absolute right. The argument would seem to run along the lines of had Parliament been made aware of a hypothetical situation which reflected the facts of *ex p Smith* at the time of enacting the Adoption Act 1976, it would have sought to qualify the right conferred by s 51. However, if we put the facts to one side and consider the case solely from the standpoint of statutory interpretation, might it not be argued that the decision reflects not so much what the law was, as what it ought to have been?

## Presumptions

**11.52** In addition to rules of interpretation, the courts have recognized the existence of certain presumptions that are to be applied when construing legislation. Thus, for example, the courts have presumed that Parliament does not intend to deny access to the courts.

> *Chester v Bateson* (1920): The Defence of the Realm Regulations 1917 were made under the authority of the Defence of the Realm Consolidation Act 1914. Regulation 2A(2) provided that: 'no person shall, without the consent of the Minister of Munitions take...any proceedings for the purpose of obtaining an order or decree for the recovery of possession of, or for the ejectment of a tenant of, any dwelling-house in which a munitions worker is living'. The regulations further provided that it was an offence for a landlord to go to court without first having sought the permission of the minister to do so. C sought to recover

possession of a dwelling-house that had been let to B. He had not first obtained the permission of the minister to take proceedings. The justices found that: B was employed in the munitions industry at the material time; that reg 2A(2) was not ultra vires; and that C ought to have sought the minister's consent. KBD held: allowing the appeal, that the individual had an 'elemental right' to seek justice in the courts. Such a right could not be taken away by anything other than the express words of a statute. Since no such words were in the 1914 Act, the regulation was invalid.

**11.53** More recently, in cases such as *R v Secretary of State for the Home Department, ex p Leech (No 2)* (1994) and *R v Lord Chancellor, ex p Witham* (1998) (see paras **3.18** and **3.19**), the courts have described access to the courts as being a 'constitutional right'. Thus in the former case, where the applicant succeeded in obtaining a declaration that a provision in the 1964 Prison Rules was ultra vires in that it went beyond the scope of the authorizing power (s 47(1) of the Prison Act 1952), Steyn LJ (as he then was) observed:

> It is a principle of our law that every citizen has a right of unimpeded access to a court… Even in our unwritten constitution it must rank as a constitutional right.

**11.54** A further example of a statutory presumption is that Parliament is presumed not to make retrospective laws. Retrospective legislation has already been considered in the context of the rule of law (paras **3.8–3.11**). In the present context, the presumption against retrospectivity is evident in the words of Lord Reid in *Waddington v Miah* (1974) when he observed: 'So it is hardly credible that any government department would promote or that Parliament would pass retrospective criminal legislation.' Given that this remark was immediately preceded in the judgment by the full text of art 7 of the ECHR (which prohibits retrospective criminal offences and penalties), it also reflects a further statutory presumption: that Parliament is presumed not to legislate in conflict with its international obligations.

**11.55** Whilst these presumptions are important, they are merely presumptions. They apply where the effect of legislation may be unclear due to vagueness or ambiguity in the words of the statute. They may be rebutted, however, where legislation is clear and unambiguous. Thus although it may be 'hardly credible' that Parliament would pass a retrospective criminal statute (although some have argued that this is precisely what the War Crimes Act 1991 amounts to), if Parliament chose to pass such a law and it was devoid of ambiguity, the courts would, as a consequence of the doctrine of the legislative supremacy of Parliament, follow the Act.

## Interpretation and the Human Rights Act

**11.56** The interpretative obligation imposed on the courts by s 3 of the Human Rights Act 1998 (paras **5.63–5.76**) represents a very significant development. As we have already seen, it has been applied by the HL in such a way as to enable their Lordships to imply a provision into an Act of Parliament: see *R v A (No 2)* (2001) (paras **5.68–5.71**). Such judicial creativity does, however, raise the question whether the courts are interpreting or making the law. If it is the latter, how can this be reconciled with the traditionally recognized limits on the constitutional role of the courts? Does s 3 of the 1998 Act call for a reassessment of those limits, at least in the context of human rights protection?

# FURTHER READING

Allan, T R S *Law, Liberty and Justice: The Legal Foundation of British Constitutionalism* (1993) Clarendon Press.

Barber, N W 'Laws and Constitutional Conventions' (2009) 125 LQR 294.

Lord Bingham *The Business of Judging* (2000) OUP.

Lord Bingham 'The Rule of Law' [2007] CLJ 67.

Brazier, R 'The Non-Legal Constitution: Thoughts on Convention, Practice and Principle' (1992) 43 NILQ 262.

Burrows, N 'This is Scotland's Parliament; Let Scotland's Parliament Legislate' (2002) Jur Rev 213.

Cabinet Office *The Cabinet Manual – Draft* (December 2010).

Lord Devlin 'Judges and Lawmakers' (1976) 39 MLR 1.

Ekins, R 'The Intention of Parliament' [2010] PL 709.

Elliott, M 'Parliamentary Sovereignty and the New Constitutional Order: Legislative freedom, political reality and convention' (2002) 22 LS 340.

Hood-Phillips, O 'Constitutional Conventions: Dicey's Predecessors' (1966) 29 MLR 137.

House of Lords Select Committee on the Constitution *The Cabinet Office and the Centre of Government* (2009–10, HL 30).

Jaconelli, J 'The Nature of Constitutional Convention' (1999) 19 LS 24.

Jaconelli, J 'Do Constitutional Conventions Bind?' [2005] CLJ 149.

Jennings, Sir Ivor *The Law and the Constitution* (5th edn, 1959) University of London Press.

Joint Committee on Conventions *Conventions of the UK Parliament* (2005–6), HL Paper 265-I, II, HC Paper 1212-I and II.

Lord Lester 'English Judges as Lawmakers' [1993] PL 269.

Mackintosh, J P *The British Cabinet* (3rd edn, 1977) Stevens.

Marshall, G *Constitutional Conventions: The Rules and Forms of Political Accountability* (1984) Clarendon.

Marshall, G and Moodie, G C *Some Problems of the Constitution* (5th edn, 1971) Hutchinson.

Munro, C 'Laws and Conventions distinguished' (1975) 91 LQR 218.

Munro, C *Studies in Constitutional Law* (2nd edn, 1999) Butterworths, chapter 3.

Pollard, D, Parpworth, N, and Hughes, D *Constitutional and Administrative Law: Text with Materials* (4th edn, 2007) OUP.

Lord Reid 'The Judge as Law Maker' (1972) 12 Legal Studies 22.

Sampford, C J G 'Recognise and Declare: An Australian Experiment in Codifying Constitutional Conventions' (1987) 7 OJLS 369.

Wheare, K C *Modern Constitutions* (2nd edn, 1966) OUP.

Lord Wilson 'The Robustness of Conventions in a Time of Modernisation and Change' [2004] PL 407.

## SELF-TEST QUESTIONS

1   Which definition of conventions provides the most satisfactory explanation of their nature and purpose?

2   What do the examples of conventions referred to in this chapter tell us about their significance in the UK constitution?

3   What is the status of conventions before the courts?

4   Professor Munro has contended: 'Dicey's court-enforcement criterion may be defended from attack. It is an adequate litmus test to distinguish laws and conventions.' Do you agree?

5   Given that conventions are non-legal rules, why are they obeyed? What is the sanction for their breach?

6   If conventions were codified, what would be the criteria for measuring the success of codification?

7   Lord Wilson has commented that: 'Our unwritten constitutional conventions are under pressure from a variety of directions, for instance because of the power of the media, constitutional change, management change and a general ignorance of, or impatience with, the constitution'. To what extent, if any, do you agree with this view?

8   Assuming that law-making is a legitimate part of the judicial function, what constitutional limits are there on the exercise of that function?

9   What do you think Lord Bingham meant when he observed extra-judicially in relation to the judicial development of the law: 'It is one thing to alter the law's direction of travel by a few degrees, quite another to set it off in a different direction'?

10   To what extent, if any, can it be argued that in *R v Registrar-General, ex p Smith* (1991), the CA overstepped the proper bounds of the judicial function?

# PART IV

## Judicial Review of Administrative Action

# 12

# The nature of judicial review

## SUMMARY

This chapter considers what is meant by the process known as a claim for judicial review. It examines the nature of a jurisdiction that is supervisory rather than appellate. Emphasis is also placed on the fact that the jurisdiction exists to control the exercise of power by public bodies. Accordingly, the distinction between public law and private law bodies has become important, as has the distinction between public law and private law matters. Both these matters are considered. This chapter also discusses the rule established by the HL in *O'Reilly v Mackman* and what effect this has had on the manner in which public law decisions may be challenged. The procedure for making a claim for judicial review under the Civil Procedure Rules (CPR) Part 54 is also considered.

## The jurisdiction

12.1 Judicial review is essentially a procedure whereby the courts are able to determine the lawfulness of the exercise of executive power. It is concerned with the legality of the decision-making process as opposed to the merits of the actual decision. We have already seen in Chapter 5 that the courts have traditionally rejected suggestions, at least since 1688, that they may review the lawfulness of an Act of Parliament. The same cannot be said of delegated legislation. It is beyond doubt that such legislation is subject to the supervisory jurisdiction of the courts. In this sense, therefore, judicial review entails the courts upholding the principle of the legislative supremacy of Parliament where the power to make legislation does not derive from the prerogative.

12.2 Parliament confers a power on a minister or a public body to make delegated legislation by inserting an appropriately worded section or subsection into an Act, the enabling or parent Act. Thus, for example, a minister may be given the power to make such regulations as he thinks fit in order to give effect to the purposes of the Act. If he chooses to exercise that power, he must ensure that he does not exceed its scope. In other words, he must ensure that he acts intra vires. Where, however, it is argued that he has acted beyond his powers (ultra vires), the courts may intervene following a claim for judicial review and grant one of the remedies considered in Chapter 14 if they find that he has acted unlawfully. Judicial review is therefore an important mechanism for ensuring that power is not abused. It may be argued, as Professor Jowell has done, that it amounts to the practical application of the rule of law (para **3.34**).

**12.3** In order for the judiciary to carry out this important task, it is essential that they are separate from and independent of the executive. Judges who could be appointed and dismissed at the whim of politicians may, in the words of Lord Atkin in *Liversidge v Anderson* (1942), become 'more executive minded than the executive'. If this were to happen, a claim for judicial review would have little chance of success and the procedure would be an ineffective bulwark against the abuse of power. Thus the effective operation of the judicial review jurisdiction is dependent upon there being a degree of separation of powers within the UK constitution, especially as between the executive and the judiciary. As we have already seen in Chapter **2**, this has recently been enhanced by the Constitutional Reform Act 2005.

## An unfettered discretion?

**12.4** The power conferred upon a minister to make delegated legislation may be extremely wide. Similarly, it may appear that he has a wide and unfettered discretion as to related matters, such as who to consult prior to exercising his lawmaking power. Where a statutory discretion is very wide, it may take on the appearance of being without limits. However, unlimited discretionary power has the potential to be abused and accordingly, when it has been claimed to exist, the courts have shown themselves willing to identify certain limits within which it must be exercised.

> **Padfield v Minister of Agriculture, Fisheries and Food (1968):** The Agricultural Marketing Act 1958 regulated the marketing of various agricultural products, such as milk. By virtue of s 19(3)(b), a committee of investigation could consider and report to the minister as to the operation of any scheme in respect of which he had received a complaint, if he so directed. A dairy farmers' association complained to the minister about the operation of a price-fixing scheme operated by the Milk Marketing Board. The minister refused to refer the complaint to a committee of investigation and the farmers accordingly sought an order of mandamus to compel him to do so. HL held: that the order would be granted. Parliament must have conferred the discretion with the intention that it should be used to promote the policy and objects of the Act. These were to be determined by the court construing the Act as a whole. The minister had misdirected himself in law as to the intention of the Act which imposed a duty upon him to have complaints investigated where they were substantial and genuine and indicated that the board had acted contrary to the public interest.

**12.5** *Padfield* therefore demonstrates that in identifying the scope of delegated powers, the courts are required to construe the relevant statute so as to identify Parliament's intention. Where the words in the statute are vague or ambiguous, it is now possible for the courts to use *Hansard*, the official report of Parliament's proceedings, as an aid to interpretation following the decision of the HL in *Pepper v Hart* (1993). The use of *Hansard* is limited, however, to ministerial statements or those of the promoter of the Bill.

**12.6** The postscript to the decision in *Padfield* also illustrates an important practical feature of judicial review proceedings: a successful challenge may not result in the desired outcome. The effect of the HL decision was that the minister had to refer the dairy farmers' complaint to a committee of investigation. He did this but subsequently declined to follow the advice which they gave him, as he was entitled to do. Having thus acted lawfully, his decision could not be the subject of further judicial review proceedings.

## Review not appeal

**12.7** It is clear from the foregoing that the judicial review jurisdiction operates within distinct limits. It is a supervisory rather than an appellate jurisdiction. Accordingly, the role of the court is to supervise the exercise of discretionary power in order to ensure that it has been exercised lawfully. In *R v Secretary of State for the Environment, ex p Hammersmith and Fulham London Borough Council* (1991), Lord Donaldson MR likened the role of the judge in judicial review proceedings to that of a referee in a football match. He remarked that:

> In football . . . the moves made by the players and the tactics employed by the teams are matters entirely for them. The referee is only involved when it appears that some player has acted in breach of the rules. The referee may then stop the play and take some remedial action, but, tempting though it may be, it is not for him to express any view on the skill of the players or, how he would have acted in their position. Still less, following a breach of the rules does he take over one of the positions of the players. So too with the judiciary.

**12.8** Similarly in *Reid v Secretary of State for Scotland* (1999), Lord Clyde observed that:

> Judicial review involves a challenge to the legal validity of the decision. It does not allow the court of review to examine the evidence with a view to forming its own view about the substantial merits of the case.

**12.9** Thus a court must not consider the merits of the particular decision, whether it was right or wrong, when hearing a judicial review claim. To substitute its own view for that of the decision-maker would, in the words of Lord Ackner in *R v Secretary of State for the Home Department, ex p Brind* (1991), amount to 'a wrongful usurpation of power by the judiciary'. Nevertheless, we shall see when we come to consider the grounds for review in the next chapter that there may be a case for arguing that some of these actually blur the distinction between the legality and the merits of a decision.

## Alternative remedies

**12.10** It is by no means uncommon for a statute to create an appeal system for dealing with disputes relating to decisions made under the Act. A right of appeal is conferred upon specified categories of persons, and the appeal itself may be heard by a variety of different bodies which include courts, tribunals, inquiries, ministers, or inspectors. Where such an appeals system exists, it is likely that the courts will require this remedy to be exhausted before allowing a judicial review application to proceed. This was described as a 'cardinal principle' by Purchas LJ in *R v Epping and Harlow General Comrs, ex p Goldstraw* (1983) and by Popplewell J in *R v Ministry of Agriculture, Fisheries and Food, ex p Live Sheep Traders Ltd* (1995).

**12.11** In exercising his or her discretion to allow a judicial review claim to proceed even where an alternative remedy is available, a judge may take into account a number of factors as described in *Ex p Waldron* (1986). These may include: the extent to which the alternative statutory remedy can deal with the matter fully; the comparative speed with which the alternative remedies can determine the matter; and the extent to which the matter requires the specialist knowledge or expertise possessed by the appellate body in order to be determined.

**12.12** Alternatively, as we have already seen (para **11.14**), the convention of ministerial responsibility may induce a court to form the view that accountability to Parliament is a sufficient safeguard against an abuse of power. Nevertheless, such accountability will not automatically defeat a judicial review claim. In the words of Lord Diplock in *R v IRC, ex p National Federation of Self-Employed and Small Businesses Ltd* (1982):

> It is not, in my view, a sufficient answer to say that judicial review of the actions of officers or departments of central government is unnecessary because they are accountable to Parliament for the way in which they carry out their functions. They are accountable to Parliament for what they do so far as regards efficiency and policy, and of that Parliament is the only judge; they are responsible to a court of justice for the lawfulness of what they do, and of that the court is the only judge.

## Procedural reform

**12.13** Judicial review has been subject to several reforms during the last 30 years or so. In 1977, for example, reforms were made to the Rules of the Supreme Court Order 53 which sought to address some of the various disadvantages which an applicant (now a claimant) faced in seeking to challenge the decision of a public body. Such disadvantages included the fact that no provision was made for discovery (now disclosure) and that declarations or injunctions were not available in proceedings under Order 53 – they could only be obtained in actions begun by writ or originating summons.

**12.14** In more recent times, judicial review has become what Cornford and Sunkin have termed 'a growth industry'. This increasing recourse to judicial review proceedings has been such that the system felt the strain. Accordingly, this fact, coupled with the changes to the civil justice system in the light of Lord Woolf's Review, acted as the catalyst for reform. A committee under the chairmanship of Sir Jeffrey Bowman was appointed by the Lord Chancellor. It set out to make recommendations as to how the judicial review procedure could be made more efficient without compromising the fairness of proceedings. Following the publication of the Bowman Report in March 2000, and a period of consultation in respect of draft rules drawn up by the Lord Chancellor's Department, new judicial review rules were laid before Parliament. These came into effect on 2 October 2000. The content of the new rules will be discussed more fully later in this chapter. For present purposes, several key features of the reformed regime can be summarized thus:

- A change in language has taken place – eg the procedure itself is now known as 'a claim for judicial review' rather than 'an application for judicial review', the party seeking review is now therefore the 'claimant' rather than the 'applicant', and the remedies which may be sought are now mandatory, prohibiting, or quashing orders rather than mandamus, prohibition, or certiorari.

- The permission stage is now inter partes rather than ex parte as was formerly the case.

- Defendants and third parties are now required to set out the detailed grounds on which they intend to rely well in advance of the hearing.

- The Administrative Court (formerly the Crown Office List) now has the power to grant two additional remedies – an interim declaration and a substitutionary remedy.

## The rule in *O'Reilly v Mackman*

**12.15** Although the result of the 1977 procedural reforms was the creation of a single procedure known as an application for judicial review, Order 53 did not expressly provide that it was an exclusive procedure. It thus became necessary for the courts to consider whether an applicant seeking a declaration or an injunction was entitled to do so by way of originating summons, or whether he must now apply for judicial review.

*O'Reilly v Mackman* (1983): Four prisoners took part in riots at Hull prison. Each was charged with an offence against prison discipline contrary to the Prison Rules 1964. An inquiry into each case was held by the board of prison visitors. The board upheld the charges in each case and imposed various penalties, including loss of remission. All four prisoners commenced actions against the board, either by writ or originating summons, seeking declarations that the board's findings and penalties were null and void due to its failure to observe the principles of natural justice. The board sought to have the proceedings struck out as an abuse of the process of the court. It claimed that the prisoners ought to have proceeded by way of judicial review under RSC Order 53. Peter Pain J took the view that the law offered the prisoners a choice and that they had not therefore abused the process of the court by opting for ordinary actions rather than judicial review. The board's appeal to the CA was upheld. HL held: dismissing the prisoners' appeal against the CA's decision, that now that the disadvantages to applicants under the old procedure had been removed by the 1977 reforms, it would as a general rule be contrary to public policy, and an abuse of the process of the court, to allow an applicant to seek to enforce public law rights by way of ordinary action rather than by way of judicial review.

**12.16** The general rule established by the HL in *O'Reilly v Mackman* (1983) is, therefore, that public law decisions ought to be challenged by judicial review, whereas private law matters are to be dealt with by ordinary action. In other words, despite the silence of Order 53 and s 31 of the Senior Courts Act 1981 on this matter, the effect of the HL ruling in *O'Reilly* was that procedural exclusivity was a by-product of the 1977 reforms. In the years that have followed, therefore, it has been necessary for the courts to attempt to make a distinction between public law and private law matters. Moreover, given that Lord Diplock stressed in *O'Reilly* that the effect of the HL decision was to establish a 'general rule' to which 'there may be exceptions', arguments have subsequently been advanced that a particular situation does indeed amount to an exception to the general rule.

---

***Cocks v Thanet District Council* (1983):** C instituted proceedings against TDC in the county court. He claimed that both he and his family were homeless and in priority need, and that the council was therefore under a duty to provide either temporary or permanent accommodation under the Housing (Homeless Persons) Act 1977. The issue on appeal was whether the proceedings were properly brought by action, or whether they could only be brought by application for judicial review. HL held: that housing authorities' functions under the 1977 Act were essentially public law functions. Whether or not they had a duty to house a person under the Act was a matter for them to decide following appropriate inquiries. If they did reach a decision that they were under a duty to house a person, that decision gave rise to rights and obligations in private law. In the present case, the housing authority had not decided the public law question in favour of C. He therefore did not have any private law rights to enforce. In the light of the principles expounded in *O'Reilly v Mackman* (1983), it would be an abuse of the process of the court to allow C to seek relief in respect of his claim otherwise than by an application for judicial review.

---

***Roy v Kensington and Chelsea and Westminster Family Practitioner Committee* (1992):** Dr R was a GP carrying out work for the NHS. The remuneration for his services was set out in regulations. These provided that a GP was not eligible for the full rate of the basic practice allowance unless the FPC considered that he was devoting a substantial amount of time to his NHS work. The FPC took the view that Dr R was not and therefore reduced his practice allowance by 20%. Dr R brought an action against the FPC claiming, amongst other things, that the committee was in breach of contract. The FPC applied to strike out his claim as an abuse of process. It claimed that he ought to have challenged their decision by way of an application for judicial review. Before the QBD, Dr R's claim was struck out. On appeal, the CA allowed the claim to stand. The FPC appealed. HL held: that an issue which was concerned exclusively with a public right should be determined in judicial review proceedings.

However, where a litigant was asserting a private law right, which incidentally involved the examination of a public law issue (the FPC's decision), he was not debarred from seeking to establish that right by ordinary action. Dr R had a bundle of private law rights, including the right to be paid for work done, which entitled him to sue for their alleged breach. It was not an abuse of the process of the court for Dr R to proceed as he had done.

---

***Mercury Communications Ltd v Director General of Telecommunications*** **(1996):** In 1984, two companies, BT and M, were granted licences to operate telecommunications systems under the Telecommunications Act 1984. In 1986, they entered into an agreement for the provision of services pursuant to a condition in BT's licence. A clause in that agreement provided for the review of the agreement after five years if either party believed that a fundamental change in circumstances had occurred. Disagreements as to terms were to be referred to the Director General (DG) for determination. An issue was referred to the DG and he made a determination. M challenged that determination and issued an originating summons. The DG and BT claimed that this was an abuse of process because the DG's determination was a public law matter which could only be challenged by judicial review. Longmore J dismissed their summonses. The CA upheld their appeal. M appealed. HL held: in deciding whether an action was properly brought by way of private law or public law, the key question was whether the proceedings constituted an abuse of the process of the court. On the facts, the dispute related to the terms of the contract between the two parties, even though the office of DG was created by statute and was subject to public law duties. The originating summons procedure was at least as well suited and possibly better suited to the determination of the issues. M's proceedings had not been an abuse of process.

---

**12.17** The decisions in these three appeals demonstrate different aspects of the rule in *O'Reilly v Mackman* (1983). Whereas *Cocks* is a good illustration of the application of that rule where the sole issue was a public law matter, *Roy* is an example of an exception to the general rule where both private law and public law matters were involved. Although the HL stopped short of describing the relationship between Dr Roy and the FPC as a contract (as the CA had done), they nevertheless felt that he did have private law rights against the committee which were capable of being enforced by ordinary action. Moreover, attention was drawn to the fact that the remedy which Dr Roy wanted, an order for the full payment of the practice allowance, could not be obtained directly in judicial review proceedings. Even if his application were successful, he would have had to institute further proceedings to obtain the money.

**12.18** In giving judgment in *Roy*, Lord Lowry referred to an argument which had been put to their Lordships by counsel for Dr Roy. This considered that two approaches could be taken to the rule in *O'Reilly v Mackman* (1983). A 'broad approach' would mean that the rule:

> *did not apply generally against bringing actions to vindicate private rights in all circumstances in which those actions involved a challenge to a public law act or*

*decision, but that it merely required the aggrieved person to proceed by judicial review only when private rights were not at stake.*

Conversely, the 'narrow approach' assumed:

*that the rule applied generally to all proceedings in which public law acts or decisions were challenged, subject to some exceptions when private law rights were involved.*

**12.19** Although Lord Lowry expressed a preference for the 'broad approach', because it was 'traditionally orthodox' and would 'have the practical merit of getting rid of a procedural minefield', the case was actually decided in Dr Roy's favour on the basis of the 'narrow approach'. The broad approach would have the effect of limiting the rule in *O'Reilly* in that it would only require an individual to proceed by way of judicial review if there were no private law rights in issue. Where there were private law rights in issue, an action could be commenced even if public law matters were also involved. The narrow approach would actually widen the scope of the rule since it would require any case which involved public law matters to proceed by way of an application for judicial review, even though private law rights may also be at issue.

**12.20** The decision in *Mercury Communications* illustrates the HL taking a relaxed approach to the rule in *O'Reilly* and recognizing that there needs to be some measure of procedural flexibility. Rather than compartmentalizing cases as either public law or private law matters which, in any event, is a difficult distinction to draw, the HL placed greater emphasis on the need to avoid an abuse of process. Thus as Professor Craig has noted, whereas *O'Reilly* assumes that to proceed by a means other than judicial review would be an abuse of process, *Mercury Communications* allows for flexibility in the choice of proceedings provided that they do not amount to an abuse of process.

## An end to the rule in *O'Reilly v Mackman*?

**12.21** In the light of the decision of the HL in *Mercury Communications* and the Civil Procedure Rules, it is open to argument whether much of the rule in *O'Reilly v Mackman* (1983) still remains. The emphasis on a strict application of the procedural exclusivity principle has now been superseded by a more liberal approach to the issue of exclusivity by the courts.

*Clark v University of Lincolnshire and Humberside (2000):* C was a student at the respondent university between 1992 and 1995. She became involved in a dispute with the university over the submission of a paper for her final examination. On the last day before the paper was due in, C lost all her data from the computer hard disk. Since she did not have a backup copy of her work, all that she was able to submit were some notes copied from a text. The paper was initially failed for plagiarism. That finding was later abandoned and the paper was marked on its merits. A mark of 0 was awarded. In 1998 C brought proceedings for breach of contract against the university. She claimed that the university appeal board had misconstrued the meaning of plagiarism, had awarded a mark beyond the limits of academic convention, and had failed to take into account her explanation of events. C's claim was struck out on the basis that breaches of contract by universities were not justiciable. On appeal, C was permitted to amend her pleadings to claim breaches of contractual rules under the university's student regulations. The university sought to argue that the judge had been correct on the question of justiciability. It also sought to contend that C should have proceeded by way of judicial review and that she had therefore abused the process of the court by suing in contract long after the time limit for bringing a judicial review application (three months) had expired. CA held: allowing the appeal, that C's claim as originally pleaded travelled deep into the field of academic judgment and could therefore be struck out on that basis rather than on the ground of non-justiciability of the relationship between student and university. However, the allegations of breaches of contractual rules pleaded by amendment were justiciable. With regard to the second issue, where a student had a claim in contract which could be brought more appropriately by judicial review proceedings, the court would not strike out the claim merely because of the procedure which had been adopted. Even though the case had been brought late, it would not be appropriate to stifle it on procedural grounds.

**12.22** In giving judgment in *Clark*, Lord Woolf MR sought to explain the effect of the Civil Procedure Rules (CPR) on *O'Reilly v Mackman* (1983) thus:

> The intention of the CPR is to harmonise procedures as far as possible and to avoid barren procedural disputes which generate satellite litigation.

In other words, the emphasis has changed since *O'Reilly* so that what really matters now is not whether the correct procedure has been followed, but rather whether the failure to follow the correct procedure amounts to an abuse of the process of the court. Thus in the context of the facts of *Clark*, Lord Woolf observed:

> Where a student has . . . a claim in contract, the court will not strike out a claim which could more appropriately be made under [Part 54] solely on the basis of the procedure which has been adopted. It may however do so, if it comes to the conclusion that in all the circumstances, including the delay in initiating the proceedings, there has been an abuse of the process of the court under the CPR.

**12.23** The principle established in *Clark* has subsequently been applied in several contexts, including the planning context. Thus in *Stancliffe Stone Co Ltd v Peak District National Park Authority* (2004), the HCt held that a delay of eight years meant that it was too late to challenge a planning decision by way of ordinary action. In subsequently confirming this decision, Buxton LJ commented that the 'need for promptitude in bringing challenges to public law decisions that, if successful, will have a wide public impact is not to be avoided by casting the complaint in a private law form, the object or (as in this case) the effect of which is to bypass the formal rules of judicial review': see the CA decision in *Stancliffe Stone Co Ltd v Peak District National Park Authority* (2005). The proceedings therefore failed as an abuse of the process of the court.

**12.24** The planning context also provides a recent example of the *application* of the exclusivity principle. Thus in *North Dorset DC v Trim* (2011), the CA held that it was an abuse of process for the respondent to challenge the lawfulness of a breach of condition planning notice in private law proceedings rather than by way of judicial review. The service of the notice had been 'a purely public law act'. Thus in the judgment of Carnwath LJ, this was 'an archetypal example of the public action which Lord Diplock would have had in mind' in *O'Reilly v Mackman*. More generally, he observed:

> Public action does not lose its 'public' character merely because it involves, as most public action does, interference with private rights and freedoms. It is only where there is an overlap with private law principles (such as contract or tort), that procedural exclusivity may become difficult to maintain.

## The public law/private law distinction

**12.25** Despite the increasingly flexible approach which the courts have taken to the issue of procedural exclusivity, it is still necessary to distinguish between public law and private law matters in the context of judicial review. However, working out this distinction is by no means an easy matter. In *R v Legal Aid Board, ex p Donn & Co (a firm)* (1996), for example, Ognall J was of the opinion 'that there can be no universal test' for determining the existence of a public law element. Whether or not there was a sufficient public law element fell 'to be decided as one of overall impression and one of degree'. From a practical point of view, therefore, where it is not clear whether a matter is essentially of a public law or private law nature, it would be advisable for a claimant to proceed by way of judicial review rather than an ordinary action since in such circumstances, there can be no question that he has thereby abused the process of the court: see *Trustees of the Dennis Rye Pension Fund v Sheffield City Council* (1998).

**12.26** Traditionally, the starting point has been to ascertain whether the decision-maker is a public or private body since judicial review only operates in respect of the decisions of public bodies. A public body will, generally speaking, derive its power either from statute or delegated legislation made under statute, or from a non-statutory source such as the prerogative. Thus local councils are clearly public bodies in that they are established under statute and many (but by no means all) of the powers which they exercise are conferred on them by statute. Private bodies, however, derive their power or authority not from statute, but from the agreement of those who are subject to their jurisdiction.

---

*R v Disciplinary Committee of the Jockey Club, ex p Aga Khan* **(1993):** The Aga Khan owned a racehorse which won the 1989 Oaks, a classic race for fillies, at Epsom racecourse. The horse was subsequently disqualified after traces of a banned substance were found in a urine sample. The Aga Khan sought to challenge the decision of the committee by way of an application for judicial review. The QBD held on a preliminary issue that the committee's decision was not susceptible to judicial review. The Aga Khan appealed. CA held: despite the fact that the Jockey Club regulated a significant national activity and had wide powers to do so, it was not in its origin, history, constitution, or membership a public body. It was barely mentioned in statute and it had not been woven into a system of governmental control. The powers which it had over those who agreed to be bound by the Rules of Racing derived from the agreement of the parties. It was therefore a private body and as such was not susceptible to judicial review.

**12.27** As is often the case when seeking to make distinctions in a legal context, it is a relatively straightforward task to identify that which occupies either end of the spectrum: bodies which are patently public at one end, and those which are equally patently private at the other, eg companies. Difficulties arise, however, the nearer we get to the middle of the spectrum. Whilst the source of a body's power will often provide the answer to the question 'Is it a public body?' this is by no means always the case.

*R v Panel on Take-overs and Mergers, ex p Datafin plc* **(1987):** The panel was a body established by the City of London to regulate takeovers and mergers. Its powers were derived from neither statute nor the common law, although it did operate within a statutory framework. D sought judicial review of the panel's decision to reject a complaint which it had made. Hodgson J refused D leave to apply on the ground that the court had no jurisdiction to hear the application. D appealed. CA held: in deciding whether or not a body is subject to judicial review, although the source of its power would normally decide the issue, it was not the sole test. A court was also entitled to look at the nature of the power which the body exercised. Having regard to the wide-ranging powers of the panel and the importance of the task that it performed, it was a body which was susceptible to judicial review. However, application for leave was refused on the facts because none of the grounds for review were present.

**12.28** The decision in *Datafin* is significant in that it recognizes that a body may rightly be described as a 'public body' because of the nature of the functions which it performs. It is also significant because the CA accepted the argument that had the City not established the panel for its own regulation, the Government would have been likely to set up a public body to perform the same function (the 'but for' test). In *R v Chief Rabbi of the United Hebrew Congregation of Great Britain and the Commonwealth, ex p Wachmann* (1993), Simon Brown J rejected the submission that in the exercise of his disciplinary functions, the Chief Rabbi was subject to judicial review. In so doing, he observed that:

> To say of decisions of a given body that they are public law decisions with public law consequences means something more than that they are decisions which may be of great interest or concern to the public or, indeed, which may have consequences for the public. To attract the court's supervisory jurisdiction there must be not merely a public but potentially a governmental interest in the decision-making power in question . . .

*where non-governmental bodies have hitherto been held to be reviewable, they have generally been operating as an integral part of a regulatory system which, although itself non-statutory, is nevertheless supported by statutory powers and penalties clearly indicative of government concern . . . it is a feature of all these cases that, were there no self-regulatory body in existence, Parliament would almost inevitably intervene to control the activity in question.*

**12.29** In a number of subsequent cases, counsel have argued this latter point. It has to be noted, however, that even where they have succeeded, it has not necessarily affected the decision. Thus in *ex p Aga Khan*, although Sir Thomas Bingham MR was 'willing to accept that if the Jockey Club did not regulate this activity the Government would probably be driven to create a public body to do so', as we have seen, the application for leave was defeated on the ground that the Jockey Club was a private body. Moreover, in *R v Football Association Ltd, ex p Football League* (1993), Rose LJ responded to the argument that if the FA did not run football, the Government would create a public body to do so with the observation that:

*On the contrary, the evidence of commercial interest in the professional game is such as to suggest that a far more likely intervener to run football would be a television or similar company rooted in the entertainment business or a commercial company.*

**12.30** In the case of *R (on the application of West) v Lloyd's of London* (2004), the CA affirmed a line of authority including *R v Lloyd's of London, ex p Biggs* (1993) in which the private law status of Lloyd's had been confirmed. Thus the decisions of that body were not susceptible to judicial review. In so holding, Brooke LJ observed:

*It seems to me that the functions of Lloyd's which are under review in this case are totally different from the functions of the Takeover Panel that were under consideration in* Ex p Datafin. *The panel exercised regulatory control in a public sphere where governmental regulatory control was absent. This case is concerned with the working out of private contractual arrangements at Lloyd's which is itself subject to external governmental regulation.*

**12.31** Since the enactment of the Human Rights Act 1998, it has become increasingly clear that there is a close correlation between the test for determining whether a body's decisions are subject to judicial review, and the test for determining a 'public authority' for the purpose of the Act.

*R (Beer (t/a Hammer Trout Farm)) v Hampshire Farmers' Markets Ltd (2004):* In 1999, the county council established farmers' markets pursuant to s 33 of the Local Government and Housing Act 1989. The claimant was accepted as a stallholder from the outset. In 2001, the running of the markets was transferred from the council to the stallholders, and a limited company was duly established to perform the task. The company's registered address was originally at the council's offices and the council provided the company with some finances and facilities, such as the use of a computer. In 2002, the claimant applied to participate in the market programme. The company rejected his application and refused to grant him a licence. The claimant sought judicial review of that decision. At first instance, the company's decision was quashed since it was held that it was acting as a 'public authority' within the meaning of s 6 of the Human Rights Act 1998, and that its decisions were therefore susceptible to judicial review. The council appealed. CA held: dismissing the appeal, that it was common ground that the company was a 'hybrid' authority rather than a 'core' public authority. Nevertheless, there were a number of factors which collectively indicated that its decision was amenable to judicial review: the markets were not statutory markets, but they were held on publicly owned land to which the public had access; the company owed its existence to the council since it had been set up by the latter using its statutory powers; the company had stepped into the shoes of the council in the sense that it was performing the same functions previously performed by the council to the same end and in substantially the same way; and the council had assisted the company, eg by providing office space, use of a computer, etc.

In delivering the leading judgment in *Beer*, Dyson LJ observed:

> It seems to me that the law has now been developed to the point where, unless the source of the power clearly provides the answer, the question whether the decision of a body is amenable to judicial review requires a careful consideration of the nature of the power and function that has been exercised to see whether the decision has a sufficient public element, flavour or character to bring it within the purview of public law. It may be said with some justification that this criterion for amenability is very broad, not to say question-begging. But it provides the framework for the investigation that has to be conducted.

## Collateral challenge

**12.32** The existence of the general principle that public law decisions ought to be challenged by way of judicial review raises a related issue: whether such a principle prevents a person from challenging the validity of a public law decision in proceedings brought against them. In short, can a public law matter be used as a shield not a sword, or does the principle require that in those circumstances, an application for judicial review should be made?

**12.33** This issue is clearly important from a practical standpoint. It also has wider ramifications in terms of justice and fairness. Is it right that an individual should be denied a defence in proceedings brought against them merely because they could have instituted proceedings themselves? Should a person be convicted under a law that would have been held to be invalid had it been challenged in judicial review proceedings? The unfairness may be greater in the event of a criminal prosecution, but the injustice would still exist in civil proceedings.

---

**Wandsworth London Borough Council v Winder (1984):** The local authority pursuant to its powers under the Housing Act 1957 resolved to increase rents generally. W, a council tenant, refused to pay the increased element of the rent. The local authority sued him in the county court for rent arrears and possession of the property. As a defence to those proceedings, W claimed that the resolutions and notices of increase were ultra vires. The local authority sought to strike out the defence as an abuse of process. It claimed that W ought to have proceeded by way of judicial review. HL held: that the reforms made to RSC Order 53 were procedural in nature. They did not prevent W from challenging the validity of the authority's decision as a defence in proceedings brought against him by the authority. W had not abused the process of the court.

---

**12.34** The decision in *Winder* thus demonstrates that a defence alleging the invalidity of a public law decision may be raised in private law proceedings. It was subsequently applied in *Wandsworth London Borough Council v A* (2000) where a parent who had been excluded from school premises on the grounds of her abusive and disruptive conduct successfully appealed against the grant of an injunction. In the judgment of the CA, the relationship between the governors or the headmaster of a school run by a local education authority (LEA) and a parent was governed by public law considerations. Accordingly, a headmaster who intended to revoke a parent's implied licence to enter the school premises was first obliged to warn the parent and to hear and consider any representations from the parent relating to the conduct which underlay the decision to exclude. In the present case, the headmaster's failure to do so could be relied upon as a defence to the private law action brought by the LEA in which it sought an injunction against the parent.

**12.35** It should be noted, however, that although such a conclusion had to be reached on the authority of *Winder*, the CA in *Wandsworth London Borough Council v A* (2000) did consider that there were 'some practical difficulties in that conclusion'. In what were obiter remarks, Laws LJ remarked that the effect of *Winder* was to 'legitimate the introduction of public law issues into a potentially wide range of private law actions'. In the opinion of the CA, such a development was not to be welcomed for two reasons relating to: (i) the proper argument of such issues; (ii) the technical difficulty of expressing the true nature of public law issues in private law actions. With regard to the latter, Laws LJ observed that:

> it is of the essence of judicial review applications that they must be brought promptly . . . and that relief accorded judicial review is discretionary. Those are not merely incidental limitations on a public law claim, but fundamental to the true nature of the interests that such a claim articulates. It is quite obscure whether either of these limitations apply to a public law defence in private law proceedings. The point does not arise in the present case . . . and there is no other reason to withhold on discretionary grounds relief that would otherwise be available . . . In another case, however, that issue of the nature of a public law claim asserted in private law proceedings might become important.

**12.36** Despite the later reservations of the CA, *Winder* remains good law. Indeed, the principle which the case establishes was applied by the SC in *Manchester City Council v Pinnock* (2010). Public law defences may therefore be raised in private law proceedings. Is the same true where the proceedings involve the alleged commission of a criminal offence?

---

*R v Crown Court at Reading, ex p Hutchinson* (1988): The defendants were protesters at the Greenham Common Air Base. They were convicted by magistrates of an offence contrary to the Royal Air Force Greenham Common Byelaws 1985. This prohibited entering, passing, or remaining in or over the protected area without permission. They appealed against their conviction on the basis that the bye-laws were invalid. The Crown Court felt that it was unable to rule on this question. The defendants therefore sought an order of mandamus to compel them to do so. QBD held: where a defendant wishes to challenge the validity of a bye-law as a defence to summary proceedings brought against them, a magistrates' court or a Crown Court (on appeal) could hear such a defence. Neither s 31 of the SCA nor RSC Order 53 had removed the jurisdiction to do so. It was neither necessary nor appropriate for summary proceedings to be adjourned so that the validity of a bye-law could be determined by the HCt in judicial review proceedings.

---

*Bugg v DPP* (1993): The defendants were convicted by magistrates of entering a protected area contrary to bye-laws made under the Military Lands Act 1892. An appeal to the Crown Court was dismissed. They appealed to the DC contending, amongst other things, that the bye-laws were invalid because the protected area to which they related had not been sufficiently identified. DC held: that bye-laws could be either substantively invalid, ie beyond the power under which they were made or patently unreasonable, or procedurally invalid, ie a procedural requirement in their making had not been complied with (eg a failure to consult).

---

**12.37** The principle which therefore emerges from these two decisions is that where D is being prosecuted for the breach of a bye-law, it is permissible to question the validity of that bye-law as a defence. In *Bugg*, the DC sought to qualify the application of this general principle by making a distinction between substantive and procedural invalidity. The significance of the distinction lay in the fact that in criminal proceedings for contravention of the bye-law, the court had the jurisdiction to determine the issue of substantive invalidity but did not have the jurisdiction to determine whether or not the bye-law was procedurally invalid.

**12.38** Subsequently, the distinction between substantive and procedural invalidity was doubted by the HL in *R v Wicks* (1998), a case concerned with D's non-compliance with an enforcement notice issued under the town and country planning legislation. In a later decision of the same court, *Bugg v DPP* (1993) was overruled.

---

*Boddington v British Transport Police* (1999): B was convicted by a stipendiary magistrate of the offence of smoking in a railway carriage contrary to a bye-law made under the

Transport Act 1962, as amended. Section 67(1)(c) of that Act conferred a power to make bye-laws 'with respect to the smoking of tobacco in railway carriages and elsewhere and the prevention of nuisances'. B appealed against his conviction. HL held: that D may raise as a defence to a criminal charge the contention that a bye-law or an administrative decision made pursuant to powers conferred by it is ultra vires. Only the clear language of a statute could take away such a right of challenge. The observations in *Bugg* were contrary to authority and principle. It was inappropriate to distinguish between substantive and procedural invalidity. The bye-law in the present case was valid since it fell within the scope of the authority under which it had been made.

**12.39**  In giving judgment in *Boddington*, Lord Steyn observed that a practical consequence of the decision in *Bugg* was that a defendant may be convicted under a bye-law which was in fact invalid. In his opinion, this was 'an unacceptable consequence in a democracy based on the rule of law'. Whilst Lord Steyn recognized that *Bugg* allowed for the possibility of challenge by way of judicial review, he felt that there were a number of factors which limited the effectiveness of such a challenge:

> *The defendant may, however, be out of time before he becomes aware of the existence of the byelaw. He may lack the resources to defend his interest in two courts. He may not be able to obtain legal aid for an application for leave to apply for judicial review. Leave to apply for judicial review may be refused. At a substantive hearing the scope for demanding examination of witnesses in the Divisional Court may be restricted. He may be denied a remedy on a discretionary basis. The possibility of judicial review will, therefore, in no way compensate him for the loss of the right to defend himself by a defensive challenge to the byelaw in cases where the invalidity of the byelaw might afford him with a defence to the charge.*

**12.40**  The *Boddington* principle was later applied in *Palacegate Properties Ltd v London Borough of Camden* (2000), where the issue was once again a collateral challenge to an enforcement notice issued under the Town and Country Planning Act 1990. It has also been applied in other contexts. Thus in *R v Searby* (2003), the appellants had been prosecuted for selling and storing pesticides without ministerial approval contrary to the Control of Pesticides Regulations 1986. At their trial, they contended that certain 'control arrangements' under the regulations were contrary to European law. The trial judge ruled, however, that this defence was not available to them and they were accordingly convicted. On appeal, the CA held, inter alia, that the trial judge had been wrong to think that the case was not covered by the general principle laid down in *Boddington*. Rather, that principle obliged the trial court to consider the defence based on the alleged invalidity of the 'control arrangements'.

**12.41**  In *W v DPP* (2005), the DC accepted that in proceedings for the breach of an Anti-social Behaviour Order (ASBO) issued pursuant to the Crime and Disorder Act 1998, it was permissible for the defence to rely on the alleged invalidity of the order in answer to the charge. However, Brooke LJ sought to limit the application of the principle as follows:

> I would stress that anything I say in this case must be understood as referring only to an order as plainly invalid as one which contains a restraint preventing a defendant from committing any criminal offence. There is great force, in my judgment, in the submission . . . that there will be a danger of opening floodgates if challenges to [ASBOs] could be made in breach proceedings, but in all these cases there are exceptions which are as plain as the exception in this case.

## Exclusion of judicial review

**12.42**  Given the importance of the courts' supervisory jurisdiction over the exercise of executive power, it is not surprising that Parliament has attempted on occasion to prevent that jurisdiction from being exercised. The mechanism for doing this has been to insert a provision to that effect in the relevant Act. Such provisions may take one of several different forms.

### Ouster clauses

**12.43**  Ouster clauses exist in various guises. Finality clauses, as their name implies, attempt to render the decision of the relevant body or tribunal final and hence beyond the control of the Administrative Court. Other examples of ouster clauses include 'no certiorari clauses' and 'shall not be questioned' clauses. The fact that a number of different alternatives have been used in statutes is symptomatic of the reluctance of the judiciary to accept restrictions on their ability to intervene. Nowhere was this more apparent than in the leading case of *Anisminic*.

*Anisminic v Foreign Compensation Commission* **(1969):** A were the owners of property in Egypt which was sequestrated by the Egyptian Government in 1956 and subsequently sold to an Egyptian organization. Under a Treaty between the United Arab Republic and the UK, compensation was paid for property which had been confiscated. This was to be distributed by the FCC which had been established under the Foreign Compensation Act 1950. A sought to challenge the FCC's decision that it was not entitled to compensation by applying for a declaration. However, s 4(4) of the 1950 Act provided that any determination by the FCC 'shall not be called into question in any court of law'. The case therefore turned on the effect of this provision. HL held: that it was a well-established principle that statutory provisions seeking to oust the ordinary jurisdiction of the court should be interpreted restrictively. Where they were reasonably capable of bearing two meanings, the meaning which preserved the jurisdiction of the court would be preferred. Section 4(4) only protected those determinations of the FCC that were not a nullity. The decision in respect of A was not a determination because the FCC had acted outside its jurisdiction. Thus it was not protected from challenge in the courts.

**12.44** Section 4(4) of the Foreign Compensation Act 1950 amounted to a complete ouster clause and yet the HL interpreted it in such a way as to preserve the court's supervisory jurisdiction. It was able to do this by asserting that this is what Parliament must have intended in enacting the provision. Nevertheless, it might be argued that in the case of complete ouster clauses, their effect is determined not by the words used but by judicial attitudes towards them. This gives rise to an inherent constitutional danger. A court which seeks to interpret ouster clauses in such a way as to preserve its jurisdiction runs the risk of acting contrary to the will of Parliament. Unchallengeable decision-making powers have the potential to be abused and therefore the courts are reluctant to stand back from them. However, where this may lead to a conflict with Parliament, the courts must tread carefully, ever mindful of the constitutional limits of the judicial role.

## Time limit clauses

**12.45** Unlike complete ouster clauses, time limit clauses do not seek to preclude legal challenge per se. Instead, they are partial ouster clauses in that they provide for the possibility of legal challenge within a prescribed time limit. In the planning legislation, the most commonly prescribed time limit is six weeks from the date of the relevant decision. Time limit clauses are therefore less iniquitous than complete ouster clauses. This helps to explain why they have been treated more favourably by the courts.

---

*Smith v East Elloe RDC* **(1956):** Under the Acquisition of Land (Authorisation Procedure) Act 1946, an aggrieved person had the right to challenge the validity of a compulsory purchase order within six weeks of the date of the confirmation or making of the order. Subject to this right, a compulsory purchase order was not to be challenged in any legal proceedings whatsoever. Property owned by S was the subject of such an order. Its validity was challenged six years after it had been made. HL held: by a majority, that the validity of the compulsory purchase order could not be impugned. It was the duty of the court to give the words of the statute their proper meaning.

---

**12.46** The decision in *Smith* illustrates the HL approaching the task of statutory interpretation as we would expect: giving effect to the plain meaning of the words used by Parliament. It should be noted, however, that *Smith* predates *Anisminic*. Thus, it later became necessary to consider whether *Smith* remained a binding authority.

---

*R v Secretary of State for the Environment, ex p Ostler* **(1977):** Under the Highways Act 1959, a person aggrieved by the making of a compulsory purchase order could challenge its validity, within six weeks of the date on which notice of its publication had been given, by applying to the HCt. Subject to this, the order was not to be questioned in any legal

> proceedings whatsoever. O sought to challenge an order when he became aware that an objection to a relief road had been withdrawn as a consequence of a secret assurance which would have had a detrimental impact on his own business. His challenge took place some months after the expiry of the six weeks. CA held: his complaint could not be considered because he had not commenced proceedings within the time limit.

**12.47** The decision in *Ostler* thus confirms that *Smith* remains a binding authority despite *Anisminic*. Lord Denning MR sought to distinguish *Smith* and *Anisminic* on a number of grounds. One such ground related to the now defunct distinction between judicial and administrative decisions (see *Ridge v Baldwin* (1964), paras **13.46–13.47**). Of the remaining grounds, the most compelling appears to relate to public policy. In short, the six-week time limit is adhered to for reasons of certainty. It enables the authority to act upon the relevant decision, in the case of a compulsory purchase order by acquiring the relevant property and demolishing it etc, without fear of the order being challenged at some later and doubtless inconvenient date.

**12.48** Although in practice it is more likely that a claimant will fall foul of a time limit clause where they seek judicial review after the expiry of that limit, it is also possible (though less common) for review to be precluded because the relevant 'window' of time has not yet started to run. Thus where an application to challenge a compulsory purchase order was made three days before the six-week 'window' had commenced, the court had no jurisdiction to hear the case: see *Enterprise Inns plc v Secretary of State for the Environment, Transport and the Regions* (2000).

## The procedure for judicial review

**12.49** The procedure for making a claim for judicial review essentially involves two stages: a permission stage which, if successful, is followed by a hearing of the judicial review. Some important aspects of the judicial review procedure will therefore be considered. However, prior to doing so, it is necessary to have regard to an important development which is intended to reduce the need for judicial review claims.

### Pre-action protocol

**12.50** The Civil Procedure Rules (CPR) contain a number of pre-action protocols relating to matters such as defamation, personal injury claims, and professional negligence. For present purposes, however, our focus of attention is the Pre-Action Protocol for Judicial Review which came into force on 4 March 2002. The aim of the protocol is set out in para 5, which provides that:

> *This protocol sets out a code of good practice and contains the steps which parties should generally follow before making a claim for judicial review. [emphasis added]*

**12.51**   One of these steps is for the parties to consider whether some form of alternative dispute resolution procedure (ADR) would be more suitable than litigation. The protocol notes that the parties 'may be required by the Court to provide evidence that alternative means of resolving their dispute was considered'. It also makes it clear that a failure to consider ADR or other parts of the protocol will be taken into account by a court when determining costs.

**12.52**   Whether or not the protocol is followed is a matter for a claimant to determine, depending upon the circumstances of their case. However, where the use of the protocol is appropriate, a court will normally expect all parties to have complied with it. Compliance/non-compliance is a matter which a court will take into account when giving directions for case management of proceedings or when making orders for costs. The protocol will not be appropriate: (i) where the defendant does not have the legal power to change the decision being made; or (ii) in an urgent case, eg where the claimant is shortly to be removed from the UK or where an interim order is necessary to compel a public body to act.

**12.53**   The pre-action procedure laid down in the protocol is essentially written. It consists of the letter before claim (sent by the claimant to the defendant) and the letter of response (sent by the defendant to the claimant). The purpose of the former is to identify the issues in dispute and establish whether litigation between the parties can be avoided. Accordingly, the letter should contain: (i) the date and details of the decision, act, or omission which is being challenged; (ii) a clear summary of the facts on which the claim is based; and (iii) the details of any relevant information that the claimant is seeking and an explanation as to its relevance. The letter should also normally contain the details of any interested parties known to the claimant. The protocol strongly advises claimants to seek appropriate legal advice before sending the letter of claim or making a claim. As a general rule, a claim should not be made until the proposed reply date in the letter of claim has passed, unless the circumstances of the case require more immediate action to be taken.

**12.54**   A letter of response should normally pass from the defendant to the claimant within 14 days of receipt of the letter of claim. A failure to meet this deadline will be taken into account by the court and sanctions may be imposed in the absence of good reasons. Where it is not possible to reply within the proposed time limit, the protocol states that a defendant 'should send an interim reply and propose a reasonable extension'. Where a claim is being conceded in full, this should be expressed in clear and unambiguous terms in the reply. If, however, the claim is only being conceded in part or not at all, this should also be stated clearly and the reply should also:

- where appropriate, contain a new decision, clearly identifying which aspects of the claim are being conceded and which are not, or, give a clear timescale within which the new decision will be issued;
- if considered appropriate, provide a fuller explanation for the decision;

- address any points of dispute, or explain why they cannot be addressed;
- enclose any relevant documentation requested by the claimant or explain why it is not being enclosed; and
- where appropriate, confirm whether or not they will oppose any application for an interim remedy.

**12.55** Fordham has argued that the requirements of the Pre-Action Protocol largely reflect what happened in practice hitherto. The advantages of such an approach are that it may result in a case being settled without the need to make a claim for judicial review. Alternatively, if no such settlement can be reached, both parties will at least be properly aware of the issues raised by the claim.

## Permission stage

**12.56** It will be remembered that following the Bowman Report, the judicial review procedure has undergone some changes. Under Order 53 of the Rules of the Supreme Court, the initial stage was the leave stage during which the applicant sought leave of the court to apply for judicial review. This was essentially a means by which unmeritorious claims, eg those clearly involving no public law element or where the time limit for making an application had expired and there was no good reason for extending it, could be filtered out. An application for leave was made ex parte, ie in the absence of the respondent. Now, however, under the Civil Procedure Rules (CPR) Part 54, the initial stage of a claim for judicial review is somewhat different. The change in nomenclature (permission rather than leave) is obvious but not especially important. What is important, however, is that this stage now involves interaction between the parties. A claimant for judicial review is required by CPR 54.7 to serve the claim form (N461) on the defendant within seven days of issue, in addition to having filed the papers with the Administrative Court. The claim form will contain a statement of a number of particulars, which include the name and description of the claimant, the grounds of the claim, and the relief sought. According to the CPR Part 54 Practice Direction, it must be accompanied by, inter alia, any written evidence in support of the claim, a copy of any order which the claimant seeks to have quashed, and copies of any documents on which the claimant seeks to rely. Any person served with the claim form who wishes to take part in the judicial review must then file an acknowledgement of service (form N462) within 21 days of the service of the claim form. Such an acknowledgement must be served on the claimant and any other person named in the claim form not later than seven days after it has been filed (CPR 54.8). A failure to file an acknowledgement of service form will prevent the relevant person from participating in the inter partes hearing to decide whether permission should be given, unless the court allows him to do so (CPR 54.9).

**12.57** It has been argued by Fordham that the rationale for these changes is twofold: (i) it will encourage defendants to properly consider the challenge from the outset and therefore concede those cases which are likely to succeed; (ii) it will ensure that the Administrative Court is well informed at the permission stage. Fordham has further argued that this 'mechanism for interaction at the permission stage is similar to what well advised parties were already doing under the old rules'. It should be noted, however, that these reforms have not been universally welcomed. Cornford and Sunkin, for example, express regret at the fact that the CPR state the need for permission but say nothing about the criteria for granting such permission. In their opinion, it is 'particularly regrettable that the opportunity to create a presumption in favour of permission has not been taken'.

**12.58** In deciding whether or not to grant permission, a judge has a considerable measure of discretion. Where permission to proceed is given, it may include directions (CPR 54.10). Such directions may include a stay of proceedings to which the claim relates. The decision to either grant or refuse permission may be made by the court on the papers without a hearing. Whether or not a hearing has taken place, the court must serve the order giving/refusing permission on: the claimant; the defendant; and any other person who filed an acknowledgement of service.

**12.59** Recent research undertaken by Bondy and Sunkin reveals, amongst other things, that claimants have been increasingly unsuccessful in obtaining permission in recent years. Thus whereas in 1996 58% of permission decisions in all categories of judicial review case resulted in the grant of permission, by 2006, only 22% achieved the same outcome. The authors suggest that the statistics show that the courts have adopted a cautious approach based on the arguability of the claim which contrasts with the more liberal approach adopted on the issue of standing (paras **12.60–12.65**). Having said that, the falling rate of permission grants may also owe something to the increasing number of cases settled prior to the permission stage. Importantly, the authors also draw attention to judicial inconsistency in relation to decisions at the permission stage. Their analysis of grant rates by individual judge reveals a 'wide variation', with the judge at the top of the table granting permission in 46% of cases, as compared with 11% for the judge at the bottom of the table. In the opinion of the authors, 'there were no obvious factors to do with the nature or type of cases involved that would readily explain this wide variation'. They believe that the issue of judicial inconsistency may become even more important following the regionalization of the Administrative Court with centres in Birmingham, Cardiff, Leeds, and Manchester, as well as London.

## Standing/Locus standi

**12.60** On receipt of a claim for judicial review, a court must consider whether or not the claimant has a 'sufficient interest' in the matter to which the application relates: see s 31(3) of the Senior Courts Act 1981. The existence of the standing or locus standi requirement means that in effect, some claimants will obtain the assistance of the courts in enforcing their rights whereas others will not. Standing will initially be determined at the permission stage, but it may also feature prominently in the hearing of the judicial review. Since the decision involves the exercise of discretion on the part of the judge (albeit based on fact and law), it is not surprising that there is some variation in the case law on this aspect of judicial review.

**12.61** Sir Konrad Schiemann has argued that the label 'exercise of discretion' 'conceals more than it reveals and prevents challenge, improvement and systemisation'. He has made the case for developing a set of clear principles on which locus standi decisions would be based. These would 'emerge with the aid of appellate courts and academic writers'. Are there any clear principles that emerge from the following cases?

---

*IRC v National Federation of Self-Employed and Small Businesses Ltd (1982):* Casual workers in the printing industry (the 'Fleet Street Casuals') had avoided paying income tax on their earnings. This practice had come to the attention of the Inland Revenue. An agreement was reached whereby the workers would register in respect of their casual employment and pay income tax in the normal way. Investigations as to unpaid tax in previous years were not to be made. The NFSESB sought an order of mandamus to compel the Commissioners to assess and collect the arrears of tax. HL held: in cases other than simple cases where it is clear that the applicant does not have a sufficient interest, the question of sufficient interest cannot be considered as an isolated point; it must be considered together with the legal and factual context. Having regard to the duties of the Revenue and the operation of the tax system itself, as a general principle, no one taxpayer has a sufficient interest in the tax affairs of another. The principle applies especially to groups of taxpayers: an aggregate of individuals each of which had no interest cannot of itself have an interest.

---

*R v Secretary of State for the Environment, ex p Rose Theatre Trust Co (1990):* The remains of the Rose Theatre were discovered in the process of developing a site for office accommodation. A group of persons, including archaeologists, formed a trust company as part of a campaign to preserve the site. The trust applied to the SoS to schedule the site under the Ancient Monuments and Archaeological Areas Act 1979 so as to protect it from development without his consent. He declined to do so and the trust sought judicial review of that decision. QBD held: the application would be dismissed since the SoS had not taken irrelevant matters into account in making his decision. On the question of standing, the trust could have no greater claim to a sufficient interest than its members had before it was formed. Since no individual member of the trust had standing, it followed that the trust created by those individuals did not have standing either.

---

*R v HM Inspectorate of Pollution, ex p Greenpeace (No 2) (1994):* The Inspectorate granted applications by British Nuclear Fuels for variations of authorizations to discharge liquid and gaseous radioactive waste from its premises at Sellafield so as to include its thermal oxide reprocessing plant. The original authorizations had been granted pursuant to s 6(1) of the Radioactive Substances Act 1960. Greenpeace (G) applied for judicial review of the inspectorate's decision..QBD held: although the court could not find for the applicant on the merits of the case, approaching the locus standi question as primarily one of discretion, the court concluded that G did have standing. G was an eminently respectable organization with a genuine interest in the issues raised by the application. It had a significant national and international membership but, more importantly, 2,500 of its members lived in Cumbria. With its access to scientific and legal expertise, G was in a position to mount a focused, relevant, and well-argued challenge on behalf of those who might not otherwise have an effective way to bring the issues before the court.

**12.62** In neither *Rose Theatre* nor *Greenpeace* was the decision on locus standi central to the determination of the case. Nevertheless, the views expressed on this point illustrate the variation in judicial opinion. Clearly the question of standing has to be determined on a case-by-case basis and it follows, therefore, that an individual or organization may have a sufficient interest in respect of one claim but not in respect of another. However, it is possible to argue that since *Rose Theatre* the judiciary have adopted a more liberal approach to standing.

**12.63** Thus in *R v Secretary of State for Foreign Affairs, ex p World Development Movement Ltd* (1995), the applicant was held to have locus standi to challenge the Government's decision to contribute financial aid to the Pergau Dam scheme in Malaysia. In reaching this conclusion, the court took into account a number of factors. These included: the importance of vindicating the rule of law; the importance of the issue raised; the likely absence of any other responsible challenger; and the national and international expertise of the applicants coupled with their interest in promoting and protecting aid to underdeveloped countries. This liberal approach to standing was equally apparent in *R v Secretary of State for Foreign and Commonwealth Affairs, ex p Rees-Mogg* (1994), where the applicant was held to have a sufficient interest to challenge the decision to ratify the Maastricht Treaty on the basis of his 'sincere concern for constitutional issues'. Might it have been possible for all students of public law to have advanced a similar argument?

**12.64** More recently, in *R (on the application of Edwards) v Environment Agency* (2004), Keith J held that the claimant had a sufficient interest to challenge the Agency's decision to issue a company with an IPPC permit (under the Pollution Prevention and Control (England and Wales) Regulations 2000) to operate a cement plant at which rubber tyre chips were to be used as a partial fuel substitute. Such a conclusion was reached despite the fact that the claimant: had not made any representations to the Agency during the extensive consultation process which took place; had not attended any of the public meetings; had not expressed his opposition to the decision by sending the Agency a pre-printed postcard provided by local campaigners; had not made himself known to the Agency at all; and appeared to have been put up to challenge the decision in order to secure public funding for the claim. Nevertheless, in the words of the judge:

> *You do not have to be active in a campaign yourself to have an interest in its outcome. If the consultation exercise ends with a decision which affects your interest, you are no less affected by that decision simply because you took no part in the exercise but left it to others to do so . . . It has been said that it is easier to identify a sufficient interest than to define it, but as a local inhabitant, Mr Edwards has a sufficient interest in the*

*decision to issue the permit even if he is temporarily homeless, because as an inhabitant*
*of Rugby, he will be affected by any adverse impact on the environment which the trials*
*on the use of tyre chips may have.*

**12.65**   In *R (on the application of Bulger) v Secretary of State for the Home Department* (2001),
Rose LJ observed that:

> the threshold for standing in judicial review has generally been set by the courts at
> a low level. This, as it seems to me, is because of the importance in public law that
> someone should be able to call decision-makers to account, lest the rule of law break
> down and private rights be denied by public bodies.

Such observations did not, however, assist the claimant in the case before the DC. In
the judgment of the court, the father of a murder victim did not have standing to challenge the decision of the Lord Chief Justice regarding the fixing of a tariff for a juvenile
detainee. In criminal cases, there was no need for a third party to intervene to seek to
uphold the rule of law; the Crown and the defendant were the only proper parties to
such proceedings.

## Reform of locus standi

**12.66**   In *Administrative Law: Judicial Review and Statutory Appeals* (1994), the Law
Commission proposed that a 'two-track system' of standing ought to be adopted (para
**5.20**). The first track would relate to those who had been personally adversely affected by
the decision which they were seeking to challenge. Thus where a person's legal rights or
legitimate expectations were adversely affected, that person 'should normally be given
standing as a matter of course'. The second track would be discretionary and would
cover cases where there was a sufficient public interest in the matter being litigated.

**12.67**   Cane has argued that the phrase 'adversely affected' is not really much of an improvement on 'sufficiently interested'. He offers the alternative of 'sufficiently personally
interested' to emphasize the personal nature of the standing. More important, however,
are Cane's criticisms of the second track. He has argued that in the law on standing, an
important distinction must be made between 'personal standing', ie on the basis of a
claimant's own personal interests, and 'representational standing'. It is this second type
of standing which he further divides into three categories:

- 'associational standing';
- 'public interest standing';
- 'surrogate standing'.

**12.68**   'Associational standing' occurs where an unincorporated group or corporation acts on
behalf of its members, whereas 'public interest standing' occurs where an individual or
group seeks to challenge a decision in the public interest rather than directly on behalf

of others. 'Surrogate standing' involves an individual acting as a nominal claimant on behalf of another individual who is the real claimant. In order for there to be genuine associational standing, Cane argues that 'the represented must have some degree of control over or some "democratic stake" . . . in the conduct of the representative'. He further argues that there is no need for a 'democratic stake' where a claim is made in the public interest.

## Time limit

**12.69**  In addition to the limitations on judicial review which have already been considered, it must be noted that the procedure is subject to a time limit. The rationale for this appears to be administrative certainty. In short, in order to allow administrative decisions to be acted upon, it is necessary that there is a point in time beyond which they can no longer be subject to challenge.

**12.70**  Where the Administrative Court considers that there has been undue delay in making an application for judicial review, it may refuse to grant leave or any relief sought (s 31(6) of the Senior Courts Act 1981). This provision must be read in the light of CPR 54.5(1). This provides that:

> The claim form must be filed – (a) promptly; and (b) in any event not later than three months after the grounds to make the claim first arose.

**12.71**  CPR 54.5(1) broadly corresponds with the old r 4(1) of the RSC Order 53. It remains possible, therefore, for a claim for judicial review to be made within three months and yet still be refused on the basis that it has not been made sufficiently promptly. This is what happened in *R v Independent Television Commission, ex p TV NI Ltd* (1991), where the CA dismissed a renewed application for judicial review where the applicants sought to challenge decisions made by the Commission relating to the grant of broadcasting licences to television companies. In giving judgment, Lord Donaldson MR stated the position thus:

> I saw it reported in the press that all the applicants had until 16 January, that is to say three months from 16 October, in which to apply for judicial review. That just is not correct. In these matters people must act with the utmost promptitude because so many third parties are affected by the decision and are entitled to act on it unless they have clear and prompt notice that the decision is challenged.

**12.72**  The fact that both s 31 of the SCA 1981 and CPR 54.5(1) make provision for time limits is unfortunate, especially when it is borne in mind that there is inconsistency between the two. For example, s 31 is concerned with delay in respect of applications for permission and substantive relief, whereas CPR 54.5(1) is only concerned with the former. Moreover, in deciding whether or not to permit an extension to the time limit, s 31 considers its effect upon the rights of any person or whether it would be detrimental to good administration, whereas CPR 54.5(1) looks at the question from the viewpoint of the claimant and whether or not there is a good reason for the delay. The position is further complicated by the fact that both the rule and the section are stated to be without prejudice to a statutory provision or a rule, respectively. In other words, by virtue of CPR 54.5(3) and s 31(7), the three-month time limit will be overridden where another provision provides for a shorter time for seeking judicial review.

**12.73**   In the leading case *Caswell v Dairy Produce Quota Tribunal for England and Wales* (1990), the HL sought to reconcile these two provisions and came to the conclusion that a failure to apply for judicial review promptly in accordance with what is now CPR 54.5(1) amounted to undue delay for the purposes of s 31(6) of the 1981 Act. The matter was subsequently returned to by the HL in *R v Criminal Injuries Compensation Board, ex p A* (1999), where Lord Slynn considered what has been described as 'the inept dovetailing' of the provisions. In his Lordship's judgment, the relationship between s 31(6) and RSC Order 53, rule 4(1) could be explained thus:

> *It seems to me that the two provisions produce the following result: (a) On an ex parte application, [permission] to apply for judicial review can be refused, deferred to the substantive hearing or given. (b) [Permission] may be given if the court considers that good reason for extending the period has been shown. The good reason on an ex parte application is generally to be seen from the standpoint . . . of the applicant . . . It is possible (though it would be unusual on an ex parte application) that if the court considers that hardship, prejudice or detriment to good administration have been shown, [permission] may still be refused even if good reason for an extension has been shown. (c) If [permission] is given, then an application to set it aside may be made, though . . . this is not to be encouraged. (d) If [permission] is given, then unless set aside, it does not fall to be re-opened at the substantive hearing on the basis that there is no ground for extending time under Ord. 53, r 4(1). At the substantive hearing there is no 'application for [permission] to apply for judicial review', [permission] having already been given. (e) Nor in my provisional view . . . is there a power to refuse 'to grant . . . [permission]' at the substantive hearing on the basis of hardship or prejudice or detriment to good administration. The court has already granted [permission]; it is too late to 'refuse' unless the court sets aside the initial grant without a separate application having been made for that to be done. What the court can do under s 31(6) is to refuse to grant relief. (f) If the application is adjourned to the substantive hearing, the question under both Ord. 53, r 4(1) (good reason for an extension of time) and 31(6) (hardship, prejudice, detriment, justifying a refusal of [permission]) may fall for determination.*

**12.74**   In the later case of *R (on the application of Burkett) v London Borough of Hammersmith and Fulham* (2001), the CA observed that:

> *It is by now clear from experience that it is only in the rare case where the rules are capable of producing one outcome and the Act another that the unfortunate*

*parallelism of these provisions needs to be explored. It is much better in almost every case to proceed . . . to examine the history of the case in the light of the extant rule, which embraces principles developed over many years by the court to meet each case on its own particular facts, and to turn to section 31(6) only where one has to and then with Lord Slynn's guidance to hand.*

**12.75** The parties to judicial review proceedings are not permitted to reach an agreement to extend the time limit: CPR 54.5(2). However, the court has a general power to extend or shorten the time limit for compliance with any of the Civil Procedure Rules, unless the Rules provide otherwise: CPR 3.1(2)(a). Such a power may be exercised where the court considers that there is a 'good reason' for the delay. This requirement, which was previously explicit in RSC Order 53, rule 4(1), is regarded by Fordham as being implicit in CPR 54.5(1) and 3.1(2)(a). Good reasons for a delay in seeking judicial review may include the exhaustion of alternative remedies or awaiting the outcome of a test case. It should be remembered, however, that whether or not the time limit is extended involves an exercise of discretion on the part of the court. In *R v Secretary of State for Trade and Industry, exp Greenpeace Ltd* (1998), Laws J identified the following factors as being relevant to the exercise of that discretion:

*(1) Have the [claimants] a reasonable objective excuse for coming late? (2) What if any is the damage, in terms of hardship or prejudice to third party rights and detriment to good administration, which would be occasioned if [permission] were now granted? (3) Even if there is substantial damage within any of those categories, does the public interest require . . . the . . . judicial review to go forward.*

**12.76** In practice, it would seem unlikely that the time limit for making a claim will be extended where delay has been brought about due to compliance with the Pre-Action Protocol (paras **12.50–12.55**).

# FURTHER READING

Beatson, J, Matthews, M, and Elliott, M *Administrative Law: Text and Materials* (4th edn, 2011) OUP.

Bondy, V and Sunkin, M 'Accessing Judicial Review' [2008] PL 647.

Bridges, L, Meszaros, G, and Sunkin, M *Judicial Review in Perspective* (1995) Cavendish.

Cane, P 'Standing up for the Public' [1995] PL 276.

Cornford, T and Sunkin, M 'The Bowman Report, Access and the Recent Reforms of the Judicial Review Procedure' [2001] PL 11.

Craig, P P *Administrative Law* (6th edn, 2008) Sweet & Maxwell.

Fordham, M 'Judicial Review: The new rules' [2001] PL 4.

Fordham, M *Judicial Review Handbook* (5th edn, 2008) Hart.

Law Commission *Administrative Law: Judicial Review and Statutory Appeals* (1994) (Law Com No 226).

Le Sueur, A 'Three Strikes and it's Out? The UK government's strategy to oust judicial review from immigration and asylum decision-making' [2004] PL 225.

Lever, A 'Is Judicial Review Undemocratic'? [2007] PL 280.

Manning, J *Judicial Review Proceedings: A practitioner's guide to advice and representation* (2nd edn, 2004) Legal Action Group.

Nason, S 'Regionalization of the Administrative Court and the Tribunalisation of Judicial Review' [2009] PL 440.

Nason, S, Hardy, D, and Sunkin, M 'Regionalisation of the Administrative Court and Access to Justice' (2010) 15 JR 220.

Part 54 of the Civil Procedure Rules–see www.justice.gov.uk/guidance/courts-and-tribunals/courts/procedure-rules/civil/contents/parts/part54.htm.

Pollard, D, Parpworth, N, and Hughes, D *Constitutional and Administrative Law: Text with Materials* (4th edn, 2007) OUP.

Schiemann, Sir Konrad 'Locus Standi' [1990] PL 342.

Sunkin, M, Calyo, K, Platt, L, and Landman, T 'Mapping the Use of Judicial Review to Challenge Local Authorities in England and Wales' [2007] PL 545.

Tanney, A 'Procedural Exclusivity in Administrative Law' [1994] PL 51.

Wade, H W R and Forsyth, C *Administrative Law* (10th edn, 2009) OUP.

Waldron, J 'The Core of the Case against Judicial Review' (2006) 115 Yale Law Journal 1346.

Lord Woolf, 'The Rule of Law and a Change in the Constitution' [2004] CLJ 317.

## SELF-TEST QUESTIONS

1   Why have the courts been unwilling to accept that discretion may be limitless?

2   How can a review be distinguished from an appeal?

3   What rule was established by the HL in *O'Reilly v Mackman*? Can it be argued that in the later decided cases, the courts have taken a pragmatic approach to the scope of this rule? Has the rule survived the introduction of the Civil Procedure Rules?

4   To what extent, if any, do you agree with Fordham that the public/private distinction is 'something of a headache'?

5   Does the decision of the HL in *Boddington* represent a welcome clarification of the position with regard to collateral challenge?

6   In *R (on the application of Richards) v Pembrokeshire County Council* (2004), Neuberger LJ stated:

> ...the advent of the Human Rights Act 1998, and in particular the consequent introduction into English law of Article 6 of the European Convention on Human Rights, may have an impact on the continuing effectiveness of the reasoning in *Ostler*.

To what extent, if any, do you agree with this view?

7   In the words of Sir Konrad Schiemann, 'does *locus standi* matter or are the courts becoming so liberal that we can forget it?'

8   An alternative to the present arrangements on standing would be to allow anyone to seek judicial review of any decision which they wished to challenge. What would be the advantages and disadvantages of such a system?

9   Applying Cane's distinction between associational and public interest standing to the *Fleet Street Casuals* case, the *Rose Theatre* case, and the *Greenpeace* case, which type of standing, associational or public interest, describes the status of the claimant?

10   To what extent, if any, do you agree with Waldron's central argument that judicial review is democratically illegitimate?

# 13 The grounds for judicial review

## SUMMARY

This chapter considers the grounds on which public law decisions may be challenged before the courts. It draws attention to the 'chapter headings' of illegality, irrationality, and procedural impropriety as stated by Lord Diplock in *GCHQ*, and considers the principles which come under these headings. Despite the fact that it is possible to identify particular principles, it should be appreciated at the outset that very often these principles overlap. Thus a public law decision may be challenged by deploying a number of arguments based on different principles. A court may conclude, therefore, that a decision was unlawful for several different but connected reasons.

## Introduction

**13.1** In considering the grounds for judicial review, two cases are of central importance: *Associated Provincial Picture Houses Ltd v Wednesbury Corpn* (1948) – the *Wednesbury* case – and *Council of Civil Service Unions v Minister for the Civil Service* (1985) – the *GCHQ* case. In neither case did the courts establish new or novel grounds for review. Their importance lies not in innovation but in their distillation of the various principles on which a decision-making process may be subject to legal challenge before the courts.

**13.2** The actual outcome in the *Wednesbury* case is not particularly important. It concerned a challenge to a decision by the corporation to attach a condition to a cinema licence whereby children under the age of 15 were not permitted into a cinema on a Sunday. It was argued by the claimant that such a condition was unreasonable and that it was therefore beyond the powers of the corporation to have imposed it. The CA concluded that the condition was in fact reasonable, although it is at least open to argument whether the same conclusion would be reached on the facts were the case to be decided in the modern day. However, the significance of the case lies in the judgment of Lord Greene MR. In that judgment, in which he stressed the supervisory as opposed to the appellate nature of the jurisdiction (see paras **12.7-12.9**), Lord Greene identified a number of principles which could form the basis of a challenge to the exercise of executive discretion. These principles, which have come to be known as the 'Wednesbury principles', can be stated thus:

- the exercise of a discretion must be real and genuine;
- in exercising a discretion, the decision-maker must have regard to relevant matters and must disregard irrelevant matters;
- a discretion must not be exercised for reasons of bad faith or dishonesty;
- a discretion must be exercised for the purpose for which it was intended.

**13.3** In addition to these principles, Lord Greene noted that, as a general proposition, a discretion must be exercised 'reasonably'. If a discretion were exercised contrary to any one of the principles, it would be possible to conclude that the decision-maker had acted unreasonably. However, in the years since the Wednesbury case was decided, 'Wednesbury unreasonableness' has been accorded a rather narrower meaning. Nowhere is this more apparent than in the other leading case on the grounds for review, the GCHQ case.

**13.4** The facts of the GCHQ case have been stated elsewhere (see para **4.27**) and will not therefore be repeated here. It will be remembered that in that case, the HL established the general principle that the exercise of prerogative power could be subject to review by the courts. Whether or not a particular exercise of the prerogative was subject to review depended upon whether it was a justiciable issue. In delivering his judgment in GCHQ, Lord Diplock opined that judicial review had reached a stage of development whereby 'one can conveniently classify under three heads the grounds upon which administrative action is subject to control'. Those three heads are: illegality; irrationality; and procedural impropriety.

**13.5** Such heads are convenient terms which encapsulate a number of different principles upon which the exercise of discretionary power may be subject to review. Moreover, the heads and the principles are not mutually exclusive. A decision will often be challenged on the basis of several different review principles, and it may be that more than one such argument is upheld by the court. Thus, for example, where a decision is based on an irrelevant consideration, that irrelevant consideration may reflect an improper purpose on the part of the decision-maker.

## Illegality

**13.6** In GCHQ, Lord Diplock observed that: 'By "illegality" as a ground for judicial review I mean that the decision-maker must understand correctly the law that regulates his decision-making power and must give effect to it.' In truth, this definition sheds little real light on the principles which fall under this head. These will now be considered.

## Relevant/irrelevant considerations

**13.7** In exercising a discretion, a decision-maker must have regard to relevant matters and must disregard irrelevant matters. The former Lord Chancellor, Lord Irvine, has argued that there are in fact three categories of consideration. In addition to the two already mentioned, he argues that there are considerations which 'may, in the decision-maker's discretion, be taken into account'. In support of this view, Lord Irvine refers to a case in which the legality of a ban on stag hunting was considered.

> *R v Somerset County Council, ex p Fewings* (1995): The local authority owned common land. Its environment committee met to consider stag hunting and resolved that it should be allowed to continue on the land. At a full local authority meeting, however, a resolution was passed banning stag hunting. Most of those who voted in favour of a ban were influenced by the argument that hunting was unacceptably and unnecessarily cruel. The claimants, who regularly hunted on the land, sought judicial review. Laws J held that the resolution was an unlawful exercise of its power under s 120(1)(b) of the Local Government Act 1972, to acquire and manage land for the 'benefit, improvement or development of their area'. In his judgment, hunting could only be banned if it were decided that there were better ways of managing the deer herd or because it was necessary to preserve or enhance the amenity of the area. The argument that hunting was morally repulsive was an irrelevant consideration. The council appealed. CA held: dismissing the appeal, that the council had not exercised its power for the object prescribed in s 120(1)(b) of the 1972 Act. It had wrongly equated itself with the position of a private landowner. It had not considered what benefit a ban would have on the area, or conversely, what detriment an absence of a ban would cause. Animal welfare and social considerations were relevant matters to take into account. Moral arguments were not necessarily irrelevant considerations contrary to what Laws J had decided.

**13.8** In Lord Irvine's opinion, by deciding in *Fewings* that moral considerations were not necessarily irrelevant, Sir Thomas Bingham MR was 'regarding such considerations as in the third category', ie as considerations which a decision-maker may, exercising his discretion, take into account.

**13.9** Frequently statute will afford some indication as to the nature of relevant considerations when conferring a discretionary power upon a decision-maker. Thus, for example, in deciding whether or not to grant planning permission, the Town and Country Planning Act 1990 requires a local authority to 'have regard to the provisions of the development plan, so far as material to the application, and to any other material considerations' (s 70(2)). Where, however, no such guidance is provided by the statute, the task of identifying relevant/irrelevant considerations is more difficult. This will require the courts to construe the statute. Where the purpose for which a discretion has been conferred is clear, relevant considerations will be those which aim to achieve that purpose. In carrying out this interpretative role, a court must be careful to avoid substituting its own view as to the appropriateness of considerations.

---

*Roberts v Hopwood* **(1925):** Poplar Borough Council had the power to pay their employees 'such salaries and wages as they may think fit'. In exercising that power, the council paid uniform wages to its employees which greatly exceeded the general wages level at the time. Moreover, the council paid equal wages to male and female employees, contrary to normal practice. When the cost of living fell, the council maintained its wage levels, despite the fact that comparable wages in the private sector were lower. The district auditor objected to the payments and accordingly surcharged those councillors who had voted for them. HL held: the councillors had taken account of irrelevant considerations – socialist philanthropy and feminist ambition – and had disregarded relevant considerations – the wage levels in the labour market and the burden which would be placed on the ratepayers as a consequence of their decision.

---

*R v Secretary of State for the Home Department, ex p Asif Khan* **(1985):** The SoS issued a circular setting out the criteria he would apply in admitting children into the UK for adoption. The claimant sought judicial review of a refusal to admit a relative's child whom he wished to adopt. He argued that the criteria had not been followed. CA held: the circular amounted to the SoS making his own rules. He had in effect stated those matters which he regarded as relevant in making a decision. Since the criteria said nothing about the natural parents' ability to care for the child – the basis of the decision by the SoS – and there was no general sweeping up clause, it followed that the decision was based on an irrelevant consideration.

---

*R v Port Talbot Borough Council, ex p Jones* **(1988):** K, a local councillor, applied for housing accommodation. She was accorded priority status and was subsequently granted the tenancy of a three-bedroomed council house despite the fact that she lived alone. The chairman of the housing tenancy committee justified the decision on the basis that: in order to carry out her council work, K needed a house in which to receive visits from members of the public; there was no prospect of a two-bedroomed house becoming available; a reasonable period of time had passed (18 months) between the decision to re-house and the grant of a tenancy; and K needed to live in the ward (Aberavon) which she represented. DC held: the council's policy was to provide suitable accommodation for those on the waiting list. The decision to grant K a tenancy in order that she could better fight an election, without regard to the needs of others on the waiting list and contrary to the opinions of the council's officers, was a clear case of a decision based on irrelevant considerations.

---

**13.10**  Although the principle of relevant considerations requires that relevant matters are taken into account in the decision-making process, it does not prescribe how much weight is to be given to competing relevant considerations; that is a matter for the decision-maker, not the courts: see *Tesco Stores Ltd v Secretary of State for the Environment*

(1995). Where a decision has been reached and both relevant and irrelevant consid-erations have featured in the decision-making process, the decision is not necessarily unlawful. Whether or not it is so will depend upon the extent to which irrelevant con-siderations have influenced the final decision. If the decision would have been the same in the absence of irrelevant considerations, it will not be unlawful. If, however, irrele-vant considerations have so influenced the final decision as to make it something other than it would have been had they not been considered, the decision will be unlawful.

> *R v Broadcasting Complaints Commission, ex p Owen* **(1985):** The applicant was the leader of the Social Democratic Party. He wrote to the BCC complaining that the broadcast-ing organizations were paying considerably more attention to the views of the Labour Party in their news and current affairs broadcasts than they were to his party, despite the fact that there was little between the parties in terms of the percentage of votes cast at the 1983 gen-eral election (see para **6.12**). The BCC responded by saying that it had no jurisdiction to hear the complaint under s 54 of the Broadcasting Act 1981. Moreover, even if it had jurisdiction, it would not have upheld the complaint for a variety of stated reasons. Held: the BCC was wrong to think that it did not have jurisdiction to hear the complaint. Of the five reasons which it gave for not upholding the complaint, four were valid in law. The fact that one was bad in law would not, however, cause the court to intervene by way of judicial review pro-vided that it was satisfied that precisely the same decision would have been reached on the other valid reasons.

**13.11**  In exercising a discretion, there are clearly certain matters which a local authority will be entitled to take into account. Thus for the individual councillor, a manifesto com-mitment, a political policy or pledge, a party whip or the views and opinions of politi-cal colleagues are all relevant considerations in the decision-making process, provided that they do not amount to a fetter on discretion (paras **13.14–13.16**). Similarly, in per-forming its various tasks and functions, it is a relevant consideration for a local author-ity to have regard to its duty under the Race Relations Act 1976 to promote good race relations in its area: see *Wheeler v Leicester City Council* (1985) (para **13.17**) and *R v Lewisham London Borough Council, ex p Shell UK Ltd* (1988) (para **13.18**). In a number of cases, the courts have taken the view that, in exercising a discretion, local authorities should have regard to the fiduciary duty which they owe to ratepayers.

## Fiduciary duty

**13.12**  Local authorities are responsible for the collection and spending of vast sums of money at the local level. Money, principally in the form of council tax, is collected so as to enable a local authority to fulfil its statutory duties and provide essential services such as education, housing, refuse collection, and the maintenance of highways. A local authority owes a fiduciary duty to those from whom it collects this money that it will not be spent thriftlessly, but that it will be used to provide these services in a way which benefits the community as a whole. Where it is shown that this fiduciary duty has been breached, the courts will be quick to intervene.

---

*Prescott v Birmingham Corpn* **(1955):** The Corporation operated trams and buses in Birmingham. It resolved to put a scheme into operation which would give free travel to women over 64 and men over 69 on six days of the week. The scheme operated for about a year before P, a local ratepayer, sought a declaration that it was illegal. Vaisey J held: the subsidizing of particular classes of society was a matter for Parliament, not the Corporation. The Corporation had no inherent power to provide such benefits to the elderly which were based on discrimination and favouritism towards a section of society, and which therefore offended against the principle of equality.

---

*Bromley London Borough Council v Greater London Council* **(1983):** Under s 1 of the Transport (London) Act 1969, the GLC was under a general duty to develop policies and encourage measures which promoted 'the provision of integrated, efficient and economic transport facilities and services for Greater London'. Section 4 of the Act placed the responsibility for implementing the policies on the London Transport Executive (LTE). In July 1981, the GLC passed a resolution implementing a commitment in the majority group's election manifesto to reduce fares charged by the LTE by 25%. To finance this policy (at a cost of £69m), the GLC required all the London boroughs to pay a supplementary rate. Bromley sought judicial review in the form of an order to quash the rate. DC refused their application. CA reversed that decision and granted the order. GLC and LTE appealed. HL held: dismissing the appeal, that both the LTE and GLC had acted ultra vires by arbitrarily reducing fares in a way which had no regard for business principles. The decision to reduce fares was a thriftless use of ratepayers' money and was in breach of the fiduciary duty that the GLC owed to its ratepayers.

---

**13.13** The breach of the council's fiduciary duty in both of these cases was enough to entitle the courts to hold that they had acted unlawfully. However, in *Bromley*, three of the five Law Lords who heard the appeal considered that the GLC had acted unlawfully for another reason: they had not properly exercised their discretion by considering themselves bound by the majority group's commitment in their election manifesto to implement the fare reduction scheme. In short, the GLC had fettered its discretion.

## Fettering of a discretion

**13.14** Decision-makers are clearly put in a position where they have a large measure of discretion as to the decision which they reach in a particular case. In exercising that discretion, they will inevitably take account of a variety of different factors. As we have already noted, they must take care to ensure that they have regard to relevant considerations and disregard irrelevant considerations. Moreover, even where a decision is based on relevant considerations, a decision-maker must ensure that such considerations have not fettered their discretion. In other words, they must not allow those considerations to so influence their thinking that they cannot be said to have exercised a discretion in the decision-making process.

**13.15**  The principle that a decision-maker should not fetter his discretion was explained as follows by Lord Browne-Wilkinson in *R v Secretary of State for the Home Department, ex p Venables* (1998):

> When Parliament confers a discretionary power exercisable from time to time over a period, such power must be exercised on each occasion in the light of the circumstances at that time. In consequence, the person on whom the power is conferred cannot fetter the future exercise of his discretion by committing himself now as to the way in which he will exercise his power in the future . . . By the same token, the person on whom the power has been conferred cannot fetter the way he will use that power by ruling out of consideration on the future exercise of that power factors which may then be relevant to such exercise. These considerations do not preclude the person on whom the power is conferred from developing and applying a policy as to the approach which he will adopt in the generality of cases . . . But the position is different if the policy adopted is such as to preclude the person . . . from departing from the policy or from taking into account circumstances which are relevant to the particular case in relation to which the discretion is being exercised. If such an inflexible and invariable policy is adopted, both the policy and the decisions taken pursuant to it will be unlawful.

It is also evident in a number of cases, of which the following are examples.

---

*R v Secretary of State for the Environment, ex p Brent London Borough Council* **(1982):** The Local Government Act 1974 introduced a system for the payment by the SoS of an annual rate support grant to local authorities to aid their general expenditure. A different government was elected in 1979 and it decided to alter the system. Pending the introduction of amending legislation, the Government encouraged local authorities to reduce their expenditure in accordance with Government targets. The SoS was dissatisfied with some of the budgets that he received from local authorities. He announced that when transitional arrangements in the amending legislation (Local Government, Planning and Land Act 1980) came into effect, he would use them against local authorities which had disregarded the Government's targets unless they could show that they had made exceptional efforts to reduce expenditure. The relevant local authorities to which this applied were informed of the last day on which they could secure exemption from the transitional arrangements. The local authorities' association wrote to the SoS asking for a meeting. He replied that he did not believe a meeting would have any practical effect. The SoS subsequently exercised his discretion under the new legislation to reduce the amount of rate support grant payable to the relevant local authorities. They sought an order to quash his decision. DC held: granting the order, that the SoS had a duty not to fetter his discretion when making a decision under the new legislation. However, he had breached that duty by refusing to meet the applicant's representatives and seeing whether they had any new suggestions to make about his policy to use the transitional arrangements against them.

---

***R v Waltham Forest London Borough Council, ex p Baxter* (1988):** A local authority resolved by vote at a council meeting to increase the general rate for the borough. At a meeting of the majority group on the council held prior to the council meeting, a number of councillors voted against the proposed rate increase. At the council meeting, however, they all voted for the increase in accordance with their party whip. Members of a ratepayer's group who opposed the increase sought judicial review of the resolution. They claimed that certain councillors had taken an irrelevant factor into account (the party whip) in voting for the increase, and that they had fettered their discretion by obeying the party whip. DC dismissed their application. They appealed. CA held: dismissing their appeal, that a councillor was under a duty to make up his own mind as to how to vote on a resolution. He must not vote blindly in support of a party policy since this would amount to fettering his discretion. On the facts, however, the councillors who voted initially against but then for the resolution had exercised a free choice.

---

**13.16** The legal position of an elected representative when exercising a discretion was conveniently summarized in the judgments in *ex p Baxter*. In the words of Sir John Donaldson MR, the duty of a councillor:

> *is to make up his own mind on how to vote, giving such weight as he thinks appropriate to the views of other councillors and to the policy of the group of which he is a member. It is only if he abdicates his personal responsibility that questions can arise as to the validity of his vote. The distinction between giving great weight to the views of colleagues and to party policy, on the one hand, and voting blindly in support of party policy may on occasion be a fine one, but it is nevertheless very real.*

Moreover, in the same case, Russell LJ observed that:

> *Party loyalty, party unanimity, party policy were all relevant considerations for the individual councillor. The vote becomes unlawful only when the councillor allows these considerations or any other outside influences so to dominate as to exclude other considerations which are required for a balanced judgment. If, by blindly toeing the party line, the councillor deprives himself of any real choice or the exercise of any real discretion, then his vote can be impugned and any resolution supported by his vote potentially flawed.*

## Improper purpose

**13.17** Where Parliament confers a power on a decision-maker, it does so intending that the power should be used for a particular purpose or purposes. In many cases, the purpose for which the power was conferred will be expressly stated in the statute. Alternatively, it may be determined by necessary implication. Provided that a decision-maker acts in accordance with the statutory purpose or purposes, he will have acted lawfully. If, however, he acts for an improper purpose, the courts will be prepared to intervene.

---

*Congreve v Home Office* **(1976):** An announcement was made that as from 1 April, the cost of a TV licence would be increased from £12 to £18. C and several thousand others took out a new licence before this date (at the old price) despite the fact that their existing licence would not expire until after 1 April. The Home Office wrote to the holders of these overlapping licences and demanded the additional fee of £6. If they refused to pay, they were threatened with the revocation of the licence. Subsequently the Home Office altered its stance and proposed that the licence would be revoked at the end of eight months. C refused to pay the £6. He sought a declaration that the revocation of his licence would be unlawful. HCt refused to grant him the declaration. CA held: the minister had no power to revoke the licences which had been granted lawfully, save where the licensee had done something wrong, eg paid by a cheque which later 'bounced'. A revocation in the present circumstances would amount to a misuse of the power conferred on him by Parliament. The demand for the £6 was also unlawful because it represented an attempt to levy a charge without the authority of Parliament contrary to the Bill of Rights 1689.

---

*Wheeler v Leicester City Council* **(1985):** Three members of the Leicester Rugby Club were invited to tour South Africa with the England rugby team. The city council was opposed to the apartheid regime which existed in South Africa at the time and it supported the policy of not maintaining sporting links with that country. It asked the club to condemn the tour and to put pressure on its players not to participate. Moreover, it put four questions to the club, each of which it wanted answered in the affirmative. Although the club sympathized with the council's stance, it was not entitled to prevent its members from going on the tour. The players went on the tour and the council subsequently passed a resolution banning the club from training on a recreation ground which the council controlled for a period of 12 months. The club sought an order to quash the council's decision. Forbes J dismissed their application. The club's appeal to the CA was dismissed. It further appealed. HL held: the ban on the use of the recreation ground was unreasonable, unfair, and amounted to procedural impropriety. Moreover, it amounted to the use of a statutory power (in the management of its property) for an improper purpose because the council were seeking to punish the club when the club had done nothing wrong.

---

*Porter v Magill* **(2002):** In 1986, the Conservative Party was returned in Westminster with a much reduced majority following the local government elections. P, the leader of the council, and her deputy developed a new policy on the sale of council-owned properties in the exercise of the council's disposal powers under s 32 of the Housing Act 1985. Since it was believed that owner-occupiers were more likely to vote Conservative, a plan was hatched to significantly increase the designated sales of council houses in eight marginal wards, thus achieving an electoral advantage. Despite legal advice to the contrary, the council's

Conservative-controlled housing committee resolved to designate for sale 74% of the eligible dwellings in the key wards as compared with 28% of the eligible properties in the non-key wards. Following complaints about the policy, an auditor was appointed to conduct an inquiry. He held a press conference in which he stated that his provisional belief was that the respondents were culpable. He later reached the final decision that the designated-sales policy was unlawful, that the respondents had known that it was unlawful, and that as a result of their wilful misconduct, the council had suffered financial loss. Accordingly, he certified under s 20(1) of the Local Government Finance Act 1982 that the respondents were liable to make good the loss, including the sum of £15.47m, which represented the difference in price between the market value of the properties with vacant possession and the discounted price at which they had actually been sold. The respondents appealed to the DC which dismissed their appeal. The CA subsequently reversed that decision and quashed the auditor's certificate. The auditor appealed to the HL. Before their Lordships the respondents contended that as councillors, they could not be expected to be oblivious to considerations of party political advantage when making decisions. They also contended that the auditor's provisional statement that he believed them to be culpable gave rise to the appearance of bias, thus infringing their right to an unbiased judge. HL held: although land could be disposed of under s 32 of the HA 1985 to promote any public purpose for which the power had been conferred, it could not be so disposed of for the purpose of promoting the electoral advantage of any party represented on the council. There had been a deliberate, blatant, and dishonest misuse of public power. With regard to the question of bias, although the auditor had made an error of judgment when deciding to publicize his provisional views, looking at the matter objectively, it had not been demonstrated that there was a real possibility that he was biased.

**13.18** In *R v Lewisham London Borough Council, ex p Shell UK Ltd* (1988), the DC held that the council's decision to boycott Shell's products because of that company's trading links with South Africa was not unreasonable. However, it did declare that the council's decision and campaign to persuade other councils not to use Shell products was unlawful because it was done for a purpose other than to satisfy public opinion or race relations, ie to put pressure on the company to sever trading links with South Africa. For a further example of the use of power for an improper purpose, see *R v Ealing London Borough, ex p Times Newspapers* (1986).

## Bad faith

**13.19** In the *Wednesbury* case, Lord Greene noted that a decision could be quashed on the basis of having been made in bad faith or dishonestly. Subsequently, in *Cannock Chase District Council v Kelly* (1978), Megaw LJ observed that:

> bad faith or, as it is sometimes put, 'lack of good faith', means dishonesty; not necessarily for a financial motive, but still dishonesty. It always involves a grave charge. It must not

*be treated as a synonym for an honest, although mistaken, taking into consideration of a factor which is in law irrelevant.*

Since bad faith involves 'a grave charge' against a public authority, it will be necessary to ensure that the matter has been clearly pleaded: see *R (on the application of Amraf Training plc) v Department of Education and Training* (2001). Only the most compelling and cogent evidence will justify a court making a finding in favour of the claimant. In practice, therefore, a finding of bad faith will be rare. It is unlikely that a public authority will have acted with malice or a sufficient degree of ill-will towards another. However, where the high evidential burden has been discharged, a claimant will succeed on this ground.

> ***R v Derbyshire County Council, ex p Times Supplements* (1990):** Under s 38 of the Education (No 2) Act 1986, local education authorities were under a duty to advertise vacancies 'in a manner likely . . . to bring it to the notice of persons . . . who are qualified to fill the post'. Articles published in *The Sunday Times* were critical of individuals and the education authority itself. The council decided to stop advertising vacancies in *The Times Educational Supplement* and any other publication owned by Rupert Murdoch, despite the fact that these publications were read by the greatest number of potential applicants for the posts. The papers sought judicial review. DC held: the council's decisions had been made in bad faith. They had not been taken on educational grounds. Instead, they were motivated by vindictiveness towards the papers.

**13.20** Thus where a decision-maker has acted dishonestly by claiming to have acted for a particular motive when in reality the decision was taken with another motive in mind, he may be said to have acted in bad faith. If, for example, a council made tree preservation orders under the planning legislation merely to justify its refusal to grant a developer planning permission, then it could be said to have acted in bad faith: see *J H Smith (Hale) Ltd v Macclesfield Borough Council* (1998), where Laws J rejected a 'serious charge' of this nature on the basis that it was not supported by the evidence.

## Irrationality

**13.21** In *GCHQ*, Lord Diplock implied that irrationality and '*Wednesbury* unreasonableness' in its narrow sense were effectively the same thing. Irrationality applied to 'a decision which is so outrageous in its defiance of logic or of accepted moral standards that no sensible person who had applied his mind to the question to be decided would have arrived at it'. In *Wednesbury* itself, Lord Greene spoke of a decision being 'so unreasonable that no reasonable authority could ever have come to it'. This formulation of words was later described as 'tautologous' by Lord Cooke in *R v Chief Constable of Sussex, ex p International Trader's Ferry Ltd* (1999). His Lordship preferred to ask 'whether the decision in question was one which a reasonable authority could reach'. In *Nottinghamshire County Council v Secretary of State for the Environment* (1986), Lord Scarman referred to an action as being 'so unreasonable as to be verging on an absurdity'. Occasionally the courts have referred to a decision which is 'perverse' or 'totally unreasonable'. Whatever the description, it is apparent that an irrational decision clearly involves the misuse of power.

**13.22** In order to succeed under the ground of irrationality, an applicant must overcome a high threshold of proof. It is not enough to establish that the impugned decision is one which a reasonable person would not have reached. Rather, it is necessary to show that the decision would not have been reached by any reasonable person. In *R v Secretary of State for the Home Department, ex p Brind* (1991), Lord Ackner noted that the test for irrationality has sometimes been criticized for being too high. However, in his opinion, this was necessary in order to underline the fact that judicial review is a supervisory rather than an appellate jurisdiction. This observation highlights the constitutional dangers inherent in the judiciary declaring decisions to be irrational. If a decision is described as being 'absurd', or 'outrageous in its defiance of logic', the merits of that decision are clearly being questioned. In effect, it could be argued that the decision has been held to be wrong. Accordingly, arguments involving irrationality have rarely succeeded before the courts, unless, that is, the decision can be said to have been totally unreasonable.

---

***Hall & Co Ltd v Shoreham-by-Sea UDC* (1964):** Under the relevant planning legislation, local authorities had the power to grant planning permission subject to such conditions as the council 'think fit'. H was granted planning permission subject to the condition that an access road should be constructed over the entire frontage of their site at their own expense. Moreover, the public was to have a right of way over it. CA held: it was not enough to say that the condition was unreasonable or unduly onerous. In order to justify a declaration that the condition was ultra vires, it must be shown that it was so unreasonable that no reasonable council could have imposed it. The condition was utterly unreasonable in that it sought to transfer the public burden of constructing a road onto the private shoulders of the developer. Parliament could not have intended such a result.

---

***Backhouse v Lambeth London Borough Council* (1972):** The council was under a statutory duty to increase the average rents charged for its dwellings by a specified amount. In purported compliance with that duty, the council achieved the average increase per dwelling by increasing the rent of one unoccupied dwelling by £18,000 per week. Held: the decision was totally unreasonable.

---

***R v Ministry of Defence, ex p Smith* (1996):** The Ministry of Defence policy regarding homosexuality was that it was incompatible with service in the armed forces. Service personnel who were known to be homosexual or who engaged in homosexual activity were discharged from the forces. The four appellants, three men and a woman, had been discharged on this basis. None of them had committed any offence or engaged in homosexual acts on service premises. They challenged the lawfulness of their discharge on the basis that it was in accordance with a policy which was irrational. CA held: the greater the policy content of a decision, and the more remote the subject matter of a decision from ordinary judicial experience, the more hesitant a court should be in holding a decision to be irrational. The existing policy could not be described as irrational at the time when the appellants were discharged. It was supported by both Houses of Parliament and by those to whom the ministry looked for professional advice. Moreover although in some countries there had been a relaxation of the ban on homosexuals in their armed forces, such changes were too recent to yield much valuable experience.

*R (on the application of B) v Worcestershire County Council* (2009): The claimants each had profound learning and physical disabilities. They had regularly attended a day centre run by the council over a period of years. As a result of a review of its provision of learning disability services, the council decided to close the centre which the claimants attended and make provision for them to attend other council-run day centres. The claimants sought judicial review of that decision on the ground that it was *Wednesbury* irrational in the sense that it had been reached without the council having made a proper assessment of staff resourcing at the other centres to meet the claimants' needs. Admin Ct held: granting the application, that the council had not been in a position to reach a rational conclusion as to whether staff resources and facilities at the other centres would be sufficient to meet the needs of the claimants. On the evidence, it was apparent that no detailed analysis had been undertaken. Accordingly, the closure decision was irrational.

**13.23**  The third of these cases, *ex p Smith*, demonstrates that the threshold of irrationality is a high one and that in the opinion of the CA, it had not been crossed in that case. When the applicants took their case to Strasbourg, however, the European Court of Human Rights reached the opposite conclusion: see *Smith v UK* (2000). In the judgment of the Court:

> the threshold at which the High Court and the Court of Appeal could find the Ministry of Defence policy irrational was placed so high that it effectively excluded any consideration by the domestic courts of the question of whether the interference with the applicants' rights answered a pressing social need or was proportionate to the national security and public order aims pursued, principles which lie at the heart of the Court's analysis of complaints under Article 8 of the Convention.

**13.24**  In more recent times, the appropriateness of this high threshold has also been questioned at the domestic level. Thus in *R v Secretary of State for the Home Department, ex p Daly* (2001), Lord Cooke opined:

> I think that the day will come when it will be more widely recognised that the Wednesbury *case was an unfortunate retrogressive decision in English administrative*

*law, in so far as it suggested that there are degrees of unreasonableness and that only a very extreme degree can bring an administrative decision within the legitimate scope of judicial invalidation. The depth of judicial review and the deference due to administrative discretion vary with the subject matter. It may well be, however, that the law can never be satisfied in any administrative field merely by a finding that the decision under review is not capricious or absurd.*

**13.25** Further criticisms have centred upon the use of the label 'irrationality'. Walker has argued that 'three difficulties may be identified: the label wrongly suggests that the test is logicality; the label ignores the important role of morals; and the label may be unnecessarily rude'. These criticisms are certainly thought provoking and they may not be without foundation since, in the words of Fordham, 'an unreasonable response does not mean an unhinged decision-maker'. If we were to dispense with 'irrationality' and opt for an alternative label which properly describes this ground of review, what do you think that label should be? 'Unreasonableness'? 'Outside the limits of reason'? 'Illogicality'? 'Immorality'? 'Proportionality'?

**13.26** The last of these alternative labels highlights the closeness of the relationship between irrationality and proportionality. It is perfectly possible that an irrational decision is also a decision which is disproportionate, and vice versa: see *R v Secretary of State for the Home Department, ex p Brind* (1991) (para **13.30**). Accordingly, we must now consider what is meant by 'proportionality' and what effect the Human Rights Act 1998 has had upon the court's approach to this concept.

## Proportionality

**13.27** In *GCHQ*, Lord Diplock acknowledged that in the future, there may be additions to the three heads which he identified. One particular ground which he had in mind was proportionality. Proportionality is a well-established principle in the administrative law of a number of EU member states, and it is a principle which is recognized in EU law. It is also a principle which is reflected in the jurisprudence of the European Court of Human Rights.

**13.28** Proportionality is sometimes explained by the expression 'taking a sledgehammer to crack a nut'. Although this is a rather graphic description, it does convey the essence of the 'ground'. To argue that a decision or a course of action is disproportionate does not amount to an attack on the objective itself. Rather, it constitutes an attack on the means by which such an objective is to be achieved. In other words, it is an argument that the same objective could have been achieved by some more proportionate means. Once again, therefore, there are constitutional dangers with this argument. For a court to hold that a decision or course of action was disproportionate would be for it to come very close to substituting its own view for that of the decision-maker. In effect, the court would be saying to the decision-maker that he had chosen the wrong option. With these constitutional dangers in mind, therefore, it is not surprising that the English courts have historically tended to approach proportionality with care. An exception occurred, however, in *R v Barnsley Metropolitan Borough Council, ex p Hook* (1976).

**13.29** The facts of *ex p Hook* are not particularly important. Suffice it to say that the case concerned a challenge to a decision to revoke a market trader's licence on the ground that bias had been present in the decision-making process. Strictly speaking, the case was decided in the claimant's favour for this reason. However, both Lord Denning MR and Sir John Pennycuick agreed that 'there are old cases which show that the court can interfere by [a quashing order] if a punishment is altogether excessive and out of proportion to the occasion'. Had it been necessary to do so, they would have quashed the council's decision on that basis alone. The third judge to hear the appeal, Scarman LJ (as he then was), made no mention of proportionality in his judgment.

**13.30** In the later case of *R v Secretary of State for the Home Department, ex p Brind* (1991), directives issued by the Home Secretary to the BBC and the IBA prohibiting the direct broadcasting of the statements of terrorists and supporters of terrorism were challenged by journalists. It was argued, amongst other things, that the Home Secretary had acted beyond his power by acting disproportionately and in a manner which was contrary to art 10 of the ECHR. In response to this argument, the HL noted that a decision which suffers from a lack of proportionality is also therefore an irrational decision. In other words, it is a decision which no reasonable decision-maker could have made. However, to accept proportionality as a ground for review in its own right would, in the opinion of the HL, unavoidably lead to an inquiry into the merits of a decision. In the words of Lord Ackner:

> *Unless and until Parliament incorporates the convention into domestic law . . . there appears to me to be at present no basis upon which the proportionality doctrine applied by the European Court can be followed by the courts of this country.*

**13.31** Now that incorporation (of sorts) has taken place in the form of the Human Rights Act 1998, it follows that the courts in this country are required to grapple with the principle of proportionality when confronted by an alleged breach of a Convention right. In considering the exceptions to such rights, the courts are required to, in the words of the former Lord Chancellor, Lord Irvine (speaking extra-judicially):

> *apply the Convention principle of proportionality. This means the court will be looking substantively at that question. It will not be limited to a secondary review of the decision making process but at the primary question of the decision itself.*

**13.32** An opportunity for the HL to consider the scope of the proportionality principle in a human rights context arose in an appeal concerning an alleged violation of a prisoner's rights relating to his legal correspondence.

---

*R v Secretary of State for the Home Department, ex p Daly* (2001): In May 1995 the Home Secretary introduced a new policy governing the searching of cells occupied by convicted and remand prisoners in England and Wales. Under that policy a prisoner was not permitted to be present during a search, and while carrying out a search, prison staff were required to examine legal correspondence thoroughly for the purpose of ensuring that it was bona fide correspondence between the prisoner and a legal adviser. D, a long-term prisoner, challenged the lawfulness of the policy. He claimed that the policy was not authorized under s 47(1) of the Prison Act 1952. In particular, he claimed that the blanket policy of requiring all prisoners to be absent when their legally privileged correspondence was being examined infringed a basic right at common law and under art 8(1) of the ECHR, and that the general terms of s 47(1) did not authorize such an infringement either expressly or impliedly. The CA held that the policy represented the minimum intrusion into the rights of the prisoner consistent with the need to maintain security, order, and discipline in prisons. D appealed. HL held: allowing the appeal, that the policy was unlawful and void. The infringement of the prisoners' right to maintain the confidentiality of their privileged legal correspondence was greater than had been shown to be necessary to maintain security, order, and discipline in prisons and to prevent crime. The degree of intrusion violated a prisoner's common law rights. It also amounted to a violation of his rights under art 8(1) that was much greater than necessity required.

---

**13.33** It is clear from the foregoing that although the HL in *Daly* were of the view that the Home Secretary's policy was based on legitimate public objectives (the maintenance of security, etc), the infringement of prisoners' rights which flowed from the application of that policy was disproportionate. In other words, those legitimate public objectives could have been met in a more proportionate manner, ie excluding from a cell those prisoners who threatened to intimidate or disrupt a search or whose past behaviour suggested that they were likely to do so. With regard to the principle of proportionality and its relationship with the traditional grounds of review, Lord Steyn observed that 'there is an overlap' between the two. His Lordship continued:

> *Most cases would be decided in the same way whichever approach is adopted. But the intensity of review is somewhat greater under the proportionality approach. Making due allowance for important structural differences between various convention rights... a few generalisations are perhaps permissible. I would mention three concrete differences without suggesting that my statement is exhaustive. First, the doctrine of proportionality may require the reviewing court to assess the balance which the decision maker has struck, not merely whether it is within the range of rational or reasonable decisions. Secondly, the proportionality test may go further than the traditional grounds of review in as much as it may require attention to be directed to the relative weight accorded to interests and considerations. Thirdly, even the heightened scrutiny test developed in R v Ministry of Defence, ex p Smith... is not necessarily appropriate to the protection of human rights... In other words, the intensity of the review ... is guaranteed by the twin requirements that the limitation of the right was necessary in a democratic society, in the sense of meeting a pressing social need, and the question*

*whether the interference was really proportionate to the legitimate aim being pursued.*
*[emphasis added]*

**13.34**  In Lord Steyn's analysis it is apparent, therefore, that although an application of either the traditional grounds for review or the proportionality approach may produce the same result, this will not necessarily be the case. In cases involving the alleged infringement of Convention rights, a more intense form of review is clearly appropriate. Such rights would in practice be afforded little protection if a defendant was able to defeat a claim simply by showing that his decision had not exceeded the bounds of reasonableness. Thus in *de Freitas v Permanent Secretary of Ministry of Agriculture* (1999), Lord Clyde was of the view that, when considering fundamental rights, a court should ask itself:

> *whether (i) the legislative objective is sufficiently important to justify limiting a fundamental right; (ii) the measures designed to meet the legislative objective are rationally connected to it; and (iii) the means used to impair the right or freedom are no more than is necessary to accomplish the objective.*

It is a moot point, however, as to whether this more intense form of review signals a shift to merits review. Lord Steyn thought not in *ex p Daly*. Do you agree with this view or with that expressed by Lord Ackner in the pre-Human Rights Act case of *ex p Brind* (1991) (para **13.30**), where his Lordship remarked that 'in order to invest the proportionality test with a higher status than the *Wednesbury* test, an inquiry into and a decision upon the merits cannot be avoided'?

**13.35**  The decision in *A v Secretary of State for the Home Department* (2005) was previously discussed in Chapter **3**. For present purposes, it will be recalled that the majority of the HL were of the view that the measures which had been taken under the authority of s 23 of the Anti-Terrorism Crime and Security Act 2001 were not strictly required in order to deal with the public emergency which they accepted was threatening the life of the nation. In other words, they were disproportionate. Thus in commenting on the lack of a power in s 23 to detain UK nationals, Baroness Hale observed:

> *The conclusion has to be that it is not necessary to lock up the nationals. Other ways must have been found to contain the threat which they present. And if it is not necessary to lock up the nationals it cannot be necessary to lock up the foreigners. It is not strictly required by the exigencies of the situation.*

The ruling of the majority on this point did not involve, however, a detailed consideration of alternative measures short of detention which might have been employed in order to address the terrorist threat. In other words, there was little comment on what would have constituted more proportionate means for achieving the legitimate aim of protecting national security.

**13.36**  The proportionality approach has been adopted by the English courts in the context of EU law, in proceedings brought under the Human Rights Act 1998, and in respect of proceedings alleging a violation of a right protected at common law. Although it remains the case, therefore, that proportionality is not a distinct ground for review in non-Convention rights cases, such a development seems highly likely in the future given the application of the principle in these other contexts. Were this not to happen, what Woolf, Jowell, and Le Seur have referred to as 'the coherence and comprehensibility of administrative law' would patently suffer. Support for this view can be found in the case of *R (on the application of Alconbury Developments Ltd) v Secretary of State for the Environment, Transport and the Regions* (2001) where Lord Slynn observed:

> I consider that even without reference to the Human Rights Act 1998 the time has come to recognise that this principle [proportionality] is part of English administrative law, not only when judges are dealing with Community acts but also when they are dealing with acts subject to domestic law. Trying to keep the Wednesbury principle and proportionality in separate compartments seems to me to be unnecessary and confusing.

**13.37** In the later case of *R (Association of British Civilian Internees (Far East Region)) v Secretary of State for Defence* (2003), in delivering the judgment of the CA, Dyson LJ commented that 'the *Wednesbury* test is moving closer to proportionality and in some cases it is not possible to see any daylight between the two tests'. However, he also expressed the view that it was 'not for this court to perform its burial rites'. Rather, it was only the HL which could finally lay the *Wednesbury* test to rest.

## Procedural impropriety

**13.38** Procedural impropriety was the third ground of challenge which Lord Diplock acknowledged in *GCHQ*. The phrase was chosen deliberately so as to encompass two areas: a failure to observe procedural rules laid down in statute; and a failure to observe the basic common law rules of natural justice.

### Procedural ultra vires

**13.39** Where a public body acting in reliance upon statutory powers has failed to comply with the procedures laid down in the relevant Act, it can be said to have acted ultra vires. Such procedures may take a variety of different forms. A common procedural requirement in an enabling Act is consultation. Thus, for example, a minister may be under a statutory duty to consult certain specified organizations or such organizations as he thinks fit prior to making a decision. Where the requirement to consult is mandatory, a failure to comply with it may mean that the procedure is thereby ultra vires.

*Agricultural, Horticultural and Forestry Industry Training Board v Aylesbury Mushrooms* **(1972):** The Industrial Training Act 1964 made provision for the establishment of industrial training boards. Prior to creating such a board, a minister was required by s 1(4) of the Act to consult any organization or association of organizations which appeared to him to be representative of people working in the relevant industry. The minister was minded to set up the plaintiff board and consulted the National Farmers Union. He did not, however, consult a subsidiary body of the NFU, the Mushroom Growers Association. QBD held: under the terms of s 1(4), some consultation by the minister was mandatory. Whether any particular organization had to be consulted depended upon a subjective test, ie the minister's own belief. Consultation amounted to the communication of a genuine invitation, extended with a receptive mind, to give advice. Since there had not been communication and the opportunity of responding, there had been no consultation.

**13.40**  It is clear from the *Aylesbury Mushrooms* case that consultation involves affording a consultee a proper opportunity to make representations. It also requires that any representations that are made are genuinely considered. It does not mean, however, that the decision-maker is bound to follow the advice which he receives. As long as the obligation to consult has been complied with, the decision-maker will not have acted in a procedurally improper manner even if his decision is in direct conflict with the advice given. Where a mandatory requirement to consult has not been complied with, the party which was not consulted may not be bound by the relevant decision. Thus in *Aylesbury Mushrooms*, the Mushroom Growers Association were not bound by the order, although the order remained effective as against those who were consulted or did not need to be consulted.

**13.41**  At one time much was made of the distinction between mandatory and directory procedural requirements with the view being that directory requirements could be safely ignored whereas mandatory requirements could not. However, in *R v Immigration Appeal Tribunal, ex p Jeyeanthan* (2000), Lord Woolf MR (as he then was) sought to play down the significance of this 'conventional approach':

> I suggest that the right approach is to regard the question of whether a requirement is directory or mandatory as only at most a first step. In the majority of cases there are other questions which have to be asked which are more likely to be of greater assistance than the application of the mandatory/directory tests. The questions which are likely to arise are as follows: Is the statutory requirement fulfilled if there has been substantial compliance with the requirement and, if so, has there been substantial compliance in the case in issue even though there has not been strict compliance? (The substantial compliance question.) Is the non-compliance capable of being waived, and if so, has it, or can it and should it be waived in this particular case? (The discretionary question.) I treat the grant of an extension of time for compliance as a waiver. If it is not capable of being waived or is not waived then what is the consequence of the non-compliance? (The consequences question.) Which questions arise will depend on the facts of the case and the nature of the particular requirement. The advantages of focusing on these questions is that they should avoid the unjust and unintended consequences which can flow from an approach solely dependent on dividing requirements into mandatory ones, which oust jurisdiction, or directory which do not. [emphasis added]

In a subsequent case concerning the proper construction of s 64(3B) of the Police and Criminal Evidence Act 1984, the HL expressly endorsed the approach advocated by Lord Woolf and by Lord Hailsham LC in *London and Clydeside Estates Ltd v Aberdeen District Council* (1979): see *A-G's Reference (No 3 of 1999)* (2001).

**13.42**  A further example of a statutory procedural requirement is the obligation to give reasons for a decision. Ministers and certain specified tribunals are under a general duty to give a statement of the reasons for a decision which they have made by virtue of s 10 of the Tribunals and Inquiries Act 1992. This general duty does not apply, however, where a specific enactment has already made provision for the giving of reasons. Under the common law, there is no general duty to give reasons. However, as we shall see, it is possible to argue that the courts are moving in the direction of imposing such a duty on decision-makers.

## Natural justice

**13.43**  The common law rules or principles of natural justice which are imposed by the courts comprise two elements: *audi alteram partem* (hear both sides); and *nemo judex in causa sua* (there should be an absence of bias with no person being a judge in their own cause). These two Latin maxims thus signify the standards which are to be met in the decision-making process. They seek to ensure that an individual is given a proper opportunity to present his side of the case prior to a decision being reached, and that the decision itself is reached in an objective manner by an independent and impartial decision-maker. There is, therefore, a clear overlap between the principles and the requirements of art 6 of the ECHR.

**13.44**  There are certain linguistic difficulties with the principles of natural justice. Whilst the manner in which they are expressed is appropriate where adjudicative functions are being performed, such as in the courtroom, they seem less suitable in respect of purely administrative decisions. A minister or panel charged with the responsibility of granting licences may not find them very helpful when they turn their minds to the question of the standards to be met in the decision-making process. Accordingly, in more recent times, it has become commonplace to talk in terms of 'fairness' or of a 'duty to act fairly'. This term has the advantage of being sufficiently wide to embrace all manner of decisions, from those which are judicial in nature to those which are rightly classed as administrative.

### The decision in *Ridge v Baldwin*

**13.45**  Historically, the courts have not always been prepared to imply the principles of natural justice in all types of decision-making process. Thus despite cases such as *Cooper v*

*Wandsworth Board of Works* (1863), where it was held that C ought to have been heard by the Board before it exercised its statutory power to demolish a house which had been built in breach of planning laws, a distinction emerged in the law between judicial or quasi-judicial decisions on the one hand, and administrative decisions on the other. The distinction was important in the present context because the principles of natural justice were held to apply to judicial (or quasi-judicial decisions) but not to administrative decisions.

---

*Franklin v Minister of Town and Country Planning* **(1948):** In order to relieve London's population density, it was proposed that several new towns should be constructed close to the capital. Stevenage was proposed as a new town by the minister, although many objections were received from the local population. Nevertheless, a draft order designating Stevenage as a new town was publicized in accordance with the New Towns Act 1946. A public local inquiry was held, but despite continued objections, the minister decided to make the order. The appellants who owned houses and land in the area sought to challenge the decision. They argued, amongst other things, that the minister was biased in that he had stated that he would make the order before considering any of the objections. Henn Collins J held for the appellants on the basis that the minister had not complied with his duty to act judicially. His decision was reversed by the CA. The appellants appealed. HL held: in agreement with the CA, that the appellants had not shown that the minister was biased. He had not been acting in a judicial or quasi-judicial capacity at the material time. Rather, his duties under the 1946 Act were purely administrative.

---

**13.46**  The distinction between judicial and administrative decisions was, in the words of Lord Denning MR in *R v Gaming Board for Great Britain, ex p Benaim and Khaida* (1970) a 'heresy' that 'was scotched in *Ridge v Baldwin*'.

---

*Ridge v Baldwin* **(1964):** R, the chief constable of Brighton, was indicted along with other officers for conspiracy to obstruct the course of justice. He was acquitted but the other officers were convicted. In passing sentence, the trial judge was critical of R, remarking that he had not set a good example to his officers and that he did not have the leadership skills necessary for office. Similar comments were made a week or so later by the judge in respect of a further charge of corruption for which no evidence was adduced. The following day, R was dismissed by the Watch Committee under a power conferred by s 191(4) of the Municipal Corporations Act 1882. He was not given any notice of the meeting, and neither was he afforded an opportunity to make representations to the committee. A subsequent appeal to the Home Secretary under the Police (Appeals) Act 1927 was dismissed. R sought a declaration from the HCt that his dismissal was unlawful and contrary to the principles of natural justice. Streatfield J held that the Watch Committee had acted in accordance with natural justice. CA held that the principles did not need to be followed because the committee had acted in an administrative rather than a judicial capacity. R appealed. HL held: after reviewing the authorities, that although they had sometimes proved to be difficult to reconcile, this was because insufficient attention had been paid to the fact that there was

> a great difference between the kinds of cases in which the principles of natural justice had been sought to be applied. There was an unbroken line of authority to the effect that an officer cannot be lawfully dismissed without first telling him what is alleged against him and hearing his defence or explanation (Lord Reid).

**13.47** For R, the outcome was important because if his dismissal were upheld, he would lose his pension rights. If he were required to resign, however, he would not. Nevertheless, from a wider perspective, *Ridge v Baldwin* (1964) is a landmark decision in that it swept away the distinction between judicial and administrative decisions and instead focused attention on what effect the decision will have on the individual. The greater the effect in terms of an individual's rights, the more likely the courts will be to require that the standards of natural justice have been complied with. However, it must be borne in mind that the principles of natural justice are not a hard and fast set of rules. What fairness requires will depend upon the particular circumstances. In the words of Lord Bridge in *Lloyd v McMahon* (1987):

> the so-called rules of natural justice are not engraved on tablets of stone. To use the phrase which better expresses the underlying concept, what the requirements of fairness demand when any body, domestic, administrative or judicial, has to make a decision which will affect the rights of individuals depends on the character of the decision-making body, the kind of decision it has to make and the statutory or other framework in which it operates.

**13.48** The decision in *Ridge v Baldwin* is also important because it emphasizes the link between the right of a person to be heard and the right to know the case brought against them. The former is a hollow right unless it also encompasses the latter. Thus in *Kanda v Government of Malaya* (1962), Lord Denning remarked:

> If the right to be heard is a real right which is worth anything, it must carry with it a right in the accused to know the case which is made against him. He must know what evidence has been given and what statements have been made affecting him: and then he must be given a fair opportunity to correct or contradict them.

## Legitimate expectations

**13.49** The phrase 'legitimate expectation' was first coined by Lord Denning MR in *Schmidt v Secretary of State for Home Affairs* (1969) to denote something less than a right which may nevertheless be protected by the principles of natural justice. In essence, a legitimate expectation amounts to an expectation of receiving some benefit or privilege to which the individual has no right. However, the phrase has been used by the courts in a number of different contexts with the result that 'there are many semantic confusions which have bedevilled this area of our law' (per Simon Brown LJ in *R v Devon County Council, ex p Baker* (1995)).

**13.50**  A body or person may have a legitimate expectation to be heard on the basis of a past practice which can reasonably be expected to continue. Thus in the *GCHQ* case (para **4.27**), the HL ruled that but for the overriding interests of national security, the court would have upheld the appellants' legitimate expectation to be consulted prior to their conditions of service being altered, since this had been the practice ever since GCHQ was established in 1947. A legitimate expectation may also be created by way of an express undertaking or promise given on behalf of a public authority by a person authorized to do so.

---

*R v Liverpool Corpn, ex p Liverpool Taxi Fleet Operators' Association* **(1972):** Under s 37 of the Town Police Clauses Act 1847, a city council had the power to license such number of hackney carriages in its area as it thought fit. The claimants, who represented 300 existing licence holders, were concerned that new licences would adversely affect the interests of their members. They were given a written assurance by the town clerk that they would be consulted if any change in the number of licences was contemplated. However, the council subsequently passed a resolution to increase the number of licences. CA held: when considering applications for licences, the council was under a duty to act fairly. It was not at liberty to disregard its undertaking without notice to and representations from the claimants. The council had acted unfairly. A prohibition order was granted to prevent the council acting on its resolutions.

---

**13.51**  The undertaking which the council had given in this case was not binding upon them. If it were so, this would have constituted a fetter on its discretion which would have been unlawful under the '*Wednesbury* principles'. Nevertheless, if the council wished to depart from its undertaking, it could only do so after it had properly considered the representations from all interested parties.

**13.52**  In *Paponette and others v Attorney General of Trinidad and Tobago* (2010), the PC emphasized the point that where a legitimate expectation is based on a promise, representation, or undertaking, the promise etc must be *clear, unambiguous,* and *devoid of relevant qualification* to be binding. The initial burden thus lies on the applicant to prove the legitimacy of the expectation by reference to these three criteria. Once they have been proved, the onus shifts to the public authority to justify why the expectation has been frustrated. In order to be able to do this successfully, it will need to establish an overriding public interest. In the words of Lord Dyson JSC in *Paponette*, 'without evidence, the court is unlikely to be willing to draw an inference in favour of the authority'. In that case, since the A-G had failed to provide the court with a statement of reasons as to why Regulations had been made which directly conflicted with assurances previously given to the applicant, the Government had failed to discharge its burden of proof. The claim therefore succeeded.

**13.53**  A legitimate expectation may also be created by an established policy. Thus in the previously mentioned case of *R v Secretary of State for the Home Department, ex p Asif Khan* (1985) (para **13.9**), the Home Office circular which the Khans received created a legitimate expectation that their case would be decided upon the basis of the published criteria. When the Secretary of State decided their application on the basis of a criterion not mentioned in the circular, he had taken account of an irrelevant consideration. He had also acted unfairly and unreasonably. The justification for the decisions in both *ex p Liverpool Taxi Fleet Operators' Association* and *ex p Khan* is that it would be contrary to the interests of good administration to allow public authorities to resile from promises or undertakings given as to procedures to be followed. Provided that such undertakings or policies do not interfere with a statutory duty, fairness requires that they are complied with. Moreover, if they are to be altered, fairness also requires that those affected by the changes are given an opportunity to be heard.

**13.54**  In the words of Taylor J in *R v Secretary of State for the Home Department, ex p Ruddock* (1987), 'the doctrine of legitimate expectation in essence imposes a duty to act fairly'. This duty to act fairly applies in the context of legitimate procedural expectations as demonstrated by *ex p Liverpool Taxi Fleet Operators' Association*. It also applies where there is a legitimate expectation of a substantive benefit. In *ex p Ruddock*, that substantive benefit was that individuals not falling within the Government's published criteria for telephone tapping would not have their telephone calls intercepted by the security services.

**13.55**  One of the most common examples of a legitimate expectation of a substantive benefit occurs in the realm of licensing. The licence itself represents the substantive benefit. The legitimate expectation to receive that benefit may arise by way of an undertaking, a policy, or a practice. Those who are responsible for issuing or granting licences are under a general duty to act fairly. However, what the duty requires in terms of the standards of fairness to be applied in a particular case depends upon whether a person is an applicant for a licence, has a legitimate expectation of receiving the licence, or already holds a licence.

> ***McInnes v Onslow Fane* (1978):** The plaintiff had held a licence to promote boxing bouts as well as a trainer's licence and a master of ceremonies licence. These licences were all withdrawn by the British Boxing Board of Control following an incident at a boxing match. Subsequently the plaintiff applied to the Board for a manager's licence. His applications were refused on six separate occasions. In respect of the last occasion, he sought a declaration that the Board had acted unfairly in that it had not informed him of the case against him and because it had not granted him an oral hearing. Sir Robert Megarry V-C held: dismissing the claims, that where the court is entitled to require that natural justice be observed, three types of decision could be identified: forfeiture cases; expectation cases; and application cases. The requirements of natural justice were different with regard to each. In the present case, since the plaintiff was merely an applicant, the duty to act fairly required that the Board act honestly and without bias or caprice.

**13.56**  The decision in *McInnes* is important for several reasons. Chief amongst these is what it tells us about natural justice or fairness. Patently this is a flexible concept the content of which will depend upon the circumstances of each particular case. In the forfeiture cases, where an existing right has been taken away, Sir Robert Megarry V-C felt that three features of natural justice were apt: the right to an unbiased tribunal; the right to notice of the charges; and the right to be heard in answer to the charges. At the other end of the spectrum, the mere applicant was entitled to very little, as *McInnes* itself demonstrates. What Sir Robert Megarry VC termed the 'intermediate category', the expectation cases, arose where the applicant had a legitimate expectation, based on what had previously happened, that his application would be granted. Thus, for example, a person seeking the renewal of a licence would have a legitimate expectation that it would be granted. Sir Robert Megarry V-C considered that these cases were more akin to the forfeiture rather than the application cases. Accordingly, at the very least, natural justice required that the individual should be informed as to why he was no longer considered to be suitable for the licence which he had previously held.

**13.57** In the case of *R v North East Devon Health Authority, ex p Coughlan* (2000), the CA held, inter alia, that an assurance given to patients that they could live as long as they chose to at a purpose-built NHS facility (to which they were to be moved) created a legitimate expectation of a substantive benefit whose frustration would be so unfair as to amount to an abuse of power. In reaching such a conclusion, Lord Woolf MR (as he then was) considered the nature of the court's role when a member of the public seeks to rely upon a legitimate expectation as against a public authority. In his Lordship's judgment:

> There are at least three possible outcomes. (a) The court may decide that the public authority is only required to bear in mind its previous policy or other representation, giving it the weight it thinks right, but no more, before deciding whether to change course…(b) On the other hand the court may decide that the promise or practice induces a legitimate expectation of, for example, being consulted before a particular decision is taken…(c) Where the court considers that a lawful promise or practice has induced a legitimate expectation of a benefit which is substantive, not simply procedural, authority now establishes that here too the court will in a proper case decide whether to frustrate the expectation is so unfair that to take a new and different course will amount to an abuse of power.

Lord Woolf continued:

> The court having decided which of the categories is appropriate, the court's role in the case of the second and third categories is different from that in the first. In the case of the first, the court is restricted to reviewing the decision on conventional grounds. The test will be rationality and whether the public body has given proper weight to the implications of not fulfilling the promise. In the case of the second category the court's task is the conventional one of determining whether the decision was procedurally fair. In the case of the third, the court has when necessary to determine whether there is a sufficient overriding interest to justify a departure from what has been previously promised.

**13.58** It is evident that the third category which was identified in *Coughlan* demands quite a high level of judicial scrutiny. Might it be argued that it runs the risk of blurring the distinction between appeal and review which is so important in the present context? In the later case of *R (on the application of Bibi) v Newham LBC* (2002), the CA suggested the following more moderate approach:

> In all legitimate expectation cases, whether substantive or procedural, three practical questions arise. The first question is to what has the public authority, whether by practice or promise, committed itself; the second is whether the authority has acted or proposes to act unlawfully in relation to its commitment; the third is what the court should do.

**13.59** Knight has commented that 'legitimate expectation is an area of administrative law that has moved quickly in a short space of time'. His discussion of the decisions in *R (on the application of BAPIO Action Ltd) v Secretary of State for the Home Department* (2008), *R (on the application of Wheeler) v Office of the Prime Minister* (2008), and *R (on the application of Bhatt Murphy (a firm) v Independent Assessor; R (on the application of Niazi) v Secretary of State for the Home Department* (2008) indicates, however, that despite the development of the law in this area, important issues remain to be resolved. Thus, for example, the precise jurisprudential basis for upholding legitimate expectations has never been clearly and unequivocally articulated by the courts. As Knight notes, 'the courts have tended to waver between justifying judicial review and its individual heads by reference to three different conceptual terms: fairness, abuse of power and the principle of good administration'. Moreover, in the context of an undertaking giving rise to a legitimate expectation, the law remains a little unclear as to by whom that undertaking must be given in order for the Crown to be bound. Thus in *BAPIO*, where the HL was required to consider the legality of guidance issued by the Department of Health relating to the eligibility of foreign doctors qualified in other countries to work in the UK, it was argued that the guidance was contrary to the Immigration Rules which had been drawn up by the Home Office. In the dissenting opinion of Lord Scott, as noted by Knight, 'one body of the Crown could not bind another'. However, as Knight also notes, Lords Mance and Rodger were of the view that undertakings could bind different government departments where the Crown was regarded as being 'an indivisible whole'.

**13.60** The argument of the majority in *BAPIO* carries particular weight where policy responsibilities have been transferred from one government to another (a not infrequent occurrence). In these circumstances, it is both fair and reasonable for an undertaking given by a predecessor to bind the successor. The position is more complicated, however, where, as in *BAPIO* itself, there is an inconsistency between the approaches of two extant government departments on the same policy issue. It may be, therefore, that Knight's contention that 'reliance upon the indivisibility of the Crown for legitimate expectation purposes should be limited at best' constitutes a sensible and pragmatic way forward.

## The right to a fair hearing

**13.61**  The right to a fair hearing is a core feature of the principles of natural justice or the duty to act fairly. Traditionally it has been expressed in the Latin maxim '*audi alteram partem*' (hear both sides). In truth, the right to a fair hearing is a broad concept which means something more than simply allowing the parties to put their side of the case. It is implicit in the principle that a person should be given sufficient notice of a hearing in order that they can prepare their case. Moreover, to be able to do this in an effective manner, it is imperative that they are properly informed of the case against them (see para **13.48**). However, there may be circumstances where the requirements of fairness are overridden by other interests.

**13.62**  Thus in *R v Secretary of State for the Home Department, ex p Hosenball* (1977), a case involving a challenge to the Secretary of State's decision to deport H on the ground that his continued presence in the UK was not conducive to the public good, it was accepted by the CA that H had been told nothing of the nature of the confidential information which formed the basis of the decision. He had not been given the opportunity of correcting or contradicting any of the information, or of testing it by cross-examination. Moreover, he had not been given sufficient information as to the charges against him so as to be able to respond to them. Nevertheless, in the words of Lord Denning MR, this was:

> a case in which national security is involved, and our history shows that, when the state itself is endangered, our cherished freedoms may have to take second place. Even natural justice itself may suffer a set-back . . . The rules of natural justice have to be modified in regard to foreigners here who prove themselves unwelcome and ought to be deported.

**13.63**  It is difficult to be precise as to what form a 'hearing' will take. The right to a fair hearing need not entail an oral hearing. It may be that the decision-maker is of the opinion that cases can be dealt with on the basis of written submissions. This may be a particularly attractive option where, for example, the decision-maker is a licensing body dealing with a great many applications. Provided that this has meant that a person has had a reasonable opportunity to put their case, fairness is unlikely to make further demands of the decision-making procedure. Where, however, a decision could have profound consequences for an individual in terms of their liberty or livelihood, it is likely that fairness will require a decision-making process which entails an oral hearing. Thus in *R (on the application of H) v Secretary of State for Justice* (2008), where the claimant successfully challenged the refusal to allow him an oral hearing in respect of a decision that he should remain a category A prisoner, Cranston J observed:

> Procedural fairness sometimes demands an oral hearing. There can be greater confidence with an oral hearing that the relevant standards have been properly applied and that

*the facts on which the decision is based are accurate. The oral hearing also gives the*
*person affected by the decision the opportunity to tailor the arguments to the concerns*
*of the decision-maker. The interests at stake are such as to trump other factors in the*
*balance such as cost and perhaps efficiency. It is clear that procedural fairness does*
*not impose the straightjacket of a quasi-judicial process and more informal procedures*
*than what one expects before the courts or even tribunals may be acceptable. An oral*
*hearing does not necessarily imply the adversarial process.*

In the judgment of Cranston J, there were five factors which justified the conclusion
that there should have been an oral hearing in this case. These included that the claimant was a category A prisoner and that his tariff for continued detention had expired.
Since both meant that his liberty was affected, they pointed 'in the direction of a particularly high standard of procedural fairness'.

**13.64** Where an oral hearing is held, fairness will require that individuals have the opportunity to contest the evidence adduced against them. Where that evidence takes the
form of witness statements, fairness may require an opportunity to cross-examine the
witnesses. However, this is not an absolute right. Whether or not cross-examination is
permitted will fall to be determined according to the circumstances of the particular
case.

## A right to legal representation?

**13.65** Where an oral hearing is held, it might be assumed that the parties have a right to
be legally represented. However, this is not the case. Thus in *R v Board of Visitors of*
*HM Prison, The Maze, ex p Hone* (1988), where the appellants alleged that the Board's
decisions not to allow them to be legally represented during disciplinary proceedings
amounted to a breach of natural justice, Lord Goff observed that:

> *I am unable to accept . . . that any person charged with a crime (or the equivalent*
> *thereof) and liable to punishment is entitled as a matter of natural justice to legal*
> *representation. No doubt it is true that a man charged with a crime before a criminal*
> *court is entitled to legal representation . . . No doubt it is also correct that a board of*
> *visitors is bound to give effect to the rules of natural justice. But it does not follow that,*
> *simply because a charge before a disciplinary tribunal such as a board of visitors relates*
> *to facts which in law constitute a crime, the rules of natural justice require the tribunal*
> *to grant legal representation.*

**13.66** Whether or not legal representation will be allowed is initially a matter for the decision-
maker to determine. In exercising its discretion, it may take a number of factors into
account. For example, if a complex point of law is at issue, it may be that the decision-
maker would allow legal representation. Conversely, a lack of legal complexity may
render legal representation unnecessary. If an individual lacks the capacity to present
his own case, fairness may require that legal representation be allowed. Thus in *Pett v*

*Greyhound Racing Association* (1969), where P faced the prospect of losing his livelihood if allegations of greyhound doping were made out against him, Lord Denning MR remarked that:

> It is not every man who has the ability to defend himself on his own. He cannot bring out the point in his own favour or the weakness in the other side. He may be tongue-tied or nervous, confused or wanting in intelligence. He cannot examine or cross-examine witnesses . . . [in a court] if justice is to be done, he ought to have the help of someone to speak for him; and who better than a lawyer who has been trained for the task? I should have thought, therefore, that when a man's reputation or livelihood is at stake, he not only has the right to speak by his own mouth. He also has a right to speak by counsel or solicitor.

The requirements of art 6 of the ECHR must also now be taken into account.

## Reasons

**13.67** We have already noted that, on occasion, a statutory provision may require a decision-maker to give reasons for a decision. Few would deny as a matter of principle that this is a reasonable and appropriate aspect of procedural fairness. It seems only right that a person ought to be informed of the reasons why a decision has gone against them. Additionally there is a case for arguing, as Fordham has done, that 'the discipline of express reasoning' assists not only the claimant but also 'the Court and even the defendant body itself'. Nevertheless, at common law, there is no general duty on the decision-maker to give reasons.

> **R v Gaming Board for Great Britain, ex p Benaim and Khaida (1970):** By virtue of the Gaming Act 1968, gaming could only take place in premises licensed by magistrates. Prior to applying for a licence, it was necessary to obtain a certificate of consent from the Gaming Board (set up under the 1968 Act). The applicants were denied a certificate and the Board refused to give reasons for its decision. They sought an order to quash the Board's refusal and a mandatory order to compel the Board to inform them of the case against them. CA held: the Board was bound to observe the rules of natural justice. It ought to be able to give an applicant a sufficient indication of the objections raised against him so as to enable him to answer them. However, it was not bound to give the reasons for its decision.

**13.68** Similarly in *McInnes v Onslow Fane* (1978), Sir Robert Megarry V-C observed that 'there is no general obligation to give reasons for a decision'. Where, for example, a board, panel, or local authority is dealing with a great many applications for licences, the fact that it is not under a duty to give reasons for its decisions may serve to ease the administrative burden which has been placed upon it. In such circumstances, a failure to give reasons may be due to entirely genuine considerations. However, difficulties arise where no reasons have been given for a decision and there do not appear to be any to justify the conclusion reached. In these circumstances, a court may be at liberty to infer that there was no good reason for the decision: see Lord Upjohn in *Padfield v Minister of Agriculture, Food and Fisheries* (1968).

**13.69** Since the *Gaming Board* case was decided, it has become possible to discern an increasing willingness on the part of the judiciary to rule in a given situation that the duty to act fairly required that reasons be given for a decision. Thus in *R v Civil Service Appeal Board, ex p Cunningham* (1991), the CA held that natural justice required that the Board should give reasons for its decision relating to an unfair dismissal claim. In reaching such a conclusion, the CA was influenced by factors such as: there was no appeal from the board's determination; in making a determination it was carrying out a judicial function; the board was susceptible to judicial review; and it was not a case where the giving of reasons would be harmful to the public interest.

**13.70** In a later case, the HL was also required to consider the legal position vis-à-vis the giving of reasons.

> *R v Secretary of State for the Home Department, ex p Doody* (1994): The applicants were serving mandatory life sentences for murder. Parole could only be considered by the Parole Board following the expiration of a prescribed period. This period was set by the Home Secretary (HS) following recommendations by the trial judges. In the present case, the HS decided not to follow those recommendations and set lengthier prescribed periods. The applicants claimed that he had acted unlawfully by failing to give reasons for his decisions. HL held: the procedure was unfair. Although the law does not recognize a general duty to give reasons for an administrative decision, such a duty may in appropriate circumstances be implied. It was contrary to the public interest not to give reasons in the present case. Moreover, since the decision of the HS was susceptible to judicial review, an effective attack on it could only be mounted if his reasoning was disclosed.

**13.71** The decision in *Doody* demonstrates, therefore, that where an individual's liberty is at issue, a duty to give reasons for his continued incarceration arises. The proposition that there is no general duty to give reasons nevertheless remains valid despite the fact that 'the trend of the law has been towards an increased recognition of the duty upon decision-makers of many kinds to give reasons': see *Stefan v General Medical Council* (1999). Accordingly, whether or not reasons should have accompanied a decision has been determined on a case-by-case basis.

> *R v Higher Education Funding Council, ex p Institute of Dental Surgery* (1994): The institute sought to challenge by way of judicial review a decision made by the Funding Council as to the institute's research rating. It argued that the council was under a duty to give reasons for its decision, and that the absence of reasons indicated that its decision was

irrational. DC held: this was an example of a decision in respect of which fairness did not demand that reasons be given.

**13.72** In *ex p Institute of Dental Surgery*, the DC acknowledged that there are a number of factors in favour of requiring reasons to be given for a decision. These included:

- concentrating the decision-maker's mind on the right questions;
- demonstrating to the recipient of the decision that this was so;
- showing that the issues have been properly addressed and how the decision has been reached; or
- alerting the recipient to a justiciable flaw in the process.

**13.73** Conversely, there were other factors in favour of not requiring reasons to be given. These included:

- it may place an undue burden on the decision-maker;
- it would demand the appearance of unanimity where there is diversity;
- it would call for the articulation of value judgments which were sometimes inexpressible; and
- it would encourage people to examine the reasons looking for previously unsuspected grounds of challenge.

**13.74** In the later case of *Stefan v General Medical Council* (1999), where it was held that the GMC's health committee was under a common law duty to give reasons for its decision to suspend S's registration as a doctor for a period of 12 months pursuant to s 37(1)(a) of the Medical Act 1983, the advantages/disadvantages of giving reasons for a decision were explained thus:

> The advantages of the provision of reasons have often been rehearsed. They relate to the decision-making process, in strengthening that process itself, in increasing the public confidence in it, and in the desirability of the disclosure of error where error exists. They relate also to the parties immediately affected by the decision, in enabling them to know the strengths and weaknesses of their respective cases, and to facilitate appeal where that course is appropriate. But there are also dangers and disadvantages in a universal requirement for reasons. It may impose an undesirable legalism into areas where a high degree of informality is appropriate and add to delay and expense.

**13.75** If the common law were to develop in such a way as to impose a general duty on decision-makers to give reasons for their decisions, the content of such a duty would clearly be important. Although his views were expressed in relation to the duty to give reasons in a planning context, the following remarks of Lord Brown in *South Bucks District Council v Porter (No 2)* (2004) as to the content of that duty may have a wider resonance:

*The reasons for a decision must be intelligible and they must be adequate. They must enable the reader to understand why the matter was decided as it was and what conclusions were reached on the 'principal important controversial issues', disclosing how any issue of law or fact was resolved. Reasons can be briefly stated, the degree of particularity required depending entirely on the nature of the issues falling for decision. The reasoning must not give rise to a substantial doubt as to whether the decision-maker erred in law... The reasons need only refer to the main issues in the dispute, not to every material consideration... A reasons challenge will only succeed if the party aggrieved can satisfy the court that he has genuinely been substantially prejudiced by the failure to provide an adequately reasoned decision.*

## The rule against bias

**13.76** It is self-evident that in order for a decision-making process to be fair, there should be an absence of bias. What amounts to bias is, however, a rather more difficult and practically important matter, especially when it is borne in mind that 'bias is an insidious thing that, even though a person may in good faith believe that he was acting impartially, his mind may unconsciously be affected by bias' (per Lord Goff in *R v Gough* (1993)). In the case of *Davidson v Scottish Ministers* (2004) (see para **13.87**), Lord Hope observed:

*The word 'bias' is used as a convenient shorthand. But it would be a mistake to approach it in this context as if its only meaning were pejorative. The essence of it is captured in the Convention concept of impartiality. An interest in the outcome of the case or an indication of prejudice against a party to the case or his associates will, of course, be a ground for concluding that there was a real possibility that the tribunal or one of its members was biased ... But the concept is wider than that. It includes an inclination or pre-disposition to decide the issue only one way, whatever the strength of the contrary argument. A doubt as to whether this is the case is enough, so long as it can be justified objectively.*

**13.77** Until relatively recently, the authorities revealed that the English courts had developed two tests for identifying bias: reasonable suspicion of bias; and real likelihood of bias. Thus in *R v Altrincham Justices, ex p Pennington* (1975), Lord Widgery favoured the former test, whereas in *R v Metropolitan London Rent Assessment Panel Committee, ex p Properties Co (FGC) Ltd* (1969), Lord Denning spoke in terms of the real likelihood of bias test. Although the distinction between bodies performing a judicial or an administrative function is no longer important in terms of the application of the principles of natural justice (see *Ridge v Baldwin* (1964), paras **13.46-13.47**) there was a school of thought that it did still have an influence on which of the tests for bias should apply. Thus in *Steeples v Derbyshire County Council* (1984), Webster J cautiously advocated the stricter standard (reasonable suspicion of bias) being applied to bodies with judicial functions and the less strict standard (real likelihood of bias) being applied to administrative bodies. Such distinctions have been rendered unnecessary, however, by subsequent developments in the case law.

---

*R v Gough* **(1993):** G was tried for conspiring with his brother to rob a betting shop. Proceedings against his brother had been dropped at the committal stage. Nevertheless, during the trial, a photograph of the brother was shown to the jury and his name was mentioned. At the end of the trial, G was convicted and sentenced to 15 years' imprisonment. His brother protested from the public gallery and, at this point, one of the jurors realized that the brother was her neighbour. G appealed against his conviction on the basis that this amounted to a serious irregularity in the conduct of the trial. His appeal was rejected by the CA. HL held: dismissing his appeal, that it was both possible and desirable that the same test should be applicable in all cases of apparent bias. That test was a real danger of bias. Real danger was preferable to real likelihood so as to encourage the courts to think in terms of the possibility rather than the probability of bias. Applying that test to the facts of the case, there was no ground for disturbing the jury's verdict.

---

**13.78**  The application of the 'real danger of bias' test to decisions of a judicial or administrative nature was confirmed in *R v Secretary of State for the Environment, ex p Kirkstall Valley Campaign* (1996). However, in *R v Local Comr for Administration in North and North East England, ex p Liverpool City Council* (1999), Hooper J held that although the 'real danger of bias' test might be applicable on an application for judicial review of a planning decision, the commissioner was entitled to apply a more stringent test set out in the National Code of Local Government Conduct. This was the test by which councillors had agreed to be bound. A subsequent appeal against Hooper J's decision was unsuccessful: see *R v Local Comr for Administration in North and North East England, ex p Liverpool City Council* (2001) CA.

**13.79**  Interestingly, as Professor Craig has noted, the *Gough* test was either not used or was modified in some Commonwealth jurisdictions. Thus in *Gascor v Ellicott* (1997), Tadgell JA in the Supreme Court of Victoria observed that:

> Although the criterion of apprehension of partiality or prejudice is possibility, not likelihood, a reasonable apprehension is to be established to the court's satisfaction: it is a reasonable and not a fanciful or fantastic apprehension that is to be established; and the apprehension is to be attributed to an observer who is 'fair minded' – which means 'reasonable'.

**13.80**  Concerns about the *Gough* test were also expressed in the domestic courts. Thus in *Re Medicaments and Related Classes of Goods (No 2)* (2001), Lord Phillips MR drew attention to the difficulties which had arisen when determining whether a decision should be set aside on the ground of bias and noted that the attempt to provide a uniform test in *Gough* had not commanded universal approval. Accordingly, Lord Phillips MR conducted a review of the relevant case law (under both domestic law and the ECHR) and concluded that:

> When the Strasbourg jurisprudence is taken into account, we believe that a modest adjustment of the test in R v Gough is called for, which makes it plain that it is, in effect, no different from the test applied in most of the Commonwealth and in Scotland. The court must first ascertain all the circumstances which have a bearing on the suggestion that the judge was biased. It must then ask whether those circumstances would lead a fair-minded and informed observer to conclude that there was a real possibility, or a real danger, the two being the same, that the tribunal was biased.

**13.81**  This modified version of the *Gough* test thus emphasizes that the standard to be applied is that of the fair-minded and informed observer. In other words, the objectivity of the test has been confirmed by requiring a court to consider not whether the facts of a case would suggest the possibility of bias to the court itself, but whether the facts would suggest the possibility of bias to a fair-minded observer. Thus in *Porter v Magill* (2002) (para **13.17**), Lord Hope remarked in relation to the modified test that:

> It represents in clear and simple language a test which is in harmony with the objective test which the Strasbourg court applies when it is considering whether the circumstances give rise to a reasonable apprehension of bias. It removes any possible conflict with the test which is now applied in most Commonwealth countries and in Scotland. I would however delete from it the reference to 'a real danger'. Those words no longer serve a useful purpose here, and they are not used in the jurisprudence of the Strasbourg court. The question is whether the fair-minded and informed observer, having considered the facts, would conclude that there was a real possibility that the tribunal was biased. [emphasis added]

**13.82**  In the more recent HL case of *Lawal v Northern Spirit* (2004), Lord Steyn noted in delivering their Lordships' judgment that the approach to the issue of bias advocated by Lord Hope in *Porter* had been 'unanimously endorsed' by the HL in that case. His Lordship continued:

> In the result there is now no difference between the common law test of bias and the requirements under art 6 of the Convention of an independent and impartial tribunal . . . The small but important shift approved in Porter's case has at its core the need for 'the confidence which must be inspired by the courts in a democratic society' . . . Public perception of the possibility of unconscious bias is the key. It is unnecessary to delve into the characteristics to be attributed to the fair-minded and informed observer. What can confidently be said is that one is entitled to conclude that such an observer will adopt a balanced approach.

Applying the modified test of bias to the facts of the case before it in *Lawal*, the HL concluded that the practice whereby part-time judges in the Employment Appeal Tribunal might appear as counsel before a tribunal having previously sat with one or more lay members of the bench hearing the appeal ought to be discontinued. In their Lordships' opinion, a fair-minded and informed observer would conclude on the facts that there was a real possibility that a lay member might be subconsciously biased due to the fairly close relationship of trust and confidence which would have been developed with the judge who was now appearing before them rather than sitting with them.

**13.83** Although Lord Steyn remarked in *Lawal* that it is 'unnecessary to delve into the characteristics to be attributed to the fair-minded and informed observer', in the Australian case of *Johnson v Johnson* (2000), it was observed that such a person's attributes included that they were 'neither complacent nor unduly sensitive or suspicious'. These comments were subsequently approved by Lord Bingham in *Davidson v Scottish Ministers* (2004) (para **13.87**). In the later case of *Gillies v Secretary of State for Work and Pensions* (2006), Lord Hope stated:

> the fair-minded and informed observer can be assumed to have access to all the facts that are capable of being known by members of the public generally, bearing in mind that it is the appearance that these facts give rise to that matters, not what is in the mind of the particular judge or tribunal member who is under scrutiny.

Cases in which the *Porter v Magill* test for apparent bias has been applied are numerous. Two recent examples will therefore suffice for present purposes.

---

*R v Pintori* **(2007):** The appellant was convicted of possessing a Class A drug (heroin) after six or seven police officers had carried out a raid at his flat. During the course of his trial, it became apparent that one of the jurors was a communications officer who worked in a command centre and who knew at least three of the officers in the case reasonably well. The trial judge was aware of the situation prior to passing sentence. The appellant appealed against his conviction on the ground that there was a real possibility that the juror and therefore the jury as a whole was biased against him. CA held: allowing the appeal, that the appellant did not have a fair trial because the fact that the juror knew the officers would of itself have led the fair-minded and informed observer to conclude that there was a real possibility of bias on her part. Such a person would have concluded that the juror was disposed to find the appellant guilty simply because she knew the officers, had worked with them, and therefore wished (consciously or unconsciously) to support them in the prosecution. Although the common law rule preventing the admissibility of jury deliberations (see *R v Mirza* (2004)) meant that there was no way of knowing what influence the juror had over the other members of the jury in reaching the verdict, the fair-minded and informed observer would conclude that there was a real possibility that she had influenced her fellow jurors.

---

*R v Abdroikov; R v Green; R v Williamson* **(2007):** Each of the three appellants had been convicted of various serious offences including attempted murder and rape. They appealed against their convictions on the ground that although the Criminal Justice Act 2003 had made changes to the rules governing the qualification/disqualification of jurors so that police officers and CPS solicitors were now eligible to sit, the presence of either a police officer or a prosecuting solicitor had deprived them of a fair trial contrary to both the common law and art 6 of the ECHR. In effect, they argued that the close connection between such individuals and the prosecution was such as to cause a fair-minded and informed observer to conclude that there was a real risk of a possibility of bias. The CA dismissed the appeals. In its judgment, the circumstances of each case demonstrated that the requirements of fairness had been met. The appellants appealed. HL held: that in the case of the first appellant, the appeal would be unanimously dismissed since it could only succeed on the basis that it was undesirable per se for police officers to serve on juries which would be contrary to the spirit of the reforms made by the 2003 Act. In the case of the second and third appellants, however, the appeals were allowed by 3:2. The majority were of the view that the instinct of a police officer on the jury to prefer the evidence of a brother officer to that of a drug-addicted defendant would be judged by a fair-minded and informed observer to be a real and possible source of unfairness beyond the reach of standard judicial warnings and directions. Moreover, in the case of the third appellant, justice was not seen to be done if one discharging the role of juror was a full-time, salaried, long-serving employee of the prosecutor.

Lord Rodger was in the minority in the second of the three joined appeals in *Abdroikov*. He sought to distinguish previous cases such as *Pintori* on the basis that there had been a clear connection between the juror and the police officers in that case whereas, in the present appeals, there was no such close connection. In his opinion, the objection in the three appeals was 'simply to the verdict of a jury which included a police officer or CPS lawyer', and the effect of the decision of the majority was to do much to reverse the reform of the law effected by the 2003 Act. Thus he stated:

> Although the fair-minded and informed observer would see that it was possible that a police officer or CPS lawyer would be biased, he would also see the possibility of the jury's verdict being biased as a result was no greater than in many other cases. In other words, the mere presence of these individuals, without more, would not give rise to a real possibility that the jury had been unable to assess the evidence impartially and reach an unbiased verdict.

## Automatic disqualification

**13.84** Occasions may arise where a person scheduled to sit in a judicial capacity would have a pecuniary interest in the outcome of the proceedings. In these circumstances, the appropriate course of action would be to declare the interest and stand down from the case since, as Blackburn J observed in *R v Rand* (1866): 'any direct pecuniary interest, however small, in the subject of inquiry, does disqualify a person from acting as judge in the matter'. Where this has not been done, the courts will be quick to set aside a decision even though there is no actual evidence of bias. Their reason for so acting is that public confidence in the administration of justice would be undermined if the decision were allowed to stand. In the words of Lord Hewart CJ in *R v Sussex Justices, ex p*

*McCarthy* (1924), it is of 'fundamental importance that justice should not only be done, but should manifestly be seen to be done'. Two cases serve to illustrate the point.

---

*Grand Junction Canal Co v Dimes* **(1852):** Lord Cottenham LC owned a substantial shareholding in the defendant canal company. He heard an appeal and affirmed an earlier decision in favour of the company. There was an appeal to the HL on the grounds that the LC was disqualified by reason of his pecuniary interest in the case. HL held: the LC was disqualified from hearing the case. The principle that no man should be a judge in his own cause was not confined to a case in which he was a party. It also applied to a cause in which he has an interest.

---

*R v Bow Street Metropolitan Stipendiary Magistrates' Court, ex p Pinochet Ugarte (No 2)* **(1999):** P was the former Head of State of Chile. Whilst in the UK his extradition was sought by the Government of Spain which wanted him to stand trial for crimes against humanity alleged to have been committed whilst he was Head of State. Warrants for his arrest were issued by the magistrates. The HL was required to consider the extent and scope of the immunity of a former Head of State from arrest and extradition proceedings. Before the appeal was heard, a committee of three Law Lords granted Amnesty International (AI) and several other interested parties leave to intervene in the appeal. AI therefore made written submissions and were represented by counsel. The HL decided by a majority of 3:2 that P was not entitled to immunity. Subsequently it became apparent that one of the Law Lords in the majority, Lord Hoffmann, was a director and chairperson of Amnesty International Ltd, the charitable arm of AI. P's lawyers therefore appealed. HL held: where the decision of a judge would lead to the promotion of a cause with which he was involved together with one of the parties, he would be automatically excluded from hearing the matter even though he had no pecuniary interest in the outcome of the case. On the facts of the present case, Lord Hoffmann was automatically disqualified from hearing the appeal. The matter would therefore be referred to another committee of the HL for rehearing.

---

**13.85**  It must be appreciated that in neither of these two cases was it alleged that there was actual bias on the part of either judge. Rather, the nature of their relationships with a canal company on the one hand and AI on the other gave rise to the presumption of bias which was sufficient to disqualify them. The decision in *ex p Pinochet (No 2)* is therefore novel in that, hitherto, a pecuniary or proprietary interest had been the basis of automatic disqualification. Lord Hoffmann had neither kind of interest.

**13.86**  Bias was also at issue in a number of appeals heard by the CA: see *Locabail (UK) Ltd v Bayfield Properties Ltd* (2000). Whilst the majority of these were rejected by the court, in *Timmins v Gormley* (2000), the appeal was allowed on the grounds of bias. The CA concluded that although there was no evidence of actual bias, the views expressed by a recorder in his writings on personal injuries claims indicated that he had strong pro-claimant and anti-insurer views. Applying a broad common-sense approach, the CA concluded, not without misgiving, that there was a real danger (now a real possibility) that a person with such views might unconsciously lean in favour of the claimant and against the defendant when determining the issues between them.

**13.87** The HL had a further opportunity to consider the issue of apparent bias in a case involving a judicial review petition brought by a prisoner in Scotland.

---

*Davidson v Scottish Ministers* **(2004):** D was a prisoner who had brought judicial review proceedings in which he claimed that the conditions in which he had been kept were contrary to art 3 of the ECHR. He sought a final and an interim order ordaining the Scottish Ministers to transfer him to conditions which were art 3 compliant. An interim order was refused at first instance and an appeal to the Extra Division of the Court of Session was refused. It later became apparent that one of the judges who had heard the appeal, Lord Hardie, had formerly been Lord Advocate (a government minister). Acting in that executive capacity, he had promoted the Scotland Act 1998 in the HL. During the course of promoting the Bill, he advised the HL as to the effect of s 21 of the Crown Proceedings Act 1947 on the remedies which might be available to the courts in Scotland against the Scottish Ministers. In effect he had promoted the protection of Scottish Ministers from judicial review. The meaning of s 21 was directly relevant to D's litigation. D applied to the Inner House for the refusal of leave to be set aside on the ground that Lord Hardie's participation in the appeal breached art 6 of the ECHR. The Inner House granted D's application. The Scottish Ministers appealed. HL held: that the test to be applied was that laid down in *Porter v Magill*, ie whether the fair-minded and informed observer, having regard to the facts, would conclude that there was a real possibility that the judge was biased. On the facts of the present case, there was a risk of apparent bias. The fair-minded and informed observer would conclude that there was a real possibility that Lord Hardie would subconsciously strive when sitting judicially to avoid a conclusion which would undermine the clear assurances he had given to Parliament.

---

When reading the speeches in the HL it is apparent that what caused their Lordships to rule in D's favour was a combination of what Lord Hardie had previously said about the legislation and the capacity in which he had said it, ie as a government minister promoting the legislation. Collectively these factors ought to have disqualified Lord Hardie from sitting as a member of the Extra Division in D's case. Lord Bingham noted that in practice, a disqualifying interest would often be recognized by a judge and then disclosed to the parties. They would then have the opportunity to object to the judge hearing the case, if they so wished. However, Lord Bingham also noted that there were 'a number of entirely honourable reasons' why a judge may not make a disclosure, eg forgetfulness or a failure to recognize the relevance of the previous involvement to the current issue.

**13.88** It is worth noting that the now retired Law Lord, Lord Steyn, did not sit on the HL panel which heard the appeal in *A v Secretary of State for the Home Department* (2005) (para **3.35**) because of a comment made in a public lecture which prompted a challenge by the Attorney-General. Although Lord Steyn has subsequently claimed that the

Government's objection that he might not be neutral was 'truly flimsy', he nevertheless stood down for the reason that 'it would be unseemly not to'.

## Actual bias

**13.89**  Patently, the decision of a judge would be quashed if it were shown that he was actually biased against one of the parties appearing before him. However, as Goudkamp has commented, 'a notable feature of the rapidly growing corpus of law on bias is that while cases involving apparent and presumed bias are in great supply, cases in which actual bias is alleged let alone proved are rare'. In seeking to explain this phenomenon, he observes:

> This is largely due to the fact that, unlike the other species of bias, actual bias requires proof of partiality. This is very difficult to establish. But even when, exceptionally, a litigant has good prospects of proving that a judge is in fact biased, a submission of actual bias is seldom made. Instead, litigants tend to take their stand on the rule against apparent bias.

**13.90**  Goudkamp offers a number of explanations as to why litigants are in practice reluctant to allege actual bias on the part of a judge. These include:

- that unless the evidence of actual bias is highly persuasive, it is far easier to demonstrate the appearance of bias;
- that to allege actual bias may insult or alienate the judge, thereby diminishing the prospects of success if the judge refuses to recuse himself;
- judges have often remarked that it is unhelpful and even damaging to inquire whether a judge is actually biased.

It is not surprising, therefore, that in many of the 'bias cases', the courts are anxious to stress that although the facts create the appearance of bias, there is no suggestion whatsoever of partiality or actual bias on the part of the judge. Goudkamp contends that such a conclusion is frequently reached in the absence of an adequate explanation, with the result that the rule against actual bias is deprived of its practical utility and is left to serve 'a purely symbolic function'.

## FURTHER READING

Beatson, J, Matthews, M, and Elliott, M *Administrative Law: Text and Materials* (4th edn, 2011) OUP.

Sir Louis Blom-Cooper 'Bias: Malfunction in Judicial Decision-making' [2009] PL 199.

Craig, P P 'Legitimate Expectations: A Conceptual Analysis' (1992) 107 LQR 79.

Craig, P P *Administrative Law* (6th edn, 2008) Sweet & Maxwell.

Fordham, M *Judicial Review Handbook* (5th edn, 2008) Hart.

Goudkamp, J 'Facing up to Actual Bias' (2008) 27 CJQ 32.

Hickman, T 'The Substance and Structure of Proportionality' [2008] PL 694.

Hilson, C 'Judicial Review, Policies and the Fettering of Discretion' [2002] PL 111.

Knight, C J S 'Expectations in Transition: Recent Developments in Legitimate Expectations' [2009] PL 15.

Law Commission *Administrative Law: Judicial Review and Statutory Appeals* (1994) (Law Com No 226).

Lord Irvine 'Judges and Decision-makers: The Theory and Practice of Wednesbury Review' [1996] PL 59.

Olowofoyeku, A A 'Bias and the Informed Observer: A Call for a Return to *Gough*' [2009] CLJ 388.

Pollard, D, Parpworth, N, and Hughes, D *Constitutional and Administrative Law: Text with Materials* (4th edn, 2007) OUP.

Reynolds, P 'Legitimate Expectations and the Protection of Trust in Public Officials' [2011] PL 330.

Rivers, J 'Proportionality and Variable Intensity of Review' [2006] CLJ 174.

Roberts, M 'Public Law Representations and Substantive Legitimate Expectations' (2001) 64 MLR 112.

Rowbottom, J 'Houses for Votes, Bias and Political Purpose' (2002) 118 LQR 364.

Steele, I 'Substantive Legitimate Expectations: Striking the Right Balance' (2005) 121 LQR 300.

Turner, I 'Judicial Review, Irrationality and the Legitimacy of Merits-review' (2008) Liverpool LR 309.

Wade, H W R and Forsyth, C F *Administrative Law* (10th edn, 2009) OUP.

Walker, P 'What's Wrong with Irrationality?' [1995] PL 556.

Watson, J 'Clarity and Ambiguity: A new approach to the test of legitimacy in the law of legitimate expectations' (2010) 34 Legal Studies 633.

# SELF-TEST QUESTIONS

1   With regard to irrationality as a ground for review, to what extent, if any, do you agree with Fordham's observation that 'there are dangers in using Olympic pole-vault height for the high-jump'?

2   It will be remembered that in *ex p International Trader's Ferry Ltd* (1999), Lord Cooke criticized the *Wednesbury* notion of unreasonableness and argued instead that the relevant test should be 'whether the decision in question was one which a reasonable authority could reach'. What purpose do you think Lord Cooke was trying to achieve by advocating the use of this 'simple test'? Assuming that it was adopted, how would it be applied in practice?

3   Why have the English courts traditionally been reluctant to embrace the doctrine of proportionality as a separate ground for review? What effect has the Human Rights Act 1998 had upon judicial attitudes towards proportionality?

4   Which, if any, of the established grounds for review blurs the distinction between the legality and merits of a decision?

5   What is the significance of the HL decision in *Ridge v Baldwin*?

6   Why do the courts prefer to talk in terms of a 'duty to act fairly' rather than the principles of natural justice?

7   To what extent, if any, do you agree with Elliott et al that: 'Giving reasons for decisions should be treated as a central facet of procedural fairness in administrative law'? Ought the common law to now recognize a general duty to give reasons, subject to exceptions?

8   To what extent, if any, have the decisions in *Re Medicaments*, *Porter*, and *Lawal* clarified the law relating to the test for bias?

9   Although the decision in *Davidson v Scottish Ministers* (2004) has been discussed in this chapter as a bias case, what does it tell us about the separation of powers?

10   Does the decision in *ex p Pinochet (No 2)* mean that in the future, a judge will not be able to hear cases involving charities with which they have a connection?

# 14

# Judicial review remedies

## SUMMARY

Assuming that a claimant for judicial review has overcome the obstacles posed by the permission stage, and has convinced the court of the substance of the allegations, the court will now be in a position to grant a remedy. However, the claimant's problems are not completely at an end. The remedies which the courts may grant are discretionary. Therefore, a court may decide not to grant a remedy where, for example, a deficiency has been resolved by a decision-maker prior to the hearing. This chapter considers the different kinds of remedy which a court has the power to grant were it to exercise its discretion in favour of the claimant.

## Introduction

**14.1** A claimant for judicial review may seek one or more of several remedies that are potentially available. These are:

- a quashing order (formerly certiorari);
- a prohibiting order (formerly prohibition);
- a mandatory order (formerly mandamus);
- declaration;
- injunction;
- interim declaration;
- substitutionary remedy.

The first three remedies are collectively referred to as the prerogative orders. At one time they were writs employed by the courts as a means of controlling the exercise of power by public bodies. Now, however, as a consequence of the Administration of Justice (Miscellaneous Provisions) Acts of 1933 and 1938 respectively, the writs have taken the form of judicial orders which may be granted on application to the Administrative Court. The power to grant the last two remedies has been conferred upon the courts by the Civil Procedure Rules (CPR).

## Damages

**14.2** A notable absentee from the list of remedies is damages. Although CPR 54.3(2) provides that a claim for judicial review may include a claim for damages, it further provides that the claim may not seek damages alone. The circumstances in which damages will be awarded in such proceedings are set out in s 31(4) of the Senior Courts Act 1981. This provides that damages may be awarded to a claimant if: (a) he has joined with his claim for judicial review a claim for damages arising from any matter to which the judicial review claim relates; and (b) the court is satisfied that 'if the claim had been made in an action begun by the claimant at the time of making the claim for judicial review, he would have been awarded damages'. Thus in *R (Kurdistan Workers Party) v Secretary of State for the Home Department* (2002), Richards J remarked: 'A claim for damages can properly be made as part of an otherwise appropriate claim for judicial review, but it is not in itself a good reason for permitting judicial review'. It may occur, for example, where it is alleged that a claimant has been falsely imprisoned by a public body. In such circumstances, it would be undesirable for a claimant to be compelled to launch two separate actions, one in public law and the other in private law, to seek redress.

**14.3** In July 2008, the Law Commission published a consultation paper, *Administrative Redress: Public Bodies and the Citizen* (CP 187), in which it sought views on a number of issues relating to state liability, including whether monetary remedies ought to be available in judicial review. Its 'provisional' view was that:

> Judicial review had developed in a way that is over restrictive in relation to the award of damages to an aggrieved citizen. This can lead to significant injustice to those citizens who are adversely affected by poor decision making. Simply quashing a decision may, without more, prove an inadequate remedy in judicial review, particularly where the claimant has suffered significant interim losses pending judgment.

**14.4** The Law Commission was also of the view that it was 'plainly anomalous that a claimant can recover damages where a public body has breached a rule of EU law intended to confer rights on individuals but not where the breach is of a rule of purely domestic law; and also that damages are available under the Human Rights Act 1998'. It therefore proposed that damages should be available as an additional, ancillary, discretionary remedy in judicial review where it could be shown that: the underlying statutory or common law regime conferred some form of benefit on the claimant; there had been 'serious fault' in the public body's behaviour; and the loss which the claimant had suffered was due to the act, omission, or decision of the relevant public body.

**14.5** In May 2010, the Law Commission published its final report, *Administrative Redress: Public Bodies and the Citizen* (Law Com. No.322). It reported that its basic proposal that monetary remedies ought to be more widely available in judicial review had met with 'either a mixed or favourable response'. Opposition to the proposals included: that wider monetary remedies were inconsistent with public law and the nature of judicial review as presently constituted; that there would be a risk of increased delay and costs in the Administrative Court were they to become available; and that they would impose an increased financial burden on public bodies. Nevertheless, the Law Commission remained steadfast. Thus it observed:

> We accept that the award of damages is not the primary function of judicial review, and that the function of judicial review may not have traditionally included the award of damages. However, in the light of recent developments in judicial review...it is unsustainable to argue that this is a good basis to continue to refuse damages to claimants.

**14.6** In the opinion of the Law Commission, the criticisms levelled against its proposals were not insurmountable. It thus adhered to its original view that 'there is a good argument in favour of reforming this area of the law'. Crucially, however, given the substantial opposition to its proposals, including a single response from the Government, it accepted that it could not take this part of its reform project any further.

## Prescriptive or permissive?

**14.7** Although each of the remedies (para **14.1**) may be granted in judicial review proceedings, CPR 54 draws a distinction between those remedies which must be sought by way of judicial review and those which may be sought in such proceedings. Thus a mandatory, prohibiting, or quashing order or an injunction under s 30 of the Senior Courts Act 1981 must be sought in judicial review proceedings: CPR 54.2. The judicial review procedure may be used where the claimant is seeking a declaration or an injunction: CPR 54.3. In the event that a claimant is seeking a remedy from each of the categories mentioned in CPR 54.2 and 54.3, the judicial review procedure must be used.

## A quashing order

**14.8** The grant of a quashing order has, as its name implies, the effect of quashing the impugned decision, thus rendering it null and void. For a claimant to be granted a quashing order, it is necessary (in common with the other remedies) that he has a sufficient interest in the matter to which the claim relates. Sometimes, in the past, the courts talked in terms of the need for the claimant to be an 'aggrieved person'. Thus in *Covent Garden Community Association Ltd v Greater London Council* (1981), it was held that a company formed to protect the interests of Covent Garden residents had standing to seek an order to quash the GLC's decision to grant itself planning permission to develop premises in the area. The application failed, however, on its merits. This relatively liberal approach to standing for quashing orders mirrors that which the courts now take in respect of the general locus standi requirement (see paras **12.60–12.65**).

**14.9** The difficulty with a quashing order (certiorari) has lain, therefore, not with the identity of the claimant but with the identity of the defendant. The question 'Against whom may an order of certiorari be sought?' appeared not to admit of a straightforward answer in the light of remarks made by Atkin LJ in *R v Electricity Comrs, ex p London Electricity Joint Committee Co (1920) Ltd* (1924). Whilst discussing the writs of certiorari and prohibition (as they then were), Atkin LJ observed that:

> *Whenever any body of persons having legal authority to determine questions affecting the rights of subjects, and having the duty to act judicially, act in excess of their legal authority, they are subject to the controlling jurisdiction of the King's Bench Division exercised in these writs.*

**14.10** If this statement is accorded a narrow meaning, it meant that at the time that it was uttered a quashing order (certiorari) had not really developed beyond its traditional role, that of quashing the decisions of inferior courts. Few other bodies could be said to be under a duty to act judicially. However, in the light of *Ridge v Baldwin* (1964) where, as we have seen (paras **13.46–13.47**), the HL sought to dispense with the distinction between judicial and administrative decisions, quashing orders are not limited to inferior courts. They have been granted against decisions made by, for example, local authorities, ministers of the Crown, rent tribunals, and a local legal aid committee. Such orders do not, however, lie against the decisions of domestic tribunals which derive their authority from a consensual submission to their jurisdiction. Neither, generally speaking, may they be sought to quash delegated legislation: see, however, *R v Secretary of State for Education and Employment, ex p NUT* (2000), where an order purporting to change the contracts of employment of teachers was quashed; and *R (C) v Secretary of State for Justice* (2008), where the Secure Training Centre (Amendment) Rules 2007 were quashed on a number of grounds, including that they were in breach of arts 3 and 8 of the ECHR.

**14.11** In common with the other prerogative remedies, a quashing order is discretionary in nature. Whether or not it is made will depend upon the particular circumstances of the case. It may not be made, for example, if a claimant has not exhausted alternative remedies, such as a statutory right of appeal. Alternatively, a court may take the view that the claimant's conduct does not merit a quashing order. In *Ex p Fry* (1954), a fireman who disobeyed an order in the belief that it was unlawful was denied certiorari (a quashing order) when he sought to challenge the decision to caution him for a disciplinary offence. The court took the view that his conduct had been foolhardy. Rather than disobeying an order, he ought to have done as he was told and then made a complaint in accordance with the prescribed procedure.

**14.12** A quashing order may also be refused where the court considers that the consequences of quashing a decision would be too far-reaching. Thus in *R v Secretary of State for*

*Social Services, ex p Association of Metropolitan Authorities* (1986), where the applicants (claimants) sought an order to quash certain regulations relating to housing benefit, Webster J declined to revoke them for several reasons. These included the fact that the regulations had been in force for six months and that by that time, local authorities would have made the necessary adaptations in order to administer them. Moreover, if they were revoked, those who had been denied housing benefit because of the new regulations would be entitled to make fresh claims, each of which would have to be determined on its merits by the local authorities.

14.13    Where the decision to amend delegated legislation is successfully challenged rather than the amending legislation itself, the likelihood of a quashing order being granted is more remote. Thus in *R (on the application of English Speaking Board (International) Ltd) v Secretary of State for the Home Department* (2011), where the claimant, a registered charity which promoted and assessed a full range of spoken English qualifications, succeeded in convincing the court that changes to the Immigration Rules and the British Nationality (General) Regulations 2003 were irrational due to, amongst other things, a lack of consultation, Wyn Williams J refused to quash the changes. There was nothing in the evidence to suggest that the changes were having an on-going deleterious effect on the accreditation process for privately run English language centres. Moreover, the effect of the rule change had not caused damage on a widespread scale for anything more than a short period after the changes came into force. Moreover, it was accepted in the witness statements that the changes were made for a legitimate and desirable purpose; to stop unscrupulous private sector providers from abusing and exploiting those who needed to be able to demonstrate English language competency. These factors therefore militated against the grant of a quashing order.

14.14    A further basis on which a quashing order and the other remedies may be refused is if the court considers that, in accordance with s 31(6) of the Senior Courts Act 1981, there has been undue delay in making a claim for judicial review and that the grant of the relief sought:

> *would be likely to cause substantial hardship to, or substantially prejudice the rights of, any person or would be detrimental to good administration.*

## A prohibiting order

14.15    Whereas a quashing order is available only after a decision has been taken, a prohibiting order is available to prevent a public body from acting or continuing to act outside its power or contrary to natural justice. In other respects, such as the bodies against whom a prohibiting order can be made and the question of locus standi, the remedy is broadly similar to a quashing order. In *R v Liverpool Corpn, ex p Liverpool Taxi Fleet Operators' Association* (1972) (para **13.50**), the CA considered the question of the relief that should be granted and decided on prohibition. Accordingly, an order was issued prohibiting the corporation from acting on its own resolutions to increase the number of taxi cab licences in its area without first hearing representations from the claimants and other interested parties on this and related matters.

## A mandatory order

**14.16** A mandatory order compels the defendant to perform a public law duty that has been imposed by law. Thus if a decision-maker is required to consult prior to making a decision and yet has failed to do so, such an order may lie to ensure that consultation takes place. A mandatory order will also be the most appropriate remedy to compel a decision-maker to exercise a jurisdiction that they have.

**14.17** As with the other prerogative orders, a mandatory order is a discretionary remedy. Thus a court may refuse to make such an order where it considers that it is not warranted. In *R v Metropolitan Police Comr, ex p Blackburn* (1968) (para **18.3**), the CA accepted that a mandatory order may lie against a chief police officer where, for example, an instruction was issued that as a matter of policy, housebreakers would not be prosecuted. In these circumstances, Salmon LJ believed that householders in the area would be able to obtain a mandatory order since the chief police officer would be failing in his duty to enforce the law. Nevertheless, the CA was anxious to stress that there were many fields in which chief officers have a discretion with which the courts would not interfere. In the circumstances of the case, a mandatory order to compel the commissioner to have his officers enforce the gaming laws was unnecessary since he had already given the court an undertaking to that effect. Similarly in *R v Chief Constable of Devon and Cornwall, ex p Central Electricity Generating Board* (1982) (paras **19.3-19.4**), the CA refused to grant a mandatory order to compel the chief constable to have his officers remove protesters from a site. The CA considered that it was for the chief constable and his officers present at the scene rather than the courts to decide when intervention was appropriate.

**14.18** Given the compulsory nature of a mandatory order, these cases illustrate that the courts will, wherever possible, avoid making such an order. Thus in the context of subjecting government ministers to mandamus (mandatory) orders, Nolan LJ (as he then was) remarked in *R v Secretary of State for Employment, ex p Equal Opportunities Commission* (1992) that:

> *In recent years when it has been successfully claimed that a minister is in breach of his legal duties, the normal practice of the court has been simply to make a declaration to that effect but not to order mandamus. The reason for this, is that ministers may be expected to carry out what the courts have declared to be their duty, and that accordingly to make an order of mandamus compelling them to do so would be unnecessary and discourteous.*

**14.19** Where an order of mandamus had been granted, RSC Order 53, rule 10, protected the respondent from any proceedings, civil or criminal, in respect of anything done in obedience to the order. There is no such explicit protection in the CPR for that which has been done to comply with a mandatory order.

## Declaration

**14.20** In his 1949 Hamlyn Lecture, Freedom under the Law, Sir Alfred Denning (as he then was) concluded by observing that:

> No one can suppose that the executive will never be guilty of the sins that are common to all of us. You may be sure that they will sometimes do things which they ought not to do: and will not do things that they ought to do. But if and when wrongs are suffered by any of us, what is the remedy? Our procedure for securing our personal freedom is efficient, but our procedure for preventing the abuse of power is not. Just as the pick and shovel is no longer suitable for the winning of coal, so also the procedure of mandamus, certiorari, and actions on the case are not suitable for the winning of freedom in the new age. They must be replaced by new and up to date machinery, by declarations, injunctions, and actions for negligence…This is not a task for Parliament…The courts must do this. Of all the great tasks that lie ahead, this is the greatest. [emphasis added]

**14.21** In the 60 or so years since these words were uttered, the courts have indeed set about the task to which Sir Alfred Denning referred with the result that declaratory relief 'has performed a crucial function in the emergence of the modern law of judicial review' (per Lord Woolf CJ in *Governor & Company of the Bank of Scotland v A Ltd* (2001)).

**14.22** Unlike the other remedies, which if granted will have a specific effect on an impugned decision, or which will require a decision-maker to act or to refrain from acting, a declaration amounts to a statement of the legal position. Although this statement does not really amount to a remedy as such, it does clarify matters for the parties and will allow them to act (or refrain from acting) accordingly. Declarations are of particular use when challenging delegated legislation. They may be issued in respect of purely domestic delegated legislation or where such legislation has been made in order to give effect to an EU obligation. In *R v Secretary of State for Employment, ex p Equal Opportunities Commission* (1995), the HL emphasized that a court has the jurisdiction to make a declaratory judgment in judicial review proceedings (assuming that the claimant has locus standi) irrespective of whether or not the court could also make a prerogative order in the circumstances of the case. CPR 40.20 confirms that: 'The Court may make declarations whether or not any other remedy is claimed'.

**14.23** The power to grant a declaration is discretionary. It may be refused, therefore, where a court considers that it is being asked to consider the legality of what might happen as opposed to what has happened. Thus in *Blackburn v A-G* (1971), where the applicant (claimant) sought to challenge the UK's accession to the Treaty of Rome (para **4.31**), Stamp LJ observed:

> it is no part of this court's function or duty to make declarations in general terms regarding the powers of Parliament, more particularly where the circumstances in which the court is asked to intervene are purely hypothetical.

**14.24**  Declarations were formerly considered to be distinguishable from other judicial review remedies in that they could be obtained against the Crown. However, given the decision of the HL in *M v Home Office* (1994), that distinction can also no longer be applied to injunctions.

## Injunctions

**14.25**  Injunctions were originally equitable remedies, but they now also operate in the public law domain. They may take one of two forms: a prohibitory injunction which, as its name implies, prohibits a party from performing a specified act; and a mandatory injunction, which orders a party to perform a specified act. It might be argued, therefore, that this form of relief is little different to mandatory and prohibiting orders. Indeed, in *M v Home Office*, Lord Woolf described these prerogative orders as being 'indistinguishable in their effect from final injunctions'. However, an advantage which injunctions have over either mandatory or prohibiting orders is that, as well as being granted as final injunctions, they may also be granted on an interim basis.

**14.26**  In *Factortame Ltd v Secretary of State for Transport* (1989), Lord Bridge reached the conclusion that an injunction could not be granted against a minister in judicial review proceedings. However, in the later case, *M v Home Office*, the facts of which were described earlier (see paras **3.27–3.28**), the HL arrived at a rather different conclusion. In overruling *Factortame* on this point, the HL unanimously decided that the language of s 31 of the Senior Courts Act 1981 was such that there was no justification for ruling that injunctions were not available against ministers and other officers of the Crown. Moreover, since injunctions were now available, it followed that interim injunctions were also available as against officers of the Crown.

**14.27**  The decision in *M v Home Office* is thus important in terms of the principle that it establishes. Nevertheless, in a public law context, whether or not an injunction will actually be granted against the Crown, or any other defendant for that matter, will depend upon the particular circumstances of the case, including whether the claimant has locus standi. Lord Woolf noted in *M v Home Office* that this newfound jurisdiction would only be exercised in the most limited circumstances and that, in the majority of situations, a declaration would be the most appropriate remedy in a claim for judicial review involving officers of the Crown.

## Interim declaration

**14.28** Formerly, it was the case that an interim declaration was a remedy not known to English law: see, for example, *Riverside Mental Health NHS Trust v Fox* (1994). In large part this was due to the belief that 'an interim declaration could have no practical purpose': see the remarks of Lord Woolf CJ in *Governor and Company of the Bank of Scotland v A Ltd* (2001). Now, however, the position has changed after developments in other jurisdictions showed this was not the situation which in turn made the case for reform in this country. Thus by virtue of CPR 25.1(b), the court has the power to grant an interim declaration at any time, including before the proceedings have started or after judgment has been given. In the case of the former, however, an interim remedy will only be made if the matter is urgent or it is otherwise desirable to do so in the interests of justice.

## Substitutionary remedy

**14.29** It will be remembered from Chapter **12** that the role of the court in judicial review proceedings is to determine the lawfulness of the decision-making process as opposed to the merits of the decision itself. It is not, therefore, for the judge to substitute his decision for that of the decision-maker. This orthodoxy is restated in CPR 54.19(2) and s 31(5)(a) of the Senior Courts Act 1981, as substituted by s 141 of the Tribunals, Courts and Enforcement Act 2007. These provide that where a court is making a quashing order in respect of a decision to which a claim relates, the court may remit the matter to the decision-maker and direct it to reconsider the matter and reach a decision in accordance with the judgment of the court. However, the orthodoxy is subsequently departed from in CPR 54.19(3), which provides that:

> Where the court considers that there is no purpose to be served in remitting the matter to the decision-maker it may, subject to any statutory provision, take the decision itself.

Section 31(5)(b) of the 1981 Act, as amended, refers in similar terms to the ability of the court hearing an application for judicial review to 'substitute its own decision for the decision in question'.

**14.30** The court's power to substitute its decision for that of the decision-maker is not, however, without limits. CPR 54.19(3) itself imposes a limit in parenthesis to the effect that where a statutory power is given to a tribunal, person, or other body, it may be the case that the court cannot take the decision itself. The power conferred by s 31(5)(b), as amended, is subject to three express limits. Thus it may only be exercised where: the decision in question was made by a court or tribunal; the decision in question has been quashed on the ground that there is an error of law; and without the error, there would have only been one decision which the court or tribunal could have reached. The sub-stitutionary remedy therefore amounts to a time-saving device rather than a significant new power for the courts. Support for this view is to be found in *R (Dhadly) v London Borough of Greenwich* (2001), where May LJ commented that: 'The circumstances in which r. 54.19(3) applies are essentially those where there is only one substantive deci-sion that is capable of being made and where it is a waste of time to send the thing back to the decision-making body'. Thus in *Thames Water Utilities Ltd (R on the application of) v Bromley Magistrates' Court* (2005), where the DC held that a district judge had wrongly determined that he did not have the jurisdiction to decide a preliminary point of law, the court resolved to determine the question of law itself in accordance with CPR 54.19 on the basis 'that no useful purpose would seem to be served by remitting the matter to the district judge'.

## Other public law remedies

**14.31** Although this chapter has focused on remedies for judicial review, it is generally recog-nized that there are two other public law remedies: habeas corpus; and quo warranto. Since neither is available in judicial review proceedings, they will not be considered further.

## FURTHER READING

Beatson, J, Matthews, M, and Elliott, M *Administrative Law: Text and Materials* (4th edn, 2011) OUP.

Bingham, Sir Thomas 'Should Public Law Remedies be Discretionary?' [1991] PL 64.

Cornford, T 'Administrative Redress: The Law Commission's Consultation Paper' [2009] PL 70.

Fordham, M *Judicial Review Handbook* (5th edn, 2008) Hart.

Fordham, M 'Monetary Awards in Judicial Review' [2009] PL 1.

Gould, M '*M v Home Office*: Government and the Judges' [1993] PL 568.

Law Commission *Administrative Law: Judicial Review and Statutory Appeals* (1994) (Law Com No 226).

Law Commission *Administrative Redress: Public Bodies and the Citizen* (2008) (Consultation Paper No 187).

Law Commission, *Administrative Redress: Public Bodies and the Citizen* (2010) (Law Com No 322).

Lewis, C *Judicial Remedies in Public Law* (4th edn, 2008) Sweet & Maxwell.

Manning, J *Judicial Review Proceedings: A practitioner's guide to advice and representation* (2nd edn, 2004) Legal Action Group.

Oliver, D 'Public Law Procedures and Remedies – Do we Need Them?' [2002] PL 91.

Pollard, D, Parpworth, N, and Hughes, D *Constitutional and Administrative Law: Text with Materials* (4th edn, 2007) OUP.

Sunkin, M 'Remedies Available in Judicial Review Proceedings' in *English Public Law* (2nd edn, 2009), edited by Feldman, OUP.

## SELF-TEST QUESTIONS

1   Speaking extra-judicially, Sir Thomas Bingham (as he then was) has answered the question 'should public law remedies be discretionary?' with a qualified 'yes'. Do you think it right that a remedy for a proven abuse of power should be a matter of discretion for the courts?

2   Does the practice of the courts in respect of mandatory orders, as described by Nolan LJ in *ex p Equal Opportunities Commission*, suggest a too lenient and deferential attitude towards ministers who have acted unlawfully?

3   What effect, if any, do you think the new remedies provided for in the CPR will have upon the courts' ability to deal with abuses of power?

4   Are the restrictions to which the substitutionary remedy is subject sufficient to prevent the courts from exceeding the scope of their supervisory jurisdiction in judicial review proceedings?

5   Commenting on the Law Commission's proposals for damages or monetary awards to be more widely available in judicial review, Fordham has suggested that they amount to 'a modest but important reform', and that in this age of 'bringing rights home', it is 'now time to bring remedies home'. Do you agree?

# PART V
## Alternative Means of Redress

PART V

Alternative Means of Redress

# 15

# Tribunals, inquiries, and the ombudsmen remedy

## SUMMARY

This chapter considers several ways in which disputes may be resolved by means other than recourse to the courts. It commences by examining tribunals and inquiries. These are now a part of everyday life given the ever-increasing role that the state plays in the life of the individual, and the potential which that creates for things to go wrong. Their characteristics are considered in a general manner, and an attempt is made to draw some distinctions both between them and between them and the courts. The important reforms made to the tribunal adjudicative system by the Tribunals, Courts and Enforcement Act 2007 will also be considered. The chapter concludes by considering the ombudsmen remedy in the public sector context. Since the office of the Parliamentary Commissioner was established in 1967, there has been an expansion in the areas in which ombudsmen may investigate complaints of maladministration. The discussion will therefore focus on some of the more established domestic ombudsmen, as well as on the European Ombudsman.

## The distinction between tribunals and inquiries

15.1 At the outset, it is necessary to distinguish between tribunals and inquiries. Whilst a tribunal is a permanent body which sits periodically, an inquiry is something which is established on an ad hoc basis. Inquiries are set up as a response to a particular event, eg the Southall Rail Crash. They may sit for many months and perhaps even years (eg the Second Bloody Sunday Inquiry), especially where their remit has been extended, but they are not permanent bodies. A further distinction which can be made relates to the decision-making powers of the two bodies. Whilst tribunals are empowered to make decisions which are binding on those parties subject to their jurisdiction, inquiries generally do not have formal decision-making powers. The end of an inquiry will often be marked by the publication of a report containing the inquiry's recommendations. It will generally be a matter for the appropriate minister to decide whether or not to act on those recommendations.

15.2 Broadly speaking, therefore, we can see that tribunals are concerned with matters of fact and law, whereas inquiries are concerned with wider policy issues. In the case of planning inquiries, however, it may be argued that they cut across the divide. They involve matters of law and policy and they are able to reach decisions rather than merely make recommendations, subject to a right of appeal to the Secretary of State.

## Tribunals

**15.3** The resolution of disputes is of course a task which the courts perform on a daily basis. However, courts are not the only forum for dispute resolution. Given the ever-increasing role of government within the modern state, as evidenced by initiatives such as the creation of the welfare state, the potential for disputes has been greatly increased. Although as Richardson and Genn have pointed out, 'Tribunals have been with us for centuries' in more recent times, it has been necessary to establish specialist tribunals to determine disputes arising in their own areas of expertise. Accordingly, there were approximately 70 tribunals in England and Wales which were administered by government departments and local authorities and which were under the direct supervision of the Council on Tribunals (now replaced by the Administrative Justice and Tribunals Council (paras **15.30–15.33**)). These included Employment Tribunals and Mental Health Review Tribunals. The creation and proliferation of statutory tribunals independent from the courts has been described by Baroness Hale as 'one of the most important and controversial features of the development of the legal system in the 20th century': see *R (on the application of Cart) v Upper Tribunal (Public Law Project and another intervening)* (2011) (para **15.26**).

### Tribunals and courts distinguished

**15.4** Although it is clear that both courts and tribunals perform an adjudicative function, they are distinct bodies. In *A-G v BBC* (1981), where the point at issue was whether a local valuation court was an 'inferior court' and hence protected by the law of contempt of court, the HL drew a distinction between the two. Lord Scarman observed that:

> I would identify a court in (or 'of') law, ie a court of judicature, as a body established by law to exercise, either generally or subject to defined limits, the judicial power of the state. In this context judicial power is to be contrasted with legislative and executive (ie administrative) power. If the body under review is established for a purely legislative or administrative purpose, it is part of the legislative or administrative system of the state, even though it has to perform duties which are judicial in character.

**15.5** It is normally the case that the name accorded to a body will indicate whether it is a court or tribunal. However, it is the nature of the function that the body performs which is important. Thus in *A-G v BBC* (1981), the HL held that a local valuation court was in fact a tribunal because it performed administrative functions. Conversely, despite its name, the Employment Appeal Tribunal is a court.

## Characteristics of tribunals

**15.6** In 1955, following the 'Crichel Down Affair' (para **11.16**), the Committee on Administrative Tribunals and Enquiries was set up under the chairmanship of Sir Oliver Franks. Its remit was to consider and make recommendations on the constitution and working of tribunals and the holding of inquiries.

**15.7** The Franks Committee reported in 1957 (Cmnd 218). It was of the opinion that the tribunal system should reflect what it described as three 'closely linked characteristics': openness, fairness, and impartiality. The committee later expanded on this theme when it observed that:

> In the field of tribunals openness appears to us to require the publicity of proceedings and knowledge of the essential reasoning underlying the decisions; fairness to require the adoption of a clear procedure which enables parties to know their rights, to present their case fully and to know the case which they have to meet; and impartiality to require the freedom of tribunals from the influence, real or apparent, of departments concerned with the subject-matter of their decisions.

**15.8** Richardson and Genn have drawn attention to two particular characteristics of tribunal adjudication: independence and the routine use of oral hearings. Although the latter can be said to fall within the Franks 'fairness' characteristic, independence is, as the authors point out, a closely related but nevertheless distinct characteristic from impartiality. Thus in *Gillies v Secretary of State for Work and Pensions* (2006), Baroness Hale remarked:

> Impartiality is the tribunal's approach to deciding the cases before it. Independence is the structural or institutional framework which secures this impartiality, not only in the minds of the tribunal members but also in the perception of the public.

**15.9** With regard to the choice between either a court or tribunal as the adjudicator in a particular dispute, the Franks Committee noted that: 'tribunals have certain characteristics which often give them advantages over the courts'. These characteristics were: cheapness, accessibility, freedom from technicality, expedition, and expert knowledge of the particular subject. However, as a general principle, the committee considered that 'a decision should be entrusted to a court rather than to a tribunal in the absence of special considerations which make a tribunal more suitable'.

## Cheapness

**15.10** It is patently the case that tribunals provide a cheaper means of resolving disputes than the courts. There is no equivalent of a court fee to be paid and, often, legal representation will be unnecessary. Where an individual is legally represented, the costs are likely to be less than in respect of court proceedings given that tribunals generally resolve disputes more quickly. This is important when it is remembered that Legal Aid is not generally available for disputes dealt with by tribunals.

## Accessibility

**15.11**   Tribunals are more accessible than the courts both physically and in the way in which they conduct their proceedings. Whilst there are several tribunals which meet only in one location, it is generally the case that tribunals will endeavour to sit in places which are convenient for those who wish to use them. Thus tribunals will often form local committees which meet across the country. Alternatively, a tribunal may travel around the country hearing cases. In the *Report of the Review of Tribunals* (paras **15.16–15.17**), it was noted that:

> It should never be forgotten that tribunals exist for users, and not the other way round.
> No matter how good tribunals may be, they do not fulfil their function unless they are
> accessible by the people who want to use them, and unless the users receive the help
> they need to prepare and present their cases.

## Freedom from technicality

**15.12**   Whilst we need to be aware of the dangers of over-generalization, it will often be the case that tribunal hearings are conducted in a more informal manner than court proceedings. Tribunals do not have the power to administer oaths and, generally, they do not adhere to the rules of evidence which are applied in the courts. The actual hearing itself is unlikely to be conducted in the formal manner of a court proceeding. The parties may all sit around the one table, and legal representation will often be unnecessary where legal points are not at issue.

## Expedition

**15.13**   Court proceedings can be slow and protracted. Tribunal hearings, by contrast, are generally more expeditious. In part this is due to the fact that the remit of a tribunal is narrower than that of a court, which may have to deal with a wide range of matters. It is also due to the fact that the expertise of the tribunal may enable it to quickly identify the issues and resolve them to the satisfaction of the parties.

## Expert knowledge of the particular subject

**15.14**   With the exception of the chairperson of a tribunal, who is normally a lawyer, the other members of a tribunal are all likely to have expertise in the particular field. This expertise will often mean that the facts of the case are rapidly understood, especially where they are similar to those of cases already heard by the tribunal. Although the court system does allow for a degree of judicial specialization, judges will still be required to hear cases which cut across a number of subject areas. Moreover, it is unlikely that a judge will have expertise on the facts of a case before the court.

## The statutory framework

**15.15**  The Tribunals and Inquiries Act 1992 consolidated the Tribunals and Inquiries Act 1971 and certain other enactments relating to tribunals and inquiries. Formerly, it provided for the statutory framework relating to the composition and procedure of tribunals. It still makes provision for the judicial control of tribunals. The Tribunals, Courts and Enforcement Act 2007 has created a new simplified statutory framework for tribunals. Accordingly, it will be necessary to have regard to provisions in both the 1992 and 2007 Acts. Prior to doing so, however, it is necessary to say something about the background to the reform of the tribunal system.

## Reforming the tribunal system

**15.16**  In May 2000 the Labour Government commissioned an independent review of the tribunals system which was carried out by Sir Andrew Leggatt, a former Lord Justice of Appeal, with the assistance of specialist advisers. In the subsequent *Tribunals for Users, One System One Service: Report of the Review of Tribunals* (August 2001), the Review team was of the opinion that of all the qualities that tribunals should possess, the most important was independence. However, the team felt that:

> nowadays when a department of state may provide the administrative support for a tribunal, may pay the fees and expenses of tribunal members, may appoint some of them, may provide IT support . . . and may promote legislation prescribing the procedure which it is to follow, the tribunal neither appears to be independent, nor is it independent in fact. *[emphasis added]*

**15.17**  In order to achieve independence and coherence, therefore, the Report recommended the establishment of a unified Tribunals Service, ie a common administrative service not unlike the courts service. The advantages of such a service were set out in the Report thus:

> It would raise their [tribunals'] status, while preserving their distinctiveness from the courts. In the medium term it would yield considerable economies of scale, particularly in relation to the provision of premises for all tribunals, common basic training, and the use of IT. It would also bring greater administrative efficiency, a single point of contact for users, improved geographical distribution of tribunal centres, common standards, an enhanced corporate image, greater prospects of job satisfaction, a better relationship between members and administrative staff, and improved career patterns for both on account of the size and coherence of the Tribunals Service.

**15.18**  In March 2003 the Government announced its intention to establish an Independent Tribunals Service within the then Department of Constitutional Affairs in order to break the link between a number of major tribunals and their sponsoring departments. The service was formally launched in April 2006. However, although this represented an important development in terms of ensuring tribunal independence and making better use of existing resources, it was rather less far reaching than the proposals set out in the White Paper *Transforming Public Services: Complaints, Redress and Tribunals* (July 2004) which are now largely reflected in the Tribunals, Courts and Enforcement Act 2007. Prior to considering these, it should be noted that as of 1 April 2011, the Tribunals Service amalgamated with the Courts Service to form a new agency, Her Majesty's Courts and Tribunals Service.

## The Tribunals, Courts and Enforcement Act 2007

**15.19** The 2007 Act received Royal Assent on 19 July 2007. It has created a new unified two-tier tribunal system by establishing two new tribunals: the First-tier Tribunal (FT); and the Upper Tribunal (UT) (s 3). These tribunals now exercise the jurisdictions of most of the tribunals previously administered by central government, with the exception of the employment tribunals and the Employment Appeal Tribunal. The *Explanatory Note* to the 2007 Act justifies this exclusion thus:

> The employment tribunals and the Employment Appeal Tribunal are excluded because of the nature of the cases that come before them, which involve one party against another, unlike most other tribunals which hear appeals from citizens against decisions of the state.

**15.20** Both the FT and the UT are divided into chambers (s 7 and Sch 4 para 4). In the case of the FT, there are: the Social Entitlement Chamber; the War Pensions and Armed Forces Compensation Chamber; the Health, Education and Social Care Chamber; the Tax Chamber; the Immigration and Asylum Chamber; and the General Regulatory Chamber. Various jurisdictions come under each of the Chambers. Thus, for example, on 18 January 2010, the Tribunals Service announced that a number of jurisdictions had transferred to the General Regulatory Chamber as part of the final phase of tribunal reform under the 2007 Act. These included the Gambling Appeals Tribunal and the Immigration Services Tribunal. The UT consists of four Chambers: the Administrative Appeals Chamber; the Tax and Chancery Chamber; the Lands Chamber; and the Immigration and Asylum Chamber. Each chamber has jurisdiction to hear appeals from the relevant FT on a point of law. In the light of the foregoing, it is perhaps not surprising that Baroness Hale has commented: 'The new structure may look neat but the diversity of jurisdictions accommodated means that it is not as neat as it looks': see *R (on the application of Cart) v Upper Tribunal (Public Law Project and another intervening)* (2011) (para **15.26**).

**15.21** Each FT and UT consists of legally-qualified members (judges) and other members. Members have either transferred from existing tribunals, or have been newly appointed, or have become a member of the FT by reason of an office they hold, eg a circuit court judge is automatically a member of both tribunals (ss 4(1) and 5(1)).

**15.22** A person is eligible to be appointed as a judge of the FT where he or she has a legal qualification and at least five years' post-qualification legal experience. A period of seven years' post-qualification experience is necessary to be appointed as a judge of the UT. In both cases, persons other than legally-qualified persons may be appointed if they have appropriate legal experience but not a relevant legal qualification. As the *Explanatory Note* suggests, this may apply to 'a legal academic or someone qualified in a European or Commonwealth jurisdiction'. The tribunal judiciary is overseen and lead by the Senior President of Tribunals. The holder of the post has various statutory powers and duties. These include: the power to make practice directions (s 23); the duty to maintain appropriate arrangements for training, welfare and guidance of judges and other tribunal members (Sch 2); and the power to assign judges and other members to chambers (Sch 4). In carrying out the functions of his office, the Senior President of Tribunals is required to have regard to the following:

- the need for tribunals to be accessible;
- the need for tribunal proceedings to be fair and handled quickly and effectively;
- the need for members of the tribunals to have the necessary legal or subject-matter expertise which relates to the matters they decide;
- the need to develop innovative methods of resolving disputes within the tribunals' jurisdiction (s 2(3)(a)–(d)).

**15.23** The FT and the UT both have the jurisdiction to review their own decisions (ss 9 and 10). Where the former sets aside one of its own decisions, it must either re-decide the matter or refer it to the UT. There is generally a right of appeal on a point of law from the FT to the UT (s 9). That right is subject to the need for permission from either the FT or the UT. Some decisions are, however, excluded from the general right of appeal. These include: any FT decision in respect of an appeal made pursuant to s 5(1) of the Criminal Injuries and Compensation Act 1995; any FT decision on an appeal under s 28(4) or (6) of the Data Protection Act 1998; or any FT decision on an appeal under s 60(1) or (4) of the Freedom of Information Act 2000.

**15.24** In addition to hearing appeals, the 2007 Act confers a jurisdiction on the UT to exercise judicial review powers: see ss 15–21. This jurisdiction mirrors that of the HCt (see Chapters **12–14**). Thus an application for review may only be made if permission has been obtained from the tribunal. That permission or leave cannot be granted unless the applicant has a sufficient interest in the matter to which the application relates. The UT has the power to grant relief in the form of: a mandatory order; a prohibiting order; a quashing order; a declaration; or an injunction. In deciding which form of relief to grant, it is required to apply the same principles that the HCt would apply on an application for judicial review. The UT is able to refuse to grant permission to make an application or refuse to grant any relief sought where there has been undue delay in making the application. Where a quashing order is made the UT, like the HCt, has the power to remit the matter to the decision-maker to reconsider or substitute its own decision for the decision in question (s 17(1)). The power to impose a substitutionary remedy has limits rather like those which apply in relation to the HCt. Thus the impugned decision: must have been made by a court or tribunal; must have been quashed on the ground of an error of law; and, without that error, there must have been only one decision that could have been reached (s 17(2)).

15.25 The judicial review jurisdiction of the UT is subject to a number of limits in the form of conditions specified in s 18 of the 2007 Act. Thus, for example, an application to be heard by the UT must not call into question anything done by the Crown Court (s 18(5)). Moreover, the judge hearing the application must have the necessary and appropriate experience. Essentially this means that they must be a HCt judge in England and Wales or the equivalent in Scotland or Northern Ireland. Where an application for judicial review is made to the HCt that satisfies all the relevant conditions, that court is required to transfer it to the UT: see s 31A of the Senior Courts Act 1981, as inserted by s 19 of the 2007 Act. Similar transfer provisions also apply in Scotland and Northern Ireland.

15.26 A related issue to the foregoing concerns the extent to which the decisions of the UT are themselves subject to judicial review. The 2007 Act is silent on the matter; there is nothing in the Act which seeks to oust or exclude judicial review of the unappealable decisions of the UT. Accordingly, in *R (on the application of Cart) v Upper Tribunal (Public Law Project and another intervening)* (2011), the SC was required to decide the issue. A unanimous court consisting of 7 JSCs held that as a matter of principle, the unappealable decisions of the UT are subject to judicial review. However, the scope of that principle was not unlimited. Given the additional pressure that would be asserted on courts' resources, and bearing in mind the need for a principled and proportionate approach which was consistent with the rule of law, it was held that the supervisory jurisdiction of the HCt would be confined to those cases where an important point of principle or practice was raised, or where there was some compelling reason for the case to be heard. The HCt's jurisdiction in this context therefore mirrors the basis on which permission to make a second-tier appeal to the Court of Appeal can be granted in accordance with s 13(6) of the 2007 Act. In delivering his opinion in *Cart*, one of three appeals raising the same issue, Lord Phillips observed:

> ...I have been persuaded that there is, at least until we have experience of how the new tribunal system is working in practice, the need for some overall judicial supervision of the decisions of the Upper Tribunal, particularly in relation to refusals of permission to appeal to it, in order to guard against the risk that errors of law of real significance slip through the system.

## Judicial control

15.27 Section 10 of the 1992 Act imposes a general duty on Sch 1 tribunals (and ministers) to give reasons for their decisions. The statement of reasons may be furnished either orally or in writing. Reasons need not be given, however, on the grounds of national security or to a person not primarily concerned with the decision. The general duty may also be overridden by, amongst other things, specific statutory provision for the giving of reasons. Where reasons are given, whether in accordance with s 10 or some other statutory provision, they form part of the final decision of the tribunal.

**15.28** Section 11 confers a right of appeal on a point of law in respect of the decisions of certain of the tribunals specified in Sch 1 to the 1992 Act. The appeal is to the HCt in the first instance, although a further appeal to the CA may be brought with the leave of the HCt or the CA.

**15.29** The 2007 Act has made two further reforms in the present context which ought to be identified. First, it enables tribunal procedural rules to be made by a Tribunal Procedure Committee (s 22 and Sch 5). Since these apply throughout the FT and UT, this reform puts an end to a system whereby fragmented rules were previously autonomously adhered to by individual tribunals. Secondly, the Act has established the Administrative Justice and Tribunals Council (AJTC).

## The Administrative Justice and Tribunals Council (AJTC)

**15.30** The AJTC is a non-departmental public advisory body set up under s 43 of the 2007 Act. Section 44 of the same Act abolished its predecessor, the Council on Tribunals. Schedule 7 to the 2007 Act makes detailed provision in relation to the Council. Part 2 of Sch 7 sets out the functions which the AJTC has in relation to: the administrative justice system; tribunals; and statutory inquiries. With regard to tribunals, the general functions of the Council are:

- to keep under review and report on the constitution and workings of the listed tribunals, ie the FT and UT, and tribunals listed by order made by the Lord Chancellor and the Scottish and Welsh Ministers;

- to consider and report on any other matter that relates to listed tribunals either generally or specifically and which the Council determines to be of specific importance; and

- to consider and report on any particular matter referred to the Council by the Lord Chancellor and the Scottish and Welsh Ministers which relates to either tribunals in general or a particular tribunal.

**15.31** The Council has between 10 and 15 members appointed by the Lord Chancellor and the Scottish and Welsh Ministers. The Parliamentary Commissioner for Administration (paras **15.44-15.45**) is an ex officio member of the Council. It performs many of its functions by committee. Presently the committees include an Education Tribunals Committee, a Health Committee, a Legal Committee, and an Access to Justice

Committee in addition to the Scottish Committee, which is expressly provided for in the 1992 Act. Its membership is determined by the Scottish Ministers. They may designate members of the Council as members of the Scottish Committee, or alternatively they may appoint non-Council members to the committee.

**15.32** The AJTC produces an annual report on the various aspects of its work during the course of that year. This is then laid before the Westminster and Scottish Parliaments, and the National Assembly for Wales, pursuant to para 21 of Sch 7 to the 2007 Act. In the annual report for 2008–09, for example, the Council considered, amongst other things, the implementation of the 2007 Act. Its predecessor, the Council on Tribunals, had earlier considered the implications for tribunals of the Human Rights Act 1998 (Annual Report 1997–8, HC 45). This is clearly an important issue for tribunals given that they are required to determine cases where Convention rights have been asserted, and to interpret legislation in a way which is compatible with the Convention (s 3 of the 1998 Act). In so doing, they have to have regard to the jurisprudence of the Convention institutions (s 2 of the 1998 Act). Moreover, the definition of 'public authority' in s 6 of the 1998 Act encompasses tribunals. Therefore, tribunals must strive to ensure that they do not act unlawfully by acting in a way which is incompatible with a Convention right, unless they are required to do so by primary legislation.

**15.33** At the time of writing, the AJTC is under threat of abolition: see the coalition Government's Public Bodies Bill, cl 1 and Sch 1. In its response to the consultation paper, 'Public Bodies Bill: Reforming the public bodies of the Ministry of Justice', CP 10/2011 (July 2011), the AJTC reiterated its disappointment that it had not been consulted prior to the publication of the abolition proposals. It regarded them as 'misguided' for a number of reasons. These included: that administrative justice is fundamentally important to citizens; that the Government appeared to have accepted that the functions assigned to the AJTC are valuable and should continue to be discharged; that the proposal to abolish the AJTC was founded on the flawed proposition that the provision of independent advice could be effectively discharged within a Government department; and that the financial savings likely to arise from abolition had been considerably overstated. In short, the AJTC was of the view that:

> ... it would be perverse to abolish a well-established, well-respected and well-connected body which – at relatively miniscule cost to the public purse – brings significant experience and expertise to the overview of administrative justice in the UK and which is in a unique position to put forward suggested improvements across the entire system of decision-making, complaints and appeals as it impacts on the daily lives of ordinary citizens.

The Ministry of Justice's consultation closed on 11 October 2011. It remains to be seen whether the AJTC's response has caused the Government to change its mind.

## Inquiries

**15.34** Inquiries may take one of two main forms: statutory inquiries, ie inquiries held in pursuance of a duty imposed by a statutory provision; and non-statutory inquiries.

### Statutory inquiries

**15.35** These may be held in a variety of different contexts. For example, such inquiries are quite common in the planning arena. By virtue of s 78 of the Town and Country Planning Act 1990, an applicant for planning permission who is aggrieved by the decision of the local planning authority has the right to appeal to the Secretary of State. In order to assist him in the determination of that appeal, the Secretary of State may cause a local public inquiry to be held. Where such an inquiry is held, it will be conducted by a planning inspector in accordance with the Town and Country Planning (Inquiries Procedure) (England) Rules 2000, SI 2000/1624, as amended. If, however, a particular planning matter raises questions of national or regional importance, or the scientific or technical aspects of the proposed development are of an unfamiliar nature, s 101 of the 1990 Act provides for the referral of the matter to a Planning Inquiry Commission (PIC). Where a referral is made, the functions and procedure to be followed by the PIC are set out in Part I of Sch 8 to the 1990 Act.

**15.36** It is evident that the procedure to be followed in a statutory inquiry will often be determined in an Act of Parliament or by rules or regulations made under that Act. However, where no such provision has been made, s 9 of the Tribunals and Inquiries Act 1992 confers a general power on the Lord Chancellor to make rules regulating inquiries' procedure.

**15.37** Inquiries have generally been regarded as being a part of the decision-making process rather than as the decision-makers. However, in the case of local planning inquiries, it is now commonplace for a decision to be made by a planning inspector in the exercise of powers delegated by the Secretary of State.

**15.38** Statutory public inquiries may be established under the Inquiries Act 2005 where particular events have caused or are capable of causing public concern, or where there is public concern that particular events have occurred (s 1(1)(a) and (b)). Formerly inquiries could be established under the Tribunals of Inquiry (Evidence) Act 1921, which was repealed by the 2005 Act. Under the 1921 Act, an inquiry could only be established following a resolution by both Houses of Parliament. Now, however, inquiries will be established at the discretion of a government minister. Fewer than 30 inquiries were held under the 1921 Act. More recently they covered matters such as the shootings at the Dunblane Primary School (1996) and the deaths of Dr Harold Shipman's patients (2003). Two inquiries were held in respect of the events that took place in Northern

Ireland on Sunday 30 January 1972 (Bloody Sunday): the Widgery Tribunal which reported in April 1972 and the tribunal under the chairmanship of the Law Lord, Lord Saville of Newdigate, which began sitting in 2000 and which did not publish its report until 15 June 2010. This latter tribunal was the subject of judicial review proceedings in respect of its decision to require military witnesses to disclose their names when giving evidence despite the inquiry's acceptance that the witnesses' fears that disclosure would endanger their lives were reasonable: see *R v Lord Saville of Newdigate, ex p A* (1999). The role of the court in such proceedings was described by Lord Woolf MR (as he then was) in the following terms:

> It is accepted on all sides that the tribunal is subject to the supervisory role of the courts. The courts have to perform that role even though they are naturally loath to do anything which could in any way interfere with or complicate the extraordinarily difficult task of the tribunal. In exercising their role, the courts have to bear in mind at all times that the members of the tribunal have a much greater understanding of their tasks than the courts. However, subject to the courts confining themselves to the well-recognised role on [claims] for judicial review, it is essential that they should be prepared to exercise that role regardless of the distinction of the body concerned and the sensitivity of the issues involved.

## Non-statutory public inquiries

15.39  Such inquiries are set up by government to look into matters of public interest or concern. Usually these entail public scandals or major disasters involving the loss of life. Thus more recently, the Government has set up inquiries into amongst other things: 'Arms to Iraq' (chaired by Sir Richard Scott VC); BSE (chaired by Lord Phillips); the Paddington Rail Crash (chaired by Lord Cullen); and the inquiry into the death of Dr David Kelly (chaired by Lord Hutton). Despite the diverse nature of these inquiries, they do share a common feature; they were all chaired by senior members of the judiciary. This has been a common practice over the years. In some cases, it has meant that a senior judge has presided over a number of public inquiries. Lord Cullen, for example, who was the Lord President of the First Division of the Court of Session in Scotland, presided over the inquiries into the Piper Alpha Oil Rig Disaster (1988–90) prior to his appointment to chair the Ladbroke Grove Rail Inquiry.

15.40  The Inquiries Act 2005 provides, inter alia, that a minister may appoint a judge as a member of an inquiry panel. However, where he proposes to do so, he must first consult a senior judge. Thus where he proposes to appoint a Court of Appeal or High Court or circuit judge, he must first consult the Lord Chief Justice: see s 10(1) of the 2005 Act. The practice of appointing judges to inquiries is therefore likely to continue in the future.

## The origins of ombudsmen

**15.41**  The term 'ombudsman' is Scandinavian in origin. Essentially it means a 'grievance man' or 'complaints officer'. The first modern ombudsman appeared in Sweden in 1809. However, the most significant development in terms of the spread of the ombudsman concept occurred in 1955, when Denmark elected its first ombudsman. The initial holder of that office, Professor Hurwitz, acted as something of an ambassador during his tenure. He made several trips to Britain which so captivated the public imagination that he received complaints from British citizens about the way in which they had been treated by public bodies in this country. His visits coincided with a growing feeling in Britain that something needed to be done in order to protect the individual against the increasing power of central government and the conduct of government officials.

### Incorporation in the UK

**15.42**  During his visits, as Stacey has noted, the Danish ombudsman spoke at meetings organized by JUSTICE, a group of lawyers committed to the idea of an ombudsman for the UK. He also had discussions with Sir John Wyatt who, as Director of Research for the Justice Committee, produced a report in 1961 which recommended that the UK should have an ombudsman. The Wyatt Report stimulated considerable interest in both the academic and popular press. Nevertheless, the government of the day rejected the idea of an ombudsman on the basis that the office would interfere with the prompt and efficient dispatch of business.

**15.43**  In its election manifesto prior to the general election of 1964, the Labour Party committed itself to the establishment of an ombudsman for central government with 'the right and duty to investigate and expose any misuse of government power as it affects the citizen'. Once elected, the new government set about drawing up legislative proposals which would fulfil its manifesto commitment. However, as Stacey notes, progress on the Bill was slow. This was partly due to the fact that many of the government departments represented on the relevant cabinet sub-committee took advantage of the opportunity to make a case for excluding their own department from the ombudsman's remit. Nevertheless, the Parliamentary Commissioner Act received Royal Assent on 22 March 1967.

## The Parliamentary Commissioner

**15.44**  The first thing to note about the Parliamentary Commissioner for Administration (the PCA) is the title of the office. Despite the fact that the holder of the office performs the role and functions of what would be called an 'ombudsman' in a different juris-diction, in the UK, PCA is the preferred official title. In the years following the crea-tion of the PCA, the ombudsman concept has spread domestically with the result that ombudsmen have appeared in other fields such as local government and the National Health Service. The holders of these offices are also known as commissioners rather than ombudsmen. More recently, however, we have seen the advent of ombudsmen in name as well as function. Thus, for example, the Courts and Legal Services Act 1990 established the office of the Legal Services Ombudsman.

## The functions of the PCA

**15.45** The role of the PCA is to investigate complaints of 'injustice' resulting from 'malad-ministration'. Despite the key nature of these concepts, neither is defined by the 1967 Act. However, during the passage of the Bill before Parliament, the minister responsi-ble, Richard Crossman, observed in the HC that 'maladministration' meant:

> *Bias, neglect, inattention, delay, incompetence, ineptitude, perversity, turpitude, arbitrariness and so on.*

## Maladministration

**15.46** The 'Crossman catalogue' represents the classic statement on the meaning of 'malad-ministration'. Nevertheless, as the words 'and so on' clearly indicate, it is not an exhaus-tive definition. Other forms of conduct not expressly referred to may also come within the definition of maladministration. A precise statutory definition would seem to have been avoided on the ground that it may have been unduly restrictive. Thus in the absence of a statutory definition, the PCA has a measure of flexibility in the conduct of investigations. Doubtless each person who has held the office since its creation has had his or her own working definition of what constitutes maladministration.

**15.47** In *R v Local Comr for Administration for the North and East Area of England, ex p Bradford Metropolitan City Council* (1979), the CA gave some consideration to the meaning of 'maladministration'. Although each judge expressed himself slightly differ-ently, a common thread emerges from the judgments: maladministration is concerned with the manner in which decisions are reached and the manner in which they are either implemented or not implemented. It is not concerned with the nature, quality, or reasonableness of the decision itself.

**15.48** Criticisms have been levelled at the term 'maladministration'. In the JUSTICE–All Souls report, *Administrative Justice* (1988), it was noted that the Commission for Local Administration in England felt that councillors and officials disliked the term. Moreover, that body argued that the term meant little to those who wished to lodge a complaint. One alternative may be to dispense with the term and instead allow the PCA to investigate any action which is 'unreasonable, unjust or oppressive' like her

New Zealand counterpart. This suggestion was made by JUSTICE in its publication *Our Fettered Ombudsman*.

**15.49** Recently, the present PCA has embarked upon what Kirkham has described as 'the most forthright attempt yet to demystify the concept of maladministration' with the publication of the *Principles of Good Administration*. These six principles, which were published to coincide with the PCA's 40th anniversary, may be summarized as follows:

- getting it right;
- being customer focused;
- being open and accountable;
- acting fairly and proportionately;
- putting things right;
- seeking continuous improvement.

**15.50** Behind each of these 'headline' statements lies a fuller evocation of the relevant principle. Thus, for example, the fourth principle, 'Acting fairly and proportionately', consists of the following:

- treating people impartially, with respect and courtesy;
- treating people without unlawful discrimination or prejudice, and ensuring no conflict of interests;
- dealing with people and issues objectively and consistently;
- ensuring that decisions and actions are proportionate, appropriate, and fair.

**15.51** In the foreword to her Annual Report for 2006–7 (HC 838), the present PCA described the principles as 'broad statements of what I believe bodies within the Ombudsman's jurisdiction should do to deliver good administration and customer service'. Continuing on the same theme, the PCA commented that the principles 'show the sorts of behaviour we expect and the tests we apply when determining complaints'. In other words, as well as reflecting good administrative practice, the principles also provide a benchmark against which maladministration may be judged. Thus as Kirkham has observed:

> The expectation must be that from now on ombudsman reports will ordinarily refer back to elements of the Principles in explaining findings of maladministration.

## Injustice in consequence of maladministration

**15.52** By definition, the wording implies that maladministration may exist without injustice and that injustice may occur in the absence of maladministration. However, in order for a complaint to be investigated, it is imperative that the complainant has personally suffered injustice as a consequence of maladministration. The link between the two concepts is therefore vitally important. It limits the class of persons who may have a complaint of maladministration investigated by the PCA and in this sense acts in a not dissimilar manner to the need to demonstrate a sufficient interest in order to bring a claim for judicial review (see Chapter **12**).

## Jurisdiction of the PCA

**15.53**  The bodies that are subject to the jurisdiction of the PCA are listed in Sch 2 to the 1967 Act. They include central government departments such as the Ministry of Defence, the Foreign and Commonwealth Office, the Home Office, and the Ministry of Justice, together with ministers and officials of such departments. Also included in the Schedule are a variety of other organizations, such as the Charity Commission, the Inland Revenue, and the Royal Mint, all of which are subject to a degree of ministerial responsibility.

**15.54**  The PCA's jurisdiction also extends to non-departmental public bodies which have executive or administrative functions that directly affect individuals and which would have been within the PCA's jurisdiction if carried out by a government department. In addition to these requirements, the bodies must also be subject to some degree of ministerial responsibility. Included in this category, therefore, are the Commission for Equality and Human Rights, the Arts Council, and the English Tourist Board. From time to time, as bodies are either established or abolished, references to them may either be inserted or deleted from Sch 2 as appropriate: see, for example, the Parliamentary Commissioner Order 2009, SI 2009/1754. Alternatively where a body is already listed, the description of that body may be altered. The PCA's office must therefore ensure that it remains up to date in respect of changes to the machinery of government, especially at a time when the coalition Government proposes to abolish a significant number of public bodies in a bill which is before Parliament at the time of writing.

## Matters excluded from the PCA's jurisdiction

**15.55**  These are provided for in s 5 of and Sch 3 to the 1967 Act. Essentially they fall into two categories: matters where a complainant has an alternative remedy available to him from a tribunal or court; or the matters specified in Sch 3. Certain matters may of course be excluded on both grounds. In the case of the former category, the bar on an investigation does not apply if the PCA is satisfied that the circumstances are such that it is not reasonable to expect the person aggrieved to resort to the alternative remedy. Clearly, therefore, the PCA has a discretion in the matter. In *R v Comr for Local Administration, ex p Croydon London Borough Council* (1989), Woolf LJ (as he then was) observed that in exercising this discretion, the ombudsman should not be concerned with whether or not the complainant would succeed in court, but rather with whether the court was the appropriate forum. Moreover, the availability of an alternative remedy was a matter to be considered both before and during the course of an investigation.

**15.56** Writing extra-judicially on the same theme, Lord Woolf has expressed the view that the PCA and her local government counterpart ought to have the power to refer a matter to court either before, during, or on the completion of an investigation. Such a power would be exercisable where a significant point of law was involved or where the courts were in a better position than the ombudsman to grant a remedy. In the PCA's annual report for 1980, the then holder of the office explained that:

> As a matter of practice, where there appears on the face of things to have been a substantial legal wrong for which, if proved, there is a substantial legal remedy, I expect the citizen to seek it in the courts and I tell him so. But where there is doubt about the availability of a legal remedy or where the process of law seems to be cumbersome, slow and expensive for the objective to be gained, I exercise my discretion to investigate the complaint myself.

## Schedule 3 matters

**15.57** Some matters are regarded as being outside the jurisdiction of the PCA even though, on the face of it, they fall within the scope of her function. They are exhaustively set out in Sch 3 to the 1967 Act. For present purposes, they may be summarized as follows:

- foreign affairs, including consular matters, matters relating to the dominions, and extradition;
- action taken by or with the authority of the Secretary of State for investigating crime or protecting state security (including passport matters);
- the commencement or conduct of civil or criminal proceedings before any court;
- the prerogative of mercy;
- action taken by or on behalf of the Minister of Health or Secretary of State by a Regional, Area, or District Health Authority or various specified hospital boards;
- contractual or commercial transactions of a government department or authority to which the Act applies, except (i) the compulsory purchase of land, or (ii) the disposal of land so acquired;
- personnel matters; or
- the grant of honours, awards, or privileges within the gift of the Crown.

**15.58** Whether or not all of these exclusions are justified is a moot point. In the case of the prerogative of mercy, for example, the effect of the exclusion is lessened by the fact that in principle, its exercise is justiciable in the light of *R v Secretary of State for the Home Department, ex p Bentley* (1994) (para **4.29**). Personnel matters are more problematic. The justification for their exclusion is that they may be resolved by other means, eg before a tribunal. In the words of the PCA in his Annual Report for 1988, his 'proper concern was with complaints qua citizen, and not with complaints qua employee, or qua supplier of goods or services to a department or public body'. Nevertheless, on several occasions, the Select Committee on the PCA has recommended that public service personnel matters should fall within the PCA's jurisdiction, as they do in the case of her New Zealand counterpart.

**15.59**   The exclusion of commercial and contractual issues from the PCA's jurisdiction has also attracted criticism, especially now that the contracting out of the provision of public services has become commonplace. Thus as Kirkham has opined:

> ...*in an era when private sector provision has become an increasingly important feature of government, the exclusion on contractual and commercial arrangements needs to be monitored to ensure that this governance technique is not used as a means by which to prevent accountability.*

## The 'MP filter'

**15.60**   By virtue of s 5 of the 1967 Act, a person who claims to have suffered injustice in consequence of maladministration must complain in writing to an MP. An investigation by the PCA will only take place, however, where the MP has referred the complaint to her (with the consent of the complainant) and has requested an investigation. Thus in an application for judicial review of the PCA's decision not to respond to a previous complaint, it was held that the failure to make the complaint through an MP was a 'complete answer' to that part of the proceedings: see *R (on the application of Senior-Milne) v The Parliamentary and Health Service Ombudsman* (2009). Normally, the expectation would be that an aggrieved person would complain to his constituency MP. This view is reinforced by the PCA's website which helpfully provides a list of all MPs, by name and constituency, for those who may be in doubt as to the identity of their MP. It also accords with the convention that MPs do not involve themselves in the affairs of another constituency. Nevertheless, since the 1967 Act is not prescriptive on this matter, it follows that a complaint could be made to an MP other than the complainant's constituency MP.

**15.61**   Unlike almost all other ombudsmen (Sri Lanka and France have a similar stipulation), the public have no direct access to the PCA. In the White Paper which preceded the 1967 Act, the government of the day stressed that it had no intention to 'create any new institution which would erode the functions of Members of Parliament'. Instead, by creating the PCA, it wished to provide MPs with 'a better instrument which they can use to protect the citizen'. In effect, therefore, the purpose of the MP filter was to allay fears that the PCA would disturb the relationship that had traditionally existed between an MP and his constituents. The requirement does ensure that an MP is kept in touch with the problems which his constituents are faced with in their contact with the machinery of the state. Additionally, it may serve as a means of sparing the PCA from needless work since complaints which are received may be capable of being resolved by the MP himself.

**15.62**  In its First Report of 1993–4 (HC 33), the Select Committee on the PCA noted that in response to a questionnaire which it sent to MPs, 38.4% of the 333 who responded were in favour of direct access to the PCA, whereas 58% were against it. On this basis, the Select Committee observed that:

> many Members value their role as champions of their constituents' complaints and are unwilling to see this constitutional function in any way by-passed or diminished.

**15.63**  Ten years later, however, the position appeared to have changed. A survey conducted jointly by the Public Administration Select Committee and the PCA's office revealed that 66% of the MPs who responded were in favour of the removal of the MP filter. However, since the response rate for the later survey was only 32% of eligible MPs, its findings should be treated with caution. Nevertheless, it is clear that there is growing support within the HC for the removal of the MP filter.

**15.64**  There is also extra-parliamentary support for affording direct access to the PCA. Thus in delivering the Gabriel Ganz Lecture at Southampton University, (October 2009), Ann Abraham, the then PCA, stated:

> I suggest that the Government should accept the recommendations of successive Parliamentary Committees and more recently of the Law Commission that the MP filter should now be removed. This need not, indeed must not, in any way detract from the central relationship between my office and Parliament but it will, I believe, signal the importance of direct citizen access for any modern ombudsman institution, both as an instrument of transparent accountability and as a sign of commitment to equal and unfettered entitlement.

**15.65**  More recently, the PCA has drawn attention to the fact that due to the filter, the dissolution of Parliament prior to the May 2010 general election meant that the service had to be suspended for five weeks: see the foreword to the *Annual Report 2010–11*. A general public survey (2,070 face-to-face interviews) and a survey of PCA customers (90 people who had previously approached the PCA with a complaint) were carried out on behalf of the PCA in late 2010. Their findings suggest that there is also some public support for allowing direct access to the PCA: see *The MP Filter: Summary of Opinion Surveys* (June 2011). Thus 19% of the 2,070 respondents in the public survey stated that the MP filter would make them less likely to use the PCA. Their reasons for this included: that it would delay the case; that they would rather deal with the case themselves; that they did not trust MPs; that they did not support their MP's political party; and that it was 'too much hassle'. It should be noted, however, that 11% of respondents said that the MP filter would make them more likely to use the PCA. Their main reasons for this view were that an MP's involvement would ensure that their case was given proper consideration, and they would prefer someone else to advocate their case.

**15.66**  The Law Commission has also contributed to the debate surrounding the utility and future of the MP filter. In its consultation paper, *Administrative Redress: Public Bodies and the Citizen* (2008) (Consultation Paper No 187), it took the preliminary view that 'there is a strong case for abolition of the MP filter' based on a number of reasons, including that the filter is no longer necessary to control the flow of complaints to the PCA, and that MPs could be kept in touch with their constituents' concerns simply by being notified when a complaint has been made to the PCA. In its final report, it noted that there was more support for a dual-track system, ie where the MP filter would be retained but not as a requirement, than there was for outright abolition. It further noted that, 'given the importance of the issue, this is a subject that requires more thought': see *Administrative Redress: Public Bodies and the Citizen* (2010) (Law Com No 322). In a later consultation, it provisionally proposed a dual-track system: see *Public Services Ombudsmen* (2010) (Consultation Paper No 196). Although some consultees, most notably JUSTICE, wanted the proposals to go further and abolish the filter, the Law Commission ultimately decided to recommend that the MP filter be repealed in its current form and replaced by a dual-track system. This was seen as an acceptable compromise in that it would make direct access possible whilst at the same time allowing those who wished to involve their constituency MP to continue to do so: see *Public Service Ombudsmen* (2011) (Law Com No 329).

**15.67**  If the MP filter is to be reformed or abolished, it is likely that primary legislation will be required. In the meantime, where the PCA's office receives complaints directly from members of the public, it will continue to inform the complainant that the matter must be referred to the office by an MP.

## An under-utilized remedy

**15.68**  Since 1993 there has generally been a steady increase in the number of new complaints that the PCA has received annually. The annual figures have nevertheless not achieved the expected caseload of 6,000–7,000 complaints per annum when the office was first established. This may well suggest that the PCA is an under-utilized remedy.

**15.69**  The under-utilization of the PCA remedy may be explained on the basis of a lack of public awareness of the office. The publication of annual reports does help to keep the public informed of the nature and scope of the PCA's work, but in truth these are unlikely to be read by people other than those with a particular interest in the field. Occasionally, a particular investigation may generate interest amongst the media, as was the case with the report on occupational pension schemes (paras **15.78–15.81**). Additionally, maintaining pages on the internet represents a further means by which the work of the PCA can reach a wider audience. Nevertheless, in 2003, MORI carried out an Ombudsmen Awareness Survey on behalf of the PCA, the Health Service Commissioner, and the Local Government Commissioners, which revealed, inter alia, that of those surveyed (focus groups and approximately 1,900 interviewees), more than half had not heard of any of these ombudsmen. Awareness of the PCA (37%) was less than for the other two ombudsmen: Health Service (45%) and Local Government (44%). These figures compared unfavourably with public awareness of other bodies which deal with complaints: Citizens' Advice Bureau (95%); Police Complaints Authority (as it then was) (72%); and OFSTED (69%). Recognition of the ombudsmen was found to be particularly low amongst the younger, unskilled/unemployed, and black and ethnic minority groups. It is clear, therefore, that further initiatives may be necessary in order to make the general public properly aware of the ombudsman remedy.

## Time limit

**15.70** Section 6(3) of the 1967 Act provides that a complaint must be made to an MP no later than 12 months from the date on which the person aggrieved first had notice of the matter alleged in the complaint. This time limit, which is more generous than the three months provided for in respect of bringing a claim for judicial review (para **12.69**), runs from when the person became aware of the matter rather than from the date on which the matter arose. Several months may therefore pass before the person aggrieved has the relevant knowledge.

**15.71** The PCA has the discretion to investigate complaints not made within the 12-month time limit where she considers that special circumstances make it proper to do so. If, for example, the aggrieved person's poor health has prevented him from making the complaint within 12 months, the PCA may nevertheless decide to investigate the complaint. The danger in extending the time limit too greatly is that the complaint loses its freshness. Memories may fade and the facts of the complaint may become distorted with time. In practice, it is likely that the PCA will carry out a preliminary examination of a time-barred case, to determine whether it has any merit, before exercising her discretion to overlook the time limit.

## Screening and investigation

**15.72** Once a complaint has been referred to the PCA by an MP, a decision must be made as to whether or not to carry out a full investigation. This will be preceded by an initial screening of the complaint by the PCA's officers. In April 2005, the PCA's office adopted a new approach for handling complaints. Thus a distinction is no longer made between a formal investigation and a complaint which is dealt with more informally. Moreover, throughout the investigation there is a greater emphasis on dialogue with the complainant than was formerly the case. This is in order to ensure that the PCA's office fully understands the nature of the complaint at the outset and to make the complainant more aware of the investigation process.

## Procedure for investigating a complaint

**15.73** Where the PCA has determined that a complaint has been duly made under the 1967 Act, she may propose to conduct an investigation. If this is the case, s 7(1) requires her to afford an opportunity to those who are the subject of the allegations either personally, or as principal officer of the department or authority concerned, to comment on the allegations contained in the complaint. The PCA and her officers therefore carry out an active investigation into the complaint. Unlike court proceedings, which typically involve a judge hearing representations on both sides of an argument and then adjudicating on the matter, the complainant need play no further role in the investigation once it has begun. Moreover, an investigation also differs from court proceedings, which are generally held in public, in that it is conducted in private.

**15.74** In terms of the conduct of the investigation itself, the PCA has a wide discretion as to the procedure to be followed. She may require any person, including any minister or officer of the department or authority concerned, who is able to furnish information or produce documents relevant to an investigation, to do so. She also enjoys the same powers as the courts in terms of the attendance and examination of witnesses and the production of documents. It is an offence to obstruct an investigation without lawful excuse or to behave in a manner which would, if the investigation was a court proceeding, constitute a contempt of court (s 9).

## Reports

**15.75** On the completion of an investigation, s 10 of the 1967 Act requires the PCA to send a report of her findings to the MP who referred the complaint to her or, if that person is no longer an MP, to another appropriate MP. This requirement ensures, therefore, that the MP is kept informed of the outcome of his constituent's complaint. Similarly, an MP will receive a statement of reasons from the PCA when it has been decided not to investigate a complaint. In both cases, the MP will need to make this information available to the complainant since the Act does not require the PCA to provide the complainant with a report. In practice, the PCA sends the MP an additional copy for him to send on to the complainant. Where an investigation has been conducted, a report of its findings must also be sent to the head of the department or authority concerned and to any person alleged to have been responsible for the action which was the subject matter of the complaint. In practice, final reports are preceded by draft reports from the PCA's office which are shared with complainants as well as with the bodies complained against (Annual Report, 2004–05).

**15.76** Generally speaking, where an investigation has found in favour of the complainant, ie that there has been injustice in consequence of maladministration, that injustice will be remedied by the relevant public authority or department. Nevertheless, it should be noted that the PCA does not have enforcement powers to ensure that her recommendations are complied with. If the PCA believes that an injustice has not or will not be remedied, she may lay before Parliament a special report on the case (s 10(3)). This additional publicity may have the desired effect.

**15.77** In 2005, the PCA laid a special report before Parliament pursuant to s 10(3) in respect of an MOD ex gratia compensation scheme for those interned by the Japanese during the Second World War: see HC 324, 13 July 2005. In the opinion of the PCA, the scheme, the criteria for which changed at a late stage thus making 1,000 British subjects no longer eligible for compensation, fell short of the standards of public administration that citizens are entitled to expect from public bodies. The report was laid because the Government accepted some but not all of the PCA's recommendations.

**15.78** On 15 March 2006, the PCA published a further special report, *Trusting in the Pensions Promise: Government bodies and the security of final salary occupational pensions*, HC 984, in which it was found that the Department of Work and Pensions (and the Department of Social Security before it) had been guilty of maladministration that had caused injustice to as many as 125,000 people who had lost all or part of their final salary occupational pensions due to the winding up of their pension schemes. The PCA made a number of recommendations including that the Government ought to consider making arrangements to restore core pension entitlements to those adversely affected. In its response published in June 2006, the Government rejected virtually all of the PCA's findings and recommendations.

**15.79** The HC Public Administration Select Committee subsequently examined the issues surrounding what was the Government's second rejection of a PCA report in less than a year: see *The Ombudsman in Question: the ombudsman's report on pensions and its constitutional implications*, HC 1081, sixth report of 2005–6, 20 July 2006. In that report, the Committee quoted the PCA who acknowledged that the Government may 'reject recommendations that I may make, after proper consideration of the public interest, and other calls on the public purse, and any other relevant matters'. However, both the Committee and the PCA were concerned by 'the government's increasing willingness not just to dispute her recommendations, but her findings of maladministration as well'. While the former is an inevitable consequence of the PCA's lack of enforcement powers and the non-binding nature of her recommendations, the latter raises important constitutional issues since if the Government were to routinely reject the PCA's findings of maladministration, it would cast serious doubt on the continuing role of the PCA. Moreover, it would potentially cause a fracture in the relationship between the executive and Parliament since the PCA is Parliament's ombudsman.

**15.80** The pensions scheme dispute between the PCA and the Government subsequently transferred to the courts when four of those adversely affected by the winding up of their pension schemes sought to challenge the Government's decision to reject the PCA's findings. In *R (on the application of Bradley) v Secretary of State for Work and Pensions* (2007), the Admin Ct quashed the Secretary of State's rejection of the PCA's finding of maladministration in relation to the provision of misleading information and directed the minister to reconsider the PCA's first recommendation relating to the restoration of core pension entitlements. Other parts of the claim were, however, rejected. Thus Bean J upheld the Secretary of State's rejection of the PCA's first finding in so far as it related to her conclusion that the maladministration that had been identified had caused injustice to all those individuals who had suffered losses after the winding up of their occupational pension schemes. Had the finding:

> been limited to the causation of injustice to any scheme member who had read the offending leaflets, or who relied on advice from colleagues or others who in turn relied on the leaflets, it would not be open to challenge.

In other words, it was the breadth of the PCA's finding that made it susceptible to challenge. Importantly, on the question whether the PCA's findings of fact are generally binding, Bean J concluded that like the Local Government Commissioners, they are binding, unless they 'are objectively shown to be flawed or irrational, or peripheral, or there is genuine fresh evidence to be considered'.

**15.81**  The Secretary of State subsequently appealed against the quashing of his decision to reject the PCA's first finding, and the claimants appealed against the upholding of the Secretary of State's decision to reject the other two findings: see *R (Bradley and others) v Secretary of State for Work and Pensions* (2009). In dismissing the Secretary of State's appeal, the CA was of the view that his decision to reject the PCA's finding of maladministration in relation to potentially misleading government information had been irrational. The claimants' appeal succeeded in part. The CA was of the view that the judge had erred in upholding the Secretary of State's rejection of the PCA's finding that maladministration had caused some injustice. In its opinion, the minister had acted irrationally in rejecting that finding.

**15.82**  A final instance of conflict between the PCA and the executive to note concerns a PCA investigation into the prudential regulation of the Equitable Life Assurance Society. On 16 July 2008, the PCA laid a report before both Houses of Parliament 'following perhaps the most complex investigation ever undertaken by my office': see *Equitable Life: A Decade of Regulatory Failure*, HC 815-I. In it, the PCA made 10 findings of maladministration that had led to injustice in the form of: financial loss; lost opportunities to make informed savings and investment decisions; and a sense of outrage amongst the complainants. Accordingly, the PCA recommended that the Government: apologize to those adversely affected by serial regulatory failure; and establish and fund a compensation scheme. These recommendations were subsequently endorsed by the Public Administration Select Committee. In response, the Government accepted in full five of the PCA's findings of maladministration, accepted a further four in part, and rejected one. Additionally, whilst it was prepared to apologize to policy holders, it was not prepared to establish and provide for a compensation scheme. Instead, it envisaged making some ex gratia payments to some of the affected persons: see Cm 7538. Not unreasonably, the PCA was 'deeply disappointed that the Government chose to reject my findings that I had made, when I was acting independently on behalf of Parliament and after a detailed and exhaustive investigation'. Thus the PCA observed:

> Within the scheme governing the operation of my office as Parliament has established it, whether the response of the Government to my report is adequate or whether instead it constitutes an inappropriate attempt to act as judge and jury in its own cause is now a matter for Parliament to consider and debate.

**15.83** The Equitable Life saga finally drew to a close when the Equitable Life (Payments) Act 2010 became law. In the opinion of the PCA, the coalition Government's decisions relating to the payment of compensation were not incompatible with her earlier recommendations. She did comment, however, that 'having heard many accounts of hardship from policyholders over the years, I understand the disappointment of those whose circumstances mean they are excluded from the compensation scheme' (foreword to her Annual Report 2010–11).

**15.84** Section 10(4) of the 1967 Act requires the PCA to lay an annual report before Parliament detailing the work of the office during that year. The figures presented in the 2010–11 Annual Report relate to various matters, including the public bodies falling within the PCA's jurisdiction which are most complained about. During 2010–11, the government departments most complained about were: the Ministry of Justice; the Home Office; the Department for Work and Pensions; and the Department for Environment, Food and Rural Affairs.

## Ombudsmen of the devolved institutions

**15.85** The electoral arrangements, composition, structure, and powers of the devolved institutions in Scotland and Wales have previously been discussed in Chapter **8**. For present purposes, it should be noted that the establishment of a national Parliament or Assembly also created the need for a parliamentary ombudsman in both countries. The powers and responsibilities of the ombudsmen are broadly similar to those of the PCA and are set out in either primary or secondary legislation. In respect of the Scottish PCA, see the Scotland Act 1998 (Transitory and Transitional Provisions) (Complaints of Maladministration) Order 1999, SI 1999/1351. In the case of Wales, the Office of the Welsh Administration Ombudsman was established by virtue of s 111 of and Sch 9 to the Government of Wales Act 1998. Now, however, this office has been abolished along with various other Welsh ombudsmen offices and a new unified ombudsman service is provided for: see the Public Services Ombudsman (Wales) Act 2005. Despite national differences relating to the bodies subject to the ombudsmen's jurisdiction, eg the Scottish PCA is able to consider complaints against a number of cross-border public bodies where the action complained of relates to a devolved matter, the concept of maladministration causing injustice lies at the heart of these ombudsmen schemes as it does in relation to the English public sector ombudsmen. In Northern Ireland, the establishment of the office of the PCA (now known as the Assembly Ombudsman for Northern Ireland) predates the 1998 devolution legislation.

# The Health Service Commissioner

15.86 Complaints relating to the National Health Service hospitals were excluded from the jurisdiction of the PCA by Sch 3 to the 1967 Act. This was by no means a popular decision. In the years that followed, bodies such as the Select Committee on the PCA recommended that the Commissioner should be entitled to investigate complaints about hospitals. However, when the Government decided to act, it chose a different option to that advocated by the Select Committee. Instead of extending the jurisdiction of the PCA, the Government opted to establish a separate Health Service Commissioner for Scotland, England, and Wales. This was achieved by the National Health Service (Scotland) Act 1972 and the National Health Service Reorganisation Act 1973, respectively. Ironically, despite the creation of the separate posts, they have in fact been held jointly by the PCA since 1973. This is due to the fact that the office of the PCA has received fewer complaints than was originally expected (para **15.68**).

## Jurisdiction

15.87 The jurisdiction of the Health Service Commissioner (HSC) was originally somewhat limited. In addition to the customary exclusion in respect of personnel matters, the HSC was excluded from investigating complaints relating to clinical decisions or family health service practitioners, ie general medical practitioners, dentists, opticians, and pharmacists. The exclusion of clinical decisions meant that from the outset, the HSC had to reject large numbers of complaints that he received. More recently, however, the jurisdiction of the HSC has been expanded. The consolidating Health Service Commissioners Act 1993 was amended in 1996 with the result that the HSC may now investigate complaints relating to clinical decisions and family health service practitioners. In the case of the former, internal professional advisers (a GP, hospital consultants, a nurse, a dentist, and a pharmacist) play a crucial role in the consideration of a case. They identify cases where external professional advice needs to be obtained which, according to the HSC's Annual Report 1998–9, will always be necessary where a clinical investigation is carried out. When considering the clinical judgments of clinicians, the HSC is 'not looking for leading edge practice'. The standard which she applies 'is whether they have acted reasonably, in a way that a patient has a right to expect from a competent clinician' (Annual Report 1998–9, para **3.4**).

15.88 In his 1998–9 Annual Report, a former HSC expressed concern about his 'inability to investigate complaints against GPs who retire or cease NHS work after the events complained of – or even during my investigation'. That inability arose from the wording of the 1993 Act which precluded such investigations. The clear injustice which could result from this lacuna was a matter which attracted the attention of the Consumers' Association. Accordingly, it drafted a Bill to amend the 1993 Act so as to provide for the possibility of an investigation into an action of a person who was a health service provider at the relevant time, but who had since ceased to be either due to retirement or otherwise. The Bill, which was introduced as a Private Members' Bill, subsequently became the Health Service Commissioners (Amendment) Act 2000. The end of this anomaly was subsequently welcomed by the HSC.

15.89 In common with the PCA and the Local Government Commissioners, the HSC is not entitled to conduct an investigation where a complainant has a right of appeal to a tribunal or a remedy before a court of law. However, she may do so if she considers that in the particular circumstances, it is not reasonable to expect the complainant to pursue an alternative remedy. Potential difficulties arise here given that complaints relating to clinical decisions may also form the basis of a medical negligence action. The HSC has taken the view that in these circumstances, it is for the complainant to decide which route to take. If the complainant expresses an intention to take legal proceedings, this precludes an investigation by the HSC.

15.90 Although the HSC has a wide discretion as to whether or not she should embark upon or continue an investigation, it is not a discretion without limits. The HSC does not have the power to conduct investigations at large. Moreover, the scope of an investigation is limited by the matters stated in a complaint; the ambit of a complaint cannot be extended beyond what it contains.

*R (Cavanagh) v Health Service Commissioner for England (2006)*: The third claimant's daughter suffered from epilepsy and learning and communication difficulties. She was diagnosed as having a vitamin B12 deficiency and started on a course of injections which, in her parents' view, had a tangible beneficial effect. The unit in which she was treated was subsequently closed down because of doubts over the integrity of its management. The third claimant made a complaint to the HSC about the Trust's decision to close the unit. The HSC carried out an investigation and rejected the complaint. She found that the shortcomings in the treatment of the girl were the combined fault of her doctors (the first and second claimants). She based this finding on two reports produced by consultants which were damning in their judgment of the doctors' professional competence. The claimants' sought judicial review of the HSC's findings. They contended that the investigation: exceeded the HSC's powers; had been conducted unfairly; and had reached some untenable conclusions. At first instance the first two grounds were completely rejected and the third was accepted in part. The claimants' appealed. CA held: allowing the appeals, that the HSC had exceeded her powers in carrying out the investigation. The scope of that investigation was limited to the matters complained about, ie the closure of the unit. The question of how vitamin B12 therapy came to be prescribed and administered lay outside the complaint and the Trust's response to it. Since the report had exceeded the HSC's powers not technically or marginally but substantially, it was vitiated in its entirety.

## Alternative complaints procedure

**15.91** There is also a presumption in the 1993 Act that a complaint should first be pursued through the NHS complaints procedure (the Local Authority Social Services and National Health Service Complaints (England) Regulations 2009, as amended) before the HSC can investigate the matter. Once again, however, this presumption may be overridden if the HSC considers that it is not reasonable to expect this to have happened. In practice, the HSC receives many complaints that have not exhausted and may not even have embarked upon the NHS procedure. These are seldom investigated unless the HSC takes the view that the NHS procedure is unlikely to resolve the complaint.

## Procedure for complaints

**15.92** A complaint must be made in writing to the HSC either by the person aggrieved or, where that person has died, by a personal representative, a family member, or some other suitable representative of the deceased. Thus unlike complaints to the PCA or the Local Government Commissioners, complaints to the HSC do not have to be made through an elected representative. The time limit for making a complaint is one year from the date on which the complainant became aware of the matters complained of. This time limit may be extended if the HSC considers that it is reasonable to do so. An investigation may follow if the complainant has suffered injustice or hardship due to:

- a failure in a service provided by a health service body;
- a failure of such a body to provide a service which it was the function of the body to provide; or
- maladministration connected with any other action taken by or on behalf of such a body.

**15.93** Assuming that an investigation is carried out and that the complaint is found to be justified, the HSC may seek an apology for the complainant. Alternatively, she may seek to ensure that a decision is changed or that an administrative practice is no longer followed. Damages are not a remedy recommended by the HSC and therefore if this is what a complainant really seeks, they ought to pursue legal proceedings.

# The Local Government Commissioners

**15.94** Complaints relating to local authorities were not included in the jurisdiction of the PCA under the 1967 Act. This amounted to a significant void which was the subject of criticism from JUSTICE, amongst others. Eventually that void was filled by the establishment of the Commission for Local Administration in accordance with Part III of the Local Government Act 1974. In practice, therefore, complaints against local government are dealt with in England by three Commissioners who operate on a regional basis, and in Wales by the unified Public Services Ombudsman.

## Jurisdiction

**15.95** The Local Government Commissioners (LGCs) exercise functions which are broadly comparable with those of the PCA. Like the PCA, they are empowered to investigate complaints where it is alleged that a member of the public has sustained 'injustice in consequence of maladministration'. Originally, complaints had to be referred to a LGC by a member of the local authority involved with a request that the matter be investigated. Now, however, as a consequence of an amendment made by the Local Government Act 1988, it is possible to by-pass this equivalent of the 'MP filter' and complain in writing direct to the LGC.

**15.96** As with complaints to the PCA, there is a 12-month time limit on the bringing of a complaint, although this can be extended where the LGC considers it reasonable to do so (s 26(4) of the 1974 Act). Prior to initiating an investigation, the LGC must be satisfied that the complaint has been brought to the attention of the authority to which it relates and that the authority has been given a reasonable opportunity to investigate, and reply to the complaint (s 26(5)(a)). Alternatively, as a consequence of an amendment made by the Regulatory Reform (Collaboration etc between Ombudsmen) Order 2007, SI 2007/1889 (paras **15.108–15.110**), an investigation may be commenced where 'in the particular circumstances, it is not reasonable to expect the complaint to be brought to the notice of that authority or for that authority to be afforded a reasonable opportunity to investigate, and reply to, the complaint' (s 26(5)(b)).

## Restrictions on the conduct of investigations

**15.97** The LGCs are precluded by statute from carrying out an investigation into a complaint where:

- there is a right of appeal to a tribunal or minister (s 26(6)(a) and (b));
- the person aggrieved has a remedy by way of proceedings in a court of law (s 26(6)(c));
- it affects all or most of the inhabitants of the local authority area (s 26(7)); or
- it involves a matter or subject specified in Sch 5 to the 1974 Act (s 26(8)).

**15.98** Schedule 5 matters can be summarized as follows:

- the commencement or conduct of civil or criminal proceedings before any court of law;
- action taken by an authority in connection with the investigation or prevention of crime;

- action relating to contractual or certain specified commercial transactions;

- action in respect of appointments or removals, pay, discipline, superannuation, or other personnel matters; or

- action concerning the giving of instruction or conduct, curriculum, internal organization, management, or discipline in any school or other educational establishment maintained by the local education authority.

**15.99** Whether or not an LGC decides to entertain a complaint is a matter for their judgment, subject to the supervisory jurisdiction of the courts. Thus in *R (on the application of M) v The Commissioner for Local Administration in England* (2006), where the complainants had laid a formal complaint before the LGC relating to the way in which an allegation about the ill-treatment of their son by a school teacher had been investigated by the local authority, Collins J held that the LGC's initial view that he was precluded from investigating the complaint by virtue of Sch 5, para 5(2) had been the correct one. Thus he observed:

> The investigation of what happened in the school is . . . in my view, clearly covered . . . because what the authority was doing was to take action, that is to say, to investigate matters which concerned the conduct in the school. It seems to me that the principle behind para 5 was to preclude the Ombudsman from looking into matters which did concern what went on in local authority schools.

## Result of an investigation

**15.100** Assuming that a LGC has decided to carry out an investigation into a complaint, the procedure to be followed is much the same as that relating to PCA investigations. In many cases, a local authority will accept that it has acted wrongly, and the matter can be settled locally. Where it does not accept that it is in the wrong, it will be necessary to publish an adverse report. Like the PCA, the LGCs do not have the power to enforce their reports. However, these reports will be drawn to the attention of the public because the local authority is under an obligation to give notice in newspapers that copies are available for public inspection. A local authority has three months from the date of issue of the report to inform the LGC of the remedial action which it proposes to take. If the LGC is not satisfied with this, he may publish a further report containing recommendations for remedial action. A local authority is required to reply to this further report. If the LGC is still not satisfied after considering the reply, he may require the authority to publish a statement in a newspaper setting out his findings and why he takes the view that the authority's response is unsatisfactory.

## Good practice guidance

**15.101** Since 1989, the LGCs have been in a position to issue guidance to local authorities on good practice in the light of their investigations. Currently, three such guides exist.

They deal with: running a complaints system; good administrative practice; and remedies. There is also a briefer guidance note on 'unreasonably persistent complainants' and 'unreasonable complaint behaviour'.

## Complaints

**15.102** The most recent Annual Report reveals that during 2010–11, the LGCs received 21,840 complaints. These fell into the following categories: benefits and tax (12%); housing (20%); planning and building development (15%); transport and highways (10%); education and children services (19%); environmental services, public protection, and regulation (10%); adult social care (8%); and corporate and other services (6%). Thus, not surprisingly, a substantial proportion of the complaints received related to two key responsibilities of local authorities: housing and planning. During 2010–11 10,792 complaints were determined. Excluding the 750 adult and social care complaints, of the remainder, some 4,012 were rejected on the basis that there was no or insufficient evidence of maladministration. A combined total of nearly 3,800 were rejected by the LGCs either in the exercise of their discretion not to pursue a complaint or on the basis that they were beyond their jurisdiction. Given that local settlements accounted for 2,215 complaints, the actual number where maladministration was found to have caused injustice was 25 (0.3% of the total excluding those outside jurisdiction).

## Ombudsmen and the courts

**15.103** Whether or not ombudsmen are subject to judicial review in the exercise of their functions has been an issue in a number of cases in addition to those already mentioned. In *Re Fletcher's Application* (1970), for example, the CA decided that the appellant should not have leave to move (as it then was) for a mandatory order (as it now is). The appeal committee of the HL subsequently refused leave to take the application to the HL. It did so on the ground that there was no jurisdiction to investigate a complaint because s 5(1) of the Parliamentary Commissioner Act 1967 conferred a wide discretionary power of investigation on the PCA.

**15.104** Two later cases concerned the office of the Commissioner for Local Administration. In *R v Comr for Local Administration, for the South, the West, the Midlands, Leicestershire, Lincolnshire and Cambridgeshire, ex p Eastleigh Borough Council* (1988), the CA ruled that where the ombudsman had exceeded his jurisdiction in reporting a complaint against a local authority, his report was subject to judicial review. The CA arrived at this conclusion on the basis of the public law character of the ombudsman's office, and because the Local Government Act 1974 did not provide a right of appeal against the findings in an ombudsman's report. Judicial review was thus available to fill the statutory void. In *R v Comr for Local Administration, ex p Croydon London Borough Council* (1989), the QBD granted the authority a declaration that the ombudsman's report was void where, on the facts, there was no justification for his finding of maladministration.

**15.105** These two cases were essentially concerned with the exercise of the ombudsman's powers. In both cases, it was alleged that he had contravened the requirements of the Local Government Act 1974. Thus in neither case did the courts address the issue of whether the exercise of the LGC's discretionary powers was subject to review. It appears to be the case, however, in the light of the ruling in *R v Parliamentary Comr for Administration, ex p Dyer* (1994) and certain obiter remarks made in the judgment, that both the PCA and the LGC's decisions are subject to judicial review. In *ex p Dyer*, in answer to the proposition that the 1967 Act indicated that the PCA was solely answerable to Parliament for the way in which he performed his functions, Simon Brown LJ noted that there was:

> nothing about the PCA's role or the statutory framework within which he operates so singular as to take him outside the purview of judicial review.

**15.106** The decision in *ex p Dyer* is less far reaching than might at first glance appear to be the case. It establishes that the PCA, and by analogy the LGCs, are subject to review, but it does not establish that all ombudsmen fall within the supervisory jurisdiction of the courts. Thus in *R v Parliamentary Comr for Standards, ex p Al Fayed* (1998), the CA rejected the argument that the Parliamentary Commissioner for Standards was subject to review. Although the CA accepted that there were a number of similarities between his office and that of the PCA, such as the fact that they are both subject to supervision by committees of Parliament and that they both report to Parliament, a 'significant distinction' existed between the two roles: the PCA investigates administrative matters, the activities of government; the Commissioner for Standards investigates the activities of Parliament. The courts are thus constitutionally debarred from using their powers of review in respect of the Commissioner for Standards by virtue of art 9 of the Bill of Rights 1689.

**15.107** Equally as important as the foregoing is the fact that although *ex p Dyer* establishes that the courts have the jurisdiction to review the decisions of the PCA, it is a jurisdiction that will rarely be invoked. Applications for judicial review are unlikely to succeed, save in exceptional cases, because the courts readily acknowledge the wide measure of discretion accorded to ombudsmen by Parliament. Thus in *R v Comr for Local Administration, ex p H (a minor)* (1998), Turner J upheld a decision of the LGC not to investigate a complaint where a remedy had already been sought by judicial review proceedings. In these circumstances, it was thought that Parliament could not have intended that the applicant should have an additional right to ventilate a grievance by complaining to the LGC. Also, in *R (on the application of Senior-Milne) v The Parliamentary and Health Service Commissioner* (2009), where the PCA had concluded that she had no jurisdiction to investigate a complaint in which it was alleged that the Financial Services Authority had failed properly to supervise the demutualization of Scottish Widows Assurance Company, the Admin Ct held that, on the facts, the PCA had been entitled to take that view. Moreover, even if the PCA had been wrong on the jurisdictional issue, there were further reasons why the judicial review application would have failed, eg it had been brought long after the expiry of the three months' time limit for making a judicial review claim and there were no good reasons for extending the time limit. For examples of successful applications, however, see *R v Parliamentary Comr for Administration, ex p Balchin (No 1)* (1996), *R v Parliamentary Comr for Administration, ex p Balchin (No 2)* (1999), and *R (on the application of Balchin) v Parliamentary Comr for Administration (No 3)* (2002), where successive reports by the PCA relating to the same complaint have been quashed by the courts.

## Reform

**15.108**  Pursuant to the Regulatory Reform Act 2001, the Labour Government made the Regulatory Reform (Collaboration etc between Ombudsmen) Order 2007, SI 2007/1889, which came into force on 1 August 2007. In consulting on the proposed Order, the Government stated that its intention was to:

> improve and streamline the complaints handling processes for the complainant in instances where the circumstances of a particular complaint crosses the jurisdiction of more than one Ombudsman, enabling the relevant Ombudsmen to work together collaboratively to address the issues raised by the case.

**15.109**  The Order made various amendments to the Parliamentary Commissioner Act 1967, the Local Government Act 1974, and the Health Service Commissioners Act 1993. It provides for the conduct of joint investigations by the PCA, HSC and the LGCs, subject to the complainant's consent: see ss 11ZAA, 33ZA, and 18ZA, of the 1967, 1974, and 1993 Acts, respectively. It also provides for the sharing of information for the purposes of a complaint and the issuing of joint reports following an investigation. Although the Order does not specify when a joint investigation may be appropriate, in a fact sheet produced jointly by the PCA and LGCs, it is suggested that complaints relating to the provision of health and social care, the administration of housing and welfare benefits, and planning and environmental issues are most likely to be investigated jointly. A further noteworthy point about the Order is that it confers new powers on the PCA, HSC, and the LGCs to appoint and pay a mediator or other appropriate person to assist them in the conduct of an investigation.

**15.110**  It might be thought that one consequence of a joint investigation would be the bypassing of the MP filter (paras **15.60–15.67**). Thus, for example, if a complaint was made to one of the LGCs and they considered a joint investigation with the PCA to be appropriate, and provided that the complainant consented, the MP filter would seem not to have been applied. In practice, however, the filter has continued to operate with the PCA assisting the complainant to make a complaint to their MP.

**15.111** In July 2011, the Law Commission published a report, *Public Services Ombudsmen* (Law Com No 329), in which it sought to develop provisional proposals contained in an earlier consultation paper. The report covered all of the public sector ombudsmen referred to in this chapter and one which is not, the Housing Ombudsman. Prior to identifying several of the report's key recommendations, it is worth noting that the Law Commission did not consider the creation of new ombudsmen or the amalgamation of existing roles. Neither did it consider the subject matter of the ombudsmen's work or the meaning of 'maladministration'. Instead, it focused on matters such as access to the ombudsmen, the ombudsman process, and independence and accountability.

**15.112** With regard to access to the ombudsmen, the Commission made a number of recommendations. Thus, for example, it took the view that it was inappropriate in the modern world for it to be a legal requirement that complaints to some of the ombudsmen must be made in writing. In its view, this acted as a barrier to some citizens and precluded the ombudsmen from being able to respond to technological developments. It was therefore recommended that statutory written complaint requirements be repealed. The Law Commission also recommended that the 'statutory bars' on ombudsmen receiving complaints that either could involve, or have involved, recourse to the courts ought to be abolished. Given the overlap between the work of the ombudsmen and judicial review, it was felt that citizens should be free to choose the avenue for redress which most suits their complaint. As was noted previously (para **15.66**), the Commission also recommended the creation of a dual-track system for access to the PCA rather than the MP filter alone.

**15.113** Some of the Law Commission's proposals will require legislation if they are to be given effect. Others, however, may be achieved merely by a change in policy, eg the publication of the criteria by which decisions are made as to whether or not a complaint should be the subject of a 'fast track' investigation. It remains to be seen to what extent, if any, the Commission's recommendations will be embraced by government and those to whom they apply.

## European Ombudsman

**15.114** By virtue of art 228(2) of the Treaty on the Functioning of the European Union (TFEU) (formerly art 138(2) of the EC Treaty), the European Parliament is required to elect an ombudsman after each election of the Parliament for the duration of its term of office. On 2 July 1995, the Parliament complied with this obligation when it elected Jacob Söderman (formerly the Finnish National ombudsman) as the first European Ombudsman.

**15.115** The European Ombudsman is required to be completely independent in the performance of his duties. He must not take instructions from any body as to the performance of those duties, and during his term of office he is not allowed to engage in any other occupation, whether paid or not. He is assisted by a staff which comprises a secretary-general, principal legal officers, legal officers, an information officer, assistants, and secretaries. The ombudsman's principal office is in Strasbourg, with a branch in Brussels.

## Jurisdiction

**15.116**  By virtue of art 228(1) of the TFEU, the ombudsman is:

> *empowered to receive complaints from any citizen of the Union or any natural or legal person residing or having its registered office in a Member State concerning instances of maladministration in the activities of the Union institutions, bodies, offices or agencies, with the exception of the Court of Justice of the European Union acting in its judicial role. [see also art 2(2) of the Statute of the Ombudsman, European Parliament Decision 94/262]*

'Maladministration' is therefore a central concept with regard to the work of the ombudsman. Nevertheless, in common with UK legislation, the term has not been defined by either the EU Treaty or the TFEU. By implication, therefore, this is a matter for the ombudsman to determine. It has been noted by the ombudsman himself that the experience of national ombudsmen suggests that it is better not to attempt a too rigid definition of what amounts to maladministration. However, in response to a European Parliament resolution calling for a clearer definition of 'maladministration', the ombudsman stated in his 1997 Annual Report that the term could be applied to:

> *administrative irregularities, administrative omissions, abuse of power, negligence, unlawful procedures, unfairness, malfunction or incompetence, discrimination, avoidable delay and lack or refusal of information.*

**15.117**  It was also stated in the 1997 Annual Report that: 'Maladministration occurs when a public body fails to act in accordance with a rule or principle which is binding upon it'. More recently, it has been suggested that maladministration arises where 'a Community institution fails to respect a legal rule or principle; fails to respect human or fundamental rights; or fails to respect principles of good administration'.

**15.118**  In several important respects, the jurisdiction of the ombudsman is wider than that of the PCA. Thus a complaint for which there is an alternative remedy is not beyond his remit. Moreover, unlike the PCA, the ombudsman may act on complaints made directly to him (as well as through a member of the European Parliament) and he also has the ability to act on his own initiative (art 228(1)). This ability is in common with most national ombudsmen. In the ombudsman's first Annual Report, it was explained that own initiative inquiries would only occur where many complaints had been received on the same issue and it was considered to be an effective way to seek a possible solution. One such own initiative inquiry into public access to documents held by EU institutions and bodies has resulted in the adoption of rules on public access by the institutions and bodies concerned.

## Petitions and complaints

**15.119** The 'right' to complain to the ombudsman is in addition to the right enjoyed by all EU citizens and any natural or legal person residing in or having its registered office in a member state to address 'a petition to the European Parliament on a matter which comes within the Union's fields of activity and which affects him, her or it directly' (art 227 TFEU). Any petitions that are received are assigned to the Parliament's Committee of Petitions. Given that there is a close relationship between a petition and a complaint, it has been necessary for the ombudsman and the committee to clarify their respective functions and to cooperate fully with one another. It is therefore possible for cases received by either to be transferred to the other provided that the complainant or petitioner agrees. Moreover, it has been agreed that the ombudsman will not accept complaints which are, or have been, before the committee.

**15.120** Once a complaint has been received by the ombudsman, it will be necessary to determine whether or not it is admissible. A complaint may be ruled inadmissible because the body or institution against which it was made does not fall within the ombudsman's jurisdiction. Further reasons for declaring a complaint inadmissible include:

- the object or matter of the complaint was not identified;
- the two-year time limit for bringing a complaint has been exceeded;
- internal remedies have not been exhausted in staff cases; or
- the case is being dealt with or has been settled by the Court of Justice.

**15.121** Writing in his Annual Report for 2010, the ombudsman has noted, amongst other things, that of the 2,667 complaints which were received in 2010, only 27% were found to be within his mandate. In other words, more than 70% of the complaints which he received were outside his mandate. It is also notable that nearly 58% of the complaints received were submitted using the internet. Where a non-admissible complaint is received, it would seem that the ombudsman seeks to transfer it to a competent body, or give advice as to where or whom to contact in order to find an effective solution to the problem. Many of the non-admissible complaints appear to have related to EU law issues, but at the national, regional, or local level. This high incidence of inadmissibility suggests a lack of understanding of the role of the ombudsman on the part of the majority of complainants. This is despite the ombudsman's website which contains, amongst other things, an interactive guide relating to complaints etc.

**15.122** Where a complaint is admissible, an investigation will follow. To date, many such investigations have resulted in a finding of no maladministration. Where, however, an instance of maladministration is revealed, the Statute of the Ombudsman obliges him to seek a friendly solution between the parties (art 3(5)). If this cannot be reached, the ombudsman may either close the file with a critical remark to the institution or body concerned, or make a formal finding of maladministration accompanied by draft recommendations. The body or institution has three months to respond. If it refuses to accept the recommendations and no other solution to eliminate the maladministration can be found, the ombudsman may send a special report with possible recommendations to both the Parliament and the body or institution concerned (art 3(6)). In his 2008 Annual Report, the ombudsman explained that this amounts to his 'ultimate weapon' and is the last substantive step that he takes in relation to a case. On receipt of the ombudsman's report, the Parliament is thus presented with an opportunity to look for a way to solve the maladministration. In common with the PCA, the ombudsman has no powers of enforcement.

**15.123** Where the ombudsman has investigated a complaint, the General Court (see Chapter 7) has the jurisdiction to hear a case involving a motion for damages against him. Moreover, the fact that the ombudsman is subject to a process of review conducted by the Parliament does not preclude him from being subject to judicial review: see Case C234/02 P, *European Ombudsman v Lambert* (2004).

# FURTHER READING

Beatson, J 'Should Judges Conduct Public Inquiries?' (2005) 121 LQR 221.

Buck, T, Kirkham, R, and Thompson, B *The Ombudsman Enterprise and Administrative Justice* (2011) Ashgate.

Buck, T, Kirkham, R, and Thompson, B 'Time for a "Leggatt-style" Review of the Ombudsman System?' [2011] PL 20.

Sir Robert Carnwath 'Tribunal Justice – A New Start' [2009] PL 48.

De Leeuw, M 'The European Ombudsman's Role as a Developer of Norms of Good Administration' (2011) 17 EPL 349.

Elliott, M 'Asymmetric Devolution and Ombudsman Reform in England' [2006] PL 81.

Gregory, R and Giddings, P *The Ombudsman, the Citizen and Parliament* (2002) Politicos Publishing.

Hadfield, B 'R v Lord Saville of Newdigate, ex p anonymous soldiers: What is the Purpose of a Tribunal of Inquiry?' [1999] PL 663.

Kirkham, R 'The Latest from the UK Ombudsman' (2004) 26 J Soc Wel & Fam L 417.

Kirkham, R 'Auditing by Stealth? Special Reports and the Ombudsman' [2005] PL 740.

Kirkham, R 'Challenging the Authority of the Ombudsman: the Parliamentary Ombudsman's Special Report on Wartime Detainees' (2006) 69 MLR 792.

Kirkham, R *The Parliamentary Ombudsman: Withstanding the test of time*, 4th report 2006–7, HC 421.

Kirkham, R 'Explaining the Lack of Enforcement Power Possessed by the Ombudsman' (2008) 30 J Soc Wel & Fam L 253.

Kirkham, R, Thompson, B, and Buck, T 'When Putting Things Right Goes Wrong: Enforcing the recommendations of the ombudsman' [2008] PL 510.

Kirkham, R, Thompson, B, and Buck, T 'Putting the Ombudsman into Constitutional Context' (2009) 62 Parliamentary Affairs 600.

Leino, P 'The Wind is in the North: The first European Ombudsman (1995–2003)' (2004) 10 EPL 333.

Parpworth, N and Thompson, K 'The European Ombudsman' [1998] CIL 157.

Peters, A 'The European Ombudsman and the European Constitution' (2005) 42 CML Rev 697.

Pollard, D, Parpworth, N, and Hughes, D *Constitutional and Administrative Law: Text with Materials* (4th edn, 2007) OUP.

Quane, H 'Challenging the Report of an Independent Inquiry under the Human Rights Act' [2007] PL 529.

Segal, Z 'Tribunals of Inquiry: A British Invention Ignored in Britain' [1984] PL 207.

Seneviratne, M 'Ombudsmen 2000' (2000) 9 Nottingham Law Journal 13.

Seneviratne, M *Ombudsmen: Public Services and Administrative Justice* (2002) Butterworths.

Seneviratne, M 'A New Ombudsman for Wales' [2006] PL 6.

Seneviratne, M 'Updating the Local Government Ombudsman' [2008] PL 627.

Stacey, F *The British Ombudsman* (1971) Clarendon Press.

Suksi, M 'Case C-234/02 P, *European Ombudsman v Frank Lamberts*, judgment of the Full Court of 23 March 2004, [2004] ECR I-2803' (2005) 42 CML Rev 1765.

Tsadiras, A 'Unravelling Ariadne's Thread: The European Ombudsman's investigative powers' (2008) 45 CML Rev 757.

Lord Woolf *Protection of the Public – A new challenge* (1990).

Wynn, G 'The British PCA: Ombudsman or Ombudsmouse?' [1973] 35 Journal of Politics 45.

## SELF-TEST QUESTIONS

1   Does the right of appeal from a decision of a tribunal to a court have the effect of negativing the advantages inherent in the tribunal system?

2   Why do you think it is a common practice for senior judges to be appointed to chair public inquiries? What advantages might such individuals bring to the conduct of an inquiry?

3   The outgoing PCA, Ann Abraham, has commented that 'in the early days the Parliamentary Ombudsman's customers were considered to be MPs'. To what extent, if any, do you think that such a view still prevails?

4   Should the MP filter be retained, or is it time that complainants had direct access to the PCA?

5   Is there a case for arguing that the PCA ought to be able to carry out investigations on her own initiative rather than having to wait to receive a complaint?

6   Kirkham has contended that although the test of maladministration 'has proved to be a powerful and adaptable tool for the task to which the [PCA] was assigned', the 'lack of clarity as to the meaning of the maladministration test is problematic . . . as it effectively grants the [PCA] a high degree of autonomy'. Do you agree?

7   What might be the arguments for using an alternative to the term 'maladministration' to indicate when the public sector ombudsmen may investigate a complaint?

8   Shortly after the establishment of the PCA's office, one commentator suggested that the office amounted to an 'Ombudsmouse' rather than an ombudsman. Is there any truth in this jibe?

9   To what extent, if any, do you agree with Kirkham's judgment that 'the Parliamentary Ombudsman has proved to be an effective addition to the system of administrative justice in the UK'?

10   With regard to the jurisdiction of the LGCs, could it be argued that the restriction imposed by s 26(7) of the Local Government Act 1974 is anomalous?

11   Should the ombudsmen have enforcement powers? If so, what form should those powers take?

# PART VI
## Civil Liberties

# 16

## Freedoms and liberties in the UK

## SUMMARY

In this chapter we are concerned with how freedoms and liberties might be protected in the UK. The chapter commences with an attempt to distinguish between rights and liberties whilst recognizing that this is by no means a straightforward task. Some consideration is also given to the way in which rights and liberties have been traditionally protected in English law. The main body of the chapter is concerned with the European Convention on Human Rights (institutions, rights, procedures, and jurisprudence) and the Human Rights Act 1998. The main constitutional aspects of the 1998 Act have already been considered in Chapter **5**. The treatment in this chapter therefore looks at the Act from a protection of rights perspective.

## Human rights and civil liberties distinguished

16.1 There are essentially two schools of thought as to where human rights are derived from. On the one hand, the 'natural law' school believes that human rights are derived from natural law; they are rights which people enjoy simply by virtue of being human. On the other, the 'legal positivist' school holds that rights are derived from legal systems; they are conferred by positive laws.

16.2 It is important to appreciate that human rights and civil liberties are extremely closely related. In some cases, it may be difficult to distinguish one from another, to identify where one ends and the other begins. The closeness of this relationship is further evidenced by the fact that the terms are often used interchangeably, implying that they are synonymous. However, is it possible to distinguish between a 'right' and a 'liberty'?

16.3 There have been many attempts to analyse what we mean by 'rights' and 'liberties'. In the case of a 'right', it is acknowledged that we may distinguish between a right which is moral and a right which is legal. Moreover, as Dworkin has noted in *Taking Rights Seriously* (1977), by asserting that one has a 'right' to do something, we are using the word 'right' in a stronger sense than if we were to observe that a particular course of action was the 'right' thing to do. The variety of meanings which lawyers may ascribe to the word 'right' have been analysed by Hohfeld. He contends that when we talk of a 'right', we may mean: right or claim; privilege; power; or immunity. For Hohfeld, the essential characteristic of a 'right' or 'claim' is that it imposes a duty on another. He underlines the point with the aid of an example. A person who owns land has a right to exclude others from entering that land. Those who are thereby excluded are under a corresponding duty not to enter that land. In the Hohfeldian analysis, this is the only proper use of the word 'right'.

16.4 The concepts of 'power' or 'immunity' need not detain us further. For present purposes, it is 'privilege' which is of interest. This is because in Hohfeld's analysis, a privilege amounts to a freedom to do something, the exercise of which cannot be prevented by another because they do not have the right to do so. It differs from a right because there is no corresponding duty on another to act or refrain from acting. In this sense, therefore, it may be argued that Hohfeld's 'privilege' closely resembles a 'liberty'.

16.5 In the light of this, it may be possible to distinguish between 'rights' and 'liberties' on the basis that rights are of a more fundamental nature than liberties. They impose duties on others rather than merely requiring that they are not interfered with. Thus when we talk of the 'right to life', we are concerned with a fundamental human right which imposes a duty on others not to take that life away. It may be argued, therefore, that respect for human rights demands more of the individual and society as a whole than does respect for civil liberties.

16.6 The suggestion made in the previous paragraph is necessarily tentative. It may be possible to distinguish between human rights and civil liberties, but it is by no means certain that this is the case. What is clear is that English courts and lawyers have traditionally talked in terms of liberties and freedoms rather than human rights when faced with claims that the 'rights' of the individual have been infringed. This thinking is in the process of evolution given the enactment of the Human Rights Act 1998.

## Political and social or economic rights

16.7 Political rights are a common feature of human rights documents. They involve matters such as: the right to life; equality of treatment before the law; freedom of expression; freedom of peaceful assembly and association; and freedom from discrimination. It will later become apparent that the European Convention on Human Rights (ECHR) is primarily concerned with the protection of civil and political rights.

16.8 Social and economic rights are rather different in nature. They are concerned with matters such as: the right to work; the right to equal pay for equal work; and the right to education. The Universal Declaration of Human Rights, which was adopted and proclaimed by the General Assembly of the United Nations on 10 December 1948, is an amalgam of political and social and economic rights. In addition to those social and economic rights already mentioned, the Declaration states in art 24 that:

> *Everyone has the right to rest and leisure, including reasonable limitation of working hours and periodic holidays with pay.*

Moreover, art 25(1) of the Declaration provides that:

> *Everyone has the right to a standard of living adequate for the health and well-being of himself and of his family, including food, clothing, housing and medical care and necessary social services, and the right to security in the event of unemployment, sickness, disability, widowhood, old age or other lack of livelihood in circumstances beyond his own control.*

**16.9**   The key distinction between political rights and social and economic rights is evident in this provision. Whilst the former tend not to require much in the way of government expenditure for their enjoyment, social and economic rights clearly place financial burdens on the state. In order for the terms of art 25(1) to be fully complied with, a comprehensive welfare and social security system would need to be in place.

## The traditional means of protecting civil liberties in the UK

**16.10**   The task of protecting civil liberties in the UK has traditionally fallen to both Parliament and the courts. However, given the susceptibility of Parliament to the dictates of a strong executive, it is unwise to think of it as playing anything more than a minor role in this connection. Thus we must turn to the courts.

**16.11**   Civil liberties have been protected in the UK by the courts (see paras **11.40–11.42**). Judges have long been concerned by attempts on the part of the executive to interfere with the rights of the individual. Thus the courts have shown themselves willing, on occasion, to act as defender of the individual against unauthorized state intervention. We have already seen in the case of *Entick v Carrington* (1765) (paras **3.26** and **3.29**) how the lack of legal authority ensured that the King's Messengers were trespassers at the relevant time. A rather more recent example of the courts acting to protect the rights and freedoms of the individual is to be found in a case concerned with freedom of speech.

*Redmond-Bate v DPP* **(1999):** Mrs R-B was preaching to passers-by on the steps of Wakefield Cathedral. She was approached by a police officer who informed her and other preachers that they were not to stop people. On his return, the officer found that a crowd of more than 100 had gathered and that some of the people were behaving in a hostile manner towards the preachers. He feared that a breach of the peace would occur if they did not stop preaching. The preachers refused to comply with his request to stop and were accordingly arrested. They were convicted by magistrates of wilfully obstructing an officer in the execution of his duty contrary to s 89(2) of the Police Act 1996. An appeal to the Crown Court was unsuccessful. DC held: whether or not the offence had been committed depended upon whether the officer was acting within the execution of his duty at the material time. This itself turned on whether there were reasonable grounds for apprehending a breach of the peace. It was both illiberal and illogical to proceed from the fact that the women were preaching about God and morality to the view that there was a reasonable apprehension that violence would erupt if action were not taken. There was nothing in the situation as perceived by the officer which entitled him to apprehend a breach of the peace.

16.12 The concept of breach of the peace will be considered in Chapter **19**. The decision in *Redmond-Bate v DPP* highlights how the courts might protect freedom of speech, a freedom which Lord Denning once referred to, in conjunction with freedom of assembly, as 'among our most precious freedoms'. It has not always been thus. In *A-G v Guardian Newspapers Ltd* (1987), Lord Bridge remarked that the decision of the majority of the HL to uphold an interim injunction preventing the sale of the *Spycatcher* book had 'severely undermined' his confidence in the 'capacity of the common law to safeguard the fundamental freedoms essential to a free society including the right to freedom of speech'.

# European Convention on Human Rights

## Introduction

16.13 The European Convention on Human Rights and Fundamental Freedoms (ECHR) was very much a by-product of the Second World War and the desire to promote unity within Europe and to ensure that human rights were properly respected and protected thereafter. Its drafting by the Council of Europe marked a shift in attitude from the pre-Second World War belief that human rights and fundamental freedoms were internal political matters beyond the reach of the wider international community. The original text of the Convention, which owed much to the efforts of British draftsmen, was signed in Rome by 15 states on 4 November 1950. It did not take effect, however, until it had been ratified by 10 of its signatories. This was achieved on 3 September 1953.

16.14 It ought to be stressed at the outset that the Council of Europe is not an institution of the EU and that, therefore, the ECHR does not amount to an EU Treaty. Although all 27 member states of the Union have signed the Convention, it has also been signed by 20 non-EU states such as Iceland, Albania, Serbia, and Montenegro which are nevertheless members of the Council of Europe. The ECHR is therefore served by its own institutions which are separate from and independent of those which serve the EU.

## Institutions

**16.15** The ECHR was originally served by three institutions: the European Commission of Human Rights; the European Court of Human Rights; and the Committee of Ministers. Each performed its own particular functions (although there was some overlap) which to a greater or lesser extent assisted in ensuring that rights guaranteed by the Convention were upheld within the signatory states. The Commission, for example, was the initial point of contact for all those who claimed to be the victim of an infringement of a Convention right. It registered the complaints that were received, it investigated them, and it determined whether a complaint satisfied the admissibility criteria. In this sense, therefore, the Commission acted as a filter. Where a complaint was ruled admissible, the Commission was charged with the responsibility of brokering a friendly settlement between the parties (paras **16.55–16.57**). If no settlement could be reached, the complaint would sometimes be referred to the European Court of Human Rights (ECtHR) for its determination, but not before the Commission had itself expressed an opinion as to whether there had been a violation of the Convention.

## Institutional reform

**16.16** The years that followed the ratification of the ECHR saw a steady and, more recently, a rapid increase in the workloads of both the Commission and the Court. This can be attributed to a number of different factors, including the widespread acceptance of the right of individual petition (paras **16.49–16.50**) and the growing public awareness that Strasbourg may provide a remedy for a grievance when all the domestic avenues have been exhausted. Almost inevitably, increasing workloads were attended by delays. Both the Commission and the Court were confronted by a backlog of cases which meant that in practice, disputes could take between five and six years to pass through their various stages at Strasbourg. Delays of this length were unacceptable and therefore institutional reform became a necessity.

**16.17** A number of states advocated the retention of a two-tier system with the Commission becoming a Court of First Instance and the original Court acting as a Court of Appeal. However, the preferred option of the majority was the creation of a single unified Court which would perform the functions of both the Commission and the original Court.

## Protocol 11

**16.18** On 1 November 1998, Protocol 11 to the ECHR entered into force. This introduced major procedural and institutional changes to the Convention machinery, not least of which was the demise of the Commission. This occurred on the expiry of a one-year transitional period during which the Commission continued to deal with applications pending at the time that the protocol was implemented. Accordingly, the ECHR is now served by two institutions: the Committee of Ministers and the Court of Human Rights.

## The Committee of Ministers

**16.19** The Committee of Ministers is essentially a political body. It is composed of the ministers of foreign affairs for each of the states which is a member of the Council of Europe. When it is not in formal session, ministerial deputies act as state representatives. Despite the political nature of the Committee, it performed a judicial function prior to the entry into force of Protocol 11. This entailed determining whether the Convention had been violated in those cases where it had received a Commission report as to the merits of the case and the case had not been referred to the Court. Although in practice the Committee did not deal with important cases, it was at the very least questionable whether a political body ought to be performing a judicial function. Accordingly, under the new system, the Committee of Ministers no longer has the jurisdiction to determine cases not going to the Court. Its role under the ECHR is therefore now confined to supervising the execution of the Court's judgments (art 46). If the Committee considers that its task is hindered by a problem of interpretation of the judgment, it may refer the matter to the Court. The decision to refer requires a two-thirds majority of the representatives entitled to sit in the Committee. The same majority is required where the Committee wishes to exercise another new power conferred on it by Protocol 14, the power to refer to the Court the question whether a state has failed to fulfil its obligation to comply with a Court ruling. Such a power may only be exercised, however, after a formal notice has been served on the state indicating that the Committee considers that it has refused to abide by a final judgment of the Court. This new power is not unlike the power which the European Commission has in relation to the judgments of the ECJ (para **7.29**).

## The European Court of Human Rights

**16.20** A key reform introduced by Protocol 11 has been the establishment of a single unified European Court of Human Rights which functions on a permanent, full-time basis. The Court consists of a number of judges equal to the number of High Contracting Parties (47), all of whom sit in their individual capacity. In order to stand for election by the Parliamentary Assembly, a candidate must be of high moral character and 'must either possess the qualifications required for appointment to high judicial office or be jurisconsults of recognised competence' (art 21). During a term of office, a judge is forbidden from engaging in any activity which is incompatible with their independence, impartiality, or the demands of full-time office.

**16.21** Judges are elected for a period of nine years (formerly it was six), with no prospect of re-election (art 22). Before taking up office, each elected judge must either swear or declare: 'I will exercise my functions as judge honourably, independently and impartially and that I will keep secret all deliberations.' Once in office, a judge enjoys security of tenure. He is required to retire when he reaches the age of 70, but he cannot be dismissed from office unless the other judges agree by a two-thirds majority that he has ceased to fulfil the required conditions (art 24). Rule 7 of the Rules of the Court further elaborates on the subject of dismissal. Before being dismissed, a judge must first be heard by the Plenary Court. Moreover, any judge of the Court may set in motion the dismissal procedure.

**16.22** It is worth noting that, in Mowbray's opinion, the original appointment of judges to the new Court 'did not operate with sufficient rigour, consistency or smoothness'. He identifies two main reasons why this was the case. First, because individual governments were given a wide measure of discretion as to the selection and prioritization of their judicial candidates. Secondly, Mowbray argues that the Parliamentary Assembly's 'scrutiny of candidates was rather secretive and selective'.

**16.23** With regard to the former, it is unfortunate that the independence of some candidates can be questioned given the emphasis that both the ECHR and the judicial oath place upon the need for independence. The danger of a politicized Court is self-evident. The decisions of the Court should be based on legal considerations alone. If it was widely believed that decisions of the Court were as much dependent upon the identity of the state concerned and the national mix of the judges hearing the case as upon the force of the legal argument, the Convention system would fall into disrepute.

**16.24** The second criticism of the appointment process, that the scrutiny of the candidates was not what it ought to have been, relates to the first in that it may have resulted in some bad appointments. Concerns were sometimes expressed in the past about the old Court and whether or not all of its members had the necessary qualities to be good judges. In the UK, Government criticism of the Court reached its zenith following the decision in *McCann v United Kingdom* (1995), where it was held that the UK had breached art 2 of the ECHR in relation to the killing of three suspected IRA terrorists by the SAS on the island of Gibraltar. Protocol 11 thus represented an opportunity for thoroughgoing reform of the Court.

## Plenary Court

**16.25** The function of the Plenary Court is not to determine cases brought under the Convention. Instead, it is concerned with matters such as: the election of a President of the Court and one or two Vice-Presidents for a period of three years; the setting up of chambers for a fixed period of time and the election of their Presidents; and the adoption of the Rules of the Court (art 26). Under these Rules, the Court is divided into five sections. The composition of each section reflects a geographical and gender balance, and takes account of the different legal systems of the various High Contracting Parties. The Presidents of the sections are the two Vice-Presidents of the Court and the three Presidents of the Chambers. A section will exist for a period of three years. The judicial business of the Court is undertaken by committees, chambers, and the Grand Chamber.

## Committees

16.26 These are set up by chambers within each of the Court's sections for a fixed period of 12 months. They consist of three judges who have the jurisdiction to determine the admissibility of individual applications brought under art 34 of the ECHR. Acting unanimously, a committee may declare an application inadmissible or strike it out of its list of cases. Any decision that it does reach is final (art 28). In this sense, therefore, the committees carry out the task of filtering applications which was formerly undertaken by the Commission. Where the committee does not reach a unanimous decision, the admissibility of an application will be determined by a chamber.

## Chambers

16.27 As has been noted (para **16.25**), chambers are established by the Plenary Court. They consist of seven judges and will include: the President of the section to which the case has been allocated; an ex officio member, the judge elected in respect of the state party concerned (or an equivalent); and such other judges from the relevant section as are appointed by the President. Chambers decide on the admissibility and merits of individual and state applications. The decision on admissibility is to be taken separately, unless the Court decides that the exceptional nature of the case demands otherwise (art 29).

16.28 In certain specified circumstances, and subject to neither party objecting, a chamber may relinquish its jurisdiction in a case in favour of the Grand Chamber at any time before it has given judgment (art 30). The specified circumstances are that:

- the case raises a serious question affecting the interpretation of the Convention or the protocols thereto; or

- the question before the chamber might have a result inconsistent with a previous judgment of the Court.

Mowbray has noted that:

> Chambers have been circumspect in relinquishing cases to the Grand Chamber. From the beginning of 2002 until the end of 2005 only 21 cases were relinquished: five in 2002 and 2003, seven in 2004 and four in 2005.

16.29 The judgment of a chamber is not necessarily final. It only becomes so:

- when the parties declare that they will not request that the case be referred to the Grand Chamber under art 43 (paras **16.30–16.31**); or

- three months have passed since the judgment was delivered and no request for a referral has been made; or

- the panel of the Grand Chamber has rejected the request for an art 43 referral.

## Grand Chamber

**16.30**  This is the most important of all the Court's guises. The Grand Chamber consists of 17 judges together with an ex officio member. It includes the President of the Court, the Vice-Presidents, the Presidents of the Chambers, and other judges chosen in accordance with the Rules of the Court. In addition to having the power to determine individual or inter-state applications passed to it by a chamber, the Grand Chamber may hear cases referred to it under art 43 of the ECHR. This provides that in exceptional cases, either party may request within three months of the date of a chamber's decision that the matter be referred to the Grand Chamber. A panel of five judges of the Grand Chamber is required to accept the request if it:

- raises a serious question affecting the interpretation or application of the Convention or the protocols thereto; or

- raises a serious issue of general importance.

**16.31**  Where a request is accepted (as it was prior to the decision in *Hirst v UK (No 2)* (2005), (para **6.6**)), the Grand Chamber will give judgment in the case. If the panel rejects the request, the decision of the chamber is thereby rendered final. There is no right of appeal against a panel's determination. By virtue of art 31, the Grand Chamber also has the power to consider requests for advisory opinions submitted in accordance with art 47 of the ECHR (paras **16.36–16.38**).

## Jurisdiction and functions of the Court

**16.32**  The Court's jurisdiction extends to all matters concerning the interpretation and application of the Convention and the protocols thereto. In the event of a dispute as to whether or not the Court has jurisdiction, the Court will decide the issue (art 32).

**16.33**  By virtue of art 36, a High Contracting Party whose national is an applicant has the right to submit written comments and to take part in hearings before either a chamber or the Grand Chamber. At any stage in the proceedings, the Court may strike out an application from its list of cases if, for example, the matter has been resolved or the applicant does not intend to pursue his application. An application which has been struck out may be restored to the list if the Court considers that the circumstances justify such a course of action.

**16.34**  The procedure before the Court is adversarial and the Court's hearings are held in public, unless exceptional circumstances justify sitting *in camera*. Similarly, documents deposited with the Court's registrar are accessible to the public unless the President of the Court decides otherwise. Where the Court finds that there has been a violation of the Convention, and the domestic law of the High Contracting Party concerned allows for only partial reparation to be made, art 41 empowers the Court to award 'just satis-faction'. The practice of the Court thus far has been that 'satisfaction' is achieved by the award of monetary compensation.

**16.35** Article 45 of the ECHR requires that reasons shall be given for judgments of the Court as well as for decisions as to the admissibility of an application. Where the whole or part of a judgment is not the unanimous decision of the Court, any judge is entitled to deliver a separate opinion.

**16.36** Articles 47–49 of the ECHR make provision for the Court to give advisory opinions. These opinions, which are given at the request of the Committee of Ministers, are on legal questions relating to the interpretation of the Convention and its protocols. They are not concerned with the content or scope of the substantive rights and freedoms defined in s I of the ECHR (paras **16.39-16.43**). Whether or not the request for an advi-sory opinion falls within the Court's competence is a matter for the Court to decide (art 48). Thus in response to the first request for an advisory opinion under art 47, the Court concluded unanimously in June 2004 that it was not within its competence to consider the coexistence of the Convention on Human Rights of the Commonwealth of Independent States and the ECHR. Writing in 2007 Mowbray commented:

> *Given the narrow scope of this jurisdiction, coupled with the Committee of Ministers' restraint in seeking them, it seems very likely that the Grand Chamber will not be burdened by its advisory opinion responsibilities in the coming years.*

**16.37** Where an opinion is given in a particular case, it will be accompanied by reasons and it will be communicated to the Committee of Ministers. In February 2008, the Grand Chamber was asked to provide an advisory opinion on certain legal questions con-cerning the list of candidates which had been submitted with a view to the election of judges to the Court itself. Although there were two questions, the answer to the first question rendered it unnecessary to answer the second. Essentially, the question con-cerned whether a list of candidates submitted by a Contracting Party for the post of judge at the ECtHR, which satisfied the criteria set out in art 21 of the ECHR, could be refused solely on the basis of gender-related issues. Malta had submitted a list of three candidates from which a judge was to be appointed. However, all of the candidates were male. The Parliamentary Assembly had rejected Malta's list on the basis that there were no female candidates contrary to Assembly Resolution 1366 (2004), as modified by Resolution 1426 (2005). On a preliminary point, the Grand Chamber ruled that it had jurisdiction to hear the matter because the issue in question was of a legal character.

**16.38** With regard to the substance of the matter, the Grand Chamber noted that the inclu-sion of a member of the under-represented sex on a list was not the only criteria applied by the Assembly which was also not laid down in art 21 of the ECHR. Additionally, the

Assembly required that candidates should have a sufficient knowledge of at least one of the two official languages (French and English). However, in the Grand Chamber's opinion, whereas this criteria flowed implicitly from art 21, in that a sufficient knowledge of at least one of the official languages was necessary to enable a judge to make a useful contribution to the work of the Court, the same could not be said of the criteria relating to a candidate's gender. Accordingly, although a gender-equality policy was legitimate in the present context, it must not have the effect of making it more difficult for a Contracting Party to put forward a list of candidates who all satisfied the art 21 requirements. Thus in the opinion of the Grand Chamber, the policy ought not to be pursued without provision being made for exceptions designed to enable a Contracting Party to choose national candidates who satisfy the art 21 requirements, and that the exceptions ought to be defined as soon as possible.

## Substantive rights

**16.39** Section I of the ECHR details the various rights and freedoms which the High Contracting Parties are required to guarantee to everyone within their jurisdiction. These rights and freedoms may be summarized as follows:

- the right to life (art 2);
- freedom from torture and inhuman or degrading treatment (art 3);
- freedom from slavery and forced labour (art 4);
- the right to liberty and security of the person (art 5);
- the right to a fair trial (art 6);
- freedom from retrospective criminal laws or increased sentencing (art 7);
- the right to respect for private and family life (art 8);
- freedom of thought, conscience, and religion (art 9);
- freedom of expression (art 10);
- freedom of assembly and association (art 11);
- the right to marry and found a family (art 12);
- the right to an effective remedy in national law where Convention rights or freedoms have been violated (art 13); and
- freedom from discrimination in the enjoyment of Convention rights and freedoms (art 14).

**16.40** It is apparent from this catalogue that the rights and freedoms contained in the ECHR are essentially civil and political in nature. The document is therefore concerned with rights and freedoms which are, as Lord Bingham observed in *Brown v Stott* (2003), 'of real importance in a modern democracy governed by the rule of law'. There is no real mention in the ECHR, however, of social or economic rights, such as the right to work or the right to be paid a fair wage, which sometimes feature in other human rights documents. Neither, as Sir Stephen Sedley has pointed out, does the ECHR say anything about 'a right to enough food and shelter to keep body and soul together', or 'a wholesome environment' which he regards as being a 'fundamental human right'.

16.41  To state the nature of the rights and freedoms which are contained in the ECHR in this manner is partly misleading since it implies that all such rights and freedoms are absolute. This is by no means the case.

16.42  The only absolute freedoms in the ECHR are the freedom from torture and inhuman or degrading treatment (art 3) and the freedom from slavery or servitude (art 4). All other rights and freedoms are subject to some form of qualification. Thus in the case of the right to life (art 2), a person may be deprived of this right 'in the execution of a sentence of a court following his conviction of a crime for which this penalty is provided by law'. Similarly, there are various exceptions to the right to liberty and security of the person (art 5). These include imprisonment after conviction by a competent court and the lawful arrest or detention of a person for the purpose of bringing him before a court. In the case of arts 8–11 of the ECHR, provision is made for quite wide-ranging exceptions to the rights and freedoms contained therein. Thus these rights and freedoms may be interfered with, limited, or restricted in accordance with or as prescribed by law where it is 'necessary in a democratic society in the interests of': national security or public safety; or for the protection of health or morals; or to protect the rights and freedoms of others.

16.43  These exceptions are common to arts 8–11. Further, more specific exceptions exist in respect of these articles. Thus the right to respect for private and family life (art 8) may be interfered with in accordance with the law where it is necessary for the 'economic well-being of the country'. Similarly, art 11 (freedom of assembly and association) does 'not prevent the imposition of lawful restrictions on the exercise of these rights by members of the armed forces, of the police or of the administration of the State'.

## Protocols

16.44  To end a discussion of the substantive rights guaranteed by the Convention at this juncture would be to overlook an important factor, namely that these rights have been added to over the years by a number of protocols. Protocols thus allow the ECHR to reflect changing attitudes towards the content and protection of human rights. In Protocol 1, for example, arts 1, 2, and 3 are concerned with the protection of property and the rights to education and free elections, respectively. This protocol was ratified by the UK a number of months after it was opened for signature in early 1952. The importance of the property right protected by art 1 of Protocol 1 is demonstrated by the fact that between 1959–2009, just under 15% of all the cases in which the ECtHR found a violation of a Convention right related to a violation of this particular right. Protocol 6, which provides for, among other things, the abolition of the death penalty, was only rat-ified by the UK on 20 May 1999 despite the fact that it had been made in 1983. Protocols 4 and 7, which are concerned with matters such as: a prohibition on imprisonment for debt; freedom of movement; a prohibition on the expulsion of nationals; procedural safeguards relating to the expulsion of aliens; the right to an appeal in criminal mat-ters; compensation for wrongful conviction; the right not to be tried or punished twice in respect of the same offence; and equality between spouses, have never been ratified by the UK although they were opened for signature in 1963 and 1984, respectively.

**16.45** At the time of writing, Protocol 12, which imposes a general prohibition on discrimi-nation on any ground in respect of the enjoyment of 'any right set forth by law', has not been ratified by the UK. Conversely, Protocol 13 has been ratified by the UK and a sufficient number of other states to enter into force. It is concerned with the abolition of the death penalty in all circumstances, ie including in relation to acts committed in time of war or of imminent threat of war. As such, therefore, it represents an exten-sion of Protocol 6 where the abolition of the death penalty is confined to peace-time executions.

**16.46** The protocols which have not been mentioned in this section were largely concerned with amending the enforcement machinery of the ECHR. They ceased to have effect when Protocol 11 came into force.

## Derogation

**16.47** In times of war or other public emergency threatening the life of the nation, a Contracting Party may, by virtue of art 15 of the ECHR, take measures derogating from its obligations under the Convention. Article 15 thus represents, in the words of Cavanaugh, 'an additional, codified margin of appreciation afforded during states of exception'. Derogation is only permitted to 'the extent strictly required by the exigencies of the situation' and the measures adopted must not be inconsistent with a Contracting Party's other obligations under international law. In the case of art 2, except where death results from a lawful act of war, and arts 3, 4(1), and 7, no derogation is permit-ted under art 15. Where a Contracting Party wishes to exercise the right to derogate, it must keep the Secretary-General of the Council of Europe fully informed of the meas-ures taken and reasons for them. When such measures have ceased to operate and the convention rights have been fully restored, the Secretary-General must be informed.

**16.48** Article 15 has been invoked by the UK on a number of occasions in the context of Northern Ireland. Despite several legal challenges to such derogations, eg *Ireland v United Kingdom* (1978), the Strasbourg authorities have ruled that they have been justi-fied by the circumstances. In so doing, it is apparent that the Court has accepted that a state should be allowed a wide margin of appreciation (paras **16.58–16.60**) in such mat-ters. Formerly the Human Rights Act expressly provided for the retention of a deroga-tion in respect of art 5(3). The UK Government subsequently withdrew the derogation, however, and the Act was amended to reflect this development: see the Human Rights Act (Amendment) Order 2001, SI 2001/1216.

## Right of individual petition

16.49 Originally, the right of an individual to petition the Commission where they claimed to be the victim of the violation of a Convention right was not automatically available following ratification of the Convention. Rather, it was dependent upon a declaration from a Contracting Party that it recognized the competence of the Commission to deal with petitions from its citizens. Thus in the case of the UK, declarations were issued on a five-yearly basis following the Wilson Government's original acceptance of the right of individual petition in 1966. There were occasions when it was suggested that a declaration ought not to be renewed, most notably following the decision in *McCann v United Kingdom* (1995) (para **16.24**). However, when it came to reforming the Convention system, the Conservative Government advocated the retention of an optional and renewable right of individual petition to the new Court. The reformed arrangements do not allow for this.

16.50 By virtue of art 34, the right of individual petition has been elevated to the status of a compulsory requirement. Thus 'any person, non-governmental organisation or group of individuals' claiming to be the victim of a violation of a Convention right now enjoys a mandatory right of access to the Court and the Contracting Parties have undertaken 'not to hinder in any way the effective exercise of this right'.

## Inter-state applications

16.51 Article 33 of the ECHR states that:

> Any High Contracting Party may refer to the Court any alleged breach of the provisions of the Convention and the protocols thereto by another High Contracting Party.

This provision largely restates the original art 24 of the ECHR, although the reference is now made to the Court rather than to the Commission. A state will not be the 'victim' of an alleged breach of the Convention by another state, but it may be that one of its citizens has been. Accordingly, this article provides for the possibility of the state acting on the citizen's behalf.

16.52 In practice, inter-state applications have been made extremely rarely. An example under the original art 24 was *Ireland v United Kingdom* (1978), where the Irish Government alleged, inter alia, that detention without trial and the use of various interrogation techniques on suspected terrorists in Northern Ireland were contrary to arts 5 and 3, respectively, of the ECHR. More recently, the ECtHR heard *Cyprus v Turkey* (2001) under art 33. However, given that such applications have the potential to threaten the unity of the Council of Europe, it seems unlikely that they will ever be much pursued. It is far more likely that human rights disputes between Contracting Parties will be resolved behind closed doors, away from the glare of publicity which would inevitably attend an inter-state application.

## Admissibility criteria

**16.53**  As we have already noted, the admissibility of an application was formerly a task for the Commission. This task is now performed by a chamber of the Court in the case of inter-state applications, or by a committee or chamber of the Court for individual applications, in accordance with the criteria laid down in art 35 of the ECHR. The decision as to whether an individual application is dealt with by a committee or a chamber is made by a Judge Rapporteur following a preliminary examination of the case.

**16.54**  For the Court to be able to deal with an application:

- all domestic remedies must have been exhausted; and
- no more than six months must have passed from the date on which the final decision was taken.

In the case of individual applications made under art 34, further admissibility criteria apply. These require that an application must not be:

- anonymous;
- substantially the same as a matter that has already been examined by the Court or has already been submitted to another international investigative body;
- incompatible with the provisions of the Convention or the protocols thereto; and
- manifestly ill-founded or an abuse of the right of application.

The admissibility criteria which apply to both types of application are essentially procedural. In the case of individual applications, however, the requirements that the application must not be manifestly ill-founded or an abuse of the right of application will involve considering the merits of the case, even though art 29 of the ECHR refers to admissibility and merits as separate issues.

## Friendly settlements

**16.55**  Where the Court has declared an application admissible, it must then examine the case which may entail undertaking an investigation. At any stage of the proceedings, the Court may:

> place itself at the disposal of the parties concerned with a view to securing a friendly settlement of the matter on the basis of respect for human rights as defined in the Convention and the Protocols thereto. (art 39(1))

**16.56** Friendly settlement negotiations are confidential and without prejudice to the parties' arguments before the Court. By virtue of r 62(2) of the Rules of the Court, no written or oral communication and no offer or concession made whilst trying to secure a friendly settlement may be referred to or relied on before the Court. Such settlements thus amount to a resolution of the case short of a formal court hearing. An applicant who is concerned about the expense or length of time that his case is taking may be attracted by a friendly settlement. It may involve the applicant being financially compensated by the state and, in addition or as an alternative to compensation, the state may undertake to amend an offending law or change an administrative practice.

**16.57** For the state, the attraction of a friendly settlement lies in the fact that it is a way of avoiding a formal court hearing and the possibility of being found to have violated the Convention. The publicity which would inevitably surround such a ruling may be damaging to a state's reputation as a guarantor of human rights. Moreover, friendly settlements often include a clause at the insistence of the state to the effect that the settlement is without prejudice to its submission that there has been no violation of the Convention. In other words, a settlement has been reached without admission of liability.

## Doctrine of a margin of appreciation

**16.58** This doctrine, which has evolved in the jurisprudence of the ECtHR, was, in the words of Cavanaugh, 'born out of the derogation regime'. Its importance lies in its recognition of the fact that a Contracting Party may be in a better position than the Court to determine when a departure from a Convention right is justified by the circumstances. In *Handyside v United Kingdom* (1976), the Court observed that:

> By reason of their direct and continuous contact with the vital forces of their countries, state authorities are in principle in a better position than the international judge to give an opinion on the exact content of those requirements [of morals] as well as on the 'necessity' of a 'restriction' or 'penalty' intended to meet them.

**16.59** The doctrine of a margin of appreciation is particularly significant in terms of the exceptions to arts 8–11 (paras **16.42–16.43**). It also has a role to play in the context of art 15 of the ECHR. In *Brannigan and McBride v United Kingdom* (1993), the Court noted that the Contracting Party was best placed to decide on the presence of an emergency situation and to determine the nature and scope of the measures necessary to avert it. The Court therefore felt that with regard to art 15, 'a wide margin of appreciation should be left to the national authorities'.

**16.60** Clearly there is an inherent danger with the doctrine: if a Contracting Party is allowed too much latitude, it is possible that it may ride roughshod over the rights which it purports to have guaranteed to its citizens. Accordingly, it ought to be noted that the operation of the doctrine is subject to supervision by the ECtHR. Where necessary, the Court will be prepared to rule that a state measure has gone beyond that which was required by the circumstances, ie that it is disproportionate to the legitimate aim pursued.

## Reform of the European Court of Human Rights

**16.61** Since 1998, there has been an 'exponential growth' in the number of applications received by the Court, with the result that as of July 2011, the backlog of cases stood at over 150,000. This figure is partly explained by the fact that the Convention system is available to 800 million people in Europe. However, it is also attributable to the limited successes of previous attempts at institutional reform.

**16.62** Protocol 14 represents one such attempt. It sought to address the problem of the Court's increasing workload by amending the ECHR in three key areas: the Court's filtering capacity; the admissibility criteria; and measures for dealing with repetitive cases. With regard to the first of these, the amended Convention now provides that the task of determining whether or not an individual application is admissible can be carried out by a single judge rather than a minimum of three judges as was formerly the case. This new mechanism thus upholds the principle that the filtering of applications ought to be undertaken by judges whilst at the same time increasing the capacity of those judges to carry out the task.

**16.63** Protocol 14 also amends the ECHR by inserting an additional admissibility requirement into art 35 (para **16.54**). At first glance, the 'significant disadvantage' criterion appears to be an important development, However, it is subject to two provisos: it does not render an application inadmissible where respect for human rights requires that it is determined on its merits; neither does it allow the rejection of an application which has not been duly considered by a domestic tribunal. Thus the new admissibility requirement remains true to the principle that any citizen of a High Contracting Party ought to have the right to apply to the Court where they believe that one of their Convention rights has been violated.

**16.64** Repetitive applications, ie applications raising identical or very similar issues to those previously determined, have been a significant contributory factor to the ever-increasing workload of the Court. Protocol 14 therefore amends the ECHR so as to enable a three-judge panel to declare an application admissible and at the same time reach a decision on its merits 'if the underlying question in the case, concerning the interpretation or application of the Convention or the Protocols thereto, is already the subject of well-established case-law of the Court'.

**16.65** It would seem, however, that these reforms are insufficient to tackle the problems which face the Court. Accordingly, High Level Conferences have been held at Interlaken (February 2010) and Izmir (April 2011). At the former conference, an Action Plan was adopted. This addressed a range of issues, such as the implementation of the ECHR at national level, filtering, repetitive applications, the supervision of execution of judgments (art 46), and a special procedure for amending the ECHR. Thus, for example, in relation to filtering, the Committee of Ministers was invited to examine the setting up of a mechanism within the Court which would go beyond the new single judge procedure. At the Izmir conference, delegates were reminded that although the Protocol 14 reforms have potential which 'remains to be fully exploited', they 'will not provide a lasting and comprehensive solution to the problems facing the Convention system'. Emphasis was therefore placed on the continuing need to drive forward further reforms. States were reminded of the need to report by the end of 2011 on the measures which they have taken to implement the relevant parts of the two declarations.

16.66 In anticipation of the UK's forthcoming assumption of the Chairmanship of the Council of Europe, the coalition Government has established a Commission on a Bill of Rights whose remit includes advising ministers on the reform of the Court. At the end of July 2011, it produced an interim advice consisting of a number of recommendations. These included that the Government should:

- vigorously pursue the need for urgent and fundamental reform of the Court;

- initiate a time-bound reform programme;

- establish a new and effective screening mechanism that allows the Court to decline to deal with applications which do not raise a serious violation of the Convention; and

- revisit the meaning and effect of art 41 of the ECHR and the role of the Court in awarding just satisfaction.

16.67 The publication of the interim advice was accompanied by a letter from its chair, Sir Leigh Lewis. In it, he noted that there were a 'number of other areas for potential reform of the Court' which may or may not be discussed by the Commission in the future. One suggestion was that retired judges may be used to determine the admissibility of applications, thus freeing up the Court's judges to deal with the substantive claims. Another was to allow admissibility to be determined by Registry officials rather than judges. Further suggestions included: enabling the Court to deliver advisory opinions as an alternative to finding that a breach of the ECHR either has or has not occurred; enabling preliminary references to be made to the ECtHR by the highest national court, thus adopting an EU law practice; and requiring applications to the Court to be signed by a lawyer or NGO in the hope that this would lessen the number of manifestly inadmissible cases being sent to Strasbourg.

16.68 In the light of the ongoing initiatives, it seems only a matter of time before further reform of the court and the convention system takes place. Patently neither the High Contracting Parties nor the Convention institutions can afford to procrastinate. Indeed, it should not be forgotten that if the states properly regard the ECtHR as a court of last resort, human rights issues will be more likely to be resolved domestically, with the result that fewer applications will be sent to Strasbourg.

## Incorporation of the Convention into English law: the judges' view

**16.69** In the 45 or so years which marked the period between the ratification of the ECHR by the UK and the incorporation of its substantive rights into domestic law by the Human Rights Act 1998, attitudes amongst the senior judges appear to have changed on the question of incorporation. The Lord Chancellor at the time of ratification, Lord Jowitt, was firmly opposed to such a course of action, and yet a successor of his as Lord Chancellor, Lord Irvine, piloted the Human Rights Bill through the HL. Why the change in attitude towards the ECHR?

**16.70** There is no simple answer to this question. At one level, it might be argued that the change in attitude owes as much to individual personalities as to anything else. Lord Denning, whose judicial career in both the CA and the HL spanned approximately 30 years of the relevant period, once argued against a Private Members' Bill to incorporate the Convention on the basis that it would lead to much litigation brought by 'disgruntled people who will bring proceedings before the courts challenging the orderly system of our society'. Lord Elwyn-Jones, the Lord Chancellor at the time (1976), objected to incorporation for similar reasons and because he considered that the ECHR was 'framed in such wide and general terms'. However, his successor, Lord Hailsham, took a contrary view in his *The Dilemma of Democracy* (1978), where he considered that incorporation may be advantageous to the UK.

**16.71** At another level, it might be argued that the need for incorporation started to become apparent to certain judges when the common law, that traditional tool for the protection of liberties and freedoms, no longer seemed capable of performing the task to their satisfaction. For example, the remarks of Lord Bridge in *A-G v Guardian Newspapers Ltd* (1987) (para **16.12**), suggest a faltering confidence in the common law's ability to protect civil liberties. Such views were not confined to statements made in court. Extra-judicial writings and lectures became a vehicle for expressing views on the Convention and whether or not it ought to be incorporated into UK law. The then Master of the Rolls, Lord Bingham, forcefully argued for the incorporation of the ECHR during a lecture on the subject in 1993. In his opinion, there was no task 'more central to the judicial function, than that of seeking to protect, within the law, the basic human rights of the citizen, against invasion by other citizens or by the state itself'. The need to incorporate the ECHR was due to a number of factors which included:

- the increasing power of the executive;
- the unreliability of Parliament as a guardian of human rights in practice;
- the ever-lengthening list of occasions when the UK was found to be in breach of the Convention either by the Commission or the Court;
- the common law as it stood was unable to give citizens the same protection as the Convention; and

- the fundamental rights protected by the Convention are part of Community law which in turn is part of UK law.

**16.72** There are obviously very close links between certain of these factors. The fact that the UK's system of government has become an 'elective dictatorship' ensures that a legislature which is in theory supreme is ultimately controlled by the executive. Moreover, the inability of the common law to protect human rights to the same degree as the ECHR partly explains the adverse rulings from Strasbourg. However, the fifth factor is perhaps the most interesting of all. Whilst Lord Bingham considered it to be an argument in favour of incorporation, might it not be argued that it was just as much an argument against the need for incorporation?

## Incorporation: a brief history

**16.73** Attempts to directly incorporate the ECHR into UK law occurred quite regularly during the 1970s and 1980s as members of the HL and backbench MPs introduced Bills before Parliament to this effect. Lord Wade, for example, introduced several Bills of Rights, but all such attempts were unsuccessful. It was apparent that the prospects for incorporation would be greatly enhanced if it were to become the policy of one of the major political parties. This occurred prior to the May 1997 general election when the Labour Party published its proposals to 'bring rights home to British people'. Essentially, it argued that incorporation would reduce costs, reduce the time taken to pursue legal proceedings, and give power back to the British courts. These were all factors which made incorporation necessary. With regard to the latter, the Labour Party argued that it was not right that other European citizens could have Convention rights dealt with by the courts in their own country whilst British citizens had to go abroad to seek justice. The increasingly poor record of the UK in terms of the number of admissible cases brought against it, the occasions on which it was actually found to have violated the Convention, and the generally serious nature of these complaints was also cited as a justification for incorporation. Thus the Labour Party fought the 1997 general election with a manifesto commitment to incorporate the ECHR, if elected. Success at the polls gave the Labour Party the mandate that it desired.

## The Human Rights Act 1998

**16.74** The Human Rights Act (HRA) received Royal Assent on 9 November 1998. Many of its provisions did not, however, come into force until 2 October 2000. Such a delay is explicable in terms of the opportunity that it provided for the courts, tribunals, lawyers, and public authorities to become better acquainted with the ECHR and the obligations and duties which flow from the conferment of rights on individuals. The key constitutional aspects of the HRA have already been discussed in Chapter 5. Thus in this chapter, the focus will be upon the human rights issues raised by the Act.

## Convention rights

**16.75** Section 1 of the 1998 Act gives effect in UK law to what the Act refers to as 'Convention rights'. These are defined as being: arts 2–12 and 14 of the ECHR; arts 1–3 of the First Protocol; and, arts 1 and 2 of the Sixth Protocol. Article 1 is therefore omitted from the definition, as is art 13 of the ECHR. In the case of the former, this is not surprising given that it does not confer a substantive right on individuals. In the case of art 13, however, the same argument cannot be applied. It requires that:

> Everyone whose rights and freedoms as set forth in this Convention are violated shall have an effective remedy before a national authority notwithstanding that the violation has been committed by persons acting in an official capacity.

**16.76** The exclusion of art 13 from the definition of 'Convention rights' was defended by the former Lord Chancellor, Lord Irvine, during the passage of the HR Bill on the basis that it was otiose. In his opinion, the power which s 8(1) of the 1998 Act invests in the courts to 'grant such relief or remedy, or make such order, within its powers as it considers appropriate', rendered the inclusion of art 13 unnecessary.

## Interpreting Convention rights

**16.77** When interpreting Convention rights, s 2 of the 1998 Act requires domestic courts to 'take into account' the jurisprudence of the ECtHR together with the opinions and decisions of the Commission and the Committee of Ministers. This clearly makes sense. It would be foolhardy if judges who were not necessarily familiar with the text of the Convention did not have regard to the judgments and decisions of the Convention's institutions in respect of the rights contained therein. However, s 2 does not oblige domestic courts to reach an interpretation which is consistent with the views from Strasbourg. Nevertheless, in *R (Alconbury Developments and others) v Secretary of State for the Environment, Transport and the Regions* (2003), Lord Slynn observed:

> Although the Human Rights Act 1998 does not provide that a national court is bound by these decisions it is obliged to take account of them as far as they are relevant. In the absence of some special circumstances it seems to me that the court should follow any clear and constant jurisprudence of the European Court of Human Rights. If it does not do so there is at least a possibility that the case will go to that court, which is likely in the ordinary case to follow its own constant jurisprudence.

**16.78** Similarly, in the later immigration case *R (Ullah) v Special Adjudicator* (2004), Lord Bingham remarked:

> In determining the present question, the House of Lords is required by s 2(1) of the Human Rights Act 1998 to take into account any relevant Strasbourg case law. While such case law is not strictly binding, it has been held that courts should, in the

> *absence of some special circumstances, follow any clear and constant jurisprudence*
> *of the ECtHR...This reflects the fact that the European Convention is an international*
> *instrument, the correct interpretation of which can be authoritatively expounded only*
> *by the ECtHR. From this it follows that a national court subject to a duty such as that*
> *imposed by s 2 should not without strong reason dilute or weaken the effect of the*
> *Strasbourg case law...The duty of national courts is to keep pace with the Strasbourg*
> *jurisprudence as it evolves over time: no more, but certainly no less.*

**16.79** In both passages, the central thrust of the remarks is that although in the vast majority
of cases national courts will be inclined to reach decisions which are consistent with
the 'clear and constant' jurisprudence of the ECtHR, there may be rare occasions when
a national court is entitled to depart from a Strasbourg decision. Thus in *R v Horncastle*
(2009), the Supreme Court declined to follow a judgment of the ECtHR in a previous case (*Al-Khawaja v UK* (2009)) on the basis that it had concerns as to whether, in
reaching that decision, the ECtHR had sufficiently appreciated the relevant aspects of
the domestic criminal justice system. In circumstances such as these it was considered
permissible to depart from the ECtHR decision, provided that reasons were given for
adopting that course of action.

## Freedom of expression and freedom of thought, conscience, and religion

**16.80** Of all the Convention's substantive rights, only two are specifically mentioned in the
main body of the 1998 Act (the Convention rights appear in Sch 1 to the Act). These
are the rights enshrined in arts 9 and 10: freedom of thought, conscience, and religion;
and freedom of expression. Sections 12 and 13 of the HRA 1998 require the courts to
have particular regard to these rights when considering granting relief or allowing for
a development in the law which would have an impact on these rights. Although this
does not amount to according these rights a special status, it does reflect the fact that
they are potentially vulnerable to the development of other rights based on the terms of
the ECHR. Thus as Duffy and Stanley have noted, s 12(4) of the Act acknowledges the
impact which the development of a tort of privacy would have upon freedom of expression. It therefore requires a court to have this in mind in respect of proceedings to prevent the publication of material which the respondent claims is 'journalistic, literary or
artistic'. In *Douglas v Hello! Ltd* (2001), Sedley LJ observed that:

> *by subsection (4) [of s 12] it puts beyond question the direct applicability of at least one*
> *article of the Convention as between one private party to litigation and another – in*
> *the jargon, its horizontal effect.*

**16.81** In the case of s 13, the importance of the right to freedom of thought, conscience,
and religion is evident where an applicant seeks to enforce a 'right' which would run
contrary to religious teachings, eg where a gay couple wished to be married in church
(Duffy and Stanley). It ought to be noted, however, that Lester and Pannick consider

that s 13 'serves no sensible purpose' for a number of reasons, chief amongst which is that the Act is more likely to benefit rather than hinder religious organizations in that, for the first time, English law protects religious freedom.

## Public authorities

**16.82** By virtue of s 6(1) of the 1998 Act:

> *It is unlawful for a public authority to act in a way which is incompatible with a Convention right.*

A public authority will not be acting unlawfully, however, if the terms of primary legislation require it to act in a way which is incompatible with a Convention right (s 6(2)). For the purposes of the HRA, a 'public authority' is not exhaustively defined. However, it does include: a court or tribunal; and any person certain of whose functions are functions of a public nature. Thus the Act envisages two, perhaps even three, categories of public authorities. First, there are courts and tribunals which are expressly mentioned in the s 6(3)(a) definition. The fact that they are so mentioned may entitle them to be regarded as a separate category or, if they are not to be so regarded, then patently they fall within the second category; those bodies which English law has recognized as being public bodies, eg government departments, local authorities, prisons, and the police. In *Aston Cantlow and Wilmcote with Billesley Parochial Church Council v Wallbank* (2003) (para **16.84**), such bodies were referred to in the course of argument as 'core' public authorities. In the words of Lord Hope in that case, they are 'public authorities through and through'. The third category consists of persons or bodies certain of whose functions are of a public nature. In *Aston Cantlow* these were referred to in argument as 'hybrid' public authorities, although they may also be referred to as 'functional' public authorities. In other words, they are not public bodies through and through. Rather, they perform certain functions which are of a public nature and which hence make it appropriate for them to be subject to the terms of the HRA in respect of the exercise of those functions. They may also perform acts which are of a private nature and which do not therefore fall within the scope of the HRA: s 6(5) of the 1998 Act.

**16.83** Parliament is expressly excluded from the definition of 'public authority' in s 6 of the HRA. Thus it would not be acting unlawfully if it were to enact laws which were contrary to Convention rights. The legislative supremacy of Parliament (see Chapter **5**) is thereby preserved by the exclusion.

**16.84** Given the open-ended nature of the definition of 'public authority' in the HRA, it has inevitably fallen to the courts to determine whether or not a body is a public authority for the purposes of the Act:

> *Poplar Housing and Regeneration Community Association Ltd v Donoghue*
> **(2001):** D was provided with accommodation by the local authority as a homeless person

in compliance with the authority's duty under the Housing Act 1996. The property was later transferred to the claimant, a housing association and registered social landlord created by the local authority. D was served with a notice to quit after it was concluded that she had been intentionally homeless. At the possession proceedings before the county court, she claimed that the making of a possession order would contravene her rights under art 8(1) of the ECHR. That argument was rejected and the possession order was made. D appealed to the CA. Since D sought a declaration that s 21(4) of the Housing Act 1988 was incompatible with her Convention rights, the SoS intervened. He contended, inter alia, that the housing association was not a public authority for the purposes of s 6 of the HRA. CA held: dismissing the appeal, that there had been no contravention of D's art 8 rights since s 21(4) of the 1988 Act was necessary in a democratic society. With regard to the 'public authority' issue, housing associations were not standard public authorities and hence they could only be a public authority for the purposes of the HRA if they performed a particular function which was public as opposed to private. In the present case, the housing association's role in providing accommodation and then seeking possession was so closely assimilated to that of the local authority that it was performing a public rather than a private function. It therefore constituted a 'functional' public authority for the purposes of s 6(3)(b) of the HRA.

*R (on the application of Heather) v Leonard Cheshire Foundation* (2002): The local authority was under a duty pursuant to s 21 of the National Assistance Act 1948 to provide accommodation for the claimants. It therefore arranged with the defendant, a charitable foundation, to accommodate the claimants at public expense. Those arrangements lasted for 17 years until it was decided to close the home down. The claimants sought judicial review of that decision. They claimed that in having provided them with accommodation, the foundation had been acting as a public authority and that it had therefore violated their rights under art 8 of the ECHR when it made the closure decision. At first instance, it was held that the foundation was not a public authority within the meaning of s 6(3) of the HRA. The claimants appealed. CA held: dismissing the appeal, that the role that the foundation was performing did not involve the performance of public functions. It was not standing in the shoes of the local authority. It did not exercise statutory powers in performing functions for the claimants.

*Aston Cantlow and Wilmcote with Billesley Parochial Church Council v Wallbank* (2003): As freehold owners of certain rectorial land, the lay rectors were under a common law obligation to repair the chancel of the parish church. The chancel fell into disrepair and the Parochial Church Council (PCC) exercised its statutory power to enforce that obligation by serving notices on the rectors under the Chancel Repairs Act 1932. The rectors disputed their liability and the PCC brought proceedings against them to recover the estimated costs of the repairs. At first instance, the lay rectors were held liable. They appealed to the CA which held that the PCC was a 'core' public authority for the purposes of the HRA and that it had acted incompatibly with the lay rectors' Convention rights when serving them with the notices. Accordingly, the appeal was allowed. The PCC appealed. HL held: allowing the appeal, that the PCC was not a 'core' public authority for the purposes of s 6 of the HRA and neither did it become a 'functional' public authority when enforcing a lay rector's liability for chancel repairs. The function of the PCC was to carry out the religious mission of the Church of England, rather than to exercise any governmental power. It was not under any state supervision. Moreover, the enforcement of liability for chancel repairs involved the recovery of a civil debt which was clearly a private rather than a public act.

---

*YL v Birmingham City Council* **(2007):** The claimant was an 84-year-old woman with Alzheimer's disease living in a care home run by a private company, Southern Cross Health-care Ltd. She had been placed there by the council in accordance with its statutory duty under s 21 of the National Assistance Act 1948, and pursuant to its powers under s 26 of the same Act to enter into contractual arrangements with private providers. The contract with Southern Cross included a clause that both it and its employees and agents were at all times to act in a way that was compatible with Convention rights. YL's care was funded by the council, a primary care trust (due to her health needs) and her own family. Southern Cross served a notice to quit on YL. On her behalf a declaration was sought that in provid-ing accommodation and care for her, Southern Cross was exercising a function of a public nature for the purposes of the HRA, and that removing her from the care home would breach her rights under arts 2, 3, and 8 of the ECHR. At first instance the HCt ruled that the care home was not performing a function of a public nature. The CA agreed, following its own previous decision in *Leonard Cheshire.* YL further appealed. HL held: by a majority of 3–2, that the appeal be dismissed. A distinction could be drawn between the statutory functions and responsibilities of a council under the 1948 Act in relation to those in need of care and accommodation, and the provision of that care and accommodation by a private company pursuant to a contract with the council. The latter was not an inherently public function and therefore fell outside the scope of s 6(3)(b) of the HRA. The claimant and others like her retained public law rights against the council, but did not have Convention rights as against the care home.

---

**16.85** It is apparent from each of these authorities that the question whether or not a body is performing a function of a public nature for the purposes of the HRA is a matter to be determined according to the particular facts of the case before the court. In the absence of a single test of universal application there is ample room for argument and, as the decisions in *Aston Cantlow* and *YL* patently demonstrate, the possibility of a divergence of opinion amongst senior judges on this fundamental question. It might be thought that the tests which have been developed by the courts for the purposes of determining whether a body is susceptible to judicial review (paras **12.27–12.28**) or whether it is an emanation of the state for the purpose of the doctrine of direct effect of directives in EU law (paras **10.26–10.30**) would be influential in the present context. However, in *Aston Cantlow*, Lord Hope made it clear that this need not necessarily be the case:

> the decided cases on the amenability of bodies to judicial review have been made for purposes which have nothing to do with the liability of the state in international law. They cannot be regarded as determinative of a body's membership of the class of 'core' public authorities ... Nor can they be regarded as determinative of the question

> *whether a body falls within the 'hybrid' class. That is not to say that the case law on judicial review may not provide some assistance as to what does, and what does not, constitute a 'function of a public nature' within the meaning of s 6(3)(b). It may well be helpful. But the domestic case law must be examined in the light of the jurisprudence of the Strasbourg court as to those bodies which engage the responsibility of the state for the purposes of the Convention.*

And:

> *Whatever its value may be in the context of European Community law, it would be neither safe nor helpful to use this concept [emanation of the state] as a shorthand way of describing the test that must be applied to determine whether a person or body is a non-governmental organisation for the purposes of art 34 of the Convention.*

**16.86** In *YL*, Lord Bingham (dissenting) implicitly agreed with Lord Hope in *Aston Cantlow* when he remarked that in deciding whether a function is of a public nature, 'it will not ordinarily matter whether the body in question is amenable to judicial review'. The reason for this is that, in the words of Lord Mance in *YL*, 'section 6 has a different rationale, linked to the scope of states' responsibility in Strasbourg'. The distinction between domestic judicial review and a human rights application before the ECtHR had previously been referred to by Lord Bingham in *R (SB) v Governors of Denbigh High School* (2007), when he observed:

> *But the focus at Strasbourg is not and never has been on whether a challenged decision or action is the product of a defective decision-making process, but on whether, in the case under consideration, the applicant's Convention rights have been violated.*

**16.87** Although there is no universal or litmus test for what is a function of a public nature for the purposes of s 6(3)(b) of the HRA, the lack of a clear statutory definition has not necessarily been regarded as a deficiency in some quarters. Thus in *YL*, Lord Bingham opined:

> *Tempting as it is to try and formulate a general test applicable to all cases which may arise, I think there are serious dangers in doing so. The draftsman was wise to express himself as he did, and leave it to the courts to decide on the facts of particular cases where the dividing line should be drawn.*

**16.88** In the earlier case of *Aston Cantlow*, Lord Nicholls had contended that when deciding whether a function is public:

> *Factors to be taken into account include the extent to which in carrying out the relevant function the body is publicly funded, or is exercising statutory powers, or is taking the place of central government or local authorities, or is providing a public service.*

**16.89** The non-exhaustive nature of this list is evidenced by the presence of the word 'include'. In *YL* Baroness Hale (dissenting) quoted Lord Nicholls's remarks with approval and commented that the factors that he identified 'tell heavily in favour of s 6(3)(b) applying to this case'. For her part, Baroness Hale identified the following factors as relevant to determining a s 6(3)(b) question:

- whether the state has assumed responsibility for seeing that the task is performed;
- the public interest in having that task undertaken;
- public funding;
- whether the function involves or may involve the use of statutory coercive powers;
- whether there is a close connection between the service provided and the core values underlying the Convention rights.

## Joint Committee on Human Rights (JCHR)

**16.90**  The JCHR plays an important role in relation to rights protection. It is required by the Standing Orders of both Houses to consider:

- matters relating to human rights in the UK (but excluding consideration of individual cases);
- proposals for remedial orders, draft remedial orders and remedial orders made pursuant to s 10 of and laid under Sch 2 to the HRA;
- in respect of draft remedial orders and remedial orders, whether the special attention of the Houses should be drawn to them.

In addition, the JCHR also considers and reports on human rights issues of more general importance.

**16.91**  In its seventh report for the 2002–03 session, the JCHR examined the meaning of 'public authority' in the HRA. It came to the view that, as the law stood, a private body is likely to be held to be a 'functional' public authority under s 6(3)(b) of the HRA 1998 where: its structures and work are closely linked with the delegating or contracting out state body; or it is exercising powers of a public nature directly assigned to it by statute; or it is exercising coercive powers devolved from the state. Other factors which may indicate that the function being performed has a 'public flavour' were identified as follows:

- the fact of delegation from a state body;
- the fact of supervision by a state regulatory body;
- public funding;
- the public interest in the functions being performed; or
- motivation of serving the public interest, rather than profit.

**16.92**  In the opinion of the JCHR, 'the situation created by the current state of the law is unsatisfactory, unfair, and inconsistent with the intention of Parliament'. As far as potential solutions were concerned, the JCHR was not convinced that amending the wording of s 6(3)(b) was the way forward, and neither did it support the ideas of scheduling a list of 'functional' public authorities to the Act, or allowing ministers to designate particular bodies as public authorities for the purposes of the Act by way of subordinate legislation. Since it was firmly of the view that it would be 'unsatisfactory to leave this matter to the present state of the case law', it advocated the following approach:

> We urge the Government to intervene in the public interest as a third party in cases where it can press the case for a broad, functional interpretation of the meaning of public authority under the Human Rights Act. In the interests of the full protection of Convention human rights which the Human Rights Act was designed to achieve, what is needed is a careful application of the current section 6 test so as to prevent any diminution in human rights protection arising from contracting out of public services.

As far as the JCHR was concerned:

> a body is a functional public authority performing a public function under section 6(3)(b) of the Human Rights Act where it exercises a function that has its origin in governmental responsibilities, in such a way as to compel individuals to rely on that body for realisation of their Convention human rights.

**16.93**  The JCHR returned to the subject of the meaning of 'public authority' for the purposes of the HRA in its ninth report for the 2006–7 session. It took the view that although its previous recommendations were capable of providing an effective solution, three years of Government third-party intervention in the appeals before the courts had failed to move the law away from the narrow interpretation adopted in *Leonard Cheshire*. In the Committee's opinion:

> the current situation is unsatisfactory and unfair and continues to frustrate the intention of Parliament. It creates the potential for significant inconsistencies in the application of the HRA and denies the protection of the rights it guarantees to those who need its protection. In view of the continuing trend towards the contracting out of public functions, there is now a need for urgent action to secure a solution and to reinstate the application of the HRA in accordance with Parliament's intentions when it passed the HRA.

**16.94**  At the time that the JCHR's report was published the appeal in *YL* was pending. Nevertheless, the JCHR expressed concern that 'whatever decision is reached in the House of Lords, it is unlikely to lead to an enduring and effective solution to the interpretive problems associated with the meaning of public authority'. As it has turned out, the majority of the HL favoured the narrow construction adopted in *Leonard Cheshire* rather than the broader interpretation favoured by both the JCHR and the minority who heard the appeal in *YL*. The JCHR has therefore advocated that the Government should 'bring forward alternative legislative solutions for consideration by Parliament shortly after the decision of the House of Lords'. It sees the direct amendment of s 6 of the HRA as 'a matter of last resort'. Its preferred solution is for 'a separate, supplementary and interpretive statute, specifically directed to clarifying the interpretation of "functions of a public nature" in s 6(3)(b) HRA'. The JCHR has suggested that the interpretive statute could contain the following provision:

> *For the purposes of s 6(3)(b) of the Human Rights Act 1998, a function of a public nature includes a function performed pursuant to a contract or other arrangement with a public authority which is under a duty to perform the function.*

**16.95** The HL decision in *YL* has subsequently been nullified by s 145 of the Health and Social Care Act 2008 which deems that the provision of publicly funded residential care in private care homes amounts to a public function for the purposes of the HRA. However, this constitutes a specific solution in relation to a particular sector rather than a more far-reaching resolution of a problem about which the JCHR continues to have concerns. Its first report of session 2009–10 makes it clear that it remains of the view that a 'legislative change is necessary to restore the original intention of Parliament, that all private bodies performing public functions should be subject to the duty to act compatibly with human rights'. Importantly, the JCHR heard evidence from public law solicitors which suggested that satellite litigation was becoming increasingly necessary on the issue of what is and what is not a 'public authority' before a claimant could be sure that a claim could proceed. The JCHR noted that in *R (on the application of Weaver) v London & Quadrant Housing Trust* (2009), the CA held by a majority that the allocation and management of social housing by a registered social landlord was a public function for the purposes of the HRA. In reaching that conclusion, Elias LJ felt that there were various factors which brought the Trust within the purview of the HRA. These were:

- it was significantly reliant on public finance;
- although it had not directly taken the place of local government, nevertheless in allocating social housing, the Trust operated 'in very close harmony' with the authority helping it to meet its statutory duties and objectives;
- the provision of subsidized housing was a function which could properly be described as 'governmental';
- the Trust could properly be described as providing a public service.

**16.96** The Supreme Court denied leave to appeal in *Weaver*. It would seem, therefore, that unless or until legislation is brought forward in Parliament to clarify the uncertainty surrounding the meaning of 'public authority' in s 6 of the HRA, the law in this area will continue to develop in a piecemeal fashion in the light of cases brought before the courts. Whether it is appropriate that such a fundamental issue, concerning the operation of the HRA and the legal enforceability of the rights contained therein, should be left to be resolved on a case-by-case and sector-by-sector basis, is a moot point.

## Does the Human Rights Act have horizontal effect?

**16.97** The concept of horizontal effect is, as we have seen, of importance in connection with the enforceability of EU law rights (paras **10.24–10.25**). In the present context, the question has arisen as to whether the Human Rights Act permits an individual to enforce Convention rights against another private individual or whether such rights can only be enforced against public authorities. In the debate on the second reading of the Human Rights Bill in the HL, Lord Irvine LC (as he then was) made it clear what the Government's intention was on this point:

> We decided, first of all, that a provision of this kind should apply only to public authorities, however defined, and not to private individuals. That reflects the arrangements for taking cases to the Convention institutions in Strasbourg. The Convention had its origins in a desire to protect people from the misuse of power by the state, rather than from actions of private individuals. Someone who takes a case to Strasbourg is proceeding against the United Kingdom Government, rather than against a private individual.

**16.98** Nevertheless, the inclusion of courts and tribunals in the definition of 'public authority' in s 6(1) of the 1998 Act has caused some, most notably Professor Sir William Wade, to argue that whatever the Government's intention was, the wording of the Act is such as to permit the enforcement of Convention rights by one individual against another. The basis of this argument is as follows. Since courts are public authorities for the purposes of the 1998 Act, they must act in a way which is compatible with Convention rights when hearing cases. Accordingly, even in proceedings between private individuals, the Court would have to determine the case in a way that is compatible with Convention rights. The net result would therefore be that Convention rights are germane in the context of private law as well as public law relationships.

**16.99** Support for this view can be found, somewhat paradoxically given his earlier pronouncement (para **16.97**), in the words of Lord Irvine. In a later parliamentary response to a proposed amendment to the Human Rights Bill, his Lordship remarked that:

> We . . . believe that it is right as a matter of principle for the courts to have the duty of acting compatibly with the Convention not only in cases involving other public authorities but also in developing the common law in deciding cases between individuals . . . In preparing this Bill we have taken the view that it is the other course, that of excluding Convention considerations altogether from cases between individuals, which would have to be justified. We do not think that it would be justifiable; nor, indeed, do we think that it would be practicable.

**16.100** Ought this statement to be regarded as having impliedly repealed Lord Irvine's earlier remarks? Professor Sir William Wade clearly thinks that it should, but a range of views on the question whether the Human Rights Act has horizontal effect have been expressed in the pages of the *Law Quarterly Review* and other leading academic law journals. Indeed, in *X v Y* (2004), Mummery LJ commented that the HRA 'has generated more legal literature than litigation on the disputed question whether it applies as between private individuals'. Sir Richard Buxton (formerly a judge of the CA) is of the view that the Act does not have horizontal effect on the basis that to hold otherwise would be contrary to the wording of the Convention rights and to the jurisprudence of the ECtHR. In his opinion, both demonstrate that Convention rights are enforceable against the state rather than against an individual. In other words, such rights only have vertical effect.

**16.101** In a further contribution to this debate, Bamforth has suggested, with respect, that neither Sir William's nor Sir Richard's view is correct. In his opinion, Sir Richard's 'attempt to dissociate the Human Rights Act from any type of "horizontal effect" is unlikely to succeed, given that his argument seemingly fails to take account of the role of the domestic courts in relation to Convention rights both at common law and under the Act'. Moreover, Bamforth rejects Sir William's 'literal argument' on the basis that it 'appears to make too much of the drafting solely of section 6 and to pay too little attention to what it actually means to say that a court is obliged, or has a lawful duty, to act in accordance with Convention rights'. In Bamforth's opinion:

> In order for the 'literal argument' to work, we would need to be able to say that a court is placed under a positive obligation to act in accordance with Convention rights in all cases which come before it, whoever the parties to the case happen to be. For a court properly to be said to be under any such obligation, it would need to be subject to a clear sanction where it failed to act in accordance with that obligation. The Act, however, makes no clear sanction available against a court for failure to act in accordance with Convention rights under section 6.

For Bamforth, therefore, what he terms the 'true' horizontal effect of the HRA lies in a provision which has been overlooked by both of the other commentators: s 3 of the 1998 Act. It is this provision, together with common law authority, which provides 'a clearer and more straightforward method of giving a measure of "horizontal effect" to Convention rights than might any argument based upon section 6'.

**16.102** In their article (which contains a useful summary of these and other views), Beyleveld and Pattinson argue that the controversy over this issue must be resolved in favour of awarding full horizontal effect to the Act. They contend that, on a conceptual level, the rights and freedoms set out in the Convention are held by individuals both against the state and against other individuals who are capable of acting in ways which interfere with their abilities to enjoy those rights; that they apply horizontally. However, in order for such rights to have horizontal effect in a particular case, they 'must be recognised as or by a cause of action between individuals in that context'. Their central contention is, therefore, that 'given the concept of a right in the Convention, the way in which the Act incorporates rights of the Convention entails that they are given full horizontal effect'.

**16.103** Whether or not the issue has been conclusively resolved by the courts is a moot point. The decisions in *Douglas v Hello! Ltd* (2001) and *Venables v News Group Newspapers*

*Ltd* (2001) appear to reflect an acceptance that the HRA does have horizontal effect, even if in the former case, the point was only made in respect of s 12(4) of the Act (para **16.80**). However, in *Campbell v MGN Ltd* (2004), the majority of the HL which heard the appeal appeared to take the view that the HRA 1998 does not have direct horizontal effect. The answer may lie, therefore, in the Act being said to have indirect horizontal effect. This seems to be reflected in the words of Dyson LJ in *X v Y* (2004) when he observed:

> the interpretative duty imposed by section 3 applies to the same degree in the legislation applying between private parties as it does in legislation which applies between public authorities and individuals. There is nothing in the HRA which, either expressly or by necessary implication, indicates a contrary intention. If the position were otherwise, the same statutory provision would require different interpretations depending on whether the defendant was a public authority or a private individual.

## Proceedings

16.104  Where it is claimed that a public authority has acted contrary to s 6, or that it proposes to do so, s 7 provides that a person may bring proceedings against that authority. Moreover, in proceedings brought against a person, they may rely on the Convention right or rights concerned. Thus the claim that a public authority has acted contrary to a Convention right may be used either as a sword or a shield. However, for the purposes of s 7, the allegation that a public authority has acted unlawfully can only be invoked by a person who is, or would be, a 'victim' of that act.

## Standing under the Human Rights Act

16.105  Standing or locus standi in respect of judicial review proceedings has already been considered in this book (see paras **12.60–12.65**). By virtue of art 34 of the ECHR, complaints under the Convention can only be brought by a 'person, non-governmental organisation or group of individuals claiming to be a victim of a violation'. Under the HRA, this 'victim test' takes precedence over the sufficient interest test where the proceedings are brought in an application for judicial review (s 7(3)). In other words, an applicant alleging the breach of a Convention right would have to establish that he is a victim of that breach. He will not be deemed to have a sufficient interest unless he is able to do so.

16.106  The issue of standing under the 1998 Act is perhaps less clear-cut than might at first glance appear to be the case. Whilst the Act itself adopts the 'victim test' from the ECHR, it does not preclude the right of a person to rely upon 'any other right or freedom conferred on him by or under any law having effect in any part of the United Kingdom': s 11(a). Since fundamental human rights are principles of both the common law and EU law, it follows that a party may be able to rely upon them in legal proceedings where their standing has been determined on the basis of sufficient interest rather than the victim test. This may be an attractive option for a 'representative plaintiff' unable to satisfy the victim test.

## Judicial deference/discretionary area of judgment

**16.107**    As has previously been noted (paras **16.58–16.60**), the ECtHR has developed a doctrine known as the 'margin of appreciation' to reflect its belief that on occasion, state authorities are better placed than the Court to determine whether or not restrictions placed on human rights may be justified by the particular circumstances. Following the enactment of the HRA, the extent to which the domestic courts would defer to the views of the executive or the legislature on such matters patently became an important issue given that under the Act, the court's role 'is as the guardian of human rights' (per Simon Brown LJ (as he then was) in *International Transport Roth GmbH v Secretary of State for the Home Department* (2002)).

**16.108**    In *R (on the application of Prolife Alliance) v BBC* (2003), a case concerning a challenge to the lawfulness of the BBC's decision not to transmit an anti-abortion party election broadcast on the ground that it violated the claimant's right to freedom of expression under art 10 of the ECHR, Lord Hoffmann observed:

> Although the word 'deference' is now very popular in describing the relationship between the judicial and other branches of government, I do not think that its overtones of servility, or perhaps gracious concession, are apposite to describe what is happening. In a society based upon the rule of law and the separation of powers, it is necessary to decide which branch of government has in any particular instance the decision-making power and what the legal limits of that power are. That is a question of law and must therefore be decided by the courts… When a court decides that a decision is within the proper competence of the legislature or executive, it is not showing deference. It is deciding the law.

**16.109**    Putting to one side arguments as to whether it is more appropriate to talk of 'deference' or a 'discretionary area of judgment' in this context, it is patently the case that the role of the courts in relation to the HRA, and the debate surrounding that role, is very important indeed. Lord Hoffmann's view, which to a large extent reflects the traditional orthodoxy that due to the separation of powers (see Chapter **2**) and constitutional principle, judges should be wary about straying into the territory of the other branches of government, is not supported by others. Thus, for example, Professor Jowell has contended:

> Lord Hoffmann is right that it is for the courts to decide the scope of rights, but there is no magic legal or other formula to identify the 'discretionary area of judgment'

*available to the reviewed body. In deciding whether matters such as national security, or public interest, or morals should be permitted to prevail over a right, the courts must consider not only the rational exercise of discretion by the reviewed body but also the imperatives of a rights-based democracy. In the course of some of the steps in the process of this assessment the courts may properly acknowledge their own institutional limitations. In so doing, however, they should guard against a presumption that matters of public interest are outside their competence and be ever aware that they are now the ultimate arbiters (although not ultimate guarantors) of the necessary qualities of a democracy in which the popular will is no longer always expected to prevail.*

**16.110** Moreover, it is noteworthy that Lord Steyn has openly expressed his disagreement with Lord Hoffmann on this subject. In Lord Steyn's opinion, 'in point of principle there cannot be any no-go areas under the ECHR and for the rule of law'. Accordingly, he advocates an approach which entails a rigorous scrutiny by the courts of impugned decisions affecting the rights of the individual, and a clear reluctance to decline to decide an issue, save in exceptional circumstances. Thus 'at the risk of over-simplification', Lord Steyn summarizes his position thus:

*The rule of law requires that courts do not surrender their responsibilities. So far as the courts desist from making decisions in a particular case it should not be on grounds of separation of powers, or other constitutional principle. Deference may lead courts not to make their own judgments on an issue. The degree of deference which the courts should show will, of course, depend on and vary with the context. The true justification for a court exceptionally declining to decide an issue, which is within its jurisdiction, is the relative institutional competence or capacity of the branches of government.*

**16.111** TRS Allan has also produced a vigorous critique of the doctrine of due deference which he contends is, 'on closer inspection "non-justiciability" in pastoral colours'. In his opinion:

*A doctrine of judicial deference . . . is either empty or pernicious. It is empty if it purports to implement a separation of powers between the courts and other branches of government; that separation is independently secured by the proper application of legal principles defining the scope of individual rights or the limits of public powers. A doctrine of judicial deference is pernicious if, forsaking the separation of powers, correctly conceived, it permits the abdication of judicial responsibility in favour of reliance on the good faith or good sense or special expertise of public officials, whose judgments about the implications of rights in specific cases may well be wrong.*

## Judicial remedies

**16.112** Where a court finds that an act of a public authority is, or would be, unlawful, it may grant such relief or remedy as it considers appropriate, provided that it has the power to do so: s 8. This proviso is important because it precludes the possibility of the courts developing new remedies for acting contrary to a Convention right. It is worth noting, however, that by virtue of s 7(11), a minister may add to the relief or remedies which a tribunal may grant for the violation of a Convention right.

**16.113**  Damages may be awarded under s 8 of the Act, although there are limits on the exercise of this power. Thus by virtue of s 8(2), 'damages may be awarded only by a court which has power to award damages, or to order the payment of compensation, in civil proceedings'. In other words, the jurisdiction to award damages is restricted to those courts which currently award damages: the civil courts. If in criminal proceedings a court held that there had been a violation of a Convention right, the 'victim' could not be compensated by order of that court. He would have to pursue separate proceedings in the civil courts. Moreover, damages are not an automatic entitlement under the 1998 Act. This much is evident from s 8(3) which provides that:

> No award of damages is to be made unless, taking account of all the circumstances of the case, including –
>
> (a) any other relief or remedy granted, or order made, in relation to the act in question (by that or any other court), and
>
> (b) the consequences of any decision (of that or any other court) in respect of that act, the court is satisfied that the award is necessary to afford just satisfaction to the person in whose favour it is made.

**16.114**  Thus a court may take the view that damages are unnecessary given the nature of the relief already granted. In deciding whether or not to award damages, or the quantum of damages, a court must take into account the principles applied by the ECtHR to the award of 'just satisfaction' under art 41 of the ECHR. Thus in this respect, s 8(3) is rather like s 2 (para **16.77**) in that it requires UK courts to have regard to the jurisprudence of the ECtHR, although it stops short of compelling them to follow it.

**16.115**  It is evident from the HL decision in *R (Greenfield) v Secretary of State for the Home Department* (2005), that when having regard to the Strasbourg jurisprudence, domestic courts are more likely to consider those cases where an award of just satisfaction has been made for a breach of the same Convention article as is relevant in the domestic proceedings. It is also apparent that for damages to be awarded, it is necessary for the claimant to establish a causative link between the loss or damage complained of and the breach of the Convention right. Thus, for example, in *R (on the application of Faulkener) v Secretary of State for Justice and the Parole Board* (2011), the CA awarded the claimant £10,000 for having been unlawfully detained for a period of approximately 10 months contrary to art 5(4) of the ECHR. In arriving at this figure, Sedley LJ noted that 'there are no articulated principles, and no discernible tariff' by which such awards are set. Instead, all that a court can do is look at past awards in helping it to quantify what amounts to just satisfaction in monetary terms in the case before it.

16.116   As the definition of 'public authority' makes clear (paras 16.82–16.89), a court is a public authority for the purposes of the Act. Courts may therefore act unlawfully by acting contrary to a Convention right, in which case they may be liable in damages. However, by virtue of s 9(3), damages may not be awarded where a judicial act has been done in good faith, unless it is necessary to compensate a person in accordance with art 5(5) of the ECHR. This entitles everyone who has been the 'victim of arrest or detention' in contravention of art 5 to compensation. By necessary implication, therefore, excepting the situation covered by art 5(5), damages will only be awarded in respect of a judicial act which can be shown to have been done in bad faith. Proving judicial bad faith is likely to be a difficult task (see paras 13.19–13.20).

## Remedial orders

16.117   Subject to the provisos laid down in s 10(1)(a)(i)–(iii), which relate to appeals, if a minister believes that there are compelling reasons for doing so, he may by order amend legislation which has been declared to be incompatible with a Convention right under s 4 of the HRA. In other words, the minister has the power to amend primary legislation by making secondary legislation. Such provisions, which are known as 'Henry VIII' clauses, confer a wide and important power on members of the executive. The parliamentary scrutiny to which they are subject may be limited. Generally, a draft of the order must be approved by each House of Parliament in accordance with the procedure laid down in Sch 2 to the 1998 Act. In urgent cases, however, a draft order need not be laid before Parliament. Given the importance of this power, its use needs to be limited. In the present context, the use of remedial orders is clearly circumscribed and in any event, it is a use for the promotion of rather than a restriction on human rights. A remedial order may also be made where in the light of a ruling made against the UK by the ECtHR, it appears that a legislative provision 'is incompatible with an obligation of the United Kingdom arising from the Convention': s 10(1)(b). Thus, for example, in order to comply with the ruling in *B and L v UK* [2005], where the ECtHR held that s 1 and Sch 1 to the Marriage Act 1949 were incompatible with art 12 of the ECHR in that they prohibited a person from marrying either the parent of his/her former spouse or the former spouse of his/her own child, the Government made the Marriage Act 1949 (Remedial) Order 2007, SI 2007/438.

## Derogations and reservations

16.118   Section 14 of the 1998 Act provides for what it terms a 'designated derogation', ie a derogation by the UK from any article of or protocol to the ECHR which is designated for the purposes of the 1998 Act by an order made by the Secretary of State. As noted previously (para 16.48), the UK formerly had a derogation entered in respect of art 5(3) of the ECHR which has since been repealed. The UK has also had a derogation entered in respect of art 5(1)(f) of the ECHR. This was the chosen course of action by the UK Government in the light of the extended power of detention contained in the Anti-terrorism,

Crime and Security Act 2001, which it was felt may be inconsistent with the obligations under art 5(1)(f): see the Human Rights Act 1998 (Designated Derogation) Order 2001, SI 2001/3644. That derogation was withdrawn, however, following the repeal of the detention provisions in the 2001 Act by s 16(2)(a) of the Prevention of Terrorism Act 2005. Part I of Sch 3 to the HRA was accordingly repealed: see the Human Rights Act (Amendment) Order 2005, SI 2005/1071.

**16.119**  Reservations are permitted under art 57 of the ECHR. This provides that:

> *Any State may, when signing this Convention or when depositing its instrument of ratification, make a reservation in respect of any particular provision of the Convention to the extent that any law then in force in its territory is not in conformity with the provision. Reservations of a general character shall not be permitted under this Article.*

**16.120**  The UK has a reservation in place in respect of art 2 of the First Protocol to the ECHR. This is concerned with the right to education. The second principle of art 2 states that in exercising any functions in relation to education and teaching, the state shall respect the right of parents to ensure that such education and teaching is in conformity with their own religious and philosophical convictions. The reservation (entered in March 1952) makes it clear that the UK accepts this principle to the extent that it is compatible with the provision of efficient instruction and training, and the avoidance of unreasonable public expenditure. Since the Government has concluded that the reservation should be kept in place, s 15 makes provision for 'designated reservations'. These include the current reservation (HRA 1998, Sch 3, Part II) and any other reservations which the Secretary of State may by order make. A designated reservation which is withdrawn wholly or in part ceases to be a designated reservation.

## A Bill of Rights?

**16.121**  Writing in the fifth edition of *A Bill of Rights* (1997), Zander contended that 'until 1974 the question of a Bill of Rights for Britain was a subject that attracted little interest'. The significance of 1974 was that it was the year in which Lord Scarman delivered the first of his Hamlyn Lectures in which he 'made the subject a serious issue for debate'. Prior to 1974, however, as Zander acknowledges, Anthony (now Lord) Lester had written and campaigned for a Bill of Rights. During the course of the 1970s to the 1990s, the subject was much debated both within Parliament and amongst the wider academic community beyond. The enactment of the HRA might have been thought to have put an end to the debate since it is regarded by some as a domestic Bill of Rights. However, there is a case for arguing that a Bill of Rights could go further than the present HRA by providing better protection for human rights by, for example, also reflecting the rights set out in other human rights documents such as the International Covenant on Civil and Political Rights.

**16.122** New life was breathed into the Bill of Rights debate as a result of the publication of the Green Paper, *The Governance of Britain* (Cm 7170) in July 2007, which gave some indication of the direction that reform may take. The penultimate sub-heading in the document referred to a 'British Bill of Rights and Duties'. After commenting that the repeal of the HRA would 'prevent British citizens from exercising their fundamental rights in British courts', the Green Paper suggested that the Act 'should not necessarily be regarded as the last word on the subject'. Instead, it could be regarded as 'the first step in a journey' that might also involve the enactment of a Bill of Rights and Duties. The Green Paper contended that such a Bill 'could give people a clear idea of what we can expect from public authorities, and from each other, and a framework for giving practical effect to our common values'. It was envisaged that:

> A Bill of Rights and Duties could provide explicit recognition that human rights come with responsibilities and must be exercised in a way that respects the human rights of others. It would build on the basic principles of the Human Rights Act, but make explicit the way in which a democratic society's rights have to be balanced by obligations.

**16.123** The JCHR made its own contribution to the ongoing debate as to whether or not there should be a Bill of Rights for the UK with the publication of its 29th report of session 2007–08. In it, the committee undertook a detailed consideration of a number of issues relating to its belief that the UK ought to adopt a Bill of Rights. The kind of document which it envisaged would build upon the rights and freedoms guaranteed in the ECHR and the HRA. These earlier human rights documents were therefore regarded as being a floor rather than a ceiling. Although the committee believed that the 'case for developing domestic formulations of economic and social rights as part of a UK Bill of Rights merits further attention', it accepted the Labour Government's position that legally enforceable economic and social rights would 'carry too great a risk that the courts will interfere with legislative judgments about priority setting'. Thus in an Outline Bill of Rights (Annex 1), the JCHR proposed that a government would be subject to a 'duty of progressive realization' in relation to rights relating to: health care; education; housing; an adequate standard of living; and a healthy and sustainable environment. The more traditional civil and political rights would be given effect through an interpretive obligation imposed on the courts, which would apply in respect of legislation and the common law. The JCHR's Outline Bill of Rights also borrowed other features of the HRA. For example, it would have empowered the courts to issue a declaration where a provision of primary legislation was found to be incompatible with the Bill of Rights. It also required a ministerial statement of compatibility/incompatibility prior to the second reading of a Bill, and would empower ministers to make remedial orders where a declaration of incompatibility had been made.

**16.124** It has previously been noted that in March 2011, the coalition Government established an independent Commission on a Bill of Rights. In addition to advising the Government on reform of the ECtHR, the Commission's terms of reference require it:

> To investigate the creation of a UK Bill of Rights that incorporates and builds on all our obligations under the European Convention on Human Rights, ensures that these rights continue to be enshrined in UK law, and protects and extends our liberties.

In August 2011, the Commission published an open-ended discussion paper, 'Do we need a UK Bill of Rights?' Much of the paper was given over to a factual explanation of the UK's current system of human rights protection. However, it did seek the views of the public on a number of general questions. These included: do you think that the UK needs a Bill of Rights? What do you think it should contain? How do you think it should apply to the UK as a whole? Responses were requested by 11 November 2011. In the light of the discussion paper, and given that the Commission is obliged to produce a report by the end of 2012, it is evident that the Bill of Rights debate continues.

# FURTHER READING

Allan, TRS 'Human Rights and Judicial Review: A critique of "due deference" ' [2006] CLJ 671.

Bamforth, N 'The True "Horizontal Effect" of the Human Rights Act 1998' (2001) 117 LQR 34.

Beyleveld, D and Pattinson, S 'Horizontal Applicability and Horizontal Effect' (2002) 118 LQR 623.

Buxton, Sir Richard 'The Human Rights Act and Private Law' (2000) 116 LQR 48.

Cavanaugh, K 'Policing the Margins: Rights protection and the European Court of Human Rights' [2006] EHRLR 422.

Clayton, R 'Judicial Deference and Democratic Dialogue: The legitimacy of judicial intervention under the Human Rights Act 1998' [2004] PL 33.

Costa, J-P 'On the Legitimacy of the European Court of Human Rights' Judgments' (2011) 7 ECL Review 173.

Duffy, P and Stanley, P *Human Rights Act 1998* Current Law Annotated Statutes Sweet & Maxwell.

Erdos, D *Delegating Rights Protection: The Rise of Bills of Rights in the Westminster World* (2010) OUP.

Feldman, D 'Remedies for Violations of Convention Rights under the Human Rights Act' [1998] EHRLR 691.

Greer, S 'Protocol 14 and the Future of the European Court of Human Rights' [2005] PL 83.

Greer, S 'Reflections of a Former President of the European Court of Human Rights' [2010] EHRLR 165.

Hohfeld, W 'Some Fundamental Legal Conceptions as Applied in Judicial Reasoning' (1913) 23 Yale Law Journal 16.

Joint Committee on Human Rights, *The meaning of Public Authority under the Human Rights Act*, seventh report of session 2003–4, HL Paper 39, HC Paper 382.

Joint Committee on Human Rights, *The meaning of Public Authority under the Human Rights Act*, ninth report of session 2006–7, HL Paper 77, HC Paper 410.

Joint Committee on Human Rights, *A Bill of Rights for the UK?*, 29th report of session 2007–08, HL Paper 165-I, HC 150-1.

Joint Committee on Human Rights, *Any of our business? Human Rights and the UK private sector*, first report of session 2009–10, HL paper 5-I, HC 64-I.

Jowell, J 'Judicial Deference, Servility, Civility or Institutional Capacity?' [2003] PL 592.

Klug, F 'A Bill of Rights: Do we need one or do we already have one?' [2007] PL 701.

Klug, F and Wildbore, H 'Breaking New Ground: The Joint Committee on Human Rights and the role of Parliament in human rights compliance' [2007] EHRLR 231.

Klug, F and Wildbore, H 'Follow or Lead? The Human Rights Act and the European Court of Human Rights' [2010] EHRLR 621.

Kratochvil, J 'The Inflation of the Margin of Appreciation by the European Court of Human Rights' (2011) 29 NQHR 324.

Lord Lester, 'The European Court of Human Rights after 50 years' [2009] EHRLR 461.

Lord Lester 'Human Rights and the British Constitution' in Jowell and Oliver (eds) *The Changing Constitution* (7th edn, 2011) OUP.

Lord Lester, Pannick, D, and Carrs-Frisk, M *Human Rights Law and Practice* (2nd edn, 2004) LexisNexis Butterworths.

Marriott, J and Nicol, D 'The Human Rights Act, Representative Standing and the Victim Culture' [1998] EHRLR 730.

Morgan, J 'Privacy, Confidence and Horizontal Effect: "Hello" trouble' (2003) 62 CLJ 444.

Mowbray, A 'Proposals for Reform of the European Court of Human Rights' [2002] PL 252.

Mowbray, A 'An Examination of the Work of the Grand Chamber of the European Court of Human Rights' [2007] PL 507.

Mowbray, A 'Crisis Measures of Institutional Reform for the European Court of Human Rights' [2009] HRL Rev 647.

Oliver, D 'Functions of a Public Nature under the Human Rights Act' [2004] PL 328.

Pollard, D, Parpworth, N, and Hughes, D *Constitutional and Administrative Law: Text with Materials* (4th edn, 2007) OUP.

Sedley, Sir Stephen 'The Rocks or the Open Sea: Where is the Human Rights Act Heading?' (2005) 32 J Law & Soc 3.

Lord Steyn 'Deference: a Tangled Story' [2005] PL 346.

Lord Steyn '2000–2005: Laying the Foundations of Human Rights Law in the United Kingdom' [2005] EHRLR 349.

Lord Steyn 'Civil Liberties in Modern Britain' [2009] PL 228.

Sunkin, M 'Pushing Forward the Frontiers of Human Rights Protection: The Meaning of Public Authority under the Human Rights Act' [2004] PL 643.

Wade, Professor Sir William 'Horizons of Horizontality' (2000) 116 LQR 217.

Zander, M *A Bill of Rights?* (5th edn, 1997) Sweet & Maxwell.

## SELF-TEST QUESTIONS

1   How might we distinguish between civil and political rights on the one hand, and social and economic rights on the other?

2   What criticisms can be levelled at the traditional means of protecting rights and liberties in English law? Did their shortcomings make incorporation of the ECHR inevitable?

3   To what extent, if any, do you agree with the view expressed by Lord Steyn that 'with all its limitations the ECHR is our bill of rights'?

4   With regard to the Grand Chamber's jurisdiction to hear referrals pursuant to art 43 of the ECHR, do you agree with Mowbray that there are concerns as to the 'institutional propriety of a single court being required to operate a de facto appellate jurisdiction'?

5   Do you agree with the view that the doctrine of a margin of appreciation is 'essential to retain state confidence in the operation of the system'? Sir Stephen Sedley has suggested that following the enactment of the HRA 1998, 'the margin of appreciation was always going to be a headache'. What do you think he meant by this? Do you agree with his view?

6   Alternatively, is it the case that the margin of appreciation is a 'conclusory label which only serves to obscure the true basis on which a reviewing court decides whether or not intervention in a particular case is justifiable'?

7   To what extent, if any, has the margin of appreciation come to be seen as a matter of right by states rather than as a matter of judicial restraint and discretion exercised by the ECtHR?

8   Could the rights contained within the ECHR have been properly respected and upheld in the UK by a means other than incorporation?

9   With regard to the cases on the meaning of 'functions of a public nature' for the purposes of s 6(3)(b) of the HRA 1998, to what extent, if any, do you agree with Baroness Hale's observation in YL that: 'The law is easy to state but difficult to apply in individual cases…'?

10 To what extent is the effectiveness of the HRA 1998 in protecting human rights dependent upon judicial attitudes towards the notion of 'deference' or the 'discretionary area of judgment'?

11 Lord Steyn has opined: 'In the development of our country towards becoming a true constitutional state the coming into force of the Human Rights Act on October 2, 2000 was a landmark'. Do you agree?

12 Do you think that the UK needs a Bill of Rights independent of the Human Rights Act? If so, what would be the content of the rights contained therein?

# 17 Freedom of expression

## SUMMARY

Freedom of expression is a right guaranteed under the ECHR (art 10). It is widely regarded as being a necessary feature in any state which purports to be a democracy. In this chapter, we shall consider the extent to which English law places restrictions on freedom of expression where the exercise of that freedom would involve the publication etc of that which is obscene or indecent, or would prejudice the administration of justice. There are other examples of restrictions on freedom of expression which will not be considered here, eg the Official Secrets Acts of 1911 and 1989 and incitement to racial hatred. The present chapter is confined to the law relating to obscenity and indecency and contempt of court on the basis that they share an important characteristic: they are regulated by both statute and the common law.

## Control of obscenity and indecency

**17.1** This is not the occasion on which to embark upon a discussion of the arguments both for and against the control of obscene or indecent material. There are too many shades of opinion on matters such as pornography and whether or not it has a place in society for them to be considered here. For present purposes, it must be acknowledged that for in excess of 150 years, Parliament has seen fit to impose restrictions on access to such material and to impose criminal sanctions in the event of a person being convicted of publishing or displaying obscene or indecent material. The law on obscenity and indecency is thus to be found in a number of statutes. The principal enactment is the Obscene Publications Act 1959 (OPA 1959) as amended by the 1964 Act of the same name. This Act will therefore be the focus of our attention in the following discussion, although reference to other relevant enactments will be made, where appropriate. In addition, it should be noted that the common law offence of obscene libel has not actually been abolished by the 1959 and 1964 Acts and neither do the statutes prevent a prosecution on a charge of conspiracy to corrupt public morals or to outrage public decency.

## Publication of obscene matter

**17.2**   Section 2(1) of the 1959 Act (as amended) provides that it is an offence where:

> *any person who, whether for gain or not, publishes an obscene article or who has an obscene article for publication for gain (whether gain to himself or gain to another).*

Section 1(2) of the 1964 Act provides that where a person has been charged with an offence under s 2 of the 1959 Act, that person:

> *shall be deemed to have an article for publication for gain if with a view to such publication he has the article in his ownership, possession or control.*

Section 1(5) of the 1964 Act further provides that 'publication for gain' means:

> *any publication with a view to gain, whether the gain is to accrue by way of consideration for the publication or in any other way.*

**17.3**   It is apparent from these provisions, therefore, that the essence of the offence is the publication of an obscene article. The test of 'obscenity' will be considered (paras **17.5-17.9**). For present purposes, it is necessary to consider what is meant by 'publication' and 'article'. Section 1(3) of the 1959 Act provides that for the purposes of the Act, a person publishes an article who:

> (a) *distributes, circulates, sells, lets on hire, gives, or lends it, or who offers it for sale or for letting on hire; or*

> (b) *in the case of an article containing or embodying matter to be looked at or a record, shows, plays or projects it, or, where the matter is data stored electronically, transmits that data.*

In *R v Barker* (1962), Ashworth J observed:

> *The forms of publication included in the definition of section 1(3)(a) fall into three distinct groups: in one group, comprising the words 'sells, lets on hire, gives, or lends' publication is to an individual; in the second group, comprising the words 'distributes, circulates', publication is on a wider scale, involving more than one person; in the third group a mere offer for sale or letting on hire constitutes publication.*

**17.4**   An 'article' is defined by s 1(2) of the 1959 Act as:

> *any description of article containing or embodying matter to be read or looked at or both, any sound record, and any film or other record of a picture or pictures.*

The definitions of 'publication' and 'article' are patently quite wide. For the purposes of the Act, it is clear that there may be more than one publication. Thus where obscene material was uploaded on a website in the United States and downloaded in the UK, the

CA held that the trial court had had jurisdiction to hear a charge contrary to s 2(1) of the OPA 1959 since the uploading amounted to one publication and the downloading had amounted to a further publication: see *R v Waddon* (2002). In *A-G's Reference (No 5 of 1980)* (1980), the CA held that a video cassette was an article within the meaning of s 1(2). In order to commit an offence under s 2(1), however, an article which is published must be obscene.

## Test of obscenity

17.5 Section 1(1) of the 1959 Act provides that:

> an article shall be deemed to be obscene if its effect or (where the article consists of two or more distinct items) the effect of any one of the items is, if taken as a whole, such as to tend to deprave and corrupt persons who are likely, having regard to all relevant circumstances, to read, see or hear the matter contained or embodied in it.

The test of obscenity is therefore the tendency that the article will have to 'deprave and corrupt' the minds of those likely to read it, etc. The phrase 'deprave and corrupt' was borrowed from the case of *R v Hicklin* (1868) where Lord Cockburn defined 'obscenity' as a tendency:

> to deprave and corrupt those whose minds are open to such immoral influences, and into whose hands a publication of this sort may fall.

17.6 In *DPP v Whyte* (1972), Lord Wilberforce observed that this test requires the magistrates or jury 'to ascertain who are likely readers and then to consider whether the article is likely to deprave and corrupt them'. It is therefore no longer permissible to presume a tendency to deprave and corrupt from a finding that an article is obscene, as was formerly the case. In performing this task, the statute provides no further assistance as to what is meant by 'deprave and corrupt'. In a trial on indictment, this will be a matter which is left to the jury, although the trial judge may provide some guidance in his summing-up or in response to a request from the jury. Where a judge does give guidance, it was suggested by the CA in *R v O'Sullivan* (1995) that it should entail reading the relevant provisions of the 1959 and 1964 Acts 'without attempting to improve or re-define the wording of the Acts'. Underlying this advice is the concern that by embellishing upon the statutory definition, a trial judge may be in danger of misdirecting a jury. In *R v Penguin Books Ltd* (1961), where the publishers of D H Lawrence's *Lady Chatterley's Lover* were prosecuted under the 1959 Act, Byrne J stated that:

> To deprave means to make morally bad, to pervert, to debase or corrupt morally. To corrupt means to render morally unsound or rotten, to destroy the moral purity or chastity, to pervert or ruin a good quality, to debase or defile.

**17.7** Expert evidence will not generally be permitted as to whether a particular article was likely to deprave or corrupt, although in *DPP v A and B C Chewing Gum Ltd* (1968), such evidence was allowed where the alleged obscene matter, which depicted violence, was directed at very young children. Similarly in *R v Skirving* (1985), the CA upheld the decision of the trial judge to allow expert evidence where the case related to a pamphlet in which instructions were given on drug taking. Expert evidence was permissible in this instance since it was felt that the average person was unlikely to have knowledge or experience of the matters dealt with in the pamphlet.

**17.8** The decisions in these last two cases highlight a further feature of the obscenity test: it is not confined to the publication of sexually explicit material. Material which deals with extreme violence or drug taking, or which is racially offensive (*Britton v DPP* (1996)), may also be obscene for the purposes of the 1959 Act. As with sexually explicit material, it is not necessary to prove that such material actually depraved and corrupted its readers; it is enough that it has a tendency to do so.

**17.9** The definition or test of obscenity has been much criticized. Thus in 1954, Norman St John-Stevas (as he then was) submitted that 'the time for abandoning the *Hicklin* formula is long overdue'. In *DPP v Whyte*, Lord Wilberforce observed that: 'It can only have been the pressure of Parliamentary compromise which can have produced a test so difficult for the courts'. Similarly in *R v Metropolitan Police Commissioner, ex p Blackburn (No 3)* (1973), Lord Denning MR posed the question 'why has the legislation misfired?' and answered it thus: 'I regret to say that it is in the wording of the statute and in the way the courts have applied it'. In a later report into, inter alia, the laws of obscenity and indecency, the Williams Committee recommended that terms such as 'deprave' and 'corrupt' should be dispensed with since they were too vague and uncertain to serve any useful purpose (1979, Cmnd 7772). More recently in commenting on Government proposals to regulate the possession of 'extreme pornography' (see para **17.23**), McGlynn and Rackley have described the test as being 'generic and opaque'. Nevertheless, it has remained unaltered as is evidenced by *R v Perrin* (2002), where the CA rejected the argument that it lacks sufficient precision for the purposes of falling within the scope of art 10(2) of the ECHR. An alternative to the test may be to simply provide that an article is obscene if it relates to or is concerned with any one of a number of specified activities. This approach was adopted by the Earl of Halsbury in his Obscenity Bill which received a Second Reading in the HL on 9 March 1999. The Schedule to the Bill contained a list of some 40 or so activities, the depiction, etc of any one of which would render an article obscene. The Bill did not, however, become law.

## The likely readers, etc

**17.10** Since an article is obscene for the purposes of the 1959 Act if it has a tendency to deprave or corrupt those persons likely to read it, it follows that an article is not obscene in itself.

It is its effect on the minds of its likely readers that matters. In *R v Calder & Boyars Ltd* (1969), Salmon LJ observed that:

> This court is of the opinion that the jury should have been directed to consider whether the effect of the book was to tend to deprave and corrupt a significant proportion of those likely to read it.

**17.11**  What is a significant proportion will be a matter for the jury to determine. Although trial judges ought to refrain from redefining the words used in the Acts, in *R v O'Sullivan* (1995) the CA felt that it would be permissible to make 'some reference to the fact that the persons likely to be corrupted should amount to more than a negligible number'. In *DPP v Whyte*, Lord Cross observed that: 'A significant proportion of a class means a part which is not numerically negligible but which may be much less than half'. A study into pornography trials in the Crown Court in England and Wales carried out by Edwards has confirmed that, for the relevant period, trial judges gave no direction to the jury as to the meaning of 'significant proportion'. More recently, in *R v Perrin* (2002), the CA was of the opinion that:

> Where, as in the present case, there is and can be no suggestion that publication is for the public good . . . we see no reason why the task of the jury should be complicated by a direction that the effect of the article must be such as to tend to deprave and corrupt a significant proportion, or more than a negligible number of likely viewers. Such a direction is all too likely to give rise to a request for further assistance as to what proportion is significant, or what number is negligible, and where the direction is unnecessary it is much better, in our judgment, for the jury to be directed simply in accordance with the words of the statute.

**17.12**  A further issue arises with regard to the likely readers of an article. What if they are habitual consumers of obscene material? Does this mean, therefore, that a defence may be run to the effect that the likely readers could not be depraved and corrupted because they already were depraved and corrupted? In *DPP v Whyte*, the magistrates came to the conclusion that the relevant articles were not obscene on the basis that the booksellers' regular customers were 'inadequate, pathetic, dirty minded men . . . whose morals were already in a state of depravity and corruption'. Nevertheless, on appeal, the HL concluded by a majority of three to two that the magistrates should have convicted the defendants. In the words of Lord Wilberforce:

> The Act is not merely concerned with the once and for all corruption of the wholly innocent; it equally protects the less innocent from further corruption, the addict from feeding or increasing his addiction.

## The aversion argument

**17.13**  In several of the leading cases, defence counsel have sought to argue that far from encouraging its readers to perform the acts which it describes or depicts, an article may in fact so revolt or disgust its readers as to discourage them from participating in such activities. This line of reasoning has become known as the 'aversion argument'. In effect, it is a contention that the article has the reverse effect of tending to deprave and corrupt its likely readers: it is a 'turn off' rather than a 'turn on'. The failure to direct the jury about this argument was one of the reasons why the CA upheld the defendants' appeal against conviction in *R v Calder & Boyars Ltd*. Such a failure amounted to a 'serious defect in the summing up'. Similarly in *R v Anderson* (1971), convictions under the 1959 Act were quashed on the basis, inter alia, that the failure to properly explain to the jury defence counsel's use of the aversion argument amounted to 'a very substantial and serious misdirection'. In the later case of *R v Elliott* (1996), however, the CA thought that it would be difficult to effectively advance such an argument in respect of a private cinema showing sex videos, where the material shown 'was clearly being offered as being attractive primarily at least to men'.

## Article considered as a whole

**17.14** In determining whether or not an article is obscene for the purpose of the 1959 Act, s 1(1) requires that its effect is taken as a whole. Where, however, the article consists of two or more items, it is the effect of any one of those items when taken as a whole which matters. Accordingly, if the application of the test shows one item to be obscene, it follows that the whole article is obscene. The legal position was explained by Lord Widgery CJ in *R v Anderson* (1971) in the following manner:

> A novelist who writes a complete novel and who cannot cut out particular passages without destroying the theme of the novel is entitled to have his work judged as a whole, but a magazine publisher who has a far wider discretion as to what he will, and will not, insert by way of items is to be judged under the Act on what we call the 'item by item' basis.

**17.15** The decision in *Anderson* has subsequently been applied to films: see *R v Goring* (1999). Thus if a film contains two or more distinct items, the prosecution will be entitled to invite the court to consider the effect of one or more of such items. Whether a part of a film is capable of being treated as a distinct item is, therefore, a matter of law for the trial judge. In a comment on the decision in *Goring*, however, Ormerod has cast doubt on the distinction made by Lord Widgery in *Anderson*. In his opinion, 'a novelist has complete control over content in his novel'. Thus Ormerod argues that 'it is more likely (and appropriate) that printed matter rather than films are treated as comprising a series of distinct elements because they usually have contents pages which facilitate selective reading'.

**17.16** It is the article or articles themselves which must be the focus of attention in obscenity proceedings. They must be examined and their effect on the likely readership must be considered in order to determine whether or not they are obscene. It is not permissible, therefore, for a defendant to show that other articles which are currently in circulation are not materially different from those which are the subject of the prosecution. On the basis of the decision in *R v Reiter* (1954), these other articles are irrelevant.

## Defences

**17.17** Several defences to a charge under the 1959 Act are provided for in the statute itself. Of these, the most significant is the defence of public good (s 4). This provides that a person shall not be convicted of a s 2 offence and a forfeiture order shall not be made under s 3 if they can show that:

> publication of the article in question is justified as being for the public good on the ground that it is in the interests of science, literature, art or learning, or of other objects of general concern.

**17.18** In effect, therefore, s 4 allows for the publication of an article which satisfies the obscenity test on the basis that publication is for the public good. The burden of proof rests with the defence on the balance of probabilities. It will only arise, however, where the prosecution has established that the article is obscene within the meaning of the 1959 Act: see *Olympian Press Ltd v Hollis* (1974). Expert evidence may be allowed as to the literary, artistic, scientific, or other merits of an article, although the final decision as to whether any of these merits outweighs the obscene nature of the article is a matter for the court or jury to decide. It would seem that for the publication of an article to be justified under s 4, it would have to contain something new or special; that which merely reproduces the commonplace would not fall within the scope of s 4: *Britton v DPP* (1996). The nature of the balancing exercise was explained in *R v Calder & Boyars Ltd* as follows:

> the jury must consider on the one hand the number of readers they believe would tend to be depraved and corrupted by the book, the strength of the tendency to deprave and corrupt, and the nature of the depravity and corruption; on the other hand, they should assess the strength of the literary, sociological or ethical merit which they consider the book to possess. They should then weigh up all these factors and decide whether on balance the publication is to be justified as being for the public good.

**17.19** In *A-G's Reference (No 3 of 1977)* (1978), the CA held that 'learning' was used in s 4 as a noun rather than a verb and that it therefore meant the 'product of scholarship'. It did not include teaching or any form of education, including sex education. In *DPP v Jordan* (1977), the HL ruled that the phrase 'other objects of general concern' was a mobile phrase, the content of which would change as society changes. Nevertheless, it was related to the specified objects in s 4 and did not therefore cover pornographic material which was claimed to have a therapeutic value for some members of the public. Previously in *R v Metropolitan Police Commissioner, ex p Blackburn (No 3)* (1973),

Phillimore LJ had remarked that it was this final phrase which 'has really done the damage' by allowing 'hard porn' to be published and that it was therefore 'high time that the phrase . . . was eliminated from s 4'. In a damning indictment of the public good defence, Lord Denning MR opined:

> the 'defence of public good' has opened a door through which many a pornographer can escape . . . Under cover of this defence, experts have been allowed to come forward and say that it is good for young people to read these magazines because it removes their feelings of guilt. Such evidence is equal to saying that pornography itself is for the public good – which is quite contrary to what Parliament intended.

**17.20** A person charged with a s 2 offence may also be acquitted if he can show that he did not examine the obscene article and that he had no reasonable cause to suspect that its publication would make him liable to be convicted of an offence under the section: s 2(5) of the 1959 Act. In practice, this defence is only likely to be made out by a person who has unknowingly distributed obscene material and who was prevented from examining it by its packaging.

## Powers of search and seizure

**17.21** Under s 3 of the 1959 Act, the police may obtain a warrant to enter and search premises or to search a stall or vehicle for obscene materials. A warrant must specify that the search which it authorizes is for 'obscene material'. In *Darbo v DPP* (1992), it was held that the expression 'any other material of a sexually explicit nature' was too wide since it encompassed material which would not be obscene for the purposes of the Act. A magistrate will only grant a warrant where he is satisfied that the police have reasonable grounds for suspecting that obscene material is being kept for publication for gain. Section 3 does not apply, therefore, to a private collection of obscene material. It does apply, however, to obscene material which is destined for publication overseas: see *Gold Star Publications Ltd v DPP* (1981). During the conduct of a search, the police have the power to seize and remove any articles which they reasonably believe to be obscene and kept for publication for gain.

### Forfeiture

**17.22** Once allegedly obscene articles have been seized, three courses of action lie open to the police: the articles may be returned to the occupier of the premises or the user of the stall or vehicle; the articles may be used as evidence in a prosecution for an offence under s 2 of the 1959 Act; or, as is quite often the case, the police may decide to bring forfeiture proceedings in respect of the seized articles. With regard to the latter, if the court is satisfied that any of the articles are obscene, they shall order that those articles are forfeited. In practice, enormous quantities of allegedly obscene articles may be the subject of forfeiture proceedings. A search of a warehouse or garage, for example, may lead to the seizure of thousands of magazines, books, and DVDs. In these circumstances, as Professor Stone has noted, a sample of the materials seized by the police would be put before a magistrate. The sample itself would have been agreed by both the prosecution and the defence. However, as he points out, whilst this serves to expedite matters, it is not a practice that strictly accords with the wording of s 3. This refers to a finding of obscenity in respect of an article as the justification for its forfeiture. Forfeiting articles on the basis that they are like articles which have been found to be obscene thus strains the wording of the statute, even if it is an understandable solution to the problem of examining large quantities of material.

## A new criminal offence?

**17.23**  As a result of a consultation process that began in August 2005 and which elicited responses that were, according to the Home Office, either 'strongly supportive or strongly opposed', Parliament has enacted s 63 of the Criminal Justice and Immigration Act 2008 which makes it an offence to possess an 'extreme pornographic image'. For the purposes of s 63, an image is 'pornographic' if it appears to have been produced solely or principally for the purpose of sexual arousal. An 'extreme image' is an image of: an act which threatens a person's life; an act which results or is likely to result in serious injury to a person's anus, breast, or genitals; an act which involves sexual interference with a human corpse; or a person performing an act of intercourse or oral sex with an animal (whether dead or alive). The new possession offence adopts a categories approach rather than the potential moral harm standard to be found in the 1959 Act. The fact that the offence is concerned with the mere possession rather than the publication of the material to which it relates is justified on the grounds of the extreme nature of that material. The potential harmful impact on the private lives of individuals is such that criminalizing possession is regarded as a legitimate and necessary invasion of rights for the protection of public morals.

**17.24**  In *R v Van der Westhuizen* (2011), the CA felt that the custody threshold had been crossed where the appellant had pleaded guilty to five charges of possession of extreme pornographic images in the form of five DVDs showing women giving and receiving oral sex with animals and being vaginally and anally penetrated. The newness of the offence meant that sentencing guidelines had not yet been issued. Since the appellant had been in possession of the DVDs prior to the entry into force of s 63 (26 January 2009), his crime lay in not destroying them when the law changed. Accordingly, a sentence of 12 months' imprisonment was set aside, and a suspended sentence of 28 weeks' imprisonment was substituted.

## Further statutory provision for obscenity and indecency

### Obscenity offences

**17.25**   Parliament's battle against obscenity has not been confined to the publication of obscene articles. It has extended into other realms, such as the theatre and postal communications. Thus it is an offence under s 2 of the Theatres Act 1968 to present or direct an obscene performance of a play. The obscenity test which the 1968 Act adopts is the same as that found in the Obscene Publications Acts, ie the tendency of the performance to deprave and corrupt persons likely to attend it. The same cannot be said of the Postal Services Act 2000. Section 85(3)(a) of this Act provides that it is an offence to send by post a postal packet which encloses 'any indecent or obscene print, painting, photograph, lithograph, engraving, cinematograph film, or other record of a picture or pictures, book, card or written communication'. It is also an offence to send 'any other indecent or obscene article' through the post (s 85(3)(b)) or any postal packet which has on the packet or on its cover 'any words, marks or designs which are of an indecent or obscene character' (s 85(4)).

**17.26**   The purpose of these provisions is the same as their predecessor, s 11(1)(b) of the Post Office Act 1953, ie to preclude the use of post office services for the distribution of indecent or obscene material: *R v Bremner and Joy* (1984). It is not aimed at protecting postal workers from the risk of accidentally opening a package containing such material. Whether or not any of the items mentioned is obscene for the purposes of s 85(3) and (4) of the 2000 Act would appear to depend not upon its tendency to deprave and corrupt, but upon the dictionary definition of 'obscene'. In *R v Anderson* (1971), which concerned prosecutions brought under both the Obscene Publications Act 1959 and the Post Office Act 1953, the court accepted that 'obscene' may mean 'repulsive', 'filthy', 'loathsome', or 'lewd'. It will be remembered, however, that in a prosecution under the 1959 Act, the defence may seek to argue that an article is repulsive (the aversion argument) (para **17.13**) in order to get D acquitted. This anomaly would have the potential to confuse a jury hearing charges under both the 1959 and 2000 Acts. It would therefore need to be clearly explained by the trial judge in his summing-up.

**17.27**   In *R v Stamford* (1972), the CA noted that, in common with the Obscene Publications Acts, the task of determining whether or not an article was indecent or obscene for the purposes of the Post Office Act 1953 was a matter for the jury. The CA accepted counsel for the appellant's argument that:

> one way of expressing the test of indecency or obscenity which are at either end of the scale common to both, was that a matter is obscene if it is one that offends against recognised standards of propriety, and it may be that the same test applies to a matter alleged to be indecent, bearing in mind, as the courts have said, that those are different concepts, different steps on the scale of impropriety, obscenity being the graver of the two.

**17.28** The meaning of 'indecent' and 'obscene' for the purposes of the 2000 Act was recently considered by the Court of Appeal.

---

*R v Kirk* (2006): The appellant was a 'vigorous opponent of vivisection'. He sent packages through the post to various individuals and companies whom he considered to be connected with experimentation on animals. Both the covers and contents of the packages showed graphic images of animal experiments. One particular package was addressed: 'To the sons and daughters of Dr Joseph Mengle, @ Bloody Huntingdon Life Sciences, an Auschwitz Laboratory'. The envelope also bore a large black swastika. K was found guilty of offences contrary to s 85(3) and (4) of the 2000 Act and sentenced to three months' imprisonment. He appealed against both his conviction and sentence. CA held: dismissing the appeal, that it was not necessary to attempt to elaborate or clarify the meaning of 'obscene' and 'indecent'. The correct approach was that taken by the HL in *Brutus v Cozens* (1973) (para **19.53**), whereby the adjective 'insulting' in s 5 of the Public Order Act 1936 had been given its ordinary meaning. Since the trial judge's summing-up had as a whole stressed that the words should be applied in their ordinary sense, the conviction would stand. The appeal against sentence was also dismissed given that K had three previous convictions for public order offences.

---

## Indecency offences

**17.29** There are several further statutory offences involving indecency. Thus s 1 of the Protection of Children Act 1978 makes it an offence to take, permit to be taken, distribute, show, or have in one's possession with a view to distributing or showing, indecent photographs or pseudo-photographs of children. For the purposes of this offence, it was held in *R v Fellows* (1997) that although a computer disk is not itself a photograph, it contained data which could be converted into a screen image and then printed in such a way as to reproduce the original photograph. The data was therefore a photograph within the meaning of the Act. Moreover, in order to be convicted of this offence, it is not necessary for the prosecution to show that D knew that the indecent photograph was a photograph of a child: *R v Land* (1999). Section 1 of the 1978 Act also makes it an offence to publish an advertisement which conveys the idea that the advertiser shows or distributes indecent photographs, or that he intends to do so. In *R v Smethurst* (2001), the CA was required to consider whether the offence in s 1(1)(a) of the 1978 Act contravened the provisions of arts 8 and 10 of the ECHR. In holding that it was sufficiently certain not to contravene these provisions, Lord Woolf CJ observed that the offence:

*is there for the prevention of crime, for the protection of morals, and in particular for the protection of children from being exploited, which is undoubtedly a matter which is necessary in a democratic society.*

**17.30** Possession of an indecent photograph or pseudo-photograph of a child is in itself an offence contrary to s 160 of the Criminal Justice Act 1988. 'Indecent' is not defined in these statutory provisions and must therefore be accorded its ordinary and natural meaning. In *Knuller v DPP* (1973), Lord Reid observed that 'indecent' meant 'anything which an ordinary decent man or woman would find to be shocking, disgusting or revolting'. It would seem that knowledge is an essential ingredient of the possession offence. Accordingly, D cannot be convicted where he cannot be shown to have been aware of the existence of a cache of indecent photographs: see *Atkins v DPP* (2000). In seeking to explain such a conclusion, Simon Brown LJ observed that:

> the very fact that Parliament created a defence [s 160(2)(b)] for those possessing photographs reasonably not known to be indecent, strongly suggests that there was no intention to criminalise unknowing possession of photographs in the first place.

**17.31**   In the Home Office consultation paper on making possession of extreme pornographic material an offence (see para **17.23**), it was reported that the number of prosecutions for offences under the 1978 and 1988 Acts rose from 93 in 1994 to 1,890 in 2003. During the same period, the number of prosecutions under the Obscene Publications Act 1959 fell from 309 to 39. The paper suggests that the reduction in the prosecutions under the 1959 Act 'reflects a higher priority being given to combating the increasing availability of indecent photographs of children through the Internet'.

**17.32**   Section 1 of the Indecent Displays (Control) Act 1981 makes it an offence to publicly display or to cause or permit the public display of any indecent matter. In deciding whether any matter (not including an actual human body or part thereof) is indecent for the purposes of the Act, the section requires that any part of the matter not exposed to view must be disregarded, and that account may be taken of juxtaposing one thing with another. In *R v South Western Magistrates' Court, ex p Heslop* (1994), it was held that an Underground station manager had not committed an offence contrary to s 1 of the 1981 Act where a poster remained on public display despite being the subject of a complaint. The poster, which depicted a model in her underwear, had been defaced thus: 'I've been sitting here for six months in my underwear and my bum smells.' In the opinion of the stipendiary magistrate, with whom the QBD agreed, although this was in extremely bad taste, it was not indecent.

## The common law

**17.33**   Section 2(4) of the 1959 Act provides that:

> A person publishing an obscene article shall not be proceeded against for an offence at common law consisting of the publication of any matter contained or embodied in the article where it is of the essence of the offence that the matter is obscene.

This section is therefore aimed at the common law offence of obscene libel. Although it does not abolish that offence, it does assert the primacy of the statutory provisions. In

*Shaw v DPP* (1962), the HL effectively created a new common law offence – conspiracy to corrupt public morals. It did so on the basis that the actus reus of the offence, the conspiracy, did not consist of the publication of the booklet (a directory of the names and addresses of prostitutes), but of an agreement to corrupt public morals by means of the booklet, which might never be published. In *Knuller v DPP* (1973), the HL held that *Shaw* had been rightly decided or that if it had not, it should remain until altered by Parliament. Moreover, it was accepted by the HL that the authorities established a common law offence of conduct which outrages public decency. Their Lordships felt that it would also be an offence to conspire or agree to outrage public decency.

**17.34** In *R v Rowley* (1991), where D left notes in public places in Brighton expressing a need for a 'pretend son' or a boy 'to collect and deliver secret messages', the CA held that the offence of outraging public decency 'consists in the deliberate commission of an act which is per se of a lewd, obscene or disgusting nature'. Therefore, D had not committed the offence since there was nothing in the notes themselves that was capable of outraging public decency. Where a person is charged with this offence, the prosecution do not need to prove that D intended to outrage public decency. It is enough that D did a deliberate act which was found by the jury to outrage public decency: *R v Gibson* (1990).

**17.35** The earliest prosecution for outraging public decency appears to have been *Sedley's case* (1675), where D had appeared naked on the balcony of a house in the presence of people on whom he then urinated. Successive cases during the 19th century often involved defendants exposing themselves: see, for example, *R v Webb* (1848) and *R v Elliot* (1861). Collectively the cases established that the offence of outraging public decency consists of two elements: an act which is of such a lewd character as to outrage public decency; and that the act took place in a public place and was capable of being seen by two or more persons who were present, even if they had not actually seen it (the 'two person rule'). Thus in *R (Rose) v DPP* (2006), where D's girlfriend had performed oral sex on him after midnight in the foyer of a bank to which customers were admitted in order to use an ATM, it was held that the offence of outraging public decency had not been committed. Although the foyer was well lit and passers-by could have seen what was happening, there was no evidence that anybody did see the act, other than a bank employee who had viewed a security camera recording the following day. In *R v Hamilton* (2007), where D had surreptitiously taken video footage up the skirts of various women shoppers and a 14-year-old girl, the CA held that his conduct amounted to an outraging of public decency. In the judgment of the court, the 'two person rule' 'can…be satisfied if there are two or more persons present who are capable of seeing the nature of the act, even if they did not actually see it'. Thus although no one actually saw D filming, the videos confirmed that others had been present in the supermarkets at the relevant times and the jury had concluded that the way D filmed (a camera concealed in a rucksack with the lens hidden and pointing upwards) was capable of being seen by those others.

**17.36** The conduct which is caught by the offence of outraging public decency may sometimes be detestable. Thus in *R v Anderson* (2008), the applicant had pleaded guilty to the offence where he had committed various acts on the prone body of a dying woman, including urinating on her, over a period of about 30 minutes. A sentence of three years' imprisonment was upheld by the CA on account of the many aggravating factors.

17.37   It might be argued that given the statutory offences which have been created in respect of that which is indecent or obscene, it is unfortunate that the common law has been used as the vehicle to develop offences which are beyond the reach of the statutory safeguards. The defence of public good (s 4 of the 1959 Act), for example, does not apply to either of the common law offences. Indeed, Kearns has suggested that the offence of outraging public decency was prosecuted in *R v Gibson* 'probably disingenuously to avoid the availability to the defendants of an artistic merit defence'. Nevertheless, the common law offences were preserved by s 5(3) of the Criminal Law Act 1977 and, as we have seen, they may continue to be charged, although in the case of corrupting public morals, this rarely happens.

## Contempt of court

### Introduction

17.38   The law relating to contempt of court is diverse and by no means entirely clear. It consists of a statute, the Contempt of Court Act 1981, various substantive criminal offences, such as perjury or perverting or obstructing the course of justice, and the common law (paras **17.76–17.79**). A further distinction exists between civil and criminal contempts. Civil contempts essentially amount to disobeying a court order: see, for example, *M v Home Office* (1993) (paras **3.27–3.28**).

17.39   Criminal contempts are of greater interest in the context of freedom of expression. Essentially they amount to conduct which represents an interference with the administration of justice. Criminal contempts may therefore take a variety of forms, including publications which are prejudicial to a fair trial, publications which interfere with the course of justice as an ongoing process, and contempt in the face of the court. In exercising the contempt jurisdiction, it is necessary for the courts to strike a balance between freedom of expression on the one hand and the administration of justice on the other. The reporting by the press and the media generally of the proceedings in court, and the discussion of issues of public concern arising in those proceedings, is clearly important. However, when the effect of the publication is to prejudice the administration of justice, the courts may and often will find those responsible for the publication guilty of contempt.

### Open justice

17.40   Open justice is an important principle in English law. In the leading case *Scott v Scott* (1913), the principle was stated to require that justice be done in public. Subsequently in

*A-G v Leveller Magazine Ltd* (1979), Lord Diplock observed that there were two aspects to the application of the principle of open justice:

> *as respects proceedings in the court itself it requires that they should be held in open court to which the press and the public are admitted and that, in criminal cases at any rate, all evidence communicated to the court is communicated publicly. As respects the publication to a wider public of fair and accurate reports of proceedings that have taken place in court the principle requires that nothing should be done to discourage this.*

**17.41** Public participation in the administration of justice is therefore central to the principle of open justice. In several cases, the beneficial effect of a public presence in the courts has been vigorously asserted by senior judges. Thus in *R v Socialist Worker Printers and Publishers Ltd, ex p A-G* (1975) (see paras **17.69–17.70**), Lord Widgery CJ remarked that:

> *The great value of having the public in our courts is that discipline which the presence of the public imposes upon the court itself. When the court is full of interested members of the public...it is bound to have the effect that everybody is more careful about what they do, everyone tries just that little bit harder and there is a disciplinary effect on the court which would be totally lacking if there were no critical members of the public or press present.*

**17.42** Similarly in *A-G v Leveller Magazine Ltd* (1979), Lord Diplock observed that open justice 'provides a safeguard against judicial arbitrariness or idiosyncrasy and maintains the public confidence in the administration of justice'. In *R v Legal Aid Board, ex p Kaim Todner (a firm)* (1999), Lord Woolf MR observed that the principle of open justice was:

> *necessary because the public nature of the proceedings deters inappropriate behaviour on the part of the court. It also maintains the public confidence in the administration of justice. It enables the public to know that justice is being administered impartially. It can result in evidence becoming available which would not become available if the proceedings were conducted behind closed doors or with one or more of the parties' or witnesses' identity concealed. It makes uninformed and inaccurate comment about the proceedings less likely.*

**17.43** These comments have subsequently been endorsed by Lord Steyn in *Re S (a child) (Identification: restriction on publication)* (2004). In that case his Lordship observed that:

> *A criminal trial is a public event. The principle of open justice puts, as has often been said, the judge and all those who participate in the trial under intense scrutiny. The glare of contemporaneous publicity ensures that trials are properly conducted. It is a valuable check on the criminal process . . . Full contemporaneous reporting of criminal trials in progress promotes public confidence in the administration of justice. It promotes the values of the rule of law.*

**17.44** More recently, in *R (Mohamed) v Secretary of State for Foreign and Commonwealth Affairs (No 2) (Guardian News and Media Ltd intervening)* (2011), Lord Judge LCJ drew attention to 'a distinct aspect of the principle which goes beyond proper scrutiny of the processes of the courts and judiciary'. Thus he observed:

> The principle has a wider resonance, which reflects the distinctive contribution made by the open administration of justice to what President Roosevelt described in 1941 as the 'first freedom, freedom of speech and expression'. In litigation, particularly litigation between the executive and any of its manifestations and the citizen, the principle of open justice represents an element of democratic accountability, and the vigorous manifestation of the principle of freedom of expression. Ultimately is supports the rule of law.

**17.45** Open justice is not, however, an absolute principle. It is subject to exceptions which, in the words of Viscount Haldane LC in *Scott v Scott* (1913) are 'the outcome of a yet more fundamental principle that the chief object of the courts of justice must be to ensure that justice is done'. In other words, there may be circumstances where a departure from the principle is necessary in the interests of the administration of justice. One such departure may involve an *in camera* hearing, ie in the absence of the press or public. However, given that such proceedings represent a wide departure from the principle of open justice, they will only be justified by exceptional circumstances. Thus if a case involved trade secrets or matters of national security, for example, a court may be justified in exercising its common law power to exclude the public from the proceedings.

**17.46** In *R v Malvern Justices, ex p Evans* (1988), where D pleaded guilty to a charge of driving after having consumed excess alcohol, the magistrates decided to sit *in camera* to hear details of D's personal life which were said to explain why she had turned to drink and why she should not be disqualified from driving. The DC dismissed an application for judicial review of that decision which was brought by a journalist and a local newspaper. However, in the opinion of Watkins LJ, proceedings should only be heard *in camera* where there were 'compelling reasons' for such a course of action. Although the DC did not hold that the magistrates had been wrong to sit in private in the present case, the general tenor of the court's judgment suggests that it considered it doubtful whether it had been appropriate in the circumstances of the case.

**17.47** In *Al Rawi and others v Security Service and others* (2011), where the claimants sought compensation in civil proceedings for their alleged detention, rendition, and mistreatment at a number of locations, including Guantanamo Bay, the issue for the SC was whether a court had power at common law to order a 'closed material procedure' for the whole or part of a trial. The SC ruled by 6:3 that a court had no such power. The controversial 'closed material procedure' had been provided for in some cases under the Prevention of Terrorism Act 2005 and the Counter-Terrorism Act 2005. If it were to apply in a case such as the present, contrary to the principles of open justice and natural justice, that was a matter for Parliament, not the courts. With regard to open justice,

Lord Dyson commented that the principle 'is not a mere procedural rule'. Rather, 'it is a fundamental common law principle'. For his part, Lord Brown remarked that open justice 'is a constitutional principle of the highest importance', and Lord Mance observed that 'principles as important as open and natural justice ought to be regarded as sacrosanct, as long as they themselves do not lead to a denial of justice'.

**17.48** The cases referred to reflect the importance which domestic courts have attached to the principle of open justice. However, it should not be forgotten that art 6 of the ECHR 'recognises a prima facie rule of open justice in criminal trials': per Lord Steyn in *Re S (a child)*. Thus in *Diennet v France* (1996), the ECtHR stated:

> The Court reiterates that the holding of court hearings in public constitutes a fundamental principle enshrined in Article 6. This public character protects litigants against the administration of justice in secret with no public scrutiny; it is also one of the means whereby confidence in the courts can be maintained. By rendering the administration of justice transparent, publicity contributes to the achievement of the aim of art 6(1), namely a fair trial, the guarantee of which is one of the fundamental principles of any democratic society.

## The Contempt of Court Act 1981

**17.49** The Contempt of Court Act 1981 (CCA 1981) was introduced by Lord Hailsham LC as a liberalizing measure. It has not codified the law on contempt; instead, it provides for strict liability in respect of contempts committed within the scope of the Act. The Act itself owes a number of its provisions to recommendations made by the Phillimore Committee on Contempt of Court (Cmnd 5794 (1974)). However, the catalyst for reform was not the publication of the recommendations themselves, but the ruling of the ECtHR in *Sunday Times v United Kingdom* (1979). In short, the Court concluded that injunctions granted to prevent the publication of newspaper articles which were critical of a company which had distributed the thalidomide drug amounted to a violation of art 10 of the ECHR which guarantees freedom of expression. In order to ensure that UK law subsequently complied with the ECHR, the CCA 1981 was enacted.

## Strict liability

**17.50** The principal feature of the CCA 1981 is the strict liability rule. Section 1 of the Act thus provides that:

> conduct may be treated as a contempt of court as tending to interfere with the course of justice in particular legal proceedings regardless of intent to do so.

Thus it is unnecessary for the prosecution to prove that D intended to commit a contempt of court or that he was reckless as to whether or not a contempt would be committed in order to secure a conviction. It will have to prove, however, that D intended to publish that which constitutes the contempt. Also, a publication will only fall foul of the strict liability rule where it:

> creates a substantial risk that the course of justice in the proceedings in question will be seriously impeded or prejudiced (s 2(2)).

**17.51** This then, is the actus reus of the offence. What amounts to a 'substantial risk' is not defined by the statute, although in *A-G v BBC* (1997), Auld LJ observed that 'the threshold of risk is not high, simply of more than a remote or minimal risk of serious prejudice'.

**17.52** Similarly, the statute offers no guidance as to when proceedings can be said to have been 'seriously' impeded or prejudiced. Nevertheless, it would seem that the purpose underlying the use of the adverb 'seriously' is to ensure that the CCA 1981 only applies to contempts that are more than trivial in nature. As Jaconelli has pointed out, the test in s 2(2):

> is compounded of two elements: the size of the risk, and the severity of impact (if, indeed, it has any effect) of the publication. Neither a remote risk of serious impediment nor a substantial risk of minor impediment will suffice.

**17.53** The strict liability rule only applies to publications as defined by s 2(1) of the Act. Thus there will be certain types of contempt, such as contempt in the face of the court, which do not involve a publication and which do not therefore fall within the scope of the Act. Moreover, the Act only applies where the relevant proceedings are 'active' at the time of the publication. For the purposes of s 2, Sch 1 to the CCA 1981 states when criminal, civil, or appellate proceedings are active. Thus in the case of criminal proceedings, they will become active where, for example, a person has been arrested without warrant. Criminal proceedings will be concluded where D is acquitted or sentenced, or some other verdict is passed which puts an end to the proceedings, or the proceedings are discontinued or concluded by operation of law.

## Defences

**17.54** Where a person has been charged with contempt of court contrary to the CCA 1981, one of several defences may be raised in argument. Section 3 of the Act provides that a publisher is not guilty of contempt under the strict liability rule if at the time of the publication, having taken all reasonable care, he does not know and has no reason to suppose that the relevant proceedings are active. A distributor of a publication may rely on an equivalent defence under s 3. In effect, these defences amount to innocent publication or distribution. The real nature of these defences is underlined by the fact that the burden of proof rests with D to be discharged on the balance of probabilities. In practice, the need to take all reasonable care will mean that D will have to show that proper inquiries were made of a case at the time of publication in order to ensure that proceedings were not active. This may entail making contact with the police in order to get up-to-date reports as to the status of a criminal investigation.

**17.55**  Section 4(1) of the CCA 1981 states that a person is not guilty of contempt under the strict liability rule 'in respect of a fair and accurate report of legal proceedings held in public, published contemporaneously and in good faith'. In other words, responsible journalism will not fall foul of the contempt laws. Where an order has been made pursuant to s 4(2) (see paras **17.61–17.67**), a publication is contemporaneous for the purposes of s 4(1) if it is made as soon as practicable after the order has expired.

**17.56**  The final 'defence' is found in s 5 of the Act. This provides that:

> *A publication made as or as part of a discussion in good faith of public affairs or other matters of general public interest is not to be treated as a contempt of court under the strict liability rule if the risk of impediment or prejudice to particular legal proceedings is merely incidental to the discussion.*

In truth, it is not really a defence as such since it will be for the prosecution (in the form of the Attorney-General) to show that the risk of prejudice to a fair trial was not merely incidental to the discussion of the matter dealt with by the article.

---

*A-G v English* **(1983):** A doctor was being tried for the murder of a baby with Down's syndrome. On the third day of the trial, an article was published in the Daily Mail which expressed support for the candidature of a woman standing for Parliament who had been born without arms. It was suggested in the article that had she been born at the time of writing, 'someone would surely recommend letting her die of starvation, or otherwise disposing of her'. Proceedings were instituted for contempt and D, the editor, was found guilty despite relying on s 5 of the CCA 1981. HL held: the appeal against conviction would be allowed. Section 5 does not take the form of a proviso or an exception to s 2(2). It stands on an equal footing with it. It was clear that the article was capable of prejudicing the jury in the trial, but it was also clear that it fell within s 5.

---

## What is a court?

**17.57**  The 1981 Act is, as its short title indicates, concerned with contempt of court. By virtue of s 19 of the Act, a 'court' is defined as including:

> *any tribunal or body exercising the judicial power of the State.*

The key aspect of this definition is thus that the body in question must be exercising a judicial function. In *A-G v BBC* (1981) (see paras **15.4–15.5**), the HL made it clear that labels can be misleading. The mere fact that a body is called a court, in that case a local valuation court, does not necessarily mean that it is a court for the purposes of the 1981 Act. What matters is the nature of its function. Thus a body which is performing an administrative function will not be a court. Tribunals may exercise the judicial power of the state and hence be courts within the meaning of s 19. In *Pickering v Liverpool Daily Post and Echo Newspapers plc* (1991), for example, a Mental Health Review Tribunal was held to be a court. Similarly in *Peach Grey & Co v Sommers* (1995), an industrial tribunal was a court for the purposes of the law of contempt. However, in *General Medical Council v BBC* (1998), the CA held that a Professional Conduct Committee of the GMC was not a court despite the fact that it performed a recognizably judicial function.

## Restrictions on reporting

**17.58** The CCA 1981 provides for two types of order which constitute restrictions on the reporting of legal proceedings. By virtue of s 4(2), a court may:

> where it appears to be necessary for avoiding a substantial risk of prejudice to the administration of justice in those proceedings, or in any other proceedings pending or imminent, order that the publication of any report of the proceedings, or any part of the proceedings, be postponed for such period as the court thinks necessary for that purpose.

**17.59** Section 11 of the Act provides that:

> In any case where a court (having power to do so) allows a name or other matter to be withheld from the public in proceedings before the court, the court may give such directions prohibiting the publication of that name or matter in connection with the proceedings as appear to the court to be necessary for the purpose for which it was so withheld.

**17.60** Several distinctions can thus be made between these two orders. The first of these concerns the duration of the relevant order. A s 4(2) order amounts to a postponement of the reporting of the legal proceedings; that postponement is at the discretion of the court and may last for some time where it has been made in order to protect proceedings which are pending or imminent. However, there will be a point in time in the future when reporting will be permitted. In practice, where a s 4(2) order is made, it is required to state the time at which it will cease to have effect. A s 11 order, by contrast, imposes a prohibition on the reporting of the particular matter, eg the identity of a victim or witness. It is not likely to cease to have effect at some point in time in the future. A further distinction relates to the scope of the orders, which must be stated in the orders themselves. The potential scope of a s 4(2) order is clearly wider than that of a s 11 order. It precludes 'any report of the proceedings' whilst it is in force and as such amounts to a 'blanket ban' on media coverage of the case. Section 11 is rather narrower in that the proceedings may still be reported, provided that the matter to which the order relates is not disclosed. In practice, however, this distinction between s 4(2) and s 11 may not always be so clear-cut. Thus at the conclusion of *R v E* (2004), the CA stated that:

> For the avoidance of doubt we make an order under section 4(2) of the Contempt of Court Act 1981, that pending final verdicts, on the trial of the appellant and his co-accused, no report of this judgment may be published which tends to identify either the appellant or his co-accused, or the Crown Court, at which they are to be tried. This order is not intended to prohibit or postpone a law report of the judgment provided that therein the appellant is identified by an initial other than his own, and the Crown Court is not identified.

## Section 4(2) orders

**17.61** In *MGN Pension Trustees v Bank of America National Trust and Savings Association* (1995), Lindsay J held that in considering whether to make an order under s 4(2), a court should adopt a three-stage approach. This would entail asking itself whether: there was a substantial risk of prejudice to the administration of justice in the proceedings; an order was necessary for avoiding the risk; and the court in its discretion ought to make any and, if so, what order.

**17.62** In the later case of *R (on the application of Telegraph Group Plc) v Sherwood* (2001), the CA advocated the use of a broadly similar three-stage test in respect of a s 4(2) order. With regard to the third stage, Longmore LJ noted that even if a trial judge concludes that a s 4(2) order is the only way of eliminating a perceived risk of prejudice, 'it still does not follow necessarily that an order has to be made'. It was at this stage, therefore, that 'value judgments' would need to be made between the competing public interests of freedom of expression and the proper administration of justice.

**17.63** As was previously noted in the context of s 2(2) of the 1981 Act, 'substantial risk' means more than a remote or minimal risk: *A-G v BBC* (1997). Once it has been concluded that reporting would result in a substantial risk of prejudice to the administration of justice, the second stage requires a court to consider whether an order is in fact necessary to avoid that risk. This involves a balancing exercise on the part of the court taking into account the need for a fair trial by an unprejudiced jury on the one hand, and the requirements of open justice and freedom of expression on the other. The mere fact that an individual faces several trials does not necessarily mean that a s 4(2) order will be granted in respect of the first trial.

> ***R v Beck, ex p Daily Telegraph plc* (1993):** Three social workers were charged with serious offences involving the sexual and physical abuse of children in local authority care. The number of charges was such that the case was divided into three indictments. At the trial of the first indictment, the judge made a s 4(2) order at the request of B's counsel. The

order extended to the reporting of the first trial up to and including the verdicts. A number of national newspapers appealed against the order under s 159 of the Criminal Justice Act 1988. CA held: that there was a substantial risk of prejudice to the administration of justice if the trial on the first indictment were to be reported. However, given the widespread public concern caused by the trial and the issues which it raised about local authority care, it would not be right for the trial to proceed without the public having an opportunity of knowing what was going on.

**17.64**  The decision in *Beck* illustrates the CA carrying out the balancing exercise and deciding it in favour of open justice and legitimate public concern as to the nature of the allegations. It also illustrates the fact that the press as 'a person aggrieved' have the right to appeal against a s 4(2) order by virtue of s 159(1)(a) of the Criminal Justice Act 1988. In determining such an appeal, the CA is required not merely to review the trial judge's decision to impose reporting restrictions but also to form its own independent conclusions on the material placed before it: see *R (on the application of Telegraph Group Plc) v Sherwood* (2001). The test advocated in *Sherwood* was applied in *R v B* (2006) where the CA allowed an appeal by the BBC, *The Times*, and Associated Press against a s 4(2) order which postponed the reporting of the conviction and sentencing of a terrorist until the conclusion of the trial of his co-defendants. In the judgment of the CA, 'the responsibility of the media to avoid inappropriate comment which may interfere with the due administration of justice . . . and the entire trial process, including the integrity of the jury itself', made the order unnecessary.

**17.65**  The press may also have a role to play in the actual process of deciding whether or not to grant a s 4(2) order.

---

*R v Clerkenwell Metropolitan Stipendiary Magistrates, ex p Telegraph plc* (1993): The Serious Fraud Office laid an information before a stipendiary magistrate alleging that T had committed an offence contrary to s 2(13) of the Criminal Justice Act 1987. The information was heard in private. T's counsel applied for a s 4(2) order to be granted on the basis that T had already been charged with other offences and that publication of the s 2(13) charge would involve a substantial risk of prejudice to those proceedings. The order was made. The newspapers believed that the s 2(13) proceedings were a matter of public interest and that reporting them would not involve such a risk. They sought to make representations to the magistrate as to why the order should be discharged. The magistrate declined to hear their representations on the basis that he had no power to hear anyone other than the parties to the proceedings. The newspapers sought judicial review of the decisions to make the s 4(2) order and to refuse to hear their representations. QBD held: the court had a discretionary power to hear representations from the press or the news media when considering whether to make a s 4(2) order. However, given that they were best qualified to represent the public interest in reporting the proceedings, a court ought normally to hear representations from the press or news media whenever they asked to be heard and whenever the court was of the opinion that their representations would be of assistance.

---

**17.66** The ruling in *ex p Telegraph Plc* is now largely reflected in part of a Practice Direction issued by the former CJ, Lord Woolf, in 2002: see Part I, para **3.2**. In addition, that Practice Direction requires that s 4(2) orders be formulated in 'precise terms' and that they be expressed in writing. Such an order must state: its precise scope; the time at which it shall cease to have effect; and the specific purpose of making the order.

**17.67** Where there is no substantial risk of prejudice to the administration of justice in proceedings, it follows that a s 4(2) order should not be granted: *MGN Pension Trustees Ltd v Bank of America National Trust and Savings Association* (1995) and *Re Central Independent Television plc* (1991). In the latter case, where a trial judge made a s 4(2) order prohibiting the reporting of a trial by radio or television whilst the jury had to spend the night in a hotel, so that the jurors could watch television or listen to the radio free from the possibility of being prejudiced by media reports, the CA held that such an order had not been appropriate. Had there been a substantial risk of prejudice, which there was not, it would have been possible to insulate the jury from the media by more proportionate means than a s 4(2) order, eg deprive them of television and radio for the night.

## Section 11 orders

**17.68** Section 11 of the CCA 1981 does not confer a power to make a direction prohibiting the publication of a name or other matter; it merely recognizes that it may be exercised by a court which has the power to do so. Thus in *Re Attorney-General's Reference (No 3 of 1999)* (2009), the House of Lords recognized, amongst other things, that although it was doubtful that s 11 had given their Lordships the jurisdiction to make an anonymity order in respect of D's acquittal on a rape charge, the court had an inherent jurisdiction to make such orders as were necessary for the purpose of the proceedings before it. Moreover, in delivering the unanimous judgment of the Supreme Court in *Guardian News and Media Ltd v Ahmed* (2010), Lord Rodger observed in an obiter remark:

> *Section 11 is dealing with the particular situation where a court, having power to do so, allows a name or other matter to be withheld from the public in proceedings before the court. An obvious example is a court allowing the victim to withhold his name when giving evidence for the Crown in a prosecution for blackmail. Section 11 then gives the court the ancillary power to give directions prohibiting a newspaper which actually knows the name of the individual from publishing it. The section resolves any doubt about the power of the court in these circumstances to prevent persons, other than the parties, from naming the individual or mentioning the matter outside court.*

**17.69** At common law, the power has been used, as Lord Rodger's remarks make clear, to confer anonymity on witnesses in blackmail trials or where matters of national security are involved.

---

***R v Socialist Worker Printers and Publishers Ltd, ex p A-G (1975):*** During D's trial for blackmail, the judge directed that the two victims of the alleged blackmail be referred to as Mr Y and Mr Z. Prior to the end of the trial, the names, addresses, and other particulars of the victims were published in the *Socialist Worker.* The A-G sought orders of committal for contempt of court against the publishers of the article and its author. DC held: by publishing the names of the victims in defiance of the judge's direction, the respondents were committing a blatant affront to the authority of the court. They were therefore in contempt of court.

---

***Re Times Newspapers (2008):*** Five soldiers had been charged with the offence of conspiracy to defraud. The trial judge ordered that the proceedings ought to be heard *in camera*, and that no report of the proceedings should be published, save for the nature of the offence charged. The order was made pursuant to s 11 of the CCA 1981 and s 94(2) of the Army Act 1955 on the grounds that: there would be a substantial risk of prejudice to national security, in terms of the safety of the individuals and on operational effectiveness, if the soldiers' identities were revealed; and there would be a substantial risk of prejudice to the administration of justice because the defence would not be able to pursue certain lines of questions and inquiries. The media appealed pursuant to s 103(2)(nn) of the 1955 Act and para 90(1) and (2) of the Courts Martial (Army) Rules 2007. Courts Martial Appeal Court held: that the claim to anonymity rested on the risk to the lives of two of the soldiers and that their service history made it clear that there would be a real and immediate risk if they were identified. Although three soldiers did not fall into this category, there was a real risk that if they were identified, the other two would be identified. Granting anonymity to all had therefore been a reasonable and proportionate action to take.

---

**17.70**  In delivering the judgment of the court in the *Socialist Worker* case, Lord Widgery CJ noted that anonymity for victims in blackmail cases had been commonplace for many years. It was justified:

> not out of any feelings of tenderness towards the victim of the blackmail, a man or woman very often who deserves no such consideration at all. The reason why the courts in the past have so often used this device in this type of blackmail case where the complainant has something to hide, is because there is a keen public interest in getting blackmailers convicted and sentenced, and experience shows that grave difficulty may be suffered in getting complainants to come forward unless they are given this kind of protection.

**17.71**  It is apparent from Lord Widgery's remarks, therefore, that a s 11 order is only to be granted where it is necessary in the interests of the administration of justice. Thus in *R v Evesham Justices, ex p McDonagh* (1988), where magistrates made an order under s 11 in respect of D's home address because he feared that he would be further harassed by his ex-wife, the DC granted a declaration that the magistrates' decision was unlawful. In the words of Watkins LJ:

> There are undoubtedly many people who find themselves defending criminal charges who for all manner of reasons would like to keep unrevealed their identity, their home address in particular . . . But s 11 was not enacted for the benefit of the comfort and feelings of defendants.

**17.72**  The view expressed by Watkins LJ in *ex p McDonagh* was subsequently reflected in a case concerned with child pornography.

---

*Re Trinity Mirror plc* **(2008):** An anonymity order was made in respect of D who had pleaded guilty to 20 counts of making or possessing indecent images of children. It had been made by the trial judge on account of D being the father of two young children whom, it was believed, would be likely to suffer significant harm were the matter publicized. During the trial, however, D's surname had been published in the court list and referred to in open court. A court reporter appealed against the s 11 order. CA held: although it had sympathy for D's children, it was sad but true that the criminal activities of a parent can bring misery, shame and disadvantage to their innocent children. Had the court upheld the s 11 order so as to protect the art 8 rights (ECHR) of the children, it would have countenanced a substantial erosion of the principle of open justice, to the overwhelming disadvantage of public confidence in the criminal justice system, the free reporting of criminal trials, and the proper identification of those convicted and sentenced therein.

---

**17.73**  In *R v Dover Justices, ex p Dover District Council* (1991), where it was alleged that D's restaurant had breached food hygiene regulations, the DC rejected economic loss to the business as justifying the grant of a s 11 order. The situation in relation to professions is, therefore, that in general they will not be granted anonymity even where they are concerned that publicity will cause damage and may seriously prejudice a reputation.

**17.74**  Thus in *R v Legal Aid Board, ex p Kaim Todner (a firm)* (1999), where a firm of solicitors sought to challenge a decision of the Legal Aid Board to terminate its franchise and applied to have its identity kept secret in the judicial review proceedings, the CA dismissed an appeal against a refusal to grant a s 11 order. In delivering the judgment of the court, Lord Woolf MR (as he then was) stated nine reasons as to why Kay J had been correct in refusing to grant the order save on an interim basis. The eighth reason is of particular interest in that Lord Woolf sought to draw a distinction between a plaintiff, a defendant, and a third party with regard to the grant of an order of anonymity. In the case of the plaintiff, he contended that 'it is not unreasonable to regard the person who initiates the proceedings as having accepted the normal incidence of the public nature of court proceedings'. A defendant was in a slightly better position given that he had not initiated the proceedings. However, it was the witness who had no interest in the proceedings who 'has the strongest claim to be protected by the court if he or she will be prejudiced by publicity'. Nevertheless, in Lord Woolf's opinion, the general approach was that:

> parties and witnesses have to accept the embarrassment and damage to their reputation and the possible consequential loss which can be inherent in being involved in litigation. The protection to which they are entitled is normally provided by a judgment delivered in public which will refute unfounded allegations.

**17.75** Where the names of the main participants in a trial have been given in open court during the course of the proceedings, the CA has no power to make a s 11 order restraining the publication of evidence when hearing an appeal against the trial judge's verdict: see the decision of the HL in *R v Hasan* (2005). Unless a court deliberately exercises its power to allow a name or other matter to be withheld, s 11 is not engaged: see *Re Trinity Mirror plc* (2008) (para **17.72**).

## The common law

**17.76** Despite the enactment of the CCA 1981, the common law may still apply in respect of publications that are 'intended to impede or prejudice the administration of justice': s 6(c) of the CCA 1981. Clearly the need to prove intention on the part of D makes it more difficult for the prosecution to secure a conviction under the common law than under the strict liability rule. However, there are certain advantages in bringing a prosecution under the common law.

**17.77** The first of these relates to the status of the proceedings in respect of which a contempt has allegedly been committed. Whereas those proceedings must be 'active' under the CCA 1981, under the common law there is some uncertainty as to whether proceedings must be 'pending or imminent' for a contempt to have been committed. In *A-G v News Group Newspapers* (1989), Watkins LJ appeared to doubt whether this was a necessary requirement and in *A-G v Sport Newspapers* (1992), Bingham LJ (as he then was) and Hodgson J reached different conclusions on this issue. This uncertainty is by no means satisfactory from the point of view of an editor or publisher of a newspaper who is contemplating whether or not to publish a particular article.

**17.78** With regard to the risk of prejudice to legal proceedings created by a publication, the common law requires that the risk must be 'real': *R v Thomson Newspapers Ltd, ex p A-G* (1968). This is therefore a less stringent standard than that required under the CCA 1981, where the risk must be 'substantial'. Finally, where proceedings are brought under the common law for contempt, the statutory defences under ss 4 and 5 of the CCA 1981 will not apply. In *A-G v Hislop* (1991), for example, it was held that the intention to impede or prejudice the administration of justice by publishing an article amounted to common law contempt. The existence of the intention was also held to negative the 'good faith' aspect of the defence under s 5 of the 1981 Act. Since the defences under ss 4 and 5 amount to important constraints on the scope of contempt and hence serve to uphold the freedom of the press, it is unfortunate that they may be by-passed in this manner.

**17.79** Thus common law contempt may apply in circumstances where the strict liability rule may not. However, it need not necessarily be simply an alternative. Where proceedings are 'active', it would be possible for an article to fall foul of both the common law and the CCA 1981: *A-G v Hislop* (1991).

## FURTHER READING

Akdeniz, Y 'Possession and Dispossession: A critical assessment of defences in possession of indecent photographs of children cases' [2007] Crim LR 274.

Bailey, S and Taylor, N *Bailey, Harris & Jones: Civil Liberties Cases and Materials* (6th edn, 2009) OUP.

Barendt, E *Freedom of Speech* (2nd edn, 2005) OUP.

Barendt, E *Media Freedom and Contempt of Court* (2009) OUP.

Beloff, M 'Fair Trial – Free Press? Reporting Restrictions in Law and Practice' [1992] PL 92.

Edwards, S 'On the Contemporary Application of the Obscene Publications Act 1959' [1998] Crim LR 843.

Hirst, M 'Cyberobscenity and the Ambit of English Criminal Law' (2002) 13 Computer Law 25.

Hofler, A 'Are the Victims of Lust Expendable?' [2006] Crim LR 3.

Home Office 'Consultation: On the possession of extreme pornographic material' (August 2005).

Jaconelli, J 'Defences to speech crimes' [2007] EHRLR 27.

Kearns, P 'Obscene and Blasphemous Libel: Misunderstanding Art' [2000] Crim LR 652.

Kearns, P 'The Ineluctable Decline of Obscene Libel: Exculpation and Abolition' [2007] Crim LR 667.

McGlynn, C and Rackley, E 'Striking a Balance: Arguments for the criminal regulation of extreme pornography' [2007] Crim LR 677.

McGlynn, C and Rackley, E 'Criminalizing Extreme Pornography: A Lost Opportunity' [2009] Crim LR 245.

McGlynn, C and Ward, I 'Pornography, Pragmatism, and Proscription' (2009) 36 J Law & Soc 327.

Miller, C J 'Some Problems of Contempt' [1992] Crim LR 107.

Murray, A 'The Reclassification of Extreme Pornographic Images' (2009) 72 MLR 73.

Ormerod, D 'Case Comment' [1999] Crim LR 670.

Ormerod, D 'Act of Outraging Public Decency: Whether public constituent of the offence proved' [2006] Crim LR 993.

Rowbottom, J 'Obscenity Laws and the Internet: Targeting the Supply and Demand' [2006] Crim LR 97.

St John-Stevas, N 'Obscenity and the Law' [1954] Crim LR 817.

Stone, R *Textbook on Civil Liberties and Human Rights* (8th edn, 2010) OUP.

Watkins, D 'The Influence of the Art for Art's Sake Movement upon English Law, 1780–1959' (2007) 28 J Leg Hist 233.

## SELF-TEST QUESTIONS

1   What are the arguments both for and against the retention of the statutory definition of 'obscenity' in the Obscene Publications Act 1959? Is the compilation of a list of activities the depiction, etc of any one of which would be obscene a better alternative?

2   Kearns has contended: 'The legal sense of obscenity was once confined to sexual immorality whereas in more recent times it has been rather artificially extended to cover the favourable presentation of drug-taking and acts that incite violence. The consequence is that it is difficult to predict what further unpleasant portrayals will be found to come under "obscenity" as a now burgeoning legal term of art: in view of the current hostility to smoking tobacco, that exercise might soon be legally subsumed under the obscenity label.' Do you agree?

3   Is it acceptable in a trial for an offence contrary to the 1959 Act that the defence may seek to establish that the publication was deliberately repulsive so as to discourage people from the activities described rather than promote them?

4   On what basis might it be argued that Professor Stone is correct when he asserts that: 'The English law relating to the control of obscenity and indecency is a mess'?

5   To what extent, if any, do you agree with the view expressed by McGlynn and Rackley that: 'There are strong arguments for the need to consider a complete overhaul of the legal regulation of pornography, including the repeal of the OPA, perhaps by establishing a review committee similar to that of the Williams Committee'?

6   What are the arguments both for and against the new criminal offence of possessing 'extreme pornographic' material?

7   If you were asked to make a case for the reporting by the press and media generally of court proceedings and the discussion of issues arising in those proceedings, what arguments would you advance?

8   Conversely, what are the arguments for restricting comments or reports on actual or pending legal proceedings?

9   What is the actus reus of contempt under the CCA 1981?

10   Will it always be the case that any prejudice to proceedings brought about by a newspaper report will have a detrimental effect on the defence alone? Can you think of any circumstances in which the prosecution may be prejudiced by a report in the press?

11   What do the cases on s 11 of the CCA tell us about the likelihood of an anonymity order being made in legal proceedings? Do you think that *Re Trinity Mirror plc* (2008) was rightly decided?

# 18

# Police powers

## SUMMARY

The principal focus of this chapter is on the powers of the police to: stop and search; arrest; and enter, search, and seize items. Although it is acknowledged that specific powers to do any of these things may be provided for in other enactments, the chapter will examine the Police and Criminal Evidence Act 1984 (PACE) powers. In addition, the exercise of police discretion will be considered together with the extent to which this is subject to review by the courts. The chapter ends by looking at two specific offences which may be committed against a police officer: assaulting an officer; or wilfully obstructing an officer, both of which can only be committed if the officer is acting within the execution of his or her duty at the relevant time.

## Police discretion

18.1 It will become apparent from the discussion that follows that the Police and Criminal Evidence Act 1984 (PACE) confers many powers upon the police. Whether or not a particular power is exercised will, of course, be a matter of discretion for an individual officer. Thus, for example, he may decide to stop and search a person or to arrest them where he believes that either course of action is appropriate in the circumstances. However, although the powers of the police are wide, they are not unlimited. Their exercise is subject to the supervisory jurisdiction of the courts. Thus where a police officer has exceeded his or her powers, the courts will be prepared to intervene.

*Lindley v Rutter* (1981): D was arrested for disorderly behaviour whilst drunk and taken to a police station. She was placed in a cell and, following a struggle, searched. Two women police officers removed her brassiere. They did so in purported compliance with a standing order from the chief constable. This recommended such a course of action so as to prevent a defendant from harming herself. In respect of the struggle D was charged and convicted of assaulting a police officer in the execution of her duty. She appealed. DC held: that the police officer had failed to properly exercise her discretion in the present case. No account had been taken of D's particular circumstances before deciding to remove her brassiere. At the material time, therefore, the police officer was not acting within the execution of her duty.

**18.2** Judicial review of police action on the basis of the *Wednesbury* principles (paras **13.2** and **13.3**) is, therefore, a possibility. In *R v Chief Constable of Sussex, ex p International Trader's Ferry Ltd* (1999), where ITF sought to challenge the chief constable's decisions on the policing of animal rights protesters at a port which had a detrimental impact on their business of exporting livestock, Lord Slynn observed that:

> My Lords, it is clear that, although the duty to keep the peace is that of the chief constable, what he does may be reviewed by the courts; if his act is clearly unlawful it will be quashed and he may be ordered to do something else; he may have to pay damages.

On the facts, the HL concluded that the police were acting within the scope of their discretion. Restricting the days on which the port would be policed was justified given the financial and manpower resource implications of policing the port in the face of large-scale demonstrations.

**18.3** In addition to considering the lawfulness of police conduct, the courts are also prepared to hear challenges brought against police inactivity. Indeed, there may be circumstances in which a court will compel the police to perform a duty that they owe to the general public.

---

*R v Metropolitan Police Comr, ex p Blackburn* (1968): The Commissioner issued a policy decision to his officers stating that they were not to attempt to enforce a provision of the Betting, Gaming and Lotteries Act 1963. The rationale for this was the uncertain state of the law at the time and the resource implications of keeping gaming clubs under observation. B sought an order of mandamus (now a mandatory order). The DC dismissed the motion. B appealed. CA held: that the wide discretionary powers enjoyed by the police were not beyond the review of the courts. Mandamus was not necessary in the present case since the Commissioner had given an undertaking to the court that the policy decision would be revoked. However, had this not been the case, the court would have been prepared to grant the order sought on the basis that the police are under a clear legal duty to enforce the law.

---

**18.4** In *R v Chief Constable of Devon and Cornwall, ex p Central Electricity Generating Board* (1982) (paras **19.3–19.4**) the CA took the view that the circumstances of the case made it inappropriate to grant an order of mandamus. Lord Denning MR observed that it was 'of the first importance that the police should decide on their own responsibility what action should be taken in any particular situation'. Applying this general principle to the circumstances of the case, Templeman LJ stated that:

> it is for the police and the board to co-operate and decide on and implement the most effective method of dealing with the obstructors. The court cannot tell the police how and when their powers should be exercised, for the court cannot judge the explosiveness of the situation or deal with the individual problems which will arise as a result of the activities of the obstructors.

## The Police and Criminal Evidence Act 1984 (PACE)

**18.5**  When introducing a revised and amended Police and Criminal Evidence Bill before the HC in November 1983, the then Home Secretary, Leon Brittan, declared that the measure was necessary for a number of reasons:

> First, the present state of the law is unclear and contains many indefensible anomalies. Secondly, the police need to have adequate and clear powers to conduct the fight against crime on our behalf and the public need to have proper safeguards against any abuse of such powers if they are to have confidence in the police. Thirdly, these measures play an essential part in an overall strategy designed to create more effective policing.

**18.6**  The need for legislation did not mean, however, that Parliament was prepared to accept whatever it was given by the government of the day. Considerable parliamentary time was spent both on the floor of the House and in the committee rooms in moulding the second version of the Bill into what was desired. Indeed, the process of enactment has been described by Professor Zander as 'an impressive example of the democratic system working'. The resultant Act is a very important piece of legislation. Although it does not amount to a codification of police powers, it does form the basis of many of the powers exercised by the police on a daily basis.

## Codes of Practice

**18.7**  Sections 60 and 66 of PACE require the Secretary of State to issue codes of practice in connection with the exercise of various powers accorded to the police under PACE. To date, eight such codes have been drafted. They are concerned with:

- powers of stop and search (Code A);
- searching premises and the seizure of property (Code B);
- detention, treatment, and questioning of suspects (Code C);
- identification matters (Code D);
- tape-recording interviews with suspects (Code E);
- video-recording interviews with suspects (Code F);
- police officers' statutory powers of arrest (Code G); and
- detention of terrorist suspects (Code H).

**18.8**  A failure to comply with a Code does not in itself render a police officer liable to any criminal or civil proceedings: s 67(10). Neither is a breach of a Code automatically a disciplinary matter as was formerly the case under the now repealed s 67(8). Nevertheless, the Codes serve an important purpose in that they provide the police with additional guidance, which is sometimes clearer than that given in PACE itself, as to how they are to exercise their powers under the Act. Each Code must therefore be readily accessible at all police stations so that it may be consulted by anyone who wishes to do so. Moreover, the fact that they are Codes rather than statutory provisions ensures that they may be more easily revised, either wholly or in part, when the need arises. In practice the Secretary of State achieves this by laying a draft of the revised Code before Parliament, considering representations made to him about it, and modifying it accordingly. The revised Code is then brought into effect by order. The most recent versions of the Codes of Practice came into effect on various different dates between after midnight on 31 December 2005 and after midnight on 6 March 2011.

## Police powers of stop and search

**18.9**  The police have the power to stop and search persons under a variety of different enactments. Thus, for example, under s 23(2) of the Misuse of Drugs Act 1971, a police officer may search any person whom he has reasonable grounds to suspect to be in possession of a controlled drug in contravention of the Act. A similar power entitles a police officer to search a vehicle or vessel for a controlled drug. For the purposes of the 1971 Act, a 'controlled drug' is a substance or product specified in Sch 2 to the Act. A police officer has the power to seize and detain anything which he finds as a consequence of a s 23 search which appears to him to be evidence of an offence under the Act: s 23(2)(c).

**18.10**  There are several powers of stop and search available to the police which are not based on the need for 'reasonable suspicion'. Thus s 60 of the Criminal Justice and Public Order Act 1994 is concerned with powers to stop and search in anticipation of violence. Where it is believed that serious violence may take place in the locality, or that persons are carrying dangerous instruments or offensive weapons in the locality, a police officer of the rank of inspector or above may authorize the use of the s 60 search powers during the course of a 24-hour period. These entitle the police to stop and search any pedestrian, any vehicle, the driver of the vehicle or, any of its passengers for offensive weapons or dangerous instruments. There is no need for a police officer to reasonably suspect that an individual is in possession of these weapons or articles.

**18.11**  A search under s 60 is, however, subject to the requirements of s 2 of PACE. Thus a failure by police officers to supply details of their names and station rendered a s 60 search unlawful: see *Osman v Southwark Crown Court* (1999). The requirements of s 2 do not need to be complied with, however, where pursuant to s 60(8A) of the 1994 Act, a police officer asks a person to remove a mask worn to conceal their identity since such an action does not amount to a 'search': see *DPP v Avery* (2001). The power to order the removal of face coverings is limited to a specific geographical location for a limited time (24 hours), and is linked to the threat of violence. In the light of the riots and looting in London and other English towns and cities in August 2011, the coalition Government intends to empower the police to be able to remove face coverings under any circumstances, provided that they reasonably believe that they relate to criminal activity.

**18.12**   Sections 44 and 45 of the Terrorism Act 2000 provided for a police power to stop and search that was not conditional on the need for reasonable suspicion. Like the power under s 60 of the 1994 Act, it was exercisable only after an authorization had been granted by a senior officer. Where an authorization was granted, it lasted for a period of 28 days. The lawfulness of an authorization and subsequent stops and searches was challenged in *R (Gillan) v Metropolitan Police Commissioner* (2006). Like the DC and the CA before it, the HL dismissed claims that there had been a violation of rights under arts 5, 8, 9, 10, and 11 of the ECHR. In its judgment, the power to stop and search under s 44 had pursued a legitimate aim, the prevention of acts of terrorism, and had been subject to appropriate constraints. Moreover, a stop and search did not amount to a deprivation of liberty within the meaning of art 5(1) of the ECHR, and any intrusion on private life was not sufficiently serious to amount to a breach of art 8(1).

**18.13**   Following the HL rejection of their claim, and an unsuccessful attempt to obtain damages under the HRA before the county court, the claimants in *Gillan* took their case to the ECtHR: see *Gillan and Quinton v UK* (2010). That Court took a different view of the events. On the issue of whether the stops and searches amounted to a deprivation of liberty within the meaning of art 5(1) of the ECHR, the Court recalled that the provision is 'not concerned with mere restriction on liberty', which is the province of art 2 of Protocol 4 to the ECHR (not ratified by the UK). The Court also observed that:

> *although the length of time during which each applicant was stopped and searched did not in either case exceed 30 minutes, during this period the applicants were entirely deprived of any freedom of movement. They were obliged to remain where they were and submit to the search and if they had refused they would have been liable to arrest, detention at a police station and criminal charges. This element of coercion is indicative of a deprivation of liberty within the meaning of art 5(1).*

**18.14**   However, the ECtHR considered it unnecessary to authoritatively determine the issue given that it was of the view that the stops and searches were in breach of art 8. Although the HL had doubted whether art 8 was engaged, the ECtHR considered that 'the use of coercive powers conferred by the legislation to require an individual to submit to a detailed search of his person, his clothing and his personal belongings amounts to a clear interference with the right to respect for private life'. Although the UK Government sought to contend that any interference with art 8 rights fell within the scope of art 8(2), due to various safeguards which included, amongst others, the limited nature of a 28-day authorization for the use of the stop and search powers, and the availability of judicial review to challenge an authorization and the actual use of such powers, the ECtHR remained unconvinced. In its judgment, 'the powers of authorization and confirmation as well as those of stop and search under sections 44 and 45 of the 2000 Act are neither sufficiently circumscribed nor subject to adequate legal safeguards against abuse'. Accordingly, since they were 'not in accordance with the law', it followed that there had been a violation of art 8 of the ECHR.

**18.15** In the light of the ECtHR decision, it was clear that the continuing use of the s 44 stop and search powers would be unlawful. Accordingly, it was necessary for the coalition Government to take action. It instituted a *Review of Counter-Terrorism and Security Powers* (Cm 8004), which addressed a number of issues, including the need for terrorism stop and search powers to comply with the ECHR. Two main options for changing the s 44 power were considered: its complete repeal; or replacing it with a more tightly defined and specific power. The former option was rejected on the ground that there was a continuing need for stop and search powers in relation to terrorism which did not require the existence of reasonable suspicion. The *Review* therefore concluded that in exceptional circumstances, a power to stop and search individuals and vehicles *without* reasonable suspicion was 'operationally justified'. Its recommendations as to the scope of that power were given effect by the Terrorism Act 2000 (Remedial) Order 2011.

**18.16** The 2011 Order is a temporary measure pending the enactment of the Protection of Freedoms Bill, when the government reforms will be given permanent force. It provides that the 2000 Act is to have effect as if ss 44–47 were repealed. It further provides that the 2000 Act is to have effect as if three new sections, ss 47A–47C, and one new schedule, Sch 6B, were inserted. Under s 47A, a senior police officer may give an authorization in relation to a specified area or place if he reasonably suspects that an act of terrorism will take place, and considers that: the authorization is necessary to prevent such an act; and both the specified area or place, and the duration of the authorization, is no greater or longer than is necessary to prevent such an act. The new authorization may last for a maximum of 14 days rather than 28, as was originally the case.

**18.17** The tightening up of the terrorism stop and search powers is both subtle and important. The main changes are that an authorization for their use may only be issued where it is reasonably suspected that terrorism *will take place*. Also, stop and search powers have to be considered to be *necessary* rather than merely expedient for the prevention of acts of terrorism. In effecting these changes, the coalition Government has sought to strike a balance between the need to comply with the ECHR and the ECtHR's ruling in *Gillan* on the one hand, and the necessity of stop and search powers not based on reasonable suspicion in exceptional cases on the other. It remains to be seen whether these objectives have been achieved. It should be noted, however, that in his report (Cm 8003), the former DPP, Lord MacDonald, believed that the model proposed in the *Review* (and reflected in the changes to the 2000 Act), was 'unlikely to fall foul of *Gillan*'.

**18.18** It has long been recognized by the courts that searching a person is not a neutral act. Rather, it involves what has been described as a 'degradation' or an 'indignity': see *Leigh v Cole* (1853) and *Bessell v Wilson* (1853). Accordingly, since a search of a person is prima facie a trespass, it will, unless authorized by either statute or the common law, constitute an unlawful act. The courts have shown themselves willing to uphold the common law rights of personal liberty and personal security where an implied power to search has been claimed.

> **Secretary of State for the Home Department v GG (2009):** GG was the subject of successive control orders made pursuant to s 1(3) and (4) of the Prevention of Terrorism Act 2005. Since November 2005, various legal challenges had been brought against the orders. In the most recent, Collins J had confirmed the propriety of the control order. He had, however, excised a provision from the order requiring GG to submit to any search of his person which might be required for the purpose of monitoring his compliance with the other requirements of the control order. The HS appealed against that ruling. CA held: dismissing the appeal, that it was axiomatic that the common law rights of personal security and personal liberty prevent any official search of an individual's clothing or person without explicit statutory authority. The language of s 1(3) of the 2005 Act was insufficient to authorize the inclusion in a control order of a general requirement to submit to searches of the person. The absence of such a power from the list of specific obligations in s 1(4) was as consistent with deliberate as with accidental omission. Even if the omission of a power of search had been a legislative oversight, it was not the role of the courts to supply what Parliament might have inserted where fundamental liberties were at stake.

## PACE

18.19 Section 1 of PACE provides that a person or vehicle may be detained by the police (the Act does not use the word 'stop') in a public place for the purpose of conducting a search for: stolen or prohibited articles; or articles in relation to which a person has committed, or is committing or is going to commit an offence under s 139 of the Criminal Justice Act 1988; or any firework which is possessed in contravention of a prohibition imposed by fireworks regulations. For the purposes of the Act, 'prohibited articles' are an offensive weapon, ie an article made or adapted for causing injury to persons, or an article used in connection with offences such as burglary or theft, eg a jemmy.

18.20 The power to stop and search may only be exercised where a constable has 'reasonable grounds' for suspecting that he will find one of these articles. 'Reasonable grounds for suspecting' is not defined by the Act. Some guidance as to its meaning is to be found in Code of Practice A. Accordingly, there must be some objective basis for the existence of reasonable grounds for suspicion. This may consist of information received which indicates, for example, that a person has been seen carrying a type of article which is known to have been stolen recently from premises in the area. However, it can never be supported on the basis of personal factors alone, such as a person's race, colour, age, or appearance. Neither can it be founded on the basis of stereotyped images of certain persons or groups as more likely to be involved in criminal activity.

**18.21** A police officer who has detained a person or vehicle in order to conduct a search need not carry out the search if it subsequently appears that it is unnecessary or impracticable: s 2(1). However, where a search is to be conducted, a police officer who is not in uniform must, prior to its commencement, provide documentary evidence of his identity. Additionally, whether he is in uniform or not, he must take reasonable steps to bring to the attention of the appropriate person (ie the person to be searched or the person in charge of the vehicle):

- his name and the name of the police station to which he is attached;
- the object of the proposed search;
- the officer's grounds for proposing to make it; and
- that person's entitlement to a copy of the record of the search.

**18.22** A failure to comply with these requirements will render a search unlawful: see *Osman v Southwark Crown Court* (1999), *Bonner v DPP* (2004), *R v Bristol* (2007), *B v DPP* (2008), and *Michaels v Highbury Corner Magistrates Court* (2009). In *Osman*, Sedley LJ suggested that police officers might carry in their pockets slips of paper giving their name and station which they could then hand out to individuals prior to searching them. Do you consider that this amounts to a practical solution where the police wish to search large numbers of persons under s 60 of the Criminal Justice and Public Order Act 1994? In *Bonner*, in holding that a drugs search had been unlawful, McCombe J stated: 'While one has the very greatest sympathy with officers who have to confront day in and day out the realities of life rather than the black letter law which this court has to apply, that law does have to be applied'. Ought we, however, to have very much sympathy for police officers who appeared from the evidence not to have a very good understanding of the requirements of either PACE or Code of Practice A?

**18.23** PACE gives little guidance as to the nature of a search. It does state, however, that s 1 does not authorize an officer to require a person to remove any of his clothing in public other than an outer coat, jacket, or gloves: s 2(9)(a). For further details regarding the nature of a stop and search, it is necessary to have regard to Code of Practice A, once again. This provides, inter alia, that in carrying out a stop and search, every effort must be made to reduce the embarrassment that the person being searched may experience. Where it is considered necessary to require the removal of garments such as a T-shirt, this must be done out of public view, eg in a police van or at a nearby police station. Such searches must be made by an officer of the same gender as the person being searched, and may not be made in the presence of any one of the opposite gender unless the person being searched so requests. Where a person is unwilling to cooperate or resists a search, reasonable force may be used as a last resort.

**18.24** Where a police officer has carried out a search, he is required by s 3(1) of PACE to make a written record of it unless it is not practicable to do so. If it is not practicable at the time of the search, a record shall be made as soon as practicable after its completion. The record of a search must state:

- its object;
- the grounds for making it;
- the date and time when it was made;
- the place where it was made;
- whether anything, and if so what, was found;
- whether any, and if so what, injury to a person or damage to property has resulted from the search; and
- the identity of the police officer making it.

If a record of a search has been made, the person searched is entitled to a copy on request within a period of 12 months from the date of the search. A failure to provide a record of a search does not, however, make the search unlawful: *Basher v DPP* (1993).

**18.25** The powers of the police to stop and search are controversial since they involve an interference with the liberty of the individual and their exercise is dependent upon the discretion of a police officer. In practice, only about one in ten searches results in an arrest. Does this mean, therefore, that the powers are not being properly exercised? Home Office research also suggests that there are concerns about the disproportionately high numbers of young black males who are stopped and searched. Despite the fact that Code of Practice A states that a person's colour or race cannot form the basis of a reasonable suspicion, racial stereotyping does seem to occur in some cases. Is the solution to this problem to be found in a legislative initiative, eg by providing a statutory definition of 'reasonable suspicion', or is it more a matter of seeking to effect a change in police attitude by education and training?

**18.26** A further issue to note about police powers of stop and search concerns their relationship with art 5 of the ECHR. It will be remembered that this guarantees the right to liberty and security of the person, subject to certain qualifications. The question in the present context, therefore, is whether the powers of stop and search fall within the scope of art 5 and, if they do, whether they fall within the scope of one of the permitted exceptions to the general right. In *R (Gillan) v Metropolitan Police Comr* (2006) (para **18.12**), Lord Bingham (with whom the other Law Lords who heard the appeal agreed), commented in relation to a stop and search under the Terrorism Act 2000:

> ...the procedure will ordinarily be relatively brief. The person stopped will not be arrested, handcuffed, confined or removed to any different place. I do not think, in the absence of special circumstances, such a person should be regarded as being detained

*in the sense of confined or kept in custody, but more properly in the sense of kept from proceeding or kept waiting. There is no deprivation of liberty.*

**18.27** As a general principle, therefore, it would seem that stop and search encounters do not necessarily engage the protection afforded by art 5 of the ECHR. However, the presence in Lord Bingham's remarks of the qualifying 'in the absence of special circumstances' does indicate that some stops and searches may fall within the scope of art 5. Thus, for example, a stop and search which lasted for an unreasonably long period of time may amount to a deprivation of liberty which invokes the protection of art 5. At the very least, this is what the ECtHR appeared to believe in its obiter remarks in *Gillan and Quinton v UK* (2010) (paras **18.13–18.14**).

## Arrest

**18.28** The most important power that the police possess is the power to arrest members of the public. In *Spicer v Holt* (1977), Viscount Dilhorne stated that:

*'Arrest' is an ordinary English word . . . Whether or not a person has been arrested depends not on the legality of the arrest but on whether he has been deprived of his liberty to go where he pleases.*

Later, in *Holgate-Mohammed v Duke* (1984), Lord Diplock observed that:

*arrest is a continuing act: it starts with the arrester taking a person into custody (so by action or words restraining him from moving anywhere beyond the arrester's control), and it continues until the person so restrained is either released from custody or, having been brought before a magistrate, is remanded in custody by the magistrate's judicial act.*

**18.29** These statements continue to reflect the position with regard to arrest. In *Lewis v Chief Constable of South Wales Constabulary* (1991), Balcombe LJ described an arrest as 'a matter of fact'. In his opinion, 'it is not a legal concept (though it clearly has legal consequences) and is a continuing act'.

**18.30** In order for an arrest to be lawful, it is necessary for the police (and members of the public) to show that they are exercising a power that is derived from lawful authority. In the case of the police, one such form of authority may be a warrant for an arrest issued by a magistrate in accordance with s 1 of the Magistrates' Courts Act 1980. Moreover, at common law, the police have the power to arrest any person who has committed or is about to commit a breach of the peace (see Chapter **19**). However, the most common source of authority for effecting an arrest is statute.

**18.31** Under PACE as originally enacted, the police (and the private citizen) had the power to arrest for an 'arrestable offence'. Essentially these were offences for which the sentence was fixed by law and persons over the age of 21 who had not previously been convicted might be sentenced to five years' imprisonment. In short, an 'arrestable offence' involved serious criminal activity such as murder, manslaughter, rape, arson, robbery, etc. The original s 24 of PACE empowered the police to arrest where: a person was in the act of committing an arrestable offence; there were reasonable grounds to suspect that person of committing an arrestable offence; an arrestable offence had been committed and the person was guilty of the offence or there were reasonable grounds for believing them to be guilty; there were reasonable grounds for suspecting that an arrestable offence had been committed, anyone who was reasonably suspected of being guilty of the offence; a person was about to commit an arrestable offence; or there were reasonable grounds for suspecting that they were about to commit an arrestable offence. The powers of arrest of the private citizen were more limited. They were not empowered to arrest a person who was about to commit an arrestable offence or whom they had reasonable grounds for suspecting to be about to commit such an offence.

**18.32**  Section 25 of PACE conferred a power of arrest on the police (but not the private citizen) in respect of non-arrestable offences. It was exercisable where an offence had been or was being committed or attempted and an officer believed that the service of a summons would be impracticable or inappropriate because any one of the 'general arrest conditions' was satisfied. These conditions fell into two categories: the identity or address of the relevant person; or the behaviour of that person. Section 25 has been repealed: see s 110(2) of the Serious Organised Crime and Police Act 2005. Many of its provisions now feature in the criteria which may render an arrest necessary under the new s 24 of PACE.

## Section 24

**18.33**  In August 2004 the Home Office published a consultation paper, *Policing: Modernising Police Powers to Meet Community Needs*, in which it set out various proposals for reforming police powers. One of the central themes of the consultation paper was the reform of powers of arrest. In the opinion of the Home Office, it was 'not always straightforward or clear to police officers or members of the public when and if the power of arrest exists for offences at the lower end of seriousness'. Accordingly, it proposed to abolish what it termed the 'gateway of seriousness' as the criterion for the existence of a power of arrest, ie whether or not an offence was an 'arrestable offence', and instead replace it with:

> a straightforward, universal framework which focuses on the nature of an offence in relation to the circumstances of the victim, the offender and the needs of the investigation.

**18.34**  The Home Office's proposals were largely reflected in s 110 of the Serious Organised Crime and Police Act 2005, which inserted a new s 24 and a s 24A into PACE. The new s 24 is concerned with a police officer's powers of arrest without warrant. Importantly, such powers are exercisable in relation to any offence. They are still largely dependent on the requirement of reasonable suspicion (paras **18.38–18.48**). However, a key difference between the old and the new arrest powers is that the new powers are only exercisable where a police officer has reasonable grounds to believe that an arrest is *necessary* for any one of a number of specified reasons (s 24(5)). The reasons are as follows:

- to enable the person's name to be ascertained;

- to enable the person's address to be ascertained;

- to prevent the person:
  - causing physical injury to himself/another;
  - suffering physical injury;
  - causing loss of or damage to property;
  - committing an offence against public decency;
  - causing an unlawful obstruction of the highway;

- to protect a child or other vulnerable person from the person in question;

- to allow the prompt and effective investigation of the offence or the conduct of the person in question; or

- to prevent any prosecution of the offence being hindered by the disappearance of the person in question.

**18.35** There is a significant overlap between the reasons that will make an arrest necessary and the former s 25 general arrest conditions. However, the list of reasons goes further than the former provision. In addition to reasons relating to the identity or address of a person to be arrested or their behaviour, the new s 24 also permits an arrest to take place where it is necessary for the purposes of the investigation of the relevant offence or the conduct of the person in question (s 24(5)(e)). It might be argued that this amounts to a 'catch-all' provision that has the potential to be relied upon in almost any case where none of the more specific reasons apply. Code of Practice G gives some guidance on the circumstances in which s 24(5)(e) may apply. Thus, for example, an arrest may be necessary under this provision where an officer has reasonable grounds for believing that the person to be arrested: has made false statements; has made false statements that cannot readily be verified; has presented false evidence; may steal or destroy evidence; may make contact with co-suspects or conspirators; may intimidate or threaten or make contact with witnesses; or where it is necessary to obtain evidence by questioning.

**18.36** Whether or not an arrest was necessary for the purposes of s 24(5)(e) was at issue in both *Richardson v Chief Constable of the West Midlands Police* (2011) and *Hayes v Chief Constable of Merseyside Constabulary* (2011). In the former case, it was held that since there was simply no evidence as to why the arresting officer had considered it necessary to arrest the claimant, the arrest was inevitably unlawful. Such a patent defect in the arrest could not be cured by the custody sergeant's reasons for detaining the claimant, since that officer's role was to consider 'whether detention is necessary not whether arrest is necessary'. In *Hayes*, the CA preferred a two-fold rather than a three-stage test for determining the lawfulness of an arrest. Thus it held that a court should consider: whether the officer actually believed that arrest was necessary, and for a s 24(5) reason; and whether objectively that belief was reasonable. In its judgment, such a test best represented 'the balance which the law must strike in this area between practicable policing and the preservation of the liberty of the subject'.

**18.37** It is evident, therefore, that the requirement that an arrest is necessary represents an important safeguard against the abuse of the arrest power. A further important safeguard which appeared in the old s 24 and which has been retained in the new s 24 is the requirement of *reasonable suspicion*.

## Reasonable suspicion

**18.38** A number of the s 24 powers of arrest are exercisable where a police officer reasonably suspects that an offence has been, is being, or will be committed. The phrase 'reasonably suspects' is not defined in the 1984 Act. In *Hussein v Chong Fook Kam* (1970), Lord Devlin described it as 'a state of conjecture or surmise where proof is lacking'. Further guidance as to its meaning was given in *Castorina v Chief Constable of Surrey* (1988), where Woolf LJ (as he then was) suggested that if it is alleged that an arrest is unlawful, three questions need to be answered:

- Did the arresting officer suspect that the person who was arrested was guilty of the offence?

- Assuming that the officer had the necessary suspicion, was there reasonable cause for that suspicion?

- If the answer to both these questions is 'yes', then the officer has a discretion to arrest, and the question then arises whether it has been exercised in accordance with the *Wednesbury* principles (paras **13.2-13.3**).

**18.39** From this, it is clear that the answer to the first question depends upon an assessment of the police officer's subjective state of mind at the relevant time. The second question introduces an objective element into the equation in that it requires an assessment of whether or not the officer's suspicion was 'reasonable' in the circumstances. These will both be matters for the police to establish. Provided they can be established, the arrest will be lawful unless the claimant can show that the decision to arrest was *Wednesbury* unreasonable. In *Al Fayed v Metropolitan Police Comr* (2004), Auld LJ noted in the context of the old s 24(6) power of arrest that 'the more substantial the interference, the narrower the otherwise generous *Wednesbury* ambit of reasonableness becomes'.

**18.40** The 'reasonableness' of the suspicion will be a matter for the court to decide having regard to the facts of the case. It thus acts as a safeguard against the abuse of the s 24 power of arrest: see *Dumbell v Roberts* (1944). Originally, however, it seems to have been introduced to protect police officers when acting in the proper execution of their duty: see *McArdle v Egan* (1933).

**18.41** In *O'Hara v Chief Constable of the Royal Ulster Constabulary* (1997), where D was arrested under s 12(1) of the Prevention of Terrorism (Temporary Provisions) Act 1984 on the basis that a police officer had reasonable grounds for suspecting him to be a terrorist, it was held that the reasonable suspicion has to be in the mind of the arresting officer. Moreover, the HL was of the opinion that an officer's suspicion need not necessarily be based on his own observations but could alternatively be based on what he had been told in a briefing or by an anonymous 'tip-off'.

**18.42** Thus in *Buckley v Chief Officer of the Thames Valley Police* (2009), Hughes J remarked:

> There is not the slightest doubt, and O'Hara makes it crystal clear, that an arresting officer may rely on what he has been told by others who may be civilian informants, reliable or unreliable, or other officers, providing that the information thus assembled provides reasonable grounds for suspicion. Indeed if it were otherwise cooperation between officers and the management of any inquiry of any size would be impossible.

**18.43** The principle established in *O'Hara* was later applied in *Hough v Chief Constable of the Staffordshire Constabulary* (2001), where the CA held that an entry made on the national police computer by an officer could form the basis of a reasonable suspicion in the mind of another officer sufficient to entitle him to arrest the suspect.

**18.44** More recently, in *Cumming v Chief Constable of Northumbria Police* (2003), where the police had arrested six individuals on suspicion of having perverted the course of justice by dishonestly tampering with security film tapes, even though they knew that only one person could have committed the offence, the CA held that there was 'nothing in principle which prevents opportunity from amounting to reasonable grounds for suspicion'. Moreover, in the words of Latham LJ:

> there can be nothing in principle wrong with arresting more than one person even if the crime can only have been committed by one person . . . Where a small number of people can be clearly identified as the only ones capable of having committed the offence, I see no reason why that cannot afford reasonable grounds for suspecting each of them of having committed that offence, in the absence of any information which could or should enable the police to reduce the number further.

**18.45** The decisions in *O'Hara* and *Hough* were referred to in *R v Olden* (2007), where the CA had to determine whether a police officer had the necessary reasonable suspicion when effecting an arrest. In holding that the suspicion was absent at the material time, the CA emphasized that what matters is the state of mind of the officer. Since the arresting officer had not stated in evidence that he either believed or suspected that the appellant had committed the relevant offence (deception), it followed that the arrest had been unlawful. The CA was not prepared to infer that the officer had the necessary reasonable suspicion because the trial judge had found him to be a 'conscientious officer'. Had it done so, it would have seriously eroded 'reasonable suspicion' as a safeguard against the abuse of the arrest power.

**18.46** Section 41 of the Terrorism Act 2000 empowers a police officer to 'arrest without a warrant a person whom he reasonably suspects to be a terrorist'. It is therefore a further example of a statutory power of arrest where the requirement of 'reasonable suspicion' will need to be established for its exercise to be lawful.

> **Raissi v Commissioner of Police of the Metropolis (2008):** The claimants were the wife and brother of an alleged terrorist. Both were arrested pursuant to s 41 of the 2000 Act. The woman was detained for 41 hours during which she was interviewed. Her brother-in-law was detained for four and a half days during which he also underwent police interviews. Both were eventually released without charge. They brought claims for damages for wrongful arrest and false imprisonment against the Commissioner. The woman's claim failed because the trial judge ruled that the police had the necessary reasonable suspicion to arrest her. Her brother-in-law's claim succeeded. The trial judge was not satisfied that five factors identified as justifying the arrest met the 'reasonable suspicion' requirement. They were: the claimant's close relationship with his brother, the physical proximity of their homes, and the importance of family links in terrorist cases; his ability to access his brother's house; the desire to interview the claimant; public safety; and the preservation of evidence. The Commissioner appealed arguing, amongst other things, that the arresting officer's suspicion had been based on two additional factors: that he knew his superiors regarded the respondent as a reasonable suspect; and that he was entitled to infer that his superiors knew more than he did. CA held: dismissing the appeal, that the five factors identified by the trial judge did not afford the arresting officer reasonable grounds to suspect that the respondent was a terrorist. Moreover, the proposition that it was sufficient for the arresting officer to infer that his superiors must have had reasonable grounds for suspicion was inconsistent with *O'Hara*. The respondent's arrest had therefore been unlawful.

**18.47** As the facts of *Raissi* demonstrate, in practice, 'reasonable suspicion' is likely to be based on a number of factors rather than one factor alone. Where this is the case, Hughes J stated in *Buckley v Chief Officer of the Thames Valley Police* (2009) that:

> *The correct approach to judgment upon the lawfulness of arrest is not to separate out each of the . . . elements of the constable's state of mind and ask individually of these whether that creates reasonable grounds for suspicion, it is to look at them cumulatively, as of course the arresting officer has to at the time.*

**18.48** As has already been noted (para **18.26**), art 5(1) of the ECHR is concerned with the individual's right to liberty and security of his person. It is possible to interfere with this liberty, however, provided that the interference falls within the scope of a permitted exception. One such exception is art 5(1)(c), namely:

> *the lawful arrest or detention of a person effected for the purpose of bringing him before the competent legal authority on reasonable suspicion of having committed an offence or when it is reasonably considered necessary to prevent his committing an offence or fleeing after having done so.*

Following his unsuccessful appeal to the HL, O'Hara lodged an application with the ECtHR in which it was alleged, inter alia, that his arrest had violated art 5(1) of the ECHR. The Court held, however, that there had been no such violation. Nevertheless, in the earlier case of *Fox, Campbell and Hartley v United Kingdom* (1990), the ECtHR had held that the arrest of a suspected terrorist under s 11 of the Northern Ireland (Emergency Provisions) Act 1978 was contrary to art 5(1) because although the suspicion was genuine, there was insufficient evidence to support the view that the suspicion had been reasonable.

## Citizen's arrest

18.49   Section 24A of PACE is concerned with a citizen's powers of arrest. Such powers may only be exercised in relation to indictable offences, ie offences which are triable in the Crown Court. A citizen may therefore arrest anyone who is in the act of committing an indictable offence or anyone whom he has reasonable grounds for suspecting to be committing an indictable offence (s 24A(1)(a) and (b)). Where an indictable offence has been committed, a citizen may arrest anyone who is guilty of the offence or anyone whom he has reasonable grounds for suspecting to be guilty of it (s 24A(2)(a) and (b)). However, these powers of arrest may only be exercised where the person making the arrest has reasonable grounds for believing that the arrest is necessary because any one of the specified reasons applies, and because it appears that it is not reasonably practicable for an officer to make the arrest instead. The specified reasons are that an arrest is necessary to prevent the person:

- causing physical injury to himself or another;
- suffering physical injury;
- causing loss of or damage to property; or
- making off before a police officer can assume responsibility for him (s 24A(4) (a)–(d)).

18.50   Where a citizen makes an arrest on the basis that an indictable offence has been committed, if D is subsequently acquitted, the arrest will have been unlawful.

*R v Self* (1992): D was suspected of having stolen a bar of chocolate from a shop. He assaulted a shop assistant and a member of the public before he was arrested by the latter. He was charged with theft and two counts of assault with intent to prevent his lawful detention contrary to s 38 of the Offences Against the Person Act 1861. At his trial, D was acquitted of the theft charge but convicted of the assault charges. On appeal, D argued that his acquittal on the theft charge meant that there was no power to arrest under s 24(5) of PACE. He argued, therefore, that he should not have been convicted of the s 38 offences because at the relevant time, he was seeking to break free from an unlawful arrest. CA held: allowing D's appeal, that the s 24(5) power of arrest required as a condition precedent that an offence had been committed. Since no offence had been committed in the present case, there was no power to apprehend or detain D.

**18.51** Although the decision in *R v Self* relates to s 24(5) of PACE as originally enacted, s 24A(2) is expressed in essentially the same terms as its predecessor. Accordingly, *R v Self* remains good law, particularly since it also reflects the position at common law prior to the enactment of PACE: see *Walters v WH Smith & Sons Ltd* (1914), and *Dallison v Caffrey* (1965).

## Information to be given on arrest

**18.52** Where a person is arrested, s 28 of PACE requires that they are informed that: they are under arrest: sub-s (1); and the ground for the arrest: sub-s (3). This information, which broadly reflects what was required under the common law (see *Christie v Leachinsky* (1947)), is to be given as soon as is practicable so that the person being arrested has, in the words of Sedley LJ in *Taylor v Chief Constable of Thames Valley Police* (2004), an 'immediate opportunity of explanation and self-exculpation'. Where D was arrested by being detained in a car which had been specially adapted by the police to trap any person who attempted to steal it, it was held, inter alia, that s 28 had been complied with by the arresting officers who arrived quickly on the scene: *Dawes v DPP* (1994). However, Kennedy LJ was of the opinion that had the officers been slow to respond, a court might not have taken the view that the information had been given as soon as was practicable. If this were indeed the case, the arrest would have been unlawful.

**18.53** In *Edwards v DPP* (1993), Evans LJ observed that: 'giving correct information as to the reason for an arrest is a matter of the utmost constitutional significance in a case where a reason can be and is given at the time'. Thus giving a person the wrong or an invalid reason for his arrest will also fall foul of s 28 and hence render the arrest unlawful.

**18.54** In several cases, it has been necessary for the courts to determine the legal consequences of an unlawful arrest.

*DPP v Hawkins* (1988): A police officer took H by the arm and informed him that he was under arrest. A struggle ensued which made it impracticable for the officer to inform H of the ground for the arrest. It became practicable to comply with s 28(3) of PACE on H's arrival at a police station, but it was found as a matter of fact by magistrates either that he was not informed or that he was given the wrong reason. They therefore dismissed informations against him for offences contrary to s 51(1) of the Police Act 1964 and s 5 of the Public Order Act 1986. The prosecutor appealed by way of case stated. DC held: at the material time, the officers were acting in the execution of their duty. The offences were committed when it was impracticable to comply with the requirement laid down in s 28(3). The fact that compliance was later practicable meant that the arrest only became unlawful from that point in time onwards.

---

*Lewis v Chief Constable of the South Wales Constabulary* **(1991):** Two women were arrested and taken to a police station. They were not informed of the reasons for their arrest (suspicion of burglary) until they arrived at the police station. They were detained for five hours and then released without charge. They sued the chief constable for wrongful arrest and false imprisonment. They sought damages for the entire time that they were detained. The trial judge ruled that their arrests were unlawful from the time that they could have been given the reasons for their arrests to the time when they were given the reasons – 10 minutes and 23 minutes, respectively. They were each awarded £200 damages by the jury. They appealed. CA held: that the trial judge had been right. The effect of telling a person, who was initially arrested without being given the reasons, those reasons at a later time was that the arrest became lawful from that moment. The women had therefore been unlawfully arrested for a matter of minutes rather than hours.

---

**18.55** These cases illustrate the effect that the s 28(3) requirement can have upon the lawfulness of an arrest. An unlawful arrest may become lawful, and a lawful arrest may become unlawful, depending upon whether s 28(3) either has or has not been complied with. The law does not require, however, that the person who made the arrest need necessarily be the person who supplies the s 28 information. Thus in *Dhesi v Chief Constable of West Midlands* (2000), where D had been arrested by a police dog handler and had been told to walk towards another officer who then informed him of the ground for his arrest, the CA held that the arrest was lawful. In the words of Stuart-Smith LJ:

> *The importance of s 28 is that the arrested person should know that he is under arrest and the reason for it. It can make no conceivable difference by whom that information is given provided that it is given at the relevant time or as soon as practicable thereafter. It is not necessary that it should be the person who actually deprives the subject of his liberty who gives that information.*

**18.56** In practice, a failure to comply with s 28 is likely to be rectified at the police station, where the arrested person is brought before the custody sergeant. Thus in *DPP v L* (1999), where a custody sergeant recorded that L had been arrested on the grounds of 'Public Order, s 5 Public Order Act resisting arrest', the DC took the view that this 'regularized' the arrest. In other words, despite the fact that there was no evidence that L had actually been informed of the grounds for her arrest, it was presumed that this must have been the case since the entry had been made on the custody record in her presence.

**18.57** Section 28 cases tend to turn on their own particular facts. Thus in *Taylor v Chief Constable of Thames Valley Police* (2004), the CA suggested that past authorities are of little assistance to a court faced with an allegation that an arrest was unlawful due to a failure to comply with the requirements of s 28. Instead, their Lordships were of the view that all that a court hearing such a case would need to have regard to was the law as stated in s 28(3), art 5(2) of the ECHR, and para 40 of the judgment in *Fox, Campbell and Hartley v UK* (1990). Article 5(2) states:

> Everyone who is arrested shall be informed promptly, in a language which he understands, of the reasons for his arrest and of any charge against him.

Commenting on this provision in *Fox, Campbell and Hartley*, the ECtHR observed:

> by virtue of para (2) any person arrested must be told in simple, non-technical language that he can understand, the essential legal and factual grounds for his arrest, so as to be able, if he sees fit, to apply to a court to challenge its lawfulness in accordance with para (4). Whilst this information must be conveyed 'promptly' . . . it need not be related in its entirety by the arresting officer at the very moment of the arrest. Whether the content and promptness of the information conveyed were sufficient is to be assessed in each case according to its special features.

Thus it would appear that courts hearing s 28 cases should apply an objective test and decide whether the words used in effecting an arrest were such as to satisfy the statutory and ECHR requirements.

## The use of force

**18.58** As with the other PACE powers discussed in this chapter, police officers may use 'reasonable force' when making an arrest under the authority of s 24: see s 117 of PACE. What constitutes reasonable force will depend upon the particular circumstances. In *Adorian v Commissioner of Police for the Metropolis* (2010), the QBD held that although the claimant had suffered severe injuries, which included a dislocated hip and fractures to his leg, during the course of resisting arrest, the force used had been no more than reasonable.

## Powers to enter property

**18.59** It was stated by Lord Camden in *Entick v Carrington* (1765) (paras **3.26** and **3.29**) that:

> No man can set his foot upon my ground without my licence, but he is liable to an action, though the damage be nothing . . . if he admits the fact, he is bound to shew by way of justification, that some positive law has empowered or excused him.

In effect, Lord Camden's remarks encapsulate what is widely understood to be the principle of legality: that interference with a person or their property can only be justified by the existence of some lawful authority which permits such interference. This authority may take one of several forms. In relation to entering a property, this may of course occur with the express permission of the owner: see *Hobson v Chief Constable of the Cheshire Constabulary* (2003). Alternatively, the law recognizes other forms of authority, which include that a person has an implied licence to enter a property.

## Implied licence

**18.60**  All those persons with lawful business on a property will have an implied licence to enter. Thus, for example, the deliverers of milk, newspapers, or mail will all be able to enter in the absence of express permission to do so. Similarly, a police officer making house-to-house inquiries would have an implied licence to enter a property. In the Australian case *Halliday v Nevill* (1984), the High Court stated that:

> *A passer-by is not a trespasser if, on passing an open driveway with no indication that entry is forbidden or unauthorised, he or she steps upon it either unintentionally or to avoid an obstruction such as a vehicle parked across the footpath. Nor will a passer-by be a trespasser if, for example, he or she goes upon the driveway to recover some item of his or her property which has fallen or blown upon it or to lead away an errant child.*

**18.61**  An implied licence to enter does not, however, give unlimited access to the property in question. Whilst a path or a driveway may represent a 'bridge or thoroughfare' between the highway and a private dwelling (*Halliday v Nevill* (1984)), an implied licence will not extend to going beyond the front door of a house or to trying to obtain access to a rear garden. Express permission would be needed in these circumstances. Similarly in the case of a shop, the implied licence to enter would only extend to the public parts of the premises. In practice, the distinction between the public and private areas of a shop is normally made clear through the use of signs or notices.

**18.62**  An implied licence to enter may be revoked by the owner of the property. Revocation can take one of two forms: verbal; or written, ie a sign or notice. In either case, the words used must be sufficiently clear to convey the fact of revocation. If there is a misunderstanding between the parties as to the meaning of what was said or written, the courts will apply an objective test. In other words, a court will consider whether the words used would have caused a bystander (had one been present) to believe that his implied licence had been revoked: see *Fullard and Roalfe v Woking Magistrates' Court* (2005).

**18.63**  On several occasions, the courts have treated expressions such as 'fuck off' as vulgar expletives rather than as a revocation of an implied licence: see, for example, *Snook v Mannion* (1982) and *Gilham v Breidenbach* (1982). Where an implied licence has been revoked, a person who remains on the property without some other form of lawful authority will have become a trespasser.

---

*Davis v Lisle* **(1936):** Two police officers suspected that the driver of a lorry had obstructed the highway contrary to s 54(6) of the Metropolitan Police Act 1839. They entered a garage into which the lorry had been driven in order to pursue their inquiries. They did so without the express permission of the owner. Neither officer was in possession of a search warrant. The owner of the garage said to the officers 'Get outside – you can't come in here without a search warrant'. Nevertheless, the officers made no attempt to leave and one of them sought to produce his warrant card, ie his identity card. They were therefore forcibly removed from the garage. In respect of his conduct, the owner was convicted of: (i) assaulting a police officer in the execution of his duty; (ii) wilfully obstructing a police officer in the execution of his duty; and (iii) unlawfully, wilfully, and maliciously damaging a police tunic. He appealed against his convictions. DC held: allowing the appeal against the convictions for offences (i) and (ii) but upholding the conviction for offence (iii), that in respect of the first two offences, at the material time, the officers were not acting within the execution of their duty. They had been told to leave and therefore they became trespassers when they failed to do so. The act of producing a warrant card amounted to an attempt to assert a right to remain on the premises which the officers did not have.

---

**18.64** Once an implied licence has been revoked, a licensee does not immediately become a trespasser. He or she must be given a reasonable time in which to leave the property. In *Robson v Hallett* (1967), where a police sergeant who had been invited into a house was asked to leave, and was then assaulted as he attempted to do so, the DC held that he was acting within the execution of his duty at the time of the assault. This would not have been the court's finding had the sergeant attempted to assert some right to remain which he did not possess, as in *Davis v Lisle* (1936).

## Under statutory authority

**18.65** In addition to entering a property under an express or implied licence, a police officer may be authorized to enter contrary to the owner's wishes. The authority in question will normally be derived from statute, although it may be authorized by the common law where it is necessary in connection with an actual or apprehended breach of the peace: see s 17(6) of PACE.

## Entry under a search warrant

**18.66** Following the receipt of an application from the police, magistrates may issue a warrant to search premises under s 8 of PACE. The application itself must state: the ground on which it is made; the enactment under which the warrant would be issued; the premises which it is desired to enter and search; and, so far as possible, the articles or persons to be sought: s 15(2). An application is made ex parte and supported by written information: s 15(3). A magistrate may issue a search warrant under s 8(1) where he is satisfied that there are reasonable grounds for believing that:

- an indictable offence has been committed; and

- there is material on the premises likely to be of substantial value to the investigation; and

- the material is likely to be relevant evidence; and

- it does not consist of or include items subject to legal privilege, excluded material, or special procedure material; and

- any of a number of specified conditions apply.

**18.67**  Formerly, search warrants could only be issued under s 8 in respect of premises specified in the application. Now, however, as a consequence of reforms prefigured in the Home Office consultation paper *Policing: Modernising Police Powers to Meet Community Needs* (2004) and given legislative effect by the Serious Organised Crime and Police Act 2005, the police are able to apply for a 'specific premises warrant' or an 'all premises warrant'. The latter enables the police to search 'any premises occupied or controlled by a person specified in the application'. The justification for such a warrant is that it enables the police to better tackle the problem of evidence and the proceeds of crime being moved from one premises to another and hence kept out of their reach.

**18.68**  The 2005 Act has also made amendments to ss 15 and 16 of PACE which provide safeguards relating to the execution of search warrants. Thus whereas formerly a search warrant could only authorize a single entry onto the relevant premises, it is now possible for the police to enter a property on a number of separate occasions under the authority of the same warrant. Moreover, whereas the time limit for executing a search warrant was originally one month, it is now three months. It is the case, therefore, that in the absence of a maximum number of entries specified on the warrant itself, the police have the power to return to the same property on numerous occasions during the three-month period, subject only to the need for written authorization from an officer of the rank of inspector or above (s 16(3B)).

**18.69**  The 'specified conditions' referred to in s 8(1)(e) include that entry to the premises will not be granted in the absence of a warrant, or that the purpose of the search will be frustrated or seriously prejudiced if immediate entry cannot be secured: s 8(3)(c) and (d).

**18.70**  It is apparent from the terms of s 8(1)(d) that a warrant under this section cannot authorize a search for certain specified items. Those items which are subject to legal privilege are defined in s 10 of PACE. Essentially they amount to communications between a legal adviser and his client, or his client's representative, relating to the giving of legal advice or in connection with or in contemplation of legal proceedings. 'Excluded material' encompasses personal records (eg records relating to a person's physical or mental health), human tissue or tissue fluid, and journalistic material (ie material acquired or created for the purposes of journalism). 'Special procedure material' is defined in s 14 of PACE. It consists of journalistic material other than that which is excluded, and items which are neither legally privileged nor excluded material, but which have been acquired or created in the course of a person's work, or for the purpose of any paid or unpaid office, and which are held in confidence.

**18.71** Whereas legally privileged material is beyond the search powers of the police, access to excluded material or special procedure material may be obtained by the police for the purposes of a criminal investigation. The procedure for obtaining access is prescribed in Sch 1 to PACE. It involves making an application to a circuit judge who may order that the material should be produced, or access granted to it, provided that one or other of the sets of access conditions is fulfilled. These are detailed in paras 2 and 3 of the Schedule. The first set, which only apply to special procedure material, contain several conditions broadly similar to those specified in s 8(1) in respect of searches for non-protected materials. In addition, reference is made to, inter alia, the fact that other methods of obtaining the material have been tried without success and that production or access is in the public interest due to the benefits that would accrue to the investigation.

**18.72** The second set of access conditions apply to either special procedure or excluded material. They are satisfied if there are reasonable grounds for believing that the relevant material is on the premises and that, but for s 9(2) of PACE, a search for that material could have been authorized by a warrant issued under a pre-PACE enactment and that the issue of such a warrant would have been appropriate.

**18.73** Entering a person's property without their permission is prima facie a trespass. If that entry is authorized by a search warrant, a police officer will have a defence to an action in trespass provided that the warrant has been both lawfully obtained and executed.

*Redknapp v Commissioner of Police of the Metropolis* (2008): The first claimant was Harry Redknapp, currently the manager of Tottenham Hotspur FC. At the material time, he and others were suspected of various criminal offences, including conspiracy to defraud and false accounting, relating to the buying and selling of footballers. A warrant was obtained pursuant to s 8 of PACE to search R's house and seven other premises. The searches of all the properties were conducted at the same time. R's wife let police officers into the house. Their arrival was witnessed by reporters from *The Sun* newspaper. The claimants brought proceedings against the Commissioner. They claimed on various grounds that the search warrant had been obtained unlawfully, and that the entry and search of their house had also been unlawful. Admin Ct held: upholding the claims, that the obtaining of a search warrant should never be treated as a formality since it authorizes the invasion of a person's home. On the facts, the application for the warrant had failed to identify which if any of the conditions set out in s 8(3) was being relied upon. Moreover, there was nothing in the statement made by the police officer who applied for the warrant to show that the defects had been remedied orally before the magistrate. Accordingly, the warrant had been obtained unlawfully. Latham LJ was also of the obiter view that the warrant had been unlawfully executed since, on entry, the police had failed to confirm that it related to the claimant's house.

**18.74** In *R (on the application of Power-Hynes) v Norwich Magistrates Court* (2009), Stanley Burnton LJ drew attention to the fact that in cases concerning the lawfulness of the obtaining or execution of a search warrant, the courts are 'faced with two competing interests': the public interest in prosecuting and preventing crime; and the property and privacy rights of the person whose home or office is to be searched. With regard to the latter he observed:

> A police search for materials is a very real and serious intrusion into the private life of those whose premises are searched, and may be very distressing for them, and if it is to be justified, the officers seeking the warrant must take diligent steps to ensure that the statutory requirements are satisfied. In addition, they must make full and frank disclosure to the justice of the peace or district or circuit judge of the facts justifying the application . . .

## Searching persons under the authority of a search warrant

**18.75** In addition to their general powers under PACE, magistrates may also issue search warrants under other enactments, such as the Misuse of Drugs Act 1971. An important point in the present context relates to the extent of a search which a warrant authorizes. Is it confined solely to the premises, or may it also extend to searching those found on the premises?

*Chief Constable of Thames Valley Police v Hepburn* **(2002):** A warrant to search a public house for drugs and related paraphernalia had been granted by magistrates under the Misuse of Drugs Act 1971. H had sought to leave the premises when he had been prevented from doing so by two police officers. He was handcuffed and subjected to a superficial search and later a strip-search. One of the issues raised by the case was whether the search warrant included the power to stop and search persons who were on the premises at the relevant time. The trial judge had concluded that it did not. CA held: that on this issue, the trial judge's ruling was plainly correct. A power to search persons was not stated on the face of the warrant, and the CA was not prepared to accept that such a power could be implied.

*DPP v Meaden* **(2003):** Between 7 and 14 police officers entered a house under the authority of a search warrant issued pursuant to s 23 of the Misuse of Drugs Act 1971 and s 15 of PACE. The warrant authorized a search of the premises and any persons found therein. The police searched one room at a time. Once they decided that a particular room was free from drugs, etc, they allowed the occupants of the house to enter that room after they themselves had been searched. M was denied permission to move around the house freely.

He resisted being moved from one room to another and eventually became aggressive. He was charged with wilfully obstructing and assaulting a police officer in the execution of his duty contrary to s 89(1) and (2) of the Police Act 1996. Before the justices, a plea of no case to answer was accepted. The DPP appealed. DC held: allowing the appeal, that the justices had erred in relying on *Hepburn*. They had overlooked the 'crucial distinction' between the facts of the two cases: that in *Hepburn* the search warrant had been limited to the premises whereas in the present appeal, it also entitled the police to search any persons found therein.

It is clear from the two decisions, therefore, that whether or not a person can be searched where the police are executing a property search warrant depends very much on the wording of the warrant itself. In *Meaden*, the DC also made it clear that, in conducting a search, the use of reasonable force as permitted by s 117 of PACE extends beyond gaining entry to the premises to include what goes on once the premises have been entered and are being searched, and also when the occupants of the premises are being searched.

## Entry and search without search warrant

**18.76**  A warrant is by no means always required to carry out a search. Section 17 of PACE authorizes the police to enter and search any premises without a search warrant where their purpose is to: arrest a person: sub-s (1)(a), (b), (c), and (ca); recapture a person: sub-s (1)(cb) and (d); or save life or limb or prevent serious damage to property: sub-s (1)(e).

**18.77**  Since s 17 empowers the police to enter a property despite the owner's objections, it is a power which must be exercised with care. The mere possession of lawful authority does not absolve the police from the need first to request the owner's permission to enter. This is evident from the decision in *O'Loughlin v Chief Constable of Essex* (1998), where three police officers forced an entry into a house in order to speak to the plaintiff's wife about criminal damage that had been done to a neighbour's car. In giving judgment, the majority of the CA held that refusing a request to enter premises does not thereby render the use of force necessary. Force would only be necessary where: an officer has stated the grounds on which he intends to enter the premises; the grounds give him a right of entry recognized by law; and his request has been refused. In *O'Loughlin* itself, the fact that the officers wished to enter the premises to question the woman rather than to arrest her meant that their entry did not fall within the terms of s 17 of PACE. Without the necessary lawful authority, they were therefore trespassers.

**18.78**  Section 17(1)(d) of PACE empowers the police to enter premises for the purpose of:

*recapturing [any person whatever] who is unlawfully at large and whom he is pursuing.*

As Professor Zander has noted, this provision reproduces the power which formerly existed at common law. It entitles the police to enter premises in order to recapture a person who has escaped from prison, a court, police custody, or detention in a mental hospital. However, for the power to be exercisable, the police must be pursuing the escapee.

---

*D'Souza v DPP* **(1992):** Mrs D was admitted to hospital under the Mental Health Act 1983 for psychiatric assessment. Following a visit from her husband, she left the hospital without leave being granted under the Act and returned home. Several hours later two uniformed police officers went to the house to take her back to the hospital. Mrs D's daughter refused to admit them and they therefore forced an entry pursuant to s 17(1)(d) of PACE. The daughter and father then attacked the officers. They were charged with assaulting an officer in the execution of his duty. Both were convicted and their convictions were upheld by the Crown Court. The daughter's appeal to the DC was dismissed. She therefore appealed to the HL. She argued that the police did not have the power to enter under s 17(1)(d) and that therefore at the material time the officers were not in the execution of their duty. HL held: allowing the appeal, that the s 17 power was exercisable where the pursuit was almost contemporaneous with the entry into the premises. Since the officers had merely resorted to the premises where they believed that they might find Mrs D, they had not been pursuing her and therefore they were not within the execution of their duty at the time of the assaults.

---

18.79 Generally, the powers of entry under s 17(1) may only be exercised if an officer has reasonable grounds for believing that the person whom he is seeking is on the premises. No such safeguard exists, however, where the entry and search is for the purpose of 'saving life or limb or preventing serious damage to property' (s 17(1)(e)). In *Baker v CPS* (2009), Sir Anthony May observed:

> The expression 'saving life or limb' is a colourful, slightly outmoded expression. It is here used in close proximity with the expression 'preventing serious damage to property'. That predicates a degree of apprehended serious bodily injury. Without implicitly limiting or excluding the possible types of serious bodily injury, apprehended knife injuries and gunshot injuries will obviously normally be capable of coming within the subsection.

18.80 Given that the s 17(1)(e) power of entry is exercisable without the owner's consent, it is arguable whether it should be subject to the requirement that an officer had reasonable grounds for believing that its exercise was necessary. Do you think that such a safeguard ought to exist, despite the fact that there is nothing in the case law to suggest that s 17(1)(e) has been abused by the police? For examples of entries under the authority of s 17(1)(e), see *Smith v DPP* (2001) (para **18.101**), *Blench v DPP* (2004), and *Friswell v Chief Constable of Essex* (2004). In Baker, Sir Anthony May made the following remarks in relation to the exercise of the power of entry:

> A constable contemplating entering premises under s 17(1)(e) may not, of course, know for certain that someone's life or limb may be in danger, or that serious damage to

*property will or may occur, but it is implicit that his entry will be lawful if he reasonably so believes. The subsection would be unworkable otherwise. He is lawfully entitled to remain on the premises until he is reasonably satisfied that life, limb or property are not or are no longer in danger. While he is thus lawfully on the premises, he is entitled to search for anything which he reasonably believes may be used to endanger life, limb or property.*

**18.81** In the later case of *Syed v DPP* (2010), Collins J gave his own assessment of the parliamentary intention underlying s 17(1)(e) thus:

*It is plain that Parliament intended that the right of entry by force without any warrant would be limited to cases where there was an apprehension that something serious was otherwise likely to occur, or perhaps had occurred, within the house, hence the adjective 'serious' applied to any question of damage; and, although I entirely agree with May LJ that the expression 'danger to life or limb' is somewhat outmoded, it again indicates a serious matter – that what had happened in the premises, or what might happen in the premises, would involve some serious injury to an individual therein.*

**18.82** In *Syed*, the DC held that officers had acted unlawfully where they had entered a house out of concern for the welfare of someone in the premises. In the judgment of the court, the officers had applied 'altogether too low a test' to justify their entry under the authority of s 17(1)(e).

## Entry and search after arrest

**18.83** Where a person is under arrest for an indictable offence, s 18 of PACE entitles a police officer to enter and search any premises occupied or controlled by that person provided that he has reasonable grounds for suspecting that there is on the premises evidence relating to: the indictable offence; or some other indictable offence which is connected with or similar to that offence. The Act does not define what is meant by 'occupied or controlled', but the expression clearly covers the arrested person's abode and quite possibly their workplace. In *Khan v Metropolitan Police Commissioner* (2008), it was contended on behalf of the Commissioner that the 'occupied or controlled' requirement was subject to an implied qualification; that it was sufficient that the officer carrying out or authorizing a s 18 search either reasonably believed, or had reasonable grounds to believe, that the premises were occupied or controlled by the person under arrest. In rejecting that argument, a unanimous CA favoured a literal construction of s 18. The requirement of occupation or control was 'fundamental to the operation' of s 18 and therefore a lack of actual occupation or control could not be overlooked as a trivial or unimportant irregularity. The absence of expressions such as 'reasonable belief' or 'reasonable grounds' from s 18 in contrast to other provisions in PACE confirmed that their omission was not accidental.

**18.84** PACE also fails to define what are 'similar' or 'connected' indictable offences for the purposes of s 18. In *Jeffrey v Black* (1978), it was held that arresting D for the theft of a sandwich did not entitle the police to carry out a search for drugs. Since these offences were neither similar nor connected, if the police wished to search for drugs, they ought to have arrested D for a separate indictable offence in which case a s 18 search would have been permissible.

**18.85** Subject to the proviso in sub-s (5), the s 18 powers may only be exercised where an officer of the rank of inspector or above has authorized them in writing. In the light of the decision in *R v Badham* (1987), it would seem that a written record of a verbal authorization would be insufficient to comply with the requirement in s 18(4). Compliance would be achieved, however, by an independent document in which the authorization was recorded in writing. The proviso applies where the presence of the arrested person at a place other than a police station is necessary for the effective investigation of the offence.

**18.86** Whereas s 17(6) of PACE preserves the common law power to enter premises in order to deal with an actual or apprehended breach of the peace, s 18 is silent as to its effect on the common law power to search for and seize evidence once lawfully on premises. That power has been referred to by the courts in a number of cases, eg *Dillon v O'Brien* (1887) and *Ghani v Jones* (1969). In *Cowan v Metropolitan Police Comr* (2000), Roch LJ, delivering the judgment of the CA, was of the opinion that the power had survived the enactment of PACE. In his view, 'Parliament made clear its intention to abolish common law powers when it wished to do so' in PACE. Accordingly, he was not prepared to hold that the common law power had been impliedly revoked by the passing of that Act. In the earlier case of *R v Governor of Pentonville Prison, ex p Osman* (1990), the DC had held that the principle in *Ghani* applied also where the crime being investigated was alleged to have been committed abroad. That decision was subsequently confirmed by the HL in *R (on the application of Rottman) v Metropolitan Police Comr* (2002), and the scope of the common law power of search and seizure was considered in *R (on the application of Hewitson) v Chief Constable of Dorset Police & Government of France (Interested Party)* (2003). It should be noted, however, that the matter has now been put on a statutory footing: see ss 161, 162, and 164 of the Extradition Act 2003.

**18.87** Section 32(2)(b) of PACE provides a further power to enter and search premises following an arrest. Unlike s 18, the power of search is not limited to premises 'occupied or controlled' by the person under arrest. Instead, it authorizes the search of premises where D was at the time of the arrest, or immediately prior to the arrest. These premises may therefore be owned by an entirely innocent third party. The s 32(2)(b) power is only exercisable where a police officer has reasonable grounds for believing that there is evidence on the premises relating to the indictable offence for which D was arrested. Thus s 32(2)(b) is narrower than s 18 in terms of the purpose of the search.

## Reforming powers of entry

**18.88** At the time of writing, the Protection of Freedoms Bill is before Parliament. Part 3 of the Bill is entitled 'Protection of Property from Disproportionate Enforcement Action'.

Chapter 1 of Pt 3 relates to all powers of entry contained in a public general Act or an SI made under such an Act. Thus the PACE powers of entry fall within the scope of the Bill's provisions. In their current form, the relevant clauses make it possible for safeguards to be added to existing powers of entry by order. They also make it possible for existing powers of entry to be rewritten, with or without modifications. This power may not be exercised, however, to alter the effect of the relevant power of entry unless the changes are such that the safeguards in relation to the power provide a greater level of protection than they did immediately before the changes were made. Chapter 1 also imposes a duty on Cabinet ministers to carry out a review of all powers of entry for which they are responsible within a two-year period. Additionally, they must lay a report of the review before Parliament. If these provisions become law, the PACE powers of entry will therefore be included in the Home Office's review.

## General power of seizure

**18.89** Section 19 of PACE confers a general power of seizure on a police officer who is lawfully on any premises. The power of seizure is exercisable where the officer has reasonable grounds for believing that the item:

- has been obtained in consequence of the commission of an offence (s 19(2)); or

- is evidence in relation to an offence which he is investigating or any other offence: s 19(3).

**18.90** In both cases, seizure is only authorized where it is necessary to prevent the item being concealed, lost, altered, or destroyed. In the case of the s 19(2) power, seizure may also be necessary to prevent the item being damaged. 'Premises' are defined quite widely by s 23 of PACE to include any place and, inter alia, any vehicle, vessel, aircraft, or hovercraft or any tent or moveable structure. In *Cowan v Metropolitan Police Comr* (2000), where the claimant sought damages allegedly arising from the seizure and retention of his car by the police during the course of a criminal investigation, the CA held that the powers of seizure in ss 18(2) and 19(3) of PACE extended to the seizure and retention of the whole premises where it was physically possible to do so. Thus a car could be seized and retained under PACE, and practical considerations, such as the need to carry out a forensic examination or to prevent the vehicle being interfered with by others, may make such a course of action both necessary and desirable.

**18.91** Section 19(4) provides for the seizure of information stored in a computer. This is achieved by requiring the information to be produced in a form which can be taken away, eg a disk copy. The power is exercisable in the circumstances provided for in s 19(2) and (3), save that seizure will not be necessary to prevent the information being altered or damaged, but it may be necessary to prevent it being tampered with.

**18.92** Code of Practice B reinforces several of the provisions in s 19 of PACE, including the fact that no item may be seized which is subject to legal privilege. Where a police officer decides not to seize property because of an explanation given by the person holding it, but he nevertheless has reasonable grounds for believing that it has been obtained in consequence of the commission of an offence by some person, Code of Practice B requires the officer to inform the holder of his suspicions. It also requires the officer to inform the holder that if he disposes of the property, he may be liable to civil or criminal proceedings.

**18.93** Where the power of seizure has been exercised, the item may only be retained for as long as is necessary in the circumstances. It may be retained for purposes which include: for use as evidence at a trial for an offence; for forensic examination or for other investigation in connection with an offence; or, where there are reasonable grounds for believing that it has been stolen or obtained by the commission of an offence, in order to establish its lawful owner. In the case of the first and second purposes, Code of Practice B stipulates that retention is unnecessary if a copy or image would suffice.

## Additional powers of seizure from premises

**18.94** Part II of the Criminal Justice and Police Act 2001 extends the powers of the police (and other law enforcement officers) to seize items from premises and from the person. In the case of the former, the powers are exercisable if three conditions are satisfied: a person who is lawfully on premises must find an item which he has reasonable grounds for believing may be/may contain something for which he is authorized to search on those premises; a power of seizure under either the 2001 Act or any other Act to which s 50 applies (eg PACE) would entitle him to seize it; and, in all the circumstances, it is not reasonably practicable to determine on the premises whether what he has found is something that he is entitled to seize or the extent to which what he has found contains something that he is entitled to seize. If all these conditions are satisfied, the property may be seized and taken away to enable a determination to be made.

**18.95** A corresponding power to seize property following the search of a person is to be found in s 51 of the 2001 Act. Where property has been seized under either ss 50 or 51, it must be examined as soon as reasonably practicable to determine whether it may be retained. The person from whom it was seized or their representative may be present at the examination. Where it appears that the seized property is subject to legal privilege or has such an item comprised in it, the item must be returned as soon as reasonably practicable after the seizure: s 54. No such obligation arises, however, where for example it is not reasonably practicable to separate a legally privileged item from the rest of the property without prejudicing the use of the latter. An obligation to return excluded and special procedure material is provided for in s 55 of the Act, subject to exceptions similar to those which apply in respect of legally privileged material. A person with an interest in the property which has been seized may apply to the appropriate judicial authority, ie a Crown Court judge in England and Wales, for the return of the whole or part of the seized property. The grounds for making such an application include that there was no power to make the seizure. The Crown Court judge may dismiss the application, or order the return of or the retention of all or part of the seized property. A failure to comply with a direction amounts to a contempt of court.

## Assault on or wilful obstruction of a police officer

**18.96** By virtue of s 89 of the Police Act 1996, a person commits an offence where he assaults a police officer in the execution of his duty or a person assisting the officer in the execution of his duty: sub-s (1). Section 89 further provides that it is an offence to resist or wilfully obstruct a police officer in the execution of his duty or a person assisting him in the execution of his duty: sub-s (2). These offences are re-enactments of earlier statutory provisions, such as s 51 of the Police Act 1964. The same offences may be committed against a Community Support Officer: see s 46(1) and (2) of the Police Reform Act 2002, and *D v DPP* (2010).

**18.97** In order for a person to be convicted of either of the s 89 offences, it is therefore necessary that an assault or wilful obstruction occurred, and that at the material time the police officer was acting in the execution of his duty. If he was not so acting, neither offence may be committed, although D could be charged with a lesser offence such as common assault. The meanings of the terms 'assault', 'wilful obstruction', and 'in the execution of his duty' are therefore of central importance to the determination of guilt under s 89.

### Assaulting a police officer

**18.98** 'Assault' is not defined in s 89 of the 1996 Act. Accordingly, it must be accorded the meaning that it has at common law. Strictly speaking, an assault is committed where a person intentionally or recklessly causes another to apprehend immediate unlawful violence to the person. The application of force, whether that be a punch, kick, or the merest unwanted touching, amounts to a battery. It is not uncommon, however, for the term 'assault' to be used in an imprecise manner so as to denote conduct which is in truth a battery. In order to be guilty of an offence under s 89(1), it is unnecessary for the prosecution to prove that D either knew or believed that the victim of the alleged assault was a police officer: *R v Forbes and Webb* (1865). Despite the antiquity of this decision it remains good law. Indeed in *Blackburn v Bowering* (1994), Sir Thomas Bingham MR (as he then was) contended that the ruling 'makes good sense'. Do you agree?

### Wilfully obstructing a police officer

**18.99** In order to be convicted of a s 89(2) offence, it is necessary not only that D's conduct amounted to an obstruction but also that it was wilful. Since neither of these terms is defined by the 1996 Act, the courts have had to determine what is meant by 'wilful obstruction'.

*Rice v Connolly* (1966): R was approached by a police officer who believed him to be behaving in a suspicious manner in an area where there had been a number of burglaries. R only gave partial answers to the questions that he was asked and he refused to accompany the officer to a police box where it was hoped he would be properly identified. R was arrested and charged with wilfully obstructing an officer in the execution of his duty contrary to s 51(3) of the Police Act 1964. DC held: allowing his appeal, that to obstruct in the context of s 51(3) was to do any act which made it more difficult for an officer to carry out his duty. 'Wilful' meant 'intentionally' or without lawful excuse. Thus although R's conduct did amount to obstructing the police, that obstruction was not wilful. R had a lawful excuse; he was under no legal obligation to answer the questions put to him.

*Hills v Ellis* (1983): D witnessed a fight between two men whilst leaving a football ground. He intervened when he saw a police officer arresting what he believed to be the innocent party. In order to make his point he grabbed the officer's elbow. He was told to desist by another officer, but he ignored the warning and was therefore arrested and charged with a s 51(3) offence. DC held: dismissing his appeal against conviction, that a private citizen had no lawful excuse to interfere with a lawful arrest by a police officer. The fact that D had an innocent motive for obstructing the officer was irrelevant. The criminal law was concerned with intention rather than motive. D intended to do the acts which amounted to the obstruction, and he was therefore guilty of the offence.

*Lewis v Cox* (1985): D's friend was arrested by the police and placed in the back of a van. D opened the van's door to inquire of his friend where he was being taken. He was told by an officer that he would be arrested for obstruction if he continued to open the door. D ignored the warning and opened the door once again as the van was about to pull away. He was arrested and charged with a s 51(3) offence. DC held: upholding the prosecutor's appeal against the magistrates' dismissal of the charge, that the magistrates ought to have asked themselves whether, by opening the van door, D intended to make it more difficult for the police to carry out their duties even though that may not have been his predominant intention. Had they done so, they would have concluded that, on the evidence, D was guilty of the offence.

**18.100**  The actus reus of the s 89(2) offence, the obstruction, has thus been broadly defined by the courts. Often an obstruction will involve a positive act (see *Hills v Ellis* (1983) and *Lewis v Cox* (1985)), but a passive obstruction will also fall within the scope of the provision, such as where a person refuses to comply with a police officer's order: see *Johnson v Phillips* (1975). The mens rea ingredient of the offence, that the obstruction was wilful, can be further illustrated with the aid of an example. If D was asked questions by a police officer and he invented a 'cock and bull story' (see *Rice v Connolly*

(1966)), his conduct would amount to a wilful obstruction in that he had intentionally made it more difficult for the officer to carry out his duties. If, however, D answered honestly but as it later proved to be, incorrectly, any obstruction that had occurred could not be said to be wilful because it was committed with an absence of intent.

## Within the execution of his duty

**18.101** In order for a s 89(1) or (2) offence to have been committed, it is necessary that, at the time of the assault or wilful obstruction, the police officer was acting within the execution of his duty. A number of cases have therefore turned on this issue.

*Kenlin v Gardiner* **(1967):** Two schoolboys were performing an innocent errand when they aroused the suspicion of two plain clothes police officers. The officers approached the boys and one of them displayed his warrant card. The boys did not believe that they were policemen. One boy was held by the arm as he attempted to run away and a struggle ensued during which he punched and kicked the officer. The other boy was also physically restrained. They were both charged with assaulting an officer in the execution of his duty contrary to s 51(1) of the Police Act 1964. DC held: in quashing their convictions, that although the boys had undoubtedly assaulted the officers, their use of force was justified in that it was an act of self-defence in respect of earlier assaults by the officers. Since the boys had been physically detained in order to question them rather than to arrest them, the officers were acting outside their duty at the material time.

*Collins v Wilcock* **(1984):** A woman suspected of soliciting for the purposes of prostitution was asked to get into a police car. She refused and walked away. A policewoman followed D in order to question her and possibly issue a caution. D again refused to speak to the officer who consequently took her by the arm in order to prevent her from continuing to walk away. A struggle ensued during which D scratched the policewoman. D was charged with a s 51(1) offence. DC held: in allowing D's appeal against conviction, that the policewoman had taken hold of D's arm in order to restrain her. Since this was not done for the purpose of arresting D, the restraint amounted to a battery and was therefore unlawful. At the material time, therefore, the policewoman was not acting within the execution of her duty.

*Mepstead v DPP* **(1995):** D returned to his van to find that one of two policemen was issuing him with a fixed penalty notice in respect of a parking offence. D became agitated and abusive and therefore one of the officers took him by the arm and uttered reassuring words in order to calm him down. Violence ensued and D was charged with assaulting an officer in the execution of his duty. DC held: dismissing D's appeal against conviction, that the degree of physical contact in the present case did not exceed that which is permissible by the ordinary standards of everyday life, ie it was not a battery. The police officer's purpose in taking D's arm was not to detain him and thus at the material time he was acting within the execution of his duty.

> **Smith v DPP (2001):** Three police officers went to a house to investigate an abandoned 999 call that had been made from the address. S, who lived at the address, was shouting and banging on the front door of the house. Noise could be heard coming from inside and the officers asked S to step aside. One of the officers took S by the arm and led him away whereupon a violent struggle ensued. He was arrested for assaulting an officer in the execution of his duty contrary to s 89(1) of the Police Act 1996, and convicted by a stipendiary magistrate. S appealed: HCt held: dismissing the appeal, that at the material time the officers were attempting to enter the house in accordance with s 17(1)(e) of PACE. In exercising that power of entry, they were entitled to use reasonable force (s 117 of PACE) which could entail force against a person or against an inanimate object. Thus at the material time, the officers were acting within the execution of their duty.

**18.102** These four cases illustrate the considerations which need to be taken into account when determining whether or not an officer was within the execution of his duty at the time that a s 89 offence has allegedly been committed. To detain a person for a purpose other than arrest clearly takes an officer outside the execution of his duty, save where the detention takes place in order to prevent a breach of the peace: see *Albert v Lavin* (1981). Other physical contact which is, prima facie, a battery may nevertheless be permissible provided that an officer has acted with a lawful purpose in mind. It would seem, however, that the longer an arm is held (for example), the more difficult it will be to argue that detention was not the officer's purpose.

**18.103** It is possible to identify in judgments such as *Kenlin* something approaching judicial regret that defendants who have reacted violently towards police officers may nevertheless escape conviction or have their convictions quashed on appeal because the officer was outside the execution of his duty at the material time. In *Bentley v Brudzinski* (1982), a case which involved the unlawful detention of a person by a police officer for the purpose of asking further questions and eliciting an identity, Donaldson LJ suggested that prosecutors should charge D with common assault as an alternative to the statutory predecessor of the s 89(1) offence. If this approach were adopted, D might still be convicted, albeit of a lesser offence, even where the officer was outside the execution of his duty at the time of the assault.

**18.104** Despite the advice proffered by Donaldson LJ, the courts have continued to feel that there is a need to remind the prosecution about the perils of bringing the wrong charge. Thus in *C v DPP* (2003), Kennedy LJ observed:

> Where . . . there is any doubt as to whether at the particular moment when the violence was offered, the police officer was acting in the execution of his duty . . . it seems to me to follow, as the night the day, that the charge laid should be one of common assault. The prosecution should not undertake the burden of proving unnecessarily that the officer was, indeed, acting in the execution of his duty.

**18.105** Since s 89(1) and (2) provide for criminal offences, their various ingredients must be established by the prosecution according to the criminal burden of proof, ie beyond reasonable doubt. Accordingly, where magistrates found that a police officer had 'on balance' been acting within the execution of his duty at the material time, they had applied the wrong (civil) test and the appellant's conviction would therefore be quashed: see *Ahmed v Bradford Magistrates Court* (2008).

## FURTHER READING

Austin, R C 'The New Powers of Arrest: Plus ça change: More of the Same or Major Change?' [2007] Crim LR 459.

Bailey, S and Taylor, N *Bailey, Harris & Jones: Civil Liberties Cases, Materials and Commentary* (6th edn, 2009) OUP.

Feldman, D *Civil Liberties and Human Rights in England and Wales* (2nd edn, 2002) OUP.

Fenwick, H *Civil Liberties and Human Rights* (4th edn, 2007) Routledge-Cavendish.

Jason-Lloyd, L *An Introduction to Policing and Police Powers* (2nd edn, 2005), Routledge-Cavendish.

Mead, D 'The Likely Effect of the Human Rights Act on Everyday Policing Decisions in England and Wales' (2000) 5 J Civ Lib 5.

Ozin, P, Norton, H, and Spivey, P *PACE: A Practical Guide to the Police and Criminal Evidence Act 1984* (2nd edn, 2010) OUP.

Pollard, D, Parpworth, N, and Hughes, D *Constitutional and Administrative Law: Text with Materials* (4th edn, 2007) OUP.

Smith, G 'Reasonable Suspicion: Time for a Re-evaluation?' (2002) 30(1) IJSL 1.

Stone, R *Textbook on Civil Liberties & Human Rights* (8th edn, 2010) OUP.

Zander, M *The Police and Criminal Evidence Act 1984* (5th edn, 2005) Sweet & Maxwell.

## SELF-TEST QUESTIONS

1  To what extent have the courts shown themselves willing to intervene in respect of the exercise of police discretion?

2  What purpose do the Codes of Practice made under PACE serve?

3  In *Cumming v Chief Constable of Northumbria Police* (2003), Brooke LJ remarked that he had been 'very uneasy about this case throughout the hearing of the appeal' and that he remained so at its conclusion. What does the case tell us about the effectiveness of 'reasonable suspicion' as a safeguard against police abuse of their power of arrest?

4  If it is true that there was often confusion as to whether or not the police possessed a power of arrest in a given situation, was the only solution to the problem to extend the power of arrest to all offences as the new s 24 of PACE has done?

5  To what extent, if any, does the list of reasons for making an arrest necessary (s 24(5)) provide an adequate safeguard against the abuse of this 'powerful weapon in the police armoury for tackling crime'?

6  Why is it particularly important that the police are always able to demonstrate that they have authority for their actions? What might be the source of that authority?

7  What is meant by the doctrine of implied licence? How might an implied licence be revoked?

8  Where the police have a statutory power to enter premises, what does the case law tell us about how this power should be exercised?

9  Where a defendant is charged with an offence under either s 89(1) or (2) of the Police Act 1996, what requirements must be satisfied in order for the defendant to be convicted?

10  Having regard to the police powers discussed in this chapter, to what extent, if any, do they strike the right balance between the needs of the police to prevent or investigate crime on the one hand, and the rights and liberties of the individual on the other?

# 19 Freedom of assembly and public order

## SUMMARY

This chapter is concerned with freedom of assembly (art 11 of the ECHR) and the powers that the police have at common law and under statute for preserving the peace and maintaining public order. The concept of a breach of the peace is discussed, together with the circumstances in which the police may take action in order to prevent a reasonably apprehended breach from occurring. The chapter also focuses on the offences under Part I of the Public Order 1986 and the statutory powers available to the police for dealing with processions and assemblies under Part II of that Act.

## Rights and freedoms

19.1 The traditional means of protecting the rights and freedoms of the individual in English law were considered in Chapter **16**. For present purposes, it is worth noting that, from time to time, English judges have talked in terms of a 'right' to protest. Thus in *Hubbard v Pitt* (1976), Lord Denning referred to:

> the right to demonstrate and the right to protest on matters of public concern. These are rights which it is in the public interest that individuals should possess; and, indeed, that they should exercise without impediment so long as no wrongful act is done. It is often the only means by which grievances can be brought to the knowledge of those in authority, at any rate with such impact as to gain remedy.

More recently, in *Austin v Metropolitan Police Comr* (2005), Tugendhat J observed:

> Political demonstrations have long been a central feature of English life. Before the extension of the franchise in the 19th century they were the only means by which the public could make known their views. But they were generally treated as rebellions, whether they were violent or not. Out of the upheavals in the 16th and 17th centuries there came to be recognised a right of free speech and free assembly. There are repeated re-affirmations by the Courts of the importance of these rights in a democracy.

19.2 However, if we think of the 'right' to protest or to demonstrate in Hohfeldian terms (paras **16.3–16.6**), it may be that it is more appropriately described as a privilege. In truth, the individual is free to protest or to demonstrate provided that they do so in a peaceable manner and do not contravene any existing law, such as obstruction of the highway.

## Breach of the peace

**19.3**  The concept of a breach of the peace has a long history in the criminal law of England. Nevertheless, until recently, the courts had shown a reluctance to indicate what type of conduct could be said to amount to a breach of the peace. Thus in 1954, Professor Glanville Williams referred to the 'surprising lack of authoritative definition of what one would suppose to be a fundamental concept in criminal law'. The courts had a tendency to refer to the concept in a way that suggested that it was so well understood as not to require definition. Moreover, there may have been a reluctance to define the concept because the courts 'are constantly under the temptation to make it do far too much work' (Williams). However, when two differently constituted Courts of Appeal did define the concept in 1981, the result was not a uniform definition.

> *R v Howell* **(1982):** A disturbance occurred in the street due to an overspill from a party. In response to complaints made by local residents, the police warned the partygoers that they would be arrested for breach of the peace unless they returned home. H verbally abused an officer and then struck him whilst being arrested. H was convicted of assault occasioning actual bodily harm. On appeal he argued, inter alia, that the force had been necessary in order to free himself from an unlawful arrest because there had been no breach of the peace. CA held: dismissing the appeal, that both the police and the ordinary citizen have a power of arrest when there is a reasonable apprehension of an imminent breach of the peace, or where a breach of the peace has been committed. A breach of the peace occurs whenever harm is actually done, or is threatened to be done, to a person or in his presence to his property.

> *R v Chief Constable of Devon and Cornwall, ex p Central Electricity Generating Board* **(1982):** The CEGB sought to survey a piece of land for the purpose of determining whether to construct a power station. Protesters tried to prevent this by obstructing CEGB's employees by, for example, chaining themselves to machinery on the site. Despite requests from the CEGB, the chief constable refused to intervene. He claimed that the police had no statutory or common law power to arrest, not least because there had been neither a breach, nor an apprehended breach of the peace. The CEGB sought an order to compel the police to remove the protesters. CA held: not granting the remedy, that there is a breach of the peace whenever a person who is lawfully carrying out his work is unlawfully and physically prevented by another from doing so (Lord Denning).

**19.4**  The tenor of these judgments is really quite different. In *Howell*, the CA emphasized the need for harm or the threat of harm before there will be a breach of the peace. In *CEGB*,

Lord Denning considered that criminal obstruction itself amounted to a breach of the peace. This latter opinion ought to be approached with caution. It was the opinion of one judge, albeit a very distinguished judge who was at the time the Master of the Rolls, and it was not shared by the other judges who heard the appeal. In subsequent cases, the test laid down in *Howell* is the one which has been preferred by the domestic courts and accepted by the ECtHR. Thus, for example, in *Percy v DPP* (1995), a case which decided that civil trespass did not amount to a breach of the peace, Collins J observed that:

> In our judgment, breach of the peace is limited to violence or threats of violence as set out in R v Howell *and any observations which indicate something wider ought not to be followed.*

In *Steel v United Kingdom* (1998), the ECtHR held, inter alia, that the concept of a breach of the peace as defined in *Howell* was sufficiently clear in English law to satisfy the requirement of art 5(1)(c) of the ECHR.

## An offence?

**19.5** Breach of the peace is not a criminal offence since it lacks the hallmarks of a crime in that a person cannot be charged with having committed a breach of the peace and neither can they be convicted of having done so. Accordingly, a person arrested for a breach of the peace and detained at a police station does not enjoy the same statutory protections set out in PACE because they have not been detained for an 'offence': see *Williamson v Chief Constable of the West Midlands Police* (2003). Nevertheless, it is good practice for the police to apply the PACE detention provisions to a person arrested for a breach of the peace and any person so detained would have redress at common law in the event that their detention was unlawful, ie where it lasted for a period longer than was necessary to prevent a breach of the peace. Although a breach of the peace is not an offence for the purposes of PACE, it is an 'offence' for the purposes of art 5 of the ECHR: see *Steel v United Kingdom* (1998).

## Reasonable apprehension

**19.6** Where a police officer apprehends that a breach of the peace is imminent, preventive action is only justified where that apprehension is reasonable. In short, there must be some basis in fact for that apprehension; a mere assertion that a breach of the peace was apprehended is not enough. Whether or not an apprehension was reasonable in the circumstances will therefore be a matter of fact for the court to decide.

**19.7** Past events may create a reasonable apprehension of a breach of the peace. Thus previous violent confrontations between rival groups, as in *Beatty v Gillbanks* (1882) (para **19.30**), may create a reasonable apprehension. Similarly, provocative conduct at the relevant time may create a reasonable apprehension of an imminent breach of the peace.

Since the reasonable apprehension requirement is a safeguard against unjustified police interference with the freedom of the individual, it is essential that the courts interpret the requirement narrowly. This has not always been the case.

> ***McLeod v Metropolitan Police Comr (1994):*** The former husband of M had obtained a court order for the return of certain furniture and effects. Three days before the order was due to expire, he went to M's house accompanied by his brother and sister, a solicitors' clerk, and two police officers. The officers were there at the request of the husband's solicitors. M was not at the house. The party was admitted by M's mother. Furniture was loaded into a van. Whilst carrying out this operation for a second time, M returned. She demanded that the furniture be put back in the house. One of the officers intervened. He insisted that the van should remain loaded and that the husband be allowed to drive away. He indicated that any disputes should be later resolved by the parties' solicitors. M took criminal proceedings against her former husband and his relatives for theft. These were dismissed. She also pursued civil proceedings against: the solicitor; her former husband and his relatives; and the police. In the action against the police, M sought damages for trespass and breach of duty. Tuckey J dismissed the claim on the basis that the police had been carrying out their duty in order to prevent an apprehended breach of the peace. M appealed. CA held: at common law the police had the power to enter private premises without a warrant to prevent a breach of the peace occurring. This was provided that they reasonably apprehended that the breach was likely to occur. The power needed to be exercised with care. The facts supported the argument that the police had a lawful excuse for entering M's house.

**19.8** When the case was heard at Strasbourg, however, the ECtHR took a rather different view of the matter. In *McLeod v United Kingdom* (1999), it held that the police officers' entry amounted to a breach of art 8 of the ECHR. This was because it was disproportionate to the legitimate aim pursued, ie action taken for the prevention of disorder or crime. In the opinion of the Court, the officers' entry was not justified since at the material time M was not even present at the house. There was therefore no basis for forming a reasonable apprehension of an imminent breach of the peace.

**19.9** More recently, it has been possible to discern a more robust approach by English courts when determining whether or not an apprehension was reasonable in the circumstances. Thus in *Foulkes v Chief Constable of the Merseyside Police* (1998), Beldam LJ expressed the view that: 'There must, I consider, be a sufficiently real and present threat to the peace to justify the extreme step of depriving of his liberty a citizen who is not at the time acting unlawfully.' Similarly in *Redmond-Bate v DPP* (1999) (see paras **16.11–16.12**), the DC concluded that there was nothing in the situation as perceived by the police officer which entitled him to apprehend a breach of the peace.

## Private premises

**19.10** The decision of the CA in *McLeod* also illustrates the fact that a breach of the peace may occur on private as well as public premises. Thus in *McConnell v Chief Constable of*

*Greater Manchester Police* (1990), where a police officer arrested a person who attempted to re-enter a carpet store after having been asked to leave the manager's office, the CA accepted that authorities such as *R v Chief Constable of Devon and Cornwall, ex p CEGB* (1982) made it clear that a breach of the peace could occur on private land. In the words of Purchas LJ in *McConnell*:

> Clearly a purely domestic dispute will rarely amount to a breach of the peace. But, in exceptional circumstances, it might very well do so. Whether those particular circumstances which come to pass on private premises are sufficient to support a reasonable apprehension that a breach of the peace was about to occur will depend on the circumstances in which the preventive steps called for under the Justices of the Peace Act 1361 are taken.

**19.11** In *McQuade v Chief Constable of Humberside Police* (2001), the CA had to determine whether a trial judge had been right to hold that a breach of the peace either committed or apprehended on private property must involve some kind of disturbance to members of the public who were off the premises at the time. The CA concluded that although in practice there would often be a public element to a breach of the peace, it was not a legal requirement. Thus, for example, a disturbance within a house which has not been overheard by a passer-by may still amount to a breach of the peace where there is violence or damage or the threat of violence or damage. In *McQuade*, Laws LJ observed that the inclusion of a public element in a breach of the peace had a tendency:

> to confuse what are two different ideas, namely the keeping of the Queen's peace and the preservation of public order. The former no doubt includes the latter, but they are not coextensive. Public order is concerned with the tranquillity and safety of public places. Keeping the peace is concerned with the prevention of violence and damage wherever they may occur, public or private. The suggestion that there has to be found an element of public disturbance in every breach of the peace conflates these two ideas and does so unsupported by any rational policy of the law.

**19.12** Given that the police have the power at common law to enter a private house in order to prevent a breach of the peace, such a power must be exercised with care. This is especially important since any entry is likely to be contrary to the occupier's wishes.

## Power of arrest

**19.13** The police (and the private citizen) have the power at common law to arrest a person who is committing or whom they reasonably apprehend is about to commit a breach of the peace. It is, however, a power which the courts consider must be used with great care and circumspection. Thus in *Foulkes v Chief Constable of Merseyside* (1998), Beldam LJ observed that although he was:

> prepared to accept that a constable may exceptionally have power to arrest a person whose behaviour is lawful but provocative, it is a power which ought to be exercised by him only in the clearest of circumstances.

Similarly in *McQuade*, Laws LJ remarked that the power of arrest for a breach of the peace:

> like any power is capable of being abused. Because no warrant is required, because the arrest may be on private property and in anticipation of trouble which has not yet occurred and because . . . there need be no public element, special care had to be taken where any such arrest is in contemplation, though the circumstances may be urgent and changing by the second.

**19.14**  In the event that an officer decides to exercise the common law power of arrest, he must be aware that the power is being used either in respect of an actual or an apprehended breach of the peace. Arresting for an actual breach of the peace where the relevant behaviour at most suggested the imminent threat of a breach of the peace thereby rendered the arrest unlawful: see *R (on the application of Hawkes) v DPP* (2005).

**19.15**  The common law power of arrest survived the reform of the PACE powers of arrest by the Serious Organised Crime and Police Act 2005. Although the Labour Government was initially in favour of abolishing the power, it accepted the police's argument that it remains useful in the context of domestic violence and where those suffering from mental health problems need to be taken into custody in order that the processes under the mental health legislation can be commenced.

## Power to detain

**19.16**  In addition to the power of arrest, there is also a power at common law to detain a person short of arresting them in order to prevent a breach of the peace. In *Albert v Lavin* (1981), Lord Diplock described such a power as follows:

> every citizen in whose presence a breach of the peace is being, or reasonably appears to be about to be, committed has the right to take reasonable steps to make the person who is breaking or threatening to break the peace refrain from doing so; and those reasonable steps in appropriate cases will include detaining him against his will. At common law this is not only the right of every citizen, it is also his duty, although, except in the case of a citizen who is a constable, it is a duty of imperfect obligation.

**19.17**  It will be noted from this passage that the common law duty to deal with a breach of the peace is a 'duty of imperfect obligation'. In other words, there may be circumstances where it would be unreasonable to expect a citizen to take action, such as where they are in charge of a child and there is a danger that the child's safety would be compromised if they were to leave them unattended. As far as the police are concerned, however, the common law power to detain may be put to good use in a number of different situations, eg in order to preserve the peace during the course of a demonstration or to prevent a person from committing a further act of domestic violence: see *Chief Constable of Cleveland Constabulary v McGrogan* (2002).

**19.18**  The power to detain or contain persons in order to prevent a breach of the peace must now be considered in the light of two recent HL decisions.

---

*R (on the application of Laporte) v Chief Constable of the Gloucestershire Constabulary (2006):* L was one of approximately 120 passengers on three coaches travelling from London to RAF Fairford in Gloucestershire. She and her fellow passengers wished to join a demonstration at the airbase against the US-led war against Iraq. The coaches were stopped by the police in a lay-by not far from the airbase. They were searched and a number of items (masks, spray paint, shields, etc) were seized. On instructions from a chief superintendent, the coaches and their passengers were sent back to London under police escort without being allowed to stop on the way. L applied for judicial review. She claimed that the police had acted unlawfully by preventing her attending the demonstration contrary to arts 10 and 11 of the ECHR, and by detaining her and forcibly returning her to London contrary to art 5 of the ECHR. HCt held: that on the facts of the case, the police had been entitled in accordance with *Moss v McLachlan* (1985) to intercept the coaches so as to prevent a breach of the peace from occurring. L's enforced return on the coach to London was, however, contrary to art 5 because: (i) there was no immediately apprehended breach of the peace by her sufficient to justify even transitory detention; (ii) detention on the coach for two and a half hours went far beyond what could be described as transitory detention; (iii) even if there had been an apprehended breach of the peace, the circumstances and length of the detention were wholly disproportionate to the aim of preventing it from occurring. The defendant appealed and L cross-appealed. CA held: dismissing both appeals, that whilst the facts of the case disclosed a reasonable apprehension of an imminent breach of the peace which had been appropriately dealt with by intercepting the vehicles, the passengers had been virtually prisoners on the return journey to London. This had been a disproportionate approach to the legitimate aim of seeking to prevent a breach of the peace. L appealed and the defendant cross-appealed. HL held: unanimously upholding L's appeal, that both the HCt and the CA had erred in finding that the interception of the coaches had been necessary in order to prevent a breach of the peace. Instead, it had amounted to a premature and indiscriminate course of action which was accordingly disproportionate.

---

*Austin v Commissioner of Police for the Metropolis (2009):* On 1 May 2001, a crowd of demonstrators marched into Oxford Circus, London, at approximately 2.00 p.m. Their numbers steadily increased so that eventually, approximately 3,000 people had gathered.

Several thousand other persons were also present on the periphery of the gathering. From about 2.20 p.m. onwards, the police refused to allow people to leave Oxford Circus. Finally, after having been detained within the police cordon for up to seven hours, those present were allowed to disperse. The appellant had come to London in order to demonstrate. On a number of occasions she had asked police officers to permit her to leave the cordon in order that she might collect her child from a crèche. Her requests were refused. In respect of her containment she brought an action against the Commissioner for damages for false imprisonment under s 7 of the Human Rights Act 1998 in respect of her right to liberty under art 5 of the ECHR. Her claims were dismissed by both Tugendhat J and the CA. The CA was of the view that, in exceptional circumstances, the innocent bystander may have his or her freedoms restricted in order that the peace be preserved. Moreover, in its judgment, there had been no deprivation of liberty within the meaning of art 5(1) of the ECHR. A appealed on the art 5 issue alone. HL held: dismissing the appeal, that having regard to the Strasbourg case law, it is not enough that what was done could be said in general colloquial terms to have amounted to a deprivation of liberty. Except in the paradigm case of confinement in a prison cell, the absolute nature of the right requires a more exacting examination of the relevant criteria. There was a threshold that must be crossed before this can be held to be a breach of art 5(1). In a case such as the present, it was unrealistic to contend that art 5 came into play at all, provided that the actions of the police are proportionate and reasonable, and any confinement was restricted to a reasonable minimum, as to discomfort and time, as is necessary for the purpose of preventing serious public disorder and violence.

**19.19**  In *Moss v McLachlan* (1985), a convoy of 'flying pickets' had been intercepted by the police after they had turned off at a motorway junction and were heading in the direction of various Nottinghamshire collieries. As a consequence of previous incidents of violence involving striking miners, the police apprehended a breach of the peace if they were allowed to continue to their intended destination. In the judgment of the DC, the fact that the collieries were between one and a half and five miles from the police cordon did not defeat the argument that a breach of the peace was imminent in terms of being proximate in both time and place. Accordingly, those pickets who had attempted to break through the cordon had been rightly convicted of wilfully obstructing a police officer in the execution of his duty contrary to s 51(3) of the Police Act 1964 (now s 89(2) of the Police Act 1996).

**19.20**  The decision in *Moss* provoked some differences of judicial opinion in *Laporte*. In the CA, Lord Woolf had described *Moss* as being 'very much on all fours' with the facts of *Laporte*. However in the HL, Lord Bingham distinguished the two cases thus:

> *With four members of one belligerent faction within less than five minutes of confronting another belligerent faction, and no designated, police-controlled, assembly point separated from the scene of the apprehended disorder, as in the centre of Fairford, it could plausibly be held in* Moss *that a breach of the peace was about to be committed by those whose onward progress the police decided to block.*

**19.21**   Lord Rodger was of the opinion that the facts of *Laporte* would have justified the belief that a breach of the peace was imminent, had the officer in charge had such a belief, which he did not. For his part, Lord Brown regarded the decision in *Moss* as:

> (just) sustainable on what is certainly one possible view of the facts of that case, but the course of action taken by the police here in preventing Miss Laporte from proceeding further as plainly unsustainable – unsustainable, first, because Mr Lambert did not in fact regard a breach of the peace as then imminent and, secondly, because . . . no such view was in any event open to him.

**19.22**   The decision in *Laporte* demonstrates that post the Human Rights Act 1998, the intensity of review by the courts will be greater than it was prior to the Act. It is therefore no longer the case that a finding that an officer's actions were reasonable will necessarily defeat the claim that his actions were unlawful. What also matters now is whether or not his actions were proportionate. On the facts of *Laporte*, the HL (unlike the HCt and CA) considered that the initial interception of the protesters had been in breach of art 5 of the ECHR because it amounted to a disproportionate course of conduct. How might the legitimate aim of maintaining public order have been achieved in a more proportionate manner? By allowing the protestors to arrive at RAF Fairford and dealing with any threatened breaches of the peace at the base itself? By targeting preventive action in the lay-by so that only those reasonably suspected of being likely to cause a breach of the peace would be prevented from continuing on their journey?

**19.23**   The decision in *Austin* makes clear that whether or not containment of 'kettling' engages the protection of art 5 of the ECHR depends upon its purpose. In the present context, however, it should not be forgotten that the appeal to the HL was concerned solely with the art 5 issue. In other words, the CA's ruling on the common law powers of the police to contain persons who were not themselves threatening a breach of the peace was not challenged. *Austin* is thus a 'very exceptional case' which falls within the scope of the principle established in the Irish case of *O'Kelly v Harvey* (1883), where Law C observed:

> even assuming that the danger to the public peace arose altogether from the threatened attack of another body on the plaintiff and his friends, still if the defendant believed and had just grounds for believing that the peace could only be preserved by withdrawing the plaintiff and his friends from the attack with which they were threatened, it was, I think, the duty of the defendant to take that course.

**19.24**   'Kettling' is a controversial police tactic. In recent times, it has been deployed in central London on a number of occasions to deal with large gatherings of people protesting about matters such as the G20 summit, the rise in University tuition fees, and the scrapping of the Educational Maintenance Allowance. Legal challenges have been brought against the actions of the police and the outcomes of the cases have depended very much upon the particular facts. Thus in *R (on the application of Moos and another) v Commissioner of Police of the Metropolis* (2011), the QBD held that the police had acted unlawfully in containing protestors in order to avoid the mere *risk* of a breach of the peace likely to be committed by others. Unlike *Austin*, the facts of *Moos* did not make it a very exceptional case justifying this measure of last resort. Conversely, in *Castle and others v Commissioner of Police for the Metropolis* (2011), the DCt ruled that the police had not acted unlawfully even though the use of containment had resulted in the detention of vulnerable protestors, including the claimants (children aged 14–16), for a number of hours, and despite the fact that it was common ground that they had been peaceful participants in the demonstration. Crucially, the officers in *Castle*, unlike those in *Moos*, had contained the claimants in furtherance of the legitimate aim of preventing an imminent breach of the peace by persons both inside and outside the cordon. Their actions were therefore held to have been necessary, proportionate, and lawful.

## Binding over

**19.25** Where a person has been found to have breached the peace, or to have engaged in con-duct likely to cause a breach of the peace, magistrates have the power to 'bind over' that person under s 115 of the Magistrates' Courts Act 1980, under the common law, and under the Justices of the Peace Act 1361. 'Binding over' amounts to a person agreeing to keep the peace and/or be of good behaviour for a specified period of time on pain of forfeiting a sum of money (a recognizance) fixed by the court if they fail to comply with the order. A refusal to agree to a binding over order may result in the person being imprisoned. Nevertheless, the binding over order itself is not a criminal conviction: *R v County of London Quarter Sessions Appeal Committee, ex p Metropolitan Police Comr* (1948).

**19.26** In February 1994, the Law Commission published a report, *Binding Over* (Law Com No 222) in which it stated that:

> We are satisfied that there are substantial objections of principle to the retention of binding over to keep the peace or to be of good behaviour. These objections are, in summary: that the conduct which can be the ground for a binding-over order is too vaguely defined; that binding-over orders when made are in terms which are too vague and are therefore potentially oppressive; that the power to imprison someone if he or she refuses to consent to be bound over is anomalous; that orders which restrain a subject's freedom can be made without the discharge of the criminal, or indeed any clearly defined, burden of proof; and that witnesses, complainants or even acquitted defendants can be bound over without adequate prior information of any charge or complaint against them. [para *6.27*]

**19.27** In the light of these objections, the Law Commission recommended that the power to bind over be abolished. The vagueness of binding over orders was referred to by the ECtHR in *Steel v United Kingdom* (1998). In that case, which was concerned with, amongst other things, the issue of whether binding over orders were specific enough to be described as 'lawful orders of a court' within the meaning of art 5(1)(b) of the ECHR, the court observed that:

> the orders were expressed in rather vague and general terms; the expression 'to be of good behaviour' was particularly imprecise and offered little guidance to the person bound over as to the type of conduct which would amount to a breach of the order.

**19.28** Binding over orders were again at issue before the ECtHR in *Hashman and Harrup v United Kingdom* (1999), a case involving hunt saboteurs. Although the facts of the case reveal that it was concerned with behaviour which was *contra bonos mores*, ie conduct which is wrong in the judgment of the majority of contemporary fellow citizens, it is nevertheless of interest in the present context since the power to bind over extends to such behaviour. The Court's finding that the order was too imprecise to comply with art 10(2) is significant. It led to provisions in the Consolidated Criminal Practice Direction (2 April 2007) which relate to the making of binding over orders. These provide that:

> III 31.2 Before imposing a binding over order, the court must be satisfied that a breach of the peace involving violence, or an imminent threat of violence, has occurred, or that there is a real risk of violence in the future. Such violence may be perpetrated by the individual who will be subject to the order, or by a third party as a natural consequence of the individual's conduct.

> III 31.3 In light of the judgment in Hashman and Harrup, courts should no longer bind an individual over 'to be of good behaviour'. Rather than binding an individual over to 'keep the peace' in general terms, the court should identify the specific conduct or activity from which the individual must refrain.

> III 31.4 When making an order binding over an individual to refrain from specified types of conduct or activities, the details of that conduct or those activities should be specified by the court in a written order served on all relevant parties. The court should state its reasons for the making of the order, its length and the amount of the recognizance. The length of the order should be proportionate to the harm sought to be avoided and should not generally exceed 12 months.

**19.29** In *Emohare v Thames Magistrates Court* (2009), where the claimant had been bound over to keep the peace for two years, the DC quashed the order because there had been no proper basis for making it. It also drew attention to the fact that the magistrates had failed to comply with the Consolidated Criminal Practice Direction and an earlier authority, *R v Middlesex Crown Court, ex p Khan* (1997), as to when it would be appropriate to impose a binding over order following an acquittal.

## Common law preventive powers

**19.30** The duties of the police have never been exhaustively defined either by statute or the common law. Nevertheless, it is clear that one such duty is the preservation of the peace.

Once this is accepted, it follows that the police will require powers in order to carry out this duty. The existence of preventive powers raises difficult issues, not least of which is the scope of those powers. In what circumstances is it justifiable to allow an officer to interfere with the freedom of the individual when no offence has been committed? In a number of cases, the courts have accepted that interference may be justified, even where a person is not acting unlawfully, in order to preserve the peace.

*Humphries v Connor* (1864): H, a Protestant, walked through a predominantly Catholic area wearing a party emblem, an orange lily. A number of people who were provoked by the emblem followed H and threatened her with violence. C, a police officer, removed the lily from H in order to preserve the peace. H sued C for assault. Court of Queen's Bench in Ireland held: that although what H did was a perfectly legal act, C's actions, which were an assault in law, were necessary in order to prevent a breach of the peace. C therefore had a defence to the proceedings.

*Beatty v Gillbanks* (1882): B, a captain in the Salvation Army, led a procession through the streets. On previous occasions there had been violent clashes with the Skeleton Army, an organization antagonistic to the Salvationists. B was informed by a police sergeant that he must obey a magistrates' notice directing all persons to abstain from assembling, and disperse at once. He refused to comply and was arrested. B was subsequently bound over to keep the peace for 12 months. DC held: that the appeal would be allowed. The appellants were acting lawfully and therefore could not be guilty of an unlawful assembly merely because other persons were thereby induced to threaten a breach of the peace.

*Wise v Dunning* (1902): The appellant, a Protestant, preached in the streets of Liverpool dressed with beads hung around his neck and waving a crucifix above his head. He used expressions which were insulting to the Catholic population. Disturbances and riots had been caused by his conduct on previous occasions. The magistrate found that his language was provocative and bound him over to keep the peace and be of good behaviour. DC held: the decision of the magistrate was correct. The natural consequence of the appellant's conduct was illegality, ie a breach of the peace.

*Duncan v Jones* (1936): D proposed to address a gathering of about 30 persons in a street near to the entrance of a training centre for the unemployed. Approximately one year before, D had addressed a meeting on the same spot. Later that same day, a disturbance had taken place in the centre. The centre's superintendent had attributed it to the meeting. Thus a year on, when D attempted to address the gathering, she was told by a police officer that she would have to move to a neighbouring street some 175 yards away. D failed to comply with the direction and was arrested and charged with wilfully obstructing an officer in the execution of his duty. She appealed. DC held: dismissing the appeal, that the case stated clearly indicated a causal connection between the earlier meeting and the disturbance at the centre. This was a sufficient basis for the officer to reasonably apprehend a breach of the peace if D were allowed to address the gathering in the street. It was his duty to seek to prevent a breach of the peace, and he had therefore been obstructed while taking steps in accordance with that duty.

**19.31** A number of noteworthy points emerge from these cases. First, although he did not dissent from the ruling of the court in *Humphries v Connor* (1864), Fitzgerald J did express severe reservations about a principle which entitled a constable to interfere with another's person where that person was neither about to commit a breach of the peace nor perform an illegal act. In sanctioning such conduct in order to prevent a breach of the peace by others, Fitzgerald J considered that the court was making 'not the law of the land but the law of the mob supreme'. Do you agree?

**19.32** The principle established in *Humphries v Connor* (1864) has been extended by *Duncan v Jones* (1936). Whilst the former established that what might otherwise be a tort would not be so if it was done in order to prevent an apprehended breach of the peace, the latter case established that it is an offence to fail to comply with a direction given in order to prevent a breach of the peace. When viewed in this light, *Duncan v Jones* represents a significant incursion into the liberty of the individual. It accords the police wide powers for dealing with apprehended breaches of the peace, subject only to the limited safeguard that the apprehension must be reasonable. Can the decision in *Duncan v Jones* be reconciled with the more recent decision in *Redmond-Bate v DPP* (1999) (paras **16.11–16.12**)?

**19.33** The decision in *Beatty v Gillbanks* (1882) raises some interesting questions. In *Duncan v Jones* (1936), Lord Hewart CJ referred to it as a 'somewhat unsatisfactory case'. He did so on the basis that, despite the observations of Field J to the effect that an individual would be liable for the natural consequences of his own acts, the court in *Beatty v Gillbanks* concluded that the disturbances were caused not by the Salvation Army but by the antagonistic Skeleton Army. The issue of causation is a difficult one in the context of public order. Given that disturbances had occurred on previous occasions and that future disturbances were therefore a foreseeable event, could it be said that the Salvation Amy had caused those later disturbances? Is it possible to reconcile the decisions in *Beatty v Gillbanks* and *Wise v Dunning* (1902)? Might it be argued that the court's sympathies were aroused by the Salvation Army but not by Dunning?

**19.34** Whether or not the decision in *Beatty v Gillbanks* (1882) was correct on its facts, it does represent a blow in favour of freedom of expression and the 'right' to assemble. If the natural consequence of A's lawful actions is that B will act unlawfully, ought A to be prevented from acting as he intended? *Wise v Dunning* (1902) indicates that the answer to this question may be 'yes', but is there an alternative way of preserving the peace and maintaining public order?

## Public Order Act 1986

### Background

**19.35** Prior to the enactment of this Act, there had been several high-profile instances of the breakdown of public order in English towns and cities. Rioting had occurred in places such as London, Liverpool, and Bristol. These events were followed by inquiries, most notably those chaired by Lord Scarman into the Red Lion Square Disorders (1974) and the Brixton Riots (1981), which sought to identify the reasons for the disturbances and to make recommendations in order to prevent a recurrence. Additional impetus for reform came in the form of a Law Commission Report (*Criminal Law: Offences Relating to Public Order*, Law Com No 123 (1983)) and government Green and White Papers (*Review of the Public Order Act 1936 and related legislation*, Cmnd 7891 (1980) and *Review of Public Order Law*, Cmnd 9510 (1985)).

**19.36** The Public Order Act 1986 was thus greatly influenced by the various suggestions and recommendations made in these reports. Although the Act confers a number of powers on the police so as to enable them to maintain public order, it is not a codification of the law in this area. As we have already seen, the police retain the power at common law to deal with actual or apprehended breaches of the peace: see s 40(4) of the 1986 Act which expressly preserves the power. Moreover, certain public order offences are still to be found in other enactments. Section 1 of the Public Order Act 1936, for example, has survived the passage of its 1986 successor. It provides that it is an offence for a person to wear a 'uniform signifying his association with any political organisation or with the promotion of any political object' in any public place or at any public meeting. In *O'Moran v DPP* (1975), the DC was of the opinion that whether or not an article of dress amounted to a uniform depended upon the circumstances of the case. Thus the wearing of berets, dark glasses, and dark clothing by a number of men at a funeral was held to amount to the wearing of a uniform for the purposes of the 1936 Act.

### The offences

**19.37** In accordance with recommendations made by the Law Commission, s 9 of the Public Order Act 1986 abolished the common law offences of riot, rout, unlawful assembly, and affray. In their place, it created a number of new statutory offences which will be considered further. For ease of explanation, these will be divided into two categories: riot, violent disorder, and affray on the one hand, and ss 4, 4A, and 5 on the other. Those features which are common to each of the offences within a category will be highlighted, as will those features which make an offence distinctive.

## Riot, violent disorder, and affray

**19.38**  These offences have the following common characteristics:

- the conduct which they prohibit must be such as would cause a person of reasonable firmness present at the scene to fear for his personal safety;

- no such person need actually be, or be likely to be, present at the scene (ie, a hypothetical bystander);

- a person must intend their conduct to be violent or threaten violence or must be aware that their conduct may be violent or threaten violence; and

- they may be committed in private as well as public places.

**19.39**  Riot is made an offence by s 1 of the Public Order Act 1986. It is the most serious of the public order offences in that a conviction may lead to a sentence of up to 10 years' imprisonment. In the case of violent disorder (s 2) and affray (s 3), the maximum sentences are five years and three years respectively.

**19.40**  The offences of riot and violent disorder are committed in a group context. In the case of riot, where 12 or more persons who are present together use or threaten unlawful violence for a *common purpose*, each person using unlawful violence for the common purpose is guilty of the offence. The requirement of a 'common purpose' is a distinctive feature of the offence of riot. It may be inferred from the conduct of the group taken as a whole. Thus a group of persons who attack police officers during a demonstration could be said to be acting for a common purpose. In the case of violent disorder, three or more persons must be present together and must be using or threatening unlawful violence, though this need not be simultaneous. Moreover, there is no requirement that they are acting for a common purpose: see *R v NW* (2010). Unlike riot, where it is only those who actually use violence who will be guilty of the offence, violent disorder may be committed by the use or threat of unlawful violence.

**19.41**  The numerical requirement for the offence of violent disorder is vitally important. It follows, therefore, that if three persons were charged with violent disorder and one of them was acquitted, the remaining two would not be guilty of the offence (although they may be found guilty of a s 4 offence: see s 7(3) of the 1986 Act). This assumes that there were only three persons present and charged. If, however, a jury is satisfied that there were others present at the scene not mentioned in the indictment, a conviction may still stand. In *R v Mechan* (2004), Potter LJ explained that the violent disorder offence:

> depends upon the three or more persons concerned being guilty of unlawful violence. Thus, if one or two persons unlawfully attack one or more victims who lawfully defend themselves with violence which is no more than reasonable for that purpose, that will not assist the prosecution to establish the ingredient of the offence which requires three participants in the unlawful violence referred to by the section.

**19.42** In its *Offences against Public Order*, Working Paper No 82, the Law Commission observed that:

> The essence of affray lies…in the fact that the defendant participates in fighting or other acts of violence inflicted on others of such a character as to cause alarm to the public: it is essentially an offence against public order.

**19.43** The offence of affray envisages at least three persons: a person using or threatening unlawful violence; a person to whom the violence or threat was directed; and a person of reasonable firmness who need not actually be present. This hypothetical bystander represents the public. The intention of the offence is to protect members of the public from the fear of unlawful violence. Thus where an assault by A on B is witnessed by C, this will not be an affray where C fears for B rather than for himself: see *R v Blinkhorn* (2006).

**19.44** A person may be charged with affray where they have participated in a street fight, even though there is insufficient evidence to charge them with a more specific offence, such as assault occasioning actual bodily harm. Affray involves the use or the threat of violence, although for the purposes of s 3, 'a threat cannot be made by the use of words alone': s 3(3). Therefore in *R v Robinson* (1994), the making of a threat in an aggressive tone of voice did not satisfy s 3(3) because there was no conduct beyond the use of words.

**19.45** The scope of the offence of affray was considered by the HL in an appeal which raised the following questions for the opinion of their Lordships: (i) whether the overt possession of a weapon may constitute a threat of violence for the purposes of s 3 when it is not used or brandished in a violent manner; (ii) whether the threat of unlawful violence has to be directed towards a person or persons present at the scene to amount to an affray; and (iii) whether in order to constitute a threat for the purposes of affray, the threat must be perceived as such by a person against whom it is addressed.

*I, M and H v DPP* **(2001):** The police received an anonymous tip-off that approximately 30 Asian youths armed with sticks were gathering in an area in the East End of London. A marked police carrier arrived at the scene and some 40-50 youths were observed milling around. Eight or nine of the youths were carrying petrol bombs. The group dispersed when the police carrier came into view and its occupants gave chase to some of the youths. Prior to their capture by the police, each appellant had thrown away a petrol bomb that he was carrying. During a police interview, it became apparent that the petrol bombs were intended to be used in a fight with a rival gang. The appellants were convicted of affray contrary to s 3(1) of the 1986 Act by a stipendiary magistrate. An appeal to the DC was unsuccessful. They therefore appealed to the HL. HL held: allowing the appeal, (i) that the carrying of a weapon may constitute a threat of violence for the purposes of s 3(1), although whether it does so in a particular case is a matter for the tribunal of fact to decide; (ii) that a defendant cannot be guilty of affray where the threat of violence is towards persons who are not present; and (iii) since the youths had not threatened violence towards the police officers, there were no victims present.

19.46   In the light of their Lordships ruling on the first two questions raised by the appeal, it was unnecessary for them to consider the third question. It follows from the decision in *I, M and H v DPP* that to be guilty of an affray, D must have threatened violence towards another and that the victim was present at the material time. Furthermore, the threat must have been such as to cause a person of reasonable firmness also present at the scene to fear for his personal safety. Although the appellants were therefore entitled to have their convictions quashed, does this case provide an example of criminal conduct going unpunished? Do you agree with the obiter remarks of Lord Hutton that the appellants ought instead to have been charged with carrying an offensive weapon contrary to s 1 of the Prevention of Crime Act 1953, or with possession of explosives contrary to s 4 of the Explosive Substances Act 1883?

## Sections 4, 4A, and 5

19.47   These offences share the following common characteristics:

- they involve the use of threatening, abusive, or insulting words or behaviour or the display of any writing, sign, or other visible representation which is threatening, abusive, or insulting;
- they may be committed in a public or a private place, although no offence is committed where D is inside a dwelling and the other person is also inside that or another dwelling;
- the basic offences are all summary in nature; and
- they may be racially aggravated under s 31 of the Crime and Disorder Act 1998.

19.48   In order to commit an offence under s 4 of the 1986 Act, D's behaviour must be directed at another person with intent to cause that person to believe that immediate unlawful violence will be used against him or another by any person, or to provoke the immediate use of unlawful violence by that person or another, or whereby that person is likely to believe that such violence will be used or that it is likely that such violence will be provoked. By virtue of s 6(3) of the 1986 Act, D will only be guilty of a s 4 offence if he intended his words, behaviour, etc to be threatening, abusive, or insulting, or he was aware that it may have such an effect.

*Atkin v DPP* (1989): Two customs officers and a bailiff went to A's farm to recover VAT which was owed. The bailiff remained outside in a car whilst the customs officers spoke with A inside the farmhouse. A became angry when he was informed that if he could not pay the money owed, the bailiff would have to enter in order to distrain on his goods. On several occasions he stated that: 'If the bailiff gets out of the car he's a dead un'. The customs officers noticed a gun in the house and accordingly left. They informed the bailiff of the threats that had been made against him and all three left the farm. A was convicted by magistrates of an offence contrary to s 4 of the Public Order Act 1986. He appealed on the basis that for such an offence to be committed, the person against whom the threats have been made must actually be physically present at the material time. DC held: quashing his conviction, that for the purposes of s 4(1)(a), the bailiff could not be the relevant person because he was not in earshot and the words were not directed towards him. Moreover, since the words used could only be directed at the customs officers, it followed in the light of s 4(2) that no offence was committed since at the material time, all concerned were within a dwelling.

**19.49**  The terms of s 4(2) underline the public order nature of the offence. D may commit an offence where his behaviour falls within the scope of s 4(1), he is inside a dwelling, and his behaviour is directed at a person who is not in that or another dwelling. However, no offence is committed where D and the victim are in the same or different dwellings. In *Atkin v DPP* (1989), Henry J remarked that the wording of s 4(2) evidenced a clear intention on the part of Parliament to 'exclude domestic quarrels conducted within the home even in circumstances where such words or behaviour would, if repeated outside the dwelling, create an offence'. Might such domestic quarrels nevertheless amount to a breach of the peace?

**19.50**  For a s 4 offence to be committed, it is necessary that D's behaviour causes another person to fear immediate unlawful violence. In *R v Horseferry Road Metropolitan Stipendiary Magistrate, ex p Siadatan* (1991), it was alleged that Viking Penguin Books Ltd had committed an offence under s 4(1) of the 1986 Act by distributing Salman Rushdie's *The Satanic Verses*. However, the DC dismissed an application for judicial review of the stipendiary magistrate's decision not to issue a summons on the information laid by the applicants before the magistrates' court. In so doing, the DC observed that the word 'immediate' in s 4(1) prior to the words 'unlawful violence' did not mean that the violence needed to be instantaneous for an offence to be committed. Instead, 'immediate' connoted:

> proximity in time and proximity in causation, that it is likely that violence will result within a relatively short period of time and without any other intervening occurrence.

**19.51**  In the later case of *Valentine v DPP* (1997), V, whilst standing outside a prison officer's house, shouted that the 'next time you go on duty we're going to burn your house. You're all going to . . . die'. The magistrates convicted V of a s 4(1) offence and he duly appealed. It was argued on his behalf that the condition precedent on the attack taking place, the prison officer's absence from the family home, amounted to an intervening occurrence and that therefore the violence was not going to be immediate in the sense of a relatively short time interval. However, the DC held that the finding was one which the magistrates were properly entitled to reach. The factual basis supported the magistrates' conclusion that the victims did believe that immediate unlawful violence would be used on them, in the sense of during the same night as the threats were issued.

**19.52**    A more recent appeal heard by the DC provides a further useful illustration of conduct which falls within the scope of the s 4 offence.

> *Liverpool v DPP* **(2008):** The appellant had given the victim's son a lift and had offered him cannabis. The victim approached the appellant and asked him not to do either of these things again. He responded by using foul language towards her in a loud voice over a sustained period. He issued personal insults and threats and made hand gestures towards her as if firing a gun whilst stating: 'I will kill you'. The incident took place in an area overlooked by flats. A resident offered the victim refuge and the police were called. The justices found that the appellant's conduct amounted to an offence contrary to s 4 of the 1986 Act. He appealed. DC held: dismissing the appeal, that the hand gesture, together with the loud and threatening language, amply justified the conviction.

**19.53**    The words 'threatening, abusive or insulting' which are common to the offences in ss 4, 4A, and 5 of the 1986 Act are not defined in the statute. In the absence of a statutory definition, the words should therefore be accorded their ordinary and natural meaning.

> *Brutus v Cozens* **(1973):** Anti-apartheid protesters walked on to a tennis court at the Wimbledon tennis championships. They distributed leaflets, blew a whistle, and waved placards and banners in front of the crowd. Play was stopped for several minutes whilst police removed them. The appellant was charged with using insulting behaviour whereby a breach of the peace was likely to be occasioned contrary to s 5 of the Public Order Act 1936 (now repealed). The insult in question was said to have been directed at the crowd. The magistrates dismissed the information against him, but the respondent's appeal to the DC was successful. HL held: the word 'insulting' was intended to have its ordinary and natural meaning. Although their Lordships were referred to a dictionary definition of 'insulting', it was felt that an ordinary sensible man knows an insult when he sees or hears it. The conduct of the appellant was deplorable and probably it ought to be punishable. It was not, however, insulting.

> *Hammond v DPP* **(2004):** H was an Evangelical Christian who had been a preacher for 20 years. He had a large double-sided sign made bearing the words 'Stop Immorality', 'Stop Homosexuality', and 'Stop Lesbianism' on each side, and the words 'Jesus is Lord' in each of the four corners. H had preached whilst displaying the sign on a previous occasion and had received a hostile reaction. On the day in question, a group of 30–40 people gathered around him as he preached. Some of the crowd were angry whilst others appeared to be distressed. H was arrested by the police for a breach of the peace. He was later charged and convicted of an offence contrary to s 5 of the Public Order Act 1986. H appealed. DC held: dismissing the appeal, that in determining whether or not a sign of this kind was insulting, it was appropriate to have art 10 of the ECHR very much in mind. That article was also relevant when considering whether or not a defendant had established the defence of reasonable

conduct under s 5(3) of the 1986 Act. On the facts, it had been open to the justices to find that the words on the sign were insulting not least because they appeared to relate homosexuality and lesbianism to immorality. It had also been open to the justices to conclude that H's conduct was not reasonable because the interference with his right to freedom of expression had been proportionate in view of the fact that his behaviour went beyond legitimate protest, was provoking violence and disorder, and interfered with the rights of others.

**19.54**  Whilst s 5 is also a summary offence, it is a less serious offence than s 4. This is evident from the fact that in the event of a conviction, the maximum penalty is a fine not exceeding level 3 on the standard scale. The actus reus of the s 5 offence entails using threatening, abusive, or insulting words or behaviour, or disorderly behaviour, etc 'within the hearing or sight of a person likely to be caused harassment, alarm or distress thereby'. In other words, it is the mental rather than the physical reaction to the words or behaviour that matters. In *Holloway v DPP* (2004), the DC had to determine a novel issue: whether it was necessary for the conduct in question to be actually witnessed by a third party before a defendant could be convicted and not merely that the conduct could have been seen by a third party. In that case, H had stood naked in front of a video camera and had filmed himself where there were schoolchildren visible in the background. None of the children, nor anyone else for that matter, had actually seen him in a state of undress. Nevertheless, he had been convicted of a s 5 offence. His appeal against that conviction was allowed. In the judgment of Silber J, the words in s 5 'mean that some person must have actually seen the abusive or insulting words or behaviour. It is not enough that somebody merely might have seen or could possibly have seen that behaviour'. For his part, Collins J who also heard the appeal did 'not regard it as necessary for the Crown to go so far as to produce positive evidence that he was seen, or that he was heard, to do whatever amounts to the insulting words or behaviour'. Thus he saw no reason 'why a charge of this nature should not be established where the evidence makes it clear that the court can properly and safely draw the inference that there were people who could see what was going on or could hear what was going on. The fact that they may not have done, for whatever reason, seems to me to be immaterial'.

**19.55**  Of these two views, which do you consider better reflects the wording of s 5? Do you agree with Collins J that his words only represented a 'slight gloss' on what Silber J had said? In the later case of *Taylor v DPP* (2006), Keene LJ observed:

> The conflict between the two members of the DC in the Holloway case, such as it is, comes down to a question of what evidence the prosecution is required to call to prove the offence. The wording of the subsection is 'within the hearing or sight of a person'. It seems to me that Collins J was right in saying that there must be evidence that someone was able to hear or see the defendant's conduct, and that the prosecution does not have to call evidence that he or she did actually hear the words or see the behaviour. In practice, the distinction between the tests formulated by the two judges in Holloway is likely to be a very fine one.

**19.56** The mens rea of the s 5 offence consists of intending or being aware that the words or behaviour, etc may be threatening, abusive, insulting, or disorderly. In *DPP v Orum* (1988), the DC held that a police officer could be a person who is likely to be caused harassment, alarm, or distress by threatening, abusive, or insulting words or behaviour. Nevertheless, Glidewell LJ did observe that: 'Very frequently, words and behaviour with which police officers will be wearily familiar will have little emotional impact on them save that of boredom'. Whether or not the words or behaviour do cause harassment, alarm, or distress will be a question of fact to be determined by the trial court.

**19.57** In the later case of *Southard v DPP* (2006), the DC rejected a submission that because the 1986 Act is aimed at occasions of real public disorder, a s 5 charge ought not to be used where the only alleged target of the bad behaviour was a police officer. Fulford J opined:

> It is easy to think of many different situations in which police officers could be caused grave harassment, alarm or distress as a result of abusive words or behaviour – for instance, during an incident of serious public disturbance when they are particularly singled out as the target of an attack. Charging an offender under s 5 would be a singularly appropriate step in those circumstances, either if the evidence against the accused did not support other more serious offences or as a lesser alternative charge.

**19.58** Several further distinctions can be made between the s 4 and s 5 offences. The first of these is concerned with 'disorderly behaviour'. Disorderly behaviour can be the actus reus of a s 5 offence, but not of a s 4 offence. The term is not defined in the 1986 Act and therefore it has been left to the courts to determine what is meant by 'disorderly behaviour'.

*Chambers and Edwards v DPP* **(1995):** C and E were protesters against a motorway link road. On the day in question, a land engineering surveyor was using a theodolite to take measurements. It was operated by emitting an infra-red beam. C held his hand in front of the theodolite to obstruct the beam. He continued to do so after being warned by the police that his conduct was disorderly and was causing harassment, alarm, or distress to the persons working there. E walked in front of the theodolite carrying a placard. He was given the same warning by the police as that received by C. However, he repeated his protest. C and E were arrested and jointly charged with an offence contrary to s 5 of the Public Order Act 1986. They were both convicted by magistrates. Their convictions were upheld by the Crown Court. They further appealed. DC held: the absence of a statutory definition of 'disorderly behaviour' suggested that Parliament had intended that such words be given their ordinary meaning. This was the approach which had been adopted in *Brutus v Cozens* (1973). Whether behaviour on a particular occasion was properly characterized as 'disorderly' was a question of fact for the trial court to determine. There need not be any element of violence, present or threatened, for there to be disorderly behaviour. In the present case, deliberate and persistent conduct which rendered ineffective a machine which the surveyor was attempting to operate in the course of his employment was capable of amounting to disorderly behaviour.

**19.59** In *Chambers*, Keene J noted that Parliament had provided certain safeguards in respect of s 5 so as 'to avoid criminalizing behaviour unnecessarily and interfering with normal peaceful demonstrations'. In addition to the mens rea requirement (s 6(4)), he drew attention to s 5(3) of the 1986 Act. This provides that:

*It is a defence for the accused to prove –*

- *that he had no reason to believe that there was any person within hearing or sight who was likely to be caused harassment, alarm or distress, or*
- *that he was inside a dwelling and had no reason to believe that the words or behaviour used, or the writing, sign or other visible representation displayed, would be heard or seen by a person outside that or any other dwelling, or*
- *that his conduct was reasonable.*

**19.60** The defences provided for in s 5(3) thus represent a further distinction between this section and s 4. They are reverse onus defences in that they require D to prove them on the balance of probabilities. One such defence was at issue in a case concerned with a protest outside an abortion clinic.

**DPP v Clarke (1991):** Anti-abortion protesters gathered outside a licensed clinic. Each protester displayed photographs of aborted foetuses to both police officers and passers-by. They were requested to stop but failed to do so. They were therefore arrested and charged with an offence contrary to s 5 of the Public Order Act 1986. It was held by the magistrates that the protesters could not rely on the s 5(3) defence because their conduct was not reasonable. However, the informations against them were dismissed on the basis that they had not intended the photographs to be threatening, abusive, or insulting. The DPP appealed. DC held: dismissing the appeal, that the justices had applied the correct tests in respect of ss 5(3) (objective) and 6(4) (subjective).

**19.61** In addition to the statutory defences, it is now clear that D may be entitled to have a conviction for a s 5 offence quashed on the basis that such a conviction is incompatible with freedom of expression under art 10 of the ECHR.

**Percy v DPP (2001):** D protested against the American Star Wars Missile Defence System outside an American airbase in the UK. Her protest took the form of defacing the American flag; a stripe was placed across the stars and the words 'Stop Star Wars' were written across the stripes. D then stepped in front of a vehicle, placed the flag down, and stood upon it. Such acts were considered by the trial judge to be calculated to offend the mostly American service personnel and their families who witnessed them and accordingly D was convicted of the s 5 offence. In reaching such a conclusion, the trial judge determined the balance between D's right to freedom of expression and the rights of the 'victims' of the protest in favour of the latter on the basis that: there was a pressing social need in a multicultural society to prevent the denigration of objects of veneration and symbolic importance for a cultural group; and that D's conduct was not an unavoidable consequence of her protest against Star Wars. D appealed. DC held: allowing the appeal and quashing the conviction, that whilst it was legitimate to seek to prevent the denigration of objects of veneration, etc, it could find no evidence in the trial judge's reasoning to suggest that he had then proceeded to consider whether an interference with D's right to freedom of expression by criminal prosecution was a proportionate response to that aim. It was the fact that the trial judge appeared to have placed too much reliance on the view that D's insulting behaviour could have been avoided which made the conviction incompatible with D's Convention rights.

19.62   Section 4A was inserted into the 1986 Act by s 154 of the Criminal Justice and Public Order Act 1994. It is broadly similar to s 5 although in order to be guilty of the offence, D must intend to cause a person harassment, alarm, or distress. Moreover, the victim must actually be caused harassment, alarm, or distress. The more serious nature of the s 4A offence is evident in the fact that a person found guilty may be sentenced to up to six months' imprisonment. By contrast, a person convicted of a s 5 offence can only be fined.

19.63   An important contrast can be drawn between s 4 and s 4A in relation to the causal nexus of the offences. Whereas the unlawful violence must be 'immediate' for the purposes of the s 4 offence (para **19.50**), it is possible that in relation to a s 4A offence, a considerable time may separate the defendant's actions and the harassment, alarm or distress of the victim. Thus in *S v CPS* (2008), where the appellant had posted a photographic image of the victim on a website and five months had passed before the victim was shown a copy by a police officer, the DC concluded that the appellant had been rightly convicted of a s 4A offence. Neither the passage of time nor the act of the police officer had broken the necessary chain of causation.

19.64   In *R v DPP* (2006), it was held that the word 'distress' in s 4A takes its colour from its context. Although the words harassment, alarm, or distress were expressed as alternatives, Toulson J considered that 'in combination they give a sense of the mischief which the section is aimed at preventing'. As to the meaning of 'distress' in the present context, he observed:

> I would hold that the word 'distress'…requires emotional disturbance or upset. The statute does not attempt to define the degree required. It does not have to be grave but nor should the requirement be trivialized. There has to be something which amounts to real emotional disturbance or upset.

19.65   In the light of this, the Admin Ct concluded that the justices had been wrong to find that a police officer had suffered distress for the purposes of s 4A where a 12-year-old boy had made masturbation gestures and shouted 'wankers' at both him and fellow officers in a police van. In *Southard v DPP* (2006), although Fulford J agreed with Toulson J's analysis of what is required for 'distress', he did not consider that the same applied to 'harassment'. Thus he observed:

> *'Distress' by its very nature involves an element of real emotional disturbance or upset but the same is not necessarily true of 'harassment'. You can be harassed, indeed seriously harassed, without experiencing emotional disturbance or upset at all. That said, although the harassment does not have to be grave, it should also not be trivial.*

**19.66** One of the common features shared by ss 4, 4A, and 5 which was previously identified (para **19.47**) is that no offence is committed where D is inside a dwelling and the victim of the words, behaviour etc is either inside that or another dwelling. For the purposes of the public order offences, s 8 of the 1986 Act defines 'dwelling' as:

> . . . *any structure or part of a structure occupied as a person's home or as other living accommodation (whether the occupation is separate or shared with others) but does not include any part not so occupied, and for this purpose 'structure' includes a tent, caravan, vehicle, vessel or other temporary or movable structure.*

In *R v Francis* (2007), the CA held that a police cell did not fall within the scope of the s 8 definition. It was a place where a person was detained in police custody rather than being 'other living accommodation'. Similarly, in *Le Vine v DPP* (2010), it was held that a laundry which could be used by the residents of a block of flats was not part of a 'dwelling' for the purposes of s 8. In reaching its conclusion, the DC emphasized the intention underpinning the Act which was to exclude disputes in people's homes, but not otherwise.

## Racially or religiously aggravated public order offences

**19.67** By virtue of s 31(1) of the Crime and Disorder Act 1998, D is guilty of an offence if he commits an offence under s 4, s 4A, or s 5 of the Public Order Act 1986 which is racially or religiously aggravated. An offence is racially or religiously aggravated for the purposes of the 1998 Act if:

> (a) *at the time of committing the offence, or immediately before or after doing so, the offender demonstrates towards the victim of the offence hostility based on the victim's membership (or presumed membership) of a racial or religious group; or*

> (b) *the offence is motivated (wholly or partly) by hostility towards members of a racial or religious group based on their membership of that group. [s 28(1)]*

**19.68** Parliament's condemnation of racially or religiously aggravated public order offences is evident in the fact that the maximum sentence for a s 4 or s 4A offence which is racially or religiously aggravated is two years' imprisonment rather than six months for the basic offence. In the case of a s 5 offence which is racially/religiously aggravated, the penalty is still only a fine. Thus in *R v Katinas* (2010), where the Crown Court had convicted the appellant of several offences, including a racially aggravated s 5 offence, his sentence of three months' imprisonment for that particular offence was quashed on appeal on the ground that it was unlawful.

---

*R v Miller* (1999): A senior train conductor approached M and asked to see his ticket. M did not have a ticket although he pretended that he had lost it. When pressed by the conductor, M became abusive. He referred to the conductor as a 'Paki' and continued his racial abuse after he was ordered to leave the train. At one point, M observed that he felt like head-butting the conductor. The conductor had considered that he was going to be hit and was upset by the incident. He signed off sick when the train reached its terminus. M was arrested and subsequently found guilty by magistrates of using racially aggravated threatening words and behaviour and travelling on a railway without a ticket. He was committed to the Crown Court for sentencing where he received sentences of 18 months and one month respectively. He appealed against the 18-month sentence. CA held: that this was a bad example of a racially aggravated offence. Although the sentence was severe, it was justified by the need to reflect public concern about conduct which damages good race relations within the community and to take account of M's previous convictions for public order and allied offences.

---

**19.69**  Where D is tried on indictment for the racially aggravated s 4 or s 4A offence and found not guilty, the jury may nevertheless find him guilty of the basic offence: s 31(6). There is no corresponding provision to allow a magistrate to do likewise where D is tried summarily: see *DPP v McFarlane* (2002). In *R (on the application of the CPS) v Blaydon Youth Court* (2004), the DC was required to determine whether magistrates' courts could conduct a joint trial of two informations alleging the racially aggravated and the basic s 4A offence where the prosecution had brought the charges in the alternative. In holding that they could, Keane LJ observed that there will 'usually be very powerful reasons why such charges in the alternative should be tried together'. Chief amongst these was that since the charges arise out of the same facts, 'to try them separately is highly likely to give rise to quite unnecessary expense and inconvenience to everyone concerned'.

**19.70**  For the purposes of s 28, the phrase 'racial group' means 'a group of persons defined by reference to race, colour, nationality (including citizenship) or ethnic or national origins': s 28(4). In *R v White* (2001), the CA was required to consider whether the expression 'African bitch' amounted to hostility based on the victim's membership of a racial group. It concluded that it did. Although the word 'African' could not be a reference to nationality or national origins since Africa was a continent consisting of many states, and although it did not denote an ethnic group because it was capable of covering people with diverse cultural traditions, the word did have a racial connotation. In the words of Pill LJ:

> *In ordinary speech, the word 'African' denotes a limited group of people regarded as of common stock and regarded as one of the major divisions of humankind having in common distinct physical features. It denotes a person characteristic of the blacks of Africa.*

**19.71**  Expressions such as 'jungle bunny', 'black bastard', 'wog', and 'fucking Islam' have also been held to denote hostility to a victim based on the victim's membership of a racial group: see *R v Duffy* (2000), *DPP v McFarlane* (2002), and *DPP v Humphrey* (2005). What if, however, D and his alleged victim are both members of the same racial group? In such circumstances, would it be possible for D to commit a racially aggravated public order offence?

**19.72**  In *DPP v Pal* (2000), D had assaulted a community centre caretaker and had called the man 'a white man's arse licker' and a 'brown Englishman'. Both the victim and D were Asian. Although it was held that D's hostile conduct was born of resentment at being asked to leave the premises rather than racism, Simon Brown LJ did consider that it was 'somewhat surprising' that it had been argued that the hostility was based on racial grounds given that both men were Asians. Commenting on this observation in the later case of *R v White* (para **19.70**), Pill LJ noted that whilst D's racial hostility towards a member of the same racial group as himself may be an unusual event, there was no basis for holding that such hostility could not in law be shown. In his Lordship's opinion:

> *It may be more difficult in such cases to establish that the hostility is of racial, national or ethnic origin as the case may be. However, a person may show hostility to his own kind whether racial, ethnic or national.*

**19.73**  Whether or not the term 'foreigner' signifies a 'racial group' for the purposes of s 28(4) of the 1998 Act was determined in a case which was ultimately heard by the HL.

*R v Rogers* (2007): R had been charged with using racially aggravated abusive or insulting words or behaviour with intent to cause fear or provoke violence contrary to s 31(1)(a) of the 1998 Act where he had encountered three Spanish women in the street and had, during an altercation, called them 'bloody foreigners' and told them to 'go back to your own country'. He subsequently pursued them to a kebab house in an aggressive manner while at the controls of a motorized mobility scooter (he was incapacitated by arthritis). He was convicted at first instance. His appeal to the CA was dismissed. He further appealed to the HL. HL held: dismissing the appeal, that those who were not British constituted a racial group for the purposes of s 28(4) as did 'foreigners' since the scope of 'racial group' went beyond groups defined by their colour, race or ethnic origin so that it also encompassed nationality and national origins.

**19.74** Section 28(5) of the Crime and Disorder Act 1998 defines 'religious group' to mean 'a group of persons defined by reference to religious belief or lack of religious belief'. In *Norwood v DPP* (2003), where N had displayed a poster in the window of his flat which contained the words 'Islam out of Britain' and 'Protect the British People' on a reproduction of a photograph of one of the twin towers of the World Trade Center in flames on 11 September 2001, the DC held, in the words of Auld LJ, that:

> The poster was a public expression of attack on all Muslims in this country, urging all who might read it that followers of the Islamic religion here should be removed from it and warning that their presence here was a threat or danger to the British people. In my view, it could not, on any reasonable basis be dismissed as merely an intemperate criticism or protest against the tenets of the Muslim religion, as distinct from an unpleasant and insulting attack on its followers generally.

N subsequently contended before the ECtHR that the criminal proceedings brought against him had violated his right to freedom of expression contrary to art 10 of the ECHR. The Court rejected his application as inadmissible. It did so on the basis that it agreed with the domestic court's assessment and in accordance with art 17 of the ECHR, which prevents individuals or groups with totalitarian aims from exploiting the principles of the ECHR for their own purposes: see *Norwood v UK* (2005).

## Processions and assemblies

**19.75** Part II (ss 11–16) of the Public Order Act 1986 provides for the statutory control of processions and assemblies. For the purposes of the Act, a 'public procession' is defined as being 'a procession in a public place' (s 16). This circular definition sheds no light on what amounts to a procession. In *Flockhart v Robinson* (1950), where D appealed against his conviction for organizing a public procession contrary to s 3(4) of the Public Order Act 1936, the KBD held by a majority that the conviction should stand. In giving judgment, Lord Goddard CJ observed that:

> A procession is not a mere body of persons; it is a body of persons who are moving along a route. Therefore, the person who organises the route is the person who organises the procession.

When the CA heard the appeal in *Metropolitan Police Comr v Kay* (2007) (para **19.78**), the majority expressed their approval of these remarks. Leveson J considered that for the purposes of the 1986 Act, a 'procession' involved 'a movement from the rallying point during a route either to some other point or, perhaps, back to the start'.

**19.76** It is clear from this, therefore, that in order to be a procession, there must be movement of a body of persons along a defined route. This contrasts with a public assembly which is a static gathering of persons. As originally enacted, s 16 of the Public Order Act 1986 provided that a 'public assembly' is:

> *an assembly of 20 or more persons in a public place which is wholly or partly open to the air. [s 16]*

**19.77** Now, however, as result of an amendment made to s 16 by s 57 of the Anti-social Behaviour Act 2003, the numerical limit upon a 'public assembly' has been reduced from 20 to two persons. Is this a case of a statute according a meaning to a word which that word would not ordinarily be understood to have? Do you consider that two persons constitute an assembly? Why might the definition of 'public assembly' in the 1986 Act have been amended in this way? For the purposes of the 1986 Act, public processions and public assemblies are gatherings which occur in a 'public place'. A 'public place' means any highway and:

> *any place to which at the material time the public or any section of the public has access, on payment or otherwise, as of right or by virtue of express or implied permission. [s 16]*

The distinction between a public procession and a public assembly is of practical importance given that the 1986 Act imposes stricter controls over the former.

## Written notice for processions

**19.78** By virtue of s 11 of the Act, the organizer of a public procession is required to give the police advance written notice where the intended purpose of the procession is: to demonstrate support for or opposition to the views or actions of any person or body of persons; or to publicize a cause or campaign; or to mark or commemorate an event. The requirement of advance written notice does not apply where: it is not reasonably practicable to give such notice; the procession is commonly or customarily held (eg, a May Day procession); or it is a funeral procession organized by a funeral director (s 11(1) and (2)).

*Metropolitan Police Comr v Kay* **(2008):** Critical Mass events had been held in London since April 1994. They involved a group of cyclists gathering on the South Bank in the early evening on the last Friday of each month. The cyclists, who often numbered 300–400, then proceeded to cycle around London. Although they purported to have no single aim, they often headed to places where they could disrupt traffic flow. They also claimed that their events did not follow a prescribed route; the route to be followed was determined by whoever happened to be at the front. In September 2005 the cyclists received letters from a senior police officer notifying them that, in his opinion, their events fell within the scope of s 11 of the 1986 Act and therefore required prior written notice to be given. Critical Mass sought a declaration from the DC as to the lawfulness of their events. The DC held that the events were 'commonly or customarily' held for the purposes of s 11(2) of the Act. Accordingly, it was not incumbent on their organizers to give advance written notice. The Commissioner appealed. CA held: by a majority of 2 to 1, that the appeal be allowed. When deciding whether or not a procession was 'commonly or customarily' held, it was necessary to have regard to the route. Although it was not the determinative factor, a procession could not become common or customary if no route or end point was ever the same. Since the Critical Mass events did not follow the same route, they did not fall within the scope of s 11(2). They therefore required advance written notice to be given pursuant to s 11(1). Critical Mass appealed. HL Held: unanimously, that the events were commonly or customarily held and hence within the scope of the s 11(2) exemption.

**19.79**  In reaching this conclusion, their Lordships generally sought to confine their remarks to the 'narrow issue' relating to the s 11(2) exemption. Thus, for example, Lord Phillips observed:

> *Section 11 does not require notice to be given of every procession that is capable of creating a disturbance. The fact that, on their natural meaning, the words of s 11(2) are wide enough to exclude some processions in respect of which the police do not have the information that they would wish is no reason to give those words an unnatural meaning. They should be given their natural meaning so as to apply to Critical Mass as a procession that is commonly or customarily held.*

In the opinion of Lord Brown of Eaton-under-Heywood, however, the real question was whether the cycle rides were prima facie notifiable processions within the meaning of s 11. He concluded that they were not: 'Their very nature as impromptu rides to my mind takes them out of the section altogether'.

**19.80**  It is worth emphasizing that the requirement of advance written notice does not amount to a request for permission to hold a procession. The police do not have the power to permit some processions to take place and refuse others. Instead, the s 11 requirement serves as a means of establishing a dialogue between the police and the organizers of a procession so that a march can take place without public order being compromised. Given that there will be occasions when a large police presence is necessary, the 1986 Act requires that at least six days' advance notice should normally be given by the organizer of a procession. Such notice must specify: the date of the procession; the start time; the route; and the name and address of the organizer(s): s 11(3). The numbers expected to participate in the procession is a notable absentee from this list. However, in practice, it seems likely that this is a vital piece of information which the police will request of an organizer if it has not already been provided.

**19.81**  It is an offence for an organizer of a procession to fail to comply with the notice requirement in s 11 or to hold a procession where the date, start time, or route differs from that stated in the written notice: s 11(7). D may have a defence, however, if he can show that he did not know of and neither suspected nor had reason to suspect the failure to satisfy the s 11 requirements: s 11(8). Moreover, where the alleged offence relates to a difference in the date, time, or route of the procession, it is a defence to show that the difference is due to circumstances beyond D's control or that it has been done with the agreement of a police officer or by his direction: s 11(9).

## Imposing conditions on processions

**19.82** Section 12 of the 1986 Act empowers the police to impose conditions on a procession. It is a power which may be exercised either prior to a procession being held or during its course. In the case of the former, it will be exercised by the chief officer of police. Where the procession is ongoing, the most senior police officer present at the scene is invested with the power to impose conditions. Conditions may only be imposed on a procession in certain specified circumstances. Thus having regard to the time, place, and route of a procession, a police officer is only entitled to impose conditions where he reasonably believes that the procession may result in:

- serious public disorder;
- serious disruption to the life of the community;
- serious damage to property; or
- the purpose of the organizers is the intimidation of others.

**19.83** Where any one of these triggers applies, a police officer may impose such conditions as appear to him to be necessary to prevent such an eventuality. The Act itself refers to conditions relating to the route of a procession or prohibiting it from entering a specified public place: s 12(1). However, the power to impose conditions extends beyond these two statutory examples. It may be exercised, for example, in respect of the start time of a procession.

## Banning processions

**19.84** With the exception of the City of London and the metropolitan police area, the police do not have the power to ban processions. The s 13 power is generally exercised by a local council, with the consent of the Secretary of State, following an application from the chief officer of police for the area. In the City of London and the metropolitan police area, it will be exercised by the chief police officer with the consent of the Secretary of State.

**19.85** Applying for a banning order is a measure of last resort. It is only to be sought by a chief officer where he reasonably believes that the power to impose conditions (s 12) is insufficient to prevent a procession from resulting in serious public disorder. A fear that a procession will give rise to any of the other three triggers for exercising the s 12 power does not therefore justify an application for a banning order. Where a banning order is made, it will apply in respect of all public processions or all processions of a specified class within the area. A 'blanket ban' on processions is therefore permissible under the

Act. Whilst such a step amounts to a significant infringement of civil liberties, it does avoid allegations that the police are guilty of political bias when seeking a s 13 order. A banning order may last for up to three months.

**19.86** In *Kent v Metropolitan Police Comr* (1981), the Campaign for Nuclear Disarmament sought judicial review of a decision by the Commissioner to impose a ban on all processions in his area, save for those traditionally held on 1 May to celebrate May Day and those of a religious character customarily held, for a period of 28 days. In giving his judgment, Ackner LJ stated that:

> Blanket bans on all marches for however short a time are a serious restriction of a fundamental freedom, and the courts will always be vigilant to see that the power to impose such a ban has not been abused.

**19.87** Nevertheless, the CA refused to declare that the ban was ultra vires. In the court's opinion, recent disturbances at marches held in the Commissioner's area meant that it had been open to him to conclude that there was 'a tinderbox situation where a month's respite from all marches was essential to prevent public disorder'. In the light of the Human Rights Act 1998, it may now be possible to challenge the lawfulness of a banning order on the ground that it represents a disproportionate response to the threat of serious public disorder. Although a court may be unlikely to quash a banning order in its entirety, it may conclude that the duration of such an order is disproportionate to the threat posed.

**19.88** It is an offence to organize a procession which D knows to be contrary to a banning order: s 13(7). Moreover, D commits an offence where he participates in a procession which he knows to be banned under s 13, or where he incites another to participate: s 13(8) and (9).

## Imposing conditions on assemblies

**19.89** There is no equivalent of ss 11 or 13 in respect of public assemblies. In the White Paper *Review of Public Order Law* (1985) (Cmnd 9510), which preceded the 1986 Act, the government of the day felt that bans on public assemblies should not be imposed because:

> Meetings and assemblies are a more important means of exercising freedom of speech than are marches: a power to ban them, even as a last resort, would be potentially a major infringement of speech (especially at election time).

**19.90** The power to impose conditions on public assemblies is to be found in s 14 of the 1986 Act. It is activated by any one of the four triggers previously mentioned in the context of public processions (para **19.82**). Where the power is exercised, either before or during the course of a public assembly, the conditions which may be imposed under s 14 are more limited than those under s 12. They relate to: the place at which the assembly may be held; its maximum duration; or the maximum number of persons permitted to attend. Whilst a ban on public assemblies would indeed be 'a major infringement of speech', it has to be noted that in truth, something tantamount to a ban can be achieved by the imposition of very restrictive conditions. In *DPP v Baillie* (1995), where B was the purveyor of information as to the time and place of a free festival, a s 14 notice was served on him by the police. It contained a number of conditions relating to the time, place and duration of the public assembly, as well as requiring that any event must be licensed in accordance with the Local Government (Miscellaneous Provisions) Act 1982. In the opinion of the Crown Court, 'the police drafted this notice so as to stop the event, not simply regulate it'. On appeal by the DPP, the DC accepted that there was 'just sufficient evidence' that B was the organizer of a public assembly for the purposes of the 1986 Act. However, the appeal was dismissed on the basis that the uncertain nature of the arrangements with regard to time and place made it impossible to decide whether the free festival would be a 'public assembly' within the meaning of s 14(1).

**19.91** At first instance in *Austin v Metropolitan Police Commissioner* (2005) (para **19.18**), Tugendhat J expressed the view that the power to impose conditions under either s 12 or s 14 of the 1986 Act was not confined to situations where the disorder, etc resulted from the procession or assembly itself. In other words, conditions could be imposed on a peaceable crowd using those powers where the source of the disorder was the actual or threatened behaviour of another crowd. Tugendhat J did acknowledge, however, that the cases where this would be an appropriate course of action would be 'very rare indeed' and that they would 'require the most anxious scrutiny'. Perhaps of even greater interest was his observation that the police were able to justify their control of the crowd by reference to their powers under the 1986 Act even though they had not had them in mind at the relevant time – they had instead relied on their common law powers in respect of a breach of the peace. Given that a failure to comply with a condition imposed under either s 12 or s 14 amounts to an offence, is it appropriate for the courts to infer the use of the statutory powers in this way?

**19.92** Reported decisions on s 14 are rare.

*Police v Reid* **(1987):** D and approximately 20 others conducted an anti-apartheid demonstration outside the South African Embassy in Trafalgar Square. They shouted slogans and wagged their fingers at guests arriving for a reception. On the assumption that this amounted to intimidatory behaviour, a chief inspector present at the scene imposed a condition on the assembly requiring it to move to another location. D's refusal to comply fully with the condition led to him being charged with an offence contrary to s 14(5) of the 1986 Act. Metropolitan Stipendiary Magistrate held: that no offence had been committed since there had been no valid ground for imposing the condition on the assembly. The chief inspector had applied the wrong test. He had equated intimidation with discomfort when, in fact, only the former justified the imposition of a condition under the 1986 Act.

---

***Broadwith v Chief Constable of Thames Valley Police (2000):*** D did not argue that the conditions imposed upon a public assembly were ultra vires. Rather, he argued that the conditions did not apply to him since he had not been present at an initial assembly which later moved to another location in accordance with a prospective condition imposed by the Chief Constable, and because at the time that he had allegedly committed offences contrary to s 14(5) of the 1986 Act and s 89(2) of the Police Act 1996, he was separate from the main body of persons and was not therefore part of a public assembly. DC held: that both arguments would be rejected. With regard to the latter argument, it was observed that groups consisted of individuals and that it may therefore be necessary on some occasions (as in the present case) for the police to take action to control the movements of an individual. The fact that D was walking away from the group at the material time did not mean that he had ceased to be part of the assembly to which the condition applied.

---

***R (on the application of Brehony) v Chief Constable of Greater Manchester Police (2005):*** B was a member of a group which regularly demonstrated outside a store in Manchester city centre because they believed that the retailer supported the Israeli Government. The Chief Constable believed that the assembly might give rise to serious disruption to the life of the community or serious public disorder over the Christmas shopping period. He therefore imposed conditions under s 14 relating to the location, duration, and maximum numbers permitted to attend the assembly. B claimed that: the Chief Constable had been under a duty to give reasons for imposing the conditions, which he had failed to do; that his belief that the demonstration might result in serious public disorder or serious disruption to the life of the community had been unreasonable; and that the conditions imposed had been disproportionate. HCt held: dismissing the application, that although there was a duty to give reasons where conditions were imposed in advance of an assembly, the Chief Constable's explanation in a letter to B informing him of the conditions had satisfied this requirement. The Chief Constable's belief that the assembly might lead to either serious public disorder or serious disruption to the life of the community had been reasonable on the facts. Moreover, the conditions imposed had been proportionate to the legitimate aim of maintaining public order.

---

19.93   Although there is no statutory right of appeal against a s 14 (or s 12) condition, it is clear that the requirement of 'reasonable belief' in relation to the triggers for the exercise of the power to impose a condition ensures that a police officer's decision is potentially subject to judicial review. Thus breach of an ultra vires condition does not, as *Police v Reid* (1987) demonstrates, amount to an offence. It does not follow, however, that the presence of some ultra vires conditions in a s 14 notice will automatically render the whole of the notice invalid. In *DPP v Jones* (2002), the DC accepted that ultra vires conditions could be severed without invalidating the whole of a s 14 notice applying the test for severability laid down by the HL in *DPP v Hutchinson* (1990). Accordingly, D may still be convicted for breach of a condition contrary to s 14(5) even where other conditions contained in the notice are invalid.

## Trespassory assemblies

**19.94** Sections 14A, 14B, and 14C were inserted into the Public Order Act 1986 by ss 70 and 71 of the Criminal Justice and Public Order Act 1994. They make provision for: prohibiting trespassory assemblies; offences in respect of trespassory assemblies; and stopping persons from proceeding to trespassory assemblies. The phrase 'trespassory assembly' is not actually defined in these provisions, although by reading s 14A(1) and (9) together, it is possible to determine what a trespassory assembly is. Essentially it involves a gathering of more than 20 persons on land to which the public has no right of access or a limited right of access. To be a trespassory assembly it is likely to be held without the permission of the landowner, or in excess of any permission, and may result in serious disruption to the life of the community or significant damage to land, a building, or a monument which is of historical, architectural, archaeological, or scientific importance.

**19.95** The police may apply to the local council to grant an order prohibiting trespassory assemblies in their area for a specified period: s 14A(1). Where an order is granted by the council with the consent of the Home Secretary (in the City of London and the metropolitan police district it will be made by the Metropolitan Police Commissioner with the Home Secretary's consent) it is subject to temporal and spatial limits: it must not last for longer than four days; and it does not extend beyond a radius of five miles from a specified centre. It is an offence to organize an assembly which D knows to be prohibited under s 14A: s 14B(1). Moreover, it is an offence to take part in an assembly which D knows to be prohibited or to incite another to take part: s 14B(2) and (3).

> ***DPP v Jones* (1999):** The defendants were part of a gathering of more than 20 persons on a grass verge adjacent to a perimeter fence at Stonehenge. The area was subject to an order under s 14A(1) of the Public Order Act 1986. Most of the gathering had moved at the request of a police officer. The defendants refused to do so and were arrested and charged with an offence contrary to s 14B(2) of the 1986 Act. They were convicted by magistrates. On appeal to the Crown Court, the convictions were quashed. They were reinstated by the DC. The defendants appealed to the HL. HL held: by a majority of three to two, that the appeal be allowed. The public had the right to use the public highway for such reasonable activities, including peaceful protest, as were not inconsistent with and did not obstruct the general public's primary right of passage along the highway. The use in the present case had been reasonable and therefore the offence of trespassory assembly had not been committed.

**19.96** An individual's civil liberties are further restricted by the terms of s 14C of the Public Order Act 1986. This confers a power on the police to restrict a person's freedom of movement by stopping him and directing him not to proceed where the officer 'reasonably believes' that: the person is on his way to an area covered by a s 14A order; and that the assembly is prohibited by that order: s 14C(1). It is an offence to fail to comply with a direction given under sub-s (1): s 14C(3).

## Demonstrations in the vicinity of Parliament

**19.97** Special provision was made for such demonstrations under ss 132–138 of the Serious Organised Crime and Police Act 2005. Essentially, it was provided that within the 'designated area' (Parliament Square and its immediate environs), those who wished to organize a demonstration were first required to give written notification to the Metropolitan Police Commissioner. The authorization requirement was challenged before the courts on a number of occasions. Thus in *Blum v Secretary of State for the Home Department* (2006), the DC held that the requirement was not incompatible with arts 10 and 11 of the ECHR. *Blum* was later applied in *Tucker v DPP* (2007), and *Moase v City of Westminster Magistrates Court* (2008). In *R (Haw) v Secretary of State for the Home Department* (2006), the CA took the view that in enacting ss 132–138, Parliament had intended to regulate all demonstrations within the designated area regardless of when they began. Accordingly, Mr Haw's pavement vigil against government policy on Iraq was caught by the authorization requirement even though it had preceded the commencement of the Act by some four years, and despite the fact that the Act was silent on the matter.

**19.98** Although the Commissioner was under a duty to authorize demonstrations (s 134(2)), he had the power to grant wide-ranging conditions on organizers or demonstrators. These included conditions relating to: the place where the demonstration may/may not be carried on; the number of persons who may take part; the number and size of banners or placards used; or the maximum permissible noise levels. Where a demonstration was taking place, the power to impose conditions was exercisable by the most senior officer present. As with the power to impose conditions on public processions or public assemblies, the power to impose conditions on a demonstration within the vicinity of Parliament was subject to judicial review. Thus in *DPP v Haw* (2007), the DC agreed with an earlier ruling that certain conditions imposed on Mr Haw's vigil were ultra vires or incompatible with arts 10 and 11 of the ECHR because they lacked clarity. In the same case, however, Mr Haw failed to convince the DC that the Commissioner's power to impose conditions *in advance* of a demonstration could not be delegated to a subordinate in accordance with the *Carltona* principle (para **11.27**).

**19.99** Sections 132–138 of the 2005 Act were controversial. There was a strong belief both inside and outside Parliament that they went too far; that they imposed too many restrictions on the ability of protestors to make the nation's legislators directly aware of their concerns and grievances. Accordingly, prior to the May 2010 general election, the then government's Constitutional Reform Bill proposed to repeal ss 132–138 and replace them with less far-reaching provisions in an amended Public Order Act 1986. Labour's subsequent defeat at the polls did not, however, halt the reform process. Instead, the coalition Government's Police Reform and Social Responsibility Act 2011 effected the repeal: see s 141. In their place, a new legal framework has been established for demonstrations in the 'controlled area of Parliament Square'.

**19.100** For the purposes of ss 141–149 of the 2011 Act, the 'controlled area of Parliament Square' comprises the central garden of Parliament Square and the footways which immediately join it. It is, therefore, considerably smaller than the 'designated area' under the repealed provisions of the 2005 Act. Within the controlled area, various activities are prohibited. These include: operating any amplified noise equipment; erecting or keeping erected a tent; using any tent or other structure for the purposes of staying or sleeping in the area; and using any sleeping equipment for the purpose of sleeping overnight in the area. 'Amplified noise equipment' includes, but is not limited to, loudspeakers and loudhailers.

**19.101** Where a constable, or authorized officer of the Greater London Authority or Westminster City Council, has reasonable grounds to believe that a person is doing, or is about to do, a prohibited act, he may direct that person either to cease the activity or not to commence it. Such a direction may include a direction that the person does not start doing that activity again after its cessation. Where a direction relates to 'amplified noise equipment', it may only be given if it appears that the person operating, or about to operate, the equipment either is or will do so in a manner to produce sound which others in the vicinity of the controlled area either can or are likely to hear.

**19.102** A s 143 direction lasts for the period specified by the constable or authorized officer issuing it, up to a maximum of 90 days. If no period is specified, the 90-day upper limit applies. Section 143 directions may be given orally, to a single person or to two or more persons collectively, and may be withdrawn or varied by the person who gave it. It is a summary offence to fail, without reasonable excuse, to comply with a s 143 direction.

**19.103** The regime under the 2011 Act thus constitutes a new approach to demonstrations in Parliament Square. It focuses on disruptive activities and the erection of encampments more obviously than the previous regime. Moreover, it is made clear in the Act itself that its provisions apply to the use of a tent or other similar structure, or sleeping equipment within the controlled area which began before s 143 came into force. Finally, it should be noted that the repeal of ss 132–138 of the 2005 Act has another intended consequence: public assemblies in Parliament Square will once again be subject to control under the Public Order Act 1986.

## FURTHER READING

Bailey, S and Taylor, N *Bailey, Harris & Jones: Civil Liberties Cases and Materials* (6th edn, 2009) OUP.

Barendt, E *Free Speech* (2nd edn, 2005) OUP.

Bonner, D and Stone, R 'The Public Order Act 1986: Steps in the Wrong Direction?' [1987] PL 202.

Burney, E 'Using the Laws on Racially Aggravated Offences' [2003] Crim LR 28.

Card, R *Public Order Law* (2000) Jordans.

Geddis, A 'Free Speech Martyrs or Unreasonable Threats to Social Peace? "Insulting" Expression and Section 5 of the Public Order Act 1986' [2004] PL 853.

Kerrigan, K 'Breach of the Peace and Binding Over – Continuing Confusion' (1997) 2(1) J Civ Lib 30.

Loveland, I 'Public Protest in Parliament Square' [2007] EHRLR 251.

Mead, D 'Of Kettles, Cordons and Crowd Control – *Austin v Commissioner of Police for the Metropolis* and the meaning of "deprivation of liberty"' [2009] EHRLR 376.

Mead, D *The New Law of Peaceful Protest* (2010) Hart Publishing.

Pollard, D, Parpworth, N, and Hughes, D *Constitutional and Administrative Law: Text with Materials* (4th edn, 2007) OUP.

Stone, R 'Breach of the Peace: the case for Abolition' [2001] Web JCLI.

Stone, R *Textbook on Civil Liberties & Human Rights* (8th edn, 2010) OUP.

Thornton, P et al *The Law of Public Order and Protest* (2010) OUP.

Townsend, C *Making the Peace: Public order and public security in modern Britain* (1993) OUP.

Williams, DGT 'Processions, Assemblies and the Freedom of the Individual' [1987] Crim LR 167.

Williams, G 'Arrest for Breach of the Peace' [1954] Crim LR 578.

## SELF-TEST QUESTIONS

1   Why is 'breach of the peace' an important concept in English law?

2   To what extent, if any, do you agree with the view that the *R v Howell* definition of a breach of the peace is too vague and imprecise?

3   What purpose is served by the requirement that a police officer must reasonably apprehend a breach of the peace before he/she can exercise the power of arrest to prevent a breach from occurring?

4   Does the decision in *Percy v DPP* (2002) (para **19.61**) suggest that the desecration of a national flag does not amount to an offence under s 5 of the Public Order Act 1986?

5   It has been suggested that the case law demonstrates 'that the ultimate purpose of s 5 of the 1986 Act [the Public Order Act] is to act as a fulcrum at which the rights of free expression intersect with the right of a broader section of the community not to be harassed, alarmed or distressed'. What do the cases tell us about the courts' approach to balancing these competing interests?

6   Why do you think that Parliament saw fit to treat processions and assemblies differently when enacting the Public Order Act 1986?

7   How do the conditions which may be imposed under ss 12 and 14 of the 1986 Act differ? Do the criteria for their application differ?

8   In *Broadwith* (para **19.92**), it will be remembered that the DC held, inter alia, that the fact that D was walking away from a public assembly at the material time did not mean that he had ceased to be a part of that assembly. What would have been the implications for the power to impose conditions under s 14 had the DC ruled otherwise on this point?

9   Do the powers under the Public Order Act 1986 mean that the common law powers for preserving public order are now redundant? What effect, if any, has the amended definition of 'public assembly' had upon your answer?

10  Do you agree with Professor Stone that the powers in relation to breach of the peace ought to be abolished?

11  Prior to their repeal, it was argued that the provisions in the Serious Organised Crime and Police Act 2005 relating to demonstrations within the vicinity of Parliament constituted an unnecessary extension of police powers. Do you think that the new powers under Part 3 of the Police Reform and Social Responsibility Act 2011 strike a better balance between protestors' Convention rights and the need to maintain public order?

# Index

## A

**Access to justice**
rule of law 3.18–3.19
tribunals 15.11
**Acts of Parliament** *see* **Legislation**
**Actual bias** 13.89–13.90
**Administrative Justice and Tribunals Council**
(AJTC) 15.30–15.33
**Advocates-General** 7.42
**Affray**
general requirements 19.38–19.46
racial or religious aggravation 19.67–19.74
**Amendments**
constitution
entrenching provisions 1.9
general powers 1.7–1.8
implied repeal doctrine 5.21–5.25
**Appeals**
judicial review distinguished 12.7–12.9
requirement to exhaust remedies 12.10–12.12
tribunal decisions 15.23–15.24, 15.28
**Arrest powers**
arrestable offences 18.31–18.32
breaches of the peace 19.13–19.15
citizen's arrest 18.49–18.51
entry of premises afterwards 18.83–18.87
importance 18.28–18.29
new statutory powers 18.33–18.37
non-arrestable offences 18.32
provision of information 18.52–18.57
reasonable suspicion 18.38–18.48
use of force 18.58
**Assault on police** 18.96–18.98
**Assembly** *see* **Freedom of assembly**

## B

**Bad faith** 13.19–13.20
**Ballot Bills** 9.41–9.42
**Belfast Agreement** 8.60–8.61
**Bias**
actual bias 13.89–13.90
automatic disqualification 13.84–13.88
ground for judicial review 13.30

**Bill of Rights**
alternative to HRA 1998 16.121–16.124
curtailment of royal prerogative 4.3
parliamentary privilege 6.90, 6.82
parliamentary supremacy 5.8
**Breach of fiduciary duties** 13.12–13.13
**Breaches of the peace**
arrest 19.13–19.15
binding over 19.25–19.29
common law detention 19.16–19.24
common law powers
prevention 19.30–19.34
no PACE protection 19.5
private premises 19.10–19.12
reasonable apprehension 19.6–19.9
relevant conduct 19.3–19.4
**Bye-laws**
collateral challenges 12.32–12.41
secondary legislation 9.60

## C

**Cabinet** *see* **Ministers**
**Capital-C constitutions** 1.2–1.3
**Certainty** 3.12–3.15
**Chiltern Hundreds** 6.26–6.27
**Citizen's arrest** 18.49–18.51
**Civil liberties**
*see also* Human Rights; Police powers
assemblies
conditions 19.89–19.93
demonstrations near Parliament
19.97–19.103
trespass 19.94–19.96
breaches of the peace
arrest 19.13–19.15
binding over 19.25–19.29
common law detention 19.16–19.24
common law prevention 19.30–19.34
no PACE protection 19.5
private premises 19.10–19.12
reasonable apprehension 19.6–19.9
relevant conduct 19.3–19.4
ECHR substantive rights 16.39–16.43
human rights distinguished 16.1–16.6

**Civil liberties** (*cont.*)
political and social rights
distinguished 16.7–16.9
processions
banning 19.84–19.88
conditions 19.82–19.83
demonstrations near Parliament
19.97–19.103
requirement for written notice 19.78–19.81
statutory controls 19.75–19.77
public order
history 19.28–19.29
statutory offences 19.35–19.66
right to protest 19.1–19.2
traditional protections 16.10–16.12
**Collateral challenges** 12.32–12.41
**Commission** *see* **European Commission**
**Committees**
Committee of Ministers 16.19
Committee of Permanent
Representatives 7.22
devolution
Executive Committee of Northern
Ireland 8.66–8.70
Joint Ministerial Committee 8.81–8.82
European Court of Human Rights 16.26
European Parliament 7.33
House of Commons
Departmental Select Committees 6.51–6.53
importance 6.44–6.45
reform proposals 6.53–6.54
scrutiny committees 6.47–6.50
Select Committees 6.46
Joint Committee on Human Rights
16.90–16.96
legislative stage
private bills 9.32–9.34
public general bills 9.15
National Assembly for Wales 8.35–8.36
**Common law**
breaches of the peace
detention 19.16–19.24
prevention 19.30–19.34
consolidation bills 9.49
contempt of court 17.66–17.69
indecency 17.33–17.37
judicial approach to royal prerogative
4.25–4.38
origins of royal prerogative 4.2, 4.17
parliamentary supremacy
judicial approach 5.63–5.76
ministerial statements 5.77–5.79

right to protest 19.1–19.2
source of law
interpretation of statutes 11.45–11.51
scope 11.40–11.44
traditional role of judiciary 11.39
sources of UK constitution 1.31
**Commonwealth constitution** 1.20–1.22
**Concordats** 8.83–8.85
**Consolidation bills** 9.46–9.57
**Constitutions**
advantages of written constitution 1.17–1.18
amendments
entrenching provisions 1.9
general powers 1.7–1.8
change in UK 1.32–1.33
classification 1.10–1.16
Dicey's rule of law 3.23
meaning 1.1–1.3
position of UK monarchy 1.23–1.25
reform proposals for UK 1.34–1.36
role of Supreme Court 2.39
sources of UK law 1.29–1.31
UK Commonwealth 1.20–1.22
UK model analysed 1.26–1.28
unwritten UK constitution 1.19
written form of superior law 1.4–1.6
**Contempt of court**
common law 17.66–17.69
'court' defined 17.57
defences 17.54–17.56
overview 17.38–17.39
protection of open justice 17.40–17.48
reporting restrictions
banning orders 17.68–17.75
postponement orders 17.58–17.67
strict liability 17.50–17.53
**Conventions**
codification 11.31–11.35
collective cabinet responsibility 11.18–11.19
conversion into law 11.29–11.30
devolution 11.36–11.38
draft Cabinet Manual 11.23–11.25
enforcement 11.20–11.21
establishment 11.22
examples 11.8–11.12
individual ministerial responsibility
11.14–11.17
judicial recognition 11.26–11.28
meaning 11.2–11.7
ministerial responsibility 11.13
**Council of Ministers**
Committee of Permanent Representatives 7.22

composition 7.15–7.16
Presidency 7.17–7.18
qualified majority voting 7.19–7.21
**Court of Justice of the EC (ECJ)**
direct effect doctrine 10.11–10.16
establishment of specialised courts 7.50
functions and jurisdiction 7.45–7.47
judiciary 7.42–7.44
overview 7.42–7.44
requirement for clear and understandable
laws 3.15
**Courts**
*see also* Common law; Judicial review;
Parliamentary supremacy; Rule of law
access to justice 3.18–3.19
contempt of court
'court' defined 17.57
defences 17.54–17.56
overview 17.38–17.39
protection of open justice 17.40–17.48
reporting restrictions 17.58–17.79
strict liability 17.50–17.53
Court of Justice of the EC (ECJ)
establishment of specialised courts 7.50
judiciary 7.42–7.44
overview 7.40–7.41
establishment of Supreme Court 2.34–2.39
European Court of Human Rights
admissibility criteria 16.53–16.54
chambers 16.27–16.29
committees 16.26
Grand Chamber 16.30–16.31
judiciary 16.20–16.24
jurisdiction 16.32–16.38
margin of appreciation 16.58–16.60
Plenary Court 16.25
reform proposals 16.61–16.68
settlements 16.55–16.57
standing 16.49–16.52
General Court
establishment of specialised courts 7.50
judiciary 7.49
jurisdiction 7.48
judicial approach to royal prerogative
4.25–4.38
judicial recognition of conventions 11.26–11.28
parliamentary supremacy
judicial approach 5.63–5.76
ministerial statements 5.77–5.79
relationship with EU law
effect on parliamentary supremacy
5.46–5.52

normal canons of construction
10.63–10.65
overview 10.50–10.52
purposive approach 10.53–10.62
scrutiny of statutory instruments 9.81
source of common law
interpretation of statutes 11.45–11.51
scope 11.40–11.44
traditional role of judiciary 11.39
State liability 10.45–10.48
tribunals distinguished 15.3–15.5
US supreme Court role 1.6
**Criminal law**
arrestable offences 18.31–18.32
contempt of court 17.9–17.53
indecency 17.29–17.32
obscenity 17.1–17.28
origins of royal prerogative 4.2
public order offences
common characteristics 19.38–19.66
racial or religious aggravation
19.67–19.74
rule of law 3.33

**D**

**Damages**
Human Rights Act 1998 16.113–16.116
judicial review remedy 14.2–14.6
State liability 10.39–10.43
**Decisions**
direct effect 10.18
sources of law 10.5
statement of reasons 10.8
**Declarations**
incompatibility with human rights 5.80–5.85
interim remedy 14.28
judicial review remedy 14.20–14.24
**Delegated legislation** *see* **Secondary legislation**
**Demonstrations near Parliament** 19.97–19.103
**Departmental Select Committees** 6.51–6.53
**Devolution**
concordats 8.83–8.85
conventions 11.36–11.38
effect on parliamentary supremacy 5.53–5.54
importance 8.14–8.17
Joint Ministerial Committee 8.81–8.82
judicial independence 2.13
Northern Ireland
Belfast Agreement 8.60–8.61
Executive Committee 8.66–8.70
importance 8.14

**Devolution** (*cont.*)
    interpretation of legislation  8.65
    legislative powers  8.62–8.64
ombudsmen  15.85
reform proposals  8.86–8.87
Scotland
    continuing development  8.54–8.58
    history  8.40–8.41
    importance  8.15
    Memorandum of Understanding  8.81–8.82
    relationship with Union legislation  8.53
    Scottish Parliament  8.42–8.58
    'West Lothian Question'  8.71–8.74
State liability  10.46
Wales
    continuing development  8.37–8.39
    history  8.18–8.19
    importance  8.15
    Memorandum of Understanding  8.81–8.82
    National Assembly  8.20–8.27
**Dicey, A.V.**
    conventions  11.2–11.3
    criticisms of model  3.24–3.26
    rule of law  3.20–3.23
**Direct applicability**  10.10
**Direct effect**
    *see also* Parliamentary supremacy
    decisions  10.18
    directives  10.19–10.23
    ECJ doctrine  10.11–10.16
    emanations of the State  26–30
    horizontal and vertical effects  10.24–10.25
    regulations  10.17
**Directions**  9.59
**Directives**
    direct effect  10.19–10.23
    sources of law  10.4
    State liability  10.37–10.38
    statement of reasons  10.8
**Discretionary powers**
    Dicey's rule of law  3.21
    general principles for review  13.1–13.5
    grounds for judicial review
        bad faith  13.19–13.20
        bias  13.76–13.90
        breach of fiduciary duties  13.12–13.13
        breaches of natural justice  13.43–13.48
        failure to give reasons  13.67–13.75
        fair hearings  13.61–13.66
        fettering of discretionary powers
            13.14–13.16
        illegality  13.6, 13.7–13.11

        improper use  13.17–13.18
        irrationality  13.21–13.26
        irrelevant considerations  13.7–13.11
        legitimate expectations  13.49–13.60
        procedural impropriety  13.38–13.42
        proportionality  13.27–13.37
    judicial deference  16.107–16.111
    police powers  18.1–18.4
    role of judicial review  12.4–12.6
    royal prerogative  4.16
**Dissolution of parliament**  4.11
**Doctrines**
    European Union
        direct effect  10.11–10.16
        indirect effect  31–36
        margin of appreciation  16.58–16.60
    implied repeal  5.21–5.25
    ministerial responsibility  11.13
    parliamentary supremacy
        alternative analysis  5.28–5.30
        declarations of incompatibility  5.80–5.85
        effect of devolution  5.53–5.54
        effect of EU membership  5.46–5.52
        enrolled Bill rule  5.18–5.20
        entrenching provisions  5.26–5.27
        examples  5.9–5.13
        Glorious Revolution  5.6–5.8
        human rights  5.55–5.62
        implied repeal  5.21–5.25
        judicial interpretation  5.63–5.76
        limitations  5.16–5.17
        ministerial statements  5.77–5.79
        non-legal limits  5.14–5.15
        restrictions on House of Lords  5.31–5.41
        retrospectivity of human rights
            5.86–5.89
        Scottish Union  5.42–5.45
        terminology  5.1
        traditional view  5.2–5.4
        unlimited powers pre-1688  5.5
    rule of law
        access to justice  3.18–3.19
        clear and understandable laws  3.12–3.15
        contemporary significance  3.34–3.40
        criminal law  3.33
        Dicey's model  3.20–3.26
        equality before the law  3.27–3.28
        legality principle  3.29–3.32
        meaning  3.1–3.7
        natural justice  3.16–3.18
        reform proposals  3.41–3.43
        retrospectivity precluded  3.8–3.11

separation of powers
    judicial independence  2.12–2.17
    Montesquieu's influence  2.4–2.6
    origins of theory  2.1–2.3
    special position of Lord Chancellor  2.9
    UK model  2.7–2.8

# E

**Elections**
    European Council  7.14
    European Parliament  7.31–7.32
    'first past the post' system  6.12–6.15
    National Assembly for Wales  8.22, 8.21
    UK franchise  6.1–6.11
**Emanations of the State**  26–30
**English parliament**
    *see also* Legislation
    dissolution  4.11
    doctrine of supremacy  5.1–5.89
    House of Commons
        abstaining from voting  6.40
        committees  6.44–6.45
        composition  6.16–6.17
        disqualification from membership
            6.17–6.20
        election of members  6.1–6.17
        electronic voting  6.43
        Father of the House  6.33
        nodding through  6.41
        pairing  6.42
        peers  6.21–6.24
        resignation of members  6.25–6.27
        sittings  6.35–6.38
        The Speaker  6.28–6.32
        statutory time limit  6.34
        voting  6.39
    House of Lords  6.56–6.90
    parliamentary privilege  6.77–6.90
**Enrolled Bill rule**  5.18–5.20
**Entrenching provisions**
    parliamentary supremacy  5.26–5.27
    Scottish Union  5.42–5.45
    written constitutions  1.9
**Entry of premises**
    after arrest  18.83–18.87
    implied licence  18.60–18.64
    legality principle  18.59
    reform proposals  18.88
    search warrants  18.66–18.75
    statutory authority  18.65
    without warrants  18.76–18.82

**Equality before the law**
    *see also* Access to justice
    Dicey's model  3.22
    modern application  3.27–3.28
**EU law**
    direct applicability  10.10
    direct effect
        decisions  10.18
        directives  10.19–10.23
        emanations of the State  26–30
        ECJ doctrine  10.11–10.16
        horizontal and vertical effects  10.24–10.25
        regulations  10.17
    implied repeal doctrine  5.25
    indirect effect  31–36
    proportionality  13.27, 13.36
    relationship with UK courts
        effect on parliamentary supremacy
            5.46–5.52
        normal canons of construction  10.63–10.65
        overview  10.50–10.52
        purposive approach  10.53–10.62
    requirement for clear and understandable
        laws  3.15
**European Commission**
    composition  7.24
    powers  7.23
    Presidency  7.25–7.29
    relationship with Parliament  7.39
    resignation *en masse*  7.30
**European Council**  7.12–7.14
**European Parliament**
    business  7.33–7.37
    composition  7.32
    election of members  7.31–7.32
    Ombudsman
        establishment  15.114–15.115
        jurisdiction  15.116–15.118
        procedure  15.119–15.123
    powers  7.38
    relationship with Commission  7.39
**European Union**
    concordats on devolution  8.84–8.85
    effect on parliamentary supremacy  5.46–5.52
    European Convention on Human Rights
        Committee of Ministers  16.19
        institutions  16.15–16.18
        origins  16.13–16.14
    European Court of Human Rights
        admissibility criteria  16.53–16.54
        chambers  16.27–16.29
        committees  16.26

**European Union** (*cont.*)
Grand Chamber 16.30–16.31
judiciary 16.20–16.24
jurisdiction 16.32–16.38
margin of appreciation 16.58–16.60
Plenary Court 16.25
reform proposals 16.61–16.68
settlements 16.55–16.57
standing 16.49–16.52
institutions
Commission 7.23–7.30
Council of Ministers 7.17–7.22
Court of Justice of the EC (ECJ) 7.40–7.50
European Council 7.12–7.14
General Court 7.48–7.49
Parliament 7.31–7.39
recent changes under Lisbon Treaty 7.6–7.11
origins 7.1–7.5
sources of law
decisions 10.5
directives 10.4
legislative powers 10.2
nomenclature 10.7
opinions 10.6
publicity 10.9
recommendations 10.6
regulations 10.3
statement of reasons 10.8
treaties 10.1
State liability 10.37–10.49
**Exclusion clauses**
ousters 12.43–12.44
time limits 12.45–12.48
**Executive Committee of Northern
Ireland** 8.66–8.70

**F**

**Fair hearings**
ground for judicial review 13.61–13.64
legal representation 13.65–13.66
retrospectivity of human rights 5.87
**Father of the House of Commons** 6.33
**Federalism** 1.14
**Fettering of discretionary powers**
ground for judicial review 13.14–13.16
jurisdiction 12.4–12.6
**Fiduciary duties** 13.12–13.13
**Finality clauses** 12.43–12.44
**Freedom of assembly**
*see also* Processions
conditions 19.89–19.93

demonstrations near Parliament 19.97–19.103
trespass 19.94–19.96
**Freedom of expression**
contempt of court
common law 17.76–17.79
'court' defined 17.57
defences 17.54–17.56
overview 17.38–17.39
protection of open justice 17.40–17.48
reporting restrictions 17.58–17.79
strict liability 17.50–17.53
Human Rights Act 1998 16.80–16.81
indecency
common law 17.33–17.37
statutory offences 17.29–17.32
obscenity
aversion argument 17.13
complete article considered 17.14–17.16
defences 17.17–17.20
forfeiture 17.22
likely readers 17.10–17.12
reform proposals 17.23–17.24
search and seizure 17.21
statutory controls 17.1
test of obscenity 17.5–17.9
theatre and postal communications
17.25–17.28
parliamentary privilege 6.82
proportionality 13.30
traditional protections 16.12
**Freedom of thought, conscience and
religion** 16.80–16.81

**G**

**General Court**
judiciary 7.49
jurisdiction 7.48
**Glorious Revolution**
origins of royal prerogative 4.2
parliamentary supremacy
significant change 5.6–5.8
unlimited powers pre-1688 5.5
**Government bills** *see* **Public general bills**
**Grand Chamber** 16.30–16.31
**Grounds for judicial review**
bad faith 13.19–13.20
bias 13.76–13.90
breach of fiduciary duties 13.12–13.13
breaches of natural justice 13.43–13.48
failure to give reasons 13.67–13.75
fair hearings 13.61–13.66

fettering of discretionary powers 13.14–13.16

general principles 13.1–13.5

illegality 13.6

improper use 13.17–13.18

irrationality 13.21–13.26

irrelevant considerations 13.7–13.11

legitimate expectations 13.49–13.60

procedural impropriety 13.38–13.42

proportionality 13.27–13.37

# H

*Habeas corpus* 14.31

**Health Service Commissioner**

exhaustion of alternative procedure 15.91

jurisdiction 15.87–15.90

procedure 15.92–15.93

**Hereditary peers** 6.57

**House of Commons**

abstaining from voting 6.40

committees

Departmental Select Committees 6.51–6.53

importance 6.44–6.45

reform proposals 6.53–6.54

scrutiny committees 6.47–6.50

Select Committees 6.46

composition 6.16–6.17

disqualification from membership 6.17–6.20

election of members 6.1–6.17

electronic voting 6.43

Father of the House 6.33

nodding through 6.41

pairing 6.42

peers 6.21–6.24

private bills 9.29–9.33

public general bills

committee stage 9.15

first reading 9.13

monarch's consent 9.18

report stage 9.16

second reading 9.14

third reading 9.17

resignation of members 6.25–6.27

sittings 6.35–6.38

The Speaker 6.28–6.32

statutory time limit 6.34

voting 6.39

**House of Lords**

composition

archbishops and bishops 6.59

hereditary peers 6.57

life peers 6.60–6.62

Lord Speaker 6.63

'Lords Spiritual and Temporal' 6.56

reform proposals 6.64–6.76

consolidation bills 9.49

private bills 9.34

Private Members Bills 9.45

public general bills 9.19–9.21

restrictions imposed by Parliament

Acts 5.31–5.40

**Human rights**

*see also* Civil liberties

breaches of the peace

binding over 19.28

relevant conduct 19.4

civil liberties distinguished 16.1–16.6

compatibility

declarations of incompatibility 5.80–5.85

ministerial statements 5.77–5.79

contemporary significance of rule of

law 3.34–3.40

effect on parliamentary supremacy 5.55–5.62

European Convention

alternative approaches 16.73

Committee of Ministers 16.19

derogations 16.47–16.48

European Court of Human Rights

16.20–16.38

incorporation into English law 16.69–16.72

institutions 16.15–16.18

margin of appreciation 16.58–16.60

origins 16.13–16.14

protocols 16.44–16.46

standing 16.49–16.52

substantive rights 16.39–16.43

European Court of Human Rights

admissibility criteria 16.53–16.54

reform proposals 16.61–16.68

settlements 16.55–16.57

standing 16.49–16.52

fair hearings 13.66

freedom of expression

contempt of court 17.38–17.79

indecency 17.29–17.37

obscenity 17.1–17.28

proportionality 13.30

Human Rights Act 1998

commencement 16.74

consideration of Bill of Rights as

alternative 16.121–16.124

Convention rights 16.75–16.76

derogations 16.118–16.120

freedom of expression 16.80–16.81

**Human rights** (*cont.*)
  freedom of thought  16.80–16.81
  horizontal effect  16.97–16.103
  interpretation  16.77–16.79
  public authorities  16.82–16.89
  remedies  16.112–16.120
  reservations  16.118–16.120
  standing  104–106
interpretation of statutes  11.56
irrationality  13.23
Joint Committee  16.90–16.96
judicial deference  16.107–16.111
judicial independence  2.12
Northern Ireland legislation  8.64
parliamentary privilege  6.88–6.89
police powers
  arrest  18.48
  stop and search  18.26
political and social rights
  distinguished  16.7–16.9
proportionality  13.30–13.32
public and private law matters
  distinguished  12.31
remedial orders  9.69
retrospectivity  5.86–5.89
retrospectivity precluded  3.9
**Hybrid bills**  9.36–9.38

**I**

**Illegality**
  ground for review  13.6
  legality principle
    entry of premises  18.59
    rule of law  3.29–3.32
**Implied repeal doctrine**  5.21–5.25
**Improper use of powers**  13.17–13.18
**Indecency**
  *see also* Obscenity
  common law  17.33–17.37
  statutory offences  17.29–17.32
**Indirect effect**  31–36
**Injunctions**  25–27
**Inquiries**
  non-statutory inquiries  15.39–15.40
  statutory inquiries  15.35–15.38
  tribunals distinguished  15.1–15.2
**Institutions**
  EU
    Commission  7.23–7.30
    Council of Ministers  7.17–7.22
    Court of Justice of the EC (ECJ)  7.40–7.50

    European Council  7.12–7.14
    General Court  7.48–7.49
    origins  7.4
    Parliament  7.31–7.39
    recent changes under Lisbon Treaty  7.6–7.11
  European Convention on Human Rights
    Committee of Ministers  16.19
    European Court of Human Rights  16.20–16.38
    origins  16.15–16.18
  House of Commons
    abstaining from voting  6.40
    committees  6.44–6.45
    composition  6.16–6.17
    disqualification from membership  6.17–6.20
    election of members  6.1–6.17
    electronic voting  6.43
    Father of the House  6.33
    nodding through  6.41
    pairing  6.42
    peers  6.21–6.24
    sittings  6.35–6.38
    The Speaker  6.28–6.32
    statutory time limit  6.34
    voting  6.39
  House of Lords  6.56–6.90
  National Assembly for Wales
    committees  8.35–8.36
    establishment  8.20
    legislative powers  8.28–8.34
    officers  8.24–8.27
    voting  8.22
  Northern Ireland Assembly
    Belfast Agreement  8.60–8.61
    interpretation of legislation  8.65
    legislative powers  8.62–8.64
  Scottish Parliament
    composition  8.42–8.44
    legislative powers  8.47–8.51
    ministers  8.46
    pre-legislative scrutiny  8.52
    presiding officers  8.45
**Interim declarations**  14.28
**Interpretation**
  European Convention on Human Rights  16.77–16.79
  function of ECJ  7.45–7.47
  impact of EU law
    effect on parliamentary supremacy  5.46–5.52
    normal canons of construction  10.63–10.65

overview 10.50–10.52
  purposive approach 10.53–10.62
indirect effect 31–36
Northern Ireland Assembly 8.65
parliamentary supremacy
  judicial approach 5.63–5.76
  ministerial statements 5.77–5.79
rule of law 3.41–3.42
sources of law
  human rights 11.56
  presumptions 11.52–11.55
  rules of interpretation 11.45–11.51
  traditional role of judiciary 11.39
**Irrationality**
alternative labelling 13.25–13.26
threshold of proof 13.22–13.24
*Wednesbury* reasonableness
    compared 13.19–13.20
**Irrelevant considerations** 13.7–13.11

# J

**Joint Committee on Human Rights**
  16.90–16.96, 16.123
**Joint Ministerial Committee** 8.81–8.82
**Judge-made law** *see* **Common law**
**Judicial review**
appeals distinguished 12.7–12.9
collateral challenges 12.32–12.41
contemporary significance of rule of law 3.34
exclusion clauses
  ousters 12.43–12.44
  time limits 12.45–12.48
fettering of discretionary powers 12.4–12.6
grounds
  bad faith 13.19–13.20
  bias 13.76–13.90
  breach of fiduciary duties 13.12–13.13
  breaches of natural justice 13.43–13.48
  failure to give reasons 13.67–13.75
  fair hearings 13.61–13.66
  fettering of discretionary powers
    13.14–13.16
  general principles 13.1–13.5
  illegality 13.6
  improper use 13.17–13.18
  irrationality 13.21–13.26
  irrelevant considerations 13.7–13.11
  legitimate expectations 13.49–13.60
  procedural impropriety 13.38–13.42
  proportionality 13.27–13.37
importance of judicial independence 2.12

jurisdiction 12.1–12.3
ombudsmen decisions 15.103–15.107
procedure
  permission 12.56–12.59
  pre-action protocol 12.50–12.55
  reform proposals 12.13–12.14
  two-stage approach 12.49
public and private law matters
    distinguished 12.25–12.31
public law remedy 12.15–12.20
remedies
  damages 14.2–14.6
  declarations 14.20–14.24
  *habeas corpus* 14.31
  injunctions 25–27
  interim declarations 14.28
  mandatory orders 14.16–14.19
  overview 14.1
  power to substitute decision 14.29–14.30
  prescriptive or permissive 14.7
  prohibiting orders 14.15
  quashing orders 14.8–14.14
  *quo warranto* 14.31
  requirement to exhaust alternative
    remedies 12.10–12.12
requirement to exhaust alternative
    remedies 12.10–12.12
rule of law 3.43
standing 12.60–12.68
time limits 12.69–12.76
tribunal decisions 15.23–15.25
**Judiciary**
*see also* Common Law; Courts; Judicial
    review; Parliamentary supremacy
appointments 2.18–2.19
approach to parliamentary supremacy
    5.63–5.76
conflicting views on separation of
    powers 2.23–2.30
Court of Justice of the EC (ECJ) 7.42–7.44
establishment of Supreme Court 2.34–2.39
General Court 7.50
independence 2.12–2.17
partial separation 2.31–2.33
tenure 2.20
two-tier tribunal system 15.21–15.22
**Jurisdiction**
Court of Justice of the EC (ECJ) 7.45–7.47
European Court of Human Rights
    16.32–16.38
General Court 7.48
judicial review 12.1–12.3

**Jurisdiction** (*cont.*)
  obscenity 17.1
  ombudsmen
    European Ombudsman 15.116–15.118
    Health Service Commissioner 15.87–15.90
    Local Government Commissioners
      15.95–15.96
    Parliamentary Commissioner for
      Administration 15.53–15.59
  two-tier tribunal system 15.23–15.25

# L

**Law** *see* **Common law; Criminal law;**
      **Legislation; Rule of law; Treaties**
**Legal certainty** 3.12–3.15
**Legality principle**
  entry of premises 18.59
  rule of law 3.29–3.32
**Legislation**
  commencement provisions 9.50–9.52
  conflict with prerogative powers 4.17–4.23
  consolidation bills 9.46–9.57
  constitutionality 1.5
  enactment of conventions 11.31–11.35
  European Parliamentary procedure 7.33–7.37
  European Union
    decisions 10.5
    direct applicability 10.10
    directives 10.4
    general powers 10.2
    nomenclature 10.7
    publicity 10.9
    regulations 10.3
    statement of reasons 10.8
  hybrid bills 9.36–9.38
  National Assembly 8.28–8.34
  Northern Ireland Assembly 8.62–8.64
  parliamentary supremacy
    alternative analysis 5.28–5.30
    declarations of incompatibility 5.80–5.85
    effect of devolution 5.53–5.54
    effect of EU membership 5.46–5.52
    enrolled Bill rule 5.18–5.20
    entrenching provisions 5.26–5.27
    examples 5.9–5.13
    Glorious Revolution 5.6–5.8
    human rights 5.55–5.62
    implied repeal 5.21–5.25
    judicial interpretation 5.63–5.76
    limitations 5.16–5.17
    ministerial statements 5.77–5.79

    non-legal limits 5.14–5.15
    restrictions on House of Lords 5.31–5.41
    retrospectivity of human rights 5.86–5.89
    Scottish Union 5.42–5.45
    terminology 5.1
    traditional view 5.2–5.4
    unlimited powers pre-1688 5.5
  private bills
    House of Commons 9.29–9.33
    House of Lords 9.34
    limited application 9.29
    public general bills distinguished 9.30
    suspension 9.35
  Private Members Bills
    Ballot Bills 9.41–9.42
    from House of Lords 9.45
    Ordinary Presentation Bills 9.44
    scope 9.39–9.40
    Ten Minute Rule Bills 9.43
  public general bills
    fall of bill 9.25
    House of Commons 9.12–9.18
    House of Lords 9.19–9.21
    overview 9.1
    post-legislative scrutiny 9.26–9.28
    pre-legislative scrutiny 9.8–9.11
    preparatory stages 9.4–9.7
    private bills distinguished 9.30
    reform proposals 9.22–9.23
    Royal Assent 9.24
    sources 9.2–9.3
  quasi-legislation 9.82
  Royal Assent 4.9–4.10
  rule of law
    clear and understandable laws 3.12–3.15
    retrospectivity precluded 3.8–3.11
  Scottish Parliament 8.47–8.51
  scrutiny committees 6.50
  secondary legislation
    bye-laws 9.60
    Orders in Council 9.58
    regulations 9.59
    regulatory reform orders 9.61–9.68
    remedial orders 9.69
    scope 9.53–9.54
    statutory instruments 9.70–9.81
  sources of UK constitution 1.29–1.30
**Legitimate expectations** 13.49–13.60
**Liability** *see* **State liability**
**Life peers** 6.60–6.62
**Local Government Commissioners**
  exhaustion of alternative remedies 15.97

good practice guidance 15.101
jurisdiction 15.95–15.96
outcome of complaints 15.102
procedure 15.98–15.100
reform proposals 15.108–15.113
*Locus standi*
European Court of Human Rights
   individuals 16.49–16.50
   inter-state applications 16.51–16.52
Human Rights Act 1998 104–106
judicial review 12.60–12.68
**Lord Chancellor**
judicial independence 2.14–2.16
reform proposals 2.10–2.11
unique position 2.9
**Lord Speaker** 6.63

## M

**Mandatory orders** 14.16–14.19
**Margin of appreciation**
doctrine 16.58–16.60
judicial deference 16.107–16.111
**Members of parliament**
European Parliament 7.32
filter for Parliamentary
   Commissioner 15.60–15.67
House of Commons
   abstaining from voting 6.40
   composition 6.16–6.17
   disqualification from membership 6.17–6.20
   election 6.1–6.17
   electronic voting 6.43
   Father of the House 6.33
   nodding through 6.41
   pairing 6.42
   peers 6.21–6.24
   resignation of members 6.25–6.27
   sittings 6.35–6.38
   The Speaker 6.28–6.32
   voting 6.39
House of Lords
   archbishops and bishops 6.59
   hereditary peers 6.57
   life peers 6.60–6.62
   Lord Speaker 6.63
   'Lords Spiritual and Temporal' 6.56
   reform proposals 6.64–6.76
National Assembly for Wales 8.21
parliamentary privilege 6.77–6.90
Private Members Bills
   Ballot Bills 9.41–9.42

Ordinary Presentation Bills 9.44
   scope 9.39–9.40
   Ten Minute Rule Bills 9.43
Scottish Parliament 8.42–8.44
standards in public life
   Committee on Standards and
     Privileges 6.49
   statutory provisions 6.91–6.95
**Ministers**
appointment by the Crown 4.12–4.15
compatibility statements 5.77–5.79
conventions
   collective cabinet responsibility 11.18–11.19
   individual ministerial
     responsibility 11.14–11.17
   overview of ministerial
     responsibility 11.13
   scope 11.8–11.12
Departmental Select Committees 6.51–6.53
devolution
   Executive Committee of Northern
     Ireland 8.66–8.70
   Joint Ministerial Committee 8.81–8.82
   National Assembly for Wales 8.24–8.27
   Scottish Parliament 8.46
secondary legislation
   general powers 9.56
   regulatory reform orders 9.61–9.68
**Monarchy**
classification of constitutions 1.12
consent to particular legislation 9.18
origins of royal prerogative 4.2–4.3
position under UK constitution 1.23–1.25
prerogative powers
   appointment of ministers 4.12–4.15
   discretionary powers 4.16
   dissolution of parliament 4.11
   Royal Assent 4.9–4.10
Royal Assent
   prerogative powers 4.9–4.10
   public general bills 9.24

## N

**National Assembly for Wales**
committees 8.35–8.36
effect on parliamentary supremacy 5.53
establishment 8.20
Government powers 8.24–8.27
legislative powers 8.28–8.34
officers 8.24–8.27
voting 8.22

**Natural justice**
  fair hearings 13.61
  ground for judicial review 13.43–13.48
  rule of law 3.16–3.18
**Nodding through** 6.41
**Northern Ireland**
  Assembly
    Belfast Agreement 8.60–8.61
    interpretation of legislation 8.65
    legislative powers 8.62–8.64
  constitutional history 8.9–8.13
  devolution
    Belfast Agreement 8.60–8.61
    concordats 8.83–8.85
    Executive Committee 8.66–8.70
    importance 8.14
    interpretation of legislation 8.65
    Joint Ministerial Committee 8.81–8.82
    legislative powers 8.62–8.64

# O

**Obscenity**
  *see also* Indecency
  aversion argument 17.13
  complete article considered 17.14–17.16
  defences 17.17–17.20
  forfeiture 17.22
  likely readers 17.10–17.12
  reform proposals 17.23–17.24
  search and seizure 17.21
  statutory controls 17.1
  test of obscenity 17.5–17.9
  theatre and postal communications
    17.25–17.28
**Obstruction of police** 18.99–18.104
**Ombudsmen**
  devolution 15.85
  European Parliament
    establishment 15.114–15.115
    jurisdiction 15.116–15.118
    procedure 15.119–15.123
  Health Service Commissioner
    exhaustion of alternative remedies 15.91
    jurisdiction 15.87–15.90
    procedure 15.92–15.93
  incorporation into UK 15.42–15.43
  judicial review of decisions 15.103–15.107
  Local Government Commissioners
    exhaustion of alternative remedies 15.97
    good practice guidance 15.101
    jurisdiction 15.95–15.96

    outcome of complaints 15.102
    procedure 15.98–15.100
    reform proposals 15.108–15.113
  origins 15.41
  Parliamentary Commissioner for
    Administration
    initial screening 15.72
    investigation of maladministration
      15.45–15.52
    jurisdiction 15.53–15.59
    MP filter 15.60–15.67
    nomenclature 15.44
    procedure 15.73–15.74
    reports 15.75–15.84
    time limits 15.70–15.71
    under-utilized remedy 15.68–15.69
**Opinions** 10.6
**Orders**
  general secondary legislation 9.59
  Orders in Council 9.58
  regulatory reform orders 9.61–9.68
  remedial orders 9.69
**Ordinary Presentation Bills** 9.44
**O'Reilly v Mackman, rule in** 12.15–12.24
**Ouster clauses** 12.43–12.44
**Overriding laws** 1.4–1.6

# P

**Pairing** 6.42
**Parliamentary Commissioner for
  Administration**
  initial screening 15.72
  investigation of maladministration 15.45–15.52
  jurisdiction 15.53–15.59
  MP filter 15.60–15.67
  nomenclature 15.44
  procedure 15.73–15.74
  reports 15.75–15.84
  time limits 15.70–15.71
  under-utilized remedy 15.68–15.69
**Parliamentary privilege** 6.77–6.90
**Parliamentary supremacy**
  *see also* Direct effect
  alternative analysis 5.28–5.30
  declarations of incompatibility 5.80–5.85
  effect of devolution 5.53–5.54
  effect of EU membership 5.46–5.52
  enrolled Bill rule 5.18–5.20
  entrenching provisions 5.26–5.27
  examples 5.9–5.13
  Glorious Revolution 5.6–5.8

human rights 5.55–5.62
implied repeal 5.21–5.25
judicial interpretation 5.63–5.76
limitations 5.16–5.17
ministerial statements 5.77–5.79
non-legal limits 5.14–5.15
restrictions on House of Lords 5.31–5.41
retrospectivity of human rights 5.86–5.89
Scottish Union 5.42–5.45
terminology 5.1
traditional view 5.2–5.4
unlimited powers pre-1688 5.5
**Parliaments**
*see also* European Parliament
English
demonstrations near Parliament
19.97–19.103
dissolution 4.11
doctrine of supremacy 5.1–5.89
House of Commons 6.1–6.55
resignation of members 6.25–6.27
National Assembly for Wales
committees 8.35–8.36
establishment 8.20
legislative powers 8.28–8.34
officers 8.24–8.27
voting 8.22
Northern Ireland Assembly
Belfast Agreement 8.60–8.61
interpretation of legislation 8.65
legislative powers 8.62–8.64
Scottish Parliament
composition 8.42–8.44
effect on parliamentary supremacy
5.53–5.54
legislative powers 8.47–8.51
ministers 8.46
pre-legislative scrutiny 8.52
presiding officers 8.45
**Partial separation of powers** 2.31–2.33
**Peers**
House of Commons 6.21–6.24
House of Lords
hereditary peers 6.57
life peers 6.60–6.62
**Permission** 12.56–12.59
**Plenary Court** 16.25
**Police powers**
arrest
arrestable offences 18.31–18.32
entry of premises afterwards 18.83–18.87
importance 18.28–18.29

new statutory powers 18.33–18.37
non-arrestable offences 18.32
provision of information 18.52–18.57
reasonable suspicion 18.38–18.48
use of force 18.58
assault on police 18.96–18.98
breaches of the peace
arrest 19.13–19.15
binding over 19.25–19.29
common law detention 19.16–19.24
common law prevention 19.30–19.34
no PACE protection 19.5
private premises 19.10–19.12
reasonable apprehension 19.6–19.9
relevant conduct 19.3–19.4
discretionary powers 18.1–18.4
entry of premises
after arrest 18.83–18.87
implied licence 18.60–18.64
legality principle 18.59
search warrants 18.66–18.75
statutory authority 18.65
without warrants 18.76–18.82
PACE
Codes of Practice 18.7–18.8
introduction 18.5–18.6
public order
assemblies 19.89–19.96
history 19.28–19.29
right to protest 19.1–19.2
statutory offences 19.35–19.66
search and seizure
extended powers 18.94–18.95
general powers 18.89–18.93
stop and search
general provisions 18.9–18.18
PACE 18.19–18.27
wilful obstruction 18.99–18.104
**Pre-action protocol** 12.50–12.55
**Prerogative powers** *see* **Royal prerogative**
**Presumptions** 11.52–11.55
**Prime Minister**
appointment by the Crown 4.13–4.15
constitutional conventions 11.8–11.12
**Private bills**
*see also* Hybrid bills
limited application 9.29
parliamentary stages
House of Commons 9.29–9.33
House of Lords 9.34
public general bills distinguished 9.30
suspension 9.36–9.38

**Private law**
  collateral challenges 12.32–12.41
  public law matters distinguished 12.25–12.31
**Private Members Bills**
  Ballot Bills 9.41–9.42
  from House of Lords 9.45
  Ordinary Presentation Bills 9.44
  scope 9.39–9.40
  Ten Minute Rule Bills 9.43
**Privilege** *see* **Parliamentary privilege**
**Procedure**
  impropriety as ground for review 13.38–13.42
  judicial review
    permission 12.56–12.59
    pre-action protocol 12.50–12.55
    reform proposals 12.13–12.14
    two-stage approach 12.49
  ombudsmen
    European Ombudsman 15.119–15.123
    Health Service Commissioner 15.92–15.93
    Local Government Commissioners
      15.98–15.100
    Parliamentary Commissioner for
      Administration 15.73–15.74
  tribunals 15.29
**Processions**
  *see also* Freedom of assembly
  banning 19.84–19.88
  conditions 19.82–19.83
  demonstrations near Parliament 19.97–19.103
  requirement for written notice 19.78–19.81
  statutory controls 19.75–19.77
**Prohibiting orders** 14.15
**Proportionality**
  applicability 13.33–13.37
  future ground for review 13.27–13.29
  human rights incorporation 13.30–13.32
**Prospective laws** 3.8–3.11
**Public authorities**
  breach of fiduciary duties 13.12–13.13
  human rights
    horizontal effect 16.97–16.103
    meaning and scope 16.82–16.89
    retrospectivity 5.86
  public and private law matters
    distinguished 12.25–12.31
**Public general bills**
  *see also* Hybrid bills
  fall of bill 9.25
  overview 9.1
  parliamentary stages
    committee stage 9.15

  first reading 9.13
  House of Lords 9.19–9.21
  monarch's consent 9.18
  reform proposals 9.22–9.23
  report stage 9.16
  second reading 9.14
  third reading 9.17
  preparatory stages 9.4–9.7
  private bills distinguished 9.30
  Royal Assent 9.24
  scrutiny
    post-legislative stage 9.26–9.28
    pre-legislative stage 9.8–9.11
  sources 9.2–9.3
**Public law**
  *see also* Sources of law
  collateral challenges 12.32–12.41
  judicial review as the appropriate
    remedy 12.15–12.24
  private law matters distinguished
    12.25–12.31
**Public order**
  assemblies
    conditions 19.89–19.93
    demonstrations near Parliament
      19.97–19.103
    trespass 19.94–19.96
  history 19.28–19.29
  processions
    banning 19.84–19.88
    conditions 19.82–19.83
    demonstrations near Parliament
      19.97–19.103
    requirement for written notice
      19.78–19.81
    statutory controls 19.75–19.77
  right to protest 19.1–19.2
  statutory offences
    common characteristics 19.38–19.66
    impact of major public disorders
      19.35–19.36
    racial or religious aggravation
      19.67–19.74
**Purposive approach**
  impact of EU law 10.53–10.62
  rules of interpretation
    rules of interpretation 11.45–11.51

**Q**

**Quashing orders** 14.8–14.14
*Quo warranto* 14.31

# R

**Reasoned decisions**
  EU secondary legislation  10.8
  ground for judicial review  13.67–13.75
  tribunals  15.27
**Recommendations**  10.6
**Reform proposals**
  devolution  8.86–8.87
  ECHR institutions  16.16–16.18
  entry of premises  18.88
  European Court of Human Rights
    16.61–16.68
  House of Lords  6.64–6.76
  judicial review  12.13–12.14
  Local Government Commissioners
    15.108–15.113
  Lord Chancellor  2.10–2.11
  obscenity  17.23–17.24
  public general bills  9.22–9.23
  royal prerogative  4.39–4.46
  rule of law  3.41–3.43
  Select Committees  6.53–6.54
  standing  12.66–12.69
  UK constitution  1.34–1.36
**Regulations**
  direct applicability  10.10
  direct effect  10.17
  nomenclature  10.7
  secondary legislation  9.59
  sources of law  10.3
  statement of reasons  10.8
**Regulatory reform orders**  9.61–9.68
**Religious freedom**  16.80–16.81
**Remedial orders**  9.69
**Remedies**
  *see also* Inquiries; Ombudsmen; Tribunals
  Human Rights Act 1998  16.112–16.120
  judicial review
    damages  14.2–14.6
    declarations  14.20–14.24
    *habeas corpus*  14.31
    injunctions  25–27
    interim declarations  14.28
    mandatory orders  14.16–14.19
    overview  14.1
    power to substitute decision
      14.29–14.30
    prescriptive or permissive  14.7
    prohibiting orders  14.15
    quashing orders  14.8–14.14
    *quo warranto*  14.31
    requirement to exhaust alternative
      remedies  12.10–12.12
  secondary legislation  9.69
**Reporting restrictions**
  banning orders  17.68–17.75
  common law  17.76–17.79
  postponement orders  17.58–17.67
**Republican constitutions**  1.12
**Retrospectivity**
  human rights  5.86–5.89
  rule of law  3.8–3.11
**Riot**
  general requirements  19.38–19.46
  racial or religious aggravation
    19.67–19.74
**Royal Assent**
  public general bills  9.24
  royal prerogative  4.9–4.10
**Royal prerogative**
  conflict with statutory powers
    4.17–4.23
  difficulties of definition and
    classification  4.6–4.8
  discretionary powers  4.16
  examples
    appointment of ministers  4.12–4.15
    dissolution of parliament  4.11
    Royal Assent  4.9–4.10
  judicial approach  4.25–4.38
  origins  4.1–4.5
  reform proposals  4.39–4.46
  scope for adaption  4.24
**Rule of law**
  access to justice  3.18–3.19
  clear and understandable laws
    3.12–3.15
  conflict with margin of appreciation
    16.107–16.111
  contemporary significance  3.34–3.40
  criminal law  3.33
  Dicey's model
    critical analysis  3.24–3.26
    three elements  3.20–3.23
  equality before the law  3.27–3.28
  legality principle  3.29–3.32
  meaning  3.1–3.7
  natural justice  3.16–3.18
  reform proposals  3.41–3.43
  retrospectivity precluded  3.8–3.11
**Rules**
  general secondary legislation  9.59
  quasi-legislation  9.82

## S

**Scotland**
constitutional history 8.5–8.8
devolution
concordats 8.83–8.85
continuing development 8.54–8.58
history 8.40–8.41
importance 8.15
Joint Ministerial Committee 8.81–8.82
Memorandum of Understanding 8.81–8.82
relationship with Union legislation 8.53
Scottish Parliament 8.42–8.58
'West Lothian Question' 8.71–8.74
effects of Union legislation 5.42–5.45
Scottish Parliament
composition 8.42–8.44
effect on parliamentary supremacy 5.53–5.54
legislative powers 8.47–8.51
ministers 8.46
pre-legislative scrutiny 8.52
presiding officers 8.45
**Scrutiny**
English Parliament 6.47–6.50
National Assembly for Wales 8.35–8.36
Northern Ireland Assembly 8.63
public general bills
post-legislative stage 9.26–9.28
pre-legislative stage 9.8–9.11
Scottish Parliament 8.52
statutory instruments
courts 9.81
Select Committees 9.77–9.80
**Search and seizure**
see also Stop and search
entry of premises 18.66–18.75
extended powers 18.94–18.95
general powers 18.89–18.93
obscene material 17.21
**Secondary legislation**
bye-laws 9.60
European Union
decisions 10.5
directives 10.4
nomenclature 10.7
opinions 10.6
publicity 10.9
recommendations 10.6
statement of reasons 10.8
Orders in Council 9.58
regulations 9.59

regulatory reform orders 9.61–9.68
remedial orders 9.69
scope 9.53–9.54
statutory instruments
general powers 9.70–9.72
judicial scrutiny 9.81
parliamentary procedure 9.73
**Seizure** see **Search and seizure**
**Select Committees**
Departmental Select Committees 6.51–6.53
hybrid bills 9.38
reform proposals 6.53–6.54
scope 6.46
statutory instruments 9.77–9.80
**Separation of powers**
judiciary
appointments 2.18–2.19
conflicting views 2.22–2.30
establishment of Supreme Court 2.34–2.39
independence 2.12–2.17
partial separation 2.31–2.33
remuneration 2.21
tenure 2.20
Montesquieu's influence 2.4–2.6
origins of theory 2.1–2.3
significance for judicial review 12.3
special position of Lord Chancellor 2.9
UK model 2.7–2.8
**Sources of law**
see also Human rights
common law
interpretation of statutes 11.45–11.51
scope 11.40–11.44
traditional role of judiciary 11.39
constitutional conventions
codification 11.31–11.35
collective cabinet responsibility 11.18–11.19
conversion into law 11.29–11.30
devolution 11.36–11.38
draft Cabinet Manual 11.23–11.25
enforcement 11.20–11.21
establishment 11.22
examples 11.8–11.12
individual ministerial responsibility 11.14–11.17
judicial recognition 11.26–11.28
meaning 11.2–11.7
ministerial responsibility 11.13
European Union
decisions 10.5
directives 10.4

legislative powers  10.2
nomenclature  10.7
opinions  10.6
publicity  10.9
recommendations  10.6
regulations  10.3
statement of reasons  10.8
treaties  10.1
legislation
consolidation bills  9.46–9.57
hybrid bills  9.36–9.38
private bills  9.29–9.38
Private Members Bills  9.41–9.42
public general bills  9.1–9.28
quasi-legislation  9.82
secondary legislation
bye-laws  9.60
Orders in Council  9.58
regulations  9.59
remedial orders  9.69
scope  9.53–9.54
statutory instruments  9.70–9.81
**Sovereignty** *see* **Parliamentary supremacy**
**Speaker of the House of Commons**
6.28–6.32
**Standards in public life**
Committee on Standards and Privileges  6.49
European Commission  7.30
statutory provisions  6.91–6.95
**Standing**
European Court of Human Rights
individuals  16.49–16.50
inter-state applications  16.51–16.52
Human Rights Act 1998 104–106
judicial review  12.60–12.68
judicial review remedies  14.4
**State liability**
damages  10.39–10.43
devolution  10.49
non-implementation of directives  10.37–10.38
'State' defined  10.44–10.45
**Statutes** *see* **Legislation**
**Statutory instruments**
general powers  9.70–9.72
parliamentary procedure
affirmative procedure  9.75
negative procedure  9.74
overview  9.73
scrutiny  9.77–9.81
**Stop and search**
general provisions  18.9–18.18
PACE  18.19–18.27

**Supremacy** *see* **Parliamentary supremacy**
**Supreme Court**  2.34–2.39

**T**

**Ten Minute Rule Bills**  9.43
**Terrorism**
arrest powers  18.46
contemporary significance of rule of
law  3.41–3.43
**Time limits**
complaints to Parliamentary Commissioner
15.70–15.71
exclusion clauses  12.45–12.48
Local Government Commissioners  15.96
procedural  12.69–12.76
**Treaties**
direct effect  10.13–10.14
origins of EU  7.2–7.3
sources of law  10.1
**Tribunals**
Administrative Justice and Tribunals
Council  15.30–15.33
appeals  15.28
characteristics
accessibility  15.11
costs  15.10
expeditious hearings  15.13
expertise  15.14
generally  15.6–15.9
informality  15.12
courts distinguished  15.3–15.5
inquiries distinguished  15.1–15.2
procedure  15.29
reasoned decisions  15.27
statutory framework
overview  15.15
reform of system  15.16–15.18
two-tier system  15.19–15.26

**U**

*Ultra vires* acts  13.38–13.42
**Union with Scotland**
constitutional history  8.5–8.8
parliamentary supremacy
5.42–5.45
relationship with devolution  8.53
**Unitary constitutions**  1.14
**Unwritten constitutions**
classification  1.10
UK model  1.19, 1.26–1.28

## V

**Victims** *see* **Standing**

**Violent disorder**
  general requirements 19.38–19.46
  racial or religious aggravation 19.67–19.74

**Voting**
  Council of Ministers 7.19–7.21
  House of Commons
    abstaining from voting 6.40
    electronic voting 6.43
    nodding through 6.41
    pairing 6.42
    procedure 6.39
  National Assembly for Wales 8.22

## W

**Wales**
  constitutional history 8.2–8.4
  devolution
    concordats 8.83–8.85
    continuing development 8.37–8.39

  history 8.18–8.19
  importance 8.15
  Joint Ministerial Committee 8.81–8.82
  Memorandum of Understanding
    8.81–8.82
  National Assembly 8.20–8.27

**Warrants**
  arrest 18.30
  search and seizure 18.66–18.75

***Wednesbury* principles**
  defined 13.1–13.5
  irrationality compared 13.19–13.20
  police powers 18.2

**'West Lothian Question'** 8.71–8.74

**Wilful obstruction of police**
    18.99–18.104

**Written constitutions**
  advantages 1.17–1.18
  classification 1.10
  codification of conventions 11.31–11.35
  codification of royal prerogative 4.46
  drafting considerations 1.37–1.40
  reform proposals for UK 1.34–1.36